MAPS OF EXPERIENCE
The Anchoring of Land to Story in Secwepemc Discourse

In many North American indigenous cultures, history and stories are passed down, not through the written word, but through the oral tradition. In *Maps of Experience*, Andie Diane Palmer draws on stories she recorded during travels through the hunting and gathering territory of Secwepemc – or Shuswap – with members of the Alkali Lake Reserve in Interior British Columbia to examine how various kinds of discourse allow knowledge to be carried forward, reconstituted, reflected upon, enriched, and ultimately relocated by and for new interlocutors in new experiences and places.

Maps of Experience demonstrates how the Secwepemc engagement in the traditional practices of hunting and gathering creates shared experiences between individuals, while re-creating a familiar social context in which existing knowledge of the land may be effectively exchanged and acted upon. When the narratives of fellow travellers are pooled through discursive exchange, they serve as a 'map of experience,' providing the basis of shared understanding and social relationship to territory. Palmer's analysis of ways of listening and conveying information within the Alkali Lake community brings new insights into Indigenous language and culture, as well as to the study of oral history, ethnohistory, experimental ethnography, and discourse analysis.

(Anthropological Horizons)

ANDIE DIANE PALMER is an associate professor in the Department of Anthropology at the University of Alberta.

Anthropological Horizons

Editor: Michael Lambek, University of Toronto

This series, begun in 1991, focuses on theoretically informed ethnographic works addressing issues of mind and body, knowledge and power, equality and inequality, the individual and the collective. Interdisciplinary in its perspective, the series makes a unique contribution in several other academic disciplines: women's studies, history, philosophy, psychology, political science, and sociology.

For a list of the books published in this series see p. 251.

Maps of Experience

The Anchoring of Land to Story
in Secwepemc Discourse

Andie Diane Palmer

UNIVERSITY OF TORONTO PRESS
Toronto Buffalo London

ISBN 0-8020-3559-0 (cloth)
ISBN 0-8020-8435-4 (paper)

∞

Printed on acid-free paper

Library and Archives Canada Cataloguing in Publication

Palmer, Andie Diane N.
   Maps of experience : the anchoring of land to story in Secwepemc
discourse / Andie Diane Palmer.

(Anthropoligical horizons)
Includes bibliographical references and index.
ISBN 0-8020-3559-0 (bound).   ISBN 0-8020-8435-4 (pbk.)

1. Shuswap Indians – History.   2. Alkali Lake Indian Reserve No. 1
(B.C.)   3. Oral tradition – British Columbia – Alkali Lake Region
(Cariboo)   I. Title.   II. Series.

E99.S45P34 2005   971.1'7500497943   C2005-901357-5

This book has been published with the help of a grant from the Canadian
Federation for the Humanities and Social Sciences, through the Aid to
Scholarly Publications Programme, using funds provided by the Social
Sciences and Humanities Research Council of Canada.

The University of Toronto Press acknowledges the financial assistance to its
publishing program of the Canada Council for the Arts and the Ontario
Arts Council.

University of Toronto Press acknowledges the financial support for its
publishing activities of the Government of Canada through the Book
Publishing Industry Development Program (BPIDP).

Contents

List of Illustrations   vii

Preface   ix

Acknowledgments   xiii

Notes on Language, Transcription, and Pronunciation   xvii

1 Introduction: A Discourse-Centred Approach to Understanding   3

2 A Brief History of Responses to Colonialism   27

3 Living on the Land   57

4 Maps   83

5 Story   118

6 Memories   136

7 Cross-Cultural Comparisons   159

Appendix: Selected Transcriptions   170

Notes   207

References   217

Index   229

Illustrations

Photographs

1 Esḱet: Alkali Lake Indian Reserve No. 1   xi

2 Angela George at *Tsecyelkw*   40

3 Ollie Johnson dipnetting at dusk on the Fraser River   62

4 Dipnetting at The Point   63

5 Bringing salmon back to The Point trailhead   64

6 Preparing salmon for smoking   65

7 Racks of salmon in the smokehouse   65

8 Angela George picking saskatoon berries   69

9 Elaine Ignatius gently taps soapberries into an open umbrella   70

10 Angela George with a home-made soapberry whip of shredded bark   71

11 Alfie Bowie enjoying soapberries in camp   71

12 Angela George scraping the outer bark of a balsam fir   73

13 Dorothy Johnson picking sage along Dog Creek Road   75

14 Site D: A cave above the Dog Creek Reserve   104

15 Site G: Angela and her grandchildren walking between remnants of pithouses   112

16 Site G: Three pithouse rings   114

17 Jimmy George and Alfie Bowie at Gustafson Lake camp   164

18 View of the Fraser River from Dog Creek Road   169

Maps

1 Peoples of the Northwest Coast and Plateau culture areas   30

2 James Teit's map of Shuswap territory (1909: 45)   32

3 Secwepemc territory (based on information from Teit [1909] and Duff [1965])   34

4 Sketch map of Alkali Lake Reserve No. 1 (RG 10, vol. 3681, file 12395-3)   38

5 Sketch map of Harper's Lake (RG 10, vol. 3681, file 12395-3)   47

6 Alkali Lake Indian Reserves   48

7 Key sites along Dog Creek Road   117

Figures

1 Guide to pronunciation in Secwepemctsín   xxiii

2 Government notice to Indian food fishermen   66

Preface

Leaving the town of Williams Lake, British Columbia, is Highway 20, which supplanted the 'grease trail' that Interior Peoples once used as a trade route to exchange goods for the oolichan oil brought by the Nuxalk People from Bella Coola. Highway 20 stretches west across the high, semi-arid Interior Plateau all the way to a precipitous drop down to the Northwest coast. This road connects with an ancient trail just before it reaches the east bank of the Fraser River. The old foot trail along the Fraser's bank became a horse path, then a wagon road, and now parts of it are even paved.

There are many stories associated with this path. In the Elders' lifetimes they once made camp and picked berries along the ancient trail on their way to 'town,' to Williams Lake, to trade, purchase supplies, or see the big annual Stampede that came with the first white settlers. Then, they say, it could take two days to get to Williams Lake, with the family in a wagon. They took the trip slowly, stopping often, and made camp on the hill over the Stampede grounds when they arrived. They came from their houses near springs and streams on the sidehills by the Fraser River, some thirty miles, or fifty kilometres, from the grease trail.

The land, once more heavily forested with jackpine and fir, is now mostly grassland and juniper, cleared to make way for the ranchers' free-ranging cattle, later for the harvest of the trees themselves, and finally for the power lines and the houses. Travelling along this old trail further out of town, one passes split-rail and Russell and snake fences, some a hundred years old – in this dry climate, they do not rot quickly. They are built above the earth, propped on top, as the hardpan, alkaline soil is hospitable to neither postholes nor posts. This is especially true now, in the middle of a multi-year drought. Where pot-hole lakes once dotted the landscape, catching the reflections of the golden-turning leaves of the cottonwoods in the still of autumn, now the water is brackish, the edges of the lakes encrusted in white alkali, formed in ring after ring to mark the old edges of the shrinking lakes.

Curving along the old road, one encounters wooden stacks of torn-down Russell fences, a new postholing machine, bright green treated posts, and the shiny barbed wire that will hold back the deer and the cattle and other travellers. 'They are straightening the road,' the Elder, David Johnson, tells me, 'they are taking out the bends.' Now that it's easier to finance new vehicles, the people of Alkali Lake can travel more quickly on the road; one of David Johnson's grandsons made it to Williams Lake in twenty-two minutes once when he found he had to drive through town and on to Kamloops to cash a winning lottery ticket.

The town is more accessible now to the older children who take the school bus along this road every day on the way to and from Williams Lake Sr Secondary. Still, to the people who live in Williams Lake, it seems a long way out of town. They are not all ranchers anymore. Many prefer not to drive beyond the pavement of town, to risk being bogged down in the 'loonshit,' as the alkaline soil is called when it becomes mud. It seems not worth the drive anyway, out to the place they used to call 'Alcohol Lake,' for all the drinking that went on at the reserve. The road was dangerous then, too, for people returning home to Alkali. A mother and her child once froze to death on their way home along it. At 40° below, everyone is cautious on its route.

By the third cattleguard on the road is an ancient battleground, now fenced for the reserve's horses, and beyond that the road joins Alkali Creek, with its old banks grown to high basalt cliffs that seem to catch fire at sunset. The old road is little more than a cart track where it fol-lows close by the sticky mud riverbed, and a newer part of the road branches off for a while. *Tsuktsékus* that place of the newer cut road is called, the word for an animal's claws gouging something, raking along the back of the hill. The old road and the cut road rejoin and wind down into the open valley, where spread out below in the spring is the green of the fields, the gold of the grasses on the sidehills, the rich darkness of the trees on the bluff, a glimmer of the lake in the dis-tance and the stream leading down to the Fraser, and always, in mud or dust, the cluster of log cabins and government houses that are crushed into Alkali Lake / Esketemc Indian Reserve Number 1.

Esḱet: Alkali Lake Indian Reservc No. 1

Before the governmcnt gave it that new name, the people had lived here, as well as further up and down the trail, but the priests decided they should all settle in this one place, by the first ranch in the Cariboo. And one by one, the families were roundcd up, and settled in this place, brought down from their meadows into the village with its long dirt track, to stay in the squat, square houses built on top of the ground, which proceed in two long lines away from the church – or toward it, depending on who is looking.

This is a study of the people who live there, the *Secwepemc* of *Esḱet*, the Shuswap of Alkali Lake, and of the trails they travcl and the tales they tell.

Acknowledgments

I wish to thank the people of Alkali Lake for their kindness and generous hospitality during my stay. I am especially grateful to those individuals who watched out for me, and quietly taught me in ways I am still discovering now. Angela George and her husband, the late Jimmy George, and their extended family receive my sincere thanks for sharing part of their lives with me. Dorothy Johnson always made me feel welcome; Betty Belanger devoted many hours and her expertise in the language to the review of transcriptions. To Dallas and Candice George I owe thanks for sharing their dear grandmother's time with me during our travels together. Lena Paul, Debbie Johnson, and the late Lorraine Johnson all opened their homes to me. I send my thanks to them and their families. Special thanks are also due to Phyllis and Andy Chelsea for their encouragement. The staff and students of the Sxoxomic School gave me a special opportunity to observe; Freddie Johnson, as principal, and the Secwepemctsín language teachers Celina Harry and Julianna Johnson welcomed me into their classroom. I would also like to thank Sharon Johnson, the late Mary Palmantier, Joan Gentles, Wendy and Dennis Carson, Lois Thain, and Tassie Nelson and members of her family, for their encouragement and support helped me find my way in the community.

The support of my doctoral committee at the University of Washington is gratefully acknowledged. Their guidance helped to shape the dissertation on which this book is based. Eugene S. Hunn, as chair, has shared in countless ways; his generous provision of office space meant that I had both the benefit of his scholarly insights and suggestions and a ready ear for my many questions.

Many people have commented on papers I have given at professional meetings, and their insights have helped to shape those papers into the chapters of this book. The encouragement and insightful comments provided by Dell and Virginia Hymes at meetings and in letters throughout the years will always be appreciated. Pamela Amoss's mentorship, comments on papers, and thoughtful scholarship continue to serve as a guide. Jay Miller read drafts of the dissertation on which this book is based, shared his own books, and unstintingly gave of his time; his contributions have been invaluable. Generous comments by Henry Glassie and Michael Silverstein on conference papers that became two of the chapters of this book offered me much encouragement as a young graduate student. I am delighted to have met all of these scholars, who devote such care and attention to students and colleagues, and hope I can live up to the example they have set in my own professional career.

This book has benefited greatly from conversations Carl Urion, to my continued delight. He and Walter Lightning deserves special thanks for their insights on Place and Story. It is a surprise, after eight years at the University of Alberta, to realize how much colleagues and their kin have become our family here; thanks to Michael and Margaret Asch and the Urions for more than can be measured. I am grateful for the support of Regna Darnell, Lisa Valentine and Fred Gleach, and for their very insistent encouragement to publish this work. Expert suggestions from Lindy-Lou Flynn and Carolyn Butler Palmer have been extremely helpful in revising this work for publication.

Beth Suprenant generously contributed her time and skills as a graphic artist to the preparation of the figures, including hand-drafting several of the maps. David Myhrum and Georgina Saranchuk deserve thanks for their contributions: map 1 and the index, respectively. Rodney Cook receives thanks for his work on the latest version of a still-evolving Lushootseed computer font. Alex Schwartzer and my brother, David Palmer, assisted in the rendering of special characters for Secwepemctsín. Mark Ebert stood ready to assist in what ever ways were needed. The staff at the British Columbia Provincial Archives and the Royal British Columbia Museum in Victoria, and the Map Librarians at the University of British Columbia were unfailingly helpful; their skills and knowledge made my time spent in their company both stimulating and productive. Thanks are also due to John St James for his careful copy-editing and to Anne Laughlin and Virgil Duff of University of Toronto Press for their continued encouragement. Fellow wrriote girrlz – Ara, Heather, Julie, Cecily – read, commented, and cared. Thank you.

Conversations with Crisca Bierwert and Marcelle Gareau have helped me at many stages in the process of research and writing. At the University of British Columbia, Jay Powell provided encouragement and support, John Barker thoughtfully obtained library privileges for me, and Patricia Marchak provided authorization for an affiliation with the university. Brian Compton provided sage advice in the cataloguing of plant specimens, and Dwight Gardiner offered linguistic insights. I have benefited greatly from many conversations through the years with Elizabeth Furniss, and from the high quality of her publications about Alkali Lake and the Interior.

The Ronald Olson Fellowship made it possible for me to embark on a course of graduate studies. Funding for research was provided by the Social Sciences and Humanities Research Council of Canada, the Wenner-Gren Foundation for Anthropological Research, the Melville and Elizabeth Jacobs Research Fund of the Whatcom Museum Society, the Phillips Fund of the American Philosophical Society, and the University of Washington Graduate Student Research Travel Fund. Further research has been made possible by the Harriet Winspear Sheila Watson Fellowship, administered by the Faculty of Arts, the University of Alberta. I gratefully acknowledge the financial support and confidence of these granting agencies, and offer my thanks to the individuals who created the supporting endowments for these funds.

I cannot give enough thanks to my parents, Leigh and Evelyn Palmer; the head of my Lushootseed family, Vi (taqᵂšəblu) Hilbert; my husband, Alf Shepherd; and our daughter, Elizabeth. Their love and support marks every page of this work.

Notes on Language, Transcription, and Pronunciation

Shuswap, or *Secwepemctsín*, and English at Alkali Lake

Shuswap, or Secwepemctsín, is a member of the Salish family of languages. Seven of the twenty-three languages in the Salish family, including Secwepemctsín, are spoken in the Plateau area of North America, and form the Interior Salish division (Thompson and Kinkade 1990). The Salish family of languages has not been reliably linked to any larger phylum by linguists.

At Alkali Lake, most people of fifty years and over speak Secwepemctsín with a high degree of fluency. Some of the eldest of the elders, in their eighties and above, speak little English, and, especially if hard of hearing, are spoken to in Secwepemctsín by others to enhance communication. The middle-aged members of the community, in discussing relative proficiency in the language, sometimes remark that the eldest members of the community speak 'deeper Shuswap' than they. 'Deep Shuswap' includes a richer vocabulary and a pronunciation less affected by the phonemic inventory of English.

Community members between the ages of forty and sixty all speak English as well as Secwepemctsín. I heard many conversations in Secwepemctsín among middle-aged individuals in passing, but when I entered their company, their conversation shifted easily into English, so as to include me. Although I worked principally with Elders over the age of forty, most of the tape recordings I made were of English speech. As any tape recording of activities made me a focused observer of conversation, I was able to tape record conversation in Secwepemctsín mainly when someone in the group understood little English (and then translation would be provided to include all participants).

Some discrete terms such as plant or place names, and verbs associated with particular harvesting techniques, were given in Secwepemctsín, often in association with the actual places and plants, embedded in narratives that were otherwise delivered in English. The Elders followed a rule of politeness, despite my urgings to talk in Secwepemctsín for the tape recorder, that one should not speak to a person in a way that they are not capable of understanding. In this, they share with the fine Lushootseed, or dxʷləšucid, orators of Coast Salish territory an understanding that one's words should be spoken in a way that they can be remembered and understood by the entire audience.

Conflicts between the systems of discourse that my Secwepemc interlocutors and I use are sometimes apparent, and provide evidence that speakers from Alkali Lake continue to employ discourse conventions that are inherently Secwepemctsín, even when speaking English. While Ridington (1990, 1992), Brody (1981), and others have noted aspects of this phenomenon with respect to other indigenous groups in British Columbia, such conflicts have been systematically described by Scollon and Scollon (1981). The Scollons have found that for ethnic Athapaskans, features of indigenous discourse systems persist despite the use of English; whether speakers of their ancestral language or not, they are 'socialized to a set of communicative patterns that have their roots in the Athapaskan languages' (1981: 12), which has the potential to affect all linguistic communication. More recently, work on 'Indian Englishes' of Regna Darnell (1992, 1993) and Lisa Valentine (1994) has covered various aspects of these communicative patterns in Englishes of southwestern Ontario Native discourse.

The lack of pronominal reference to gender in Secwepemctsín is a readily identifiable feature of (especially older) Secwepemctsín speakers' English (cf. J. Miller 1990: xxxiii–xxxiv). This manifests itself in the interchangeability of 'he' with 'she,' and 'him' with 'her,' in references to individuals. This feature is evident throughout the narratives quoted in this book, and has not been altered in the printed text. It appears in the transcription, as this interchangeability is generally accepted in speech among speakers of English at Alkali Lake. I have observed one eight-year-old child at Alkali Lake tease another for this Secwepemctsín styling, and the other continuing its use in his peer's presence. (It can be noted that, in much of Canadian English, there is a trend toward the development of genderless language, as reflected in terms such as 'waitperson,' and the use of 'their' as a third-person singular form.) The writer and poet Jeannette Armstrong has recently discussed the ways in which speakers of another Interior Salish language, Okanagan, use a style of English that reflects an (artful) avoidance of pronomial reference (1998). I am convinced by Armstrong's work that the choice not to alter the transcription presented here to standard English is a reasonable one.

Children on the reserve all speak English as their first language, and are not generally fluent in Secwepemctsín. Although children seldom speak more than single sentences in Secwepemctsín outside of the classroom without prodding, there is evidence of passive linguistic ability in some children, who immediately respond to their elders' quickly spoken requests for assistance, given in Secwepemctsín.

Language classes are conducted several times per week in each grade at the reserve's Sxoxomic School. Children generally have good Secwepemctsín pronunciation skills, as is reflected in their English as well as their Secwepemctín. In their language classes, which begin in preschool and continue through grade 10, they are first taught the alphabet, vocabulary words, simple sentences, and phrases. Both language instructors are fluent, loving, and enthusiastic. They strive to teach the children about their culture as well as their language. For children at Alkali Lake, to 'speak good Shuswap' has connotations of cultural knowledge as well as linguistic ability.

The English spoken reflects remnants of the lexical choices (e.g., 'vehicle' for 'car') and the lilting pronunciation of the Irish nuns who instructed Alkali Lake children in English at St Joseph's Mission during the residential school era (e.g., [fíləm] for film). For the generation now in their sixties and seventies, who had the most contact with the Sisters at St Joseph's, this type of pronunciation, complete with epenthetic shwa (ə), as above, is especially noticeable in the reserve's English name, 'Alkali' ([ɛlɔkʌloy])

The variation in the pronunciation of Secwepmctsín /s/ (where /s/ = [s/š]; A. Kuipers 1974: 24) carries over to the Secwepemctsín speaker's pronunciation of English words, where [s] and [š] are often interchanged. This varies by speaker, but the tendency is strongest for the use of [š] in word-initial position in cases where [s] is used by speakers of Standard English, and toward substituting [s] for Standard English [š] intervocalicly (e.g., mission is pronounced by many as [mɪsɪn]).

A Note on Transcription Choices for Tape-recorded Speech

English speakers are accustomed to treating signals of continued

attention as background information, foregrounding the more sub-
stantive speech to such an extent that they seldom include references
to the signals of continued attention as such in their reports of conversations. In order to indicate this in print, signals of continued attention
from audience members are indicated by their placement to the right
of the narrative, in italics, as suggested by Dell Hymes (personal communication). A selection of transcripts included in the appendix
reflects all of the researcher's (typically Anglo-Canadian) signals of
continued attention. These signals originate in a system of discourse
that sometimes clashed with the Secwepemec system, and held the
potential to redirect talk. I follow Ridington's (1988) example in this
matter.

The transcription notation presented in Gumperz (1982: xi) is incorporated for the following:

[conversation overlap
( ) unintelligible word

An initial ... in a transcription indicates that the tape recorder was
turned on in the middle of a word or phrase.

Tape-recorded speech encapsulated in square brackets are orientational notes, as in the following example:

Andie: [2.6 miles past the cattleguard]

These are delivered *sotto voce*, and are not part of the conversational
exchange. They are only included in the complete transcripts in the
appendix.

The notation [*break*] in a transcription means that the tape recorder
was turned off and then on again.

Transcribed narratives are broken into lines according to pauses in
speech, following Tedlock (1983). Pauses of relatively even lengths are
marked by line breaks. Longer pauses are marked by a blank line, even
longer ones by two blank lines, and the longest are more fully
described.

Increased volume is noted by the use of capitals, as in:

and put it wherever you're sore
Your KNEES

An audible catch or quick repair in speech is marked by a dash, as in:

and we used to s–walk in there.

Where the speaker runs on rapidly without pause, for longer than the width of the page allows, the narrative phrase is continued, indented, on the next line. Lines are *not* indented to indicate verses or stanzas, *contra* Hymes (1981).

Transcripts of tapes may provide a way to ensure that the words of the people I worked with are heard, even with the inevitable layers of interpretation on my part. The appendix contains transcripts from two interviews, a small sample from the over 100 hours of tapes on which this work is based. Recorded during car rides, the words on tape are often muffled by the roar of the engine, the pounding of the car against the dirt roads, or the joyful noise of children in the back seat. Betty Belanger, Angela George's daughter, has invested many hours in checking portions of the transcripts and deciphering previously unintelligible sections of her mother's speech. The painstaking task of fully transcribing these documents is ongoing in some cases, while in others context has entirely swallowed content, and transcription must wait until technology permits us to better eliminate certain background sounds, and amplify speech. I expect to be analysing aspects of these tapes and transcripts for many years to come, but include two of them here, so that a fuller sense of the overall flow of conversation may be realized by readers. Also, I expect that these transcripts will be of interest to people of Alkali Lake who may chose to read this book.

Many of the transcripts and tapes are also being circulated, outside of this publication, within the families of individuals who consented to be recorded. The efforts of Vi Hilbert and her co-contributors to circulate transcripts and translations of Lushootseed texts (Hilbert et al. 1990) to families of storytellers, before publication of the texts with analysis, have impressed on me the importance of such action. Similarly, when *Life Lived Like a Story*, authored by Julie Cruikshank in collaboration with Yukon area Elders Angela Sidney, Kitty Smith, and Annie Ned, was published in 1990, *Tagish Tlaagú: Tagish Stories* (by Mrs Angela Sidney and recorded by Julie Cruikshank) had already been in circulation for eight years. Most recently, the warm reception given William Elmendorf's *Twana Narratives* (1993), published over fifty years after his initial fieldwork, and in the last years of his life, provides encouragement to circulate transcripts of narratives within the communities where they are recorded.

The Transcription of Secwepemctsín and Lushootseed Words

The transcription of Secwepemctsín words in this book follows Aert Kuipers's practical orthography (1975; cf. Kuipers 1974), except in passages quoted from Teit (1909), in which case transcription follows the original. Dr Kuipers designed two separate orthographies for the language, one that he designates as 'practical,' the other 'technical.' I have chosen to use the practical orthography, as it is the one most commonly employed in the classroom by native speakers at Alkali Lake. Lushootseed orthography is as presented in Hess (1976).

A guide to pronunciation of Secwepemctsín words in the text, derived from Kuipers's description of the technical orthography, follows.

CONSONANTS (C)		OBSTRUENTS (K)			RESONANTS (R)					NASALS and LIQUIDS / GLIDES
		Plos.		Fric.						
		plain	glott.		plain	glott.				
labial		p	p'		m	m'	labial			NASALS and LIQUIDS
dent.-lateral		t	t'	ll	n l	n' l'	dental			
dent.-palatal		ts	ts'	s	y i	y' i7	plain		palatal-velar	
velar	plain	k	k'	c	r	r'	velarized			GLIDES
velar	round.	kw	k'w	cw						
uvular	plain	q	q'	x	g	g'	plain	uvularized		
uvular	round.	qw	q'w	xw	gw	g'w	round.		laryngal-uvular	
laryngal	plain		7	h			—	plain		
laryngal	—				w u	w' u7	round.			

VOWELS (V)	Approximate N. American English equivalent
i	pizza or ski
e	bed
a	father
u	rude
o	for

Figure 1   Guide to pronunciation in Secwepemctsín

MAPS OF EXPERIENCE

Chapter 1

Introduction: A Discourse-Centred Approach to Understanding

I went to Alkali Lake, British Columbia, as a young student, with some idea of what my chosen field, linguistic anthropology, was supposed to be. I had the guidance of Vi taqʷšəblu Hilbert, my professor of Lushootseed Salish language and oral literature at the University of Washington, who encouraged me to go and introduce myself to the people in that place. taqʷšəblu had told me a great deal about the respectful approach to Story, including the acknowledgment that Stories may be guides, but only if the listener is mindful that the teller is far more than a mere vessel for the telling. While the ostensible focus of this work is on talk, the one who writes down talk is responsible for far more than a representation of people's words.

I received careful training from my teacher, who modelled the respectful interaction between people that is the foundation on which Story is reformulated in every telling. I am still learning to convey that very approach – that social contract between interlocutors, over and above the transcribed words through which it can be represented – in a language which communicates that emergent understanding back to my interlocutors in the Alkali Lake community, to my teachers, to my fellow linguistic anthropologists, and to my self.

This book is an examination of how various kinds of talk, situated in particular places on the landscape, and in travel between them, allow that knowledge to be carried forward, reconstituted, reflected upon, enriched, and ultimately relocated, by and for new interlocutors, in new experiences, and sometimes new places. Specific conversations, stories, and other narratives presented here are tightly bound up in the circumstances of travel to fishing, hunting, and gathering places in a specific territory and time with particular groups of family and friends.

I argue here that engagement in the traditional practices of hunting and gathering creates shared lived experiences between individuals, while recreating a known social context in which existing knowledge of the land may be effectively shared and acted upon. It is through such practices, and such shared lived experiences, that an anthropologist, engaged as both a participant and observer, can learn something of what would be important to tell back about the Stories that unfold in those circumstances. Through such experiences, a newcomer to a culture can learn to attend to the context of the words.

I suggest here that whatever the particulars of the exchanges described in this book, it is the ways of listening to information, and the ways of conveying it, which I was exposed to at Alkali Lake, that can open up some possibilities for discussions across cultures regarding the strong associations of Peoples to Place, Language, and Story. In the midst of several decades of land claims negotiations between First Nations and the Crown, I hope that providing some references to everyday discourse in hunting and gathering contexts will provide some room for more listening to occur.

Because I was not raised in Secwepemc territory, I learned about the land, the stories, and the lives of the people I travelled with there as a newcomer. I found that the exchange of talk does not necessarily lead to shared understanding, nor even to the negotiation of the terms by which meaning is constituted. This book is a continuation, on my part, of the effort to understand a social framework with reference to observed and recorded communicative practice; it is my attempt to apprehend what it is that a newcomer's ear (and eye, and heart) might at first miss as directed communication. It is also a reflection on that particular genre which was not originally apparent to me in those communicative practices, which I have learned to identify as Story. Story, with a capital 'S,' can be considered as a bundle; carried in a light, portable package, unwrapped in each telling, shared, and then wrapped up for another time, in the memories of those who attend to what it has to offer.

My initial conceptions of how Story would be shared by speakers of Shuswap, or Secwepemctsín, at Alkali Lake were influenced by my experience of taqʷšəblu's practice in another Salish culture and language, Lushootseed, or Puget Salish. taqʷšəblu has made it her life's work to foster an appreciation and understanding for the Lushootseed world and language. To accomplish this goal, she maintains a heavy schedule of storytelling engagements at universities, bookstores, museums, and festivals. As part of unwrapping the gift of Story at any event, taqʷšəblu chooses which stories she will tell based on what she learns the particular audience 'needs to hear.' She has worked to instil a respectful way of listening, to expand our capacities to recognize what is offered to each of us, and to model ways that we can contribute to the Stories' care. She steadfastly refuses to provide a program in advance of the event. Each of her tellings, each narrative, is part of the discussion she engages in with that particular group of people who have requested that she come and share with them. She often has to remind those audiences that what she is sharing with them is not 'entertainment,' but sʔyəyəhub, or Stories. Explicit references to the interpretive frame she wishes her audience to learn to use, and her understandings of both her frames and theirs, are part of the telling.[1] Often, an audience's attention needs to be directed by her labelling the social action there unfolding: 'I am going to tell you a Story ...'

Once, while relating a story about Blackberry,[2] taqʷšəblu mentioned that her own opportunity to hear a particular story came while she was visiting with her aunt as they sat in the shade after picking berries. Her aunt, Susie Sampson Peter (gʷəqʷulčəʔ), was nearly blind, and so although she could pick berries, her hands were often cruelly torn by spines and slivers. As a young girl, taqʷšəblu would sit, patiently picking the thorns out of her aunt's fingers, and listening to what she had to tell. It was this very small vignette, of a young girl and her dear aged aunt, that pulled the stories I heard from my professor, and those I read in books, away from the classroom, away from imagined settings of the campfire and the kitchen table, and out onto the land. With taqʷšəblu's experience in mind, I set out to conduct research at Alkali Lake with the goal of recording tellings of such stories in hunting and gathering contexts.

Acknowledging Contributors and Honouring Voices

Ethnographic research is a collaborative endeavour; it cannot be accomplished without the participation of the people whose world the anthropologist wishes to explore. Often in the practice of ethnographic *writing*, however, the other voices drop out. I have chosen a narrative style of ethnography to present the process of discovery that is field-work, as it is my intention that the voices of the people I worked with at Alkali Lake be heard along with mine. My wish is to contribute something of value to my collaborators as well as to my academic colleagues. I consulted with many people in the Alkali Lake community over the course of sixteen months of fieldwork, between 1987 and 1989. With regard to the tape recording of narratives, my chief consultants were Angela and Jimmy George, a married couple in their mid-sixties who speak Secwepemctsín as their first language, and English as their second. It is their words and actions that provide the material for this book, and they are quoted directly, and at length.[3] Although it had been the generally enforced practice of the Canadian government, and of the churches contracted to provide education in the early 1900s through the mid-1960s, to send children away from home to the Cariboo Mission's Indian residential school for seven to twelve years of education in English, neither Jimmy nor Angela George attended the school. They thereby avoided some of the consequences of attending, and were able to accompany their own Elders in hunting and gathering activities from an early age. Angela (along with at least three other female Elders at Alkali Lake) has never learned to read, and Jimmy learned to read at home. Their learning took other forms; stories were told in ways that could be remembered, understood, and passed on. The Georges display an intimate knowledge of and strong familiarity with the land, and were willing to share their times out fishing and gathering with me. They are also kind and generous people; along with their children and grandchildren, they put up with the stumblings of this researcher with much patience and affection. Much of what I will present in the following chapters is an attempt on my part to let them know what it is that I am still learning from them, and what it is that I am still puzzling over, after all of these years.

The reserve's English name, Alkali Lake, and the Secwepemctsín name Esket are given here rather than a pseudonym, contrary to the sometime convention in anthropology of concealing identities (cf. Szklut and Reed 1991 for a careful consideration of the topic). The unique, extremely public nature of Alkali Lake among Indian communities in Canada makes this appropriate. The community had gone from an over 98 per cent alcoholism rate to a sobriety rate of 95 per cent in twenty years, and chose to share this victory with the rest of the world. In 1987, the community made a film, The Honour of All, about their struggle with alcoholism, which has been widely shown on television in Canada and abroad. Individuals in the band chose to share their personal experiences in this way, and, in most cases, portrayed themselves in the film.

Newspaper articles and the publication of interviews with band members in numerous popular publications including the *Reader's Digest* and the *Los Angeles Times* following the airing of the film are indications of the community members' willingness to serve as examples for others struggling toward sobriety. The tremendous impact they have had in galvanizing other communities' efforts, and on the lives of the many individuals who have flooded the band office with cards and letters, are testaments to the film's effect. In the years following the premiere of *The Honour of All*, several television programs about the Alkali Lake community have aired in Canada. A CBC documentary for the television program *Man Alive* was filmed while I was resident on the reserve. It focused on how band members were coping with the after-effects of sexual abuse experienced by many who attended residential school at the Cariboo Mission up until the 1960s. The director for the *Man Alive* series, David Cherniak, returned to Alkali Lake to film a four-part documentary, *Reservation*, in 2001. Some of the figures who gained wide public attention from *The Honour of All* a generation earlier appear in the documentary.

The issues of voice and authority, and awareness of the specific power relations inherent in the role of the ethnographer, have been concerns of Americanist anthropological study since its beginnings. These issues have received renewed attention from postmodernist theoreticians, who have also placed an emphasis on multivocality in writing, and on a discourse-centred approach to ethnography (Clifford and Marcus 1986; Marcus and Fischer 1986). The works of anthropologists from Boas forward have been considered valuable by members of First Nations communities, not because of their theories and interpretations, but because of what is actually recorded of the words of the People. It is my estimation that the Secwepemc people I know do not need their culture reinterpreted for them. The audience that is appreciative of such an analysis includes those anthropologists, cultural geographers, historians, and others who have not had the privilege of knowing of their lives from first-hand experience. Aboriginal people may take an interest in seeing how others see them, and appreciate others' struggles toward a clearer perception of humanity, but I have found that it is more the detailed documentary information that anthropologists provide, rather than the anthropologists' interpretation of that information, which is appreciated as a record of their past.

It should also be noted that in British Columbia Aboriginal voices have been relatively successful in being heard (whether or not their messages have been productively acted upon) in the last twenty years.

First Nations in British Columbia, and the Salish Peoples in particular, have enjoyed substantial economic power through their political unions. The Union of BC Indian Chiefs and the BC Association of Non-Status Indians each have had as many as two hundred employees on payroll and budgets of two million Canadian dollars, thus attracting the continued interest of the popular press (Tennant 1990: 165).

There is a great difference between what outside perspectives mean to Indigenous Peoples and what they mean to members of the dominant national culture. Members of non-Native cultures may be interested in and appreciative of what others think of them, but for them, outsiders' perspectives seldom have an impact at the level of the individual. Foreign policy and domestic policy are quite different spheres to the average Canadian or US citizen, and few unmodified outside perceptions filter through the insular layers of domestic news media. Native people in Canada and the United States, however, are bombarded almost every day by people looking in, establishing governmental policies or at least offering opinions, and telling them who they are.

Entering the Community

Indian Reserves in Canada are sovereign territory, and so before my first trip to Alkali Lake, I set out to gain permission to visit. The anthropologist Robert MacLaury urged me to contact Andy Chelsea, who was then the elected Chief of the Alkali Lake Band,[4] and his wife, Phyllis Chelsea, of the band's Curriculum Development Committee. Jay Powell, who had worked with the committee to create language textbooks (e.g., Powell, Jensen, and Chelsea 1979), and Alan Haig-Brown added their encouragement. I telephoned the Chelseas, and made arrangements to meet them at the local shopping mall in the town of Williams Lake. I outlined my interests to them and they were agreeable to my proceeding with the project.

At that time, I naively thought that my familiarity with one (Coast) Salish language, Lushootseed, would go a long way toward preparing me to work in another, the Interior Salish language of Secwepemctsín. I would later find the division between Coast and Interior Salish languages to be greater than I anticipated; I was dismayed to discover I had already identified all of the common Lushootseed-Secwepemctsín cognates within my first week of fieldwork, and that the linguist Aert Kuipers listed only seventy-two paired entries for Secwepemctsín and Lushootseed in his etymological index (1974: 293).

Before I began the main work of recording, and while I was a new-comer to the reserve, I spent two to three hours of each school day in the band-run school, working on learning Secwepemctsín and getting to know the children on the reserve. They all spoke English as their first language, but Native language and culture classes were part of the standard curriculum in each grade. I am extremely grateful to the staff and students of the Sxoxomic School for permitting me to observe in their classes. I have attempted to return their kindness by providing various services and goods back to the school. I substitute taught the language class for one week, while the very fluent and enthusiastic language teachers, Elders Julianna Johnson and Celina Harry, were away at a workshop. This may have provided a break for the other teachers, but I fear the benefits to the students were dubious, as I was attempting to develop some innovative, but upon reflection, impracti-cal, lesson plans for classroom language instruction. The students bore my efforts with good humour.

Events unfolding in British Columbia in 1987 made me especially conscious of the costs and benefits to the band that might be associated with my study. Before going to Alkali Lake, I had paid a visit to the Secwepemc Cultural Society in Kamloops, to let them know I hoped to conduct fieldwork in Secwepemc territory. I arrived there at a time when a court case involving an anthropologist testifying in potential opposition to a Salish band was much in the provincial and national news. One member of the Cultural Society was quite dismayed to find another anthropologist on the doorstep. I might not have proceeded any further with the study were it not for the fact I had already made an appointment to visit members of the Alkali Lake band.

I considered James Teit, who worked with the Secwepemc and other Interior groups at the turn of the last century, to be a model ethnogra-pher. His tireless work to see Native rights recognized, his payment of consultants, his competence in the bush, and his humility and industry, as evidenced in his correspondence with Marius Barbeau, Edward Sapir, and Franz Boas, all impressed me very much.[5] Despite this record, the Salish writer Christine Quintasket, or Mourning Dove, per-ceived Teit's work of recording stories in Interior Salish territory as unfair competition to the preparation of her own work, to be published as *Coyote Stories* (1933).[6] Mourning Dove was not aware that Teit felt an obligation to pay people for their time, and that he had obtained some (very limited) outside funding to do so under the direction of Franz Boas and Edward Sapir, through the American Museum of Natural

History and the Canadian Anthropological Division, housed in the Department of Mines.[7]

Mourning Dove's response to Teit's efforts reminds me that with the best of intentions, an anthropologist's presence can create negative impacts. This has been taken into consideration by organizations with influence over the practice of anthropology. As a member of the American Anthropological Association, I am bound by their ethics guidelines (1990). As a faculty member of the University of Alberta, I am also guided by university protocols, and those laid out in the Canadian Tri-Council Statement on Ethics. Although one can never anticipate all the negative impacts of fieldwork, I endeavoured to keep the range of possibilities in mind.

The very first practical concern, the particular field site selected, at once imposed certain considerations: Would the very presence of another person have more detrimental than positive effects on a community? Could the community accommodate another person, given its very limited water supply? Would the shelter for one anthropologist in a village where many are on a long waiting list for housing (which was growing longer owing to recent legislation [cf. Joseph 1991]) oblige another soul to live in unbearable accommodations? When I arrived, the community had approximately four hundred residents, and so the addition of one individual would certainly be noted by all.[8] With these considerations in mind, I did not initially request permission to live on the reserve. In addition, I felt it would be best if people had a chance to get to know me first, and so I stayed with a Euro-Canadian family that lived near the reserve. Dennis and Wendy Carson were most gracious hosts, and I am very grateful to them for their hospitality. They lived halfway between the main reserve, Indian Reserve (IR) No. 1, and the town of Williams Lake. After four months, I was invited to stay at a house on IR No. 2, which obviated most of the concerns I had about living on the main reserve. Ultimately, I moved to the main reserve and stayed with a family there during the second course of fieldwork in 1989. On subsequent trips, I have stayed both on IR No. 1 and on other reserves. I was by then familiar to the members of the community, and was (I hope) able to manage my impacts on the community with a greater sophistication as to what could be accommodated.

I had not realized when I set out that the positive impacts of fieldwork on a community cannot always be anticipated, either. I had considered my ability to provide transportation to community members as a possible minor benefit of my research. It proved to be most important, as gasoline in the area cost fifty to sixty cents per litre even then, and the backroads' wear and tear on vehicles was considerable and costly. I was able to provide trips to 'town' (Williams Lake) for any who cared to accompany me, and transportation for Elders who wanted to go berry picking or fishing, or simply to visit friends on other reserves. The latter type of excursions related directly to my purposes, and came to be the main times when I would tape-record stories (cf. Brody 1981: xvii–xix). As we drove, I would leave the tape recorder turned on to collect whatever was said, if permission of the occupants of the vehicle could be secured; and I made copies of the tapes for the participants to do with as they wished. I thanked people for participating in taped interviews with copies of the tapes and, as appropriate, with cash or a gift.

In addition to the extended fieldwork over sixteen months, follow-up visits, each of a week or more to the reserve on my part, and visits to my home by Alkali Lake residents have continued almost every summer to the present. These trips have allowed for the clarification and refinement of certain points during the writing of this book. Elders who have rich experience in their respective, overlapping subsistence territories served as principal consultants. So as not to prejudge which was the relevant information to record, continuous streams of conversation during travel were recorded, often for the full length of a ninety-minute tape or more. When I found it inadvisable to tape record, for reasons of confidentiality, I turned off the recorder. Duplicate tapes deposited in the community archive were occasionally further edited to maintain confidentiality.

I photographed as much of our travels as I could. Although the costs of publication preclude the inclusion of a larger number of images in this document, photographs nonetheless served as important supplementary references for the identification of places and plants described in the audio recordings, and provide a record of our travels. They are also precious in that many of the dear ones photographed have since passed on, and these photographs, often taken during very happy times in travel, can serve as reminders of more than mere fieldwork.[9]

The standard anthropological technique of participant observation was employed throughout the study. Tape recordings were made during travel and at resource sites. These sites included salmon, trout, and kokanee fishing areas and associated processing camps and smoke-houses, berrying spots, medicinal plant beds, sage-picking areas, and hunting camps. All of these sites of subsistence activity required travel out of the village, and into less frequented areas, where I was to find that stories are often told about experiences on the land.

One of the reasons for using participant observation in hunting and gathering contexts as a methodological approach is that it is an effective way of investigating what might otherwise be overlooked, not because a story could not be told in another context, but because it may more likely be remembered in a context that contains natural features, places, animals, plants, or activities associated with the story. Grounded in past oral tradition and vital to the transmission of cultural knowledge, Secwepemc place names and narratives told in travel past specific sites form an oral map of the landscape and its resources, mooring remembrance and ideology to place.

The stories I heard in travel to key sites were not often explicitly marked off as such. Rather, travel often provided the occasion for narratives that included references to the presence or absence of game, or of particular plants, to water or shelter, to routes of travel, to the specific geography of the places encountered. I would later recognize the presentation of canonical creation stories and their intersection with life story narratives within the discourse of place I was exposed to, but during my first year at Alkali, I struggled just to understand what the point of much of the talk was. My imported expectations concerning the social conventions of narrative construction, and the 'proper' ordering of elements in conversation were getting in the way.

Fortunately for me, the anthropologist who studies this sphere of discourse must necessarily enter into it. In so doing, one will affect and contribute to the discourse in some way, for discourse is brought into being through interaction; it exists *between* individuals, as Greg Urban (1991) has pointed out. I was treated to an active attempt at engagement on the part of my interlocutors. What I encountered and recorded with them forced me to rapidly do away with my initial assumptions. A lot of stumbling around on the way to a nascent sense of communicative competence made even the smallest personal discovery of appropriate entry into talk in that new place an exciting event. It made me thankful that communication was possible at all.

I now smilingly tell my students that one of the reasons that linguistic anthropologists (at least, of my sort) are drawn to the discipline is that we have such a hard time communicating with anyone, we have had to make it our full-time study just to communicate clearly with others in daily life. We sometimes make this worse by using a code that is not amenable to penetration by those outside of the discipline. As one guilty party, I will now endeavour to explain a path through our metalanguage, or our language about language, which informs and influences the theories applied here. I will begin with few words about 'narrative,' about the associated term 'discourse' and about those who engage in discourse, the interlocutors.

Narrative and Discourse, Discourse Systems, and Systems of Discourse Analysis

'Narrative' and 'discourse' are, at best, slippery terms, as Charlotte Linde (1993: 223-4) has noted. They are part of a hierarchical description of language that includes the more easily defined units of phone and phoneme, phrase and sentence. The study of narrative takes as its focus a string of speech from a single or choral voice. William Labov's conception of narrative, which he defined with respect to narratives of personal experience, is 'one method of recapitulating past experience by matching a verbal sequence of clauses to the sequence of events which (it is inferred) actually occurred.' A narrative consists, at a minimum, of 'a sequence of two clauses which are *temporally ordered*' (Labov 1972: 359–60; emphasis in original). In other words, at a minimum, a state is established in a clause as uttered by the speaker, followed by some alteration in the state in the following clause.

Labov's discussion of temporal order in defining a narrative, however useful it may otherwise be, does not in itself take into account the other systems of ordering that may be referenced in the extralinguistic component of the narrative process. Such systems can include reference to the land, through the very occupation of a particular place and time by given speakers. This is not the fault of Labov's description of narrative, which focuses on language-internal phenomena, but such a focus does not encompass that very quality which separates words on the page from that which makes those words 'narrative' to a linguistic anthropologist interested in the relationship of talk to social process. That quality is the located unfolding of spoken words, which through the process of utterance in and of itself takes up a span of time. This sense of time is extralinguistic, but it cannot be separated from the words uttered without removing a fundamental quality of that which is more than just words. Just as we tease out the complexities of potentials for language, and consider syntax as a set of what is possible through a set formulated equations, we must consider other, sometimes unrecognized, potentials that can also be activated, by reference to language-external contexts that are resources to speakers of a particular language-in-culture. Social, as well as referential, meaning must be accounted for if we are to fully consider narrative as part of a system of making sense.

The scope of the term discourse, as I employ it, is tightly focused. I reserve the term *discourse* to refer to specific, reportable interchanges between individual speakers and hearers. In order to explain the interpretive framework I employ in the study of those reported interchanges, however, I must briefly account for other, interpenetrating theoretical orientations current in linguistic and sociocultural anthropology, which claim related uses of the term. In describing these uses, Roger Spielmann points out that 'at the level of discourse analysis, ... there is very little agreement between the major traditions. There are no agreed labels and fewer agreed structures' (1998: 149). This is even true of the work among linguistic anthropologists who may at first appear to be examining similar phenomena in their studies of discourse. The difference between analytical traditions is also reflected in differences in methodology and topics of analysis.

In sociocultural anthropology in general, the term discourse is increasingly used, in a broad metaphorical sense, to refer to engagement in a whole body of communicative practices and communications between and within groups as delineated by a situated observer (as many informed by the work of Michel Foucault, 1972). In order to avoid confusion, I use the terms *system of discourse* and *discourse systems* when referring to discourse in this Foucauldian sense.

Conversation analysis is another area of study often referenced in linguistic anthropology as a form of discourse analysis. In Roger Spielmann's work on Ojibwe discourse, for example, the focus is on the analysis of conversation with an emphasis on content (topic) analysis in 'extending procedures and analytical categories used in descriptive linguistics beyond the level of the sentence' (1998: 50). In Spielmann's methodological and theoretical tradition, 'LDA [Linguistic Discourse Analysis] aims to discover and describe a complete roster of the features that contribute to the purpose of a particular discourse or stretch of talk' (1998: 149). Spielmann's tradition of discourse analysis, which can be called features analysis to distinguish it from other kinds of discourse analysis, is very useful in the writing of rules that are sensitive to specific contexts in which talk is situated, including, for example, politeness rules and rules for the use of deictics. A well-known example of this kind of work is to be found in the work of Charles Frake, including 'How to Ask for a Drink in Subanun' (1966). This kind of analysis is also helpful for describing conversations as types, instantiated in particular conversations under study, with typicalities deduced in accordance with an assumption that the conversations under study are examples of widely shared types of intracultural exchange. The test of such work is to evaluate how effectively it describes the rules that will allow a non-native speaker to achieve communicative competence in a given community.

Although discourse analysts may assert in common that change is fundamental to a living communication system, tacit assumptions behind the models used differ. In some approaches, the cultural systems under study are theorized as closed, but potentially penetrable, as in Spielmann's and Frake's examples. In others, such as the speech act theory of Austin (1962) and Searle (1969, 1979), the systems are seen as closed and impenetrable. Speech act theory proceeds from the tenet that one can 'get inside the head'[10] of the native speaker – and in so doing, one can discern the locutionary, illocutionary, and perlocutionary acts performed through the utterance. This founding proposition of speech act theory is not subscribed to here.[11] In finding that covert intentionality in speech can only be guessed at, my work proceeds from the opposing tenet, following Sapir (1921), that one can never 'get inside the head' of the native speaker. Analysis is instead based on the examination of observed interlocutions *between* speakers, taking as a source of data the concrete instances of talk shared between multiple interlocutors, over time and space.

As my study is one in which the fieldworker is trying to make sense of the talk of others through direct engagement, or participatory observation, as opposed to observation of conversation in which the fieldworker takes no part, the model I use is also one of meaning as emergent and mutually constructed between interlocutors, and constantly shifting in interpretation. Cultural systems are theorized as open and actively interpenetrating, as in, for example, Robin Ridington's (1990) work on conflicting models of courtroom discourse in a British Columbia land claims case. Ridington acknowledges power differentials in an examination of concrete discourse in courtrooms and other cross-cultural fora, and studies the fieldworker's own position as contributing to the conversations under study.[12]

An investigation of discourse of this kind brings to the linguistic and cultural analysis of narrative the consideration of apprehension, interaction, and interpretation. As M.M. Bakhtin has observed with respect to discourse as text, 'the event of the life of the text, that is, its true essence, develops *on the boundary between two consciousnesses, two subjects'* (1986: 106; emphasis in original as printed in translation). Centring this inquiry on speech and social action in discourse is not to consider discourse as a lens through which to view culture, but rather, following Greg Urban (1991: 1), to consider discourse as a *locus* of culture. I am concerned here with the unfolding of human relationships and how these are constituted and negotiated by means of speech and shared silence, through time and travel, and referenced to landscape through stories. In this work, stories, as shared between individuals, are considered according to this understanding of the term 'discourse.'

I find that this approach has been best described in the writings of Urban and of Joel Sherzer, in their call for a 'discourse-centered approach to language and culture.' Sherzer refers to 'the analysis of discourse that is rooted in social and cultural contexts of language use and considers questions of speech play and verbal art to be central' (1987: 295). It is the discourse-centred approach to culture and language (Sherzer 1987; Urban 1991) that provides the theoretical framework for this book. In its attention to verbal art, it complements the foundational work of Dell Hymes (1981) and Dennis Tedlock (1983), which spurred my initial investigation. Its attention to the contexts of social and cultural interaction is accommodated by the Hymesian methodology represented in the ethnography of speaking (Hymes 1972). The advantage of using Urban and Sherzer's approach in a work so tightly centred on the production and apprehension of narrative is that it allows for attention to form and genre (especially as explored by Bauman [1977] and Briggs and Bauman [1992]), as well as to the content of cultural expression (Urban 1991: 105).

Much of the work that has been inspired by the discourse-centred approach has to do with ritual speech in more public fora (e.g.: Keane's [1997] discussions of Anakalangese performances of ceremonies, Duranti's [1994] of the Samoan *fono*, and Sherzer's work in Kuna gathering houses [1979, 1983]). While my work is related to theirs in its examination of concrete instances of speech performance, and in its attention to the social consequences of speech, the contexts in which speech is studied here lend themselves to a different sort of constellation of participants, and a different degree of public presentation. The contexts in which the speech is exchanged are generally concerned with the sharing of information within a family group in a manner that emphasizes cooperation over competition. Drawing on these contexts, I examine how meaning is negotiated through language in relationship to other aspects of culture, including the practices of hunting and gathering, and travel over the land. At Alkali Lake, hunting and gathering is generally conducted in small groups of relatives and/or friends, ranging from pairs to parties of six or so individuals, and sometimes including several age groups and both genders. In the instances recounted here, these conversations also included me, a younger married woman of mixed Euro-American ancestry.

On Interlocutors

One way to explore the necessary connectedness of spoken language to that which it references is to consider the term 'interlocutor.' This term, in its most elementary formulation, refers to one who is engaged in conversation, as a speaker, a hearer, or both. As Dell Hymes reminds us, when we focus on the speaker, we must also attend to Audience (or other Participants) and not take it for granted that we know whom the audience for particular narratives will be. Some speakers consider God, or Creator, as one who is always present, and therefore always an interlocutor. For the Salish Elders I have spoken with on this subject, interlocutors may also include others considered to be Persons, albeit of the non-human sort, including, for example, plants, trees, rocks, wind, and in particular, as shall become apparent throughout this book, Bears. Interlocutors may also be not physically present, or even metaphysically so, as mindful speech can also engage, for the speakers of Alkali Lake with whom I worked, those yet to be born, and those already passed on. *When* the words are spoken is not all-important if the speaker takes into account how those words might be apprehended at a future time. This is somewhat akin to what writers attend to with their written words: future audience. However, in what I am learning of the Secwepemc world, what one might say to what might otherwise be constructed as a 'future audience' can have immediate consequences. As I will discuss in chapter 5, where other, non-human interlocutors are recognized by members of the culture, their role is not limited to that of audience; they are also attended to as sentient communicators of meaning.

I think that an attempt to grasp a larger sense of who or what the potential interlocutors are, for certain kinds of narrative, for particular individuals, is essential to beginning to take seriously how it is that an Elder at Alkali Lake, or elsewhere in the Salish world, can, for example, respectfully approach trees, ask them that they provide bark for a basket, and later discuss with the anthropologist what they have learned from their engagement with that tree. The focus on words, which as a linguistic anthropologist I document, must remain linked to situated meaning for the speaker, however nascent my understanding of their perspective on communication might be.

At Alkali Lake, Angela George draws strength and comfort from diverse forms of communication. Several are sources of spiritual guidance: the Plains Sundance, pow-wows (Native Indian Dancing), Roman Catholicism, Christian Fundamentalism, as well as the teachings about the sweathouse she learned from her Elders. She relies on the efficacy of all of these, and her faith is reflected in many of her everyday actions, including drinking holy water for internal ailments, and the application of a vast knowledge of local medicinal plants, of which she says 'It's really / helped a lot / if you believe it.' Angela prays for her relatives and friends at the Sundance, in the Catholic church, and in the sweathouse. She has reflected on the request of her late son, a lay preacher, that she become a 'Christian' (for her, this is a distinct category from Catholic), and feels that his prayers and laying on of hands saved her life on one occasion. Similarly, among Coast Salish practitioners of Spirit Dancing, or *Seyowin*, those who call on guardian spirit powers in the longhouse may also be devout and active members of the Indian Shaker church, the Catholic church, or all three. Religious philosophies that, to some, might seem to conflict, can comfortably coexist in the spiritual understanding of many members of Salish cultures.

Strong statements against the Sundance by one of the village's former parish priests, and the disapproval of the pow-wow expressed by leaders in the 'Christian' church have not resulted in an abatement of participation in any such activities by Angela or other female Elders I have talked to. The rejection of one system of faith to raise up another is seen as highly disrespectful, and telling someone to give up a way of praying or voicing an opinion about it at all is considered a violation of the personal autonomy of the believer, and disrespectful to one's own self, as the devaluing of another's beliefs implies an incapability of seeing the worth of one's own.

Respect and Prayer

A fundamental tenet manifest in Salish discourse and personal behaviour is the respect for personal autonomy. I have learned that behaving respectfully towards all living things is an essential aspect of proper

Salish behaviour, and this respect is the pathway to knowledge. Respect involves careful observation to discern the ways of living things. Respect can include attention to how a deer grazes, or how bark attaches to a tree. In respect lies the assumption that each being has its own intentionality, such that a deer will 'let itself be killed' or bark will 'allow itself to be peeled'; if one behaves respectfully towards someone or something, one allows room for understanding potentially to follow. Once, when ṭaqʷšəblu spoke of listening to hour after hour of seemingly endless testimony at a candlelight service for a dear departed friend, she said: 'This is part of our discipline: Respect [the speaker] even if it kills you. *Even if they have nothing to say.*' Respect, then, includes a discriminating attention, whether to the habits of a deer or the motives of a speaker.

This notion of respect for personal autonomy parallels a characteristic described by Scollon and Scollon (1981) with regard to a pattern in world view, which they have extended from their observations of Northern Athapaskan discourse to include other northern Native Canadians and Alaskan people who come from hunting and gathering traditions (1981: 100). The Scollons attribute respect for the individual to Athapaskans' choice 'to rely heavily on the development of the knowledge, skills, and adaptive flexibility of each separate individual as the central means of group survival' (ibid.). In my experience, the notion of respect for the individual corresponds well to Secwepemc (and, more widely, Salish) respect for personal autonomy. Between broad Salish and Athapaskan patterns, the similarities with regard to notions of respect are strong, and common ground can also be found with regard to some aspects of narrative.

The Scollons argue that, for Athapaskans, the primary means of acquiring knowledge are from personal experience and stories of the experiences of others (1981: 101).[13] Robin Ridington, also working with speakers of an Athapaskan language, in this case the Dunne-za, or Beaver, discusses their ways of obtaining and claiming knowledge as stemming from 'the authority of individual experience' (1988: xii). For the Secwepemc narratives discussed here the similarities are evident; narratives of personal experience, and narratives of others' experiences, are appropriate vehicles for the transmission of knowledge. For all of the similarities, however, it is important not to lose sight of the centrality of this sort of transmission for all humans, and, indeed, for other creatures as well.

Keith Basso's description of the Apache practice of 'stalking with stories' (1990a) – letting the telling of stories indicate that someone is behaving in a way that requires correction, if the individual chooses to interpret the story as directed toward them – provides an example of careful, and at first seemingly undirected, instruction. As I will discuss in chapter 5, for the Secwepemc urgent directions regarding personal safety are also couched in this manner.

With Thanks to the Bears: My First Story

I first gleaned some understanding of the rules governing talk in travel from a shared experience on the side of a small dirt road between the Dog Creek Reserve and the town of Clinton. The Elder with whom I travel most frequently, Angela George, and her friend Hazel Johnson, along with Hazel's mother, Chewinik Johnson, and I, were driving back to Alkali Lake after a long hot day of picking berries. The car filled with the sweet sticky scent of berries as each bounce along the dusty hard-pan crushed a few into juice, and with all that hard driving on worn-out shock absorbers, Hazel decided she needed to step out of the car and relieve herself. This is standard roadside practice where bush and sage-brush are omnipresent and cars are rare. Hazel got out and was taking her time. The remaining occupants of the car, in the meantime, had spotted a bear. Hazel had lost her sight as a young girl, and so was warned about what the rest of us could see: 'Hazel, there's a bear!' Hazel must have thought we were teasing her for taking so long. She didn't say anything. Then, we saw something that made us even more uneasy: 'Hazel, the bear has a cub!' Hazel just laughed. Then, we saw something more alarming still: 'Hazel, the bear has *two* cubs!' Still laughing, Hazel felt her way back into the car. She had to be convinced that we weren't just teasing her after we were safely underway.

The next time I drove past the site of the bear incident, I was in the car with Angela George and some people who had not been along on the earlier expedition. I started laughing and reminisced about the event. Everyone enjoyed the story; I felt comfortable telling it and warmed by the audience's response. After once passing the site and relating the story, I found, on each subsequent passing, that I was prompted to tell it if I neglected to tell it of my own volition. Prompts came in the form of expectant glances in a suddenly quiet car, with verbal cues following only if I missed the first silent signals of attention. I had an appropriate story to tell, one that contributed to my companions' information about a particular place. By finally entering into an appropriate pattern of communication, I was able to begin to understand what it was that people from Alkali Lake considered important to recount when they travelled through their territory, and why.

Place and Story

Harry Hoijer has called the strong relationship of story to place 'spatial anchoring' (quoted in Basso 1990a: 107) in describing how meaning is layered into landscape through experience over time. To adequately consider the form of narrative discussed here, I must take into account its presentation as situated on the land and in relation to my interlocutors' particular historical and world knowledge. To consider narrative without also taking its situation in discourse into account is to decontextualize it, thereby losing some of its associated meaning.

To demonstrate briefly the rich possibilities and striking poetics open to this area of inquiry, I include here an excerpt from Keith Basso's investigation of place-related discourse in the Cibecue Apache culture:

> After Nick had taken his place on the stand, he was asked by an attorney why he considered water to be important to his people. A man of eminent good sense, Nick replied, 'Because we drink it!' And then, without missing a beat, he launched into a historical tale about a large spring not far from Cibecue – *tú nchaa halíí* ('lots of water flows up and out') – where long ago a man was mysteriously drowned after badly mistreating his wife. When Nick finished the story he went on to say: 'We know it happened, so we know not to act like that man who died. It's good we have that water. We need it to live. It's good we have that spring too. We need it to live right.' Then the old man smiled to himself and his eyes began to dance.   (1990a: 137)

In this passage Keith Basso exquisitely captures Nick Thompson's essential way of explaining how the stories referenced to the land can serve as a moral guide for the Cibecue Apache. As should be apparent from the references to 'the stand' and 'the attorney,' however, Thompson is asserting these things to demonstrate, to a judge, that the land is an essential part of culture. The increasing use of such cross-cultural discourse, as a rhetorical necessity in the courts, also figures prominently in the experiences of my interlocutors at Alkali Lake. In addition to providing the story of the way of life of a People as they are anchored morally, spiritually, and linguistically to the land, this book is about the re-anchoring of discourse and its attendant meanings in a landscape that is increasingly under pressure from logging, ranching, road construction, and the attendant increase in human settlement.

Keith Basso has called for the attention of anthropologists to place beyond place as mere location, and specifically to place names, arguing that little work has been done in this area by anthropologists or linguists since the Second World War (1990a: 105–6). Work since that time has been enriched by the contributions of cultural geographers (Yi-Fu Tuan 1974, 1977) as well as anthropologists (c.f. Hunn 1990; Kari and Fall 1987); and the burgeoning 'grey' literature of background reports submitted in support of land and resource claims by cooperative clan, band, or tribe-based research groups in Australia, Canada, and the United States. Others have lent support to the study of place in anthropological inquiry (Rodman 1992; Low and Lawrence-Zúñinga 2003), and to the linking of theoretical concepts in anthropology to particular places (Appadurai 1988; Dresch 1988). The formation of a Place and Space Group among members of the American Anthropological Association, the sponsorship of an advanced seminar of the School of American Research on 'Place, Expression, and Experience' with its associated volume (Feld and Basso 1996, with contributions by five additional writers), and publications by Basso (1990a/b; 1996), Cruikshank (1990a), Kahn (1990), Hirsch and O'Hanlon (1995), and Carlson (2001) are indicative of the growth of ethnographically centred investigations of place with an attendant focus on language.

The study of narratives of place, or place-related discourse, is rapidly expanding as an area of strong anthropological interest (Rodman 1992). Just as the work of Dell Hymes (1981), Dennis Tedlock (1972, 1983), and Jerome Rothenburg (1972) assists in the resuscitation of the smothered voices found in narratives in print, so now are anthropologists recognizing that attention to places can inform and enliven accounts. Collections of narratives cut adrift from their moorings are being re-anchored to their associated physical contexts as writers begin to learn to represent the poetics of lived space on the printed page.

'Walking and Talking'

Considering the importance of Place to Story while simultaneously taking into account the importance of interrelationships between interlocutors, which take place on the land, requires a further expansion of the interpretive framework. Fortunately, others have worked seriously to tease out these connections in a way that takes them simultaneously into account, while also recognizing that a respectful approach must permeate the communicative endeavour. Linda Akan's (1992) work with the Elder Alfred Mantiopies provides a most fruitful way to bring this connection into sharper focus. A sense of the sacredness of connection, of mindful listening, comes out in Mantiopies and Akan's work together. Their article *'Pimosatamowin Sikaw Kakeequaywin*. Walking and Talking: A Salteaux Elder's View of Native Education' examines meaning as emergent and mutually constructed between interlocutors who necessarily approach conversation from different vantage points. Akan points out that 'the powerful metaphor of good talking and good walking is more than a metaphor, [it] is also a direct and clear statement of the personal ethical responsibility of teachers and educators to care intimately for children and to live in such a way that our words reflect the way we live' (1992: 191). In other words, the conversation between Akan and Mantiopies provides a model of, and a model for, respectful communication as mutually experienced with reference to the land on which we dwell.[14]

> The text or discourse of the Elder is mindful of the environment. The firm belief that we are not responsible for or deserving of credit for such a great act or miracle as thought is always implicit in their speech ... The responsibility of using the gifts that were given to us in the best way we can goes without saying. In this way we live out our tasks by being true to ourselves. This is Pimadizewin, or a worthwhile life. Pimosatamowin, or our walk in life, is how we arrive at that knowledge or make sense of that task. (Akan 1992: 193)

Akan's interpretation makes 'our walk in life' synonymous with our development of knowledge through discourse. In my discussion of the creation of maps of experience in the Secwepemc discursive world, I endeavour to keep the work of Mantiopies and Akan in mind.

A Guide to the Chapters

The linguistic anthropologist William R. Seaburg, quoting Joan Didion, has explored the idea that 'we tell ourselves stories in order to live' (Didion 1979: 11). I have adapted that tenet as: 'we tell stories in order to make sense of our lives.' This book is a study of narratives, and how they are used by the Secwepemc people now living at Alkali Lake to make sense of their lives. It takes as its scope those occasions in travel on the land in which I was privy to their storied world. Their narratives are embedded here in an ethnography, which also comes in the form of a narrative, the organizing principle of which is the process of discovery I went through in an attempt to understand my own responsibilities to respectfully represent the individuals who invited me in.

Throughout most of this book I focus on modes of transmission of information of those 'people without history' (Wolf 1982) to demonstrate their history as mapped in the oral record of their interaction with and on the land. As a researcher and one directly engaged in discussion with the very participants in that research, I am also mindful that I have had the luxury of access to the archival records of the British Crown, while few individuals now resident at Alkali Lake have had much time or opportunity for such study. All of the means by which they were driven from their lands were not known to my interlocutors at Alkali Lake, and the ways that settlers were able to gain control of water rights and range land without any treaties being signed was part of what we puzzled through in our conversations. When I was asked such questions, and was told that what I could find out in archives might be useful to them, I worked to make a meaningful contribution to the conversation.

Chapter 2 establishes the historical context for current living conditions at Alkali Lake, and so provides a way in, for those who have not lived there all of their lives, to an understanding of how it was that group of people could be crammed onto a tiny piece of land without any treaty being signed, or even a formal survey of the land conducted. The chapter chronicles the change in Secwepemc life in the Cariboo that was brought on by trading companies, the gold rush, disease, and missionization, and the accompanying suppression of traditional stories and the cultural contexts in which they are part of everyday talk. In examining both the historical circumstances under which the people of Alkali partially incorporated sedentism and agrarianism into their lives, and the ways in which they continue their hunting and gathering lifeways, I address the phenomenon of village coalescence.

Chapter 3, 'Living on the Land,' concerns the relationship between people and the land on which they rely as a source of renewal, as well as for part of their livelihood. In examples drawn from courtroom discourse in a local hunting rights case, two Secwepemc individuals express their understandings of their relationship to the land and its resources across conflicting systems of discourse (cf. Ridington 1990, 1992). Their narratives may shed light on the perceived differences between Secwepemc and Euro-Canadian cultural attitudes toward hunting and gathering, as represented from a Secwepemc perspective.

The central chapters, 4 through 6 (on maps, stories, and memories), describe the narrative world of Alkali Lake Elders in travel, away from the main reserve. Taken as a group, the stories I heard emerged at the unique interstices of individuals, circumstances, and places. In writing about a culture where knowledge comes from personal experience, and the sharing of information is embedded in stories, it seems most appropriate to present my understanding in the order in which I came to make sense of things. These chapters examine in turn the different kinds of talk I encountered in hunting and gathering contexts.

Chapter 4, 'Maps,' examines the narratives of personal experience that I heard as an individual who had been admitted, as a newcomer, to the travel experiences of Elders and to the fishing and berry picking they engaged in. Place, and places along a key stretch of road, provides an axis of orientation for this chapter. I examine how stories told while travelling to hunting and gathering sites reflect personal knowledge of the land and its resources. Telling these stories is found to be a social obligation to those with whom one hunts and gathers. The stories form the basis of shared understanding and relationship to a territory. When the personal narratives of fellow travellers are pooled, they can function as an oral map of the area for the entire group. The structure of narrative events suggests that, in this oral culture, knowledge of the land and its resources is thereby maintained.

Anthropologists often learn their most important lessons by making mistakes. The stories I was next introduced to, discussed in chapter 5, provided admonitions against my particular actions. The stories all carry instructions about proper conduct in spiritually charged situations, including the reception of messages or portents from animals including owls and bears and, in particular, grizzly bears. In Secwepemc culture, personal autonomy is highly valued (cf. Scollon and Scollon 1981), but crucial direction, admonitions, and information must, nonetheless, be conveyed. When I unwittingly violated rules of proper conduct in this context, an interlocking set of narratives were told to advise me. The chapter concerns the patterning of instruction given in the systematic telling of these stories, and draws on Cruikshank's (1990b) explanation of the use of traditional narratives as scaffolding for the interpretation of narratives of personal experience. I also examine the continuation of particular social practices in the context of mourning, which seem to have also once been richly associated with stories, but now draw their authority from personal experience with the supernatural.

The stories heard in the overarching context of mourning were, sadly, a major part of my experience at Alkali. No fewer than nine deaths in the community marked the time of my first two years of fieldwork. I have returned to the bedsides, and to the funerals, of more dear ones in the ten years following, including those of the husband, a son, and a son-in-law of my chief consultant, Angela George. A Gwich'in woman, visiting Alkali Lake from a far northern community on the Koyukon River, observed that it was at the funerals that everyone pulled together in her community, and that was where they shared and remembered the old ways. She wished that her community directed as much energy into the living as it did into the dying. Still, where else but in mourning does a living individual so strongly need the support of community, the endurance of culture, and the comfort of memories that, though they are experienced in heartbeats, may persist beyond the passing of a single individual's life? It is the same at Alkali Lake.

In chapter 6, 'Memories,' I explore the nature of life story in place-related narrative, and contrast it with another, newer type of life story – publicly presented narratives situated in ritually defined places, such as Alcoholics Anonymous meeting rooms in the village. Both forms of life story are investigated to explore their contemporary meanings at Alkali Lake. The impact of a new collective narrative, a filmic recreation of the history of alcoholism at Alkali Lake, is also discussed.

I return to a discussion of space and place in the final chapter of the book to examine how place is differently constructed by Secwepemc and Euro-Canadian culture. The data suggest that there are possible loci of understanding that may yet smooth the conflict between Euro-Canadian and Secwepemc systems of discourse. This work, as an ethnography concerned with perceptions and experience of place, extends to an examination of displacement, as effected by encroaching settler populations and the ensuing changes in the landscape itself. Conceptions of Secwepemc identity as inextricably linked to land, story, and language have had to be rethought, for the people of Alkali Lake are increasingly disassociated from that constellation of markers, and yet they continue to mark the land on which they have experience with Story.

Chapter 2

A Brief History of
Responses to Colonialism

We had to prove that we were a people and that we had a language. It
was very strange and highly emotional at times – causing a lot of anger.
And sometimes drove me to tears when I got home. I never ever showed
it in public. I waited till I got alone and then just beat the wall and say,
'Why? Why? I'm sitting here. Can't you see me?'

Yagalahl (Dora Wilson-Kenni, 1992: 9)

Few materials can be found outside of the Canadian National and British Columbia Provincial Archives that provide any indication of how
Secwepemc people, with whom no treaties were negotiated by the British Crown, the Canadian government, or the Province of British
Columbia, found themselves only recognized by those governments as
having some claim to tiny patches of land in their vast territories. This
account is provided in order to address a critical gap in the published
histories now in general circulation; it is not a gap than can be filled
entirely, but notice can at least be given here to the still partially unanswered questions concerning the mechanisms by which particular
families were separated the from land. As Elizabeth Furniss (1999) and
Julie Cruikshank (1998) have each pointed out in addressing cultural
erasure in Euro-Canadian written histories, providing such ethnohis-
torical accounts may render the current social conflicts between First
Nations and settlers, over land claims and resource use, more intelligi-
ble. The people with whom I work at Alkali Lake are generous enough
to tell stories about their history; my aim here is to provide a brief history from a world I was more familiar with when we met: libraries,
government archives, correspondence files, and paper maps.

As Eric Wolf has observed, 'The more ethnohistory we know, the more clearly 'our' history and 'their' history emerge as part of the same history. Thus, there can be no 'Black history' apart from 'White history,' only a component of a common history suppressed or omitted from conventional studies for economic, political, or ideological reasons' (Wolf 1982: 19). Thus, the history of the archive concerned with the Secwepemc is not separable from that of the oral record; each is part of a more fully developed history, one that is now more firmly intertwined in local social action, for the original manuscript of this chapter has been read by many in the community, including those working to establish an agreement on land claims.

With a wave of his hand toward the fencelines we could see below us, the Elder David Johnson told me stories about a former owner of the Alkali Lake Ranch, who married a chief's daughter, and moved his survey stakes from the edge of the ranch to further encroach upon the reserve. Some of the means by which the rancher was able to accomplish this can be gleaned from intergovernmental correspondence written by government officials and now housed in the BC Provincial Archives. The archives also supply a partial story of how an area was marked off as the reserve, 'Indian Reserve Number One,' when no treaties had been signed, and how that reserve, known as 'Alkali Lake,' was cut off from access to the very lake for which it was named. In response to questions put to me by my interlocutors concerning the government's 'paper trail,' and how that trail corresponds to their own experiences, this chapter is concerned in part with the written historical records, including the published and unpublished materials of James Alexander Teit, an Orkney Islander working under contract to the North Pacific Expedition of the American Museum of Natural History. Teit began assembling stories, material collections, and interviews with Secwepemctsín-speaking people around Dog Creek and Alkali Lake, and elsewhere in Secwepemc territory in the 1890s. Under the direction of Franz Boas, and with the financial sponsorship of Morris Jessup, Teit and other ethnographers investigated possible links between Peoples living on both sides of the North Pacific. The years of European contact had significantly altered Secwepemc life-ways from the ethnographic present that Teit was contracted to record, and his reconstruction (Teit 1909) must be viewed with that limitation in mind.

Teit's perspective on the Secwepemc and other Interior Salish groups was undoubtedly influenced by his long-term residence in Northern

Nlha7kápmx (formerly called Thompson) territory at Spences Bridge, married to a Nlha7kápmx woman, Lucy Artko or Athello.[1] His descriptions of Secwepemc customs (Teit 1909) are often referenced to corresponding Nlha7kápmx customs (catalogued in Teit 1898, 1900). He had experience as a trapper and hunter over much of the Interior of British Columbia, sometimes in the company of his Nlha7kápmx in-laws, sometimes working as a guide to supplement his scant pay as an ethnographer.[2] This experience in the bush, and his work in support of Native land claims, especially with the Indian Rights Association of British Columbia, as an interpreter and the secretary for the association,[3] brought Teit into extended contact with Secwepemc people and their territory. His reconstruction remains the best *written* record we have of Secwepemc life in the prehistoric period, and as is evident in the citations below, I rely on his published and unpublished research for much of the information presented in this chapter.

The ancestors of the people now settled at Alkali Lake had ties to indigenous peoples up and down the Fraser River, and out to the Pacific coast. To the south were other Interior Salish groups, including the Nlha7kápmx, Lillooet, and Okanagan, with whom the Secwepemc traded, raided, and intermarried. The foot trail, which allowed the Secwepemc access to their southern neighbours, is still in evidence along sections of the Fraser River. The well-established 'grease trail,' a trade route for oolichan oil from the west coast, must have put the Secwepemc in touch with the Bella Coola as well. Raids by the Cree, who came all the way across the Rocky Mountains from what is now Alberta to capture wives, are reported in many tales I have heard at Alkali Lake. A story recorded at Soda Creek, a Secwepemc reserve north of Alkali Lake, also tells of women taken captive by the Cree or other people from far to the east (Speare 1973: 39–41). The eastern flank of the Secwepemc territory was home to the Cree, Stony, Lakes, and Kootenai. The Carrier (Dakelhne) and the Tsilhqot'in, both of which are Athapaskan groups, were established immediately to the north[4] and west[5] of the Secwepemc, respectively (see map 1).

Teit reported that there were two different forms of social organization extant at the time of European contact, a three-class system for the Secwepemc of the north and west, including Alkali Lake, and a more egalitarian system for the south. He postulated that the northern form of Secwepemc social organization had recently evolved under the influence of the Carrier and Tsilhqot'in ranking systems, which in turn

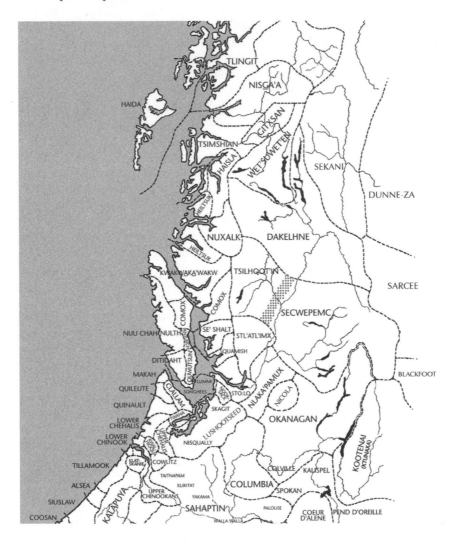

Map 1   Peoples of the Northwest Coast and Plateau culture areas. Map by David Myhrum, based on a map by Wayne Suttles, 'Native Languages of the North Pacific Coast of North America.' Copyright Cameron Suttles, 1978. The stippled area represents a shift in occupation at the time of the 1862–3 smallpox epidemic. Used and modified with permission of Oregon State University Press, from a map appearing in Robert Boyd, ed., *Indians, Fire and the Land in the Pacific Northwest* (Corvallis: Oregon State University Press, 1999), 5.

were derived from the ranking systems of their coastal neighbours (1909: 576). Teit hypothesized that a northern-style ranking system, which included a stratification into nobility, commoners, and slaves, along with crest groups and certain dancing societies, may have spread through to Alkali Lake from the Canyon Division by 1855, but very little was remembered of the system by the people Teit interviewed in 1900. Verne Ray remarked of the stratification, '[I]t was in all cases [Tsilhqot'in and Secwepemc] superficial' (1939: 29). Much of the work on ranking systems was carried out with an underlying theoretical premise that ideas about stratification diffused from the coast. What was missing in this early anthropological work was a recognition that the specifics of nation-to-nation, or group-to-group, relationships can be called upon by members of each group in response to each others' notions of power, and that these shifting adjustments of relationships do not constitute a 'superficial' adaptation, but one that is mobilized where deemed useful, and is otherwise not engaged. What might not have been apparent to the early ethnographers was how ranking systems and internal relationships of Interior Peoples were continually refashioned to respond, in the ethnographers' own times, to the local imposition of colonialist forces of church and state, as well as to individual agents of those institutions, and to prospectors and settlers flooding into their territory.

Seven culturally recognized divisions of the Secwepemc were described by Teit as extant in the early 1900s. Each was made up of relatively closely related villages that shared hunting grounds. Alkali Lake is part of what Teit called the Fraser River Division, along with the other villages on the east side of the Fraser, including Dog Creek and Canoe Creek. Teit also grouped Alkali Lake for some purposes with the Canyon Division (1909: 459), which was west of the Fraser River. When the Canyon Division was almost completely wiped out in the smallpox epidemic of 1862–3, most of the survivors settled at Alkali Lake (Teit 1909: 463–4; Duff 1965: 31).

Teit's (1909) map showing Secwepemc territory and the seven divisions is shown in map 2. It should be noted that the map contains an error in the drawing of the boundary for the Shuswap Lake Division. In a letter of 1 April 1910, Teit wrote to C.F. Newcombe, amending the boundaries on his map of 1909:

The Shuswap boundaries are all correct [in Teit's 1909 work on the Secwepemc] excepting part to the south but this is my mistake and not

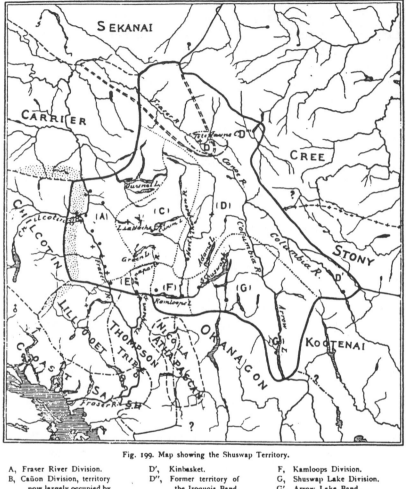

Fig. 199. Map showing the Shuswap Territory.

A, Fraser River Division.	D', Kinbasket.	F, Kamloops Division.
B, Cañon Division, territory now largely occupied by the Chilcotin.	D'', Former territory of the Iroquois Band.	G, Shuswap Lake Division.
	D''', Shuswap, Cree, and Iroquois mixed.	G', Arrow Lake Band.
C, Lake Division.		●, Villages.
D, North Thompson Division.	E, Bonaparte Division.	+, Former villages.

Dotted area, territory recently occupied by the Chilcotin. Area at head of Fraser River, enclosed by broken double lines, temporarily occupied by the Sekanai.

Map 2   James Teit's map of Shuswap territory (1909: 450). Courtesy of American Museum of Natural History.

yours ... [B]ut last year I ascertained for certain the boundaries near Arrow Lakes are wrong, I went through this region last year and made sure of this point. The country from the mouth of the Kettle River following up the Columbia and taking in the Lower and Upper Arrow Lakes north to or slightly beyond Revelstoke was occupied by the Lakes or Lake Indians, a tribe very closely related to the Chaudiere or Colville Indians and speaking a dialect very close to the Okanagon.   (PABC, Newcombe Family Papers)

Despite Teit's efforts, the error persists on some linguistic maps today. I have drawn Map 3 to provide a version of Teit's linguistic and division boundaries incorporating the changes Teit describes in his notes to Newcombe, and to show some of the locations of major Secwepemc band settlements.

Another note from Teit to C.F. Newcombe provides information on the permeability of and change in boundaries on linguistic maps of the area:

I don't know whether it would be correct to include the band of mixed Shuswap and Cree in the map. [Teit refers here to an ethnological map of BC, sent to him by Newcombe.] The nucleus of this band was Iroquois who came to B.C. in very early days in the employ of the NorthWest C.$^{oy.}$ and settled around Tête Jaune Cache. really in Shuswap territory or hunting ground. They intermarried with Shuswap and later very largely with Cree. In very recent years they appear to have forsaken that region to a considerable extent, and now make their headquarters just east of the Yellowhead Pass in Cree Territory.   (PABC, Newcombe Family Papers)

Teit's further notes to Newcombe can be read as a caution to any who wish to consider linguistic or cultural boundaries as fixed in time, or even as definable in terms of edges, rather than centres. Although Teit refers to the group as having an Iroquoian nucleus, in his published work, Teit, or his editor, Franz Boas, decided to call the above-mentioned group the Upper North Thompson Band of Shuswap (1909: 454). Teit did not go to the Tête Jaune Cache area himself, but says he met some of the people elsewhere. He provides the careful qualification, 'I cannot say to what extent the Shuswap language is spoken among them. Those I met spoke Shuswap, but were also proficient in Cree, and understood a good deal of Canadian French.' This description reinforces Silverstein's recent argument against characterizing

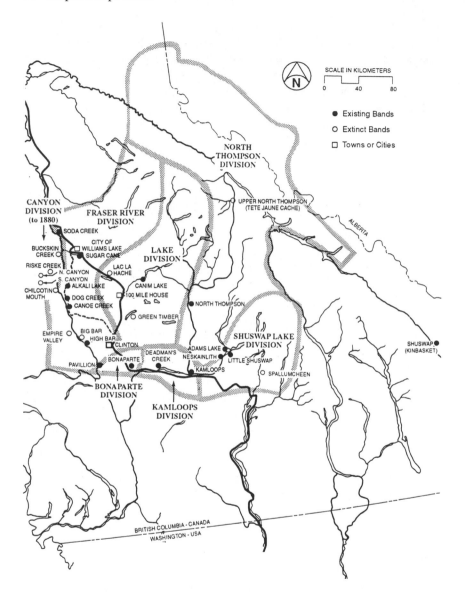

Map 3   Shuswap territory map (based on information from Teit (1909) and Duff (1965)). Cartography by Beth Suprenant.

Native American speech communities as typically monolingual (1996: 127), and holds implications for 'the role of indigenous languages in the contemporary ethnic politics of culture' (Silverstein 1996: 126). Genealogical research shows strong Cree influences at Alkali Lake, which continue with regard to intellectual exchange, the giving of gifts, and a concern for mutual relatives among individuals on both sides of the Rockies.

Contacts with Explorers and Traders

The first recorded Secwepemc-European contact in Secwepemc territory was in 1793, when Alexander MacKenzie came down from Carrier territory on his journey from Fort Chipewyan looking for the North West Passage. He briefly travelled down the Fraser River to a point between present-day Williams Lake and Quesnel before backtracking north of Quesnel to the beginning of the overland 'grease trail' that led to Bella Coola and the Pacific Ocean (Newman 1987). His venture into Secwepemc territory could not have lasted more than a day or two, and whether his party's contacts may have resulted in the spread of disease along this route is not discernible from the historical record.

In 1805 Simon Fraser founded Fort McLeod at McLeod Lake, New Caledonia, in the Peace River (Arctic) drainage. The North West Company next established a fort at Prince George, then Fort George, in Carrier territory. The new fort would have provided access to firearms and staples in exchange for pelts by 1808, but Teit remarked that before Fraser's journey down the river, only the Secwepemc people of Soda Creek had seen white men (1909: 449).

Simon Fraser first floated through Secwepemc territory in 1808, past the banks of the river where people still dip-net below Alkali Lake. James Teit mentioned that a Canyon Division Secwepemc man residing at Alkali Lake in 1900 had seen Simon Fraser's party as a boy (1909: 449), and recorded a corroborating tale from a Styne Creek Nlha7kápmx woman that 'among them [Fraser's party] was a Shuswap chief who acted as interpreter' (1912: 414). Teit wrote that Fraser 'gave presents of tobacco, beads, and knives to almost all the Indians he met' (1909: 449). Fraser's extensive contact through the length of Secwepemc territory may have included the transmission of disease, which could account for reports that on Fraser's return journey, 'boulders were hurled down at the explorers' canoes; showers of arrows met some of their attempts to land for food' (Newman 1987: 113), and the cartographer David Thompson's 1808 report of 'distemper' among the Northern Secwepemc (Boyd 1985: 376).

The Gold Rush

By 1821, the Hudson's Bay Company (which had by then acquired the North West Company) had posts established at Kamloops (Fort Thompson) and at Alexandria, in Carrier territory, near present-day Quesnel. Trade between the Secwepemc and the Bay men was then accomplished on some semblance of equal footing. The white population was still small, and interested in maintaining exchange with the Native people of the Interior. This relatively balanced relationship would soon change. In 1858, British Columbia was established as a British colony when gold was discovered on the Fraser River. The rush was on: 'between April 1 and November 30 alone, 27,000 men poured out of California bound for British Columbia' (British Columbia 1987: 4). By way of contrast, Teit's 1850 estimate for the entire Secwepemc population was 7200 (1909: 466); James Mooney's was 5300 (cited in Boyd 1985: 376).

As mining claims on the lower Fraser played out, prospectors pushed northward along the Fraser and its streams. The building of the 'Cariboo Waggon Road'[6] to the Interior was begun in 1859, bringing labourers and the Royal Engineers into the area to serve the needs of the mining industry. Some gold was found at Quesnel in 1859 (Morice 1905: 295), and in 1860 a major strike was made near Barkerville at William's Creek. It was considered to be 'the richest goldfield in the world' (ibid.: 296), and at the height of the gold rush, Barkerville claimed to have the largest population west of Chicago and north of San Francisco. Almost all of Barkerville's new citizens arrived via the new wagon road, still under construction, and so passed directly through the Fraser River Division territory.

Some newcomers did not make the trek all the way to Barkerville, but established stores or roadhouses along the wagon road. These establishments were named after their road mileage from Lillooet or Ashcroft, and included 150 Mile House, which was less than 50 kilometres by trail from the Alkali Lake village. A store where alcohol could be purchased by Native people was opened near the village in approximately 1860.[7] It is unclear from the records precisely where this store was, but A.G. Morice reports the opening of Dunlevy's store at Beaver Lake, southeast of Soda Creek, in 1861 (1905: 310). Also in 1861,

47 Mile House, now known as Clinton, was founded with the building of the road from Lillooet over Pavilion Mountain into Fraser River Division Secwepemc territory. Clinton became a major junction, as it connected the Lillooet trail, an early route of travel for the miners, to the newer Cariboo Wagon Road.

In 1860, a Mr Bowie pre-empted (laid claim to) all of the land in the valley floor from the village of Alkali Lake to the lake itself (see map 4). As there were suddenly more whites than Indians in the Interior, settlers and miners could act with impunity. They were not accountable to British law, especially as many were lately from California and were not British subjects; they claimed land without authorization, often in anticipation of extinguishment of Native claims. Although the Royal Proclamation of 1763 had made it quite clear that Native title was to be recognized, nothing had then been decided with regard to whether the new colony or the Crown should pay for the extinguishment of Native title (Tennant 1990). It may have appeared to some settlers that such action would soon be unnecessary in the Interior, as the smallpox epidemic of 1862–3 felled an estimated two thirds of the total Secwepemc population (Teit 1909: 463).

Smallpox

In 1861, smallpox was reported at Victoria. The subsequent forced dispersal of Native people encamped there (Duff 1965: 42), and the travel of many whites through Victoria, a supply point, to the Interior in search of gold provided the conditions for smallpox to spread throughout the province. Incidents of smallpox coming to the Interior from Bella Coola are reported (Teit 1909: 463), and there is an undated report in the Alkali Lake band files that 'in the Chilcotin, a white man took blankets from the bodies of the dead and sold them to other Indians,' which is corroborated by Duff (1965: 42). Morice reports the names of two men engaged in this practice, Angus McLeod and 'a certain Taylor' (1905: 317). There are stories of smallpox being brought by the miners, as in this account from Augusta Tappage of Soda Creek, a reserve north of William's Lake:

> How they got it she says was from a man on foot coming through the country.
> A white man. A miner, maybe, in those days.
> He camped near the Indians and they gave him food and they were good

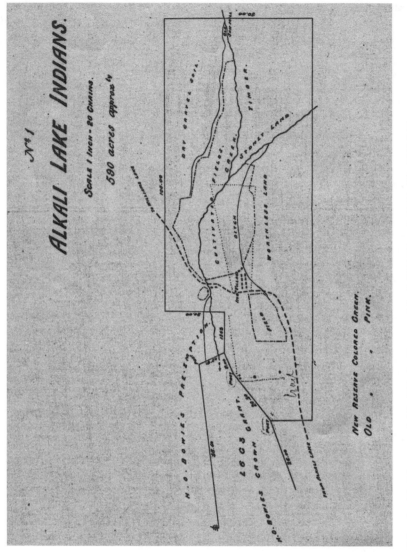

Map 4   Sketch map of Alkali Lake Reserve No. 1 (RG 10, vol. 3681, file 12395-3)

to him. And I guess he thanked them by giving them this nice blanket – a
Hudson's Bay blanket, my grandmother says.
Well, that man didn't have smallpox – no, he didn't have it. But they fig-
ured out later that he must have carried it with him in that blanket.
They all got it anyway after he left. It cleaned them out.

(Words of Augusta Tappage, as recorded in Speare 1973: 30)

A story told by the late David Johnson of Alkali Lake would indicate
that the survivors from the Canyon Division were few. It is said that a
boy and his younger sister were the only survivors of a Canyon village,
and that the boy swam across the Fraser River with his sister, to Alkali.
When they were older, they married into the group at Alkali Lake.

Tsecyelk̓w

Angela George has told me other stories about smallpox, as we have
walked the hills between Alkali Lake and the Fraser River, at a place
called Tsecyelk̓w. Tsecyelk̓w overlooks the present-day settlement on the
main reserve, as shown in the accompanying photo (p. 40). The following stories were told to me by Angela on two separate trips to Tse-
cyelk̓w; the first on a drive, and the second on a hike to the very place
shown in the photo.

Angela: There were those that musta live in the reserve
         up here

                                                      AP: Uh huh

         They say those that's was up there
         they live
         They didn't get this uh – small pox
         they get
         They all live
         what's living up here
         up on the hill
         They say when people wants to go up there and tell them
             about the
         people that was dying here
         They bow and arrow'em
         They don't let'em go up there
         And they all live what was up the mount –
         up that hill

Angela George at *Tsecyelk̓w*

AP: So they were on top of the hill here?
Angela: Yeah

                                              AP: Oh!

Angela: It's a big place up there
        I go up there a lot of times
        It's really spooky because I was there all alone
        S'where the reserve people stayed n'
        those that was down here they all die but those that's up there
            they didn't die
        Just like Lac la Hache that island

                                          AP: Mhm

Angela: The people the Indian people all live
            what was staying in the island
        They ca( )

                                          AP: Mhm

        They never let anybody go there that bad sickness was
            around
        Smallpox
        Long ago

                              (Tape 1, 24 August 1988)

Angela George speaks of the people who once lived on the hill and survived a smallpox epidemic. She may be referring to the smallpox epidemic of 1862, which, with the exception of two individuals who crossed the Fraser and joined the Alkali Lake population, decimated the entire Canyon band of Secwepemc across the Fraser River (Duff 1965). She could alternatively be referring to the next smallpox epidemic, which swept through the Cariboo in 1875. Angela compares the method of survival employed by them (i.e., killing anyone who came near them) to that of her ancestral neighbours, who remained in isolation on an island in the middle of Lac la Hache. Other people from the reserve have told me about the people on the hill rolling rocks down to keep out intruders. This hill is clearly visible from the main reserve, and must serve as a reminder to some of this history. Narratives such as Angela's, especially with the recounting of a desperate survival technique, bring the events of the past vividly into public remembrance, for at least one more generation.

The Move to Permanent Villages

The combination of the flood of incoming miners and settlers, dwindling game, disease, and alcohol reduced the numbers of Native people and their ability to defend the territory they had previously controlled by agreement or force. Groups that had formerly occupied several villages coalesced into single village sites, or into more dense settlements. The present village of Alkali Lake is referred to as a probable prehistoric village site, called *Esket* in Secwepemctsín, but the settlement pattern for the area may have formerly been much less concentrated. A rudimentary survey of the land surrounding the current village reveals surface evidence of former pithouses, not only along the sidehill that runs through the centre of the main reserve, but also on a hill above and to the east of the reserve. There is evidence that another cluster of pithouses lay to the west of the village, close to the lake and the trailhead that leads down the cliffs to a dip-netting site. This settlement pattern began to change as more and more land surrounding Alkali Lake was pre-empted by European settlers. Some families and individuals sought employment from ranchers who married or allied with Secwepemc women, and made camp at or near the rancheries that were developing in the area.[8]

The only land on which the people could be assured of remaining relatively unmolested was a forty-acre segment of what is now Alkali Lake IR No. 1. It was Governor James Douglas's policy that village sites and associated fenced acreage be reserved for the use of the aboriginal residents (Duff 1965: 61). In addition, Native people could, in theory, pre-empt land in the same fashion as whites.

R.C. Moody, Chief Commissioner of Lands and Works, writing to the Colonial Secretary on 11 June 1862, asked if it was indeed the case that Indians could pre-empt in the same manner as whites, in accordance with the Pre-Emption Proclamation. The response back, on 2 July 1862, was that according to the legislation to be passed, BC Natives could

> [H]old land under pre-emption on the following conditions:
> 1st. They reside continuously on their farms.
> 2nd. That they build thereon a house of squared logs with shingled roofs, not less than 30 by 20 feet, and side walls 10 feet high.
> 3rd. That they clear, enclose, and cultivate 1st year 2 acres of wood-land, or five acres of prairie land.
> 4th. That no power shall be given to convey such land without the consent of the Governor having first been obtained.
>
> (British Columbia 1875: 25)

(There is record of a 'Land Ordinance of 1870,' so the above restrictions may not have taken effect until that year.) Although the section was still in force and used as late as 1872, 'the practice of giving these permissions has been discontinued, lest it should interfere with the Dominion policy of concentrating the Indians upon Reserves.'[9]

With the retirement of Governor Douglas in 1864, the policy pertaining to Indian lands was radically altered. The political scientist Paul Tennant (1990) provides evidence that the official who replaced Douglas in this area made a complete and deliberate disavowal of the law with regard to Indian lands. Despite the Royal Proclamation of 1763, the new Commissioner of Lands and Works, Joseph Trutch, as administrator of Indian lands, said that Indians never owned the lands, and he barred them from pre-empting land (Tennant 1990; British Columbia 1875). Some reserves may have been marked off by the 1860s, but the schedule of all reserves *surveyed* in British Columbia by 1871 includes none north of the 114 milepost, Cariboo Wagon Road (British Columbia 1875). In 1868 John Adams, the owner of a sawmill, posted pre-emption notices at the village site of the marked-off Soda Creek reserve (ibid.: 48). On occasion, village sites were completely taken over by settlers, as in the case of the (Chimney Creek) Williams Lake Band.

The Arrival of Missionaries

The first Oblate missionary to travel through Secwepemc territory was Modeste Demers (Morice 1905: 231). In 1842 he preached to the Secwepemc of Alkali Lake, Chimney Creek, and Soda Creek, and encouraged the construction of churches (Whitehead 1981: 35) before heading north into Carrier territory. In 1867, the Oblates of Mary Immaculate purchased land twelve miles southwest of Williams Lake to establish St Joseph's Mission (Whitehead 1981).

The Chimney Creek band of Secwepemc, under Chief William, camped at the mission after their game was driven off and their land pre-empted (Whitehead 1981: 91), until land near the mission was purchased for a reserve by the government, probably in 1880.[10] The land, a ranch south of William's Lake, was purchased from a Mr Bates. The land is referred to in the government records as 'the Bates Estate,' and forms the present-day Sugar Cane Reserve.[11]

In 1879 a church was constructed by Alkali Lake residents at their crowded village site. Father Lejacq, who preached at the new St Pierre's Church in Alkali, was a firm believer in enforcing temperance and other values through the employment of Father Durieu's system of Catholicizing the Native peoples of the West.

> 'Durieu's System' (as it became known) saw the creation of a Catholic Indian state in every willing Indian village. An administration was created under the direct authority of the Bishop, with local missionaries acting as the initial supervisors. The administration consisted of: the Chief and a sub-Chief, who were responsible for keeping undesirable white men (e.g., bootleggers) away from their people; one or two watchmen who ensured that both adults and children attended religious instruction and did not return to now-forbidden Indian practices; policemen who carried out punishments – the collecting of fines or, occasionally, physical punishment for frequent repeaters – passed down by the Chief on those who lapsed into the old ways (although drunkenness was one of the gravest transgressions); catechists who were responsible for teaching religious knowledge to both adults and children and 'la cloche' men, bell-ringers, sometimes known as 'ting ting' men, who summoned the people to church three times daily. (Whitehead 1981: 18–19)

Whatever the arguments for (Whitehead 1981) or against (Haig-Brown 1988) the compatibility of Catholicism and the pre-existing spirituality of the Northern Secwepemc people, the certainty of some social order and protection from land pre-emption and alcohol at a time of extremely high mortality rates and a huge influx of settlers and miners must have made the Oblate's interest attractive to some, and so the Durieu System was adopted at Alkali Lake for a time.

Agrarian Life

In addition to encouraging a new form of social order in the face of rapid social change, the missionaries contributed to the growing pressures on the Secwepemc to remain in one place. Underlying the Durieu System of discipline was the Oblates' perception of settled agricultural life as a necessary condition for salvation and redemption. According to the Oblates' *Constitution and Rules*: 'Every means should therefore be taken to bring the nomads to abandon their wandering life and to build houses, cultivate fields and practise the elementary crafts of civilized life' (quoted in Whitehead 1981: 18). And so there was a great encouragement on the part of the Catholic church to settle. The Church further imposed a sometimes arbitrary division or regrouping on Secwepemc people. As I understand from conversations with people at Alkali Lake, the early priests sometimes pushed people to live in particular parishes when they were routed from their former homes by disease or settlers' pre-emptions, even though they may have been more properly affiliated with the people at other villages.

Settlement was further encouraged through the Oblates' pressing of land claims for the Secwepemc, generally appealing to the government to make agrarian land available in the form of secured and larger reserves. The appeal to the government and Canadians in general is concerned with farming land and rangeland, not with hunting land. The popular understanding carried over from Governor Douglas's term was that unreserved Crown lands could be hunted over by Native peoples without impediment.

In an eloquent letter sent to the *Victoria Standard* newspaper from the Okanagan Mission on 28 August 1874 by Father Grandidier, O.M.I., the Kamloops missionary appealed to the government and the public on behalf of Secwepemc interests in farming and animal husbandry. Excerpts of the letter are presented here:

At Kamloops the Shuswap Indians gathered to welcome him [the Indian Commissioner, Colonel Powell], expecting that their grievance would be redressed, they exposed to him their needs, their earnest and unanimous wish to have more land, by the improvements which they had already accomplished on their reservations, without help from anybody, by their sole efforts, and by the census of their cattle, they showed that theirs was no idle wish.

...

Their reservations have been repeatedly cut off smaller for the benefit of the Whites, and the best and most useful part of them taken away, still some tribes are corralled on small pieces of land, as at Canoe Creek or elsewhere, or even have not an inch of ground as at Williams Lake.

...

In former times the Indians did not cultivate land, now brought by the example of the Whites they see its value, they are not unwilling to let the Whites have the greater and the best portion of it, but not the whole or nearly so.

...

But will not twenty acres be sufficient for each family? What is the purpose of the Government? to civilize and make useful men of them – The first step to do it is to reclaim them from their wandering life and attach them by bonds of interest to the soil.   (RG 10, vol. 3613, file 4036)

The missionaries' goals in this respect were shared by the newly created Canadian government. In 1868, the *Act for the gradual civilization of Indian Peoples* (a.k.a. the *Indian Act*) was passed by the Canadian parliament to create reserves, set up band councils, and define who was legally considered Indian. Reserves had in some cases been surveyed, but were not yet official. Meanwhile, ranchers continued to pre-empt Indian land, and the Church and the federal and provincial governments were not living up to expectations. In fact, some actions of church officials sparked protest.

Complaints about the cruelty of Father LeJacq's replacement, Father Marchal, are made in an 1875 letter from John E. Lord of Lillooet. The letter mentions public floggings, that Marchal treats Indians as 'lower than dumb animals,' and that he whips Protestants, too, so 'it cannot be from religious principles.'[12] Lord argues: 'It seems that his particular motive is to obtain money; for the slightest offense he whips, or will let them off on the payment of a fine.' A letter from the Chief of Fountain corroborates Lord's complaint. It reports that Marchal ordered twenty-five lashes for people 'having illicit connection,' and yet the priest refused to marry one couple.[13]

The smallpox that revisited the band in 1875[14] could not have helped in the adjustment to a new way of life at Alkali Lake. The Church was falling out of favour and many were ready to revolt against the new system by the time Indian agents finally arrived to address the residents' appeals for their land claims to be settled.

The Allotment of Land Reserves

According to the surveyors' records of 1881 for Indian Superintendent James Lenihan, the Alkali Lake band members had by that time amassed 561 horses, 123 cattle, 69 sheep, and 15 pigs.[15] I would expect that one reason for adopting an agrarian way of life was that it was the surest way to secure lands against encroachment. Whether or not this was an underlying motivation, it is apparent from Lenihan's records that he was asked to secure lands for the rearing of horses and cattle, and that the reserves, no matter how inadequate their land base, were laid out in accordance with this aim, and with water rights reserved for irrigation of fields.[16] One hundred inches from Alkali Lake Creek were reserved, and all the water from Harper's Lake, as is recorded in the surveyor's sketch and notes reproduced in map 5.[17] Of the seven reserves initially granted to the people of Alkali Lake, Reserve No. 1 was designated for residential and agricultural use (see map 4), Reserves Nos. 2 to 6 for agriculture, and No. 7 as a fishery on Lac la Hache, between mileposts 122 and 123 on the Cariboo Wagon Road. Fishing, an essential part of making a living at Alkali Lake, must have also been regarded by the Indian Superintendent as important, for exclusive rights to fish the east bank of the Fraser River from the confluence of the Chilcotin to Little Dog Creek were granted in addition.[18]

In 1893, one William Wright pre-empted land where Alkali Lake people had made improvements and were growing hay.[19] The objections to his behaviour on the part of Alkali Lake residents were strong enough that, at the request of Indian Agent E. Bell, Indian Superintendent A.M. Vowell paid a visit to the reserve in 1894.[20] In 1895, Alkali Lake was awarded additional reserves, some more suitable for haying than others, numbered 8 to 14.[21]

In 1923, a re-survey of Indian reserves was undertaken in British Columbia. The surveyors' efforts are commonly known as the 'Ditchburn-Clarke cutoffs,' as the result was frequently to cut more land off of existing reserves than to convey additional lands. In the 1920s, Indian population numbers for British Columbia reached their nadir

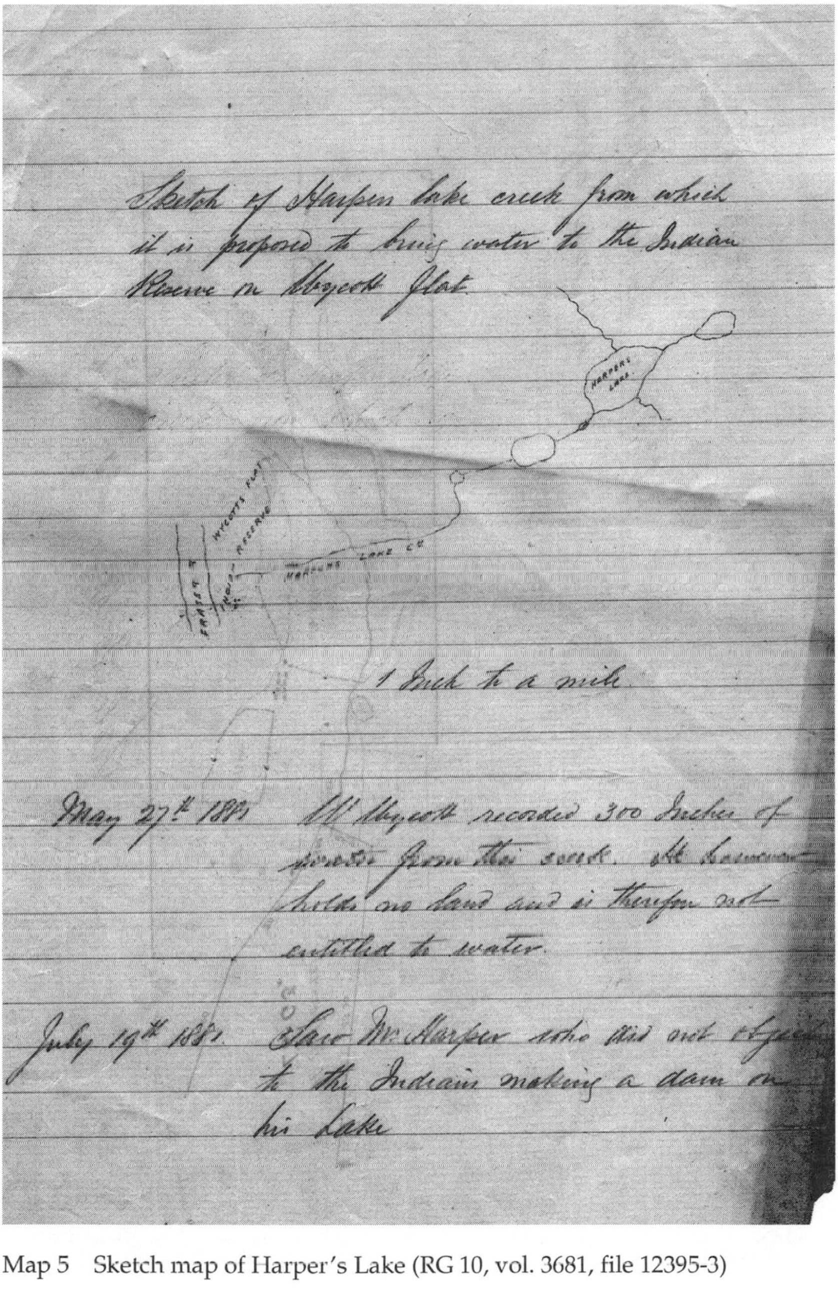

Map 5 Sketch map of Harper's Lake (RG 10, vol. 3681, file 12395-3)

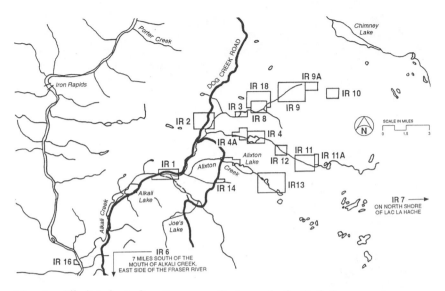

Map 6   Alkali Lake Indian Reserves. Cartography by Beth Suprenant.

(Duff 1965: 44), and the dwindling numbers provided the rationale for the re-survey. At Alkali Lake, a previously established reserve was almost disallowed, and some reserves previously marked off and applied for were not granted. However, a small amount of land was officially gained, forming reserves 16 and 18. This was to be the last government registration of lands at Alkali Lake (see map 6).

Mission Education

In 1891, the first children from Alkali Lake were enrolled at St Joseph's Mission's new industrial boarding school.[22] A new alliance was formed between church and Alkali Lake leaders when Father Francis Thomas, a strong proponent of the Durieu System, came to serve in the Cariboo. Thomas's term was to last from the late 1890s until 1940, and was paralleled by the term of the Alkali Lake hereditary chief, Sxox-omic, who was also known as Chief Sampson. The exact dates of the chief's term of office are unclear (see Furniss's queries, 1987: 124), but the Durieu System was re-established during this time.[23]

   Most of the children were removed to the residential school during the years following Father Thomas's arrival, in part through the enforcement of an 1894 amendment to the *Indian Act* that made it illegal to keep children out of school (Furniss 1992: 12). Often, the children would stay most, or all, of the year, at the school. Their experiences of Alkali were limited to occasional summers at home until they reached age sixteen or more, as the mission school they attended was forty miles from Alkali and the children were required to stay the year round to supply labour for the mission's ranching operations. This separation from their parents meant that, starting as young as age four, children had little chance to learn traditional ways in childhood, and were forbidden to speak Secwepemctsín. The girls became knowledgeable instead in the area of domestic servitude, learning to darn socks, do laundry, mop floors, and cook on stovetops, while the boys learned to work in the fields. Training in manual labour was considered by their teachers to be an important supplement to studies in reading, writing, and religion. Their training contributed to the upkeep of the mission and prepared the children for the wage labour that the mission and the government anticipated they would apply for after completing their education.

One of the justifications for residential schools cited in popular apologias is that the drinking of parents made homes on reserves unfit and dangerous for children. It should therefore be pointed out that the reserve was still under the Durieu System's iron fist of enforced temperance when the current Elders, as children, would have been in school. The band-produced film *The Honour of All* places the reintroduction of alcohol to Alkali Lake at the end of this period, in the 1940s. Andy Chelsea cites culturally recognized authorities on the subject when he says, in the film's prologue, 'as far back as our Elders can remember, there was no drinking at Alkali Lake.' The change in life on the reserve in the 1940's would have been attested to by the Elders alive at the time of the filming. Those Elders, raised in the teens and twenties of the twentieth century, probably did not experience drinking on their home reserves, although alcohol would have been available 'in town' (William's Lake) from bootleggers, trappers, and ranchers.

Many who are now Elders at Alkali grew to be devout Catholics from their religious training at the mission, but have nonetheless told me of their misery and homesickness, hunger and weariness working in the mission's kitchen and fields. Furniss (1992) describes the sorrows of the students at the school (including the running away of several boys, and the subsequent death of one of them), as do the Secwepemc participants in the 1991 documentaries on sexual abuse, *A*

Circle of Healing and *A Violation of Trust* (both by the Canadian Broadcasting Corporation). Brow reports that 'stories of severe punishment, such as beatings, the withdrawal of food, and confinement were universal among Indians from Alkali Lake, Sugar Cane, Deep Creek and Soda Creek reserves' (1967: 69).

In 1949, the *Public Schools Act* was amended to make provincial school education available to Indian children, by agreement with local school boards. Tuition fees were to be paid to the mission by the Indian Affairs Branch for another year (British Columbia 1952). The mission school switched from an 'industrial' to an academic emphasis in 1951, in accordance with the *Revised Indian Act*. Schoolchildren were not to see their parents on a daily basis at Alkali Lake until 1958, when the Department of Indian Affairs opened a one-room day school on the reserve for grades 1 through 6.[24] Some Alkali Lake children continued to be educated at the mission until 1964, when the federal government took over control of the mission school from the Oblates. From 1960 to 1970, children wishing to complete grade 12 had to travel to Prince George, or to the residential school in Kamloops.[25] When the BC public schools in Williams Lake finally opened their doors to integration in the late 1960s, children did not at first commute from Alkali Lake, but were boarded at the mission's student residence. Thus, the separation of children and teenagers from their parents and the daily influence of the church on their lives were continued to the 1970s.

In the late 1990s and early 2000s, inquiries into the treatment of children at the residential school were finally acted upon. The process was painful, as memories of abuse were relived by many in the community. As elsewhere in Canada at this time, some victims turned to suicide after giving testimony. As of this writing, a bishop has been suspended, and charges are pending in some cases.

The Reserve in the Mid-1960s

The circumstances of life at Alkali Lake in the mid-1960s were extremely bleak, according to Catherine Brow (1967). The affairs of the band seem to have been run entirely by outside administrators, and improvements to the reserve's physical plant contracted by Indian Affairs employed no one from the reserve (ibid.: 87). Many houses were drafty, uninsulated prefabricated plywood structures heated by wood cookstoves. (Brow's map of the village [161] shows some houses, now somewhat remodelled and plumbed, that are still in use at Alkali

Lake today.) Water was obtained from pumps in the central dirt track that runs through the reserve, when the water mains were not frozen or otherwise broken (Brow 1967). Electric lines were run to the reserve in 1965, but electric stoves and heaters were not then in use.

Brow reports that of the 209 people resident on the reserve in 1966, only 8 had wage-earning jobs. Although she does not provide statistics concerning hunting or gathering, she mentions that older women did some gardening and berrying, while young people seemed to purchase most of their food with social-assistance cheques. 'Potatoes and salmon, which is smoked and preserved, constitute the basic food supply of every family. Although this diet is supplemented with some purchased goods, especially bologna, cookies and eggs, most meals consist of bread (either store bought or an unleavened homemade variety),[26] potatoes and salmon' (1967: 92).

An extremely high rate of alcoholism had developed on the reserve, and Brow's thesis is full of references to drinking parties, abuse, and despair. The movie that Alkali Lake residents made of their struggle with alcoholism concurs with Brow's assessment of life on the reserve in the 1960s.

The Struggle for Autonomy from 1968 Onward

The late 1960s saw the beginnings of band control over its own housing, education, and social services. In 1968, the home schooling program was introduced, and the Indian Affairs Branch provided funding for one band member to coordinate the program on the reserve.[27] Band government changed in 1971, when chief and council were no longer elected to life terms. With the desire that chief and council be responsive to the electorate came the formation of task forces and other committees. In 1972, under the supervision of the band's Esket Education Committee, the Alkali Lake band took over the education program, and some control over disbursement of school funds, from Indian Affairs. Generations of Secwepemc children had been forbidden to speak their own language in the mission school, but in 1974 Secwepemc language studies were added to the curriculum of Alkali Lake's day school.

Beyond the reserve, Prime Minister Trudeau's administration attempted to make radical changes to Indian policy in 1969. The first attempts backfired, but galvanized organized Native response to government and led to the strengthening of the Union of BC Indian Chiefs, which became a powerful poliltical force (Tennant 1990). With a government-funded budget of two million dollars per year (ibid., 1990, reporting figures for 1972), the Union had the attention of the press, and therefore, the ear of the government. More government monies were freed up for improvements and development programs on reserves. Alkali Lake benefited from the increase in funds, which allowed for improvements to the physical plant and the startup of some small enterprises. Steady jobs funded by the federal government also permitted some band members to remain on the reserve while working for wages.

As recounted in Elizabeth Furniss's master's thesis (1987) on the Sobriety Movement at Alkali Lake, and in *The Honour of All* (1987), the 1970s were a time of intense change, spurred by the resolve of Phyllis Chelsea, the newly elected chief Andy Chelsea, and others to introduce sobriety to the reserve. The band went from a rate of alcoholism at or near 100% in 1972, to a sobriety rate of 40% in 1975, 60% in 1979, and 90% by 1985 (Alkali Lake Band Files). Newly sober band members attended alcohol treatment centres off-reserve and were rewarded with refurbished housing, the possibility of on-reserve employment, and, most importantly, the fierce support of their community to remain sober. Furniss attributes the success of the movement partly to the similarities in rigid social control of the Chelseas' tactics to those of the Durieu system.

Prosperity

When I arrived to begin fieldwork in the fall of 1987, Alkali Lake was experiencing a period of prosperity and pride. The film *The Honour of All*, chronicling the band's successful journey to sobriety, had been aired nationwide by the Canadian Broadcasting Company earlier that year, and band members were attempting to come to terms with their newfound celebrity. Many wore jackets that proclaimed their band affiliation wherever they went. In the town of Williams Lake, the perception of the general population seemed to be that Alkali Lake was prospering. People from the reserve were able to secure loans to buy pickup trucks at local dealerships, and high school students from Alkali Lake strolled around the local shopping mall, looking confident and well groomed. A band-run piggery, greenhouse, and cafe had just closed down, unfortunately, but plans were afoot for the band to purchase a sawmill. The band had control of its own school; the principal and several teachers were band members, and the Secwepemc language and cultural studies had been introduced to the curriculum. A company for the development of human potential called New Directions provided jobs on the reserve and funds for travel to other reservations and reserves in the United States and Canada.

With the relative economic prosperity that accompanied the sobriety movement, the hosting of many people of different bands at the reserve, and the opportunities for travel afforded to Alkali Lake band members, there seemed to be a considerable increase in marriages that resulted in residence at Alkali Lake – including marriages to members of the Fraser River Division bands at Sugar Cane, Canoe Creek, Dog Creek, the Lakes Division (Canim Lake), Kamloops, and, further afield, the Carrier and even Tlingit. Brow (1967) reported a high level of out-marriage from Alkali Lake in the 1960s, and this reversal in the trend can also be considered a sign of the band's prosperity.

Employment Opportunities

Cash entered Alkali Lake's mixed economy from a variety of sources, including the federal government, school disbursements, the band store and gas station, the timber and ranching industries, and band-operated businesses. Off-reserve opportunities in the timber industry included sawmill machine operation, slash burning, logging, and forest fire fighting. In the town of Williams Lake, the multi-band-operated Cariboo Tribal Council provided employment for two to three women from Alkali Lake, while the RCMP employed one officer from the band.

On the reserve, summer band development work provided regular wages to some, and provided training experience for others receiving unemployment-insurance and social-assistance funds. Housing construction was an important component of this seasonal work and training, especially because of new federal legislation that was expected to greatly increase the demand for housing on the reserve. The passage of Bill C-31 in 1985 had eliminated as discriminatory, and therefore not in accordance with the Canadian Charter of Rights and Freedoms, the section of the *Indian Act* that had excluded many from the official Indian Register, and had thereby denied them the right to live on reserves, or to claim housing entitlements. The old *Indian Act* decreed that the children of Indian women and non-Indian men had no recognition under federal law as so-called 'status' or 'registered' Indians, and that Indian women who married non-Indian men involuntarily lost their status as Indians, as did any minor children born before the marriage (Duff 1965: 46–7). Many Indian women who had married non-Indian men, and the descendants of those women, were in the process of obtaining or reinstating their legal status as Indians in 1988, and were applying for on-reserve housing.

Cowboying and haying were also important occupations in the summer, both on the reserve and in the employ of other local ranches. Many people at Alkali are excellent riders and wranglers, and some participate in, and win on, the professional rodeo circuit. Monetary rodeo prizes are generally balanced or outweighed by the costs of participating in the events, and so do not often bring much direct income to the reserve, but known ability with horses can make a difference both in securing employment on ranches and in the good opinion of businessmen who need to be negotiated with in Williams Lake.

The most significant and consistent source of employment on the reserve was funded by the federal government through the band's general operating revenues. The chief and four to five council members, the band office secretary, the medical-services nurse, the alcohol treatment counsellor and two to three other social-services employees, Homemakers (domestic help), and a summer youth coordinator were all band members.

The band-run Sxoxomic School provided employment to band members and was funded by the monies that would have gone to the larger Williams Lake School District if the band had opted to have the district run the school. Because they ran the school themselves, band officials could also offer priority hiring to band members. The principal, grade 1 teachers, daycare provider, Secwepemc language teachers, classroom helpers, home-school coordinator, and school janitor were all band members.

Offering classes from nursery school to grade 10, the band-run school has provided some considerable advantages to the community that go beyond employment. Children no longer need to live separated from their families, or commute the 100-kilometre round trip to and from Williams Lake each day. Parents are involved in the school and know the teachers as friends or family members. Teachers have knowledge of their students' families and of any difficulties they may currently be facing. The school gym is used by the full community for special events and sports activities, and the library is open to all.

Because band members have taken many workshops on alcohol-related topics, they are better versed in the manifestations of fetal alcohol effects than most teachers in mainstream school systems. Their sophistication in these matters complements traditional ways of teaching; when working in the school they show patience with slower learners and respect for each individual's efforts at school. Caring teachers from the community, and a new group of students born to sober parents, may prove to make a great difference in the education and employment opportunities of the next generation.

School and government employees on the reserve who were not band members included the band administrator, accountant, psychological counsellors, several teachers, the vice-principal, a doctor, and a nurse. A computer-science teacher in the school did not then have official status as a band member, but is of Alkali Lake ancestry. Despite a shortage of housing, the school board encourages the teachers to live on the reserve, and to participate in reserve life, so that they may come to know the families of Alkali Lake as more than simply pupils and their parents.

The band has other employment opportunities closely associated with its sobriety and the human potential movement. Andy and Phyllis Chelsea took a one-week course from Lifespring Canada in 1980 (Furniss 1987): a program to develop self-esteem, self-awareness, self-enhancement, and a sense of responsibility for one's own actions. Techniques were highly confrontational, and were based on the same core philosophy as is the more widely known Erhardt Seminars Training (also known as EST). Thirty-eight Alkali Lake band members took the Lifespring Training in Vancouver in 1981, and twenty-eight went on to a second stage of training (Furniss 1987: 67). When Lifespring Canada dissolved, one of the leading trainers came to Alkali Lake, and with band members ran a new company, called New Directions. New Directions provided on-reserve employment for band members, who acted as workshop leaders or trainers. They offered the workshops free to band members, and generated funds by charging off-reserve participants at a usual rate of four hundred dollars per week-long workshop. Trainers and volunteer assistants also had the opportunity to travel to other reserves, some in distant parts of the United States and Canada, to offer workshops. Families on the reserve would host workshop attendees and would receive cash to help with room and board costs. A company based on the reserve, called Pathways, was developed by key leaders from New Directions. In the years following the founding of New Directions, several individuals from Alkali Lake have worked as addictions counsellors for government health and human services agencies. A tourism company, Native Journeys, currently promotes cultural and recreational experiences at and around Esk̇et.

Land Claims

As should be apparent from the foregoing history, claims to land, to a decent livelihood, to control of education, and to self-governance have been actively pursued by Secwepemc people vis-à-vis Euro-Canadian colonial agents since the first contact between these groups. Secwepemc territory has never been subject to a formal treaty between the Crown and the Secwepemc people and their descendants now residing at Alkali Lake, and the title and rights to their territory have never been ceded, surrendered, or sold to the Crown. A new chapter in political relations was begun in 1993, with the entrance of the Secwepemc people into a treaty-negotiation process with the BC and Canadian governments. A treaty research and negotiations team made up of Alkali Lake band members was set up. Funding for the team and their consultants was provided largely by an advance[28] against the anticipated future claims settlement. In 1997, the signing of a Framework Treaty Agreement between the BC Ministry of Aboriginal Affairs, the federal Ministry of Indian Affairs and Northern Development, and the Esketemc First Nation (formerly the Alkali Lake Indian Band) led to the commencement of talks to set out an agreement in principle between these parties. However, no such agreement has been reached. The band reported, via the BC Treaty Commission, that in 2003 the federal government had expressed some desire to withdraw from treaty talks due to their lack of progress.

The Esketemc First Nation continues to negotiate with timber cut-block licensees and the Ministry of Forests for some control over the timber harvest within their traditional territory. The BC Court of Appeals has ruled that timber licensees have a duty to consult with First Nations regarding cut blocks on their traditional territories, whether land-claims agreements with the First Nations have been completed or not. The Supreme Court of Canada heard evidence in the Crown's appeal of this ruling in March 2004 in the case *The Minister of Forests, et al. v. Council of the Haida Nation*. The Supreme Court's ruling in this case is expected to have a significant impact on the ability of Secwepemc First Nations to control resource access and revenues within their traditional territories.

Chapter 3

Living on the Land

Subsistence activities form an integral part of life in Alkali Lake, particularly when subsistence contributions to livelihood are viewed at the level of the extended family, rather than the individual. While a wage earner today may have little time to schedule an overnight trip to fish for salmon, or a trip into the mountains to hunt, it is generally the case that some in the family will be able to take on these tasks, often with the benefit of a vehicle or gas money provided by the wage earner. In order to consider the cultural transmission of knowledge, as rooted in subsistence traditions, this chapter will address issues of economics and history, health and spirituality, identity and family support.

The degree to which hunting and gathering continue to sustain families at Alkali Lake is generally underestimated by federal and provincial agencies. Government records for Alkali Lake throughout the 1900s show only how much cash was generated from trapping and through guide services provided to hunters. The records list how many band members were unemployed and self-employed in census years as lump figures, as does Brow (1967). Of 99 reserve residents investigated by Brow in 1966, 29 people were listed as 'employed' [i.e., as wage labourers], 57 as 'unemployed or self employed,' and 13 as 'infirm.' A similar situation exists in the historic documentation of other Indian economies of British Columbia, as Hugh Brody found in the case of the Dunne-za, or Beaver Indians:

> It is not easy to gather statistics for income from all available sources. The reluctance of hunters to give full details about their hunting, the fact that Indian trappers within the Treaty 8 area are not obliged to file fur returns, and people's imprecise recollection of exact numbers, even when volun-

teered, make quantification elusive. Accused, as they repeatedly are, of overharvesting, waste, and defiance of game laws, Indian hunters suspect that numbers may be used against them. Yet they also know that they stand accused of no longer needing to hunt. Local Whites, and even some game management officials, have often said that Indians have ceased to use the bush. Conventional methods of calculating the Indian economy reinforce this notion. Wage employment and transfer payments (pensions, child allowances, unemployment cheques, welfare benefits, etc.) are recognized as income; earnings from the bush are not. Full-time hunters are, therefore, officially classified an unemployed. Their earnings from the hunt, and even from trapping, are taken to be minimal or nil or unavailable. Conventional economic analyses thus systematically misrepresent the Indian economy.   (1981: 200)

Although wild foods are not eaten in all houses on the reserve every day, my observation at Alkali Lake has been that, if desired, berries and wild meat or fish can always be found to set on the table.

Hunting and Trapping

When James Teit arrived on a pack train at Dog Creek in 1900, the land set aside for reserves in the area was still inadequate for farming and ranching, making continued fishing, hunting, and gathering an economic necessity, as well as continued custom. Deer, elk, and caribou were formerly the most commonly hunted large game. Teit reported that elk were almost extinct in the area by 1850, and the territory for caribou had diminished (1909: 513). Reports from the Alkali Lake band files indicate that the first moose in their local hunting territory was spotted in the early 1900s. Logging has provided the moose with abundant habitat, and they have grown more numerous in recent years. Moose and deer are most commonly hunted today, as they are available. Snares are set, especially by children, for smaller animals such as rabbits. Mink, marten, otter, and beaver are still occasionally trapped for their pelts, and old hide stretchers can be seen propped up against people's cabins in the meadows away from the main reserve.

People of several families at Alkali still hunt for deer and moose on the west side of the Fraser opposite their main reserve, despite the encroachment of the Tsilhqot'in in that area after 1862. Access to the other side of the river is maintained across the Farwell Canyon bridge well north and west of Alkali (approximately sixty-five miles away, by

road), and by the Churn Creek suspension bridge to the south. The
river is also sometimes crossed on the winter ice. In addition, one
Alkali Lake reserve (IR No. 16, Old Clemene's), a fishing place, is
located on the west bank of the Fraser River (see map 7, p. 117). The
lands east of the main reserve, off Joe's Lake Road and southward,
toward the Dog Creek Reserve, are also frequently hunted. Pickup
trucks provide speedier access and easier transport of meat for those
hunters who go out in the evenings but must be at wage jobs in the
morning. Still, many hunters set out on foot or horseback, or trailer
their horses to more promising hunting areas.

Fishing

Before European contact, as today, the hunting and gathering economy
has included a strong emphasis on fishing. For the Secwepemc, salmon
was (and remains) a key resource, especially in the semi-sedentary villages of the Fraser River Division. During the summer runs, the ancestors of the people of Alkali Lake dip-netted on the Fraser River at
several key eddies near their villages. Occasionally, sturgeon were also
taken from the Fraser, although they were very difficult to land, requir-
ing stout ropes, days of patience, and often the use of trees as tie-off
points for the ropes (cf. Speare 1973: 33–35). Kokanee salmon were
caught in small gill nets during their run at Lac la Hache, and trout
were taken in early spring by weir or dip net from the small streams
that feed into the Fraser near Alkali Lake.

Trout and kokanee are still caught today, and their respective fisheries are on reserved land at IR No. 4 and IR No. 7 (Windy Mouth) on Lac
la Hache. Trout are caught in streams as the spring begins and the
snow melts. On trips I went on, children laughing and splashing in
boots swirled sticks in the water to flush the trout downstream where
older people, both men and women, waited with dip nets. The trout
run is not large, and no one gets the opportunity to consume more than
a few trout each year, but as the first fresh fish of the year, and a har-
binger of spring, it is very welcome. Kokanee, which have a run in Lac
la Hache, can be caught cooperatively as well, by pairs of people walking into the lake holding a gill net spread between them.

Fishing for salmon at Alkali is now mostly done at night. This keeps
the caught fish cool, and people say the fish can't see the nets that way.
It is also more peaceful to fish at night, as troublesome Fisheries officers are less likely to interrupt. When one is standing on a slippery rock,

reaching out with a long, heavy dip net to catch something that might weigh twenty pounds, little attention can be spared to watch the river's edge for approaching strangers.

In 1987 and 1988, salmon made up a larger share of the food budget at Alkali than did deer and moose meat combined. At the height of the summer run on the Fraser in 1987, teams of three dip-netting fishermen were able to bring in well over two hundred fish in an evening. The peak of the salmon run is never entirely predictable, however, and the fishermen may invest a full night's labour, only to 'catch a lot of water.' Throughout the late 1990s the supply of fish grew increasingly unreliable. The Department of Fisheries' schedules for the Native food fishery have become increasingly restrictive, and a number of the salmon caught have had to be discarded because of unusual ulcers appearing on their flesh. Concern over these ulcers has led one Elder on the Soda Creek Reserve upriver from Alkali to give up eating salmon entirely (E. Furniss, personal communication). Ongoing treaty talks between the United States and Canada are not currently providing people involved in the fishery on the Fraser River and its tributaries with any reassurance of a continuation of a healthy population of salmon into the future. Dwindling stocks of coho salmon led to calls for restrictions, ranging from a 10 per cent harvest to a total ban on sport, commercial, and Native food fisheries for coho in 1998.

Processing the Catch

The salmon, which were formerly prepared in a fish camp adjacent to the dip-net sites, now generally rest ungutted in a stone cache through the cool of the night, and are then hauled back to the reserve by the fishermen via horse or pickup truck at first light. Fish camps, with drying racks, are still occasionally made at the dip-netting site at the Churn Creek suspension bridge.

Smoking, freezing, and canning are all common methods of preserving fish. Whereas mostly men and boys fish, now, as in the past, women do much of the processing of the fish. Most people have small (10' × 10') shed smokehouses behind their houses, and prepare the salmon there on outside tables. A smoky fire helps to keep the flies off the fish, and the preparers, during processing. Women often work together to rapidly prepare the fish for smoking. The head is removed from each salmon, and then it is slit along the belly and gutted. Each half of the fish is cut parallel to the skin, to halve its thickness and to allow for the fish to be spread out across the drying rack or sticks. The fish are then slashed in a crosshatch pattern, often characteristically enough that a woman's individual 'signature' is evident, or at least her area of origin. A shake of salt to aid in drawing out the moisture, and other spices, especially pepper, are optional touches. The salmon is then draped and spread over a rail or rafter in the roof of the smoke-house.

The guts, and sometimes the heads, of the salmon are added to the fire pan full of aged pine cones and sticks in the smokehouse, and con-tribute to the smoke. Fires need to be checked every hour or so, for if they are not kept up until the fish are dry (one to three days, depend-ing on conditions) the fish will be beset by flies. The fish are turned over during smoking, and then taken into the home for storage, and to make room for the next night's catch. The sustained effort is made eas-ier if there are many at home taking responsibility for checking on the fire. The end product is a food that can be stored for a year with little additional effort, is tasty whether eaten plain or in soup, and that is ideal for hunters to carry for nourishment when they must travel light.

In addition to putting up a stock of dried salmon, each family also cans and or freezes fish, with deep-freezers gaining in popularity and affordability ever since Alkali Lake got electricity in 1965. Fish can be speedily wrapped in aluminum foil, butcher paper, or plastic, which cost money, as do the deep-freezers and the electricity, but the savings in time over smoking, especially important for a woman who works in a day job, are tremendous. Frozen fish also lend themselves to slow baking, as they can be left in a slow oven while one is away at work during the day. Salmon prepared in this way suit the style of hospital-ity evident at Alkali Lake, where, ideally, there is always a kettle on for tea, and something in the oven or on the stove for whomever drops by.

Using a range of storage techniques seems especially prudent, as an animal may occasionally get into a smokehouse, or the smoky fire can go out and flies ruin a batch of dried fish. Freezers cannot always be relied on either. At the height of the fishing season in 1989, the provin-cial electric company, BC Hydro, deemed a week's work on the power lines south of the reserve necessary. Power was cut off daily from 8:30 to 11:40 a.m., and again from 1:00 to 3:00 p.m. Power was restored between 11:40 a.m. and 1:00 p.m., presumably to accommodate people cooking lunch. A court case was being heard on the reserve, and arrangements were made by the band's attorney for power to be on for the day court was in session, but no such arrangements were made

Ollie Johnson dipnetting at dusk on the Fraser River

Dipnetting at The Point

with respect to the fishery. I am not aware of whether appeals were made, but the consequences to some families' supplies of fish were extreme. The men would arrive back at the reserves with their catches between 6:00 and 8:00 a.m., and distribute the fish by going house to house. Women preparing the fish for freezing would gut and wrap them, and then put them in the freezer. The power would then be cut off, and the fish might, or might not, get cold enough to retard spoilage until the evening. The more fish in the freezer, the less likely they were to get cold. For families in which the adults held jobs outside the home, and so could not remain at home long enough to prepare fish for smoking, or tend to the smoke pots, it was a difficult season.

In some years, Native food fishery licences are required by the Canadian government. Obtaining a licence requires a trip to the agency office in William's Lake on a weekday. Such a licence may minimize immediate conflicts with Fisheries officials patrolling the river, but many at Alkali Lake strongly object to obtaining a licence for their fishing, and argue that to obtain licences to hunt or to fish is to compromise their rights to manage their own livelihoods. Some on the reserve actively discourage others from seeking licences. Fisheries regulations change frequently, and are to some extent dependent on how many fish are counted coming up the river by the government spotters.

Bringing salmon back to The Point trailhead

Preparing salmon for smoking

Racks of salmon in the smokehouse

Sharon Please 1) post on bulletin boards 2) make extra copies and send to families that harvest.

Government of Canada
Fisheries and Oceans

FISHERIES PUBLIC NOTICE

NOTICE TO INDIAN FOOD FISHERMEN

1989 Indian Food Fish Licences will be available from the Department of Fisheries and Oceans Office in Williams Lake effective June 12, 1989.
The Williams Lake office is located at 260 D, North Broadway, next door to ICBC.
Dept. of Fisheries and Oceans staff will be available to issue licences at the Williams Lake Office from: 8:00 AM to 12:00 Noon and 12:30 PM to 4:30 PM daily, Monday to Friday, effective June 12, 1989 until further notice.

All Indian Food Fishermen are reminded that they must be in possession of a valid food fishing licence prior to engaging in food fishing or transporting fish lawfully caught under an Indian Food Fish Licence.

The following regulations are in effect for 1989 in Williams Lake Sub-district:

1. Fishing is permitted 7 days per week by means of a dip net or gaff in the Chilcotin and Chilco Rivers upstream to Henry's Crossing and in the Fraser River from Churn Creek to Quesnel River.

2. Fishing times are subject to change by Fisheries Public Notice. Changes to normal fishing times may be required due to strength of salmon returns or harvest allocation rate.

3. Indian Food Fish Licences must be carried by the fisherman at all times when fishing and produced to a fishery officer upon request.

4. Sale, trade or barter of fish caught under authority of an Indian Fish Food Licence is strictly prohibited.

5. No person other than a registered Indian shall be in possession of fish caught under the authority of an Indian Food Fish Licence.

FOR FURTHER INFORMATION, CONTACT THE DEPT. OF FISHERIES AND OCEANS IN WILLIAMS LAKE, B.C.— TELEPHONE 398-6544.

P.C. Harvey,
Fishery Officer.

Received JUN_8 1989.

PLACE Williams Lake B.C.
DATE June 5, 1989

THIS POSTER MAY BE DISPLAYED IN POST OFFICE LOBBIES BY AUTHORITY OF POSTMASTER GENERAL.

Government notice to Indian food fishermen

In some years, there is a window of only a few days when fish can legally be caught. Regulations are usually posted at the post office in the village store, but those Elders who are non-literate do not of course read the notices. The accompanying figure provides the text of posted notice for the opening of the fishing season in 1989 as an example of these regulations.

Berries, roots, moss, and bark

When Angela George picks berries, her entire concentration is on picking rapidly, and efficiently, to fill as many buckets as possible before nightfall, while still keeping an eye on her grandchildren. The days available to pick berries are few, and the gas money to get far from the reserve to unpicked fields is costly, so berry picking is a rapid, focused activity that allows little time for talk or rest during the actual picking. There is plenty of time to talk on the long trips home. Away from berry picking, every step that Angela takes when she is gathering seems to find her reaching to touch, and name, and remember the uses for, another plant.

When we travel, she notes the changes on the landscape attributable to the introduction of livestock:

Angela: Used to be lots of berries
Saskatoons down here in this spot
And the ranchers here they don't feed their cattle
and they eat all the bushes

AP: Yes?

My mom used to come up on wagon and pick enough there
for one winter
And white people here the ranchers there ( ) they don't feed
their cattle
and they eat all the berry bushes their cattle

AP: Mmm.

( )
they make the cattle suffer

(Tape 3 b; 17 July 1989)

Cattle grazing has significantly lessened the diversity of plant life: the avalanche lily (*Erythronium grandiflorium*; called *swicw* in Secwepem-ctsín) and mariposa lily (*Calochortus macrocarpus*; *lilt'se* in Secwepemctsín), their corms once commonly dug for food, are now rarely seen in bloom. The trampling of cattle hooves has compacted the dry alkaline soils throughout the area, making those lilies that do survive exceptionally difficult to dig up. Angela George has had some experience steam-cooking layers of roots and corms in pit ovens (cf. Turner et al. 1980: 10, 1990: 72), but notes that even when enough roots can be found, this traditional mode of preparation takes a lot of work by those young and strong enough to dig the pit, and responsible enough to tend it through several days of steaming.

Other starchy foods from the bush take less work to prepare, but are nonetheless seldom eaten today at Alkali Lake. Angela George and her cohort are exceptional in that they still occasionally gather huge bags of black tree lichen (*Bryoria fremontii* or *Alectoria jubata*; called *wíla* in Secwepemctsín) to steam into pudding-like loaves. The lichen is not all that difficult to pick, and is light to pack, though bulky. It can be steamed on the stove-top or in the oven. I have found it to be delicious.

In all, over 135 species of plants are reported as being of known use as food, medicine, or construction material in the more diverse ecosystems in the Secwepemc Kamloops Division territory to the south of Alkali Lake (G. Palmer 1975a). The territory around Alkali Lake is in the Interior dry belt. Douglas fir and lodgepole pine are the main tree types, with cottonwood being common as well. Sage and grasses dominate on the hardpan, while willows, red osier dogwood, and aspen fringe the edges of springs and streams.

Entries in Turner et al. (1990), which pertain to the Nlha7kápmx in the Thompson River area, are a good source of information about traditional plant use at Alkali Lake, as the area has biogeoclimatic characteristics similar to those in the territory around Alkali Lake. In addition, many Secwepemc plant names closely resemble the names in the Nlha7kápmx language, Secwepemctsín's close linguistic relative. I will discuss the most commonly used and talked about plants at Alkali Lake below.

Berries are perhaps the most significant resource in use today as a food. The most abundant, and the most commonly collected, are the service berry (saskatoon, *Amelanchier alnifolia*), soopolallie (soapberry, *Shepherdia canadensis*), and the various *vaccinia*, or blueberries. The tiny lowbush blueberries are picked by hand, or are raked off the bush using a fine comb and catch basin implement, which looks rather like a flour scoop with spikes on the leading edge, and has a capacity of approximately one cup. The several kinds of blue or huckleberries are

Angela George picking saskatoon berries

Elaine Ignatius gently taps soapberries into an open umbrella

Angela George with a home-made soapberry whip of shredded bark

Alfie Bowie enjoying soapberries in camp

picked and eaten fresh, and may be frozen or made into pies and jams. A few people still preserve some of their supply of berries by drying them in the sun, and periodically pouring juice over them during the drying process, but this is no longer a common treatment.

Birch bark is still regularly fashioned into baby and berry-picking baskets by at least four female Elders at Alkali. The bark cradles 'breathe' better than the cradles fashioned out of cardboard in roughly the same manner as the bark ones, making for more comfortable babies. Similarly, the birch-bark berry baskets are preferred to plastic buckets, for berries can remain for a time in a bark basket without sweating and rotting. One female Elder is said to own a clump of birch trees above IR No. 1. Birch trees are sparse locally, but grow abundantly in the far wetter Lakes Division territory, and another Elder gathers her birch bark in that territory, near Canim Lake, after obtaining permission from her friends there to do so.

Medicines

All foods classified as 'Indian food' are also considered as 'Indian medicine.' An individual's health and well-being can be maintained in part through the consumption of 'Indian foods' and, occasionally, through fasting, or abstinence from consumption, through the production of food by fishing, hunting, and gathering, through the preparation and sharing of food, and by learning about the land, plants, and animals through participation in these activities. The larger category of 'medicine' (*melamens*), however, also includes plants that are not strictly 'foods' and the practices used to treat illnesses and maintain health.

Brow (1967) has noted that until changes were made to the *Indian Act* in 1951, no one from Alkali Lake was treated in hospital, except for those with cases of tuberculosis. Tuberculosis cases for the Interior and Lower Mainland of British Columbia were managed at Coqualeetza, an all-Indian sanitarium in the Fraser Valley near the US-Canadian border. The lack of Western medical-care facilities available to Indians until as recently as the 1950s has perhaps contributed to the fact that traditional remedies continue to be remembered by Elders and middle-aged people. Yet this is certainly not the only, or necessarily the most significant, reason. For many, I would suggest, the spiritual value of these medicines is also important.

Individuals who have knowledge of traditional and Western reme-

Angela George scraping the outer bark of a balsam fir

dies can weigh the costs and benefits of each, based on their particular circumstances, and choose accordingly. One example of a change in treatment concerns the preferred cure for toothaches. In the traditional remedy, the small, red root of the yarrow plant is mashed onto an infected tooth. Within a day, the tooth should shatter and fall out. This was formerly a reasonable course of action, as the alternative to a bad tooth infection is sometimes death. When over-the-counter remedies could be obtained, it was found that Absorbine Jr. had the same effect as the sometimes hard-to-find root. Now, a dentist in town is available through Indian Health Services, so teeth are sometimes filled, instead of being shattered.

Major ailments that would require surgery and several days of hospitalization if treated by doctors in town are sometimes treated with home remedies. Gallstones, for example, are sometimes successfully treated with an infusion of boiled juniper berries, drunk several times a day for several days. Minor ailments such as cuts and sores can be treated with salves of balsam tree sap, and chewing the pitch from lodgepole pines helps a sore throat. Eyewashes and teas 'to purify the blood' are in common use.

In reserve kitchens, coffee tins and other containers often sit on the back burners of stoves, slowly simmering up medicines, including juniper and Labrador tea, to purify the air in the room or to drink as a tea. Ground, dried big sage leaves from the local sidehills and red cedar scales collected at nearby Horsefly are handled with great respect, and are used in a purifying smudge. This may be left to smoulder in a shell on the table, especially at night, if one is plagued by bad dreams, or if there is a heavy feeling in the house. Wild-rose brambles pinned over doorways also offer spiritual protection.

Traditional medicines for physical and spiritual purification and general well-being are used on a daily basis on the reserve, and are often employed in association with the sweat bath. These sweats are held at Alkali almost daily, and complement the Plains-style Sacred Sweats, which are also held on the reserve. Several individuals make important contributions to the community through the running of the Plains-style Sweatlodge Ceremonies, but I do not have the kind of knowledge that would permit me to discuss these here. In the local-style sweats, specific healing ingredients may be infused into water to assist with the cure of a particular ailment. The water is usually drawn from the creek, and heated next to the sweat-bath fire in a clean oil drum. Wild rose bushes and other plants are also cooked into the drum of water, to be used as a

Dorothy Johnson picking sage along Dog Creek Road

general wash. The water prepared in this way is fragrant and imparts softness to skin and hair. A fresh mat of Douglas fir boughs covers the floor, inside the sweat house, and bent green willow branches form the ribs of the lodge. Dried sage leaves are sprinkled over the heated rocks in the sweatlodge during prayer, sending fragrance into the air, and steam from the water over the rocks fills the lungs. Songs may be sung, and difficult problems talked out, and friendly support offered, in the warm, darkened space of the sweatlodge.

Traditional Foods

The interchangeable classificatory labels 'Indian food' and 'traditional food' as used at Alkali Lake provide a rich topic for investigation. Beyond the consideration of these foods as medicine, it should also be noted that they are important markers of identity. At feasts and banquets (and there were many – four held for the whole community and visitors from off-reserve in the space of three weeks one November, for example), foods perceived as traditional were in high demand, and were often finished, while other foods, such as store-bought cold cuts, languished a while on the buffet tables. Soopolallie juice, 'Indian ice cream,' all kinds of berries and berry pies, and homemade jams are included as traditional foods on the feast table. Although freshly gathered roots and shoots and other traditionally harvested plant foods seldom appear on feast tables, they are occasionally gathered in small quantities by some Elders, and are served in household dinners, or cooked up and sent over to the houses of friends and relatives. In this way, these foods are shared, even though they may not be harvested in quantities appropriate for presentation as feast dishes. All these foods indicate hospitality and self-reliance on the part of the host. Other frequently consumed 'Indian foods' include stews and other dishes made from deer, moose, elk, and salmon.

Traditional foods are advocated as part of a healthy diet by instructors for the alcohol treatment program at Poundmaker's Lodge at St Albert, Alberta, which many of the Elders have attended, and at the University of Lethbridge, to which some have travelled to participate in a nutrition program. Several Elders point to these programs as influencing their cooking.

Bannock, or frybread, is considered 'Indian food' throughout much of North America. Made mostly of flour and oil, it is easy to prepare, and much less costly than store-bought bread. Flour, along with sugar and tea, was a part of the fur-trade economy long before cash was used between traders and Native peoples in the west. In a workshop on the Alkali Lake Reserve, Native health advocates visiting from the US Indian Health Services based in Rockport, Maryland, discounted the value of frybread to the diet. When they talked about the health risks associated with its high fat content, the rhetoric used to strengthen their position was that frybread was 'not Indian food.' Yet, many Elders tell me that they get sick on 'Whiteman's foods,' and that they are much happier eating wind-dried salmon and bannock every day. It is also the case that salmon, bannock, berries, and other 'Indian foods' are locally prepared by people whom one knows, and under known circumstances. Such food, 'prepared with love,' provides far more than physical nourishment.

Obstructions to Current Hunting and Gathering Practices

The ability to hunt and gather, and to continue these practices in the context of their mixed economy, is seen by the people of Alkali Lake as essential to their livelihood. Currently, several problems with ranchers and with fish and game officials are topics of discussion on the reserve. Many men and women lament that land is being fenced by ranchers, that cattleguards are being replaced by gates, and that gates are being locked. Land where berries are picked and hunting is carried on, or land that is simply necessary to cross to get to a good place to do so, is rendered inaccessible. Even in an area where people thought they were on good terms with the ranchers, gates are sometimes locked without notice. People warn each other of what they have discovered when they return to the reserve, but on several occasions, when I have been travelling in a car with people to pick berries, we have encountered new barricades on accustomed trails, and different routes, often many miles out of the way, had to be taken instead. With this transformation, laments of lost land and locked gates have come to be part of the place-related discourse, as well. As Angela George relates in the following narrative:

Angela: Long ago we used to go around in here
        we used to go round that ( ) lake

AP:Yeah?

    Now we got to ask the rancher
    if we wanted to do that

(Tape 3a; 17 July 1989)

When the recreational hunting season opens each fall, Alkali Lake's subsistence area is flooded with recreational vehicles and campers from the Lower Mainland of British Columbia and from the United States, which further encourages ranchers to lock their gates, and routes the newcomers to new areas where they intrude even farther into Alkali Lake territory. Hunters from Alkali Lake often travel with few supplies, whether on horseback or by truck, as they have access to cabins, left open and stocked with bedding, utensils, and firewood by friends and relatives. These cabins are now sometimes ransacked by intruders during the recreational hunting season or even earlier in the year, during the summer tourist season. Where once the common practice in the Interior was to use any cabin, replace what was used, and leave something extra, now padlocks are sometimes placed on doors, and the most valuable supplies may be removed to houses on the main reserve at the end of a stay. Planning for each hunting trip becomes more involved, and the risk of finding oneself with no available shelter or food is much increased.

The current obstructions to subsistence activities are common topics of discussion in the reserve community. Discussions with outsiders, including ranchers and government officials, can lead to unpredictable, and often very unpleasant, outcomes for Alkali Lake people, including diminished access to lands, physical confrontations, jail, and fines. While understandings may be reached, and mutually agreeable outcomes established in some cases, the risks associated with initiating such conversations with outsiders are high, and may increase the costs of subsistence activities. Passive resistance is practised by many individuals, including strategies such as avoidance of reading posted fishing notices (which communicate a regulation, but brook no exchange) and finding ways to make a living on the land without observation by officials and ranchers, including conducting usual activities at unusual hours. Often, however, interactions with outsiders, in negotiation and confrontation, become unavoidable.

Discourse in the Courtroom

Since at least the beginnings of the colonial period, Alkali Lake people have been involved in an ongoing, and ever-increasing, obligatory discourse with the settlers, missionaries, government officials, and even lawyers and anthropologists working in the courts. As in the historical past, many people at Alkali Lake today are strongly aware of, and sometimes participate in, the battles waged in the courts over hunting and fishing and land-use rights. This experience, along with the associated type of discourse between politically dominant groups and Indigenous peoples, is common throughout the world today. In British Columbia, the Gitksan and Wet'suwet'en Land Claims case, *Delgamuukw v. British Columbia*, has garnered much notice in the press, and has held the attention of Native Peoples and non-Natives alike, through to its review by the Supreme Court of Canada in 1997. Locally, two cases concerned with hunting and government-imposed seasons, *Dick v. The Queen* and *Regina v. Alphonse*, directly involved members of the Alkali Lake band throughout the full course of the 1980s. During the 1990s, direct action through the preparation of a land claim has meant that much attention has been paid to mapping where and how people use territory for hunting and gathering. Increasingly, practices must be explained and justified to outsiders in an attempt to defend and maintain a way of life, as in the examples provided here of such Secwepemc discourse, taken from testimony given in the BC Provincial Court in William's Lake.

The argument has been made in the courts, and by government officials, that hunting and gathering are no longer essential to Native life, and are obsolescent practices, given the introduction of a cash economy. Cash may be more accessible on reserves now than it was in the 1960s, but the change is recent, and much depends on government budgets that are not directly controlled by First Nations. Wage-earning jobs may come and go, but the ability to put meat on the table means that a family will never be poor. Even men on the Alkali Lake Reserve who hold day jobs go out to fish and hunt at night occasionally, sharing the activity with their friends, teaching their children, and participating in the distribution system whereby they can provide meat and fish to relatives and Elders in the village. The Elder Charley Johnson, testifying in court on behalf of a Secwepemc hunter from a nearby reserve, described the importance of this way of life:

> The difference in buying a package of meat and the hunting for meat, is the fact that hunting in my case goes even further. It's my livelihood for all my children. My whole life depends and my childrens' whole existence depends on my hunting, as a means of raising them, whereas buying a package of meat over the counter at the supermarket or any store, does not complete the circle of training, the hunting. This package of meat that I buy over the counter, only exists as a meal and there's no value in this piece of meat, as a means of rearing my children.   (*Regina v. Alphonse* transcript, 65–6, 6 August 1987)

Mr Johnson expressed his conviction that 'existence,' 'livelihood,' and the process of raising children cannot be accomplished through the mere input of calories. The value of hunting is more than the meals it provides. To hunt is to learn, it is to 'complete the circle of training.' The activities associated with hunting teach his children what it is they need to know in order to live their lives properly.

Later in his testimony, Mr Johnson also spoke of the distribution system in place: 'It has been understood long before, within the elders, that in the hunting tradition, the sharing of the game was very common among the people. The one that bagged the game, really did not keep all the game, but shared it among within the community. Yes, it is this sharing that is most significant within the community' (ibid.). Traditional practices of sharing food and the associated interreliance of a community's members are extremely important components of a hunting and gathering way of life (cf. Mauss 1967 [1925]). The food shared is the medium through which community and family relationships are expressed, verified, and strengthened. The sharing process itself is part of the traditional 'circle of training.'

Alice Abbey, then the Chief of the William's Lake Band, elaborated on what hunting means in Secwepemc culture during the same trial. A lawyer for the defence had asked her why, considering that 'it's not always fun' to do so, 'why do the men in your village, in the band, insist on going out and hunting deer?' Chief Abbey responded:

> To fully answer your question, I would have to comment that fun – we don't look at it as fun. Okay, so that's totally out of the question, fun. It's a spiritual – okay? And it all depends on – sometimes we have gatherings and we have feasts and we have celebrations. You always have that relationship and that contact with everything around you and when you're walking through the bush, you're passing not only – you're not – for it to be snowing or for it to be raining is irrelevant. It's hard for me to explain it to you. Like, you have relations. The rock people you're passing, you know, like the limb people. You know, the people – and all our relations within that whole environment are communicating. Okay? Like, they communicate if there is danger. Wildlife knows this danger, if you're walking through the forest, they know that, and then when a deer comes by you, when you come upon a deer, that particular species knows that you're there, it's all been communicated, they know, and if you, yourself, have that type of relationship, you read all those signs and you know the winged people are communicating to the four legged people, that there is danger in the air, and when you come and kill that, it's a spiritual with everything. Okay? So it's not – it's so much more than just going to Safeway or Overwaitea, you know, and it's our gift, it's a nourishment for us, a total nourishment. It's healthy. When you go to Safeway or you go to Overwaitea, that's totally different. Our people are not accustomed to those foods, and what is more, they are not accustomed to – that relationship isn't there, the relationship that you have in your own traditions and your own cultures. It's so different, so you could have Safeway Stores every thirty feet that are abundant with beef. You would not get the same nourishment you would get if you walked to nurture yourself, to nurture yourself. (*Regina v. Alphonse* transcript, 39–40, 11 February 1987)

Chief Abbey, as well as Mr Johnson, is attempting to explain to an outside audience, the Provincial Court of British Columbia, what it is about practice of subsistence that is valued and essential to the

Secwepemc way of life. These two witnesses are attempting to bridge a gap between cultures, to explain to the court something of the Secwepemc system of transmitting cultural knowledge, and of Secwepemc ways of knowing associated with hunting and gathering.

Chief Abbey makes many points to the court about the value of hunting (and, implicitly, gathering) to her people, as she understands it. She responds to a question from the lawyer, who is 'on her side,' in that he is defending someone from the reserve, and so should be sympathetic to her system of discourse. Before she even begins to address the lawyer's intended question, she must define what she is *not* talking about, to extinguish a preconception the lawyer may hold concerning whether an activity is, or is not, 'fun.' (In the Secwepemc system, his was a completely inappropriate comment because it evaluated the quality of a situation in negative/positive terms, and is, in addition, off topic, as the concept of 'fun' might only be applied to some other realm of experience and existence.) Her words come tumbling out. There are so many concepts to explain, and so few shared points of reference. In order to make the court understand, she not only describes how the Secwepemc are situated in a hunting and gathering life-way, she also attempts to describe a parallel system of relationships and knowledge that she indicates must exist in the white world as well.

An examination of her narrative shows that she makes several points about the Secwepemc lifeway, as follows:

1 Hunting is spiritual.
2 Hunting may be undertaken to supply food for the community or for communal activities that include more people than are in the village, such as gatherings, feasts, and celebrations.
3 Walking through the bush, an activity that is part of hunting, allows for *contact* with a certain world that may not otherwise be accessible.
4 There is a *relationship* fostered between humans and that certain world, through this contact.
5 The relationship involves communication with other beings that are in some way sentient, and these beings communicate with each other as well.
6 One can participate in that communication if one knows how to read/interpret the signs available in this context.
7 Although one could ingest meat from the supermarket, the deer offers *total* nourishment, for body and spirit, and as such, the consumption of it is part of a healthy process; to eat of the deer is

to nurture yourself, and to walk in the bush where that deer is found
is to nurture yourself.

8 Hunting is a gift; it is something that has been given to the
Secwepemc people.

Chief Abbey's points about what the Secwepemc life-way does *not*
include are as follows:

1 Secwepemc people are not accustomed to supermarket food; it is not
part of their culture, and it does not nurture them.

2 Secwepemc people have no relationship with that place which is the
supermarket and the things found there.

3 By inference, there is no communication, and no communion, with
that other world if one gets one's food from the supermarket.

4 Eating food from the supermarket does not contribute to the health
of the individual, and supermarket food does not contribute to a
feast.

Finally, she attempts to explain her understanding that Euro-Canadians
have some system of special relationships, traditions, and knowledge
that parallel those found in a Secwepemc way of life. She suggests that
these include other ways of obtaining sustenance (including visiting the
supermarket) that might permit Euro-Canadians to understand something more of the Secwepemc system.

Anthropologists have begun to examine Native – Euro-Canadian
courtroom discourse in detail, to glean from it what understandings
can possibly be negotiated across 'conflicting models of discourse'
(Ridington 1990: 189), and discern what gaps must still be bridged (e.g.,
Ridington 1992: 12–24; Cruikshank 1992: 25–42; Miller 1992: 55–65). Mr
Johnson's and Chief Abbey's testimonies reveal that these speakers
hold certain conceptions, grounded in experience, of what it is, they
find, that the outsiders have *not* understood. Their explicit and implicit
references to difference can serve as a guide to topics worthy of inquiry
that might otherwise remain incomprehensible to an observer from
another culture. How, what, and why they communicate *across* systems
of discourse provides an indication of what information they consider
culturally significant about hunting and gathering within their own
model of discourse. Their words provide a guide to the respectful pursuit of knowledge about hunting and gathering discourse, which I
endeavour to discuss in the following chapters.

Chapter 4

Maps

The paradox of memorized history that is spoken and heard is that while it can preserve intimacy and locality over astonishing time depths, it seems to be only one generation away from extinction. It is a fragile linkage of spider strands across time. For it to endure someone somewhere must continue to bear witness, must intuitively resist the demands of media and archive in favor of the interactive, oral narrative. For this sort of history to preserve the economy and actuality of memory, it roots its actions in place, not dates. It neglects time to inject energy instead into the human and supernatural neighborhoods of its tales. It is called into being during and for interpersonal situations. It nurtures the family and community and cosmic continuities of which it speaks.

                                                        Peter Nabokov (1987: 145)

Looking for Patterns

For the people of Alkali Lake, stories that reflect a knowledge of the land and its resources are often told in association with particular places during travel. In this chapter, I examine such narratives, and the contexts in which they are told, so as to investigate what they reveal about patterns of discourse, and what the band members I travelled with find to be significant features to describe in their world. This attention to resources is an outstanding feature of discourse in travel, and, as I was to learn, could range from simple remarks to elaborately detailed narratives. The structure of such discursive events suggests that, in this oral culture, knowledge of the land and its resources, and of how to act in relation to them, is maintained and passed on through such stories.

Hunting, gathering, and fishing are activities that require travel away from the very public and densely occupied space of Alkali Lake Reserve No. 1. When people travel out for such purposes from Alkali Lake, they assemble the appropriate equipment, such as a rifle and hunting knife, or baskets, or a dip net and burlap sacks, to tuck into the back of a vehicle next to a lunch basket and other supplies. They invite companions with a mention that they might travel out to 'see if they can catch anything,' to 'have a look down that way,' or to 'see what might be around,' being careful not to mention what is being sought, lest such arrogance be noted by some creature, and their chances spoiled (cf. Brody 1981: 35–7).

Conversation during travel includes many topics that are also appropriate topics of talk in the village, including upcoming and current events and discussions about members of the family and people in the community. Confidences can be shared with a select group, and will not inadvertently include anyone who might happen to walk in on a place of talk, as can frequently happen in the village. Also, in travel, an additional kind of narrative, particularly appropriate to hunting and gathering contexts, interweaves with the rest of the conversation, and takes precedence in directing the flow of talk.

According to H.P. Grice's theory of conversational implicature,[1] participants cooperate in conversations to contribute 'such as is required, at the state at which it occurs, by the accepted purpose or direction of the talk exchange in which [they] are engaged' (Grice 1975: 45). Determining what the 'purpose or direction' of the travellers' talk might be was difficult for me at first. I assumed, according to Grice's maxims, and based on the fact that all others travelling had a sense of the flow of conversation, even when I did not, that such cooperation was taking place. Talk caromed off in directions that made little sense in terms of the discourse rules of my own culture. For example, on a berry-picking trip, Angela George, well along in a discussion of visitors coming up for a pow-wow, suddenly changed topic, and then changed it again (topic shifts indicated by italics):

He comes up for pow-wows sometimes or the Gathering in Alkali
He come lots of years here
That's how come I come to know him
eating with him and –
Well I guess that's how come I know lots of people by talking to them
I travel this with Jimmy on foot lots of times

We used to go hunting on foot sometimes
Sometimes I think he wanted to go to town
I'd tell him, 'Let's go hunting'
We'd come up
But I never do it now two years
I was thinking maybe I was just in his way
Let him do what he wants
Maybe I was just too bossy
I was thinking.
Oh, look at the nice boughs.

[Tape of 10 July 1989][2]

Deixis (that is, the pragmatic aspect of discourse in which reference relies entirely on context), in the form of such verbal pointing to places and plants as they are passed, marks the shifts to different topics, which are often made with no more than a breath being drawn between the shifts. I found, imbedded in the course of a ninety-minute session of taped travel with Angela George, numerous examples of these shifts made in reference to places and resources, including no fewer than twenty that were employed to point out that we were passing berry bushes, including *sxúsem* (soapberries) and huckleberries, as italicized in the following examples:

Angela: I wouldn't I would be dry if it was today I can't even sew
        I used to sew gloves before
        Eh, there's not many sxúsems, see?
AP: No not many
Angela: Maybe we have to go down Chase or Quesnel
        Last year they say there was none in Quesnel musta been
          someplace here

        There we come with a tractor one time around here
        We was hauling wood
        Another time we was hunting on foot hunting
        It was deep snow yet in the spring when we come through
          here

AP: Mmm

Angela: Took us four hours from the reserve to get to our cabin
        [*laughter*]
        We didn't walk fast we didn't run we just walked slow

> *Look there's no sxúsem around here*

(Tape of 10 July 1989)

Angela: It didn't rain up here I guess
just down the reserve
Used to be lots of huckleberries back in there
Long ago we used to camp in there

(ibid.)

Such mentions of berries are interjected into longer narratives, or may be given at the end of one narrative, with another narrative beginning after the mention of the berries. This style of switching from topic to topic as new places come into the travellers' view holds not only in the case of berry bushes, but for other resources as well, as can be seen in the shifts to other topics in the narratives quoted above (e.g., 'I travel this with Jimmy on foot lots of times'; 'There we come with a tractor one time around here'; and 'Long ago we used to camp in there'). Beyond these brief examples of how topic shifts are triggered by the passing of particular sites, the reader can also refer to the selected transcripts in the appendix to attain a sense of a full conversation over the course of a trip in the car, and of the wide range of topics discussed on such a trip. Hunting places, camping spots, and many other resource sites are pointed out during travel, sometimes in brief orienting statements, and sometimes in richly developed narratives. The fact that these statements displace other topics in longer streams of speech suggests that pointing out places and such resources as berries, or their bushes, is the most pertinent or, to employ Grice's maxims and terminology, relevant speech (1975: 46) to the activity at hand, and may be appropriate whenever such places or resources come into view. The span of time within which such topics are most relevant is, in part, dependent on the mode and speed of transportation used in travel.

Angela George's observations on the condition of berry bushes provide some of the briefest examples of place-related topic shifting in discourse that I recorded in hunting and gathering contexts. It can be argued that all of these references to berries may be defined as narratives in and of themselves, regardless of their degree of elaboration. The mere passing of the berry bush, brought to the audience's attention with the wave of Angela's hand, serves as an extralinguistic form of orienting statement, and is followed by a commonly employed phrase, such as 'used to be lots,' indicating both that something (berries) was there before, according to her personal experience, and that a change to the impoverished bush now in view has occurred. Such phrases may be laconic, but the experience of place they indicate is rich indeed. Allowing for the extralinguistic information to be considered as part of the context, these brief references fit Labov's definition of narratives of personal experience (1972: 359–60), as discussed in chapter 1.

The ability to describe the bushes, and their former (and therefore, potential) bounty with such economy does not preclude the occurrence of more elaborate descriptions. Sometimes, the mentions of the bushes are more detailed, as in the following three examples recorded on the same trip:

(1) Angela: Yeah one time we come up here
                  and we get looots of *sxúsem*
                  and up the meadow up
                  tocqtocqcqcnk we get lots and that
                  and that uh Jimmy's mom got mad at us
                  we had nowhere to put this *sxúsem*

(2) Angela: There was lots of *sxúsem* you could see it from far
                  s' just red.
                  We did go down on that trail
                  This was just red this bush one year when we come.

(3) Angela: Yeah that's where you used to go get *sxúsem*
                  here on them opens

                                                          AP: Hmm

      Angela: You know on them there's lots of it.
                  But if there's none there'll be none
                  One time we come up with the wagon it was red all over
                  Holy smokes
                  we get some 'til we had enough
                  we go home and we tell the people
                      lots of people come up.

On the particular day's tape recording from which these examples are drawn, Angela mentioned each of the places she had picked berries as we passed them on our way to her cabin, and again on the return to the reserve. The identification of an unnamed narrative genre specifically associated with hunting and gathering contexts allows for its further investigation. It is part of the discourse that accompanies what Chief Abbey has described as a central feature of Secwepemc life: travelling out in the bush to obtain nourishment.

Named Places and Unremembered Names

While travelling past specific places on hunting and gathering expeditions, travellers from Alkali Lake often comment on the features of the land, and relate what is remembered about those places. There are many places that are passed on the road which are associated with such talk, especially on the main routes of travel to traditional resources. Angela George, while in the midst of pointing out one of those places, a trailhead called *psekweku7*, after the rosehips found there, said:

I guess eh people names the roads where
wherever they go you know, they name it, so they know
which way they're going or their partners you know
   to tell them where they were going.
The names
I just about forget all the names in Alkali you know
   going up the meadow
The same up – up going down Dog Creek
   and Canoe Creek they have names
every little place.

(Tape of 10 July 1989)

Angela George remembers some of the names for the places she travels past and is always sure to mention them on each passing. (See the transcripts in the appendix for 10 July 1989, for Secwepemc place names along Joe's Lake Road, and for 24 August 1988, for place names on Dog Creek Road in her repertoire.) Even when the names of places have been forgotten, stories about those places may persist, and so the lack of a remembered lexical identifier will not be considered here as necessarily indicating that a place has fallen out of use, or is no longer salient to the Alkali Lake community. Furthermore, new names can come into use, and different names may be used by different groups of travellers to describe the same place.

One particularly heavily used section of road and the associated

Secwepemc territory will serve as a guide to the way the people of Alkali Lake tell stories about resources, and indicate how these stories constitute the dominant feature of discourse in travel. Comparisons to other parts of the territory and associated discourse will be drawn after demonstrating the type, density, and content of discourse over this stretch of road by a variety of interlocutors on many different occasions, travelling for many different purposes.

The Trail: Dog Creek Road and the Territory it Crosses

The geographic focus of the narratives discussed below is a part of Secwepemc territory along the Fraser River between Alkali Lake Indian Reserve No. 1 and the Churn Creek suspension bridge, approximately eighteen miles to the south (see map 7, p. 117). The area is traversed by Dog Creek Road, a dirt road that winds along the cliffs and creeks on the eastern side of the Fraser River, following the route of a foot trail that was well established by at least the time of Fraser's voyage of 1808, and was probably long in use before that. This stretch of road, despite its poorly banked twists and and unrailed turns, 10 per cent grades, washouts and washboards, and numerous opportunities for unforgiving plunges into the chasm of the Fraser River far below, in very heavily used by people living at the Alkali Lake, Dog Creek, and Canoe Creek reserves. It is the road to Williams Lake and Alkali Lake for people living in Dog Creek and Canoe Creek, and when the back ways to the towns of 150 Mile House and Lac la Hache are hit by heavy rain or snow, it can be the easiest road to use to reach paved highway, and the services of the towns beyond. For people from Alkali Lake, it is a road to salmon-fishing and berry-picking spots, to the homes of relatives on the other reserves, and to the suspension bridge across the Fraser that leads to the Gang Ranch and the Chilcotin Plateau.

The choice of this section of Alkali Lake hunting and gathering territory for study allows for greater accuracy in mapping sites associated with narratives; the currently available maps of Dog Creek Road provide adequate reference to pinpoint particular places of talk. Because the conversations discussed here were recorded before civilian-owned global positioning system (GPS) units were programmed to give error-free positions, and because even the most current maps still supply errors evident when they are 'ground-truthed' against GPS readings (that is, checked with known, fixed points), it was useful to find a riverside road with numerous distinctive physical details to conduct a check on the relationships of story to key places. Many of the other roads travelled in Alkali Lake hunting and gathering territory offer up rich opportunities for story, but most are little more than cart tracks, and sometimes are unmarked or have sections mismarked on government topographic maps. New roads, bulldozed for logging trucks or hydroelectric-line maintenance, often cut across the old roads, or modify their routes. Some of the logging roads we travelled were created on an ad hoc basis off the principal logging roads; as one section becomes muddy and impassable, another section of road can be blazed through by the caterpillars and other heavy equipment used in logging. These logging roads are often not long in commercial use, but they are easily followed and are kept open by the passage of four-wheel-drive vehicles and pickups, and by the recreational vehicles of fall-time recreational hunters. These new roads are travelled by Secwepemc people when the old ones are made impassable to their vehicles by heavy machinery, when new gates from the ranchers block access, or when recent logging has changed the characteristics of the land, the plants and animals who frequent it, and the degree of accessibility to all travellers.

The new roads alter the characteristics of familiar territory, and are not customary routes of travel. They may be relatively unfamiliar or completely new to the experience of people at Alkali Lake. In contrast, Dog Creek Road permits the investigation of narratives associated with particular places over a long time span, as there is a long record of Secwepemc experience with the places along the road. The most recently modified major section of Dog Creek Road south of Alkali Lake is over forty-five years old. As indicated by the airport marked on map 7, this newer section of road veers away from the river and across the top of the plateau toward the Second World War–era military airstrip, and then returns to its former route along the Fraser.

This particular choice of geographic area along Dog Creek Road for close analysis also allows for a concentrated focus on a segment of the territory that contains multiple resources such as berries, medicinal plants, important salmon dip-netting sites along the Fraser River, and the houses of friends and relatives on two reserves close to Alkali Lake, at Dog Creek and Canoe Creek. Along Dog Creek Road, south of Alkali Lake Reserve No. 1 and north of the main Dog Creek Reserve, Alkali Lake people pass by numerous frequently remarked-upon places, including a pithouse site called *Tsecyelk̓w*; the men's and women's sweatlodges (the *sq̓ilye*); a trailhead down to a Fraser River dip-netting site and an associated campsite; a berry-picking place called *Tsecreptsen*; the place of a cold spring where wild rhubarb grows, called *Nukláwt*; Echo Mountain, or *Tsexqwmeṁles* (where fish, meat, and berries were once dried and cached, and grass was pulled for horses); a trail leading to a deer-hunting area across the Fraser; another dip-netting trail at Little Dog Creek or *Stegtsetsulqw*; and a gulch and pithouse site called *Cklutetátu7s*. In addition to trails, camps, water, food, and medicine, graves and sites of tragic accidents are also passed and remarked upon. This list of significant places along Dog Creek Road is not exhaustive. As Angela George has observed, not all the names of places are remembered. This list refers only to some of the sites mentioned in the six transcripts discussed below. The sites along Dog Creek Road associated with the particular narratives discussed in this chapter are shown on map 7, with reference letters that correspond to those given in the text. Each noted dip-netting site along the Fraser River is indicated on the map.

The Transcripts: Selection of Narratives

The travel associated with the taped narratives discussed in this chapter was undertaken by individuals from Alkali Lake travelling with me to collect particular plant and animal resources at sites in the area, and, on one occasion, explicitly to record place names and take photographs with reference to mileage markers, for later transfer to a topographic map. Conversations were taped during travel on foot and in the car while travelling on Dog Creek Road and in the surrounding countryside, and at places where we stopped to fish, hunt, or gather. Travel through this heavily exploited territory, and time spent along the way to clean berries, to cook, and to eat, yielded narratives about the land and its resources, although talk generally ceased when people were actively picking or fishing.

I was fortunate to travel Dog Creek Road on numerous occasions with a variety of individuals who consented to be tape-recorded. Other routes of travel also yielded a good selection of narratives associated with hunting and gathering, including the narratives quoted earlier in this chapter. However, the majority of the narratives recorded on other routes were presented by a single individual, Angela George. It is the Dog Creek Road area for which I have been able to collect the most representative sample of narratives, recorded with several different speakers travelling together, in varying combinations of age and sex, on different trips. These narratives constitute a geographically related segment of the corpus of texts that document the types of stories, and the sense of place, encountered throughout the Alkali Lake hunting and gathering territory.

The narratives quoted in the remainder of this chapter were recorded on six days between 24 August 1988 and 28 September 1989. The set of interlocutors varies, assuring in so far as possible that the observed narrative patterning is a shared feature within the Alkali Lake speech community. The variations between sets of interlocutors in terms of numbers, ages, and genders represented, and the main purpose of each trip compare as follows:

Tape 1, 24 August 1988:
- Angela George and Andie Palmer
- Trip to record place names
- Recorded while driving south of Alkali IR No. 1 on Dog Creek Road, and return

Tape 2, 9 July 1989:
- Angela George, her husband Jimmy George, friend Hazel Johnson, and Andie Palmer
- Trip to visit relatives and pick sage
- Recorded while driving south on Dog Creek Road to the Churn Creek suspension bridge, and return

Tapes 3a and 3b, 17 July 1989:
- Angela George, and her grandchildren, Dallas George and Candice George, and Andie Palmer
- Trip to pick saskatoon berries at *Cklutetátu7s*, and to visit relatives at Dog Creek Reserve
- Recorded while driving south on Dog Creek Road, while walking at *Cklutetátu7s*, and return

Tape 4, 21 July 1889:
- Jimmy George, Ollie Johnson, and Andie Palmer
- Trip from Alkali Lake to Churn Creek to dip-net for salmon
- Recorded while driving south on Dog Creek Road, and at the Churn Creek dip-netting site

Tape 5, 27 July 1989:
- Jimmy George and Andie Palmer
- Trip from Alkali Lake to Churn Creek to dip-net for salmon
- Recorded while driving south on Dog Creek Road

Tape 6, 28 September 1989:
- Angela George and Andie Palmer
- Trip to collect medicinal plants
- Recorded while walking on the hill overlooking Alkali Lake Reserve
  No. 1, just west of Dog Creek Road, and return

To facilitate comparison of the narratives recorded on six trips through the Dog Creek Road area, with several different interlocutors, the narratives are discussed together in the text with respect to their geographic referents of eight key sites. Map 7, found at the end of this chapter, provides a guide to the general location of the sites discussed. Selected narratives are quoted at length, but readers are encouraged to consult the appendix, to confirm how these narratives are situated with respect to the general stream of discourse over the course of separate journeys.

Having chosen the transcripts from this set of expeditions as a base on which to draw for exemplary narratives, and having defined and delimited the territory under investigation, we can now turn to an investigation of the recorded speech, and to considering what specific narratives reveal at a particular intersection of language and culture – Secwepemc discourse in hunting and gathering contexts. My focus here will be to draw out the most fundamental, utilitarian aspects of the narratives in order to provide the broadest framework possible for understanding how they function in the system of discourse. Even here, the poetics of the narratives, with their spare style and many parallelisms, may be appreciated.

Site A: Trailhead of Alkali dip-netting area

Jimmy George and Ollie Johnson, who is a relative of the Georges, and I were driving south in the late afternoon of 21 July 1989 from Alkali Lake IR No. 1 to the west bank of the Fraser at the Churn Creek suspension bridge, to dip-net for salmon. I had a tape recorder running as we neared the trailhead that leads down to one of Alkali Lake

Reserve's principal dip-netting areas. We were driving down the dirt road, speaking about a burial site we had just passed.

AP: ... We found a grave
         as well
Jimmy: Yeah
         Strange to go down there

Jimmy then changed the topic of conversation to point out a trailhead.

Jimmy: We used to go way down over there
         We start down that steep gulch
         and we used to s–walk in there
         Clifford used to come with one horse and you know
         put all our lunch and s–stuff on there and we
         walked down
         and for carrying just a net
         Big load on that old horse remember that little Whitey?
Ollie: Yeah
Jimmy: Then he had a big
         frown after that
         Boy, that little horse he used to be really packed
         [*laughter*]

                                             (Tape 4; 21 July 1989)

Bringing out the humour of the situation, Jimmy George's focus was on the little horse struggling up the trail. His narrative also indicates that the catch there was good, since the horse 'used to be really packed.' Jimmy did not mention *what* was packed up, choosing a graceful and, I think in this case, deliberate way to speak of that which we were on our way to catch that very trip. Hunters from Secwepemc territory and elsewhere often employ circumlocution in such cases, the prescriptive rule being not to name the animal hunted for. I often forgot the rule, as in an instance earlier that same day. Before we set out on the trip, I told Jimmy that I had rigged a tarp in the back of my station wagon 'to hold the fish.' He countered, 'If we catch something.'

Jimmy George would typically point out trailheads as we passed them. On our next tape-recorded trip to dip-net for salmon, we passed the same spot. Jimmy was talking about the grave of a baby, found elsewhere by workers digging holes for silage, and how he had learned of this from someone on the reserve. He then coughed, paused, and pointed out the trailhead:

Jimmy: ... Charlie's mom told her about it.
           It was Lorraine's granny I told that to
           [*cough*]

           You never –
           Oh yes you said you went down there before
           Down this fishing place?
AP: Yeah.
           On that 'road.'[3]
           [*laughter*]
Jimmy: Yeah it used to be nice here when Buster used to run it ( )
           Those guys they don't care you know it's only
              you have to go and roll it
           just once with a bulldozer, eh?

                                    AP: Mhm?

           Don't cost them hardly anything that time
           I think it was only eighteen cents or something for ( )
              the pieces, eh?

                     (Tape 5; 27 July 1989)

Jimmy continued with a long narrative about the late Buster Hamilton's grading of the steep road down to the river, making it safe for the cattle that used to be taken down to the river each fall.

    The same trailhead to the Alkali dip-netting area was also mentioned by Angela George each time we passed it. Angela and I had been speaking of how she used to cut hay for the Alkali Lake Ranch as we approached the site. Here are her words:

... cut the hay
and we used to camp
Lots of us used to camp here
Make salmon at the same time as we work here
for the ranch
Quite a few – fifteen years ago now they don't
nobody
All the reserve used to work here
long ago

But now they have machineries to do it
Long ago they used to have horses to do it
the haying

(Tape 1; 24 August 1988)

In each narrative, the speaker has pointed out what the site is by speaking of personal experience associated with it. While Jimmy spoke of packing (salmon) up the trail, Angela's emphasis was on how they used to 'make salmon' at the camp (that is, to process the fish for storage after they have been caught). This was her personal experience of fishing associated with the site.

In the cooperative efforts toward making a living, the differing personal and gendered experiences of Alkali Lake women and men are reflected in their respective emphases on activities mentioned in their narratives associated with given sites. Narratives of personal experience necessarily reflect the experiences of, and so the activities undertaken by, the speaker. This difference in emphasis is also demonstrated in narratives that make reference to the deer-hunting area on the west side of the Fraser River.

Site B: Trailhead to deer hunting area

South of the trailhead to the Alkali dip-netting area is an old trail that leads down to the Fraser River and crosses to a hunting area in view across the river. Years ago the hunting area was approached by crossing over the frozen river on foot, trailing packhorses. Today, Alkali Lake hunters travelling as far as the other side of the Fraser generally take a vehicle, and so do not cross the river there via the old trail, but drive farther south on Dog Creek Road, cross at the Churn Creek suspension bridge, and double back to the hunting area. Jimmy George made reference to the hunting area in view across the river as I travelled with him and Ollie Johnson:

Jimmy: I hung all around across there before

AP: Uh huh?

Jimmy: One time we used to cross from camp
          way over there somewhere
AP: How long would you stay over there?
Jimmy: 'Bout 10 days
          two weeks

Angela's mom was
drying
My father-in-law me an him we go to hunt
One time we kill five
five deer n' eight does sometime

Pretty scarce now again
Too many hunters

(Tape 4; 21 July 1989)

Jimmy's mention of thirteen deer killed is typical of Secwepemc hunters' explicit quantification of game, and contrasts with the indirection employed in speech before a hunt. Alkali Lake hunters and fishermen generally mention the quantity of their catch, whether fish or game, and can often remember how many fish or deer were taken in a given night years before, with a high degree of agreement on the numbers among hunters or fishermen who participated in the catch.[4] News of how many salmon made up the total night's catch for various fishing parties circulates through the village as men[5] return from the dip-netting sites. I have not heard any mention of how many fish were caught by any one man, but the numbers tend to be fairly even, as the fishermen take turns with the net, and as a rule do not hand over the dip net until they have caught at least one fish. The landing of Chinooks and of two or three fish caught on a single stroke of the net are now uncommon events, and are remarked upon. Men fishing divide up each catch evenly, with the exception of the huge Chinook salmon sometimes caught with the regular run, which are taken home by the men who caught them.

Plant resources harvested are not quantified in the same way as salmon or game. Numbers of baskets collected is not as significant a topic of village conversation on return from a gathering expedition as is the quantity of berries still available on the bushes. As was mentioned previously, when Angela noted that significant quantities of berries were found in a given area in the past, she would say, with a wave of her hand across the area, 'Used to be lots.' Apparently, the quantity available on the bush was more relevant information to share than the number of baskets picked. A public indication of how good the potential for harvest is comes in the form of branches bearing representative samples of berries, broken off by the pickers and distributed to their neighbours on returning to the village. Angela has told me that when they used to carry baskets on foot or by packhorse, branches laden with berries would be carefully folded over the individually picked berries, and these branches served in addition to keep the cargo cool and restrained from bouncing out.

Jimmy's extremely condensed account of a full two-week-long hunt ends with a lament that there are now too many hunters, resulting in a scarcity of game. On another occasion, Jimmy mentioned that on one hunting expedition originating at that place, they were able to get a deer at the bottom of the trail without even having to cross the river:

Yeah I hunt around here lots of times
Way down down long the down at the bottom

AP: Mmm

Before we went I shoot a deer and we went down there
Angela and I down way down
Boy, we sure have a hard time
She wanted to come too, you know
We had a wagon that's long ago

(Tape 5; 27 July 1989)

What may be implied here, too, is that the game is growing increasingly scarce, for when this event occurred, he and Angela George 'had a wagon that's long ago.' His accounts are found to be especially laconic when compared to Angela George's narrative concerning her activities associated with the site; for instance, as we passed the trailhead together:

Angela: Long ago when we used to go and dry,
        dry meat for three months
        we never waste anything we used to
        dry the
        everything you know the lungs, the liver,
          the throat of the deer
        the heart, we used to dry.
        The legs of the deer we skin it and
        boil it and make butter out of that fat
        and we keep the bones
          but we had left you know the
        smashed up bones
          we make butter out of the deer legs

and keep it for our soup next year next spring
we don't waste nothing
When we dry meat we keep the bones in the meat
   we don't throw away the bones
      we keep it on the meat
when we dry it
we used to cut the hair off the
fur you know that
the hide we used to cut the fur and s–s–dry it
and whip it with a big stick
take off the fur you know
as it gets dry
clean it off like that 'n we
we make holes around the
hide 'n we
we make a rope you know 'n lace it
lace it together
put our meat in between
lace it together that meat
you know
step on it till it settles the meat
then they it'd be nice 'n flat
and when we come back from across the river
we'll have loads of this
eh dried meat on our
on the sleigh when we come back then
then we have pack horses too.

When we go across the river long ago we used to
take lots of vegetables and potatoes and bury it
As we going where where we camp
   we buries them there
On a sack buried there then next time we camp
   again we buries some more food there.
As we come back we have food from the
   what we bury
      we stay there for two or three days
as we come home.
We stay across the river 'til 'til you see the the
   mountains way back starting to get

>   you know we have a ways of looking the country if
>   its gonna get cold.
> AP: Uh huh? How do you
>   [
> Angela: Then we start home.
>   You know it used to get foggy, quite foggy
>   across the river
>   you know across the high mountains
>   *sqwelq̓wélt*, they call
>   and it get gray that fog.
>   Then we started home.
>   We come home then.
>   We just make it home in four days and it gets cold.
>   (Tape 1: 24 August 1988)

Both Angela and Jimmy George have given accounts of what they have done to contribute to their livelihood, and have in so doing provided information to their respective audiences about how to gain access to a particular resource. Jimmy would kill the deer; Angela and her mother would dry it for packing out and storage. Jimmy's information is terse, whether in the presence of Ollie, another hunter who might benefit from knowing something of the hunt, or when travelling with only me, a non-hunter.

Angela George, in contrast, provides an extremely detailed description of her experience. Her narrative, very long and full of important information about the hunting and gathering way of life, contains numerous parallelisms that at once contribute to the poetic aspect while assisting in the audience's remembrance of the information (cf. Ong 1982; Goody 1977; A. Palmer 1985) and its segmentation into smaller units of information. Dell Hymes (1981) and, more recently, Joel Sherzer (1987) and Greg Urban (1991) have paid particular attention to parallelism in narrative structure – that is, in a general sense, to 'similarities between discourse segments that are sequentially juxtaposed' (Urban 1991: 60) – and beyond this, to parallel structuring in like narratives, and to parallel structures in action and speech (Urban 1991). Angela George's narrative of personal experience concerning drying meat provides many examples of parallelism, as she has woven together short phrases with several repetitions within each of the sections. I have identified seven sections that make up her narrative, as based on described action and as circumscribed by sets of repetitions.

She begins with a description of how they saved and dried all the parts of the deer, and continues with a section concerning how they would lace it into newly made parfleches to pack it. She then explains the means for carrying the meat back across the river, how they would store provisions for the hunt at the camp, and how they would know when to come home.

After the establishing clause ('Long ago when we used to ...'), which situates the narrative for the audience with respect to time as they have already been oriented with respect to place, the first section includes the repetition of the words 'dry meat' and 'waste anything/every-thing/nothing' in parallel phrases, on both ends of a listing of parts to be saved, in an imbedded parallel structure marked each time by the article 'the.' In order to briefly demonstrate the parallelism inherent in the narrative, I treat the first section of the narrative here by marking the parallel phrases that encompass the listing of deer parts (presented here in italics), in bold and underlined fonts.

Long ago when **we used to** go and **dry,**
dry meat for three months
we <u>never waste anything</u> **we used to**
dry <u>the</u>
<u>everything</u> you know *the lungs, the liver,*
    the throat of the deer
the heart, **we used to dry.**
The legs of the deer **we skin it** and
boil it and **make butter** out of that fat
and <u>we keep</u> *the bones* but we had left
    you know *the*
smashed up bones we **make butter**
    out of *the deer legs*
<u>and keep it</u> for our soup next year next spring
<u>we don't waste nothing</u>
When **we dry meat** <u>we keep</u> *the bones in the meat*
    <u>we don't throw away</u> *the bones*
        <u>we keep it</u> on *the meat*
when **we dry it**

This technique provides a more visual, albeit experimental, way of marking some of the parallelisms in this narrative fragment, and of making the patterns touched upon more readily apparent.

Site C: Trailhead to Little Dog dip-netting site

There are several trailheads that lead to dip-netting sites on Dog Creek Road. One, now seldom used by Jimmy George, drops down to the Fraser near Little Dog Creek.

Jimmy: I want to go down that Little Dog Creek eh, Ollie?
Ollie: heh heh
          Boy
          S'too hard
Jimmy: We hardly make it up there
AP: With horses
Ollie: Steep

(Tape 4; 21 July 1, 1989)

The exchange was brief, squeezed into the conversation as we passed, but the place was marked by Jimmy's spoken reference to this barely accessible fishing site, and the barest tip of his lip and incline of the head toward the site.

I spent a considerable amount of time driving in reverse to missed cart-tracks before I realized Jimmy was cueing me to turn in ways more subtle than the use of directives I was accustomed to. Angela George was more explicit than this on one occasion, but still incorporated indirection in her suggestion that 'if I was bossing myself, well, I'd go left. The other road that way' (recording of 10 July 1989); later on the same trip she said, 'if I was bossing this car ...' This use of the term 'boss' is borrowed from the cowboy vernacular, which includes terms like 'straw boss' and 'range boss.' Angela and other Alkali Lake people have great experience working for local ranches on open range where herds of cattle must be driven, or bossed, along trails to the railroad yard in Williams Lake. Angela's delicate suggestions as to where my car might go are couched in terms that allow us to consider the car as if it were a cow, straying from the trail, rather than a vehicle under the control of someone who was frequently confused by the network of cart tracks and dirt roads.

Angela had told me that the Secwepemc names for Little Dog Creek is *Stegtsetsulqw* (tape 1; 24 August 1988). In addition to mentioning that a camp near the trailhead was where they used to dry salmon, she, as did Jimmy and Ollie, made a reference to the trail and its steepness:

Angela: One time I was going back to Al– Dog Creek
            and we seen a moose there
AP: Right there?
            At the curb?
Angela: And we kill him right in that gulch
            in that steep gulch where he was lay and die
            That gulch we had a hard time to pack him out
            then when we port him up

(Tape 3b; 17 July 1989)

On other occasions, Jimmy mentioned the trailhead in passing and it became incorporated into the discussion (see tape 4; 27 July 1989, beginning with 'That's a reserve too down there where those guys fish'). Angela also gave a terse indication of its presence on one trip:

Jimmy and CY we go down every day
Afternoon they fish all night and I dry it.

(Tape 1; 24 August 1988)

In the latter case, considering the speaker was Angela George, the brevity of the remark may have been influenced by the fact that we had come to the end of our trip south as we approached this place, and made a quick turn back towards Alkali Lake, just as it was coming into sight.

Site D: A Cave above the Dog Creek Reserve

Occupants of the car would often give signals of attention to a raconteur in anticipation of a story to be told around the next bend. These are generally pauses and silence, with some or all members of the audience turning toward the potential storyteller. As I began to appreciate and anticipate the repetition of stories, I grew fond of hearing a story from Jimmy about a cave in the cliffs that we passed on Dog Creek Road. On this particular trip, the car had become quiet as Ollie, Jimmy, and I rounded the corner by the steep, crumbling basalt outcroppings that Dog Creek cuts through. I saw the mouth of the cave and started to ask:

AP: Where was it your dad ran up to get that ice?
                [
Jimmy: Just up here

Site D: A cave above the Dog Creek Reserve

We stopped right around here
Get some ice from up there in summertime
Mustn't be far he wasn't long and he come back
Supposed to be another one across there somewhere

(Tape 4; 21 July 1989)

Jimmy had been ready to tell us about the cave site, as is evident from the overlapping speech, and I had issued an unnecessary prompt. Sometimes a storyteller is distracted and misses the spot to tell the story. If this happens, someone in his company who knows that a story could be forthcoming might prompt the storyteller. This prompting is what first drew my attention to the shared responsibility to tell the story. When I found that I would prompt, too, I realized that I had, unawares, grown accustomed to the rhythm of such discourse. I can only wonder how many times I had trampled on non-verbal cues to begin stories when they were directed toward storytellers on earlier journeys. Although Charles Briggs's (1986) discussion of theory and methodology directs readers to 'learn how to ask,' for my work I am continually reminded by the good example of Salish Elders that the more fundamental enterprise here is to learn how to listen.

Jimmy tells of his personal experience in this narrative. Although he did not gather the ice himself, he remembers standing on the road, waiting for his father. On other occasions he has told me of his regret that he did not go right into the cave with his father, the better to learn where to get the ice. I have not been able to determine whether the cave was used as an icehouse for ice hauled from the creek in the winter, or if the ice was naturally formed in the cave. Jimmy is the only person I have worked with who has seen the ice, and he was not sure of its origin. Teit (1909: 589) provides information about another use of the cave by the people then settled at Dog Creek. He reports that young Secwepemc men formerly went into seclusion there as part of their spiritual training during puberty, and followed this with nightly sessions of dancing and praying. Although Teit emphasizes this was a former use, it should be noted that there are some young men from Alkali Lake today who include such practices in their training, at sites unknown to me.

Site E: *Nukláwt*

Other narratives associated with other resources seldom or no longer in use remain in circulation, including the following account given by

Angela about a place called *Nukláwt*, where wild rhubarb (*Heracleum lanatum*, also known as cow parsnip [Turner et al. 1980]) was once gathered, and where fresh spring water can still be found.

Angela: This is a place too
         They call it *Nukláwt*.
         That's where we get
         wild rhubarb in the spring time

                                              AP: Ooh ...

Angela: Then we get some
         eh
         them greens from the spring?
         greens to eat?

                                              AP: Mhm?

Angela: in the spring water
AP: [This is on the right at 1.3][6]
Angela: Get to cook in the springtime from there I learn it from
         elders
         but wild rhubarb

         Used to
         live on it long ago
         Make soup out of wild rhubarb
         boil it 'n
         eat it all the time
         But now
         we don't
         go out and make it now.
         But we still
         think of the wild rhubarb
         It's good for Indian medicine too
         it's the roots
         boil it
         and put it wherever you're sore
         your KNEES
         Then
         fades away the sore from on your knees
         the wild rhubarb roots
         use it in sweats too.
         It's really

helped a lot

if you believe it.

AP: Mhm

Angela: You wouldn't be crippled for your life if you were –
if you use it some
that wild rhubarb roots.

(Tape 1; 24 August 1988)

Angela's narrative sums up how memories of these sites remain important. Secwepemc people still think of these places, and remember them with stories. Angela says, 'But we still / think of the wild rhubarb.' She identifies the site as a 'place' and one with a name, *Nukláwt*. That she gives fairly explicit medicinal information with the site identification indicates that the wild rhubarb might someday be used again. To a lesser degree than was found in her narrative about the deer-hunting area, she incorporates parallelisms that provide a rhythm and, I would argue (following Milman Parry and Albert Lord [Lord 1960]), assist in the remembrance of her narrative's information: her four repetitions of 'wild rhubarb,' and two of 'wild rhubarb roots,' and her parallel mentions of sore knees.

Nukláwt is, or was, a multiple-use site. Angela has mentioned on other occasions that there is a spring at the site where the rhubarb shoots come up. Other consultants are familiar with the name and location of the site, which has a current use as a source of drinking water, whether or not the rhubarb is harvested by anyone at Alkali Lake today.

Site F: Accident Site

In addition to narratives that stress the positive attributes of sites, some stress the negative – the dangers of a site. Jimmy and Ollie's reference to the Little Dog trail, above, alludes in part to the hazards of travel. Many packhorses, fully laden with sacks of salmon and supplies, have fallen off the steep trails to be lost in the Fraser River.

Other place-related discourse memorializes terrible loss. Jimmy George had been talking about building a root cellar, lapsed into silence, and then pointed to the site of a tragic accident:

Jimmy: Where ah Frank[7] went over down here

Right here down
AP: Did Frank put him there himself? Frankie, er?
Jimmy: Frank and a couple womens
One of them two sisters
I guess he was bringing her bring her
for fishing down to Dog Creek
and that's the one that died

AP: Mhm

Guess was only one wheel left on that car
when they get down the bottom
Wheels come off
Well it's steep

AP: Mhm

Don't know how he live

(Tape 4; 21 July 1989)

Angela George told a story about the event too. She had been telling us a story about why one should not tell children how much they should eat, but she changed topic to point out the site:

Don't tell them not to eat too much
That's where Frankie Wilson fall down in there
    [*half line deleted*]
    that woman that's staying with us' sister died

AP: Mmm

He musta been there overnight before they
talk about the tracks going in there
and them guys come up to look and there they was

AP: Uh huh

This guys that was coming the night
before he seen the tracks go over the hill
and he didn't bother to look
'til next day before he said
we should have looked for that car went over the bank and we
you know we went to look and there was Frankie Wilson
he was badly hurt on his leg

AP: Mhm

This woman there he was hurt
and the sister was dead.

(Tape 3b; 17 July 1989)

Several sites of fatal road accidents were inevitably mentioned by people on each passing of the sites. In the case of the accident involving Frank Wilson, Angela was among the group that found the car and its occupants the night after the crash; in the small reserve communities in northern Secwepemc territory, all such losses are deeply personal. The accident mentioned here had occurred at least ten years before, and the road at that place remains extremely steep and treacherous.

Site G: *Cklutetátu7s*

Cklutetátu7s is the site of both contemporary and early historic uses, and although it is a favoured camping site of Angela George, it is also associated with great tragedy. The combination of these strongly negative and positive attributes are manifest in many of the narratives and discussions recorded with regard to the site. Before turning to specific examples from associated discourse, I will summarize what I have learned about *Cklutetátu7s* from the Georges.

Angela and Jimmy have explained to me that *Cklutetátu7s* was a place where the Secwepemc once lived in pithouses. The pithouses were probably occupied in the late 1800s; eight raised earthen circles and saucer shaped depressions left by the pithouses are still quite evident, and indicate that the settlement was substantial. It is likely that the place's appeal as a village site was based on the same characteristics that make it a favourite of Angela George.

Angela has remarked on this place: 'It's a really nice place to camp there' (tape 1; 24 August 1988), and 'the best camping ground we ever had' (tape 3a; 17 July 1989) Angela found it to be an excellent place to dry fish, and remarked, 'There are no flies there or nothing,' (tape 1), which leads me to suspect that the afternoon breeze that blows up the gulch there helps to wind dry the salmon, while keeping the flies at bay. *Cklutetátu7s* is very close to the trailhead of the Little Dog dip-netting site, and so would have provided a convenient place to process salmon, and also to protect the community's interests in a key dip-netting site. During Angela's earlier years the gulch was a very popular place for picking wild raspberries, and Angela reports that one Elder used to pick soopalalie berries there as well. The spring associated with the site would only run for part of the day in the lower section of *Cklutetátu7s*. As Angela described it, 'that creek comes down here and daytime / he dries up but in night comes / later in the afternoon he comes' (tape 3a; 17 July 1989). There was also a grassy area that Angela said provided lots of browse for the horses when they would camp there.

Angela has told me that the people who lived at *Cklutetátu7s* in the pithouses were wiped out by an epidemic of either influenza or small-pox about one hundred years ago. As no one could go near their pit-houses without becoming infected, the afflicted were left where they died, and their houses eventually caved in on top of their bodies, becoming their graves. Immediately adjacent to one of the pithouses is a rock cairn that Angela identified as a grave. If the house and grave were contemporaneous, the grave's inappropriate placement would imply that the occupants of the pithouse were too weak to bury a body any further from their house.

The site bears some reminders of its former occupation beyond the large structures. The ground also yields stone and bone projectile points, some of which were collected by members of the George family years ago. The projectile points are at once interesting and important links to a past heritage, and both Jimmy and Angela have referred to the points when we have passed there. However, the projectile points were made by people now dead, and in accordance with Secwepemc (and larger, Salish) traditions, such personal belongings should either be bur-ied or 'sent up' to the dead in a fire, but not used by the living without special precautions being taken to purify them. Jimmy George made a brief reference to the place, in between pointing out a location where people used to raise sheep and a trail to the Little Dog dip-netting site:

Jimmy: ... that cross used to be a big old log there
         just to keep the sheep there at night time.
         Right over there.

         Call this one *Cklutetátu7s* this this little gulch.
                                     AP: Mmm   [at a corral]
Jimmy: I find a little bit of a scraper there some kind
            I don't know
               I'll show you when we get back
                                              AP: Mmm
         Where I find it.

         That's a reserve too down there where those guys fish
                                     (Tape 5; 27 July 1989)

On another trip with Jimmy, the reference to *Cklutetátu7s* became part of a conversation as I made a reference to the place we were passing:

AP: [Ange]la took me up here the other day
Jimmy: Oh yeah?
         Way up there?
         You see where them Indians used to live before?
AP: Yeah
Jimmy: Way over there
         Didn't find any uh arrowheads around there?
AP: Not a one
Jimmy: I used to find'em
         Musta pick it all up I guess
AP: Yeah

AP: It was really beautiful
Jimmy: Yeah
         Yeah we camped up there a couple times
         Twice
                                          (Tape 4; 21 July 1989)

As I introduced the general topic of place in this conversation with Jimmy George, I have no way of determining whether he would have mentioned the site on his own. He did, however, direct the questions with regard to the old pithouses and arrowheads, and volunteered that he and Angela had camped there.

Angela's narratives from *Cklutetátu7s*, below, were recorded on two other trips. She includes references to the projectile points, the people who lived there, and the campsite, but her narratives are more detailed and reflect the ambiguities and eeriness of the place:

Angela: I guess those er underground Indians[8]
             used to live up there
         long ago you still could see the holes
             where they would stay up there.
         Up there I guess
             where the water comes comes in there
         in the evening the water comes out
             but in the later in the day
                 they had to go way up to get water.

Site G: Angela and her grandchildren walking between remnants of pithouses

They call it *Cklutetátu7s*,
    says it's really nice place to camp there
to dry fish there's no flies or nothing.
                                    (Tape 1; 24 August 1988)

Angela: Yeah everybody that's living in them holes like this
             they all die
         Musta been long ago
         That's where Ethel and them used to pick up
             them good spearheads
         them bow and arrow
                                    (Tape 3a; 17 July 1989)

In these two narratives, knowledge of events long past is qualified by the use of 'I guess ... long ago' and 'Musta been long ago.' The references to the past are paired with mentions of current direct experience of the site, in the declaratives 'it's really nice place to camp there / to dry fish there's no flies or nothing' and 'That's where Ethel and them used to pick up them good spearheads / them bow and arrow.'

Angela's personal knowledge of this place came to include a more

immediate experience of the ancestors whom she had carefully qualified her knowledge of earlier.

Me and the kids I think
Earl was a baby then
We used to stay at the camp all the time
    but Jimmy goes down
All that trouble for me working on that salmon
and the baby staying awake all night fishing
    and ( ) the salmon

At first Dorothy and Ethel and Betty
    were playing outside
        and they hear these people
            laughing in the *ishken*[9]
and they stayed in the tent
we have a coal oil lamp
'Go fix my bread!' I had some bread
    cooking around the campfire
And they say
'We can't go and fix your bread,' they say,
    'them people come alive, they're laughing
        at the place over there.'

                                        (Tape 3a; 17 July 1989)

Years ago
'Bout ten, fifteen years ago
we camped there n'
Ethel n' my daughters
used to hear it
Betty and them used to hear it
The
the people laughing
up in them holes
underground houses
She say they hear them laughing early in the afternoon
But I don't hear it
Because the girls used to go and collect them
bow and arrowheads
from that

Site G: Three pithouse rings

the mounds where they must of make
   the bow and arrowheads
And its what the girls used to collect
And they hears them people laughing
after

(Tape 1; 24 August 1988)

These narratives recount the consequences of collecting things from people who have passed away, and also serve as vivid reminders of those ancestors and their passing.

Site H: *Tsecyelk̓w*

Tsecyelk̓w overlooks the present-day settlement of Alkali Lake Reserve No. 1, and was discussed in chapter 2. When considered in relation to the narratives recorded at the auto accident site and at *Cklutetátu7s*, the overall discourse on this site suggests a time continuum linking various kinds of stories of personal experience to group experience and, eventually, to group history.

The narrative is historical in its use of indirect reference to the source of the information (e.g., the use of 'they say' as a qualifier). It shares qualities of a personal narrative in that Angela provides access to the story by mention of her ancestral ties to, and supernatural encounters with, the people on the hill, as well as by her many visits to the place. On a trip to collect tree pitch later in the summer, we walked right onto the hill to gather plants and to view the holes in the ground that mark the remains of the old pithouses. Angela's narrative on that occasion was also filled with references to a time past, as is evident in her reference in the first line to 'long ago' and her reference to other authorities in the use of 'they say':

It was long ago
I guess when they say when a
First time when the white people come and they
the smallpox come
They all die they say who live they have
holes on the face and the skin
Holes
they say
those that live

(Tape 6; 28 September 1989)

The act of relating a narrative to an audience includes them in the narrator's experience of the place in some way, and turns personal knowledge into knowledge shared by the group. Just as the Secwepemc use personal narratives in part to make sense out of their lives and experiences, so it is important for individuals, as members of the culture, to make sense of the experience of the group. To bear witness to the narrators' stories is to share the experiences in part of the narrator's own ancestors, and to claim their experiences for the living group.

Findings

A corpus of texts has been identified for the Secwepemc of Alkali Lake that constitutes what may be called narratives of place. These narratives of place are highly context-sensitive; they are most appropriately told at the actual site of the occurrence highlighted in the narrative. The narrator is expected by the audience to contribute anecdotes that relate to personal experience and knowledge of the land, its resources, and its potential dangers.

Audience members who are aware of a potential narrator's experience at a site through previous journeys over the territory with that person may prompt the person to speak of his or her experience if the narration does not appear to be forthcoming. Prompts by the audience include signals of attention such as silence on approach to a site and questions about the site. The stories are generally retold on each passing of the site, although some elements of the stories may be highlighted or downplayed on different journeys, and another's talk may interfere with their mention.

Personal experience associated with specific sites is appropriate material for narratives of place. Directives (e.g., 'there is the fish trail you should stop at' or 'be careful here') are not generally used. Instead, personal experience of the site, conveyed in narrative, supplies both the cautions and the orientations. In Secwepemc society, where men and women often contribute in different ways to hunting and gathering, experiences of sites tend to be discussed differently. Hence, the person who is telling a story at a site might have carried out activities there that will never be likely to be conducted by some other members of the group, yet all who are present to hear a narrative will thereby share in knowledge of the resources found there.

An individual may incorporate stories into their personal repertoires about events for which they do not have first-hand experience. Almost always, the manner in which the knowledge was acquired, the degree of certainty of an event's occurrence, and the source from which the speaker draws knowledge and authority to speak are qualified and identified. This precision in speech, in sources of knowledge, is a highly significant characteristic of Secwepemc discourse, both in hunting and gathering contexts and elsewhere.

Each participant familiar with the territory contributes his or her narratives of personal experience to the set of key sites as the sites are passed. The strings of anecdotes in each participant's repertoire may be seen as comprising a personal map of the landscape travelled. All such narratives acquaint those present who are less familiar with that part of the territory with the resources to be found there; personal and ancestral knowledge of the land is thereby pooled among groups of hunters or gatherers. The result is a shared cognitive map of the area, where personal experience becomes group experience. Together with historical narratives and creation stories, these personal narratives of place interweave to form a rich and intricate map of the experience and survival of the people of Alkali Lake.

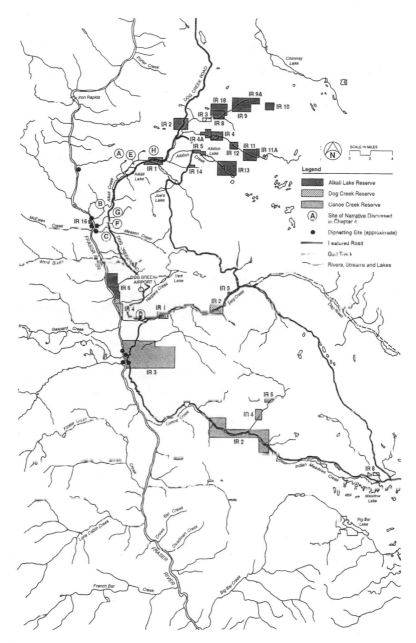

Map 7   Key sites along Dog Creek Road. Cartography by Beth Suprenant.

Chapter 5

Story

When I first remember, about sixty years ago, the people of my tribe had very many stories, far more than they have now. [...] Many of the stories which were commonest when I was a boy are now seldom told, or have been forgotten altogether. Thus the number of stories have decreased, and no new stories have taken their place, excepting (of late years) some Bible stories introduced by the priests. These are looked upon, however, as forming a different class, and are not considered the same as the myths of the speta'kuł [i.e., stories of the time of the world's transformation]. Tales of every kind are not told as often as formerly among the people. When I was a boy, very many stories were told about the Old-One or Chief, who travelled over the country teaching people, and putting things to rights. Many wonderful tales were related of him; but the men who told these stories are now all dead, and most of the 'Old-One' tales have been forgotten. The majority of the Coyote tales have survived, however, and are often told yet, for they are funny, and children like to hear them. Formerly Coyote stories were probably commonest of all.

Sixwi'lexken (quoted in Teit 1909: 621)

Sixwi'lexken's lament, quoted above, is echoed today in the concerns of his relatives in Alkali Lake, and in other parts of the wider Salish world. Darwin Hannah and Mamie Henry, recording Nlha7kápmx tellings of Interior Salish stories nearly one hundred years later, heard from many Elders that stories were told at night when they were young, but that many were forgotten: 'One elder jokingly stated, "Ask by the graveyard," for when the elders die, they take with them their encyclopedia of knowledge' (Hanna and Henry 1996: 11). Fortunately, stories are still told, at times, by some, as Hannah was to find in Nlha7kápmx territory around Lytton, and I was to find a bit farther up the Fraser River, at Alkali Lake.

Story and Landscape

The earliest written record of Secwepemc speta'kuł is provided by the geologist George Dawson (1892), who worked in Secwepemc territory, especially in the Kamloops area, from the mid-1870s through at least 1889. His beautiful hand-coloured maps, some of which are housed at the University of British Columbia's map library, are covered with place names that he learned from Secwepemc people. Dawson's list of Secwepemc place names in the Kamloops area includes over seventy proper names that are descriptive of general physical features (e.g., using Dawson's orthography: Spil-ma-moos, Little Flat; Shloot, The Eddy; and Pil-te'-uk, White Earth [now Clinton]), as recorded in the Geological Survey of Canada's *Annual Report* (Dawson 1894: 401B–404B). His diaries (Cole and Lockner 1989) indicate that he came as close to Alkali Lake as Pavilion and Hat Creek. He reports that, of the stories he collected from the Secwepemc, most are from Kamloops and some are from Lytton. (The latter settlement is in fact in Nlha7kápmx, and not Secwepemc, territory.) He published the collection of stories in 1892, including two Coyote stories, and several about animal-monsters, which formerly took men as their prey, but came to be the food of humans. A Trout-Husband story Dawson recorded is similar to one told by the late Charley Draney of Deadman's Creek (Kamloops Division of Secwepemc), published in Bouchard and Kennedy 1979 (47 56). Thunder and Mosquito, another story in Dawson (1892), was later told by Charley Draney to the linguist Aert Kuipers in 1970 (Kuipers 1974: 96). Of the stories he heard, Dawson reports, '[s]everal ... are already forgotten by the younger Indians, or, if not forgotten, they cannot be induced to speak of them' (1892: 28).

J.A. Teit provides a published set of creation stories he heard near Alkali Lake, especially downriver at Dog Creek. Teit, as did Dawson, found that in the part of Secwepemc territory he visited, 'the number of stories has decreased, and no new stories have taken their place' (1909: 621). Teit wrote down as many of the tales as he could. Of his time with the Fraser River Division, Teit writes: 'During the season of 1900, I collected the bulk of my information from several old men in the vicinity of Canoe Creek and Dog Creek, and especially from a

very intelligent man called Sixwi'lexken, who was born near Big Bar'
(447).

In 1900, Teit collected eighty-three stories for the Fraser River Division at Canoe Creek and Dog Creek (and some more from the North
Thompson River Secwepemc at a later date), two about Old-One,
twenty Coyote tales, twelve 'brief stories of transformation,' and forty-
six others. New stories, though of a different kind, were finding their
way into the Secwepemc repertoire from the Catholic church, and as
adaptations of European folk tales. Teit unfortunately did not record
any of these newer stories in the Secwepemc repertoire, but did so with
respect to the Nlha7kápmx in his 1912 publication. The 'brief stories of
transformation' he recorded from the Fraser River Division bear some
resemblance to some of the short stories from Kamloops that Dawson
published. The stories collected by both men share much with stories
told throughout the Pacific Northwest and the Plateau (cf. Thompson
1946; Boas 1917).

In the case of many indigenous cultural groups in the Pacific Northwest and Plateau, including the Secwepemc of Alkali Lake, a key time
for telling traditional stories was the winter. In the evenings, the old
people would instruct the young: 'About bed-time mythological tales
were told by some old person until the people all fell asleep. On the
following evening another elderly person told stories, and thus all the
people who knew any myths took turns at relating them throughout
the winter. These were the times when the old people would address
the young, and when they would admonish them to follow the rules of
proper ethical conduct' (Teit 1909: 617).

Opportunities for such evening interchanges had perhaps diminished when the Secwepemc began to move from winter pithouses to
European-style single-family dwellings, as encouraged by the Catholic
priests.[1] But perhaps it is the age and status of the potential audience,
as well as the lack of traditional setting, that contributes to reticence. I
was, eventually, to hear stories in a context comparable to the one Teit
describes. When I brought my daughter as a toddler to Alkali Lake,
years after my initial fieldwork, Angela George would take her on her
knee in the eventings, and tell her some of the stories I had thought
were no longer told.

Teit's monograph on the Secwepemc begins with a photographic
plate of a boundary marker in Secwepemc territory. It is a weathered
and hollowed boulder, called 'Coyote's sweat-house' (1909: 454). Many
of the stories in Teit's collection contain references to apparently gener-

ically defined settings, such as 'a lake' with 'grassy shores' (638). Such a description may, however, in some cases refer not to the nonce form (Hunn 1994: 81) but to the proper names for a place in Secwepemc.

A number of stories reported by Teit refer to events that occurred at specific locations, most notably the story of *Tlee'sa and His Brothers* (1909: 644–51; cf. Dawson 1892: 31–5). *Tlee'sa and His Brothers* traces the travels of four brothers from near Kamloops, past Savona, by Deadman's Creek, up the Bonaparte River to Chasm (near Clinton), down the Bonaparte to Hat Creek, overland to the Marble Canyon and Pavilion, and thence up the Fraser River to a place near High Bar. This version of the story names places close to Canoe Creek Reserve, where Angela George, and many other people from Alkali Lake, have close relatives. (It should be mentioned that most people once living at Canoe Creek Reserve No. 1 have since moved north to the Dog Creek Reserve, the location of the elementary school and combined band offices for the two reserves.)

> Then the brothers, following up the Fraser River toward High Bar, passed west of Pavilion Mountain, over a high bluff, on the flat top of which they saw a Chipmunk, who was also a pubescent girl. She was dancing, and they stopped to look at her. The brothers tried to transform her, but could not manage it properly. They walked forward, but found their feet getting heavy. After a few more steps, they became transformed, and gradually turned to stone where they stood. The Chipmunk girl became changed into stone of a red color, for she was painted red at that time; and the stripes, like those on a chipmunk, may still be seen on her back. The place where she stands is called Luti't. The place where Tlee'sa and his brothers stand is called Siemmi'y. The former may be seen a little distance to the rear of his brothers, for he was behind them when they all became transformed.   (Teit 1909: 650–1)

Physical features, including caves and canyons, places to find arrowstones, eagles, and other resources, are specifically located in the story at particular places along the Brothers' path. The attention paid in the story to the Brothers' experiences with various creatures and dangers in relationship to places where important resources are found parallels the narratives of personal experience and the historical narratives I discussed in the previous chapters, and provides evidence that, for the Secwepemc, such stories can serve as another source of authority, which can be incorporated when talking about places and their resources.

In the version of *Tlee'sa and His Brothers* that Teit recorded, the tale begins in Kamloops Division territory, but the Brothers travel up the Bonaparte River into North Thompson Division territory. It ends with the brothers transformed into red rocks on the edge of the North Thompson River above the Red Trees Reserve. This transfer of story locale to locally accessible places and corresponding physical features is not uncommon. In Lushootseed Salish territory, the Snoqualmie and the Upper Skagit each locate the place where a rope fell from the sky world (in their Star-Child creation stories) and piled up in a heap at the centre of the earthly world, near their respective villages. Much farther afield, Miriam Kahn has discussed how the people of different villages of Papua New Guinea tell the same stories but the locations of events shift to reflect and claim the villagers' respective local landscapes (1990: 59). The area around High Bar, where the stone Chipmunk and Brothers are said to stand, is no longer on the life-path of the people I travel with, although it was in their childhood. This shift has occurred within the lifetime of living Elders, as Canoe Creek people have moved north to consolidate at Dog Creek, and as High Bar is no longer the location of a band settlement.

Jimmy George once made reference to *Tlee'sa and His Brothers* on a fishing trip. References to the power of pubescent girls are common, and dancing is still considered a way of demonstrating that power in Salish cultures. In Coast Salish tradition, this power is most commonly displayed in Seyowin ceremonies (Amoss 1978); in the Interior it is now demonstrated in pow-wow dancing. Staring into someone's eyes or staring directly at them, as Tlee'sa and his brothers did, is considered more than rude; it is considered to be dangerous. Eyes, particularly of a dancer full of their power, and menstrual flow, also indicative of power according to the instruction of some Elders, are said to be conduits or openings to the spirit world. Despite their many adventures and clever tricks, Tlee'sa and his brothers were no match for Chipmunk at the height of her powers.

Jimmy George and Angela George both tease and laugh about not staring at chipmunks, apparently meaning members of the opposite sex. Their brief reference to the story in this way, and their mention of the pillars farther down the Fraser River, show their awareness of the story. The story also incorporates general social knowledge about how to act as respectful beings (i.e., by not staring). Although the stories I have quoted here from the pages of writings by Teit and Dawson make direct reference to the land, and attempt the fullest possible accounting of details, they seem enervate when contrasted with the way the smallest references can be brought to life through the words given in passing by the Georges.

Story and Mourning

The first story ever told me by the late David Johnson of Alkali Lake was the biblical tale of Noah and his ark. He has translated this into Secwepemctsín, and a copy of it may be found at the school on the reserve. David Johnson was a devout Catholic, the altar boy at Alkali Lake for as long as he was physically able (see Brow 1967: 125), and very proud of his part in constructing St Pierre's Church in the village. Over his living-room sofa was a large commemorative document of the blessings bestowed by the pope on David Johnson and his late wife, Celestine, on the occasion of their seventy-fifth wedding anniversary. He told me the story of Noah and his ark as we sat in his living room, looking out of his front window directly at the church. This was a story of importance to him.

When I asked for stories about Coyote, he said he did know some 'fairy tales,' but the folk tale he told next was a European-derived one about a princess. The term Teit recorded as 'speta'kuł' (1909: 621) from the storyteller Sixwi'lexken is transcribed as *stseptékwll* by Kuipers (1975: 13) and is glossed by people at Alkali Lake today as 'myth' or 'fairy tale' (cf. Kuipers 1974: 135). (*Stseptékwll* contrasts with *slexéyem*, which is glossed as 'a realistic story' [Kuipers 1975: 13].)[2] For David Johnson, a European fairy tale and a Secwepemc 'myth' were of the same kind, leaving aside what meaning he may have imparted to *stseptékwll* as a class. Or, at least, this was the kind of story David Johnson would tell me.

David Johnson was an amicable conversationalist. Mostly, when we visited, he told me how he was 'doing all right' and discussed the projects he was working on, including building a three-wheeled cycle to allow him to get around the reserve more speedily, creating drainage for the reserve's muddy main road, and building a shelter for his wood pile. Our contact, though comfortable, was not based on any history of shared experience, and did not provide us many occasions to puzzle through life's difficulties together.

After I had known David Johnson for several months, he did ask if he could rely on me for a favour. He asked if I would drive him to town, so that we might join in a funeral procession as it made the long drive from a mortuary in Williams Lake, bringing home a body to Alkali Lake. On our drive to town, he pointed out the window at some pothole lakes between IR No. 1 and IR No. 2. He told me that giant serpents had once appeared in one lake, and had then disappeared, coming up in the next one. He said that the lakes must be somehow connected by a tunnel or hole underneath. This is the only time he ever spoke to me about such creatures.[3] I did not then have the experience to know that the reference may have been brought out by the circumstances of a death on the reserve.

On the occasion of my driving David Johnson to town, we waited in Williams Lake for several hours, with many delays, for the body to be released from the funeral home so the processional could form. A coroner's report must be filed in the case of any death that occurs outside of a hospital, and in the case of a community so remote from such a facility, most deaths require such investigation. Bodies must be shipped as far as Prince George for examination, and in the meantime, the phone calls are placed, messages are sent to band offices on other reserves, and word of the death passes quickly. Most older people are very aware of how their village members are related, and when word of a death is sent to their reserve, they are consulted to ensure that all local kin receive the news. While we waited, David told me the story of bringing his own brother's body home. His brother had died far to the north one winter, and he had to bring the body home by sleigh. The journey took several days, and when the weather began to warm, the scent drew wild animals, which pursued him back to Alkali. I could understand his wish to support those coming home. A tarp, which was to be burned later, was finally secured in the back of the pickup truck to protect the coffin from dirt and dust on the fifty-kilometre trip back to Alkali. Other people waited in cars just off the main reserve, and joined the processional there. From the reserve, the rumble of the approaching vehicles, and the dust in the air, can cause one to look up, as far off on *Tsuktsékus* a seemingly endless chain of headlights begins its slow winding down the hill.[4]

People who have been off in the bush or away at cabins in the meadows sometimes show up at the reserve, subdued, and pay calls on friends and relatives to sit and hear if there is any news. Something about the manner of a particular animal they saw in the bush may be interpreted as a message. A deer coming up to them with no fear, and looking directly at them, or an owl flying close may be viewed as a sign that they ought to go see their relatives at the reserve. Not wishing to invite ill fortune, the reasons for paying an unexpected visit, or returning home early, are usually left unrevealed by the individual, until the sad reason is made apparent. As Chief Abbey stated in her testimony, quoted earlier, '[A]ll our relations within that whole environment are communicating [...] [I]f you, yourself, have that type of relationship, you read all those signs.'[5]

When word of a death is sent out, people make plans to travel to the reserve where the funeral and burial will take place. Some will be staying for up to four days, and the extended family of the deceased makes plans to feed them all. A special friend of the family will be asked to serve as head cook, and other women will come forward to volunteer their help, or will be asked, as friends, to do so.

Grieving family members do not prepare food. I have been told that one's sentiments are shared through the food they prepare, and that 'angry food,' and food prepared in grief, is to be avoided. If a woman is menstruating, she will not volunteer to cook, as a woman is considered especially powerful at that time, and her connection with the spirit world strong enough that, in a time of death, she might render those who eat what she cooks, especially family members of the deceased, vulnerable to its pull.

Part of food preparation is hunting and gathering, and depending on the closeness of the relative who died, an individual might refrain from these activities for anywhere from a few days to a year after the funeral. When people are in mourning, they bear watching closely. The restrictions, in my experience, oblige those who are grieving to have contact with the living, who, according to custom, stand ready to offer all the support that they can. Those who are restricted in their procurement of sustenance are fed by others, and this love and attention, as well as the actual food, provides nourishment for the mourning family members and assists in their recovery.

Teit (1909) provides extensive information on old taboos on hunting and gathering after the death of a family member. Some of the restrictions he reports regarding the preparation of food, picking berries, and hunting and fishing by the family of the deceased for a period after the death are still observed. These restrictions are not absolute, however, and certain precautions may be taken if the restricted activities are to be practised. For example, I learned from Angela George that if a man must fish in the year after his wife has died, he must find some way to make the salmon think he is not fishing for them. She said that one way to accomplish this is to take dead leaves and scatter them into the river, and pretend to be dip-netting for leaves, instead of fish.[6] This practice may in some way be associated with the following excerpt from *Coyote and Grisly Bear*, which Teit heard told in the Fraser River and North Thompson Divisions of Secwepemc territory: 'It was now winter-time, and Coyote thought he would play another trick on Grisly-Bear-Woman. Taking some dead leaves, he threw them into the river, and they changed into salmon. Then he took some dry service-berries from the trees and threw them at the bushes, thus making them green, and laden with many fresh berries. He then went into the house, and informed Grisly-Bear-Woman that many salmon were running and the service-berries were ripe' (1909: 631).

Non-relatives are given money to go to the grocery store, and women prepare the food in their homes or in a central kitchen, to be taken to the house where all those helping with the project may take their meals for several days. Young men from outside of the family are quietly given gas money, firearms, or other assistance that will allow them to go out and hunt. A grave will not be dug by the men until the morning of the funeral, but they will begin to build a wooden cover to put over the coffin, and construct a cross or plaque for a grave marker. The kitchen is busy, under the direction of a head cook, and the family makes plans and receives visitors in the parlor.

When the body is sent back from the coroner, it goes to one of the Williams Lake funeral homes for embalming. The funeral home cremates any substances that are not put in the coffin, and this practice is locally acceptable, as burning is seen as one proper way to send remains on to the person they were part of. Even in day-to-day life, people are expected to be careful of what they leave of themselves lying around, whether hair, or fingernail clippings, or other such things. Burial or burning are considered appropriate means of sending them on, so that one need not come back later to look for what was left behind in this world. These practices are seen as fundamental indicators of self-respect.[7]

Children are considered to be particularly vulnerable to ghosts that might come to welcome the deceased, and it is at these times that Elders tell stories to teach the children about protecting themselves from the spirits of the dead. Through often chilling narratives, the children are cautioned against yelling around the funeral fire, and are warned not to walk at night on the pathways that lead to the village graveyard, and to stay close to their homes. They are admonished by the Elders not to run around outside with any food or drink from the feast table, for the food will become 'empty,' as the nourishment will be taken by the spirits gathering around. People say that the dead come at this time to welcome their relative, and food is offered up in the bonfire to feed them.

The Events of August 1989

I returned to the field in the summer of 1989 to focus my work specifically on the oral mapping process discussed in chapter 3. I had been back at Alkali Lake for three weeks when the woman with whom I was staying and her brother were tragically killed in a traffic accident. The woman was very dear to me; she was a confidant about my mother's age, and we were coming to be 'like family' to each other. Her brother was regarded as a kind of a son-in-law by my chief consultant, Angela George. The suddenness of the deaths, the double funeral, and many other circumstances contributed to Angela's strong desire to escape from the sadness of the reserve, and go up to her old territory near Lac la Hache to camp and pick berries. The combined weight of my grief and having to cope with my responsibilities as a member of a deceased person's household contributed to my readiness to go away with her for a few days.

We travelled toward Timothy Mountain from Lac la Hache, about three hours by road from the main Alkali Lake reserve. We had gone there together before, and Angela had told me stories about her times working there on a ranch with her husband. In the days following the funeral, the stories recorded in that territory had a different bent. References to the land and its resources continued, but the most salient elements of the stories were no longer references to specific sites, and were brought out by the overarching context of mourning.

We spent a day picking blueberries and raspberries, and that evening found us driving away from the fields, our baskets full of berries bouncing around in the back of the station wagon. While we travelled, Angela spoke of the children she had lost in childbirth and illness. We were visiting a territory she and her husband had lived in many years before – she said she had not been out there since their old ranch boss, a man she had been very fond of, had died. She spoke of all these losses as we drove into the dusk.

She then recalled that when we started picking early that day, we found the bushes were trampled as if someone had just picked before we arrived. The person must have been a little taller than we, for he could break the branches off and lean a little further in to pick the berries.[8] I had teased the rancher who had directed us to the raspberry patch, saying that he had gotten to them all before us. He swore he did not, and then he remembered to tell us that there had been bears in the field all morning.

Tape of 6 August 1989

(The style of the written transcript presented here, with the ethnographer's silent reflections interleaved into an unbroken stream of recorded speech, is based on Ridington's [1988] treatment of narrative.)

We were travelling. Angela began to speak of the trampled raspberry bushes, and their lack of fruit, as if someone had picked just before we arrived. I turned on the tape ...

Angela: ... bushes.
       Musta been a bear.
AP: Yeah.
       It did look like a man, didn't it?
Angela: Yeah.
       Yeah they say it was an old woman
         that changed into a bear long ago.
       That was a story.
       They say one old woman went out with his
         his grandson musta been like Dal.[9]
       And
       He couldn't find him.
       And
       next two days when they
       they lost him and
       they find his tracks,
       next two days n',
       third day they found his tracks again
         where he killed his grandson bury him under
       you know a
       old root?

                              AP: Uh huh?

       Well, it must a been an old
       Stump

where she dug a hole then bury his grandson.
And they coulda see him when he was –
   when he went from there his feet was a bear.
But they didn't see him.
Third day and they see him.
And his ... his head was a woman yet.
   Didn't change in a bear just his body.
     They left him alone when they seen he was a bear.
Fourth day when they see him he was bear all over

                                  AP: Mmm

and his head.
So they let him go.
And them bears come after two years there.
Old Woman that change into a bear.

Her last sentence had the finality of the end of a story in its rhythm, but after drawing one quick breath she launched into another tale:

Angela: And the same with the grizzly bear
          they say it was a young boy.
          He used to be mean that boy.
          And his dad and his mother want him to come be a good boy.
          They took out his heart and they taken it to big rocks n'
          flat rocks n'
          and they took out his heart and put it between hot rocks
          And they put it back into him. He tell him he should
          'We fixed your heart, t'
            to come be a good boy.'
          They say that they say that
          Swicw[10] they called the ones that were half dried.
          They say they were laying there. *Swicw.*
          Stuck it in his mouth
          say he growled like a bear and he jumped way up and he
          bite that tree and he splinter.
          When he hit the ground he was a grizzly bear.
          And he walked away.
          And his mother musta tell him don't hurt nobody now d' you
            gotta
          have a reason to attack somebody.
          Now it's like that.

Grizzly bear he have a reason to attack
people.

AP: Mmm

She knows that.
Same with the bear.
Same with the cows or bulls or whatever.
She'll have a reason to attack you.
To get mad at you.
And to be wearing them dead peoples clothes
  or whatever you get from dead people?

AP: Mhm?

You wearing it that's why the bear come and get mad at you.
Or the bulls or the cows.
And if you get your period. They come attack you anything
( )
If you're travelling
your period.

AP: Uh huh?

Same if you're wearing dead person's clothes.
Same if you walk in a graveyard and you come you go
  somewhere.
Bears will attack you
  for this dirt from the graveyard on your shoes.

AP: Mmmmm

[*Long pause*]

*It occurred to me that two people had borrowed shoes from me on the day of the
funeral.*

Angela: Yeah them even them sa'
         even them them gentle cows are.
         They say one poor old lady must have tell his daughter,
         'fill this pail.'
         And she used to carry water for this cow

AP: Uh huh?

         to water him.
         Buckets.
         Fill it up in the tub.
         Wo musta tell his daughter 'let's look at that cow.'
           Well he was a gentle cow.

'Let's look at him.' When it happened
    to get the water from that creek and fill up that that tub.
( )
If it's true you know that the girl will have her period
    if it's some of-some animal will attack her.
They say the minute that girl fill up that tub
and that cow jump on that
on that tub and he horn it.
Squash it to nothing.

                                            AP: Mmmm

He make noise loud and he horn it against the fence.
Squashed the tub.

They say them little bears, well, used to
One time somebody get little bears in the reserve and
They that that one man musta say we'll see
them little bears knows that.
They say they want to cover up with blankets
    when there's lots of mosquitoes.
He give'em a blanket to cover up
    and they cover up and they enjoy that blanket
        when there's lots of mosquitoes.

                                            AP: Hmm

[Angela gets a laugh in her throat.]
Angela: Chee.
    They get a dead person's coat and they give'em.
    Put it on'em.
    Oooh they say they make noise them little bears
        they're just a few months old.
    Say they really make noise like a bull
        and they dug a biiiig hole.

                                          AP: Uh huh?

And they tear up this coat in little pieces
    and he put it in a hole and he bury it.

                                          AP: Yeah?

Dead person's coat.
Even little bears know.

                                          AP: Mmm

Some Elders tell a story about a man from the reserve who took a dead person's blanket in his wagon into the bush, and was attacked by bears. When he threw them the blanket, they left him alone, and ripped up and buried the blanket. Another story relates that people travelling with a dead person's things held up a rosary to protect themselves, stopping a bear in its tracks and turning it away.

Angela: That's why I was thinking you know,
       I travels a lot.
       And I watch what I'm doing I don't
       I don't take things from the second hand store
         and use it when I go somewhere in case
           somebody might a'–
             somebody's clothes you know that dies
               maybe they sell'em in second hand.

AP: Mmhmm

       Same with your shoes you gotta watch what you're using
         when you're traveling like this
       out in the bush.

I knew from stories I had heard from other Elders that shoes worn to the grave-yard had to be brushed off with juniper boughs, as the dirt clinging to them could enrage bears.

Angela: The minute you holler at a bear or whatever you holler at
         then you had something you know
           that they could attack you for it to come after you.

Children, especially the grandchildren of Angela, are told not to scream and cry or fight with each other, or 'the bears will come'; 'might be a bear will come and take you away.' Bears, we learn from Angela, have to have a reason to attack. Hollering, she says, is one of those reasons. (In Tlee'sa and His Brothers, *James Teit records, 'Henceforth the grisly bear shall be a mere animal, able to kill people only at times they are foolish' [1909: 646].)*

Angela: Same with
       you see a deer or you see a moose if he come and attack you.
       Your family's gonna go late at night or that day, they
       If a deer comes after you.
       If you see deer a standin' there
       and he sees you
       and well he breathes on you.

AP: Uh huh?

Like if they spit on you and they jump,
it's a bad sign somebody's gonna die in your family
    or whoever you're staying with.

AP: Mmm

Angela: What happened when we was up the mountain hunting.
Dennis went an' hunting and Victor's mum musta died.
Dennis seen a big buck.
She was standing good that buck.
He could of be able to shoot it.
He was hunting.
See that buck just like of he spit on him
'Wwhwx !'
and he jump.
Dennis knows he – even if he try to shoot him
    I guess he'll come after him.
Say it must have been hard
out of luck. He say that
'Buck,' he say, 'just like he spit on me and he jump.'
Dorothy get up there he say,
'We come for you guys we gotta go home,' he say
'Victor's mum died.'

A personal narrative about a coyote sending a sign of death to Angela's family followed. It parallels the narrative about the buck, above, but it must currently be considered as confidential information. As such, it is not transcribed here.

Angela's information is presented with the authority of personal experience, and through stories that reference the experiences of others, to obliquely suggest proper behavioural models for the audience, in a manner typical of Secwepemc ways of teaching. Her advice provides a set of exmaples of Secwepemc ways of knowing, as well as an explanatory framework for unfortunate events. The stories she tells are similar in form and content to ones I have heard told to children by other Elders on the reserve, to caution children to behave properly at funerals, and to avoid dangerous interactions at times of mourning.

Angela's advice is presented in a highly condensed and patterned form. It includes a sequence of two well-known stories of transformation, two examples of attacks she has heard about, and the relation of two family experiences associated with death. Her narrative provides a rationale for animal behaviour witnessed today that is rooted in the past, imbedded directives about proper comportment around animals, and an interpretation of their actions as that of messengers.

Brown Bear and Grizzly Bear are closely associated with death, with the violence that sometimes accompanies death, and with respect for the dead. These stories concerning Bears communicate appropriate behaviours during times of mourning. They provide vehicles for carrying important cultural information in ways that the information can be remembered and understood, often through elegant patterning and dramatic renderings. Angela's narrative contained cultural information she considered crucial to our spiritual and physical well-being. She pulled out all the stops in her narrative pacing, explaining through the barest outlines of story, personal actions and personal experience what she felt I needed to understand immediately, and also what she needed to remind herself of. The information we are given altogether is that animals need a reason to attack, what those reasons for attack can be, how to avoid being attacked, and the inevitability of death in the messages the animals bring.

Despite Teit's information labelling the winter as the appropriate time to tell such stories (1909: 621), it seems to be the case now (and perhaps in Teit's time as well) that particular stories, such as those concerning Grizzly Bear, and others associated with death, were also told in times of mourning. The tradition of winter storytelling seems to have ceased or at least markedly diminished, while the cultural information that at least some of the stories provide can still prove to be a helpful guide to action. Whatever the case may have been formerly, as they are employed today by Angela George, the stories and cautionary personal narratives provide crucial cultural information and instructions in a culturally appropriate manner, where explicit directives or observations regarding the suitability of another's behaviour are considered to be unacceptable violations of personal autonomy.

In times of mourning, people at Alkali Lake still cleanse their houses with juniper, purify the air with burning sage, and hang rose branches over their doors. They are careful not to buy clothing they might travel out in from thrift stores, and to burn the things that belong to the dead. They are respectful of the spirit world, as is apparent in their many precautions during menstruation, and their avoidance of food preparation during mourning. When hunting or gathering, whether for funeral feasts or in general, they pay careful attention to the world around them and to the signs that may appear to them. Younger peoples' linking of these practices to a shared system of knowledge is now mostly accomplished through hearing others' narratives of personal experience, as well as legend or historical stories, and through their own experiences. The stories may not be referred to as in old times, but many of the social practices the stories reinforced are still considered meaningful and are carried out.

These observations hold significance for social practices outside of the context of mourning as well, as was discussed earlier with respect to the knowledge referred to, and the social practices implied in, the story *Tlee'sa and His Brothers*. Narratives of personal experience may be more comprehensible, more immediately accessible to young people, and where stories, as ways of knowing, may have once been employed, they may no longer be used in most cases as authoritative support for practice.

For the Secwepemc, to travel out, or to hunt and gather after a death requires a type of traditional knowledge additional to the typically presented oral map of the landscape and its resources. In both our travelling and gathering Angela and I were violating several taboos, which are observed by most people at Alkali Lake to the present day, by picking berries so soon after a death (cf Teit 1909: 592–4). Considering our state of grief and close relationship to the immediate family, ours was a questionable activity. There was also a possibility that my shoes carried with us some of the dirt and scent of the graveyard, as they had been borrowed by someone for the day of the funeral. In addition, I had been menstruating, although I did not realize this until we finished picking berries for the day. (See *The Woman Who Became a Grizzly Bear*, in Teit 1909: 715–18, for further information on appropriate conduct in such a circumstance.)

According to Secwepemc traditions, our activities put us in danger of being attacked by bears or other animals. In order to protect us from potential misfortunes, Angela wanted to leave the woods where we had planned to camp, to stay with others in a house instead. She first needed to make sure I was aware of our circumstances. Her observation of trampled berry bushes, and the belated realization of the presence of a bear, considered in the context of the recent deaths, had sparked Angela to deliver a particular kind of narrative on the night of August 6th. In this overarching context our situation urgently required my comprehension. Angela did her very best to teach me about protecting myself out on the land, and in the process provided a model of guidance for social action in a Secwepemc world.

Chapter 6

Memories

Anthropological life-story work is a fundamentally collaborative endeavour, in that it involves the construction of a narrated version of a self, negotiated into coherence through understandings between the recorder-anthropologist and the person whose story is ostensibly being put to paper. With any transmission of a life story, as Charlotte Linde has noted, 'coherence must be understood as a cooperative achievement of the speaker and the addressee; it is not an absolute property of a disembodied, unsituated text' (1993: 12). I found that at Alkali Lake, to listen to life stories was to enter a treasured relationship where learning something of how to perceive and act in a particular social world comes through the transmission of another's life experience. This discovery was not, for me, immediate; I first had to learn what the role of the addressee was in the 'cooperative achievement' Linde has discussed.

I have heard two distinct narrative styles employed in the telling of life histories by the Secwepemc of Alkali Lake. Each style of life history is well developed, context-sensitive, highly valued, and frequently used in the culture. One is a stylistic adaptation of a non-Indigenous form and involves the careful retelling of a life story in a chronologically linear style with minimal audience participation. The other, which Angela George has called 'telling my life,' invites listener interaction and is told in many discrete segments, each strongly linked to place. This chapter compares the two styles, so as to explore what Margaret Blackman calls 'the specific cultural conventions of life story discourse' (1991: 56).

The Newer Form of Personal Narrative

The newer form of life history requires careful and oblique presentation, for it is the highly confidential narrative shared in the fellowship of Alcoholics Anonymous. Narratives told within the context of Alcoholics Anonymous meetings are to be held in strictest confidence, are not to be quoted or recorded, nor may they be reiterated outside of an Alcoholics Anonymous (AA) meeting. All in attendance at AA meetings are customarily reminded of these restrictions, which I will honour here. Thus, only general descriptions of the usual content of AA narratives are mentioned here. Members of the Alkali Lake Indian Band may tell their life stories privately at AA meetings, but as a community they have chosen to make public a collective history of their struggle to overcome alcoholism on their reserve, through their film *The Honour of All* (1987). I view their film as a meta-narrative of the AA personal narrative, and will address its impacts on the community later in the chapter.

An AA personal narrative is an orally presented account of an individual's struggle with alcohol delivered within the context of an AA meeting. The body of the narrative typically begins with a mention of life before the narrator discovered the bottle, the first drink, the development of problems in life associated with alcohol, the lowest point in the person's life, the decision to quit drinking, and then the struggle toward recovery. A publicly available and AA-sanctioned document, popularly known as the AA 'Big Book' (*Alcoholics Anonymous: The Story of How Many Thousands of Men and Women Have Recovered from Alcoholism, by Bill W.*, 1976) provides a sample of life stories similar in topic to those discussed at the confidential AA meetings.

The AA narrative is generally chronologically linear in presentation, and at Alkali Lake it often touches on events over virtually the entire life span of the narrator, as people in the community were often introduced to alcohol at a very early age. The histories frequently end or begin with a mention of the length of time since the narrator last had a drink, and often the formulaic closing line is used: 'Thanks for my sobriety.' The progression of linear time in the narratives is further marked by the importance placed on AA 'birthdays,' the anniversary of a person's entry to sobriety, which is celebrated with a birthday cake at the meeting. At Alkali, when an adult mentions that it is their birthday, this is generally the kind of birthday they mean.

For older adults, birthdates, as opposed to AA birthdays, become important in the context of receiving pensions. Visiting priests often recorded dates of baptism, but dates of home births were not necessarily recorded. It is also the case that a baptismal certificate for one child might be saved, and if the child subsequently died, the next same-sex child born was given the same baptismal, English or French, name. In this way, many written records of birth and baptism have been mixed together. I found my questions about specific dates of events in people's past often went unanswered.

Strongly active in the Alcoholics Anonymous fellowship, community members regularly attend AA meetings, and participate by witnessing others,' and by telling their own, personal narratives of their struggles. The AA personal accounts are confessional and often deeply moving, to the narrator and the audience. The pattern and dynamics of the AA narrative suggest that it may be part of a larger genre of conversion stories, common in Coast Salish country as well. Pamela Amoss (personal communication) finds these characteristics of AA personal narratives shared with Pentecostal conversion stories and Indian Shaker church conversion narratives.

The format of the AA meeting as a whole has been learned from the outside world, and slightly adapted at Alkali to better suit the needs of the community. AA meetings on and off the reserve have chairmen (or women) and people responsible for taking up a collection and making coffee, and setting out the chairs. At Alkali, the chairs are arranged in a circle, rather than in rows, to accommodate all on a more equal footing. The AA meeting is held at different houses on the reserve each week, meaning that the AA narrative is not grounded in place in the sense of a constant physical location for the meeting, but rather it is ceremonially contextualized; whatever place is selected for the meeting is an appropriate ground for telling AA narratives and conducting the other business appropriate to AA.

In an AA personal narrative, the particular history of an individual with respect to alcohol is arranged chronologically. It is a performance that can benefit the narrator and listener on personal, emotional, communal, political, and social levels. It serves on the level of affect to allow a person to explain what they have come to be, as they understand their life at that moment. The stories present a way to make sense of one's life. Thus, I would consider AA personal narratives to be representative of a type of life history.

Community Knowledge and Personal Identity

At all AA meetings, fellowship and support in sobriety can be found, but the form and political significance of AA meetings at Alkali Lake differ somewhat from those held off the reserve. Attendees at Alkali

Lake meetings need not be alcoholics, nor even particularly anonymous. Virtually all participants have known each other since birth, and all community members are urged to attend, including this anthropologist. Audience, then, has a high degree of correspondence with the community the narrator will encounter outside of the AA meeting. Relationships outside of the meeting are of course in some ways affected by what occurs within.

Being an adult member of the community means being able to participate fully in the meetings, and this involves, for each member from time to time, presenting an AA personal narrative. A speech act common to all AA meetings in my experience on and off the reserve is the use of a formulaic floor-opener to begin a narrative. The floor opener, which at once gives a person licence to speak and affirms his or her membership in the group, is: 'Hi, my name is [e.g.] Bill, and I'm an alcoholic.' The appropriate response from the full audience is: 'Hi, Bill.' At Alkali Lake, this floor opener is a particularly fundamental statement of both personal identity and community membership, beyond the context of the meeting.

At all AA chapter meetings, a formal reading aloud of AA regulations takes place. In one of the texts read, AA members are advised to 'take what you need, and leave the rest.' This advice aligns with the existing Secwepemc presentational strategy concerning instruction, where a narrative of personal experience may be recounted to direct advice to some or all members of the audience, should they chose to notice what was offered for their consideration. No comment on the personal narratives presented in AA is permitted under AA regulations, and none is given, in accordance with Secwepemc rules of oral communication for both the first speaker and the addressee. Respect for another's personal autonomy precludes both phrasing advice as a suggestion, or for commenting on it as such. This rule holds in some Athapaskan speech communities (cf. Basso 1990; Scollon and Scollon 1981) as well, as was discussed in chapter 1. Ironically, the very reading aloud of 'take what you need, and leave the rest,' as it is phrased as a directive, may seem a violation of the rule in itself. In the context of a document read out loud and written by some unknown person, however, it is unlikely to be so construed by the addressees.

While the AA narratives are held in confidence, they cannot be held entirely separate from other aspects of community interaction, which have become absorbed into AA meetings. As anything said in a meeting is said in an ostensibly 'safe place,' if there are certain things a person wants to make known about experiences with other family members, they may choose to use the AA meeting as the forum by embedding the information in their AA narrative. Extreme social pressure can be brought to bear by what people 'know' from the meeting, even if they are honour-bound not to discuss that knowledge.

Just as Alkali Lake community members are known to each other inside and outside of the AA meeting, with little possibility of maintaining anonymity, in the aftermath of making the film *The Honour of All* aspects of their lives and the state of their community became well known beyond the reserve. Some individuals chose to make their stories public to the point of portraying their former selves on film, and grew famous as their story was shown on VCRs at community halls throughout Indian Country, and then was broadcast to a wider audience, nationally on Canadian television, and in the United States on the Discovery Channel and the Public Broadcasting System. Prominent members of the community were soon deluged with requests from around the world to come and tell of their personal achievements, and to present their film. These sought-after community members gained much experience through public-speaking engagements and demonstrated high levels of competence in making presentations, which although not necessarily performed in the venue of AA meetings, were in the style of AA personal narratives.

The Problem of Participation at Alkali Lake AA Meetings

The issue of how young people may seek to gain entrance into the adult world through drinking is a very serious one. The young person at Alkali is caught in a bind. He or she has learned as an audience member at AA, and through intense observation and traumatic interaction with drinkers, that drinking is dangerous and unacceptable behaviour. Youth does rebel, however, and many young people who have recently begun drinking have no current interest in associating with many outside of their age group. For those who have remained sober throughout their young lives, and who do wish to associate with the older adults, we must consider that without drinking and becoming sober, these young people have no story for the AA meeting and no way of announcing 'My name is Bill, and I'm an alcoholic.' One young man who knows he is an alcoholic, but has never taken a drink, does not contribute to the meetings in terms of telling stories. Another went on a very public 'drunk' for one night at a reserve dance, assured everyone that he was drunk, and then returned to sobriety, and began active participation in AA meetings thereafter.

Beyond identification as an adult member of the Alkali Lake community, through the pow-wow, Sundance, and other Native organizations that eschew the use of alcohol, a larger identity as an Indian, or traditional, person is maintained. A line of dialogue in *The Honour of All* shows just how strongly the people of Alkali hold the notion of 'Indian as alcoholic.' Their response to alcoholism as separating them from non-Natives is summed up in the response given in their film (Alkali Lake Indian Band 1987) to the white bootlegger trying to make a living: 'Your way of living is our way of dying.'

Consequences of the Film

Many people at Alkali Lake turn on their VCRs and watch the film for a very private source of encouragement when they feel depressed or discouraged. Reviewing their earlier selves on film, and seeing on film the people who have inspired them, can be a source of great comfort. Viewing the film in these circumstances can be like visiting a place, in that remembrance of past events that transpired over the course of filming, and of the places where they occurred, can be vividly recalled. On a few occasions when I have visited people on the reserve who happened to be watching the film, I have heard them tell stories about its making.

Despite the positive aspects of the film, *The Honour of All*, as a meta-AA narrative, also has had some unforeseen negative consequences. These can instruct both anthropologists and community members on the potential pitfalls and benefits of writing down narratives, or of otherwise fixing them to some permanent medium, as on celluloid.

Because the story is fixed on film, and widely accessible, selection of audience cannot be taken into account by the storytellers. When people from Alkali Lake travel to present the film or give workshops, or welcome visitors to the village, they face an audience from the outside world that understands the film as representing the real and relevant version of the people of Alkali Lake. The outside audience knows them as they had come to understand or, at least, present themselves in 1985. The film is not accepted as 'history' because people keep discovering it and experiencing it anew. This temporal aspect of the telling cannot be controlled by the storytellers. People told the story to make sense of their lives, but now find that the story talks back to them. The storytellers have moved on from that point, but find themselves exhausted by the expectations placed on them to live up to, rather than beyond, their selves as cast in the film. The chief at the time of the film's release, Andy Chelsea, chafed at being labelled, in an article in *Reader's Digest*, 'the savior of the Shuswap.' As one exhausted teenager put it, 'I'm so *tired* of being a role model!'

The film as text takes on an authority that may supplant that of the speaker. An Alkali Lake person, speaking at AA meetings or gatherings with people from outside of the community, may feel obliged to structure their personal narrative in a way that fits into the collective vision of band sobriety and prosperity offered by the film. In the course of repeated tellings over time, the presenter of an AA narrative will recount the same events with different emphases, bringing new insights into play to make sense of the present. For people from Alkali Lake, these newer narratives are nonetheless referenced to the meta-narrative of the film. Disempowerment by one's own (in this case, collective) narrative is indeed ironic, especially in light of anthropology's interest in authority and power in voice.

The film has attracted visitors to Alkali Lake who seek inspiration for their own sobriety through attendance at Alkali Lake AA meetings to listen to the narratives of community members. There is in this community considerable pressure to maintain sobriety. Children from other reserves are occasionally brought by their relatives into the safety net that Alkali seems to represent. In addition to visitors seeking inspiration from the community there were frequent visits from the press in the year following the release of the film. The increased lack of anonymity in the AA meetings, with so many outsiders visiting, allows little room for the confession of relapses, or 'backsliding.' To backslide conflicts with the synchronic/quasi-mythic narrative of the film. As a result, some people who backslide may come to avoid AA meetings in their own community entirely.

For the full adult, the consequences of deviation from the ideal may be severe. Band employees who are caught drinking alcohol may be fired according to the directives of the band council. Band members who return to drinking, however briefly, do violence to the dream of community-wide sobriety expressed in *The Honour of All*, and risk the disappointment of and rejection by those within and outside of the community who cling to the hopeful images of the film. At Alkali Lake, even in the confidential confessions of the AA meeting, the outside may look in.

Taping a Personal Narrative with Angela George

Angela George is one of the individuals at Alkali Lake who has occasionally been asked to speak at conventions. She has told me that she held forth for over an hour on the subject of her life as an invited guest at one such gathering. At that event she was given many thanks, was much honoured as an Elder, and was presented with an exquisitely beaded walking stick. Her reflections on that speech, and her description of the audience's appreciation of it, had become an important part of her larger narrative about her life. In my experience, when people admired the beaded walking stick, Angela would tell them how she came to possess it. I knew she was aware of the value others place on her life story, and on her community's story.

I had travelled a few times with Angela George to fishing places, and to visit her relatives, before I felt comfortable asking if I might tape-record some of what she had to say. After we had about six months of acquaintance, I asked her if she would come driving with me, to record place names close to Alkali Lake, just south on Dog Creek Road. I made the request on a day that I felt less shy around her than usual, on an auspicious occasion in my own culture, my own birthday.

I proudly announced that it was my birthday to Angela George and others around me. It did not occur to me until years later that my statement might have been interpreted to refer to an AA birthday. Yet, in considering a general Secwepemc perspective on such an announcement, this would have been a logical interpretation of my remark. An AA birthday is a mighty achievement for an individual, and, as I have already noted, is a marked event in the community. Alternatively, being born is something everyone does, whether a particular date is noted on record to mark the event or not. My proud announcement of the date of my birth would have seemed foolish; I must have meant the other kind.

Angela assented to my request to tape-record her. I asked her if we could record place names, in association with the sites. I wanted to record her saying the names, and make an accompanying photographic record of the sites. She had told me the Secwepemc names of places as we had travelled before, without the tape recorder, and as this was important information for the community to have on record, it seemed a good project to develop with her. We set out south on Dog Creek Road the next day to commence our work. A transcript of that day's recording is appended to this book, and a few of her comments on named places from that trip appear in chapter 5. In addition to the narrative Angela supplied, the recording and transcript include all of my pestering requests for place names, and their repetition for the tape recorder, the sound of the car screeching to a halt, the whir of the camera, and our laughter as I repeatedly leapt from the car to take photographs, only to be tripped, strangled, or otherwise detained by errant microphone cords entangled in the seatbelt, stick shift, or steering wheel.

As we were returning from several hours of investigation, my requests for place names had diminished. I had taken my last photograph, and we were returning to the reserve. Angela then told me a version of the story that she had told at the convention. I present some of it here, but have removed sections that might compromise the anonymity of others:

Angela: Don't know how old I was when I first remember
I musta been around two I guess
My granny I was raised with my granny
used to
live in a –
live in a tipi[1] like
was built up like a tipi this house and
dirt on top and you know er all the way down
it was built like a tipi with rails
and we used to have a hole on top
and that's where the smoke goes out
we used to have a campfire in the middle of the – this tipi
that's where – where I grew up and where I was raised
We used to have a – beds all around it
tipi like and
lots of – swamp hay I guess for a mattress
and that's what we used to sleep – sleep on
And there was no pots no forks no – no cups then
when I first remember
and my granny used to cook that –
our food in the campfire in the ashes
used to cook that the vegetables
and the potatoes[2] into the campfire
or fish and rabbits or whatever we eat
we just cooked on the sticks beside the fire
Then when he cook that and he finish cooking then –

my granny used to put boughs
   on the on the ground on the floor
that's where he puts what's cooked and
looked delicious food for us to eat
then he'd kneel down and pray
pray first before we eat
they pray when they get up
they pray when before they eat
they pray before they sleep
first thing in the morning they pray

that's when I first remember

and I didn't know
that people would have a father
'Til I was 18 before I asked my mom
[*five lines deleted*]
I was raised by my mom and my granny that's all
my grandpa musta died long ago
So I was raised by my uncles

it was hard life for me n –
'Til I start living with white people when I was eight

earned my own living
worked
It started when I was eight I never go to school
I worked every day
'til I was 22
I still didn't make no money
I was paid every day of working
My mom spend all my money on the food
My sisters' and brothers' clothing
That's where I learned
everything to support my – my family my kids
even now I still do the same
I'm 65 I'm
I'm still supporting myself
and still uh – learned a lot more about my life
I never drink 'til I was 25

Because I loved my kids I wanted to be with my kids
I want to raise them up first
before –
[*line deleted*]
So many years before I start drinking
Liquor was open for four years for the Indians before I
started drinking and four years
because everybody drinks
[*eight lines deleted*]
it was over and over
my life

then I guess I was stupid in my life I
[*line deleted*]
I got old before I think of myself
breathed ( ) my tracks
look over myself
In a big country
and I was sitting in Alkali Lake
treated like a dog
and I don't even know
I still sit there
[*line deleted*]
it's what happened for so many years before I
before I started paying back
[*two lines deleted*]

I didn't know I was strong
'til I would be
fight back 'til I find out
[*line deleted*]
I didn't know I was strong
All my boys
My three boys tried to

tried to stop me
they couldn't stop me
[*eleven lines deleted*]

'n so

But now that I stayed sober for ten years
   and I see lots of things
Lots a nice things that I seen lots of good friends
lots of nice people
all the places I travel
since I since I was a Native dancer in pow-wows
seeing lots of people
see lots of friends going Sundancing lots of other people
from different countries, friendly people
get
get my
give me lukewarm on my feelings on my heart
when I hear that drumming
my heart goes dancing first before my feet goes dancing
AP: Mmm

I really have good feelings from drumming
dancing
I sees lots of things in
dancing and sweats
ceremonial sweats
I sees lots of things
Lots of good things and I have warm feeling
get a – get well on sweats lots of times
Try it on my elders and they got
better.
Have a bad cold
Taking them for sweats
I was scared first to give them sweats to get better but
try it
believe it.
(Tape of 24 August 1988)

The narrative Angela produced has characteristics of an AA narrative in its structure, temporal orientation, topic, and sentiment. It is also a version of the story she had told at the convention, where AA-style narratives were appropriate. It does not include the formulaic opener ('Hi, my name is ...') or closing (typically, 'Thanks for my sobriety') one would expect to find only in an AA meeting. It does begin with the kind of orientational information that typically follows the formulaic opener in an AA narrative ('Don't know how old I was when I first remember /

I musta been around two I guess'). It gives an account of life before the discovery of the bottle (to 'I never drink 'til I was 25'); the first drink at age twenty-five (in this narrative, noted but not further elaborated); the development of problems associated with alcohol (deleted lines); the lowest point ('and I was sitting in Alkali Lake / treated like a dog / and I don't even know / I still sit there'); the decision and reason to quit drinking (lines deleted); the struggle toward recovery (from 'I didn't know I was strong' to 'But now that I stayed sober for ten years and I see lots of things'); and on into her recovery and taking up of spiritual pursuits through her participation in pow-wow dancing, the Sundance, and the ceremonial sweat lodge. Her sacred activities today parallel the religious devotions of her family in her childhood.

The temporal ordering of the narrative is accomplished through reference to years of age at the time of an event. Despite the precision they seem to imply, these are inexact, as was discovered when Angela attempted to draw her pension at what should have been age sixty-five. The ages mentioned can instead be considered as ordinals, marking order, while not being set to specific calendrical dates. This considered, the relative ages still serve to orient us, and the progression of her narrative is orderly, even in the embedded times mentioned, such as her reference back to 'when [she] was eight.' The narrative marks the order of life events and makes reference to her current number of years of sobriety, and her ages at different stages in the process of alcoholism, in the phrases:

when I first remember ...
I musta been *around two* I guess ...
when I first remember ...
'Til I was 18 before I asked my mom ...
did I start living with white people *when I was eight.* ...
It started when I was eight I never go to school ...
I worked *every day / 'til I was 22* ...
I'm 65 I'm / I'm still supporting myself ...
I never drink *'til I was 25* ...
Liquor was open *for four years* for the Indians *before I...*
started drinking and four years ...
I got old before I think of myself ...
But now that I *stayed sober for ten years* and I see lots of things ...

I have long puzzled over why she chose to deliver such a (relatively) long and rich narrative in my company on that particular day, at that time. It might have been occasioned by the first use of the tape recorder, my birthday and its association with AA, or the newness of our relationship. Although I had then known Angela George for several months, the trip marked the first time we had gone on an outing without bringing other people along. The memories that the trip had brought her as we travelled may have contributed, as well. In fact, one particular story that she had told earlier, seemed as if it could fit into the longer narrative just described. We had just left the reserve, and were passing the communal women's sweat lodge when Angela started talking:

Ah this is the sweats
Where they used to sweats year round
   all winter and all summer
      to keep people to keep clean
They make sweats even doesn't matter in the cold weather
Bath in the creek
To be strong
Keeps their health happy the sweats
I guess they been using the sweats for years and years
That's where they

Long ago
My granny wanted me to sweats
Four months I sweats
I was about 13, 14
And he tell me to not use any
any soap or anything for me to get clean
   just to rub myself with bough you know
      to rub myself all over with a bough
And don't use soap to wash my hair
   just use a bough you know
To get clean
I sweats every day for four months
That's how I keep my
my m'granny tell me I keep my looks
The same'til I'm old n'
You know to keep my looks
Look natural

AP: Uh huh

Natural Indian woman

AP: Yeah

That's how I look now
Never used a –
anything on my skin
Just my natural looks

(Tape of 24 August 1988)

This life-story fragment is situated in time by the mention of duration (four months), her age (13 or 14), which indicates its significance in her life as the special training received at puberty. Although it was delivered at the beginning of our trip, it seems as if it would mesh neatly into the longer narrative Angela delivered later, where she speaks of her life before the bottle, but does not mention her adolescence. One prompt or mnemonic for the story was the sweat lodge we passed, or the place of the sweat lodge. It may or may not be the case that Angela would have incorporated this story in a more elaborate AA narrative.

How an Elder 'Tells Her Life'

A short session at her kitchen table a month later was to be my only other opportunity to record Angela George that summer. I left her with copies of the tapes, and hoped I would be able to see her again when I returned the next summer. I saw her next on my first day back at the reserve in 1989. That day she told me she had dreamed that she would tell her life, and I would record it for her. When she told me this, I was pleased to comply with what I thought was her request. Based on what I had previously heard from her about her public-speaking engagement, and having listened to the narrative she presented in my car the summer before, my assumptions were that she would present a chronological account that we could assemble in her house, and as an audience I would be a conduit, a mostly passive listener operating a tape recorder. To further fill out and clarify the narrative, which I assumed would be stylistically similar to AA narratives I had heard from community members at Alkali Lake meetings, I formulated a set of questions.

I sat at her kitchen table the next day, ready to begin, with tape-recorder levels set to receive her words. However, the narrative I had anticipated was not delivered. Her life story was not what she wanted to discuss at her kitchen table. I decided to be helpful, and suggested she mention all the children she had, their names, and when she had them. She balked; she seemed reticent, as if she were unable to understand the questions. Providing a neatly ordered chronology was apparently not what she had in mind.

Charles Briggs has pointed out that 'interview techniques smuggle outmoded preconceptions out of the realm of conscious theory and into that of methodology' (1986: 3).[3] What I had attempted to do in Angela's kitchen was a formal interview, with all the baggage of questions I thought should inform it. My 'conscious theory' concerned my expectation that Angela and I had a common understanding of what kind of narrative a life story is. My questions followed from that interpretive framework, rather than from an understanding of what it might mean to Angela to 'tell her life.' I had forgotten, again, what Vi Hilbert continues to teach me about 'learning how to listen.'

Our interview went no further. I felt awkward and disappointed that I had somehow not lived up to my role as recorder of life history. After a cup of tea and something to eat, Angela suggested we go pick berries the next day. We took her young grandchildren, Candice and Dallas, in the car with us. Angela and I took Joe's Lake Road, a familiar route that leads near her family cabin. We were near Joe's Lake when we passed a place where she and her husband, Jimmy George, had once encountered some bears:

Angela: One time me and Jimmy was going around in there
   hunting we was on foot
    and the one bear had three little ones there
   playing on them trees them
   He had two black ones and one white one
   I would like to get the white one

                   AP: Yeah

Angela: But Jimmy wouldn't want to kill him
   Oh, he say,
    'He must have like his kids just like you.'
   [*laughter*]
   I wanted the white one they were nice and small yet.
   He say, 'That bear loves his little ones just like you.'
                 (Tape of 10 July 1989)

Finding a mother bear with three cubs is an event worthy of remark. To find a white cub is even more remarkable. Angela may have wanted to take home the little bear, but Jimmy was unwilling to kill its mother to make this possible. It is doubtful that the two black cubs would have survived without her. Angela's empathy and identification with the mother bear, through Jimmy's observation 'That bear loves his little ones just like you,' is also significant. She had to forgo the novelty of having a white bear cub, because a mother loves her 'little ones.' Angela was telling me what we both knew; how important that kind of love can be. (In a sense, there are little bears in Angela's family, too. Angela's daughter Dorothy has a Secwepemc name, *Kenkeknem*, meaning black bear.) This is a story of a decision not to act on impulse, and one of sweet sentiment, delivered with laughter, told at a specific place, by Angela to me. One minute later, after mentioning that she 'had all of [her] skirts ready for the Sundance,' and a pause, she came back to the story:

Oh, we used to come through in there when we hunt
   and there's a lake in there
     and other lake back in there.
That's where we seen this bear
   with his three little ones
Pretend to be eating the grass around
he keep on looking at his little ones
   playing on the tree

We had now passed a bit beyond the lake, which had been visible a minute earlier, hence her deictic remarks, which oriented my attention to the place once more. The bear was acting like a person, 'pretending' and looking at its 'little ones.' And next:

He's just like a human person that bear
he say when his little ones fight
That one that starts to fight
   he'll take him and he'll spank him.

(Tape of 10 July 1989)

And so the bear even disciplines her children as a human person might. It also should be noted that the use of the binomial, 'human person,' contrasts humans with other kinds of persons, including bears, or, when viewed another way, includes humans and bears in the hierarchical category of 'person.' (This is the same kind of reference to personhood that Chief Abbey made in her speech, quoted in chapter 3.)

The story Angela George told had an internal consistency, but was never linked in her narrative to other events, or to longer sequences of events. I find Linde's notion of life story as a 'discontinuous narrative unit' (1993: 216) to be very helpful here as a conceptual tool. It falls to me, in part, as addressee, to discern the links between what I perceive as fragments. In the Euro-Canadian storytelling style I am most familiar with, a life story segment can be presented with respect to a larger story told earlier, through the use of *orientation clauses* (ibid.: 70). (E.g., 'Remember when I was away in Germany?') This allows the hearer to think about the life story already related, mark the place in the account already loosely woven into coherency, and mentally push apart the threads, to accommodate another piece of the tale. If there is a shared cultural understanding on the part of the speaker and addressee as to the cues appropriate for such orientation, the accommodation is successful. If such orientation is not part of the discourse structure of the language used, it is possible that some other linguistic, or perhaps even extra-linguistic, cue is being employed. On that day, I was not able to discern the indexical features that might orient me with respect to Angela's narrative. I was not even aware then that this story was an important part of 'telling her life.'

The next week found us travelling to another place, and then coming home with two cranky grandchildren in the back seat:

Angela: My mom musta shoot some bear in there
         Round there there were two bears and he kill them
         My stepfather wasn't supposed to kill it
         and my mom kill it herself
         She shoot it with a big rifle
AP: How come he wasn't supposed to shoot it?
Angela: Just like in olden days
         Jimmy didn't believe it you're not supposed to kill a bear
         and he did kill a bear and our boy died
         It's supposed to be like that

                                                              AP: Oh

Angela: Like my –
Candice: Uh!
Angela: Don't start kicking Dal!

                                              (Tape of 17 July 1989)

Much of Angela George's life story is beyond my capacity, as a person from another culture, and a younger person who has experienced far less personal suffering than she, to fully comprehend. The question I had asked at her kitchen table, about how many children she had, was one of consequence. At Alkali, such a question necessarily carries another question, nested within it: How may children have you lost?

My question in the car, 'How come he wasn't supposed to shoot it?' cut in on her story, and caromed the conversation off in a different direction than I think she had intended. A native Secwepemctsín speaker would have shared with Angela an underlying cultural understanding of why men do not kill bears, and of the relationship between humans and bears. Her references to the time, 'Just like in olden days,' and Jimmy's lack of belief in it, 'Jimmy didn't believe it you're not supposed to kill a bear,' are also indicative of prevailing attitudes against such stories, or of their discounting as 'fairy tales,' which was encouraged by the local Catholic priests. The story that she had been telling about her mother shooting a bear, meanwhile, was left unfinished as the children began to fight in the back seat. It was not resumed, and we drove on to other places, and into different stories.

Telling Stories to Make Sense of Life

Angela's way of explaining her son's death, 'and he did kill a bear and our boy died / it's supposed to be like that,' is a very different way of making sense out of one's life, actions, and outcomes than the one I knew. What Angela presented was indexed to a larger, canonical story. Her brief reference to 'olden days' indicates a similar anchoring of events to parallel orderings in another world, and leaves room for an understanding of the otherwise unthinkable, the loss of a son.[4]

For Tagish and Inland Tlingit Elders, Julie Cruikshank has found that stories with motifs common to many North American groups, such as the Star Husband Story, are used to explain events in storyteller's lives (1990: 339). Where such stories can serve as models relevant to a person's life, they may be drawn upon for the support and comfort they provide through their explanatory power. Similarly, references to the model of Christ's story of suffering and the stories of mythical women warriors were used by Ruth Behar's Mexquitican consultant, Esperanza, to refer to the way her life is lived (Behar 1993: 11–12). Greg Urban has explored the structural oppositions of life and death to show how the irreversibility of death is explained in Shokleng myth as being caused by the failure of individuals to properly carry out instructions (1991: 66–7). For Angela George, the moral ordering of the world is still in some ways referenced to canonical stories, which have relevance for the way she lives her life.

The Conflict between Orientational Axes in Two Traditions of Discourse

Angela George and I travelled together often for the rest of that summer. It was important to her to travel to the places where she had spent her days, to introduce me to her kin and to her former employers, and to show me the places where she had lived and worked. We travelled several times to Timothy Mountain, about 160 kilometres from the reserve, where she and her husband had once worked as a camp cook and hunting guide. We also visited her friends and relatives near Lac la Hache, where she had once worked for a rancher. Within the context of travel, Angela George told me about many key life events, including her marriage to her first husband; her time working on the ranch; her illness, cured by her son's prayers; her visions and subsequent participation in Sundances; her trips to pick berries; and her time spent at the family cabin. At first, I thought the stories were told during travel simply because her house afforded no quiet (children running, TV blaring), and there was no way to record without distractions.

Sitting at Angela's kitchen table at the start of the summer of 1989, I had been attempting to impose that sort of chronological order on her story with the kinds of questions I was asking, and which Angela was not answering. Joel Sherzer provides a caution against this approach: 'Given the temporal organization of most narratives told in European languages, it is not surprising that narrative theorists, often without knowledge of non-European narrative traditions, define narrative universally in terms of temporal sequence' (1985: 303). I find her own expression, 'telling my life,' a most appropriate descriptor of Angela's narratives, because it does not indicate in any sense that chronology is an essential component of an ordered account. As I discussed in chapter 4, for the Secwepemc the telling of spatially anchored narratives can be considered together as a 'map of experience,' their telling being a way of maintaining knowledge of the land and its resources by the group. Until Angela explicitly categorized those narratives as 'telling her life,'[5] I was unaware that this kind of life story, for the Secwepemc, is also bound up with place.

It seems that this association of life story with place may be useful in the study of other cultures' oral histories and life stories as well. In her work with Haida Elder Florence Edenshaw Davidson, Margaret Blackman states that Davidson began the story about her life with 'the drowning of her brother Robert, one month before her birth,' but '[f]rom that point on ... there was little chronological order to the narrative' (1982: 16). In Cruikshank's work on place names with the Tlingit/Tagish Elder Mrs Angela Sidney, she found that Mrs Sidney would tell stories to explain the place names, and that 'by imbuing place with meaning through story, narrators would seem to be using locations in physical space to talk about events in chronological time' (1990b: 347). Cruikshank (1990a) has also examined the work of Keith Basso and Renato Rosaldo with respect to narratives of place to show that life-story accounts are often evoked by place, or even by the mention of a place name. Perhaps the strongest example of the latter phenomenon recorded in the literature can be found in Edward Schieffelin's *The Sorrow of the Lonely and the Burning of the Dancers* (1976; see also Feld 1995), in which the Bosavi are described as driven to extreme sorrow and rage when a place longingly remembered is called up through the singing of its name. All of these orientational frameworks to story or song, whether documented or implied, indicate that temporality is only one of many ways of coherently referencing past events.

Linda Akan, in her work with Alfred Manitopeyes, spoke of the importance of 'walking and talking,' which takes simultaneously into account an organization according to place and the differing perspectives of the speaker and hearer in their co-creation of the discursive event. 'The sentence "she was given good counsel" and "she received a powerful teaching" describes a process of give and take that is implicit in the discourse. Similarly, walking and talking are metaphors that describe this process, which the Elder refers to as traditionalist Salteaux education. If we can imagine a visual representation of this process, we would see two acts occurring simultaneously from different perspectives' (1992: 192). Akan's interpretation of narratives recounted to her in this way also takes into account time as unfolded between interlocutors 'simultaneously' and from two different perspectives, as derived from the interlocutors' different understandings of the teachings available to us in the stories from differing vantage points of age, experience, and culture.

As other ethnographers have found related phenomena in their research, I am left with several, only partially answerable, questions: Why are there at least two different forms of life story for the

Secwepemc? How are they used differently to make sense of life, for the narrator and the audience? Does the Western style of biography used in the Secwepemc culture for the AA personal narrative convey to them the same meaning as it does to members of Western culture?

Contrasting Form and Use of Life-History Narratives

I have found that 'telling my life' concerns the passing on of life experiences, themselves not temporally ordered, to another individual over time at shared intersections of experience and place. Hence, the temporally organizing element of 'telling my life' is actually the shared time of storyteller and audience, as audience comes to know and understand more about the narrator through time. Within this framework, the narrative accounts that comprise 'telling my life' refer to various points in time, in conjunction with place, and with relationships, in order to weave together a new understanding of self, and then to remake it continually.

'Telling my life' involves *repair*. Through recounting memories of the land and the stories the landscape contains, a narrator and audience knit their experience of a place into a new whole. It is a creative process. This has led me to consider that life stories may not be best represented in print in the order of occurrence of the events, as the shared experience of the narrator and audience should be taken into account as well.

I have also found that, when listening to someone 'telling their life,' being the *audience* requires, on my part, a complete engagement. I have to listen with great attention in order to determine what might be meant for me to understand with respect to my own life, or to my relationship with my consultant, and what might be important for others to hear later. As a writer/recorder/conduit, I need to pay attention so that I can be the ears for the Elders' grandchildren and others who will be reached through their tape recordings. In Angela's case, she wanted me to record these stories for her as well. She would like other people to know about how she has lived her life. My organization of the stories must reflect an accounting for that audience as well.

In contrast to 'telling my life,' the chronologically sequenced and tightly designed AA personal narratives, as told at Alkali Lake, leave no room for other than a passive audience. The AA narratives are fixed in one time and place, the context of the AA meeting, with strict cautions against reinterpretation, appropriation, or discussion by the audience (W. 1976). The audience is always advised at the meeting to 'take what you can use, and leave the rest.' The stories themselves may internally be temporally ordered, but they are static.

I suggest that AA narratives are used for maintenance of identity within the group. Part of the way an individual maintains identity as a recovering alcoholic within the group is by finding strength through his or her own and others' personal narratives, so as not to drink and to help others not drink. The performance of the AA narrative situates the narrator as a fully adult member of the community.

At Alkali Lake, alcoholism and sobriety are closely tied to group identity. Although the stories told at AA meetings are linear, forward-progressing, chronological texts, they all end with the same *now*, the maintenance of a sober life. In telling us who we are, the stories, respond to the questions What made me drink and How can I draw on that now to keep me from drinking again? The stories for some who have quit drinking, and who wish to remain in good standing as members of the successful, sober community of Alkali Lake, end with that. They are static, they remain in stasis; it is not good to fall off the wagon. In this one place in life, it is *not* good to have new stories to tell. It is the other, non-chronological type of narrative that is concerned with growth and interaction. With 'telling my life' there will always be new stories to tell. The arrangement of those stories, however, is more like a bouquet of flowers, which can be appreciated from different angles, individually or as a group.

Chapter 7

Cross-Cultural Comparisons

Social Constructions of Place

Throughout the pages of this book I have considered how particular places are imbued with social meaning by and for the Secwepemc, how spaces become places through human action on the landscape, and how people come to know the land through personal experience. Despite my attention to these matters, I found that in doing my fieldwork I imposed some social constructs of my own onto the landscape, and created some boundaries and amalgamations with my verbalized categories where none exist for the Secwepemc, or exist with different boundaries than mine.

One winter day at Alkali Lake, when the snow was deep, a newcomer from a Manitoba reserve amusedly remarked, 'I think it's real cute the way you guys park all over the sidewalks.' I had to laugh at her assumption that there was something under all that snow; I knew that during the spring breakup nothing but endless mud would emerge, and in the summer's heat, dusty flattened earth would stretch unbroken from house to house. 'Myrtle,' I laughed, 'there *aren't* any sidewalks!' She tolerated my response with mild amusement of her own. What struck me as so funny was that, even though there were no sidewalks separating driving area from walking area and house path from house path, I had always behaved as if they were there, or ought to be. While children sauntered down the middle of what I constructed as the 'road,' I walked a certain distance from the houses, where a sidewalk *could* go, in my estimation, and would park my car a corresponding distance from the houses. People from the reserve would park up close to the houses, sometimes right against the doorstep, or, in the summer, anywhere they could find shade: in the 'back,' 'front,' or 'side' of the house (my constructions also). I had been making room for things that did not exist.

Such differing cultural constructions of place draw attention to other Euro-Canadian definitions of features on the landscape with respect to discourse and action. How the environment is categorized as 'human' or 'built,' versus 'natural,' may reflect how members of that culture behave with respect to the earth. For example, in the United States this perceived dichotomy can be found codified in the administrative rules implementing the National Environmental Policy Act and its counterparts at the state and local level. These regulations prescriptively structure the 'elements of the environment' that should be addressed in the contents of an environmental impact statement, subdividing them between the 'natural environment' and the 'human,' or 'built environment' (United States 1969; Washington State 1984). The perceptual stance reflected in this analytical structure may conflict with the views of some Native peoples. Thus, my experiences and observations may be indicative of the type of differing culture-based perceptions that environmental planners encounter when evaluating the impacts of projects involving Native interests relating to land and resources.

In Euro-Canadian culture, concepts of the 'built environment' are multiple, intricate, and heavily layered with the baggage of social rules and expectations (cf. Lawrence and Low 1990), in contrast with the broad level of categorization of the 'natural environment.' There are fewer Euro-Canadian cultural assumptions made about the social uses of the 'natural environment,' and so, fewer expectations to cloud the ethnographer's observations of how other peoples use that space. Just as an urban culture may attach rich social meanings to aspects of cities, for hunter-gatherer and pastoral societies, their complete territory is also rich and immensely variable in its constructions. Through my fieldwork, Secwepemc notions of place came to some extent to replace what I had first experienced as 'wilderness,' or the 'natural environment.'

Shifting the boundaries of my initial constructions included doing away with my designation of a four-sided, roofed structure, with kitchen and beds in it, as a place called a 'home.' At Alkali Lake, when people ask where a person resides on the reserve, they do not inquire, 'Where do you live?' but rather, 'Where do you stay?' Those structures are where people 'stay.' Even when I attempted to label them more generically as 'houses,' I still held certain notions of the uses of such places, and of the rooms within them, as private places. It became very evident, however, that at Alkali Lake people behaved differently toward houses than I did. For many, virtually any room could serve as a place to sleep, the top of a roof could be used for storage, and doors were not generally knocked on to gain entrance. Lived spaces, those places that fit my notion of 'home' and what a home provides, with attendant connotations of domesticity, are labelled as 'Angela's place' or 'Irene's place,' for example, and include places in close proximity to the house, the 'junk house' (or *ctsillentn* – a small building detached from the house where useful tools and other things are kept), the smokehouse where fish is cured (the *ckecmelcw*), and outdoor tables and other workplaces where meat is processed and fish are cut.

Beyond these places, people also stay 'up the meadow,' that is, away from the village on the main reserve, in seasonal camps and cabins upstream on other Alkali Lake reserves, and some locations in customary use off the official reserves. Many of these reserves were set aside by the government because the land would produce swamp hay for the reserve's livestock, as was mentioned in chapter 3. Hay harvested in the meadows is still used as feed for the reserve's horses and cattle, but the meadows are also important to the people of Alkali Lake in that they are places away from the dense settlement of the village. They provide solitude and relief from the village's intensity of human interaction, and access to food resources that was once afforded by small family encampments as part of the seasonal round. The meadows, camps, and cabins, along with the junk houses, smokehouses, and the government-built structures on IR No. 1, are all home places; they are geographically separated constituent units that constitute a home when considered as a whole.

The maintenance of sets of home places, and Alkali Lake peoples' uses of them, is comparable to that found in other traditionally hunting and gathering societies. Hugh Brody has described one Dunne-za Elder's use of space as follows:

> Beside Joseph's house is all the paraphernalia of an encampment, so much so that the house itself is diminished, and becomes a far less dismaying sight than if it were a home as such, a place to which domestic life is restricted. The appearance of poverty has its place in a more complicated system of life; Joseph's Reserve home is one of several camps, cabins, and accumulations of equipment that together are far more important than the condition, size, or furniture of the house we are now visiting. (Brody 1981: 3)

The Dunne-za and other indigenous societies in British Columbia share in common with the Secwepemc the experience of a relationship to a series of colonial, national, and provincial governments, which laid out villages and expropriated their lands, defined a defensible claim to staked land as including 'improvements' (British Columbia 1875: 25) such as a squared log structure of certain dimensions, and, along with the early priests, encouraged people to abandon their winter *c7ístken*, or pithouses. The colonial and post-colonial governments have, to a large extent, dictated where Indian people will 'stay,' but have not been able to entirely alter, or indeed, to even recognize, where it is that the people *live*.

Secwepemc homes, as realms of domesticity, are not entirely fixed to place. The sense of home is also strongly anchored to time: winters are spent in the village, summers (or weekends) in the meadow and in the fishing camps and back, in the present-day mixed economic life-way that includes aspects of the ancient seasonal round. Without a complete change in where a family's 'home' is culturally situated, one cabin may fall out of use and another be built in a more advantageous location; a person from Alkali Lake might temporarily set up a home place in the city of Vancouver for employment or education, revealing a flexibility in the set of home places' physical locations. I have earlier discussed place as providing the most salient axis of orientation for making sense of life and experience for the Secwepemc, in contrast with Euro-Canadian society's orientation in life-story narrative to the shared experience of events in time, including key events in national history (cf. Linde 1993). Different associations with time and place also hold with respect to Secwepemc and Euro-Canadian conceptions of home. For Euro-Canadians, it is *home* that is strongly anchored to place, creating identity with respect to settlement, to neighbourhoods, and to hometowns.

The political history of British Columbia is filled with justifications for the denial of the importance, and knowledge, of place for First Nations in British Columbia by the people who came afterward. An example comes from one Mr Nind, writing to the Colonial Secretary about the Secwepemc living near Kamloops in 1865:

> These Indians do nothing more with their land than cultivate a few small patches of potatoes here and there; they are a vagrant people who live by hunting and fishing and bartering skins; and the cultivation of their ground contributes no more to their livelihood than a few days of digging

wild roots; but they are jealous of their possessory rights, and are not likely to permit settlers to challenge them with impunity; nor, such is their spirit and unanimity, would many settlers think it worth while to encounter their undisguised opposition. This, then, has the effect of putting a stop to settlement in these parts.   (British Columbia 1875: 29)

This attitude continues its entrenchment in the recent decisions of the courts, including *Apsassin v. the Queen* (as discussed in Ridington 1990: 186–205); the *Calder* case (as discussed in Tennant 1990); and the McEachern decision in *Delgamuukw v. British Columbia* (as discussed by Cruikshank, Ridington, and others in B. Miller, ed., *B.C. Studies* 95 [1992]: 3–92, as well as in Culhane 1997).

Although anthropology is only beginning to come to terms with the association of landscape to narrative, most people in Canada and the United States, even 'rootless' folk of mixed European ancestry, remember and reminisce about home places in their childhood and settings that lent shape to key life events. Newcomers' claims that Indians 'weren't using the land' or 'weren't improving the land' have been augmented and superseded by the claims of the newcomers' grandchildren, such as 'Our family has been on this land for three generations,' accompanied by narratives of their own. Narratives of place based in personal experience provide points of access as well as conflict for a wider audience across cultures. They can provide a starting point for developing an understanding of members of other cultures, to see them in terms of their relationship to the land.

Displacement

The people of Alkali Lake have been displaced from much of their territory. They have been granted reserves, but their land base for hunting and gathering has been severely diminished. Eugene Hunn's finding that there is a correlation between 'toponymic density – the number of named places per square mile within the range of a linguistic community' (1994: 81) and the population density of a community, allowing the prediction of an estimate of place names remembered by an individual as numbering approximately 500, has some implications for the remembrance of place names for the Secwepemc. Given Hunn's attention to population density (measured insofar as was possible with respect to 'traditional use areas'), as the Secwepemc land base continues to decrease, it is possible that the Secwepemc may condense the

Jimmy George and Alfie Bowie at Gustafson Lake camp

area over which places are named, and describe the same absolute number of places within a smaller area. As their territory becomes more and more restricted to the main roads and the town of Williams Lake, the names that go with the places, and the associated stories, may come to focus more and more on new ways of making a living.

In the early years of Euro-Canadian contact, introduced diseases caused the number of Secwepemc people who once carried the memories of the land to shrink suddenly and dramatically. The movement of people over the land has since been severely restricted by confinement to residential school in their youth, by the increasing fencing and locking of gates on lands claimed by ranchers, and by the changing mode of transportation that limits much of the travel to roads and cart tracks. Secwepemc lived space, and so their narrative space, continues to be compressed.

Narratives of place that contain laments passed down through the generations include Jimmy George's account, below, delivered at the former boundary fencepost of IR No. 1. It concerns European ranchers who married Alkali Lake women in order to appropriate reserve land:

David Johnson here he was telling me about it
   he knows quite a bit.
So they lose that
I guess he took a woman from here
that he registered on his claim, eh?

                         AP: Mhm?

But the people here, old chief you know
   I guess he didn't know to do that
[*to register a counter claim*]

                         AP: Oh

The same thing happened with this ranch here
   to those Indians
all went badly, I guess
then again that Moore, old Harry
He get a woman from here too
and then they – and the old chief
   I guess that's the main reason
they lose that too
so there we were
I ( ) bad about it like
it's all a long time ago, eh?
Must be a hundred years or more ago I guess.

                   (Tape 5; 27 July 1989)

Jimmy and Angela George's narratives of place are deeds, based on personal experience and past history, to parts of their territory that they are now prevented from using. These acts of claiming are comparable to Wet'suwet'en Athabascans recountings of their histories and relationship with the land through songs called *kungax* 'As the Wet'suwet'en follow the trails to their territories, so they seek to capture the songs that go with their titles to their territories' (Gisday Wa and Delgam Uukw 1989: 30). Each *kungax* is a 'trail of song,' or spirit power song, that is traditionally brought out at feasts (Gisday Wa and Delgam Uukw 1989). Some were brought out in a Western context that parallels their feasts, at their land claims case (*Delgamuukw v. British Columbia*), in an effort to establish for the court their rights to the land through personal knowledge of its use and their longtime association with it (Ridington 1992).

In chapter 5 I discussed how narratives of personal experience and historical narratives can be seen as forming an oral map that corresponds to the landscape. Many cultures that map through such stories can transfer some of this information to drawn maps. Paper maps of registered traplines have come to be very significant, with respect to Euro-Canadians and their competing land interests, as evidence of held territories for many Indian people in British Columbia today (Brody 1981; Gisday Wa and Delgam Uukw 1989: 60). Some Dunne-za dream maps first, and then draw them out. From what I am able to discern from the literature (Brody 1981; Ridington 1988), these maps show at once the 'trails to heaven' and the tracks and trails of animals with which they are intertwined, the same tracks men follow on the hunt. Ridington also discusses the Dunne-za 'trail to heaven' as a 'trail of song' (1988: 279). Of the Adnyamathnha of Australia, Dorothy Tunbridge writes: 'For the people, the stories are the land. In the language Yura Ngawarla, "telling (someone) a story," *yarta wandatha*, means simply "telling (someone) the land (*yarta*)," or "linking (that someone) to the land"' (1988: xxxv). As diverse as these stories and the cultures they come from are, spatially-anchored stories reveal a tendency for humans to identify in the land ways to remember, to teach and to learn through their own experiences and those of their friends and ancestors, and to respect the land they live on for what it has to teach.

Maps and Memories

Place-related canonical stories may carry a moral force, as Keith Basso has demonstrated with respect to the Cibecue Apache (1990a). However, the dwindling number of canonical stories told by the people at Alkali Lake, and the apparent decrease in the number of such stories that are specifically anchored to place, should not be considered as indicative of a loss of any moral compass on the part of individuals. The association of story fragments with current Secwepemc social practices suggests that if knowledge, which is spatially anchored to places now outside of the newly limited Secwepemc territory, is still of use, that knowledge will continue to be effectively transmitted, even in disassociation from the known places of reference.

Because of the rhetorics of identity and difference associated with an ineluctable attachment to land, language, and story, rhetorics created by and about First Nations, the separation of members of Native cultures from these important elements might be seen by some as evidence of a lack of Native identity. It is not the case, however, that Secwepemc identity resides solely in these connections. These are features that Chief Abbey and others have identified as different in some fundamental way from those of the dominant culture of Canada. They are salient points of difference that evidently require explaining across cultures, and that seem to be at odds with competing ideologies, such that there is a need to press land-claims cases, to demand that children be educated in their home communities, and to insist that customary lands not be removed. It is because this is the intersection at which systems of discourse both meet and conflict that clarifications must be made, and the differences elaborated. When separations from land, language, and story are enforced, individuals still use whatever tools are available to them to make sense of their lives. This should be obvious in the simple observation that members of groups that were exposed to a policy of forced assimilation have somehow managed to persist as distinct groups. There is good evidence, then, that people will survive, that their cultures will endure, despite deprivations of land, language, and story through the dissociative forces of state, church, and school, if the human link between generations that allows for the cultural transmission of knowledge is somehow maintained. I will close this chapter with some observations on how the resources available to speakers at this moment are used as fully as possible.

Angela and Jimmy George have recounted in story two places on the landscape where people were turned to stone; both sites are located in areas where I have not travelled in their company. These places are also mentioned in *Tlee'su and His Brothers* (Teit 1909: 644-51). One site is on the Fraser River south of the Churn Creek suspension bridge, and the other is at Chasm, near Canim Lake Reserve. Jimmy's narrative, quoted below, which was delivered after we almost ran over a chipmunk on Dog Creek Road, is at once a fragment of that story, disassociated from place, and a lament for what has been lost to him:

This was supposed to be two guys or something
Standing across and there's supposed to be a
good looking girl there dancing across on the hill
this guy's standing watching
I don't know it's some kind of a story, eh?
I wish I'd know you know
My grandfather used to tell me about it
Now I missed all that
There's lots of stories

(Tape 5; 27 July 1989)

Just as oral maps of the landscape are made up of narratives of history and personal experience, maps may extend into the time Jimmy speaks of here as well. *Tlee'sa and His Brothers* and other stories indicate that at least some of the stories once told, and possibly some still told, were anchored to the landscape. *Tlee'sa and His Brothers* charts supernatural beings' routes of travel through the territories of the Kamloops, Bonaparte, North Thompson, and Fraser River Division Secwepemc in a systematic and densely organized narrative frame. Eugene Hunn has noted the importance of a similarly arranged story for the Sahaptin culture (1994: 82; 1990: 68-71) found in Jim Yoke's account of Coyote naming the places on the land, as recorded in 1927 by Melville Jacobs (1934, 1937). Each of these stories, with their systematic recountings of significant places in a culture's territory, and their links to another time, establish charters of moral force in their claims to knowledge and use of the land for the cultures in which they originate.

Parts of both of these longer narratives can also be unpacked into a series of separately told, detailed stories about mythological beings with respect to particular places and creatures. This is also the way in which Coyote stories are told across the Plateau area (cf. Boas 1917; Mourning Dove 1933). Taken together, some Coyote stories constitute a linked chain of events that correspond to happenings in particular places in Coyote's travels, as he made his way up a river or across the hills, where the people who tell the stories now roam. The stories form a chain, but are seldom told in sequence. Instead, on given occasions, and for particular audiences, a part is pulled out for telling, and the guide to the whole of the stories remains on the land. In a similar manner, 'telling my life' for the Secwepemc may consist of highly compressed, densely organized, and systematic tellings, and is also made up of separately told stories related to places on the land, told over a long period of time (cf. Linde 1993: 4). In the Secwepemc case, I find that while many stories provide the oral map to resources on the land, *the land itself* becomes the map of human experience by which 'telling one's life' is remembered.

The narratives written down here provide a small record from the storied landscape, but the stories themselves are 'called into being during and for interpersonal situations' (Nabokov 1987: 145). The information they provide can come from personal experience or through the chain of oral history and mythology, but 'it is rooted in place not dates' (ibid.). Even a simple trip to town from Alkali Lake with an Elder is productive of such narratives, if one has time and knows how to bear

View of the Fraser River from Dog Creek Road

witness. There was once more time to tell these stories, in the years when people travelled at a slower pace, on horseback or foot. I am not good with horses, but for my first year at Alkali, I had an old car with a bad carburetor. The sorry old thing could barely do thirty miles an hour downhill. Occasionally, when I would drive an Elder to town to do some shopping, a young person would catch a ride. One girl smilingly told me that, in my car, 'you get a chance to enjoy the scenery.' And the talk. In a slower vehicle, there is time to notice the places, and to tell the stories. For this kind of knowledge to endure, people need to continue to travel, to listen, and to tell stories on the land.

Appendix

Selected Transcriptions

Transcript of Tape Recorded on 24 August 1988

Driving with Angela George to record place names south of Alkali Lake IR No. 1 on Dog Creek Road.

Angela: There were those that must have live in the reserve
        up here
                                                               AP: Uh huh

Angela: They say those that's was up there
        they live
        they didn't get this uh-small pox
        they get
        they all live
        what's livin up here
        up on the hill
        They say when people wants to go up there
          and tell them about the
        people that was dyin' here
        They bow and arrow em
        They don't let'em go up there
        and they all live what was up the mount –
        up that hill

AP: So they were on top of the hill here?

Angela: Yeah
                                                                AP: Oh!

Angela: It's a big place up there
        I go up there lotta times

It's really spooky because I was there all alone
S'where the reserve people stayed n'
Those that was down here they all die
   but those that's up there they didn't die
Just like in Lac la Hache that island

AP: Mhm?

Angela: The people the Indian people all live
   what was stayin in the island
They ca –

AP: Mhm?

Angela: They never let anybody go there that bad sickness was
   around
Smallpox
Long ago.

AP: So, what was the name of the top of the hill there?

Angela: I think it's *tsecyelk̓w* they call 'em, *tsecyelk̓w*
You know that *ḉyil*¹ there
Kinda hole it's *tsecyelk̓w*?
AP: What does, what does that word mean?
Angela: You know it's a kind of the
you know like if it's this one you know
AP: Oh sort of a curved –
Angela: Yeah curved
AP: Okay
Angela: Yeah that's what they named that
AP: Oh, okay so there were people living on that hill
Angela: Yeah
AP: [So straight out from the main road at reserve at what we're
   gonna call mile zero.]
Okay that's great
Lets head on a little
We should go this way er?
Angela: Yeah
AP: Okay
[So we're turning right onto the main road, or left, rather, past
   the fence.]
Were there always sweats right along here?
Angela: Ah this is the sweats

Where they used to sweats year round
  all winter and all summer to keep people to keep clean
They make sweats even doesn't matter in the cold weather
Bath in the creek
To be strong
Keeps their health happy the sweats
I guess they been using the sweats for years and years
That's where they

Long ago
My granny wanted me to sweats
Four months I sweats
I was about thirteen fourteen
And he tell me to not use any
any soap or anything for me to get clean
  just to rub myself with bough you know
    to rub myself all over with a bough
And don't use soap to wash my hair
  just use a bough you know
To get clean
I sweats every day for four months
That's how I keep my
my m'granny tell me I keep my looks
The same till I'm old n'
You know to keep my looks
Look natural

                          AP: Uh huh

Natural Indian woman

                          AP: Yeah

That's how I look now
Never used a –
anything on my skin
Just my natural looks

AP: Did anybody live along this stream right along here through
        the ranch?
Angela: Oh they fish a lot here in the spring
        They fish
        They use this creek for fishing

Springtime

AP: Do you remember the name of this creek in Shuswap?

Angela: *tswec*[2]

tswec

All these creeks you know where they come from from way
up there's a fishin place
way up ahh ...
Enoƙit[3] that uh what do you call that

I forgot the name of that
the name of this
where it starts from
there's three lakes up above where this lake this creek
comes from before it come from
[

AP: is that up #4?

Angela: there's lakes

I guess we use it as a fishing place way up
long ago when the fish comes down in the creek and
then they gets into the lake again up *tsextseqeqenk* then he
comes down
then we fish from there again
when they *tsyuct* that
písell[4] they call *písell* they *tsyuct*
fish there
then they come here
and they fish comes up
and we fish n'
they say long ago they used to fish goin down there
from this other end of the lake goin down they
they set the net there to fish
they call them *stsaqừsten*
These ones their pickin place they call it
tsecréptsen[5]
that first place here
is *tsecréptsen* where they cook – where they pick
berries them elders

AP: [This is at mile 1.0.]

Angela: *tsecréptsen* and *sxest* they call it *sxest* where they pick

That's that rocky place they call *sxest*

AP: What are they picking there?

Angela: They pick saskatoons and chokecherries

The same there they pick saskatoons and cherries and
    stseqwem

They call em *stseqwem* in Shuswap them high bush
    saskatoons

AP: Mmm

Angela: They makes *lekemín*[6] out of it

you know Indian soup flour

lekemín you put berries in there

AP: Ah

Angela: same with them

with the fish ah eggs them make soup out of it

they they put berries in there n' boil it

and when they dry the fish eggs they boil it

you know they soak it then boil it

and mix it with with berries

then that's what they eat long ago.

Long ago we never did buy food to eat when we travelled

we cook our Indian food to travel with

like the the fish

dry fish that's what we have n'

and we used to have broth for tea long ago

our Indian tea

we never did live on coffee and what we buy

we never did buy tea or juice long ago

our kids was raised by dry fish and little pieces of fat you
    know

from fall time

meat we dry

we raised our kids from that to suck on this piece of fat

or piece a salmon a piece a dry dry meat

and we live on berries you know

kids get sick we boil our dry berries

and give em the juice to drink

we never did have

juice like today we live on juice but long ago we live on berry
    juice

AP: Mhm

Angela: I guess it was our top food when we kill porcupine long ago
         and cook the porcupine n' eat it

                                                        AP: Hmm

Angela: Porcupine and rabbit
AP: I'm gonna take a couple pictures of the two places you just
         mentioned for berry picking so we can have a picture of
         em so I'll do that real quick.
Angela: Spring water real cold water this water that's comin down its
         what the Rieterman's house have in their house

                                                        AP: Oh

Angela: and this one what's comin down over here it's steady comin
         that spring water ...
         esxest spring water
         s̓tekektkwe they call
         spring water's *s̓tekektkwe*[7]
Andie: Uh huh?
Angela: that comes real cold
             [
AP: Okay, so I wanna take a to take a
Angela: *s̓tekektkwe s̓tekektkwe*
AP: *s̓tekektkwe*
Angela: Yeah
AP: So the first berry place over here is called? what again? just
         over here?
Angela: eh *tsecreptsen* and *sxest*
         then way over by the river that that's
         tyememqo they call it
AP: Ok well I'll use up picture number 14, 15 14 and 15 on these
         two so I'll be quick ...

[*break*]

                                            AP: ... Uh huh?
Angela: Me and Betty we both cry when I finish singing it and it come
         through the tape.

                                            AP: Uh huh?

Angela: I guess she listens to it but eh Dorothy says she's gonna tape
         the kids and us and send it to Betty
AP: Yeah
Angela: Yeah that would be nice

AP: Well I can take a I can make a tape like that for you any time
                you want
                [
Angela: yeah um
          This is a place too
          They call it *nukláwt.*
          That's where we get
          wild rhubarb in the spring time

                                                      AP: Ooh...

Angela: Then we get some
          eh
          them greens from the spring?
          greens to eat?

                                                      AP: Mhm?

Angela: in the spring water
AP: [This is on the right at 1.3.]
Angela: Get to cook in the springtime from there I learn it from
                Elders
          but wild rhubarb

          Used to
          live on it long ago
          Make soup outa wild rhubarb
          boil it n'
          eat it all the time
          But now
          we don't
          go out and make it now.
          But we still
          think of the wild rhubarb
          It's good for Indian medicine too
          it's the roots
          boil it
          and put it wherever you're sore
          your KNEES
          Then
          fades away the sore from on your knees
          the wild rhubarb roots
          use it in sweats too.
          It's really

helped a lot

if you believe it.

AP: Mhm

Angela: You wouldn't be crippled for your life if you were –
if you use it some
that wild rhubarb roots.

AP: What what kind of greens from the springs do you get?
Angela: Oh it's them – it grows thick on top of the on top of the
water
you fish it out with stick
and clean it

AP: Oh

Angela: Then you can just use it with your sandwiches
or you cook it n' eat it
AP: Is it a plant or? is it is it the
Angela: grass yeah
AP: It's a grass
Angela: Yeah
It grows on top of the springwater
[*silence*]
AP: Were there any houses along the creek here?

Angela: And long ago they say they used to pick berries on that
behind this Echo Mountain
Pick berries and dry it up on top of the hill
Elders used to come down they say from the from up the
mountain come down on the creek and get water in their
baskets pack it up there
They stay up there'til their berries is dry they dry it on the –
they pull grass and they dry it on the grass
They say long ago that
we don't have pots to boil the berries we have a way of ber –
boilin it
and the elders they say that he peels this spruce with no no
limbs and he he makes a fire beside the creek to
steketqwen[8] heat up rocks there
and he put that spruce there on top of these two two sticks on
each end to hold it up

and he puts the berries in there and he puts the hot rocks in
     there he washes it in the creek
the rocks and he puts it in the berries til they start to boil
and when the juice comes out of the berries you don't put
     water in it
but the the own juice of the berries comes out of the
and he slacks down one end and the juice goes in a in a
     baskets
he takes all the juice out from the berries
then he puts it on the grass on the side hill to dry
He pats it you know pats it

AP: Mhm

Angela: Big enough to handle and he as they gets dry he puts the back
     the juice on there 'til it's all gone
and that's what they
long ago
they don't have containers to take along with them to take
     water they used to just put this berries in the container
          and and that's what they suck on that all day and not
               get dry and not get hungry
Seems delicious but I never did
make it
to eat yet like that

AP: So is this Echo Mountain up here or is it the one around
     there?

Angela: Yeah that's Echo Mountain
That's where they pick the saskatoons
     and they pick their choke cherries[9]
They smash it up like
smash up the you know the the stones with the berries n'
then they dries it like that
He says that
you know what the insides of the choke cherries say
the seeds of the choke cherries and the seeds inside
     they say it's the one that
he lives in the berries
and they smash it up
and dry it like that
they say it's the one that's
They calls it

nekept te s7illen[10] like like that

if you eatin' piece of fat

they say the inside of the cherry it's really good to leave it in
   on there and smash it up and dry it up and eat it

and it gets dry

AP: So they don't keep the skin of the cherry?

Angela: N – yeah they –

No they keep everything in choke cherries they smash it up
   and they

You know when they shape it up and they dries it on some

and that's what they eat in the winter

I guess people live like when I first remember in this world

we live on my my mum used to pick lots of berries of three or
   four kinds of berries and we used to live on berries live
      on dry meat live on dry salmon dry fish

We hardly see a store to buy something to eat we just live on
   our own food

Like I guess we

early in Fall we go to Williams Lake and

we buy lots of flour a wagonload full of flour

That's what we have all winter

What we buy

50 it used to be in 50 pound bags the flour long ago and come
   in the flour sacks

we make use of the sacks we we wash it

and uses a dish towel

or whatever we wanted to use it for

underclothes or whatever for the womens or the kids

this flour sacks

but nowadays they have paper

paper bags for the flour because it's all you could use it as a
   startin' up your fire

this bags of flour or everything is in paper bags nowadays but
   long ago they have it in in in this material container

everything was in material container this

this sugar and the

salt and everything was in material

and you could make use of the material container they have
   long ago

but now they have paper boxes and paper of everything

you can't even make use of it
just some plastic
when they start usin' this plastic we can keep the plastic con-
    tainer and use it
This what they call *xtsqeẃsten*[11] they say that's where they
    catch fish when they come down from the lake in spring
what they call *xtsqeẃsten* this

AP: Should we go down there?

Angela: That's *xtsqeẃsten*. That's the you set your net there for the fish
         and they comes down at night.

AP: Shall we go down and look at the spot?

Angela: Eh?

AP: Should we go down there?

Angela: I don't know if we should go down.

AP: Oh let's check it out. Oh! It says no tresspassing.
              [

Angela: Yeah we'll go down.

AP: 'kay
         [This is at 3.2 and we're going off the road. There's a turnoff
             down here.]

Angela: What kind of a bird was that?

AP: Looked like a grouse, didn't it?

Angela: *spyu7*.[12]

AP: Some *spyu7*.

Angela: The people who you eh they have two names of this you
             know where the fish goes down *yuct– yuctkikne*

AP: Let's back up to this trailer.

Angela: Look like J.

AP: Oops can't back up with this. Do you wanna hold the micro-
             phone?
         [*Laughter*]

AP: Looks like there it is Hi J.
         [*Sound of tractor engine cutting out*]
         How you doin'?

J: Fine.

AP: Angela and I are making a a tape of spots along here the old
             names of the fishing spots as we go.

J: Oh!

AP: Is it okay to come down this way and do that?

J: I guess it is you see, oh yeah. Just down the creek here?
AP: Yeah.
J: Yeah.
AP: I wasn't sure what the rule was if we stayed on the roads if it
              was okay or what.
J: Yeah.
AP: Okay. Thanks.
J: You bet.

AP: Glad it was J.
Angela: Yeah.
          [*laughter*]

AP: What was the other name again?
Angela: uh *yuctkiknes*. 'Where the fish goes down.'

Angela: Yeah they say that's where they used to
          catch fish long ago them
          people used to come down
          the reserve and *xtsqewsem*[13] here with the net all night.
                                                        AP: Oh
Angela: They don't do it anymore.
AP: How long ago did they stop doing that?
              [
Angela: It was quite a while ago.
          It's a it must have been about thirty years ago.
                                                        AP: Mmm
Angela: When Victor's Granny was alive that.
          Yeah that's where they used to come down and fish and come
              and catch fish through the night.

          Gee there used to be looots of berry bushes there but they
          they take it off and make a field out of it this new rancher.
AP: Oh the <u>new</u> one.
Angela: Yeah that eh
          But years ago people used to come down here with wagons
              and pick.
          Choke cherries or saskatoons or whatever they picked long
              ago when 'bout twenty years ago.

AP: Uh huh?
Angela: That's the sage growin' up there.
         Victor's granny musta
         planted some sage over there 'bove that sp –
         Over there and it's a big spot where they come out the sage
            what he used to plant.
         What they planted but the eh I go and pick some when I
            really
         needed some when I'm out of sage.
         [*camera click*]
AP: [So picture 16 is the field where people used to pick. It's now
            developed by the ranch.]
         So they <u>planted</u> sage?
Angela: Eh?
AP: They <u>planted</u> sage?
Angela: Yeah up there. I'll show – you know above the ranch used to
            be a store there?
                                                              AP: Mhm?

Angela: They planted sage there and they
         It's a big spot there where they come out but I go and pick
            some when I really need it.
AP: [Mm that's picture 17.]
         Huh.
         Tell you what I'll turn the car around here.
         [So we're at 3.6 miles we've doubled back on a road onto the
            ranch and ... I'm just gonna back up.]

AP: Everything's so green after that rain.
         Any special spots on the hills up there?
Angela: Oh.

AP: So can you show me which one
               Echo Moun –
               [
Angela: This place they call them Moore Ranch here.
                                                              AP: Mhm?
Angela: *necitsmeṅ.*
AP: Which place is that?
Angela: *necitsmeṅ* is them – where you cut hay.

AP: Oh!
Angela: In Shuswap.

AP: So which one
                      [
Angela: Is Echo Mountain's eh Indian name
                          is *tsexqwmemles*
          Is Echo Mountain
AP: Is it the one straight ahead of us?
Angela: Yeah.
          That's eh this hill in the middle of the *tsexqwmemles*
AP: Hmm. So is is Echo Mountain this whole place
                                              [
Angela: Yeah.
AP: or is it just that one peak er?
Angela: No. It's er there's a road comin behind there.
AP: Oh. Can we get to it from the main road?
Angela: I don't know if you can get through it with this car but with a
              pickup you can go through good.
AP: Mm maybe we can take a look.
          Still down this way the road?
Angela: Yeah. You come around over there
              [
AP: Oh so –
Angela: You come around the other side too.
AP: Okay! Let's go take a look.
          [So we're back on the main road at 4.0 after that gate onto
          Alkali Ranch's property. Just in case someone listening to
          this is totally lost – right after this at 4.1 is a sign that says
          'Caution open range cattle at large' and that's at, for us,
          4.1.]

AP: What are those little fences for do you know?
          You know how sometimes there's just a piece of fence stuck in
              the middle of the field?
          Do you see that little piece of fence that's over there?
Angela: Oh that's just a stack yard
AP: It's a what?

Angela: That's where they stack the hay.
AP: What's the little fence for?
Angela: I guess it's just to keep the keep the snow from piling in that
             into the stack.
AP: Oh! Okay!

Angela: Yeah that's what I think he keeps the fence there for.
             There the snow would not pile in there.

Angela: Used to be big house here. Moore Ranch, long ago.
AP: [Mile 4.5]
Angela: It burned down about 10 years ago or 5 years ago.
                                                        [
AP: Mmm
Angela: When that house big house burned down they had the
             upstairs.
             Yeah that's where they got their water from across over there.
                See you still could see that.
             You see the water comin' from over there?
AP: Yeah.
Angela: Get the spring water to come to that house.
AP: Was the house here or just up here?
Angela: Used to be people livin here to feed cattle in winter or people
             staying here to
             to cut the hay
             and we used to camp
             Lots of us used to camp here
             Make salmon at the same time as we work here
             for the ranch
             Quite a few – fifteen years ago now they don't
             nobody
             All the reserve used to work here
             long ago
             But now they have machineries to do it
             Long ago they used to have horses to do it
             the haying

Angela: The point of the fishin place there *tyenmémqs*[14]
             and going down the river it's

yegmímen they call em way down the river there's a spring
 water there
they call em
dirty water *xteqwtéqw xteqwtítqw*
they call em way down the river where there's a flat there
 for
a fishin' place
along *cpelutsin*
the Indian name of it *cpelutsin* that's *xteqwtitqw cpelutsin*
The *yegmímen* on top of the hill that's where you go down the
 river

AP: So *yegmímen* is sort of the entrance?

Angela: Eh yeah *yegmímen* is a sounds like it's something grinded that
    you know the ground that's the name of the ground that's
    you know where it's
    look like if it's if you go around and around and around on
    it n'

AP: Oh sorta scrubbed?

Angela: Yeah in it yeah. I was gonna
    And that place way over there where you go up the hill and
    go over it.
    The Indian name of it is *tsencwlelóls.*

AP: That's that hill we see way in the distance, the one the road
    goes up?

Angela: Yeah. That place over there *tsencwlelóls.*
    The name of that cut you know when that on the road goin'
    up that hill.

                      AP: Mm

Angela: And that's after that that you know that after this that turn in
     there *cklutetátu7s* they say it's name in Shuswap
      cklutetátu7s then before you leave Little Dog Creek.
    Little Dog Creek is *stegtsetsetsulqw* in Shuswap.

AP: Can you say that again?

Angela: *stegtsetsetsulqw*

AP: Okay. Lemme take –

Angela: And after, after Little Dog Creek
    that they call em *ctseqwmimentmes*
    [*camera click*]

AP: So number 18 is this is what do you call this place where you
          go over again?
Angela: It's a *tsencwlelóls* that.
AP: Okay.

          Have we come yet to that place yet where the spring comes
          up and disappears?
          That place where people used to live?
Angela: You mean that you mean way up past Alkali?
          That *stscelwáwtkwe*?
AP: Nnn ...
Angela: You know, Hideout Creek? There used to be grass on top of
          that the creek on top of that little creek.
          stscelwáwtkwe they called.
          There's lots of other names that Indian names past Alkali that
          other way.

AP: There's a place you told me about where ah you went
              camping once with the kids and they heard voices you said
                  the spring would come out for part of the day and part
                      of the day it would be
                      [
Angela: Yeah that's that's where
                      they call em *cklutetátu7s*.
AP: Oh.
Angela: You know there.
          I don't know what's there.
          There's lot of people I guess live there before
              before they die on smallpox.
          I guess there was lots of Indians even living across there.
                                                        AP: Mmm
Angela: Charlie Johnson was saying he was pushing some dirt
              with a bulldozer
          and he seen some some people underground I guess
              staying you know they pushing off their stuff
                  and so he quit and he move it away.
          c7esístken̓ they call it *c7esístken̓* is their underground homes
              long ago.
          They live underground you know
              and they don't get cold in there cold weather.

AP: I like that rock.
Angela: Yeah that that's where them Indians used to camp down
          there long ago when they when their workin at the ranch
          here.
          They camp there lots of them.
AP: [6.6] Oh.

AP: This whole valley's really pretty.
Angela: Yeah There that's Echo Mountain
          it's a call'em
          That old Elder where I learned a lot of things from her
          is Victor's granny
          she used to go up there
          and stay up there
          and dry berries long ago
AP: [so 19's Echo Mtn.]
Angela: Come down she say when the sun goes down and carry water
          from the creek and go up there.
          Stay up there all the
          til the berries is dry
          and they come down
          bring it down to foot of the hill
          and they bury it around in them baskets
          They dug it up in springtime
          they have it in baskets with covers and they
          buries it
          She say it's be just like fresh s–berries in the spring when
          they
          dug it up.
                                                    AP: Hmm
Angela: They make salmon they
          bury it here and there
          you know for their food in spring
          ah see that's what they used to do and over there they used
          to it
          That's what used to do you know long ago I used to make
          jam
          and dry fish or dry s– meat you know we'd keep it up the
          meadow
          We'd keep it there next time we come we eat from there

but now you can't even keep nothin.
People steals it from you.
You would think it's enough food now
[*laughter*]
Long ago it was different.
We used to go down the river long ago and get salmon with
    horses
As we go down we pull grass for our horses to eat.
We pull grass and we load it up in the wagon
As we go down we pick up our wood and we go down
get salmon with our own wood what we gather
What food we have left over we bury it down there for next
    time we get salmon we eat that.

Long ago when we used to go and dry,
dry meat for three months
we never waste anything we used to
dry the
everything you know the lungs, the liver, the throat of the
    deer
the heart, we used to dry.
The legs of the deer we skin it and
boil it and make butter out of that fat
and we keep the bones but we had left you know the
smashed up bones we make butter out of the deer legs
and keep it for our soup next year next spring
we don't waste nothing
When we dry meat we keep the bones in the meat we don't
    throw away the bones we keep it on the meat
when we dry it
we used to cut the hair off the
fur you know that
the hide we used to cut the fur and s–s–dry it
and whip it with a big stick
take off the fur you know
as it gets dry
clean it off like that 'n we
we make holes around the
hide 'n we

we make a rope you know 'n lace it
lace it together
put our meat in between
lace it together that meat
you know
step on it 'til it settles the meat
then they it'd be nice 'n flat
and when we come back from across the river
we'll have loads of this
eh dried meat on our
on the sleigh when we come back then
then we have pack horses too.

When we go across the river long ago we used to
take lots of vegetables and potatoes and bury it.
As we going where where we camp we buries them there
On a sack buried there then next time we camp again
    we buries some more food there.
As we come back we have food from the what we bury
    we stay there for 2 or 3 days
as we come home.
We stay across the river 'til 'til you see the the mountains
    way back starting to get
you know we have a ways of looking the country if its
    gonna get cold.

AP: Uh huh? How do you
                            |
Angela: Then we start home.
You know it used to get foggy, quite foggy
across the river
you know across the high mountains
sqwelqwélt, they call
and it get grey that fog.
Then we started home.
We come home then.
We just make it home in four days and it gets cold.

                                        AP: Mmm

Angela: That's what they call *cyeyamímen* that's goin down the river
         over there.

AP: [Okay we just passed the the high point on the road at the
          first turn arrow.]
Angela: That one's *tyenmémqs* that's
AP: What's *tyenmémqs?*
Angela: *Tyenmémqs cyeyamímen.*
                  [
AP: Which is? Okay. I'll get a picture of [*cye*]*yamímen.*
Angela: And down that hill there's a spring water they call it
              cteqwtitq̓w
          and a across the river there
          that Indian Reserve there they call em *cklutank.*
          'The green grass on the sidehill' [*laughter*] *cklutank.*
                                              [
AP: Oh is that what it means?
                                              That's neat!
Angela: That's where they were gonna to stay catchin salmon. That's
          where we maybe we should camp over there.
                            [
AP: Mmm. How do y–
Angela: Get salmon. Louie wants to camp out tonight to camp to get
          salmon
          3 or 4 days campin I don't know
          and I'm here
          I should be gettin ready
                                                          AP: Yeah
Angela: But I don't know what I'll do
          Dorothy was sayin maybe it's better you guys to stay here
              and then settin up a camp settin up everything to dry
                  fish.

AP: So can you say again the name of this place right here?
Angela: Yeah that's the fishin place there. *Cyéẁmen* they calls *cyéẁmen*
          is the fishin place.
AP: Okay. [I'll take a picture of that number 19.]
          [*car door slam*]
          And then that other place over there what did you call it
              again?
          [picture 21. 20, rather.]

[Mile 7.8]
Angela: We used to use this for as a pickin place
        this *cklutetátu7s* we called it

End of Side 1

Side 2

Angela: You wouldn't know there was a raspberries used to grow in
        that gulch long ago.
                                        AP: Mm
Angela: We start all of us we used to pick there. Raspberries n' I don't
        know who used to go to pick em ( ).
        Every time we come there somebody's ahead of us so we quit
        comin.
        Not too long down there we used to always pick raspberries
        in em.
        That oldchill, Eileen [?] used to come and pick some *exiitum* in
        there long ago.
        Here we make Indian medicine out of this little deal here.
AP: Out of which?
Angela: Them *segwsesegwt* they call we used to pick them there n
        have to start the one out pretty soon, make Indian medicine.
AP: [That's at point 82] What what do you use from the hills for
        the medicine? What plant is it er?
Angela: Eh *segwsesegwt*. That's you boil it and you you drink it and
        you bath yourself in it if you get sore legs or
        Used to use it as Indian medicines
        Lots of ways of gettin better
        the *segwsesegwt*.
        [*camera click*]
AP: I guess I dont see which one *segwsesegwt* is.
        Is it the red the little red ones er?
Angela: No its eh that one's got purple flowers early in the spring like
        bell? You know like
                                     AP: Oh yeah
Angela: you get red.
        You get purple flowers
        that look like them them little bells.

AP: Mhm? Okay I know the way [the road forks here]
Angela: Yeah I don't know which way.
         I guess those er underground Indians used to live up there
         long ago you still could see the holes where they would stay
            up there.
         Up there I guess where the water comes comes in there
         in the evening the water comes out but in the later in the day
            they had to go way up to get water.
         They call it *cklutetátu7s* says it's really nice place to camp
            there
         to dry fish there's no flies or nothin.
AP: [That's picture number 23. It's right across from a corral at
            mile 8.4].
         This is this is where your son got scared right? Where your
            grandson got scared?
Angela: Don't look like if there's any not even chokecherries here.
AP: You see any?
Angela: ( )
AP: Any chokecherries for us?
Angela: Around here all the ways up that gulch
AP: Wanna stop and grab some?
Angela: Used to be lots over there you know below that
         we used to go pick on this this bushes long ago.

Angela: Years ago
         'Bout ten, fifteen years ago
         we camped there n'
         Ethel n' my daughters
         used to hear it
         Betty and them used to hear it
         The
         the people laughin
         up in them holes
         underground houses
         She say they hear them laughing early in the afternoon
         But I don't hear it
         Because the girls used to go and collect them
         bow and arrowheads
         from that

the mounds where they must of make the bow and arrowheads
And its what the girls used to collect
And they hears them people laughing
after.

Underground it comes out over here but it dissappears
   again.

AP: So it comes from this – oh there's two springs here.
Angela: No he comes out over here but it disappears again
       must comes underground.

AP: To this spot?

Angela: Well I guess it's is the end of it.
AP: Okay let's just turn around at that cattleguard then.

       Oh yeah this grove of trees I remember you telling me about
         it
       coming through here.

Angela: That's where we used to let go our horses where there's lot's
       of
       Lots of feed.
AP: Uh huh?
Angela: Daytime we used to let go our horses there and come and eat
       lunch here.

AP: So did you want to do any more recording or did you want to
       head back?
       [adjusting air conditioning]
       How's that? It's on '4.' I'll shut my window.
       That'll make it cooler.

Angela: Well I don't know what we should do. Maybe we should turn
       back from here.
AP: Okay. I'll turn this thing off a sec.
       [Car is overheating with fan and a/c.]

Angela: It disappears again
            Used to be lots of chokecherries in that gulch.
            Where we used to pick long ago
               and we never come there for a long time

AP: ( ) there's a little side road here to turn off
            I like this rock face here, this is pretty.

Angela: I don't know where Louise wants to camp.
            She say 'we'll see where we'll camp.'
            A few weeks we camp there and we dry salmon.
            Jimmy and CY we go down every day
            Afternoon they fish all night and they come back and I dry
               it.
            I know there's a road goin up up the hill and goes down
               Alkali.
                                         AP: Uh huh?

Angela: It's the road.
AP: Oh that road here?
Angela: Yeah.
AP: Can we get back in on that road er how would my car do on
               it?
Angela: He goes down and that
            Slappin' Lake they calls *sṭeqwstem*
            Say it again?
            S-sṭeqwstem Slappin' Lake
            Somebody bath there and slap hisself.
                                              AP: Mm

Angela: In that lake up here.
            We used to go up there with a wagon lots of times.
            Sometimes we'd go down to the river we'd have no no
              salmon then we'd go up there and hunt up the meadow.
AP: Uh huh?
            [*camera click*]

Angela: Don't know how old I was when I first remember
            I musta been around two I guess
            My granny I was raised with my granny

used to
live in a –
live in a teepee like
was built up like a teepee this house and
dirt on top and you know er all the way down
it was built like a teepee with rails
and we used to have a hole on top
and that's where the smoke goes out
we used to have a campfire in the middle of the – this
    teepee
that's where – where I grew up and where I was raised
We used to have a – beds all around it
teepee like and
lots of – swamp hay I guess for a mattress
and that's what we used to sleep – sleep on
And there was no pots no forks no – no cups then
when I first remember
and my granny used to cook that –
    our food in the campfire in the ashes
used to cook that the vegetables and the potatoes into the
    campfire
or fish and rabbits or whatever we eat we just cooked on the
    sticks beside the fire
Then when he cook that and he finish cooking then –
my granny used to put boughs on the on the ground on the
    floor
that's where he puts what's cooked and
looked delicious food for us to eat
then he'd kneel down and pray
pray first before we eat
they pray when they get up
they pray when before they eat
they pray before they sleep
first thing in the morning they pray

that's when I first remember

and I didn't know
that people would have a father
Till I was 18 before I asked my mum

[*five lines deleted*]
I was raised by my mum and my granny that's all
my grandpa musta died long ago
So I was raised by my uncles

it was hard life for me n –
'Til I start livin with white people when I was eight
earned my own livin'
worked
It started when I was eight I never go to school
I worked every day
Till I was 22
I still didn't make no money
I was paid every day of working
My mum spend all my money on the food
My sisters and brothers clothing
That's where I learned
everything to support my – my family my kids
even now I still do the same
I'm 65 I'm
I'm still supporting myself
and still uh – learned a lot more about my life
I never drink till I was 25
Because I loved my kids I wanted to be with my kids
I want to raise them up first
before –

[*line deleted*]
So many years before I start drinking
Liquor was open for four years for the Indians before I
started drinking and four years
because everybody drinks
[*eight lines deleted*]
it was over and over
my life

then I guess I was stupid in my life I
[*line deleted*]
I got old before I think of myself
breathed ( ) my tracks

look over myself
In a big country
and I was sitting in Alkali Lake
treated like a dog
and I don't even know
I still sit there
[*line deleted*]
it's what happened for so many years before I
before I started paying back
[*two lines deleted*]

I didn't know I was strong
'Til I would be
fight back 'til I find out
[*line deleted*]
I didn't know I was strong
All my boys
My three boys tried to
tried to stop me
they couldn't stop me
[*eleven lines deleted*]

n' so

But now that I stayed sober for 10 years and I see lots of
    things
Lots a nice things that I seen lots of good friends
lots of nice people
all the places I travel
since I since I was a native dancer in Powwows
seeing lots of people
see lots of friends goin sundancing lots of other people
from different countries, friendly people
get
get my
give me lukewarm on my feelings on my heart
when I hear that drumming
my heart goes dancing first before my feet goes dancing
                                                    AP: Mmm
I really have good feelings from drumming

dancing
I sees lots of things in
dancing and sweats
ceremonial sweats
I sees lots of things
Lots of good things and I have warm feeling
get a – get well on sweats lots of times
Try it on my elders and they got
better.
Have a bad cold
Takin them for sweats
I was scared first to give them sweats to get better but
try it
believe it

AP: So do you want to go to Dorothy's er?
Angela: And they let me know themselves and I find out
         it was really nice.

End of Side 2

Selection from a Transcript of Tape Recorded on 10 July 1989

Travelling on Joe's Lake Road and beyond. A berry-picking trip with Angela George, Dallas and Candice George. Alfred Bowie, Marcella Bowie, and Jimmy George are in an accompanying vehicle.

Angela: ... If I was bossin' myself well I'd go left.
         The other road that way.
                                              AP: Mm
Angela: This one goes riiight around the mountain that road.
         Go to our cabin.
AP: The one on the other side?
Angela: This road. This road goes right around the mountain
             and comes to our cabin.
         This road.
AP: Oh.
CG: ( )

Angela: One time me and Jimmy was going around in there
        hunting we was on foot
          and the one bear had three little ones there
        playing on them trees them
        He had two black ones and one white one
        I would like to get the white one

                                            AP: Yeah

Angela: But Jimmy wouldn't want to kill him.
        Oh, he say, 'He must have like his kids just like you.'
        [*laughter*]
        I wanted the white one they were nice and small yet.
        He say, 'That bear loves his little ones just like you.'
AP: Mmm. [14.2 miles. Past the turn and we're past the turnoff for
        Joe's Lake, and we're just by the lake.]
Angela: I had all my skirts ready for Sundance

                                        AP: Mhm?

        [*pause, 30 seconds*]
        Oh, we used to come through in there when we hunt
        and there's a lake in there
          and other lake back in there
        That's where we seen this bear with his three little ones
        Pretend to be eating the grass around
        he keep on looking at his little ones playing on the tree

                                    AP: Mmm

Angela: He's just like a human person that bear
        he say when his little ones fight
        That one that starts to fight he'll take him and he'll spank
          him.

        Yeah that's where we went to in there when we go home
        On foot
AP: Where?
Angela: Eh go home in there. Short cut.
AP: Just right here?
Angela: Yeah.
AP: [14.6 miles]
Angela: Jimmy must've –
        Dennis must've been sneaking up to them ducks to get them
        And I went over there to see
        This was water in there

AP: Yeah

Angela: Dennis must have been sneaking up to them ducks and they
           run over there
         Eh he was mad at me
         Dennis. Scare his ducks
         [*pause, 30 seconds*]
         Another road going down that way

AP: [14.8 miles]. *Hmm*

CG: [*voice in background*]
Angela: I think I'll go and see my son to pray for my breath.
         Roger?

AP: *Mhmm?*

Angela: Pray for my healing.
         There's an empty bottle must have been somebody drinking
           around here

         Long time ago.
         [*pause*]
         It was something funny when
         say when the first time when we bring the liquor out here
         It used to be a dollar a big bottle of whiskey

AP: *Yeah?*

Angela: He say and
         womens sews glove, work glove,
           to sell for 25¢ to the white people
         An'e sews four pairs to buy a bottle
         [*laughter*]
         I wouldn't I would be dry if it was today I can't even sew
         I used to sew gloves before
         Eh there's not many *sxúsems* see?
AP: No not many
         Maybe we have to go down Chase or Quesnel
         Last year they say there was none in Quesnel
           musta been someplace here

Angela: There we come with a tractor one time around here
         We was hauling wood
         Another time we was hunting on foot hunting
         It was deep snow yet in the spring when we come through
           here

AP: Mmm

Angela: Took us four hours from the reserve to get to our cabin
           [*laughter*]
           We didn't walk fast we didn't run we just walked slow
           Look there's no *sxúsem* around here

AP: Ah I saw a little on that bush
Angela: Oh one time we was going along here and gee it was just
               red
           them *sxúsem* all over
           Might be some gooseberries
           stcwelcwucwel[1]
AP: *stcwelcwucwel*?
Angela: Look at the cows!
DG & CG: Mooo! Moooo!
AP: Is *stcwelcwucwel* uh, *stcwelcwucwel*, is that gooseberries?
Angela: Eh?
AP: Is *stcwelcwucwel* is that gooseberries?
Angela: *stcwelcwucwel*
AP: *stcwelcwucwel*?
Angela: Yeah that's like goose berries.
           tqitqe is strawberries.
           tqitqe in Shuswap.
           tqitqe
           Raspberries is
           what was it?
           s7aytsqwem,[2] *s7aytsqwem* them raspberries
AP: *s7aytsqwem. s7aytsqwem.*
Angela: I really loves them raspberries.

AP: Mmm

Angela: To pick
           You can't pick too much in a day it keeps settling and
               settling them raspberries I used to pick all day
           I used to try to pick it, clean you know
               so I wouldn't have to clean it too much

AP: Mhm?

Angela: I think it must have been good to pick you know when its
               ripe
           and put rag underneath and touch it and it'll come down

AP: Mmm

Angela: them raspberries.
          That was where Jimmy laughed at me when we were on
             foot
          Jimmy had a lonely shirt on I had a coat, thin coat on
          And it rain really hard
          And I was cold but Jimmy he wasn't cold
          he tell me, ' I'll lend you my shirt if you cold.'
          [*pause*]
          Hey there's a few here and there that's *sxúsems* not that
             many
AP: Yeah here's a few
Angela: Might of gone down from the rain
          *tsert*³
          [*pause*]
          [*ten lines deleted*]
Angela: And his dancing all the time it doesn't matter
             if he's up the camp
          he's dancing when the drumming is on.
                                                    AP: Mhmm
Angela: Oh it really bring me up to have a good – good ( )
          You really feel good insida him to
          hear that drumming
          [*pause*]
          What I uses them old old trees – you know them boughs
             really old *tsyoq̓wi* for smoking my hide
AP: Which ones?
Angela: get them really powdery old tree
          that's what I use for smoking
AP: Why is that good?
Angela: Heh?
AP: Why why that kind?
Angela: Because its got no pitch
                                                    AP: Oh!
Angela: It's old powdery
AP: [Open fields. 8.1]
Angela: It's like them cones when they use the cones gotta be them
             black old ones can't use them fresh ones because its
                pitchy.
          Now we see'n pretty – Pretty *spelṗélum,*⁴ *spéṗlum*

AP: What's that?
Angela: Its a little open they call it *spelpéṗlum*
AP: spilpeplum?
Angela: *spep-spélem* this little open

                                                  AP: Oh

   [*long pause*]

Angela: Yeah that's where you used to go get *sxúsem* here on them
        opens
                                            AP: Hmm

Angela: You know on them there's lots of it.
        But if there's none there'll be none
        One time we come up with the wagon it was red all over
        Holy smokes
        we get some'til we had enough
        we go home and we tell the people lots of people come up.

AP: So is Alkali just down there?
Angela: Eh?
AP: Are we on top of the mountain over Alkali?
Angela: Yeah. Alkali is over here down the river.
        Alkali reserve is down here.
AP: Straight ahead.

Angela: Yeah it took a long time before my breath get good again
           when I was talking to ( ) to do that.

        Yeah short cut to Dog Creek horseback
           we used to go through this way
                                            AP: Mmm
        [16.8]
Angela: *pesekwekwu7*[5]
        is the name of the place
        through here *pesekwekwu7*
        eh eh them rosebush berries
                                       AP: Uhhuh?

AP: This place is named after rosebush berries?
Angela: Yeah *pesekwekwu7*
AP: *pesekwekwu7*

Angela: I guess eh people names the roads where
   wherever they go you know, they name it, so they know
   which way they're going or their partners you know
    to tell them where they were going.
   The names
   I just about forget all the names in Alkali you know
    going up the meadow
   The same up – up going down Dog Creek
    and Canoe Creek they have names
   every little place.
   Them old boughs like that when its red
    that's what you use to start a fire.
   q̓welxw, q̓welxw

                 AP: Umhm?

Angela: And them old dry limbs that's what you use for starting
   fire.
AP: [We're going through a gate.]
Angela: Poison Lake they call.
AP: Poison Lake?
Angela: *k̓setkwe*[6]
AP: *k̓setkwe?*
Angela: You know them Indian they say long ago the Indians used to
   come up here to wash their blankets
AP: What –
Angela: I forgot about my water

                AP: Mmm

   Why do they call it Poison Lake?
Angela: *k̓setkwe* that's them
   them bleach. Indian bleach
AP: Oh that's why they washed their blankets here.
Angela: Yeah that's where they washed their blankets long ago
AP: [So we're at a fence Jimmy's just opened for us 17.3 miles]
Angela: If I was bossin the car – I'd come around
        [
AP: Do you want me to get you a big
           thing of water from the back?
Angela: Yeah
   That's where we come from that that lake in'it?
   We come all the way around.

AP: Oh yeah Joe's Lake is right there.
JG: [*in background*] along the fence that way? In'it? This
                   way?
               Way over where that ( ) ten used to be
Another voice: Yeah I think so
AP: Put your seatbelt on Cand –

End of Side 1

Notes

Chapter 1   Introduction

1 Greg Sarris provides a description of how his aunt and teacher, the renowned Pomo basket maker Mabel McKay, plays with frames in her discussion of Medicines with a non-Pomo university audience. Sarris and I both borrow the notion of framing, as it is used here, from the sociologist Erving Goffman. Sarris's insights led me to re-examine the ways in which taqʷšəblu negotiates with her audiences at storytelling events.

2 This is a favourite story of taqʷšəblu's. Some years later, she related it to Peggy Dunn, whose transcription of part of the story appears in Hilbert et al. 1995: xiii–xiv.

3 The Georges' storytelling ability also deserves mention, so I have followed Hymes's (1981: 142) example of prominently naming narrators. In some cases I have changed the references to people not present who are mentioned in the narratives to pseudonyms, for people do not necessarily give their consent to be talked about.

4 Alkali Lake Indian Band was the name in use during my initial fieldwork. The band is now called the Esketemc First Nation in official correspondence between the band and the Crown, from the Secwepemctsín place name for Alkali Lake, Esket. Because most people on reserve still refer to the place itself by its English name, I continue to use the term in this way when speaking of the lake, village, and surrounds. For references to the current the governance council and the official reserve lands, I use the terms Esketemc and Esket.

5 Provincial Archives of British Columbia (PABC), Newcombe Family Papers; Canadian Geological Survey (CGS), Sapir-Teit Correspondence.

6 Mourning Dove speaks of this in a letter written to her mentor, L.V.

McWhorter, in 1918: 'I am sure it will be hard for me to get any more legends without paying hard cash for them, A Whiteman has spoiled my feild [*sic*] of work, He is a Canadian and lives at Spences-Bridge B.C. I wish you would write to him and find out about his works, he claims he is a true friend to the Indians here and all of Canada but we are so suspicious of the Whiteman that to be frank with you, and I know that you feel Indian so I will speak freely. I have some doubts about him. [...] What I started to tell you was, that this Mr. James Tait [*sic*] has collected folklores among the Indians and has been paying five dollars apiece for good Indian legends and naturally that has spoiled the natives and of course they wish the same price from me whether the story is worth a nickel to me. A lot of times the same stories are told to me a little differently from one party and another will say, that is not true fact, but I know the straight of it and will tell me with a little addition which is no help but only waste of time listening and taking note' (as quoted in Brown 1990: 118–19).

7 CGS, Sapir-Teit Correspondence; Darnell 1990.

8 The population living on Esketemc reserves (formerly called the Alkali Lake reserves) in 2004 was approximately 650.

9 A grant from Academic Technologies for Learning (ATL) at the University of Alberta has allowed me to design a computer database archive of images on compact discs (CDs), creating a digital record that will not deteriorate as quickly as the original slides. Thanks to ATL's $10,000 investment in the creation of the archive, photo CDs of family pictures can be produced for the individuals and families from Alkali Lake, Lillooet, Canim Lake, Lac la Hache, and Fountain, who appear in some of the 800 photographs in this collection. I mention this here in part to alert any from the communities who would like to search the collection for photographs of loved ones or fondly remembered places.

10 Cf. Spielmann's use of the phrase (1998: 148).

11 Alessandro Duranti has provided an expanded critique of this aspect of speech act theory in his *Linguistic Anthropology* (1997), and it is prominently challenged in Hill and Irvine's discussion of 'Responsibility and Evidence in Oral Discourse' (1993), as well as by other contributors (Duranti 1993; Du Bois 1993). Nonetheless, speech act theory and related theories of pragmatics developed by philosophers of language have had a continued influence in philosophy by way of writers such as Jürgen Habermas (1996).

12 Another practitioner of this type of discourse analysis is Jane Hill, who examines language-in-use as an index of social power differentials across class and socially constructed categories of race (1998).

13 Much of the published information on discourse in recent years for groups
    in subsistence economies in the plateau and lower subarctic regions has
    pertained to Athapaskans, as is reflected in the cited literature throughout
    this work (but see Hanna and Henry 1995, York et al. 1993, Robinson 1989,
    Bouchard and Kennedy 1979, and Carlson 2001 for narratives from the Sal-
    ish area). Therefore, it is also important to note that aside from the discus-
    sion they provide concerning personal autonomy, I do not find the
    descriptions of Athapaskan discourse patterns, particularly the 'integrated
    knowledge' and 'entropy' that Scollon and Scollon describe, to be applica-
    ble to individuals' speech that I heard at Alkali Lake.
14 Tim Ingold's 'dwelling perspective' (2000) shares these ends, but Ingold's
    work takes a more generalist, 'top down' approach to theory, and is more
    concerned with the interpretation of discourse at the broadest level. I prefer
    Akan's 'bottom up' approach, which anchors discourse theory to concrete
    instances of speech.

Chapter 2   A Brief History of Responses to Colonialism

1 PABC, no. 16265, file 4227; Maud 1982: 63–4
2 PABC, Newcombe Family Papers; CGS, Sapir-Teit Correspondence, 21 Nov.
   1911
3 CGS, Sapir-Teit Correspondence, 16 May 1911; PABC, no. 56433
4 Teit's (1909) map shows Sekani territory as encroaching on Secwepemc territory to the north. Duff notes that this situation was temporary: 'The
   Sekani and Beaver both formerly lived in Alberta, but about 1874 the Beaver obtained muskets and forced the Sekani up the Peace River into the
   Interior of British Columbia' (1963: 60).
5 After a smallpox epidemic in the 1860s, the Tsilhqot'in would come further
   east to inhabit formerly Secwepemc territory just across the Fraser River
   from Alkali Lake (Teit 1909; Duff 1965).
6 I will hereafter modernize the old spelling of 'waggon,' as applied to the
   road. It is still occasionally referred to as a wagon road, despite being paved
   over most of the surface that is still in use.
7 Alkali Lake Band Files, n.d.
8 The published reminiscences of Hillary Place (1999) contain many references to Secwepemc families working on the ranches near Dog Creek and
   Alkali Lake, and elsewhere in the Cariboo-Chilcotin region.
9 British Columbia 1875: 4, in the section entitled 'Report of the Government
   of British Columbia on the Subject of Indian Reserves.'

10 A telegram from I.W. Powell in 1880 reads, in part, '... have purchased Bates Estate' (National Archives of Canada, RG 10, vol. 3681, file 12395-2). However, the date of 1881 appears in the official correspondence of W.E. Ditchburn, Indian Commissioner for BC, in which he writes: 'In fact, I must say such a procedure was not necessary in 1881 when the Bates estate was purchased by the department' (ibid.). Both sources are at odds with the 1879 date Whitehead (1981: 91) gives for the purchase.

11 RG 10, vol. 3681, file 12395-2

12 RG 10, vol. 3617, file 4606

13 Ibid.

14 Alkali Lake Band Files, n.d.

15 RG 10, vol. 3681, file 12395-3. The numbers of livestock are scrawled marginalia on the notes of the surveyor.

16 Ibid.

17 Ibid.

18 Ibid.

19 RG 10, vol. 3917, file 116524

20 Ibid.

21 Letter from P. O'Reilly, Indian Reserve Commissioner, 26 Sept. 1895

22 Alkali Lake Band Files, n.d.

23 Alkali Lake Band Files, n.d. See Furniss 1987 for an insightful discussion of the impact of the Durieu system on the form of the Sobriety Movement at Alkali Lake in the 1970s and 1980s.

24 Alkali Lake Band Files, n.d.

25 Ibid.

26 Brow refers here to frybread.

27 Alkali Lake Band Files, n.d.

28 In 1999, the BC Treaty Commission's annual report stated: 'Since opening its doors in May 1993, the Treaty Commission has allocated $122.5 million in negotiation support funding to First Nations, $97.7 million as loans.' The funding allocations in 1999, and those projected by the BC Treaty Commission for future years, were characterized as 'inadequate' and it was noted that '[e]ven those First Nations nearing completion of agreements in principle or otherwise making negotiation progress will find it difficult if not impossible to sustain the pace of negotiations.' The Treaty Commission's findings have been borne out at Alkali Lake, where no significant negotiations with the Crown have taken place since 1999. Internet source: BC Treaty Commission 1999 Annual Report, at http://www.bctreaty.net/annuals_2/99funding.html.

Chapter 4   Maps

1 Grice has been criticized in linguistic anthropology for his theoretical
notions concerning intentional meaning (see especially Duranti 1992 and
Du Bois 1992). However, I find that his Conversational Maxims (1975) do,
in fact, provide an opening for ethnopragmatic inquiry. For example, his
Maxim of Quantity (i.e., don't give too much or too little information)
allows me to ask: in a given speech genre for a given culture, what *is* too
much or too little information? How are violations noted by the speaker
and the addressees? And, finally, is quantity not in any way subject to
restriction in a given genre? In considering Grice's maxims as pointing to
potential parameters for four areas of interest in speech, and pointing up
those norms that might be discovered in part by being alert to possible
violations noted by speakers through metacommentary, I am also able to
attend more closely to ways in which I might align my speech with that of
the group. As I must ruefully note, this is an area in which I require any and
all assistance available.

2 All examples in the section entitled 'Looking for Patterns' are drawn from
one tape, recorded on a berry picking expedition near Joe's Lake Road on
10 July 1989. These examples capture the particular clarity of purpose of the
trip (to pick berries), and offer the reader some examples of narrative
outside the narrow focus area of Dog Creek Road discussed later in the
chapter.

3 It bears explaining that the 'road' we are laughing about is a precipitous
trail that can be negotiated by a vehicle in some years, when it is maintained, but that quickly washes out. On the one occasion I went down it as a
passenger in an old, full-sized pickup, rather than walking, I feared for my
life at the same time as I admired the spectacular vistas of the Fraser River,
and the adept manoeuvring of the vehicle by a driver who seemed able to
make his way down with only two wheels in contact with the earth at any
given moment. To me, the trip down under any circumstances seems more
of a controlled fall than a drive.

4 Harvey Feit (1973) discusses the indirect counting of game animals by
northern Cree hunters through the record of bones and antlers of the animals consumed being hung with care on trees (cf. Jones and Konner 1976
for a comparable example concerning San hunters in the Kalahari). One
Rock Cree hunter interviewed by Brightman characterized the hanging of
bones as a 'reminder' (1993: 118).

5 Some younger women, and women who have no male familial support,

dip-net today, but most women assert that dip-netting is the province of men.

6 This quiet remark into the tape recorder indicates that we are 1.3 miles south of the road entrance to the main reserve.

7 'Frank (Frankie) Wilson' is a pseudonym. The name has been changed throughout the transcription.

8 Angela is referring here to Secwepemc people who lived in pithouses.

9 This is an Anglicization of the Secwepemctsín word for pithouse, *c7ístken* (cf. Kuipers 1975: 15).

Chapter 5 Story

1 Housing shortages on the reserve sometimes belie that fragmentation: during my fieldwork in 1989, as many as fifteen memebers of an extended family were obliged to share sleeping areas, including living-room couches and floor space, at one particular frame house at Alkali Lake. Housing shortages are severe on many other reserves, as well. Ron George argues that of the 77 per cent of all status Indians living off-reserve, most do so 'as a direct result of lack of services, housing, and land' (quoted in Joseph 1991: 76).

2 The one narrative recorded by the late Secwepemc Elder Augusta Tappage of Soda Creek (in Speare 1973: 56) that I would categorize as a creation story is entitled for the purposes of Speare's *Days of Augusta* (1973) as 'The Woman Who Was Prisoner of the Bear (Children's Story).'

3 Dawson (1892) includes stories associated with particular lakes, where water people or monsters lived.

4 A detailed description of funerary practices current at Alkali Lake can be found in A. Palmer (1994: 119–25). The account given there contrasts dramatically with Brow's (1967) account of approximately 20 years earlier.

5 *Regina v. Alphonse*, transcript p. 40, 11 February 1987

6 Jay Miller notes that in Tsimshian mythology, Salmon People are said to fish for cottonwood leaves that are floating in the river. The leaves are said to be 'salmon' to the Salmon People (1984: xvii). This practice aligns with observations of salmon in the everyday world, as well, as spawning salmon do not eat on their journey, but will snap at leaves in the water and other disturbances.

7 I was told that it is different for white people, when I asked about blood donation and organ donation. Still, the people I was talking to blanched when I mentioned my own beliefs about such things. So as not to cause alarm or have anyone think I was not self-respecting in this way, I was then as careful as I could manage to follow their practices, especially with regard

to the long blonde hair that clearly did not belong to anyone else on the reserve.

8 For detailed footage of bear foraging behaviour, and a comparison to human gross motor movements, see the film *The Bear* (Annaud 1988).

9 The reference is to Angela's (then) seven-year-old grandson, Dallas.

10 According to Angela George, *swicw* is a kind of dried root that looks like the tooth of a grizzly bear (*Erythronium grandiflorium*). The English common name for the plant is Yellow Dog-Tooth Violet, or Yellow Avalanche Lily. Turner et al. (1980: 45–6) provides information on the harvesting of the lily corms by another Salish group, the Okanagan-Colville.

Chapter 6   Memories

1 Angela began her narrative with her first memories of life in a pithouse, which she describes as being shaped like a tipi with 'dirt on top.' She has since taken me out to Gustafson Lake, and we have looked at the old depressions in the ground, which mark the places where her family's pithouses and, in the case of smaller depressions, the pit ovens stood.

2 'Potatoes' could refer to either indigenous roots and corms or to introduced potatoes, which were grown by many Secwepemc families then, and continue to be grown by the older women at Alkali Lake. The growing of potatoes is seen as a virtuous activity by some of these Elders, who sometimes point out that certain younger women have no interest in growing them.

3 I am grateful to an anonymous reviewer for the *Journal of Linguistic Anthropology* for directing me to Briggs's (1986) volume. Briggs's cautions, I continue to find, do not apply only to interview techniques. For example, part of the interpretive frame that I brought to the field concerned a notion of professional self, and within that, some ideas of what it was to 'do (good) fieldwork.' I now have to ask myself what I think it is that an anthropologist *does*, and then ask if that is bound up with some idea of 'collecting data,' or with actually getting useful information. Some part of my notion of what 'doing fieldwork' meant in 1989 included asking questions. It has taken me a long time to realize that most fieldwork (at least, in Salish territory) is undertaken to discover what the 'right question' is. And then one needs to have the sense, rather than to ask, to consider how people have been providing me with the answer all along.

4 Salish tales of Bears associated with death, which include mentions of extremely violent acts by Grizzly Bear Woman, can be found in Hannah and Henry 1995, and Elmendorf 1993. For Clackamas versions of these stories, see Jacobs 1960.

5 I would agree with Crapanzano (1984) that 'the life history ... is the result of a complex self-constituting negotiation,' whose dynamic must be taken into consideration, but I am surprised by his statement that the life history 'is the product of an arbitrary and peculiar demand of another – the anthropologist.' In my case, it was the consultant who made the demand that was first misunderstood, and the persistence of the consultant that led to the eventual work of recording, transcription, and interpretation. I did make what were interpreted as arbitrary and peculiar demands in my initial misunderstandings of what 'telling her life' would consist of, but these were generally met by confusion, reticence, and/or laughter.

It is a mixed blessing that this dear Elder is hard of hearing; when we drove, she often misunderstood what I had asked over the car and road noise, or talked right over my questions, telling me whatever she wanted to. I have watched her guess at what others have said as well. Although sometimes questions that required immediate answers were misinterpreted, her responses to supposed questions were often much more interesting than the responses to my actual questions would have been. I suspect she may at times have guessed at what I had asked, and inferred that I had asked a culturally/situationally appropriate question.

Appendix

Transcript of 24 August 1988

1 To q̓ílye is 'to take a sweatbath.'
2 *Tswec* is the general term for 'creek' (Dixon and Kuipers 1974: 8).
3 *Enok̓it* is called Swan Lake in English, according to Betty Belanger.
4 *Písell* is the term for 'trout' (Kuipers 1975: 8).
5 This word might be related to *reptsens̓*, 'to put meat on a stick,' as in Kuipers (1975: 23).
6 *Lekemín* is a soup made from flour. *Lekelét* (bread) is a related term.
7 'Fresh water' is *sewllkwe*; *sɬekektkwe* is probably 'spring of water,' although it varies from Kuiper's entry of *sqwléltkwe* (1975: 6). The root, 'water,' is *(et)kwe* (Kuipers 1974).
8 *Étsqwem; étsqwens* – to bake (Kuipers 1975: 23)
9 Chokecherries are called *tkwló7se* in Shuswap.
10 *S7illen* is 'food.'
11 *Xtsqew̓sten* may be the generic term for 'dip-netting place' as well as the proper name for this place.
12 *Spyu7* – 'bird.'

13 To pit-lamp for fish is to *tsétsk̇weṁ* (Kuipers 1975: 27).
14 A generic term for a point of land is *tk̇meqs* (Kuipers 1975: 5).

Transcript of 10 July 1989

1 *Stcwelcwucweḷ* are gooseberries.
2 *S7aytsqwem* are raspberries.
3 *Tsert* is Shuswap for the falling of a tree (note from Betty Belanger).
4 *Spelṗéṗlum* is a little valley, small prairie or 'little open.' This is the reduplicated form of *spélem* (prairie) (cf. A. Kuipers 1975: 5). Angela George's varied pronunciation is transcribed as heard.
5 *Pesekwekwu7* is named for rose hips, which are called *sekwekwu7*, according to Betty Belanger.
6 *K̇setkwe* means that the water isn't any good to drink, hence, the English name 'Poison Lake' (note from Betty Belanger.) The high soda content of the lake bottom, which Angela George calls 'Indian bleach,' was once used for washing clothing and blankets.

References

Archival Materials

Alkali Lake Indian Band. No date. Band Files. Unpublished records.

Canadian Geological Survey. Correspondence of Edward Sapir and James A. Teit, regarding ethnology, linguistics, and politics, 1911–22.

National Archives of Canada. Record Group 10, Government of Canada, Indian Affairs. Black Series Headquarters Files, 1872–1950. Field Office Correspondence and Miscellaneous, circa 1833–1954.

Provincial Archives of British Columbia (PABC). Newcombe Family Papers, 1870–1955. Charles F. Newcombe: Correspondence Inward, series A, volume 5, folder 143. Contains 54 items, mostly letters of correspondence with James A. Teit, 1900–18.

– Province of British Columbia. With special division, volume, and file numbers listed.

Willard, Ike, and Gary Green. 1972. Description (in English) of life in an underground house and other customs. Told by Ike Willard. Taped on the Neskainlith Reserve, Chase, BC, in September 1972 by Gary Green of the BC Provincial Museum. Catalogued with BC Indian Language Project materials as SHU-T-001.

Court Cases

Delgamuukw v. British Columbia (1991), 79 Dominion Law Reports (4th), 185–640 (Supreme Court of British Columbia]).

Dick v. The Queen (1985), 23 Dominion Law Reports (4th), 33–63 (Supreme Court of Canada).

Haida Nation v. British Columbia (Minister of Forests) (2004), 245 Dominion Law
    Reports (4th), 33 (Supreme Court of Canada).
Supreme Court of British Columbia. 'Reasons for Judgment of His Honour
    Judge C.C. Barnett [*Regina v. Alphonse*],' 22 February 1988.

Government Publications

British Columbia. 1875. *Papers Connected with the Indian Land Question, 1850–75.*
    Victoria: Government Printer.
– 1952. Provincial Advisory Committee on Indian Affairs. *3rd Annual Report.*
    For the Year Ended December 31st 1952. Victoria: Queen's Printer.
– 1987. Ministry of Tourism, Recreation and Culture. *The Gold Rush Trail Guide.*
    Victoria: BC Provincial Government.
Canada. 1985. Indian and Northern Affairs Canada. *Chiefs and Councilors, Band
    Administration Offices, British Columbia Region.* April 1985.
United States. 1969. *The National Environmental Policy Act.*
Washington State. 1984. *The State Environmental Policy Act of 1971.* Chapter
    43.21C, Revised Code of Washington. SEPA Rules, Effective April 4, 1984;
    Chapter 197-11, Washington Administrative Code (as revised).

Articles, Books, and Presented Papers

Akan, Linda. 1992. '*Pimosatamowin Sikaw Kakeequaywin.* Walking and Talking:
    A Salteaux Elder's View of Native Education.' *Canadian Journal of Native Edu-
    cation* 19(2): 191–214.
American Anthropological Association. 1990. 'Revised Principles of Profes-
    sional Responsibility.' In letter of 15 March 1990, from Eugene L. Sterud,
    executive director, to members of the Association.
Amoss, Pamela. 1978. *Coast Salish Spirit Dancing: The Survival of an Ancestral
    Religion.* Seattle: University of Washington Press.
Appadurai, Arjun. 1988. Putting Hierarchy in Its Place. *Cultural Anthropology*
    3(1): 36–49.
Armstrong, Jeannette. 1998. 'How Narrative Is Body Present in Oral Tradition:
    Experiences of an Okanagan Storyteller and Writer.' Paper presented to the
    Perspectives on Native American Oral Literature Conference. Vancouver,
    University of British Columbia, 5–8 March.
Austin, J.L. 1962. *How to Do Things with Words.* Cambridge: Harvard University
    Press.
Bakhtin, Mikhail Mikhailovich. 1986. 'The Problem of the Text in Linguistics,
    Philology, and the Human Sciences: An Experiment in Philosophical Analy-

sis.' In C. Emerson and M. Holquist, eds, *Speech Genres and Other Late Essays*, 60–102. Trans. V.W. McGee. Austin: University of Texas Press.

Basso, Keith H. 1990a (1984). '"Stalking With Stories": Names, Places, and Moral Narratives among the Western Apache.' In *Western Apache Language and Culture: Essays in Linguistic Anthropology*, 99–137. Tucson: University of Arizona Press.

– 1990b (1988). '"Speaking with Names": Language and Landscape Among the Western Apache.' *In Western Apache Language and Culture*, 138–73.

– 1996. *Wisdom Sits in Places: Language and Landscape among the Western Apache*. Albuquerque: University of New Mexico Press.

Bataille, Gretchen M., and Kathleen M. Sands. 1984. *American Indian Women: Telling Their Lives*. Lincoln: University of Nebraska Press.

Bauman, Richard. 1977. *Verbal Art as Performance*. Prospect Heights, IL: Waveland Press.

Behar, Ruth. 1993. *Translated Woman: Crossing the Border with Esperanza's Story*. Boston: Beacon Press.

Bierwert, Crisca. 1999. 'Figures in the Landscape.' In *Brushed by Cedar, Living by the River: Coast Salish Figures of Power*, 36–71. Tucson: University of Arizona Press.

Blackman, Margaret B. 1982. *During My Time: Florence Edenshaw Davidson, A Haida Woman*. Seattle: University of Washington Press.

– 1989. *Sadie Brower Neakok: An Inupiaq Woman*. Seattle: University of Washington Press.

– 1991. 'The Individual and Beyond: Reflections on the Life History Process.' *Anthropology and Humanism Quarterly* 16(2): 56–62.

Boas, Franz. 1917. *Folk-Tales of Salishan and Sahaptin Tribes*. American Folklore Society Memoirs, vol. 11. Ed. Franz Boas. Lancaster, PA: G.E. Stechert & Co.

Bouchard, Randy, and Dorothy I.D. Kennedy, eds. 1979. *Shuswap Stories*. Vancouver: CommCept Publishing Ltd.

Boyd, Robert T. 1985. 'The Introduction of Infectious Diseases among the Indians of the Pacific Northwest, 1774–1874.' Doctoral dissertation in Anthropology, University of Washington.

Briggs, Charles. 1986. *Learning How to Ask: A Sociolinguistic Appraisal of the Role of the Interview in Social Science*. Cambridge: Cambridge University Press.

Briggs, Charles, and Richard Bauman. 1992. 'Genre, Intertextuality, and Social Power.' *Journal of Linguistic Anthropology* 2(2): 131–72.

Brightman, Robert A. 1993. *Grateful Prey*. Berkeley: University of California Press.

Brody, Hugh. 1981. *Maps and Dreams: Indians and the British Columbia Frontier*. London: Jill Norman and Hobhouse Ltd.

Brow, Catherine Judith. 1967. 'A Socio-Cultural History of the Alkali Lake
    Shuswap, 1882–1966.' Master's thesis in Anthropology, University of Wash-
    ington.
Brown, Alanna Kathleen. 1990. 'Mourning Dove's Recovery Years, 1917–1919.'
    In W.H. New, ed., *Native Writers and Canadian Writing*. Vancouver: UBC
    Press.
Carlson, Keith Thor. 2001. *A Stòl:ō-Coast Salish Historical Atlas*. Vancouver: Dou-
    glas and McIntyre.
Clifford, James, and George E. Marcus, eds. 1986. *Writing Culture: The Poetics
    and Politics of Ethnography*. A School of American Research Advanced Semi-
    nar. Berkeley: University of California Press.
Cole, Douglas, and Bradley Lockner, eds. 1989. *The Journals of George M. Daw-
    son: British Columbia, 1875–1878*. Vols. I and II. Vancouver: University of Brit-
    ish Columbia Press.
Crapanzano, Vincent. 1984. 'Life-Histories.' *American Anthropologist* 86: 953–59.
Cruikshank, Julie. 1988. 'Myth and Tradition as Narrative Framework: Oral
    Histories from Northern Canada.' *International Journal of Oral History* 9(3):
    198–214.
– 1990a. 'Getting the Words Right: Perspectives on Naming and Places in
    Athapaskan Oral History.' *Arctic Anthropology* 27(1): 52–65.
– 1990b. *Life Lived Like a Story: Life Stories of Three Yukon Native Elders*. Lincoln:
    University of Nebraska Press.
– 1992. 'Invention of Anthropology in British Columbia's Supreme Court: Oral
    Tradition as Evidence in *Delgamuukw vs. B.C.* Common Sense and Plain Lan-
    guage.' *BC Studies Special Issue* 95(2): 25–42.
– 1998. *The Social Life of Stories: Narrative and Knowledge in the Yukon Territory*.
    Lincoln: University of Nebraska Press.
Culhane, Dara. 1997. *The Pleasure of the Crown: Anthropology, Law and First
    Nations*. Burnaby, BC: Talonbooks.
Darnell, Regna. 1990. *Edward Sapir: Linguist, Anthropologist, Humanist*. Berke-
    ley: University of California Press.
– 1992. 'The Inadvertent Muffling of Native Voices in the Southwestern
    Ontario Media.' In W. Cowan, ed., *Papers of the Twenty-third Algonquian
    Conference*, 91–106. Ottawa: Carleton University.
– 1993. 'Functions of English in Southwestern Ontario Native Discourse: The
    Basis of Traditional Language Survival.' In W. Cowan, ed., *Papers of the
    Twenty-fourth Algonquian Conference*, 81–96. Ottawa: Carleton University.
Dawson, George. 1892. 'Notes on the Shuswap People of British Columbia.' In
    Proceedings and Transactions of the Royal Society of Canada, vol. 9: 3–44.
Didion, Joan. 1979. *The White Album*. New York: Simon and Schuster.

Dixon, May, and Aert H. Kuipers. 1974. *A Shuswap Course*. Leiden: University of Leiden.

Dresch, Paul. 1988. 'Segmentation: Its Roots in Arabia and Its Flowering Elsewhere.' *Cultural Anthropology* 3(1): 50–67.

Du Bois, John W. 1993. Meaning without Intention: Lessons from Divination. In J.H. Hill and J.T. Irvine, eds, *Responsibility and Evidence in Oral Discourse*, 48–71. Cambridge: Cambridge University Press.

Duff, Wilson. 1965. *The Impact of the White Man*. The Indian History of British Columbia: Volume 1. Anthropology in British Columbia, Memoir #5. Victoria, BC: Provincial Museum of British Columbia.

Duranti, Alessandro. 1993. 'Intentions, Self, and Responsibility: An Essay in Samoan Ethnopragmatics.' In J.H. Hill and J.T. Irvine, eds, *Responsibility and Evidence in Oral Discourse*, 24–47. Cambridge: Cambridge University Press.

– 1994. *From Grammar to Politics: Linguistic Anthropology in a Western Samoan Village*. Berkeley: University of California Press.

– 1997. *Linguistic Anthropology*. New York: Cambridge University Press.

Elmendorf, William. 1993. *Twana Narratives: Native Historical Accounts of a Coast Salish Culture*. Seattle: University of Washington Press.

Feit, Harvey. 1973. 'The Ethno-ecology of the Waswanipi Cree: Or, How Hunters Can Manage Their Resources.' In B.A. Cox, ed., *Cultural Ecology: Readings on the Canadian Indians and Eskimos*, 115–25. Toronto: McClelland and Stewart.

Feld, Steven. 1995. 'Wept Thoughts: The Voicing of Kaluli Memories.' In R. Finnegan and M. Orbell, eds, *South Pacific Oral Traditions*, 85–108. Bloomington: University of Indiana Press.

Feld, Steven, and Keith H. Basso, eds. 1996. *Senses of Place*. Santa Fe: School of American Research Press.

Foucault, Michel. 1972. *The Archaeology of Knowledge*. Trans. A.M. Sheridan Smith. London: Tavistock.

Frake, Charles O. 1964. 'How to Ask for a Drink in Subanun.' *American Anthropologist* 66(6, pt 2): 127–32.

Furniss, Elizabeth Mary. 1987. 'A Sobriety Movement among the Shuswap Indians of Alkali Lake.' Master's thesis in Anthropology, University of British Columbia.

– 1992. *Victims of Benevolence: Discipline and Death at Williams Lake Indian Residential School, 1891–1920*. Williams Lake, BC: Cariboo Tribal Council.

– 1999. *The Burden of History: Colonialism and the Frontier Myth in a Rural Canadian Community*. Vancouver: UBC Press.

Gisday Wa and Delgam Uukw. 1989. *The Spirit in the Land: The Opening State-

ment of the Gitksan and Wet'suwet'en Hereditary Chiefs in the Supreme Court of British Columbia. Gabriola, BC: Reflections.

Goody, Jack. 1977. *The Domestication of the Savage Mind.* Cambridge: Cambridge University Press.

Grice, H.P. 1975. 'Logic and Conversation.' In P. Cole and J.L. Morgan, eds, *Syntax and Semantics Vol. 3, Speech Acts,* 41–58. New York: Academic Press.

Grimes, Joseph. 1975. *The Thread of Discourse.* The Hague: Mouton.

Gumperz, John J. 1982. *Discourse Strategies.* Cambridge: Cambridge University Press.

Habermas, Jürgen. 1996. *Between Facts and Norms: Contributions to a Discourse Theory of Law and Democracy.* Trans. William Rehg. Studies in Contemporary German Social Thought. Cambridge, MA: MIT Press.

Haig-Brown, Celia. 1988. *Resistance and Renewal: Surviving the Indian Residential School.* Vancouver: Tillacum Library.

Hanna, Darwin and Mamie Henry, eds. 1996. *Our Tellings: Interior Salish Stories of the Nlha7kapmx People.* Vancouver: UBC Press.

Hess, Thom. 1976. *Dictionary of Puget Salish.* Seattle: University of Washington Press.

Hilbert, Vi (ṭaqʷšəblu). 1980. *Huboo: Lushootseed Literature in English.* Seattle: Private printing.

Hilbert, Vi (ṭaqʷšəblu) et al. 1990. *Lushootseed Texts: sʔyəyəhub ʔi kʷiʔ sʔyəcəb dxʷʔal tiʔiʔəʔ ʔaciłtalbixʷ.* Transcribed by Vi Hilbert, Thom Hess, and Dawn Bates. Trans. Vi Hilbert, Thom Hess, and Crisca Bierwert. Stories told by Martha Lamont, Hagan Sam, and Susie Sampson Peter. Seattle: Lushootseed Research.

– 1995. *x̌ačusədəʔ ʔə gʷəqʷulčəʔ: Aunt Susie Sampson Peter; The Wisdom of a Skagit Elder.* Trans. Vi (ṭaqʷšəblu) Hilbert and Jay Miller. Recorded by Leon Metcalfe. Seattle: Lushootseed Press.

Hill, Jane H. 1998. Language, Race, and White Public Space. *American Anthropologist* 100(3): 680–9.

Hill, Jane H., and Judith T. Irvine, eds. 1993. *Responsibility and Evidence in Oral Discourse.* Studies in the Social and Cultural Foundations of Language, no. 15. Cambridge: Cambridge University Press.

Hirsch, Eric, and Michael O'Hanlon. 1995. *The Anthropology of Landscape: Perspectives on Place and Space.* Oxford: Clarendon Press.

Hunn, Eugene S. 1994. 'Place-Names, Population Density, and the Magic Number 500.' *Current Anthropology* 35(1): 81–5.

Hunn, Eugene S., and David H. French. 1981. 'Lomatium: A Key Resource for Columbia Plateau Native Subsistence.' *Northwest Science* 55 (2): 87–94.

Hunn, Eugene S., with James Selam and Family. 1990. *Nch'i-Wàna, "The Big*

River": Mid-Columbia Indians and Their Land. Seattle: University of Washington Press.

Hymes, Dell. 1972. 'Models of Interaction of Languages and Social Life.' In J.J. Gumperz and D. Hymes, eds, Directions in Sociolinguistics: The Ethnography of Communication. New York: Holt, Rinehart, and Winston.

– 1981. 'In vain I tried to tell you': Essays in Native American Ethnopoetics. Philadelphia: University of Pennsylvania Press.

Ingold, Tim. 1986. 'Territoriality and Tenure: The Appropriation of Space in Hunting and Gathering Societies.' In The Appropriation of Nature: Essays on Human Ecology and Social Relations, 130–64. Manchester: Manchester University Press.

– 2000. The Perception of the Environment: Essays on Livelihood, Dwelling and Skill. New York: Routledge.

Interagency Advisory Panel on Research Ethics, Canada. 1998. 'Tri-Council Policy Statement: Ethical Conduct for Research Involving Humans. 1998.' With 2002, 2003 updates.

Jacobs, Melville. 1934. 'Upper Cowlitz Geographic Notes; Upper Cowlitz Myth and Geographic Text.' In Northwest Sahaptin Texts. Part I, 198–204; 205–11. New York: Columbia University Press.

– 1937. 'Upper Cowlitz Geographic Notes; Upper Cowlitz Myth and Geographic Text.' In Northwest Sahaptin Texts. Part II, 228–37, 238–46. New York: Columbia University Press.

– 1960. The People Are Coming Soon. Seattle: University of Washington Press.

Joseph, Shirley. 1991. 'Assimilation Tools: Then and Now.' In In Celebration of Our Survival: The First Nations of British Columbia, 65–79. Vancouver: UBC Press.

Jones, Nicholas Blurton, and Melvin J. Konner. 1976. '!Kung Knowledge of Animal Behavior (or: The Proper Study of Mankind Is Animals).' In R.B. Lee and I. DeVore, eds, Kalahari Hunter-Gatherers: Studies of the !Kung San and Their Neighbors, 325–48. Cambridge, MA: Harvard University Press.

Kahn, Miriam. 1990. 'Stone-Faced Ancestors: The Spatial Anchoring of Myth in Wamira, Papua New Guinea.' Ethnology 29(1): 51–66.

Kari, Jim, and James A. Fall. 1987. Shem Pete's Alaska: The Territory of the Upper Cook Inlet Dena'ina. Fairbanks: Alaska Native Language Center.

Keane, Webb. 1997. Signs of Recognition: Powers and Hazards of Representation in an Indonesian Society. Berkeley: University of California Press.

Kuipers, Aert H. 1974. The Shuswap Language: Grammar, Texts, Dictionary. The Hague: Mouton.

– 1975. A Classified English-Shuswap Word-List. Lisse, Belgium: Peter De Ridder Press.

Labov, William. 1972. *Language in the Inner City: Studies in the Black English Vernacular.* Philadelphia: University of Pennsylvania Press.

Lavie, Smadar, and Ted Swedenburg, eds. 1996. *Displacement, Diaspora, and Geographies of Identity.* Durham, NC: Duke University Press.

Lawrence, Denise L., and Setha M. Low. 1990. 'The Built Environment and Spatial Form.' *Annual Review of Anthropology* 19: 453–505.

Lightning, Walter. 1992. Compassionate Mind: Implications of a Text Written by Elder Louis Sunchild. *Canadian Journal of Native Education*, 19(2): 215–42.

Linde, Charlotte. 1993. *Life Stories: The Creation of Coherence.* New York: Oxford University Press.

Lord, Albert. 1960. *The Singer of Tales.* Cambridge, MA: Harvard University Press.

Low, Setha M., and Denise Lawrence-Zúñinga, eds. 2003. *The Anthropoligy of Space and Place: Locating Culture.* London: Blackwell Publishing.

Marcus, George E., and Michael M.J. Fischer. 1986. *Anthropology as Cultural Critique: An Experimental Moment in the Human Sciences.* Chicago: University of Chicago Press.

Maud, Ralph. 1982. *Myth and Legend: A Short History of Myth-Collecting and a Survey of Published Texts.* Vancouver: Talonbooks.

Mauss, Marcel. 1967 (1925). *The Gift: Forms and Functions of Exchange in Archaic Societies.* Trans. I. Cunnison. New York: W.W. Norton.

Miller, Bruce. 1992. 'Common Sense and Plain Language.' *BC Studies Special Issue* 95(2): 55–65.

Miller, Jay. 1984. Introduction to J. Miller and C.M. Eastman, eds, *The Tsimshian and Their Neighbors of the North Pacific Coast*, xi–xxii. Seattle: University of Washington Press.

– 1990. Introduction to J. Miller, ed., *Mourning Dove: A Salishan Autobiography*, xi–xxxix. Lincoln: University of Nebraska Press.

Monet, Don, and Skanu'u (Ardythe Wilson). 1992. *Colonialism on Trial: Indigenous Rights and the Gitksan and Wet'suwet'en Sovereignty Case.* New Society Publishers: Philadelphia.

Morice, A.G. 1905. *The History of the Northern Interior of British Columbia.* Toronto: William Briggs.

Mourning Dove (Christine Quintasket). 1933. *Coyote Stories.* Ed. Heister Dean Guie. Caldwell, ID: Caxton Printers.

Nabokov, Peter. 1987. 'Present Memories, Past History.' In C. Martin, ed., *The American Indian and the Problem of History*, 144–55. New York: Oxford University Press.

Newman, Peter C. 1987. *Caesars of the Wilderness.* Company of Adventurers, vol. 2. Markham, ON: Penguin Books Canada, Ltd.

Ong, Walter J. 1982. *Orality and Literacy: The Technologizing of the World*. London: Meuthen.

Palmer, Andie. 1985. 'Translation and the Spoken Word of Rock and Coyote.' Unpublished M.A. research, University of Washington.

– 1994. 'Maps of Experience: Shuswap Narratives of Place.' Doctoral dissertation in Anthropology, University of Washington. Ann Arbor, MI: University Microfilms International.

Palmer, Gary. 1975a. 'Shuswap Indian Ethnobotany.' *Syesis* 8: 29–81. British Columbia Provincial Museum, Victoria: Queen's Printer.

– 1975b. Cultural Ecology in the Canadian Plateau: Pre-Contact to the Early Contact Period in the Territory of the Southern Shuswap Indians of British Columbia. *Northwest Anthropological Research Notes* 9(2): 199–245.

Place, Hillary. 1999. *Dog Creek: A Place in the Cariboo*. Surrey, BC: Heritage House.

Powell, Jay, Vickie Jensen, and Phyllis Chelsea. 1979. *Learning Shuswap: Book One*. Alkali Lake: Shuswap Language Committee.

Ray, Verne F. 1939. *Cultural Relations in the Plateau of Northwestern North America*. Publications of the Frederick Webb Hodge Anniversary Publication Fund. Vol. 3. Los Angeles: Southwest Museum Administrator of the Fund.

Ridington, Robin. 1988. *Trail to Heaven: Knowledge and Narrative in a Northern Native Community*. Iowa City: University of Iowa Press.

– 1990. *Little Bit Know Something: Stories in a Language of Anthropology*. Iowa City: University of Iowa Press.

– 1992. 'Fieldwork in Courtroom 53: A Witness to Delgamuukw v B.C.' *BC Studies Special Issue* 95(2): 12–24.

Robinson, Harry. 1989. *Write It on Your Heart: The Epic World of an Okanagan Storyteller*. Comp. and ed. Wendy Wickwire. Vancouver: Talonbooks/Theytus.

Rodman, Margaret C. 1992. 'Empowering Place: Multilocality and Multivocality.' *American Anthropologist* 94(3): 640–56.

Rothenburg, Jerome. 1972. *Shaking the Pumpkin: Traditional Poetry of the Indian North Americans*. Garden City, NY: Doubleday and Co.

Sapir, Edward. 1949 (1921). *Language: An Introduction to the Study of Speech*. New York: Harcourt, Brace & World.

Sarris, Greg. 1993. 'Part One: The Verbal Art of Mabel McKay: Talk as Culture Contact and Cultural Critique' and 'The Woman Who Loved a Snake: Orality in Mabel McKay's Stories.' In *Keeping Slug Woman Alive: A Holistic Approach to American Indian Texts*, 17–48. Berkeley: University of California Press.

Schieffelin, Edward L. 1976. *The Sorrow of the Lonely and the Burning of the Dancers*. New York: St Martin's Press.

Scollon, Ron, and Suzanne B.K. Scollon. 1981. 'The Bush Consciousness and Oral Narrative Discourse.' In *Narrative, Literacy and Face in Interethnic Communication*. Advances in Discourse Processes, vol. 7. Norwood, NJ: Ablex Publishing Corp.

Searle, John R. 1969. *Speech Acts: An Essay in the Philosophy of Langugage*. London: Cambridge University Press.

– 1979. *Expression and Meaning: Studies in the Theory of Speech Acts*. New York: Cambridge University Press.

Sherzer, Joel. 1979. 'Strategies of Text and Context: Kuna *kaa kwento*.' *Journal of American Folklore* 92: 145–63.

– 1983. *Kuna Ways of Speaking: An Ethnographic Perspective*. Austin: University of Texas Press.

– 1987. 'A Discourse-Centered Approach to Language and Culture.' *American Anthropologist* 89: 295–309.

Shostak, Marjorie. 1981. *Nisa: The Life and Words of a !Kung Woman*. Cambridge, MA: Harvard University Press.

Sidney, Angela. 1982. *Tagish Tlaagú: Tagish Stories*. Whitehorse: Council for Yukon Indians and the Government of Yukon.

Silverstein, Michael. 1996. 'Encountering Language and Languages of Encounter in North American Ethnohistory.' *Journal of Linguistic Anthropology* 6(2): 126–44.

Speare, Jean E., ed. 1973. *The Days of Augusta*. Vancouver: J.J. Douglas, Ltd.

Spielmann, Roger. 1998. *'You're So Fat!': Exploring Ojibwe Discourse*. Toronto: University of Toronto Press.

Szklut, Jay, and Robert Roy Reed. 1991. 'Community Anonymity in Anthropological Research.' In C. Fluehr-Lobban, ed., *Ethics and the Profession of Anthropology: Dialogue for a New Era*, 97–114. Philadelphia: University of Pennsylvania Press.

Tanner, Adrian. 1979. *Bringing Home Animals: Religious Ideology and Mode of Production of the Mistassini Cree Hunters*. New York: St Martin's Press.

Tedlock, Dennis. 1972. *Finding the Center: Narrative Poetry of the Zuni Indians*. Trans. D. Tedlock. New York: The Dial Press.

– 1983. *The Spoken Word and the Work of Interpretation*. Philadelphia: University of Pennsylvania Press.

Teit, James Alexander. 1898. *Traditions of the Thompson River Indians of British Columbia*. Memoirs of the American Folklore Society, vol. 6. New York: Houghton, Mifflin and Co.

– 1900. *The Thompson Indians of British Columbia*. Memoir of the American Museum of Natural History, New York. Vol. 2, Anthropology. Vol. 1, part 4. Ed. Franz Boas. New York: Knickerbocker Press.

– 1909. *The Shuswap*. The Jessup North Pacific Expedition. Memoir of the American Museum of Natural History, New York. Vol. 2, part 7. Ed. Franz Boas. New York: G.E. Stechert. (Repr. New York: AMS Press, 1975.)

– 1912. *Mythology of the Thompson Indians*. The Jessup North Pacific Expedition. Memoir of the American Museum of Natural History, New York. Vol. 8, part 2. Ed. Franz Boas. New York: G.E. Stechert. (Repr. New York: AMS Press, 1975.)

– 1917. *Folk-Tales of Salishan Tribes*. Folk-Tales of Salishan and Sahaptin Tribes. American Folklore Society Memoirs, vol. 11. Ed. Franz Boas. Lancaster, Pa.: G.E. Stechert & Co.

Tennant, Paul. 1990. *Aboriginal Peoples and Politics: The Indian Land Question in British Columbia, 1849–1989*. Vancouver: UBC Press.

Thompson, Laurence C., and M. Dale Kincaid. 1990. 'Languages.' In Wayne Suttles, ed., *Handbook of North American Indians, Vol. 7, Northwest Coast*, 30–51. Washington: Smithsonian Institution Publications.

Thompson, Stith. 1946. *The Folktale*. New York: Dryden.

Tuan, Yi-Fu. 1974. *Topophilia: A Study of Environmental Perception, Attitudes, and Values*. Englewood Cliffs, NJ: Prentice-Hall.

– 1977. *Space and Place: The Perspective of Experience*. Minneapolis. University of Minnesota Press.

Turnbridge, Dorothy 1988. *Flinders Ranges Dreaming*. Canberra: Aboriginal Studies Press.

Turner, Nancy J., Randy Bouchard, and Dorothy I.D. Kennedy. 1980. *Ethnobotany of the Okanagan-Colville Indians of British Columbia and Washington*. Occasional Paper of the British Columbia Provincial Museum, no. 21. Victoria: British Columbia Provincial Museum.

Turner, Nancy J., Laurence C. Thompson, M. Terry Thompson, and Annie Z. York. 1990. *Thompson Ethnobotany. Knowledge and Usage of Plants by the Thompson Indians of British Columbia*, Royal British Columbia Museum Memoir no. 3. Victoria: Royal British Columbia Museum.

Urban, Greg. 1991. *A Discourse-Centered Approach to Culture: Native South American Myths and Rituals*. Austin: University of Texas Press.

Valentine, Lisa Phillips. 1995. *Making It Their Own: Severn Ojibwe Communicative Practices*. Toronto: University of Toronto Press.

– 1994. 'Performing Native Identities.' *Papers of the Twenty-fifth Algonquian Conference*, 482–92. Ottawa: Carleton University.

W., Bill. 1976. *Alcoholics Anonymous: The Story of How Many Thousands of Men and Women Have Recovered from Alcoholism*. New York: Alcoholics Anonymous World Services.

Watanabe, John M. 1992. *Maya Saints and Souls in a Changing World.* Austin: University of Texas Press.

Whitehead, Margaret. 1981. *The Cariboo Mission: A History of the Oblates.* Victoria, BC: Sono Nis Press.

Wilson-Kenni, Dora (Yagalahl). 1990. 'Time of Trial: The Gitksan and Wet'suwet'en in Court.' *BC Studies Special Issue* 95(2): 7–11.

Wolf, Eric R., 1982. *Europe and the People without History.* Berkeley: University of California Press.

York, Annie, Richard Daly, and Chris Arnett. 1993. *They Write Their Dreams on the Rocks Forever: Rock Writings in the Stein River Valley of British Columbia.* Vancouver: Talonbooks.

Films and Videotapes

Alkali Lake Indian Band. 1987. *The Honour of All, Parts I and II.* Produced by the Alkali Lake Indian Band, Chief Dan George Memorial Fund, Four Worlds Development Project, and Phil Lucas. Alkali Lake, BC.

Annaud, Jean-Jacques. 1988. *The Bear.* Jean-Jacques Annaud, director. North American Release: TriStar Pictures.

Canadian Broadcasting Corporation. 1991a. 'A Violation of Trust.' *The Fifth Estate.* David Kaufman, producer.

– 1991b. 'A Circle of Healing. Part One: Breaking the Silence.' *Man Alive.* Louise Lore, executive producer.

– 1991c. 'A Circle of Healing. Part Two: When the Eagle Lands on the Moon.' *Man Alive.* Louise Lore, executive producer.

Cherniack, David. 2002. *Reservation.* Parts 1–4. Produced and directed by David Cherniack in association with VisionTV.

Index

Introductory note: Page numbers referring to illustrative materials are followed by (A) for the appendix, (f) for figures, (m) for maps, (p) for photographs, and (T) for tapes. Secwepemctsín names and words are indexed in first- and second-level headings along with their English translations.

Abbey, Alice (Chief of William's Lake Band), 80–2, 125, 152, 167, 212n5

Adams, John, 42

Adnyamathnha of Australia, 166

Akan, Linda, 23, 156, 207n14

Alberta, 29, 34 (m), 76, 209n4

alcohol, use and sobriety: alcohol treatment program (Poundmaker's Lodge), 76; alcoholism, rates of, 6, 51, 52, anonymity, loss of, 137, 140, 142; availability of, effect on lives, 41, 44, 49, 136–42, 147–9, 157–8, 200 (A); 'backsliding,' 142; Durieu System, 43–4, 48, 49, 52, 210n23; fetal alcohol syndrome, recognition of, 54–5; film about, consequences, 26, 141–2; group identity, 158; The Honour of All, 6–7, 49, 52, 137, 140, 141, 142; Indian as alcoholic, 141; New Directions, 53, 55; Pathways, 55; sobriety, 'AA birthday,' 137; sobriety, pressure to maintain, 142; sobriety, rates of, efforts for, 6, 52, 53, 54–5, 55–6, 137–42, 158; Sobriety Movement at Alkali Lake, 52, 210n23; white bootlegger, 141; youth, reactions of, 140–1, 142

Alcoholics Anonymous (AA), at Alkali Lake. AA 'Big Book' (*Alcoholics Anonymous: The Story of How Many Thousands of Men and Women Have Recovered from Alcoholism*, by Bill W.), 137; 'AA birthday,' 137, 143; AA meetings, context, format, 26, 137–42, 157–8; AA personal narratives, 137–42, 147–58; *The Honour of All*, 6–7, 49, 52, 137, 140, 141, 142; meta-narrative in *The Honour of All*, 137, 141, 142

'Alcohol Lake,' x

'Alkali' (ɛləkʌloy), xix

alkali: hardpan, alkaline soil, ix, 68;

'loonshit,' x; pothole lakes, white alkali, x, 124

Alkali Creek, x, 46

Alkali Lake (*Esket*): Alkali Lake, 6, 7, 8, 29, 31, 38 (m); Alkali Lake territory, roads, 57–60, 68, 76–8, 89–90, 163–5; Alkali Lake village (IR 1, *Esket*) 26, 36, 37, 38 (m), 41, 209n7; *Esket*, in Secwepemctsín (Alkali Lake in English), 6, 41, 56, 207n4; Interior dry belt, territory around, 68

Alkali Lake Indian Band, people and life of: access to land, displacement from, problems, 76–8, 79, 90, 163–5; Alcoholics Anonymous meetings at, 26, 136–42, 157–8; Alkali Lake Indian Band (now, Esketemc First Nation), 207n4; band circumstances, 24, 50–1, 210n26; children (births, deaths) 127, 154; discourse, contexts of, xvii, xviii, 16–17, 24–6, 78–82, 83, 84, 86, 115, 116, 119, 120, 123–4, 136–42, 143–4, 157–8, 159–69; Durieu System, 43–4, 48, 49, 52, 210n23; economy of, 53, 57, 59–60, 76–8, 79, 163–4; education, school on reserve, xix, 9, 50, 51, 54–5, 167; employment, programs, workshops, 41, 52, 53–6, 57–8, 63, 76, 79, 102, 209n8; Esket Education Committee, 51; Esketemc First Nation, 28, 56, 207n4, 208n8; Framework Treaty Agreement, 56; funerals, behaviours, preparations, mourning, 26, 123–5, 126–7, 134, 135, 212n4; 'home(s)' of, 160–2; hunting, fishing, land-use rights, court cases, 17, 57–67, 78–82, 84, 88, 95,

97; intermarriage, outmarriage, 33, 53; land claims by, resources, revenues, 46, 67, 56; land claims by others, ranches by Alkali Lake, 21–2, 24, 37, 38 (m), 41, 209n8; livestock owned in 1881, in surveyor's records, 46, 210n15; Native Journeys, 56; New Directions, 53, 55; Pathways, 55; plant use, 67–72; prosperity (in 1980s), 52–3; religion, spirituality, 18, 26, 134–5; *Secwepemc* of *Esket*, xi; Shuswap of Alkali Lake, xi; settlement in villages (village coalescence), xi, 24, 41–2, 44–5, 59, 161, 162; smallpox, 37, 39–41, 209n5. *See also* Canadian government; English; First Nations; fishing; food; hunting and trapping; missionaries, missions; narratives from Alkali Lake; Native(s); place(s), of the Secwepemc people; province of British Columbia; religion, spirituality; reserves; residential schools; Secwepemc (Shuswap people); Secwepemctsín (Shuswap language); stories of the Secwepemc people

Alkali Lake Indian Reserve: Alkali Lake/Esketemc Indian Reserve No. 1, x, xi (p), 28, 38 (m), 41, 46, 48 (m), 84, 89, 92, 93, 114, 170 (A); Framework Treaty Agreement, 56; Harper's Lake, 46, 47 (m); Indian Reserve (IR) No. 1 (and No. 2), 10, 28, 72, 124, 164; location, name, x–xi, 203 (A); map of Alkali Lake Indian reserves, 48; Reserve No. 7, 46; Reserves Nos. 8 to 14, 46, 210n21; Reserves Nos. 16 to 18, 48,

48 (m); Reserves Nos. 2 to 6, 38
(m), 46; sketch map of Alkali Lake
Reserve No. 1, 38; sketch map of
Harper's Lake, 46, 47 (m); St
Pierre's Church (built in 1879), 43;
Sxoxomic School, xix, 9, 54, 167.
See also reserves
Alkali Lake Ranch, 28, 95, 183 (A)
American Anthropological Associa-
tion, 10, 22
American Museum of Natural His-
tory, 9–10, 28
Amoss, Pamela, 122, 138
Armstrong, Jeannette, xviii–xix
Arrow Lakes, Lower and Upper, 33
arrowheads. *See* projectile points
Athapaskans, languages and people,
xviii, 19; 'the authority of individ-
ual experience,' 19; Carrier
(Dakelhne), 29, 30 (m), 31, 32 (m),
35, 36, 43, 53, 209n4; discourse,
xviii, 19, 207n13; Dunne-za, or
Beaver, 19, 57–8, 161, 162, 166,
209n4; Gisday Wa and Delgam
Uukw, 165, 166; Gitksan and
Wet'suwet'en land claims case,
Delgamuukw v. British Columbia, 78,
163, 165; indigenous discourse systems, xviii; peoples of the Northwest Coast and Plateau culture
areas, 30 (m); personal autonomy,
respect for, 139; 'trail of song' (*kungax*, spirit power song), 165; 'trails
to heaven' (maps of the hunt), 166;
Tsilhqot'in, 29, 30 (m), 31, 58,
209n5; Wet'suwet'en Athabascans, 165. *See also* Basso; Brody;
Ridington; Scollon, Suzanne and
Ron
Austin, J.L., 15

avalanche lily, yellow (*swicw* in
Secwepemctsín), 67–8, 213n10. *See
also* food

Bakhtin, M.M., 15–16
Barbeau, Marius, 9
Barkerville, 36
Basso, Keith, 19–20, 21–2, 139, 166
Bauman, Richard, 16
BC Association of Non-Status Indi-
ans, 8
Bear, The, 213n8
Behar, Ruth, 154
Belanger, Betty (daughter of Angela
George), xxi, 113, 175 (A), 214n3,
215nn3, 5, 6
Bell, E. (Indian Agent), 46
Bella Coola, ix, 29, 35, 37
berries. *See* food
Blackberry, 5, 207n2
Blackman, Margaret, 136, 156
black tree lichen (*wíla* in Secwepem-
ctsín), 68. *See also* food
Boas, Franz, 7, 9, 28, 33, 168
Bonaparte territory, 168
Bowie, Alfie, 71 (p), 164 (p), 198 (A)
Bowie, Marcella, 198 (A)
Boyd, Robert, 30
Briggs, Charles, 16, 105, 151, 213n3
British Columbia. *See* province of
British Columbia
British Columbia Provincial
Archives. *See* Provincial Archives
of British Columbia
British Crown, 24, 27
Brody, Hugh, xviii, 11, 57–8, 84, 161,
166
Brow, Catherine, 50, 51, 53, 57, 72,
123, 212n4
California gold miners, 36, 37

Canadian Anthropological Division, Department of Mines. *See* Canadian Geological Survey

Canadian Geological Survey (CGS), 119, 207n5, 208n7, 209nn2, 3

Canadian government: Bill C-31 (reinstatement of rights, 1985), 53–4; Canadian Charter of Rights and Freedoms, 53; Crown lands, unreserved, 44; Department of Fisheries, 60; Department of Indian Affairs, 50, 51, 56; employment, funding, records of, 52, 53–6, 57–8; expropriation of lands by, 162; Fisheries Public Notice, 66 (f); Framework Treaty Agreement, 56; *Indian Act (Act for the gradual civilization of Indian Peoples)*, 45, 48–9, 53, 72; Indian agents, 46; Indian economy, analysis of, 57–8, 79; Indian Register, 53; land claims negotiations, 4, 46, 56, 167; Ministry of Indian Affairs and Northern Development, 50, 56; mission school, control of, 50; Native food fishery licences, 63, 66, 67; recognition of Secwepemc, 27; reserve, naming of, x–xi; reserves, creation of, records about, 46–8, 57; residential schools, 6; *Revised Indian Act*, 50; 'status' or 'registered' Indians, 53–4; Supreme Court of Canada, 56, 78; Treaty 8, 57; treaty-negotiation process, 56; Trudeau, Pierre Elliott (prime minister), 51. *See also* First Nations; Native(s); province of British Columbia; reserves

Canadian Tri-Council Statement on Ethics, 10

Canim Lake Reserve, 72, 167

Canoe Creek Reserve, 31, 53, 89, 121

Canyon Division, 31, 32 (m), 34 (m), 35, 39

Cariboo, xi, 6, 24, 41, 48

Cariboo Mission (residential school), 6, 7. *See also* residential schools

Cariboo Tribal Council, 53

Cariboo Waggon Road, 37, 209n6; 47 Mile House (Clinton), 20, 36–7, 119; mileposts (122 and 123), 46; 150 Mile House, 36, 89; 114 Milepost, 42; 122 and 123 mileposts, 46

Carlson, Keith Thor, 22

Carrier (Dakelhne; Athapaskan people), 29, 30 (m), 31, 32 (m), 35, 36, 43, 53, 209n4

Carson, Dennis, 10

Carson, Wendy, 10

Catholic church. *See* missionaries, missions

CBC (Canadian Broadcasting Corporation), 7, 50, 52, 140

Chasm, 167

Chaudiere or Colville Indians, 33

Chelsea, Andy (Chief of Alkali Lake Band), 8, 49, 52, 55, 142

Chelsea, Phyllis (Curriculum Development Committee), 8, 52, 55

Cherniak, David, 7

Chief of Fountain, 45

Chief Sampson (Sxoxomic, Alkali Lake hereditary chief), 48

Chief William (Chimney Creek Secwepemc), 43

Chilcotin Plateau, 37, 46, 89

Chimney Creek Secwepemc (Williams Lake Band), 42, 43

c7ístken (pithouses, winterhouses),

41, 109–14, 112 (p), 114 (p), 120,
162, 186 (A), 212n9
Churn Creek suspension bridge, 59,
60, 89, 92, 93, 96, 167
Cibecue Apache, 19–20, 21–2, 166
Cklutelátu7s (a place of pithouses),
41, 109–14, 112 (p), 114 (p), 186 (A),
191 (A), 212nn8, 9
Clinton (47 Mile House), 20, 36–7,
119
Columbia River, 33
conversations, analysis, 14–17, 84,
211n1. *See also* discourse; narrative;
narratives from Alkali Lake
Coqualeetza (all-Indian sanitarium
for tuberculosis), 72
Coyote Stories, 9, 207–8n6. *See also*
Mourning Dove
Coyote stories, tales, 119, 120, 123,
125–6, 168
Crapanzano, Vincent, 214n5
Cree, 29, 33, 35, 211n4
'creek' (*tswec*), 173 (A), 214n2
Cruikshank, Julie, xxi, 22, 25, 27, 82,
154, 156
cyéwmen (fishing place), 190 (A)

Darnell, Regna, xviii
Davidson, Florence Edenshaw
(Haida Elder), 156
Dawson, George, 119, 120, 121, 122,
212n3
deixis (reference by context), 85, 152.
See also discourse; narrative; narra-
tives from Alkali Lake
Demers, Modeste (Oblate mission-
ary), 43
Dick v. The Queen (hunting court
case), 78
Didion, Joan, 23

dip-netting. *See* fishing
discourse: anchoring, re-anchoring,
of, 21–2; Bakhtin, 15–16; communication across systems of, 82; conflicting models of, 25, 82; contexts
of, 3–4, 16–17, 21–3, 136; conversations, analysis, 14–17, 84, 211n1; in
the courtroom, hunting, 78–82;
cross-cultural, 21, 166–7; deixis
(reference by context), 85, 152;
described, explained, 12, 13–14,
15–16; discourse analysis, 14–16,
207n12; discourse-centred approach to language and culture,
16–17, discourse theory, 23,
209n14; discursive event, interlocutors, 156; Duranti, 16, 208n11,
211n1; Foucault, 14; Frake, 14–15;
Grice (theory of conversational
implicature, Conversational Maxims), 84, 86, 211n1; hunting and
gathering discourse, 78–82, 83, 84,
86, 116; Hymes, 16, 17, 100; life
story discourse, 136, 150–8, 214n5;
locus of culture, 16; place-related
discourse, 21–2, 26, 89, 168; respect
for, 18–19; Ridington, Robin, xviii,
xx, 15, 25, 82, 128; Sherzer, Joel, 16,
100; sociocultural anthropology,
14; speech act theory, 15, 208n11;
Spielmann, 14; as text, 15–16;
Urban, 12, 16, 100; 'walking and
talking,' 22–3, 156. *See also* interlocutors; narrative; narratives
from Alkali Lake
Discovery Channel (US), 140
Dog Creek Reserve, 20, 28, 31, 53, 58,
59, 89, 103–5, 117 (m), 121
Dog Creek Road: cave in cliffs, 41,
104 (p); description, location, 89–

91, 103, 117 (m), 143, 170 (A); Little
Dog Creek (*Stegtsetsuĺqw, stegtset-
setsuĺqw*), 46, 91, 102–3, 185 (A);
map of key sites along, 117; old
foot trail, 89; roads, logging, other,
90–1; sage, growing along road, 75
(p)

Douglas, James (Governor), 41–2, 43,
44

Draney, Charley, 119

Du Bois, John W., 211n1

Duff, Wilson, 37, 209n4

Dunlevy's store, 36

Dunn, Peggy, 207n2

Dunne-za, or Beaver Indians, 19,
57–8, 161, 166, 209n4

Duranti, Alessandro, 16, 208n11,
211n1

Durieu System, Father Durieu, 43–4,
48, 49, 52, 210n23. *See also* alcohol;
missionaries, missions

Echo Mountain (*Tsexqwmeȟles*), 91,
177 (A), 178 (A), 182 (A), 183 (A),
187 (A), 214n8

Elmendorf, William, xxi, 213n4

English: adults, fluency in, use of,
xvii, xviii, xix; children, fluency in,
use of, xix; Canadian English,
xviii; Cariboo Mission Indian residential school, 6; epenthetic shwa
(ə), xix; 'Indian Englishes,' xviii;
pronunciation of, xix; Secwepemctsín, effect of on English, xviii;
Sisters at St Joseph's Mission (Irish
nuns, teachers), xix; Standard
English, xix; Sxoxomic School, xix,
9, 54. *See also* Alkali Lake Indian
Band; residential schools;
Secwepemctsín

Enoḱit, lake above fishing creeks
(Swan Lake), 173 (A), 214n3

environment. *See* place; place(s) of
the Secwepemc people

epenthetic shwa (ə), xix

Erhardt Seminars Training (EST), 55

Esḱet, in Secwepemctsín (Alkali Lake
in English), 6, 41, 56, 207n4. *See also*
Alkali Lake (*Esḱet*)

Esḱet: Alkali Lake Indian Reserve
No. 1, xi (p). *See also* Alkali Lake
Indian Reserve

Esḱet Education Committee, 51

Esketemc First Nation, 56, 207n4. *See
also* Alkali Lake Indian Band

Esperanza (Mexquitican consultant),
154

ethnographic writing, 5

étsqwem, étsqwens, to bake, 214n8

Farwell Canyon bridge, 58

fences (split-rail, Russell, snake), ix, x

Feit, Harvey, 211n4

First Nations: Aboriginal voices, 7–8;
and anthropological study, 7–8, 9–
10; BC Association of Non-Status
Indians, 8; BC Treaty Commission, 56, 210n28; British Columbia,
7–8, 162–3; British Columbia First
Nations names, 30 (m); conflicts,
cultural erasure, 27; and the
Crown, 4, 37, 56; Framework
Treaty Agreement, 56; Indian
Reserves, sovereign territory, 8;
land claims, 22, 27, 29, 37, 56, 78;
map of First Nations of British
Columbia, 30; People(s), 7–8, 28;
Salish Peoples, economic power, 8;
and resources, 56; timber cut-block
licensees, 56; treaty-negotiation

process, 56; Union of BC Indian Chiefs, 8, 51–2. *See also* Canadian government; Native(s); province of British Columbia; reserves

fishing: Alkali Lake IR No. 16, Old Clemene's (fishing place), 59, 117 (m); catch, division and quantity of, 63, 97, 211n5; Churn Creek suspension bridge, 59, 60, 89, 92, 93, 96, 167; Department of Fisheries, licences, 60, 63, 66–7; dip nets, 59, 60; dip-netting, at Little Dog Creek (on Fraser River), 102–3; —, at The Point, 63 (p); —, on Fraser River, 35, 41, 59–60, 62 (p), 91, 93–6, 97, 211–12n5; 'dip-netting place' (*xtsyetbulun*), 180 (A), 214n11; Farwell Canyon Bridge, 58, fish, as food, 51, 57, 58, 60; fish processing, preserving, 60–5, 65 (p), 95, 96, 102, 103, 109, 187–8 (A); fish stocks, 60; fisheries, Lac la Hache, 46, 59, Fisheries Public Notice, 66 (f); fishery, problems with, 60; fishing, at night, 59–60, 62 (p), 79; a fishing place (*cyébmen*) 190 (A); fishing place (The Point, *tyenmemqs*), 104–5 (A), 189–90 (A), 215n14; fishing rights, granted, 46; gill nets, 59; lake above fishing creeks (*Enokit*, Swan Lake), 173 (A), 214n3; mourning period restrictions, 125–6, 212n6; pit-lamp for fish (*xtsqebsem*), 181 (A), 215n13; The Point trailhead, 63 (p), 64 (p); salmon (chinook, coho, kokanee) fishing, 57, 59–60, 64 (p), 97; sturgeon fishing, 59; trout (*písell*) fishing, 59, 214n4; weir, 59; 'Where the fish goes down' (*yuct-*

kiknes) 180 (A), 181 (A). *See also* food; hunting and trapping; narratives from Alkali Lake

food: 'angry food,' 125; bake food (to), (*étsqwem, étsqwens*), 214n8; bannock, 76; baskets, birch bark, 72; berries and narratives, 84–8, 211n2; berries, picking and quantity ('used to be lots'), ix, 67, 68–72, 85–8, 97–8, 174 (A); berries, preserving, 177–9 (A), 187–8 (A); berry-picking place (*tsecreptsen*), 91, 173 (A), 175 (A), 214n5; bird, grouse (*spyu7*), 180 (A), 214n12; black tree lichen, 68; blueberries, huckleberries, 68, 72, 127; bread (*lekelét*), 214n6; cattle, effect on plants and soil, 67–8; choke cherries (*lkwlo7sr*), 178 (A), 179 (A), 181 (A), 192 (A), 194 (A), 214n9; corms, roots, 67–8, 76, 213n10, 213n2; diet, nourishment, 76, 81–2, 88, 125, 127; Echo Mountain (*Tsexqwmemles*), 91, 177 (A), 178 (A), 182 (A), 183 (A), 187 (A), 214n8; 'food' (*s7illen*), 214n10; food, from the supermarket, 79–82; —, taken by the spirits, 126–7, —, trips to Williams Lake, 179 (A); foods as medicines, markers of identity, 75–6; frybread, 76, 210n26; gooseberries (*stcwelcwucwel*), 201 (A), 215n1; greens, on the springwater, 177 (A); 'Indian food,' 72, 75, 174–5 (A); 'Indian ice cream,' 76; Indian soup flour (*lekemín*), 174 (A), 214n6; Indian tea, 174 (A); plants as food, 67–8, 72, 76; porcupine and rabbit, 175 (A); potatoes, 51, 144, 213n2; raspberries (*s7aytsqwem*), 109, 127, 128,

191 (A), 201–2 (A), 215n2; rosebush berries, place named for (*pesekwekwu7*), 203 (A), 215n5; rosehips (*sekwekwu7*), 88, 215n5; saskatoon berry (service berry, *stseqwem*), 68, 69 (p), 174 (A), 178 (A), 181 (A); soapberry, soopolallie berries (*sxúsem*), 68, 70 (p), 71 (p), 76, 85, 86, 87, 109, 191 (A), 200 (A), 201 (A), 203 (A); strawberries (*tqitqe*), 201 (A); 'traditional food,' 75–6; 'used to be lots' (quantity remaining), 67, 97; 'Whiteman's foods,' 76. *See also* fishing; hunting and trapping; medicines, treatments

Fort Chipewyan, 35

Fort McLeod, 35

Foucault, Michel, 14

Frake, Charles O., 14–15, 15

Fraser, Simon (explorer), 35–6, 89

Fraser River, ix, x, 29, 31, 39, 41, 46, 58, 59, 89, 96, 107, 119, 122, 167, 169 (p), 209n5; Cariboo Waggon Road, 36, 37, 42, 46, 89, 209n6; Churn Creek suspension bridge, 59, 60, 89, 92, 93, 96, 167; dip-netting on, 35, 41, 59–60, 62 (p), 63 (p), 91, 93–6, 97, 211–12n5; explored by Simon Fraser, 35–6, 89; Fraser River Division, 31, 32 (m), 34 (m), 36, 37, 53, 59, 168; gold discovered on (1858), 36

Fraser Valley, 72

Furniss, Elizabeth: on Durieu System, 48, 49, 210n23; ethnocultural accounts, accuracy of, 27; on residential schools, 48–9, 49–50; on sobriety movement among Shuswap Indians of Alkali Lake (thesis), 52

Gang Ranch, 89

George, Angela: accident, story about, 108–9, 212n7; ancestors, stories about, and spiritual encounters, 39–41, 109–15; 'Angela's place,' 161; on bear as a 'human person,' 151–2; on bears, beliefs and stories about, 128–33, 135, 151–2, 153–4, 213n4; berry picking, quantity of berries ('used to be lots'), 67, 69 (p), 71 (p), 85–8, 97–8, 109, 127–8; children (births, deaths, names of), 113, 127, 154; consultant on research, 26, 127, 214n5; daughter Dorothy (*Kenkeknem*, Black Bear), 113, 152, 175 (A); employment (on ranches), 95, 102, 127, 155; grandchildren (Candice, Dallas), 6, 112 (p), 128, 132, 151, 153, 198 (A), 205 (A), 213n9; hunting and gathering narratives, 84–6, 95–6, 98–101, 102–3, 106–7, 109; on Indian medicine, treatments, 106–7; land, access to, stories about, 77, 95–6; learning, from Elders, on the land, 6; life experiences, losses, storytelling, 6, 18, 26, 107–9, 122–3, 134, 207n3; and names of places, use of, 88–9; smallpox, stories about, 39–41, 110, 115; and sobriety narrative, analysis of, 147–50, 200 (A); son, death of, 153, 154, 213n4; spiritual practices (prayers, pow-wows, sweats), 18, 84–5, 106, 145, 147, 148, 154–5, 199 (A), 200 (A); 'telling her life,' 127–34, 143–55, 157, 213n1, 214n5; tipi (teepee), life in, 144, 195 (A), 213n1; at *Tsecyelkw*, 39–41, 40 (p), 114–15; and work, from young

age, 145. *See also* Appendix;
Belanger
George, Jimmy; accident, story
about, 107–8, 212n7; and bears,
beliefs and stories about, 151–2; on
Cklutetátu7s (a place of pithouses),
109, 110–11; cues, manner of, 102;
fishing experiences, 93–5, 102, 107;
at Gustafson Lake, 164 (p); hunting experiences, as guide, 96–7, 98,
100, 155; land, stories about, 164–5,
167; and learning, from Elders, on
the land, and reading, 6; life experiences, storytelling, 6, 103–5, 122–
3, 207n3
Gisday Wa and Delgam Uukw, 165,
166
Goffman, Erving, 207n1
gold, discovery of, rush, 24, 36–7
gold miners, 36, 37, 39, 41
'grease trail,' ix, 29, 35; Bella Coola,
ix, 29, 35, 37; Cariboo, xi, 6, 24, 41,
48; history, use, of, ix–xi; Interior
Plateau, ix; Nuxalk People, ix, 30
(m), oolichan oil, ix, 29; to Williams Lake, ix, x, 10, 11, 49
Grice, H.P. (theory of conversational
implicature, Conversational Maxims), 84, 86, 211n1
Gumperz, John, J., xx
Gustafson Lake, camp, 164 (p), 213n1

Habermas, Jürgen, 208n11
Haig-Brown, Alan, 8
Haig-Brown, Celia, 43
Hamilton, Buster, 95
Hanna, Darwin, 118–19, 213n4
Harper's Lake, 46, 47 (m)
Harry, Celina (teacher), 9
Henry, Mamie, 118, 213n4

Hess, Thom, xxii
Hideout Creek (*stscelwáwtkwe*), 186
(A)
High Bar, 121, 122
Hilbert, Vi (ṭaqʷšəblu): and audience, 5, 207n1; aunt, Susie Samp-
son Peter (gʷəqʷulćə?), 5; and
Blackberry, 5, 207n2; interpretive
frames for stories, 5, 207n1; 'learn-
ing how to listen,' 3–5, 151; as listener, showing respect, 19; and
Lushootseed (Puget Salish language), 3, 4; and Lushootseed
texts, xxi; professor, storyteller, 3,
4–5, 207n1; Stories (sʔyəyəhub), 5;
Story, gift of, care of, 3, 4, 5. *See also*
interlocutors; Lushootseed
(dxʷləšutcid); Salish
Hill, Jane, 208n11, 208n12
Hirsch, Eric, 22
Hoijer, Harry, 21
Honour of All, The, 6–7, 49, 52, 137,
140, 141, 142
Hudson's Bay Company, 36
Hunn, Eugene, 163, 168
hunting and trapping: access to land,
displacement from, problems, 76–
8, 79, 90, 163–5; Alkali Lake territory, roads, 57–60, 68, 76–8, 89–90,
163–5; catch, quantity of, 97, 211n4;
completes the 'circle of training,'
79; court cases about, 78–82, 212n5;
custom, spiritual, subsistence
activity, 57, 58–9, 76–7, 78, 79–82;
distribution of, sharing, 79–80;
game, killing, preserving, use, 58–
9, 96–101, 103; hunters, recreational, 77, 90; hunting and gathering discourse, narratives, 78–82,
83, 84, 86, 116; hunting practices,

77, 78; logging, effect on moose, 58; and mourning period, restrictions, 125; parfleches (dried hides), 101; porcupine and rabbit, 175 (A); and relationship with nature, 80, 81–2; supply, scarcity, 97, 98; trapping, 58; value of, as more than food, 79–82. *See also* Abbey; fishing; food; Johnson, Charley; narratives from Alkali Lake

Hymes, Dell, xx, xxi, 16, 17, 22, 100, 207n3

Ignatius, Elaine, picking soapberries, 70 (p)

Indian Act (*Act for the gradual civilization of Indian Peoples*), 45, 48–9, 53, 72. *See also* Canadian government

'Indian bleach,' 204 (A), 215n6

'Indian Englishes,' xviii. *See also* English

Indian reserves. *See* reserves

Indian Rights Association of British Columbia, 29

Ingold, Tim, 209n14

Interior Peoples, ix, 29, 31, 77

Interior Salish division, xvii

Interior Salish language, Okanagan, xix

Interior Salish peoples, stories, 29, 118. *See also* Salish

interlocutors: audience (or other participants), 17, 136, 157; communication, respectful, 23; cooperative achievement, 136; cues, linguistic, extra-linguistic, 13, 102, 153; defined, speaker, listener, 17; future audience, 17; God, or Creator, 17; human, non-human, 17–18; Hymes on, 17; interrelationships, social contract, 3, 22–3, 136, 153, 156–7; repair in 'telling my life,' 157; 'walking and talking,' 22–3, 156. *See also* Hilbert

Iroquois, in Shuswap territory, 33

Jacobs, Melville, 168, 213n4

Joe's Lake Road, 59, 88, 151, 198 (A), 205 (A), 211n2

Johnson, Charley, 79–80, 80–1, 82, 186 (A)

Johnson, Chewinik, 20

Johnson, David, x, 28, 39, 123–4, 165, 212n4

Johnson, Dorothy, picking sage, 75 (p)

Johnson, Hazel, 20, 92

Johnson, Julianna (teacher), 9

Johnson, Ollie, 63 (p), 92, 93, 96

Kahn, Miriam, 22, 122

Kamloops (Fort Thompson), 36, 50, 53, 119, 120, 121, 122, 168, 210n25

Keane, Webb, 16

Kettle River, 33

Kootenai (people), 29, 32 (m)

Koyukon River, 26

ksetkwe ('Poison Lake'), 204 (A), 215n6

Kuipers, Aert H.: etymological index, 8; orthography, 'practical' and 'technical,' xxii; pronunciation variations, xix; on *slexéyem* ('a realistic story'), 123; on *stseptékwll* ('myth' or 'fairy tale'), 123, 212n2; and Thunder and Mosquito story, 119

Labov, William, 13, 87. *See also* narrative

Lac la Hache, 40, 41, 46, 59, 89, 127
Lakes Division or Lake Indians, 29, 33, 53, 72
'Land Ordinance of 1870,' 42
lekelét (bread), 214n6
lekemín, Indian soup flour, 174 (A), 214n6
Lenihan, James (Indian Superintendent), 46
Lifespring Canada, Training, 55
Lillooet, trail, 36, 37
Lillooet people, 29, 32 (m)
Linde, Charlotte, 13, 136, 153, 162
linguistic anthropology, 3, 14
Little Dog Creek (*Stegtsetsulqw, steglsetsetsulqw*), 46, 91, 102–3, 185 (A). *See also* Dog Creek Road
Lord, John E. (letter), 45
Lushootseed (dxʷləšutcid); Coast Salish language, 8; Coast Salish people, xviii; L. Salish (Snoqualmie, Upper Skagit), 122; L.-Secwepemctsín cognates, 8; as orators, xviii; orthography, xxii; Puget Salish, 4; Star-Child creation stories, 122; texts, xxi. *See also* Hilbert; Salish
Lytton, 119

Mackenzie, Alexander, 35
MacLaury, Robert, 8
Mantiopies, Alfred (Elder), 23, 156
mariposa lily (*lill'se* in Secwepemctsín), 67–8. *See also* food
McKay, Mabel, 207n1
McLeod, Angus (and 'a certain Taylor'), 37
medicines, treatments: alcohol treatment program (Poundmaker's Lodge), 76; Coqualeetza (all-Indian sanitarium for tuberculosis), 72; foods as medicine, 75; 'Indian' food and traditional food, 72, 75–6; Indian Health Services, 74; 'Indian' medicine, 72, 106–7, 191 (A); local-style sweats, 74–5; *Nukláwt* (place of wild rhubarb, spring water), 105–7; Plains-style Sacred Sweats, Sweatlodge Ceremonies, 74; sage, 74, 75, 75 (p), 182 (A); *segwsesegwt* (purple bell-shaped flowers), 191 (A); sweat baths, 18, 74–5, 106–7; traditional remedies, plant use, 72–5, 73 (p), 75 (p), 115, 191 (A); trees, food and medicinal uses of, 72, 73 (p), 74–5, 115, 202 (A); US Indian Health Services (Rockport, Maryland), 76; wild rhubarb, wild rhubarb roots (cow parsnip), 106–7. *See also* food
metalanguage (language about language), 13
Miller, Jay, 212n6
mission education. *See* residential schools
missionaries, missions: Cariboo Mission, 7; Catholic Indian state, administration, 43, 46; Catholicism and Northern Secwepemc, 43–4; Chief of Fountain, 45, *Constitution and Rules* (Oblates'), 44; Demers, Modeste (Oblate missionary), 43; 'Durieu's System' (Father Durieu), 43–4, 48, 49, 210n23; Grandidier, Father, 44–5; LeJacq, Father, 43, 45; Lord, John E. (letter), 45; Marchal, Father, 45; mistreatment, at missions, 45, 48–9; Oblates of Mary Immaculate, 43, 50; Okanagan mission, 44; settlement of Secwe-

pemc, xi, 44–5, 162; St Joseph's Mission, xix, 43; St Pierre's Church (built in 1879), 43, 123; Thomas, Father Francis, 48–9. *See also* religion, spirituality; residential schools

Moody, R.C. (Chief Commissioner of Lands and Works), 42

Mooney, James, 36

Moore (Harry) Ranch, 164–5, 182 (A), 184 (A)

Morice, A.G., 36, 37, 43

Mourning Dove (Christine Quintasket), 9; Coyote stories, 9, 168, 207–8n6; McWhorter, L.V. (mentor), 207–8n6. *See also* Salish; stories of the Secwepemc people; Teit

Myhrum, David, 30 (m)

Nabakov, Peter, 83, 168

narrative: cooperative achievement, 136; cues, references, linguistic and extralinguistic, 13, 102, 153; deixis (reference by context), 85, 152; described, explained, 13–14; 'discontinuous narrative unit,' 153; historical narratives (legends), 135, 165; 'map of experience,' 25, 116, 155, 168; narrative process, making sense, 13–14, 23, 115, 141, 154; narratives of personal experience, 13, 19, 25, 87, 96, 116, 135; narratives of place, 22, 83, 88–9, 107, 115–16, 156, 162, 163; orientation clauses, 153, 155; repair in 'telling my life,' 157; 'telling my (her, their) life,' 136, 153, 155, 157, 158; temporally ordered (clauses), 13; temporal sequence (by events), 148–50, 155–6; 'walking and talking,' 22–3, 156.

See also Briggs; discourse; Grice; Labov; Lunde; Nabakov; narratives from Alkali Lake; stories of the Secwepemc people; Story narratives from Alkali Lake: AA personal narratives, 137–42, 147–58; accidents, losses, 92 (T3b), 92 (T4), 107–9, 212n7; ancestors, relating to, 39–41, 109–14, 114–15; cave (Dog Creek Reserve), 92(T4), 103–5, 104 (p); *Cklutetátu7s* (a place of pithouses), 92 (T1), 92 (T3a), 93 (T5), 109–14, 112 (p), 114 (p), 212n9; context, context-sensitive, structure of, 83–4, 115–16; continuum, of time, of people, 114–15, 116, 166–9; conversations, shifts in topics, topics, 84, 85, 86, 154, 211n2; cues, verbal and non-verbal, prompts, 102, 105; on deer hunting, 92 (T1), 92 (T4), 93(T5), 96–101, 211n4; on dip-netting, at Churn Creek suspension bridge, 92 (T4), 93 (T5), 93–6, 211nn3, 5; —, at Little Dog Creek, 46, 91, 92 (T1), 92 (T3b), 92 (T4), 102–3, 185 (A); Dog Creek Road, 89–91; experiences of place, 86–7, 116; hunting narratives, court cases, 80–2; on land, resources, 83, 86, 87, 88–9, 90–1; 'map of experience,' 25, 116, 155, 168; narrative patterning (shared), 92; *Nukláwt* (place of wild rhubarb, spring water), 91 (T1), 105–7; oral tradition, culture, 12, 83; parallelisms in narratives, 93, 100–1, 107; of personal experience, 13, 19, 25, 87, 96, 116; place-related topic shifting, 86; on roads, logging, old and new, 89–91; story, silent signals of attention

to, 20, 103, 116; styles (two), 136;
taped narratives, explanation
about, xxi, 91–3; temporal sequence (of events), 148–50, 155–6;
trailhead, 41, 64 (p), 88, 91, 93, 94,
95, 96, 98, 102, 103, 109; travel, conversations, 25, 83–4, 88; —, hunting
and gathering contexts, 11, 12, 25,
84, 86; *Tsecyelkw* (pithouse site), 39–
41, 40 (p), 92 (T1), 93 (T6), 114–15.
See also George, Angela; George,
Jimmy; Grice; narrative; place(s) of
the Secwepemc people; stories of
the Secwepemc people
National Archives of Canada, 27
National Environmental Policy Act
(US), 160
Native Journeys, 56
Native(s): and Crown, 4, 37, 42, 56;
and environment, 160; fur-trade
economy, 76; Gitksan and Wet'-
suwet'en land claims case, 78, 165;
Indian Rights Association of British Columbia, 29; Native land,
land-use, claims, 22, 27, 29, 37, 56,
78; Native title, 37, pre-emption of
land by, restrictions, 42. *See also*
Canadian government; First
Nations; pre-emption of land (land
claim); province of British Colum
bia; reserves
necitsmeń (hay cutting place), 182–4
(A)
Ned, Annie (Yukon Elder), xxi
New Directions, 53, 55
Newcombe, C.F., 31, 33
Nlha7kápmx, 35, 68, 118–19, 120. *See
also* Teit
Nind, Mr (letter to Colonial Secretary, 1865), 162–3

North Thompson (Upper), 29, 33, 168
Northwest Company, 33, 35, 36
Northwest Passage, 35
Nukláwt (place of wild rhubarb,
spring water), 105–7
Nuxalk People, ix, 30 (m)

O'Hanlon, Michael, 22
Okanagan, Interior Salish language,
xix, 33
Okanagan people, 29, 32 (m)
'Old-One' tales, Old-One (Chief),
118, 120
oolichan oil, ix, 29. *See also* 'grease
trail'

Pacific Ocean (Northwest coast), ix,
29, 30 (m), 35
parflŵ hea (dried hides), 101
Peace River, 209n4
pesekwekwu7 (place named for rosebush berries, rosehips), 88, 203 (A),
215n5
Peter, Susie Sampson (gʷaqʷulćaʔ), 5
pithouses (*c7istken*, winterhouses),
41, 109–14, 112 (p), 114 (p), 120,
162, 186 (A), 212n9
place: and anthropology, study of
place, 3–4, 5, 10, 12, 21, 22, 163;
Cibecue Apache culture, 19–20
21–2, 166; and cultural geographers, 22; Euro-Canadian home,
162; 'grey literature' (land claims),
22; human or built environment,
160; and language, 22, 166, 167;
'map of experience,' 25, 116, 155,
168; memories of places, 12, 88–9,
107, 166–9; Place and Space Group,
22; place-related discourse, 21–2,
26, 89, 168; place names, impor-

tance of, meaning, study of, 12, 22, 88–9, 156; Place to Story, importance of, 21–3; spatial anchoring, 21, 155, 166; toponymic density, 163. *See also* place(s), of the Secwepemc people

Place, Hillary, 207n8

place(s), of the Secwepemc people: berry-picking place (*tsecréptsen*), 91, 173 (A), 175 (A), 214n5; *Cklutetátu7s* (a place of pithouses), 41, 109–14, 112 (p), 114 (p), 186 (A), 191 (A), 212n8, 9; 'creek' (*tswec*), 173 (A), 214n2; cultural, social meaning, 26, 159, 160, 162; 'dip-netting place' (*xtsqeẃsten*), 180 (A), 214n11; Echo Mountain (*Tsexqwmeṁles*), 91, 177 (A), 178 (A), 182 (A), 183 (A), 187 (A), 214n8; a fishing place (*cyéẃmen*), 190 (A); fishing place (The Point, *tyenméṁqs*), 184–5 (A), 189–90 (A), 215n14; hay cutting place (*necitsmen*), 161, 182–4 (A); Hideout Creek (*stscelwáwtkwe*), 186 (A); homes, named, temporary, varied, 160–1, 162; lived space (homes, territory, compressed), 161, 163–4; 'junk house' (*ctsillentn*), 161; lake above fishing creeks (*Enokit*, Swan Lake), 173 (A), 214n3; 'little open,' little valley, small prairie (*spelpéplum*), 202–3 (A), 215n4; meadows, use of ('up the meadow'), 88, 161; narrative space, compressed, 26, 164; narratives of place, 162, 163, 164–5; natural environment or wilderness, 160; *Nukláẃt* (place of wild rhubarb, spring water), 105–7; pit-houses (*c7ístken*, winterhouses),

41, 109–14, 112 (p), 114 (p), 162, 186 (A), 212n9; place for rosebush berries, rosehips (*pesekwekwu7*), 88, 203 (A), 215n5; place for sweatbaths, 171 (A); The Point, trailhead, 63 (p), 64 (p); 'Poison Lake' (*ksetkwe*), 204 (A), 215n6; seasonal homes, 162; Slappin' Lake (*sṫeqwstem*), 194 (A); smokehouse (*ckecmelcw*), 161; 'spring of water' (*sṫekektkwe*), 175 (A), 214n7; toponymic density, 163; trailhead, 41, 64 (p), 88, 91, 93, 94, 95, 96, 98, 102, 103, 109; *Tsecyelkw* (pithouse site), 39–41, 40 (p), 90, 114–15; 'up the meadow,' 88, 161; *yuctkiknes* ('Where the fish goes down'), 180 (A), 181 (A). *See also* narratives from Alkali Lake; place; Secwepemc (Shuswap people)

Point, The, trailhead, 63 (p), 64 (p). See also *tyenméṁqs*

'Poison Lake' (*ksetkwe*), 204 (A), 215n6

Poundmaker's Lodge (St Albert, Alberta), 76

Powell, Colonel (Indian Commissioner), 44–5

Powell, I.W., 210n10

Powell, Jay, 8

pre-emption of land (land claim): Land Ordinance of 1870, 42; by Native people (legislation), 42; protection from, 44; by settlers, 37, 41, 42, 43, 44, 46. *See also* Douglas; Moody; Trutch

Pre-Emption Proclamation, 42

Prince George (Fort George), 35, 124

projectile points (arrowheads), 110–11, 113–14

province of British Columbia:
Apsassin v. the Queen, 163; BC Court
of Appeals, 56; BC Ministry of
Aboriginal Affairs, 56; BC Ministry
of Forests, 56; BC Treaty Commission, 56, 210n28; British colony
(1858), 36; Calder case, 163; 'Ditchburn-Clarke cutoffs,' 46; expropriation of lands by, 162; First Nations
names, 30 (m); Framework Treaty
Agreement, 56; Gitksan and Wet-
suweten Land Claims case, 78, 163,
165; gold rush, 35–6; Indian population numbers, 46, 47; Interior of,
209n4; land-claims agreements, 56;
The Minister of Forests, et al. v. Coun
cil of the Haida Nation, 56; pre-
emption of land, by BC Natives,
legislation, 42; Provincial Court of
British Columbia, 78, 80; public
schools, integration of, 50; Public
Schools Act, 50; recognition of
Secwepemc by, treaties, 27; report
on Indian reserves, 209n9; reserves
surveyed in (by 1871), 42; timber
cut-block licences, 56; treaty-
negotiation process, 56. See also
Canadian government; First
Nations; Native(s); reserves
Provincial Archives of British Columbia (PABC), 24, 27, 28, 207n5,
209nn1, 2, 3
Provincial Court of British Columbia, 78, 80
psekweku7 (place named for rosehips), 88, 203 (A), 215n5

Quesnel, 35, 36, 85, 200–1 (A)
Quintasket, Christine (Salish writer),
9. See also Mourning Dove

qyil, sweatbath (q̓ílye, 'to take a
sweatbath'), 171 (A), 214n1

Ray, Verne, 31
Regina v. Alphonse (hunting court
case), 78–82, 212n5
religion, spirituality: ancestors, relating to, 39–41, 109–14, 114–15; baptism, certificates for, dates of, 137–
8; biblical tale, Noah and his ark,
123; burial, cremation, 125, 126,
212n7; Catholics, devout, Elders
as, 49; Christ, canonical stories
about, 154–5; 'Christian,' Christian
Fundamentalism, 18; conversion
stories, 138; creation stories (Teit),
116, 119–20; dead, deaths, beliefs
about, respect for, 124–5, 126–7,
130–2, 133, 135; funerals, behaviours, preparations, 26, 123–5, 126–
7, 134, 135, 212n4; Indian Shaker
church, 18, 138; longhouse, 18;
mourning periods, activities during, restrictions of, 26, 125–6, 133,
134–5; Plains Sundance(s), 18, 141,
147, 148, 152, 155; pow-wows
(Native Indian dancing), 18, 84,
122, 141, 147, 148; priests, 18, 137–
8, 154; Roman Catholic church
(Catholicism), 10, 120; St Pierre's
Church, 43, 123; Spirit Dancing
(Seyowin), 18, 122; spiritual training of young Secwepemc men,
105; sweathouse, sacred sweatlodge, sweats, 18, 74–5, 90–1, 106,
147, 148, 149–50, 171 (A), 214n1.
See also missionaries, missions
Reservation (Man Alive series), 7
reserves: Alkali Lake Ranch, 28, 95;
Alkali Lake reserves, 28, 208n8;

Alkali Lake Reserve No. 1, xi, 38
(m), 46, 48 (m), 84, 89, 93, 114;
'Bates Estate,' 43, 210n10; Crown
lands, unreserved, 44; diminished,
restricted, 26, 76–7, 78, 163–4;
'Ditchburn-Clarke cutoffs,' 46;
Dominion policy, 42; for farming,
livestock (swamp hay), 44–5, 161;
fishing rights on, 46; and *Indian
Act* (*Act for the gradual civilization of
Indian Peoples*), 45, 48–9; Indian
reserves, as sovereign territory, 8;
livestock, surveyor's records of
(1881), 46, 210n15; map of Alkali
Lake Indian reserves, 48; Moore
(Harry) Ranch, 164–5, 182 (A), 184
(A); report of Government of British Columbia on Indian reserves,
209n9; reserve land, appropriated,
164–5; reserves surveyed in British
Columbia (by 1871), 42; re-survey
of reserves, 46, 48; size of, 41, 44–5;
sketch map of Alkali Lake Reserve
No. 1, 38; sketch map of Harper's
Lake, 46, 47 (m); Sugar Cane
Reserve, 43, 50, 53; survey of
reserves, 45, 46–8, 48 (m), 210n21.
See also Alkali Lake Indian
Reserve; Canadian government;
Douglas; First Nations; Native(s);
province of British Columbia
residential schools: Cariboo Mission,
6, 7; Durieu System, 43–4, 48, 49,
52, 210n23; and *Indian Act*, amendment to, 49; 'industrial' (boarding
school), 48, 50; Kamloops residential school, 50; loss of language,
culture, in, 48, 51; mission education, 48, 50; mistreatment of students in, 49–50; and *Public Schools*

Act (British Columbia), 50; reasons
for, 48–9; and *Revised Indian Act*,
50; separation from parents, 48–50;
sexual abuse in, 48–9, 50; St
Joseph's Mission, xix, 43, 48,
210n22; training, educative and
religious, 49. *See also* English; missionaries, missions; sexual abuse
Ridington, Robin, xviii, xx, 15, 19, 25,
82, 128, 163, 165
Rosaldo, Renato, 156
Rothenberg, Jerome, 22
Royal Engineers, 36
Royal Proclamation of 1763, 37, 42

Sahaptin culture, 168
St Joseph's Mission, xix, 43, 48,
210n22. *See also* English; residential schools
Salish: bears, tales about, 213n4;
Coast Salish, xviii, 18, 122, 138;
fieldwork in Salish territory, 105,
213n3; Interior Salish division,
xvii; Interior Salish language,
Okanagan, xix; Interior Salish peoples, stories, 9, 29, 118; interlocutors, views of Salish Elders, 17–18;
Okanagan-Colville group, 213n10;
personal autonomy, respect for, 19;
respect and prayer, 18–19; Salish
discourse, 18–19; Salish Elders
(learn how to listen), 105; Salish
Peoples, economic power, 8; Salish
writer (Christine Quintasket), 9;
Spirit Dancing (*Seyowin*), 18, 122.
See also Hilbert; Lushootseed;
Mourning Dove
Salmon People (Tsimshian mythology), 212n6
Sapir, Edward, 9, 15

Sapir-Teit Correspondence, 207n5, 208n7, 209nn2, 3

Sarris, Greg, 207n1

saskatoon berry (service berry). *See* food

s7aytsqwem (raspberries), 109, 191 (A), 201–2 (A), 215n2

Schieffelin, Edward, 156

Scollon, Ron, xviii, 19, 25, 139, 209n13

Scollon, Suzanne B.K., xviii, 19, 25, 139, 209n13

Seaburg, William R., 23

Searle, John R., 15

Secwepemc (Shuswap people): AA 'birthdays,' 137, 143; 'Alcohol Lake,' x; alcohol, use and sobriety, *see* alcohol; Alkali Lake/Esketemc Indian Reserve No. 1, x, 20; an thropological study, response to, 7–8, Bella Coola (Nuxalk People), ix, 29, 35, 37; Canadian French, understanding the language, 33; Catholicism and Northern Secwepemc, 43–4; *Cklutetátu7s* (a place of pithouses), 41, 109–14, 112 (p), 114 (p), 186 (A), 191 (A), 212nn8, 9; class stratification, social organization of, 29, 31; Cree, contact with, intermarriage with, language, influences of, 29, 33, 35, 211n4; cultural, linguistic, territorial divisions (7), maps, 31, 32 (m), 33 (m); discourse, differences by gender, 116; 'distemper' among Northern Secwepemc, 36; employment on ranches, 41, 102, 209n8; employment opportunities, 53–6, 79, 95–6; 'grease trail,' life experiences along, ix–xi, 29, 35; *The Honour of All*, 6–7, 49, 52, 137, 140, 141, 142; hunting practices, value of, 58–9, 76–82; intermarriage, outmarriage, 33, 53; Iroquois, in Shuswap territory, 33; land claims, negotiations, treaties, 24, 27, 28, 56, 210n28; map of Shuswap Territory (Palmer), 33, 34 (m); — (Teit, 1909), 31, 32 (m), 209nn4, 5; narratives of place, 115–16, 163–9; oral communications, rules of, 139; oral map, tradition, 12, 168; oral record, culture, 24, 28, 83; personal autonomy, respect for, 19, 25, 139; personal narratives, importance of, 19, 115, 136–42, 157–8; pithouse residents, 111, 186 (A), 212n8; pithouses (*c7ístken*, winterhouses), 109–14, 112 (p), 114 (p), 120, 162, 186 (A), 212n9; populations of (Teit, Mooney), 36, 208n8; protection from pre emption of land, 44; religion, spirituality, 18; *Reservation* (*Man Alive* series), 7; *Secwepemc of Esket* (Shuswap of Alkali Lake), xi; Secwepemc-European contact, early, 35–6; settlement in villages (village coalescence), xi, 24, 41–2, 44–5, 59, 161, 162; sketch map of Alkali Lake Reserve No. 1, 38; smallpox, 37, 39–41, 209n5; social organization, class stratification, 29, 31; 'status' or 'registered' Indians, 53–4; trade with others, ix, 29; Upper North Thompson Band of Shuswap, 33, 34 (m); ways of knowing, teaching, 116, 133–4. *See also* Alkali Lake (*Esket*); Alkali Lake Indian Band; English; fish-

ing; food; 'grease trail'; hunting
and trapping; medicines, treatments; narratives from Alkali
Lake; religion, spirituality;
reserves; residential schools;
Secwepemctsín (Shuswap language); sexual abuse; smallpox;
stories of the Secwepemc people
Secwepemc Cultural Society (Kamloops), 9
Secwepemc of *Esket* (Shuswap of
Alkali Lake). *See* Secwepemc
(Shuswap people)
Secwepemctsín (Shuswap language):
adults, fluency in, use, xvii, xviii,
xix, 9; children, fluency in, language classes, xix; children forbidden to speak S. at residential
schools, 49; 'Deep Shuswap,' xvii;
gender, lack of pronominal reference to, xviii; guide to pronunciation in Secwepemctsín, xxiii (f);
Interior Salish language, xvii, 8;
Nlha7kápmx language, close
linguistic relative, 68; 'speak
good Shuswap,' xix; Sxoxomic
School, xix, 9, 54. *See also* English;
transcription of tape-recorded
speech
segwsesegwt (purple bell-shaped
flowers), 191 (A)
Sekani (people), 32 (m), 209n4
sekwekwu7 (rosehips), 88, 215n5
service berry (saskatoon berry). *See*
food
sexual abuse: at Cariboo Mission
Indian residential school, 6, 7; *A
Circle of Healing* (CBC documentary), 49–50; *Reservation* (*Man Alive*
series), 7; *A Violation of Trust* (CBC

documentary), 49–50. *See also* alco-
hol; residential schools
Sherzer, Joel, 16, 100, 155
s7illen ('food'), 214n10
Shokleng myth, 154–5
Shuswap Lake Division, 31, 32 (m)
Shuswap language (Secwepemctsín),
33, 35. *See also* Secwepemctsín
Shuswap people (Secwepemc):
Shuswap territory, linguistic,
division boundaries, maps, 31, 32
(m), 33, 34 (m); Upper Thompson
Band of Shuswap, 33. *See also*
Secwepemc
Sidney, Angela (Yukon, Tlingit/
Tagish Elder), xxi, 156
Silverstein, Michael, 33, 35
Sixwi lexken (storyteller), 118, 120,
123
Slappin' Lake (*steqwstem*), 194 (A)
slexéyem ('a realistic story'), 123
smallpox: account of, by Augusta
Tappage, 37, 39; blankets spread
disease, 37, 39; at Bella Coola, ix,
29, 35, 37; Canyon band decimated, 39, 41; Cariboo epidemic
(1875), 41, 46, 210n14; *Cklutetátu7s*
(a place of pithouses), 41, 109–14,
112 (p), 114 (p), 186 (A), 191 (A),
212nn8, 9; epidemic (1862–3), 37,
41, 209n5; at Lac la Hache, 40, 41,
46, 59, 89, 127; and miners, 37, 39;
spread of, 37, 39–41; survival,
methods used for, 39, 41; *Tsecyelkw*
(pithouse site), 39–41, 40 (p), 114–
15, 170–1 (A), 171 (A); at Victoria
(1861), 37
Smith, Kitty (Yukon Elder), xxi
soapberry (soopolallie berry,
sxúsem). *See* food

sociocultural anthropology, 14
Soda Creek reserve, 29, 35, 36, 37, 42,
    43, 50, 60
Speare, Jean E. 39, 212n2
spelpéplum ('little open,' little valley,
    small prairie), 202–3 (A), 215n4
Spences Bridge, 29, 207–8n6
Spielmann, Roger: discourse analy-
    sis, 14, 15, 208n10; 'LDA' (Linguis-
    tic Discourse Analysis), 14; and
    Ojibwe discourse, analysis of con-
    versation, 14. *See also* 'discourse'
Spirit Dancing (Seyowin), 18. *See also*
    religion, spirituality
spirituality. *See* religion, spirituality
spyu7 (bird), 180 (A), 214n12
sqilye (sweatlodges), 90–1
Standard English, xix
Star Husband Story, 154
stcwelcwucwel (gooseberries), 201
    (A), 215n1
Stegtsetsulqw, stegtsetsetsulqw (Little
    Dog Creek), 91, 102–3, 185 (A)
siekektkwe, ('spring of water'), 175
    (A), 214n7
steqwstem (Slappin' Lake), 194 (A)
stseptékwll ('myth' or 'fairy tale'),
    123
Stony, 29, 32 (m)
stories of the Secwepemc people:
    animal-monster stories, 119, 212n3;
    animals, messages of death in, 133;
    bears, about, attacks by, 127–35,
    154, 213nn8, 9, 10; biblical tale,
    Noah and his ark, 123; 'brief sto-
    ries of transformation,' 120; Brown
    Bear, Grizzly Bear, 126, 133, 134,
    135; Chipmunk girl, 121, 122, 167;
    contexts, styles of stories, 134–5;
    Coyote and Grizzly Bear (Teit), 126;

Coyote tales, 118, 120, 123, 125–6,
    168; creation stories (Teit), 119–20,
    212n2; cultural, social knowledge
    in stories, 122–3, 126–7, 133–5;
    dead, deaths, in stories, 124–5,
    126–7, 130–2, 133, 135; dead per-
    son's clothing, 130, 131–2; deer
    story, 132–3; European folk/fairy
    tales, 120, 123; 'fairy tales,' 120,
    123, 154, 212n2; graveyard story
    (shoes), 130, 132, 135; Grizzly Bear
    Woman, 126, 135, 213n4; menstru-
    ation, effect, power of, 122, 125,
    130, 131, 135; mourning periods,
    125–6, 133, 134–5; narratives of
    personal experience, 134, 135;
    'Old-One' tales, Old-One Chief,
    118, 120; pothole lakes, serpents in,
    x, 124, 212n3; recording of stories,
    by George Dawson, 119, 120, 121,
    122, 212n3; —, by James A. Teit,
    118–26, 132, 134, 135; shoes
    (graveyard story), 130, 132, 135;
    Sixwi'lexken (storyteller), 118, 120,
    123; *slcxéyem* ('a realistic story'),
    123; 'speta'kuł' (myth or fairy
    tale), 118, 123; stories to make
    sense of life, 23–6, 154–5, 157, 166–
    9; stories as narratives of personal
    experience, 133, 134, 135; storytell-
    ing, in evening, winter, 120, 212n1;
    stseptékwll ('myth' or 'fairy tale'),
    123, 212n2; 'telling my (her, their)
    life,' 136, 153, 155, 157, 158, 168;
    Thunder and Mosquito story
    (Dawson), 119; *Tlee'sa and His
    Brothers*, 121–2, 132, 135, 167, 168;
    Trout-Husband story (Dawson),
    119; water people (Dawson sto-
    ries), 212n3; 'The Woman Who

Became a Grizzly Bear,' 135; 'The Woman Who Was Prisoner of the Bear,' 212n2. *See also* Johnson, David; Mourning Dove; narratives from Alkali Lake; Story; Teit

Story: *audience*, role of, 17, 136, 157; defined, 4; in context, place, 3–4, 21, 83, 155, 168; culture/knowledge sharing, 3–4, 12; Euro-Canadian storytelling style, 153; interlocutors, interrelationships and social contract between, 3, 22–3, 153, 156–7; life story(ies), 136, 155, 214n5; Place, importance of to Story, 21–3, 155–6; reformulation of, with each telling, 3, 136; repair in 'telling my life,' 157; respect for, 3–5; signals of attention to, 20, 103; spatial anchoring in, 21, 155–6; Stories, as guides, 3; talk, exchange, importance of, 3, 4; teller of story, importance of, 3; 'telling my (her, their) life,' 136, 153, 155, 157, 158, 168; temporal order of (by events), 148–50, 155–6; *See also* discourse; Hilbert; interlocutor; narrative; narratives from Alkali Lake; stories of the Secwepemc people

stscelwáwtkwe (Hideout Creek), 186 (A)

stseptékwll ('myth' or 'fairy tale'), 123, 212n2

stseqwem, saskatoons, high bush, 174 (A)

Styne Creek (Nlha7kápmx), 35

Sugar Cane Reserve, 43, 50, 53

Suttles, Wayne, 30 (m)

sweatbath (*q̓yil*), 171 (A), 214n1

sweatlodges (*sq̓ilye*), 90–1

Swicw (dried root of Yellow Avalanche Lily), 129, 213n10

Sxoxomic (Chief Sampson, Alkali Lake hereditary chief), 48

Sxoxomic School, xix, 9, 54

sxúsem (soapberry, soopollalie berry), 68, 70 (p), 71 (p), 76, 85, 86, 87, 109, 191 (A), 200 (A), 201 (A), 203 (A)

Tagish stories, xxi, 154, 156

Tappage, Augusta, 37, 39, 212n2

t̓aqʷšəblu. *See* Hilbert

Tedlock, Dennis, xx, 16, 22

Teit, James Alexander: and American Museum of Natural History, 9–10, 28; Athello (Lucy Artko), Nlha7kápmx woman, wife, 29, 209n1; on cave at Dog Creek Reserve, 104 (p), 105; estimate of Secwepemc population, 36; as ethnographer, records of, xxii, 9–10, 28–35, 58, 209n2; Indian Rights Association of British Columbia, work with, 29, 209n3; map of Shuswap Territory (1909), 31, 32 (m), 209nn4, 5; Native land claims, support of, 29; Nlha7kápmx in-laws, 29; North Pacific Expedition, 28; stories of Secwepemc, recording of, 118–26, 132, 134, 135; *Tlee'sa and His Brothers* story reported by, 121. *See also* Mourning Dove; stories of the Secwepemc people

Tennant, Paul, 37, 42

tepee. *See* tipi

Tête Jaune Cache, 33, 34 (m)

Thompson, David, 35–6

Thompson River area, 68

Timothy Mountain, 127, 155

tipi (teepee), life in, 144, 195 (A), 213n1

tkwló7se (choke cherries), 178 (A), 179 (A), 181 (A), 192 (A), 194 (A), 214n9

Tlee'sa and His Brothers, 121–2, 132, 135, 167, 168

Tlingit, 53, 154, 156

tqitqe (strawberries), 201 (A)

trailhead, 41, 64 (p), 88, 91, 93, 94, 95, 96, 98, 102, 103, 109. *See also* narratives from Alkali Lake; place(s) of the Secwepemc people

transcription of tape-recorded speech: explained, xix–xxii; practical orthography, xxii; signals of continued attention, xix–xx. *See also* Belanger; Gumperz; Hymes; Kulpurs, Ridington; Tedlock

trees, uses of, food and medicinal, 72, 73 (p), 74–5, 202 (A)

trout fishing, 59

Trudeau, Pierre Elliott, 51

Trutch, Joseph (Commissioner of Lands and Works), 42

Tsecreptsen (berry-picking place), 91, 173 (A), 175 (A), 214n5

Tsecyelkw (pithouse site), 39–41, 40 (p) 114–15, 170–1 (A), 171 (A)

tsert (falling of a tree), 202 (A), 215n3

Tsexqwmemles (Echo Mountain), 91, 177 (A), 178 (A), 183 (A), 187 (A), 214n8

Tsilhqot'in (Athapaskan people), 29, 30 (m), 31, 58, 209n5

Tsimshian mythology (Salmon People), 212n6

Tsuktsékus (part of new cut road), x, 124

tswec ('creek'), 173 (A), 214n2

Tunbridge, Dorothy, 166

Turner, Nancy J., 68, 213n10

tyenmémqs (fishing place, The Point), 184–5 (A), 189–90 (A), 215n14

Union of BC Indian Chiefs, 8, 51–2

University of Alberta, Academic Technologies for Learning (ATL), 10, 208n9

University of British Columbia (map library), 119

University of Lethbridge (Alberta), 76

Urban, Greg, 12, 16, 100, 154

US Indian Health Services (Rockport, Maryland), 76

Valentine, Lisa, xviii

Victoria (British Columbia), 37

Victoria Standard, newspaper, 44

Vowell, A.M. (Indian Superintendent), 46

'walking and talking,' 22–3, 156

Whitehead, Margaret, 43–4

white settlers, ix, 24, 27, 36, 41, 42, 44, 45

Williams Lake: Band (Chimney Creek), 42; Cariboo Tribal Council, 53; Dog Creek Road, from Alkali Lake, 89; fishing licences, 63; food, trips to Williams Lake for, 179 (A); railroad yard, cattle, 102; relations with Alkali Lake, 52, 53; School District, 54; Sr Secondary School, x; Stampede, ix; 'town,' travel to, ix, x, 10, 11, 49

Windy Mouth (IR No. 7, on Lac la Hache), 59

Wolf, Eric, 24, 28

Wright, William (pre-emption of land), 46

xtsqełsem (pit-lamp for fish), 181 (A), 215n13
xtsqełsten ('dip-netting place'), 180 (A), 214n11

Yagalahl (Dora Wilson-Kenni), 27

Yellow Avalanche Lily (*swicw* in Secwepemctsín), 67–8, 213n10. *See also* food
Yellowhead Pass, 33
Yoke, Jim, 168
yuctkiknes ('Where the fish goes down'), 180 (A), 181 (A)
Yura Ngawarla (language), 166

ANTHROPOLOGICAL HORIZONS

Editor: Michael Lambek, University of Toronto

Published to date:

1 *The Varieties of Sensory Experience: A Sourcebook in the Anthropology of the Senses*
  Edited by David Howes
2 *Arctic Homeland: Kinship, Community, and Development in Northwest Greenland*
  Mark Nuttall
3 *Knowledge and Practice in Mayotte: Local Discourses of Islam, Sorcery, and Spirit Possession*
  Michael Lambek
4 *Deathly Waters and Hungry Mountains: Agrarian Ritual and Class Formation in an Andean Town*
  Peter Gose
5 *Paradise: Class, Commuters, and Ethnicity in Rural Ontario*
  Stanley R. Barrett
6 *The Cultural World in Beowulf*
  John M. Hill
7 *Making It Their Own: Severn Ojibwe Communicative Practices*
  Lisa Philips Valentine
8 *Merchants and Shopkeepers: A Historical Anthropology of an Irish Market Town, 1200–1991*
  Philip Gulliver and Marilyn Silverman
9 *Tournaments of Value: Sociability and Hierarchy in a Yemeni Town*
  Ann Meneley
10 *Mal'uocchiu: Ambiguity, Evil Eye, and the Language of Distress*
  Sam Migliore
11 *Between History and Histories: The Production of Silences and Commemorations*
  Edited by Gerald Sider and Gavin Smith
12 *Eh, Paesan! Being Italian in Toronto*
  Nicholas DeMaria Harney
13 *Theorizing the Americanist Tradition*
  Edited by Lisa Philips Valentine and Regna Darnell
14 *Colonial 'Reformation' in the Highlands of Central Sualwesi, Indonesia, 1892–1995*
  Albert Schrauwers

15 *The Rock Where We Stand: An Ethnography of Women's Activism in Newfoundland*
Glynis George

16 *Being Alive Well: Health and the Politics of Cree Well-Being*
Naomi Adelson

17 *Irish Travellers: Racism and the Politics of Culture*
Jane Helleiner

18 *Writing and Colonization in Northern Ghana: The Encounter between the LoDagaa and the 'World on Paper,' 1892–1991*
Sean Hawkins

19 *An Irish Working Class: Explorations in Political Economy and Hegemony, 1800–1950*
Marilyn Silverman

20 *The Double Twist: From Ethnography to Morphodynamics*
Edited by Pierre Maranda

21 *Of Property and Propriety: The Role of Gender and Class in Imperialism and Nationalism*
Edited by Himani Bannerji, Shahrzad Mojab, and Judith Whitehead

22 *Guardians of the Transcendent: An Ethnography of a Jain Ascetic Community*
Anne Vallely

23 *The House of Difference: Cultural Politics and National Identity in Canada*
Eva Mackey

24 *The Hot and the Cold: Ills of Humans and Maize in Native Mexico*
Jacques M. Chevalier and Andrés Sánchez Bain

25 *Figured Worlds: Ontological Obstacles in Intercultural Relations*
Edited by John Clammer, Sylvie Poirier, and Eric Schwimmer

26 *Revenge of the Windigo: The Construction of the Mind and Mental Health of North American Aboriginal Peoples*
James B. Waldram

27 *The Cultural Politics of Markets: Economic Liberalization and Social Change in Nepal*
Katherine Neilson Rankin

28 *A World of Relationships: Itineraries, Dreams, and Events in the Australian Western Desert*
Sylvie Poirier

29 *The Politics of the Past in an Argentine Working-Class Neighbourhood*
Lindsay DuBois

30 *Youth and Identity Politics in South Africa, 1990–1994*
Sibusisiwe Nombuso Dlamini

31 *Maps of Experience: The Anchoring of Land to Story in Secwepemc Discourse*
Andie Diane Palmer

SCREAMPLAYS

Edited by
RICHARD CHIZMAR

BALLANTINE BOOKS

NEW YORK

A Del Rey® Book
Published by Ballantine Books

http://www.randomhouse.com

Library of Congress Catalog Card Number: 97-93152

ISBN: 0-345-39429-1

Cover design by David Stevenson
Cover illustration by David McKean
Interior design by Ann Gold

Manufactured in the United States of America
First Edition: September 1997
10 9 8 7 6 5 4 3 2 1

CONTENTS

INTRODUCTION
Dean Koontz   vii

GENERAL
Stephen King   1

THE LEGEND OF HELL HOUSE
Richard Matheson   41

MOONLIGHTING
Harlan Ellison   185

KILLING BERNSTEIN
Harlan Ellison   209

DEAD IN THE WEST
Joe R. Lansdale   257

TRACK DOWN
Ed Gorman   365

THE HUNTED
Richard Laymon   469

INTRODUCTION

- - - - - - - - -

BY

DEAN KOONTZ

Great Art and Muppet Hatred

Writing the first draft of a screenplay is not as enjoyable as making love or eating a big plateful of kibby with garlic-flavored yogurt sauce, but it's close behind those activities on the list of Experiences that Prove God Exists.

The screenplay format is so flexible, allowing for such easy revision, that it has a special appeal for obsessive-compulsive scene polishers like me. Totally restructuring a 100-page film script to accommodate an inspired new twist to the story is a breeze when compared to the nightmare of performing the same task with a 500-page novel.

Furthermore, a screenplay is not meant to be published and read by the public, as is a novel. One is relieved of the need to refine the prose in which one sets a scene or describes the action; only the dialogue must be spot on, while all else is written with telegraphic brevity in respect of the interpretations that will come from the director, the DP (director of photography), the set designer, the visual-effects specialists, and other creative elements in what is, after all, a collaborative medium.

Although a novelist has the luxury of going internal with his characters, the screenwriter is limited by the inherent shallowness of film and cannot reveal the thoughts of characters — short of the clunky device of a voice-over, which is long out of fashion. This presents the pleasant challenge of revealing characters *solely* through the actions they take, while freeing the writer from the complex task of directly portraying the numerous — and revealing — harmonies and contradictions between the characters' internal and external worlds.

In addition, the word count of a screenplay is but a small fraction of the word count of the average novel. Hallelujah.

As the author of a novel, even if you are treated well by 90 percent of reviewers, you can count on being savaged occasionally by a reviewer who 1) wants to be a novelist himself but can't sell his work and loathes you because you're published, or 2) is a published novelist who sent you his new script for an endorsement and didn't get one and loathes you because you either didn't have time to read his book or didn't like it, or 3) is a deranged literary stalker who has been striving to kill you with words in every publication that will allow him space for the past fifteen years, solely because he has fixated on you much as that sociopathic slasher fixated on the actress Teresa Soldana. This never happens to screenwriters because even the most famous film critics seem to be oblivious of their contribution and think that every frame was extemporaneously conceived by the auteur director and his cast. Screenwriters are often anguished about this lack of respect, but anonymity ensures against the assaults to which novelists are subjected.

And though a novelist occasionally catches reviewers in the act of criticizing a book without having read it (their fecklessness revealed when they confidently cite inaccurate plot and character details from a publisher's error-riddled press release), *no* film critic has such a short attention span that he cannot sit two hours in a dark theater before expressing his opinions.

In the course of performing his work, the screenwriter has a shot at meeting Sandra Bullock, Peter O'Toole, Winona Ryder, Gene Hackman, or even whatever wonder dog has most recently starred in a box-office-shattering canine epic. Novelists mostly sit alone in their studies.

Screenwriters can have names like Babaloo Mandel and be hugely successful. Novelists must have more serious names if they wish to sell books.

Screenwriters can look like Joe Esterhaz and be acclaimed as great talents. But novelists who look like Joe Esterhaz are under continual surveillance by state and federal police agencies.

By now you probably believe that I would exhort every aspiring young writer to focus his or her efforts entirely on the screenplay and to forgo writing novels at all costs. If this is what you think, you did not sufficiently ponder the words "first draft" in the opening sentence of this introduction, and when you read the third paragraph, you did not give the proper ironic edge to the words "collaborative medium."

The first draft is the sole effort of the screenwriter, the joyous exploration of his heart and soul, the exuberant expression of his talent. Then he gets notes from producers, directors, studio executives, and ultimately actors. The fate of the project — whether it languishes in development hell or eventually goes before the cameras — and the quality of the finished film depend on the talent, intelligence, perceptivity, sensitivity, humility, mental health, sobriety, and personal grooming habits of those who become the writer's collaborators on the second and all subsequent drafts. Because the actors, studio executives, directors, and producers are human beings — well, most of them, anyway — it is a rare project indeed that does not require the writer to be involved with at least one megalomaniac, or incoherent cokehead, or homicidal sociopath. Only one is required to wreck either a five-million-dollar art film or a hundred-million-dollar extravaganza.

Allow me a single anecdote:

After writing the first-draft screenplay based on one of my novels, I was delighted when the studio green-lighted the project, conditional only on the signing of an acceptable director. Often, the green light is also — and primarily — conditional upon the signing of a name actor for the male lead, which is much more difficult than nailing down a good director. The producers sent the script out to major talent agencies, expecting eight or nine directors to express strong interest, of which three might prove acceptable to the studio. Instead, twenty-two directors responded enthusiastically, and twelve were of sufficient caliber to excite the studio brass. Perversely, the producers rejected all the Oscar-nominated, critically acclaimed directors and all those with box-office hits to their credit, asking the studio to accept, instead, a director whose body of work included one obscure film with minor cult status and a truckload of direct-to-video shlock that made Ed Wood appear the equal of Orson Welles. More perversely still, the studio agreed.

In my first telephone conversation with this director, he was literally incoherent. His voice repeatedly slid away into a wordless mumble and strange quiet laughter — as if voices in his head were not yet urging him to kill the President of the United States but were telling him jokes. During a torturous forty-five-minute conversation, I got from him only the observation that he wanted the script "pumped up," to ensure that our project would be "the bloodiest, sexiest, craziest fucking movie ever made." As the original story involved very little blood, no sex, and a meticulously logical storyline, I grew alarmed. He told me he wanted to "emphasize the themes of incest and buggery," and when I noted that no such elements existed in the script, he said, "so we'll put them in, and then we'll emphasize the hell out of them."

Subsequently, when I phoned the producers to express my concerns about the director, they told me not to worry. "He's eccentric," they said, "but he's a genius. We know how to control his eccentricities and elicit his brilliance." They cajoled me into taking a meeting with them and the genius.

This meeting, which the director was too busy to schedule for two months, lasted more than ninety minutes. The genius excused himself to use the bathroom five times, and each time that he returned, his eyes were more blood-shot and watery than before. He was even more incoherent than he had been on the telephone months earlier. He spoke of the "incestuous, sodomizing, fascist bastards" who would be exposed and held up to scorn by this film, and he envisioned "massive gut-ripping machine entities blasting through buildings with such dramatic realism that we'll blow the heads right off the candy-ass audience."

Half an hour into the meeting, he noticed that both his shoes were untied. He gave me a baleful look and said, "Did you do that?"

I assured him that I had not been tampering with his laces.

Not twenty minutes later, noticing his untied shoes again, he leaned forward in his chair to frown down at them. "This again," he said with a weary sigh, as though plagued to distraction by trickster gremlins, but he made no effort to tie new knots.

As he was leaving, he caught sight of his loose laces once more, gave me a look of high suspicion, and said, "Okay, enough of this." Scowling, he pointed a finger at me and said, "Neither of us wants this to be a fucking Muppet movie, do we?"

"No," I assured him.

"I hate those cute, furry-assed little bastards," he said — and departed.

When the director was gone, I expected the producers to burst into laughter or, at least, to shake their heads in despair at their poor colleague's decline. Instead, they were solemnly enthusiastic about the prospects of the film.

As none of this — from the incestuous fascists to the gut-ripping machine entities to the Muppets — seemed to relate to either my novel or the script that I had based on it, I asked the producers — call them Tweedledum and Tweedledee — if they had understood anything that this pitiful man had said during the meeting. "No," Tweedledum replied, "not really. But the guy's a genius. We don't operate on his level." When I calmly suggested that a blazing genius, by virtue of his superior intelligence, should be a more effective communicator than the average Joe, not an incoherent rambler with blood-shot eyes and body odor, both producers disagreed with me. "Geniuses," said Tweedledee, "usually don't make sense to the rest of us — until we see their finished work, of course, and then we understand and we're humbled by it." And Tweedledum said, "Like Mozart or Andrew Lloyd Webber."

I decided that life was too short to work with our genius and to wait for that humbling moment, so I left the project. This infuriated Tweedledum and Tweedledee, because it was my script the studio had conditionally green-lighted, and the responsible executive would at least temporarily pull the green light if another writer came aboard. "You will," said Tweedledum, "never work in this town again." And Tweedledee said, "Worse, when this picture becomes a monument to art, you won't have a chance to be associated with it, because we'll leave your name out of the advertising."

Two years later, after numerous drafts by another writer, the project died. The director moved on to more direct-to-video shlock. The monument to art was never constructed, and the world is richer for that. I am still working in this town — and have endured numerous variations of this story.

I keep subjecting myself to this torture because the screenplay offers a supple format with enormous promise. And because, once in a while, a project goes well. As I write this, my screenplay, based on my novel *Phantoms*, is in production at Miramax/Dimension, under the guiding hand of Joe Chappelle, a talented young director. Joe has shot my script 98 percent as written. When Peter O'Toole wanted to change just one pronoun in a speech, he called me and talked about it for half an hour. The dailies and all the early assembled sequences are dazzling, even without music or special effects yet laid in, and I'm confident that Joe's cut will be terrific. I'm even willing to hope that the studio's cut, after Joe, will be respectful of my words and his vision — though nothing is certain until the day the finished film is actually released. Whatever the outcome, I've had a chance to work with people I respect, not only Peter and Joe but Bob Weinstein, one of the legendary founders of Miramax, and a great producer named Joel Soisson — instead of sitting alone in my study. Oh, yeah, and I've got a great *Phantoms* crew T-shirt.

I've no doubt that all of the novelists in this book are driven, like me, to write the first drafts of their screenplays out of the sheer love of the form. They persevere through the vicissitudes of the development process in the hope of working with a special team, like ours on *Phantoms*, that will be free of megalomaniacs, incoherent cokeheads, and homicidal sociopaths. When things go wrong, the dream is never visualized, and the script lies on a shelf, unproduced: all that passion expended and hard work done for nothing. Courage is required to risk precious time and one's heart in the writing of a screenplay when a novel is far more of a sure thing; therefore, when you read the scripts herein, I hope you'll make a special effort to visualize the stories — both those that have been produced and those that have not — on the authors' terms and, by doing so, give them a life in the theater of your mind that is as similar as possible to their creators' original intentions.

GENERAL

BY

STEPHEN KING

FADE IN:

1   *EXT. — A HOUSE — NIGHT*

It's a nice white duplex in an upper-middle-class neighborhood. The hour is late, the neighborhood quiet.

We can see curtains fluttering outward from one upstairs window, which has been partially raised. Below this window is an ivy trellis.

2   *INT. — AMANDA'S ROOM — NIGHT*

It's the room of an eight-year-old girl, not messy but definitely overstuffed with all the worldly goods a doting mommy and daddy can provide. We see a big dollhouse, a small sewing machine, a TV, a smallish stereo, etc. There are pictures of horses on some walls and teeny-bop rockers on others.

Against one wall: a birdcage on a floor stand, now covered for the night.

Against the opposite wall: a large Dolls of All Nations collection sitting on the floor with their backs against the baseboard.

CAMERA PANS ALL THIS SLOWLY, SILENTLY, and then focuses on the focus of the room: the child's canopy bed in the

(MORE)

(CONTINUED)

2   *CONTINUED:*

center. AMANDA'S bed, and she's sleeping in it, but we can only
see a lick of her hair over the pulled-up comforter. Curled up near
the foot of the bed is a large gray-black tomcat: GENERAL.

SOUND: A peculiar RIPPING, SPLINTERING NOISE — LOW.

3   *INT. — THE BIRDCAGE, CU — NIGHT*

It's covered, but the parakeet inside has heard the noise — it
CHEEPS.

4   *INT. — THE BASEBOARD OF ONE WALL — NIGHT*

This is the wall against which the Dolls of All Nations are sitting.
THE CAMERA PANS SLOWLY along them: Chinese lady, Dutch
doll in clogs, Kenyan tribeswoman, Mexican boy and girl with linked
hands — they sit there with their legs poked out in front of them,
staring into the darkness with their dead dolly eyes.

The RIPPING NOISE stops for a moment, then STARTS AGAIN,
LOUDER. One of the dolls, a Russian lady in a babushka, topples
into the lap of a rabbi doll.

In the blank space revealed by the falling Russian lady doll, we see a
crack appear in the wood. RIPPING SOUND CONTINUES as the
baseboard slowly rips itself open, revealing a gap of first an inch . . .
then two . . . then five. A very *dark* gap.

5   *INT. — THE BIRDCAGE, CU — NIGHT*

The parakeet cheeps again. The cage SHAKES A LITTLE.

6   *INT. — AMANDA'S BED — NIGHT*

RIPPING SOUND continues; PARAKEET CHEEPS AND
FLUTTERS. AMANDA stirs a little in her sleep, and that's all.
GENERAL, however, wakes up. He looks around, eyes green in the
darkness. Toward:

7   *INT. — THE BASEBOARD, GENERAL'S POV — NIGHT*

All of the dolls have been shaken up a little — they lean against
each other this way and that, as though tipsy. In the gap where the
Russian lady was sitting before she fell indecorously into the rabbi's
lap we see that hole in the baseboard. Dark. *Very.*

8   *INT. — THE MASTER BEDROOM — NIGHT*

AMANDA'S parents, HUGH and SALLY-ANN, share a big double
bed. She stirs partly awake.

>   SALLY-ANN
>   Did you hear something fall in Amanda's room?

>   HUGH
>   Huzzit. . . .

>   SALLY-ANN
>   Well, I thought I did.

>   HUGH
>   Vuzzzzz. . . .

>   SALLY-ANN
>   And Paulie was cheeping . . . did you put
>   General out?

HUGH pulls the covers up even farther, so he's completely buried.

>   SALLY-ANN
>   I don't want that cat sleeping with her. That's one
>   new wrinkle that's going to get ironed out in a
>   hurry. My mother always said cats can steal a
>   sleeping child's breath. Smother it.

>   HUGH
>   That's ridiculous. And I don't hear a thing.

SALLY-ANN'S not convinced.

>   SALLY-ANN
>   Maybe it's ridiculous. Maybe not. And I *know* I
>   heard Paulie. Be a love and check on her, Hugh?

From beneath the covers on HUGH'S side, a SNORE.

SALLY-ANN looks annoyed . . . but not quite annoyed enough to
get up and check for herself, it seems. She listens a moment longer,
then rolls over onto her side and goes back to sleep.

9   *INT. — THE PARAKEET'S CAGE, CU — NIGHT*

Silent. Paulie has gone back to sleep.

10   *INT. — AMANDA'S BED, WITH GENERAL — NIGHT*

GENERAL has not. He's wide awake, staring at:

11   *INT. — THE CRACK IN THE BASEBOARD — NIGHT*

Not just dark now. Malevolent yellow eyes with slit pupils are
staring out of the darkness between the dolls.

12   *INT. — GENERAL — NIGHT*

With a cat's limber, almost soundless grace, GENERAL leaps down
from the bed. THE CAMERA tracks him across the floor to the
jagged hole in the baseboard.

13   *INT — THE BASEBOARD, A CLOSER SHOT — NIGHT*

The glittery eyes disappear a second before GENERAL gets there.
He paws into the dark the way a cat will paw at a mouse hole
(although this hole is quite a bit bigger than your average mouse
hole). He even tries to stick his head inside. His tail is switching
angrily.

There is a fast, ugly CHITTERING SOUND from inside —
almost the sound of a mongoose. GENERAL draws back, and we
see that the paw which was inside the hole is bleeding.

Suddenly a tiny, twisted hand — almost a claw — holding a queer
little dagger licks out of the hole in the baseboard. It stabs at
GENERAL'S feet, barely missing them.

GENERAL draws back, HISSING.

14   *INT. — THE PARAKEET'S CAGE — NIGHT*

A few more CHEEPS, LOW.

15   *INT. — AMANDA, SLEEPING — NIGHT*

She stirs a little, then sleeps soundly again.

16   *INT. — BY THE BASEBOARD, WITH GENERAL — NIGHT*

He's sitting prudently away from that hole, ears laid back, tail
twitching. The hand reaches out twice more, eerily fast, stabbing at
the floor, leaving small splintery digs in the wood. The unseen

(MORE)

(CONTINUED)

16   CONTINUED:

owner of the hand — and the dagger — makes that dangerous CHITTERING SOUND.

At last it withdraws.

The GRINDING SOUND begins again. The edges of the ragged hole move toward each other a little, stop, then move a little more.

GENERAL backs off a pace, puzzled and very much on alert.

The baseboard slides suddenly closed. The hole is gone. There's not even a crack where it was. This is some sort of magic.

GENERAL sniffs at those little digs in the wood.

17   INT. — THE MASTER BEDROOM — NIGHT

Both parents sound asleep.

18   INT. — AMANDA'S ROOM, FEATURING THE BED — NIGHT

GENERAL leaps easily onto AMANDA'S bed and lies down again . . . but his green eyes sparkle watchfully.

19   INT. — THE BASEBOARD — NIGHT

Smooth and complete. No sign anything has happened, except for those tiny digs in the wood of the floor, the Russian lady's head in the rabbi's lap, and the tipsy look of the formerly neat line of dolls.

SOUND: ANGRY CHITTERING, MUFFLED.

20   EXT. — AMANDA'S HOUSE — DAY

It's a beautiful sunwashed morning on a neat-as-a-pin suburban street. Anything strange seems a million miles away from this place.

21   EXT. — THE SIDE LAWN — DAY

Here is GENERAL, creeping along on his belly in the dewy grass. His green eyes are intent on something we can't see. He stalks . . . pauses . . . and stalks again.

22   INT. — THE KITCHEN — DAY

AMANDA is at the table in the breakfast nook with a bowl of Alpha-Bits in front of her. She's watching cartoons on a portable TV. HUGH is buried in *The New York Times*.

(CONTINUED)

22   *CONTINUED:*

SALLY-ANN comes over from the stove with a plate of scrambled eggs for HUGH and another one for herself. She reaches around his newspaper with his plate and it disappears.

> HUGH (behind the *Times*)
> Thanks, Sal.

She sits down. There's something on her mind.

> SALLY-ANN (to AMANDA)
> Turn that off, honey. I want to talk to you.

> AMANDA (deep in a cartoon-induced daze)
> Hmmmm?

SALLY-ANN reaches past her and turns the TV off firmly. AMANDA looks at her. She, AMANDA, is a beautiful kid with blond hair and a delicate, vulnerable look just under the skin.

> SALLY-ANN
> You had General in with you again last night, didn't you?

> AMANDA
> Welll . . .

> SALLY-ANN
> No *welllll* about it. I scatted him out of there while you were in the shower. This time he sharpened his claws on the floor and left a bunch of marks.

> AMANDA
> But Mom —

> SALLY-ANN
> Also, he scares Paulie. Birds and cats don't get along so well, in case you never watched Sylvester and Tweetie-Bird on TV.

> AMANDA (protesting)
> General *loves* Paulie!

23   *EXT. — THE SIDE YARD, WITH GENERAL — MORNING*

It's a sparrow he's been stalking. He's on the sparrow's blind side, and as we watch, GENERAL pounces on the hapless bird.

24   INT. — THE BREAKFAST NOOK — MORNING

AMANDA is obviously distressed. HUGH has lowered his paper
and is observing his daughter with some sympathy.

SALLY-ANN
General used to stay out nights and we were all
perfectly fine. Including *you*.

AMANDA (low)
That was before I started getting the bad dreams.

HUGH
Exactly what *are* these famous bad dreams that
started last month, Mandy?

AMANDA is looking down at her cereal, dragging her spoon through
it. It's clear she's lost her appetite. Her hair mostly conceals her face.

AMANDA (lower still)
I don't know. I only know General keeps
'em away.

SALLY-ANN
Well, General goes out again as of tonight,
Amanda. We've indulged you on this one long
enough.

25   INT. — AMANDA, CLOSE — MORNING

When she looks up we see she is really, actively *scared*.

26   INT. — THE BREAKFAST NOOK WITH ALL THREE —
      MORNING

SALLY-ANN softens a little. She's not going to give in, but she does
soften a bit. Reaches across and takes her daughter's hand.

SALLY-ANN
Honey, he sheds. Your coverlet's going to have to
go to the cleaner's. He digs at things with his
claws, he knocks your dolls over —

HUGH (dryly)
Also, Nanny told your mother that cats steal kids'
breath.

(CONTINUED)

26   *CONTINUED:*

AMANDA drops her spoon into her cereal and goggles first at her
father, then at her mother, who now looks a bit discomfited.

> AMANDA (giggling)
> Why would General steal *my* breath when he has
> his own?

HUGH either does not see or chooses to ignore the *extremely* dirty
look SALLY-ANN throws his way. Instead, he falls into a burlesque
accent that suggests "Nanny's" Russian or Polish ancestry.

> HUGH
> You haf to put *all* ennimals out in da night,
> Aminda! Erspecielly da *ket* ennimals! Or dey
> climb up on your chest in de night end such your
> breat oud . . . *like dis* . . . !

He has come over the table more and more toward his giggling
daughter, all the time waggling his eyebrows up and down and
scrunching up his face. Now, his face close to hers, he *sucks:*
WHOOOOOSH-GULP! AMANDA collapses into helpless giggles.

> SALLY-ANN (coldly)
> Well now, Hugh. That was very, very helpful.

She gets up and begins to rattle her dishes together, although she
hasn't eaten a thing.

> HUGH
> Aw, honey, sit down and eat.

> SALLY-ANN
> Jokes about my mother's accent at breakfast have
> a way of killing my appetite. Sorry.

AMANDA has stopped laughing and is looking at her mom,
concerned and unhappy. SALLY-ANN turns toward her, dishes in
her hands.

> SALLY-ANN
> Your father can joke about Nanny all he likes, but
> General is *not* going to spend his nights in your
> room, Amanda. And that is *it*.

(CONTINUED)

26   *CONTINUED: —2*

She crosses to the sink and puts her dishes down on the counter. She looks out the window and glimpses something. She draws the curtains back to see better.

27   *EXT. — THE SIDE LAWN, SALLY-ANN'S POV — MORNING*

GENERAL trots by with the dead sparrow in his mouth.

28   *INT. — SALLY-ANN AT THE COUNTER — MORNING*

Well, that's it; everybody out of the pool. This lady is *never* going to change her mind.

AMANDA runs to her, hugs her.

> AMANDA
> I'm sorry we laughed at Nanny, Mom. But can't General —

> SALLY-ANN
> Uh-uh, honey. Subject's closed. No more coaxing, Bus in fifteen minutes.

She gives AMANDA a gentle pat on the butt to get her started, and AMANDA leaves the room with one final, troubled glance over her shoulder.

As she leaves, HUGH joins SALLY-ANN at the counter.

> HUGH
> For what it's worth, I'm sorry, too. I guess I overcranked.

> SALLY-ANN
> Well, I guess you did.

> HUGH
> Forgiven?

> SALLY-ANN (kisses his cheek)
> Well . . . probation.

> HUGH
> I'll see the damn cat's put out, if it's what you
> (MORE)

(CONTINUED)

28   *CONTINUED:*

              really want . . . but for the record, babe, they
              don't steal breath.

SALLY-ANN glances toward the window.

                          SALLY-ANN
              Maybe they don't . . . but they kill birds.

29   *INT./EXT. — THE FRONT LAWN, THROUGH AMANDA'S*
      WINDOW — MORNING

      A school bus pulls up. AMANDA runs across the lawn toward it, her
      school dress billowing, and gets on board. The bus pulls out.

      SOUND: That LOW, UGLY CHITTERING NOISE.

30   *EXT. — THE SCHOOL BUS, FROM BEHIND — DAY*

      It rolls down the street to the corner.

31   *EXT. — GENERAL, ON THE SIDE LAWN — DAY*

      He stands watching the bus go, his green eyes alert.

      The dead bird is between his paws.

32   *INT. — PAULIE'S CAGE IN AMANDA'S ROOM — DAY*

      The cover is off now and we can see inside. PAULIE is your
      average parakeet, now drowsing on his perch.

      SOUND: That LOW, UGLY CHITTERING SOUND.

      PAULIE doesn't like it. He starts flying around in his cage,
      cheeping his agitation.

33   *INT. — THE BASEBOARD WITH THE DOLLS — DAY*

      CHITTERING SOUND CONTINUES.

      Slowly, the Russian lady doll falls back into the rabbi's lap.

34   *INT. — PAULIE'S CAGE — DAY*

      He's flying wildly around in his cage; that noise is driving him crazy
      with fear.

                                              (CONTINUED)

34   *CONTINUED:*

                                                                    DISSOLVE TO:

35   *EXT. — AMANDA'S HOUSE — NIGHT*

It's not terribly late. There are still plenty of lights on in the house.

                              HUGH (voice, faint)
                          Time to brush your teeth, Mandy!

The front door opens and SALLY-ANN deposits GENERAL on
the front step . . . none too gently either. The door slams shut.
GENERAL, freshly cast out of Eden, stands there on the step for a
moment, tip of his tail switching. Then he moves off into the dark.

36   *INT. — THE UPSTAIRS BATHROOM — NIGHT*

AMANDA, wearing fuzzy pink pajamas, is brushing her teeth. She
is an extremely dejected kid tonight.

                                  AMANDA
                      Mommy, may I *please* have General sleep with
                      me tonight?

                              SALLY-ANN (brisk)
                      No. Be sure to get the back ones, honey. That's
                      where most of the food builds up.

                               AMANDA (low)
                                 Okay, I will.

She drops her eyes and goes on brushing her teeth, obviously trying
for the back ones. Before she drops her gaze, we see she is very
near tears. SALLY-ANN sees it too, and looks troubled.

37   *INT. — AMANDA'S BEDROOM — NIGHT*

She's tucked in. HUGH is sitting beside her on the bed. The room
is deep with shadows. We can see the Dolls of All Nations ranged
against the wall; someone has set that Russian hussy back up again.
The window is open a bit, as on the previous night; the curtains
flutter outward. PAULIE'S cage is covered. Everything is as it was
when we first peeked into AMANDA'S room . . . with one obvious
exception. GENERAL is gone.

                                                              (CONTINUED)

37   *CONTINUED:*

> HUGH
>
> It might be easier to get General back in the
> house if you could tell me what your bad dreams
> were about.

> AMANDA
>
> I can only remember that there's a monster. Like
> in that story you read me about the bridge.

> HUGH
> Billy Goat's Gruff?

> AMANDA
>
> Yes, that one! Only this one lives in the wall!
> *My* wall!

> HUGH
> Listen, Mandy —

She sits up, scared, urgent, pretty, pleading, charming.

> AMANDA
>
> Can't General *please* come back inside? Sleep
> with me? I'll buy him a cat bed out of my
> allowance so he won't get his hairs on the bed!

She really is crying now. HUGH gently brushes her hair off her
forehead.

> HUGH
>
> You know what your mom can be like when she
> gets an idea in her head.

> AMANDA
>
> Yeah, I know. Like brushing your back teeth. And
> cats stealing kids' breath.

She starts wiping her eyes on the sheet. Amused, HUGH hands her
his handkerchief.

> HUGH
> Making fun of Nanny's accent at the breakfast
> (MORE)

                                                        (CONTINUED)

37   *CONTINUED: —2*

>   table this morning wasn't exactly the best way to
>   start. I might be able to talk your mom around —
>   no promises, but maybe. I —

She gives him a fierce hug and a resounding kiss.

>   AMANDA
>   Thank you, Daddy!

>   HUGH
>   No promises, remember.

>   AMANDA (lies down)
>   No promises.

He goes to the doorway and then looks back at her.

>   HUGH
>   You know it's just a dream you have sometimes,
>   don't you, Mandy?

>   AMANDA
>   I guess I do . . . but in the dreams it sure seems real.
>   (Pause)
>   Mom doesn't like General, does she?

>   HUGH
>   Mom likes General just fine, babe. Now go to
>   sleep . . . no bad dreams.

He blows her a kiss and gently closes the door.

38   *INT. — AMANDA, IN BED — NIGHT*

Just lying there, alone and frightened. She looks up for awhile, then
looks left, toward:

39   *INT. — THE DOLLS, AMANDA'S POV — NIGHT*

They stare at THE CAMERA — at AMANDA — with their dead
dolly eyes.

40   *INT. — AMANDA — NIGHT*

She turns hurriedly over onto her other side, to the right, so she
>   (MORE)

                                                        (CONTINUED)

40   *CONTINUED:*

doesn't have to look at those spooky dolls. She closes her eyes; on her face is a resolute I'm-making-the-best-of-it expression.

41   *INT. — THE DOLLS AGAINST THE BASEBOARD — NIGHT*

Very faintly, that CHITTERING SOUND comes, and some of the dolls (the Russian lady, the rabbi, the Mexican children) tremble.

42   *INT. — AMANDA, IN BED — NIGHT*

Some time has passed, and AMANDA is fast asleep.

43   *EXT. — THE FRONT DOOR — NIGHT*

GENERAL trots up onto the stoop. He paws lightly at the closed door, as if puzzled that he can't get in . . . or this is, perhaps, concern. He paws at the door again and then *waows*, LOW. He turns reluctantly away.

44   *INT. — THE MASTER BEDROOM — NIGHT*

The lights are off, HUGH and SALLY-ANN are in bed, but both are still awake.

>   HUGH
>   She was crying when I kissed her good-night.

>   SALLY-ANN (sighs)
>   Cheer me up.

>   HUGH
>   Maybe we'll talk about this again tomorrow, what
>   do you think?

>   SALLY-ANN
>   Well — maybe we will. But I don't trust that cat,
>   Hugh. Not a bit.

She rolls to one side; HUGH to the other.

45   *INT. — AMANDA'S ROOM — NIGHT*

SOUND: The baseboard ripping open.

46   INT. — THE DOLLS RANGED ALONG THE BASEBOARD —
      NIGHT

They jiggle against each other and the Russian lady falls aside as
before. The baseboard rips open in a wide, jagged hole.

CHITTERING SOUND.

For a moment nothing more happens; then THE CREATURE
comes out. Exactly what is it? A gremlin or an elf of some sort, I
suppose. The director and the special effects guy will make him
look the way he should look. He's about five inches high, humanoid,
and wearing a breechclout or a loincloth. He has yellow eyes and an
ugly expression — but it's not a stupid expression, oh no.

He's carrying that strange crooked knife in one hand.

He turns toward the dolls, grins, and suddenly slashes the Russian
lady so that her stuffing bleeds out across her stomach. He cocks his
head and grins. He CHITTERS. This might be laughter. Yeah, he
sounds like he's laughing. This is one very mean little being.

With incredible speed, THE CREATURE lopes across the floor to
the foot of AMANDA'S bed; THE CAMERA TRACKS HIM.

SOUND: PAULIE chittering.

THE CREATURE'S head snaps around with the speed of a striking
panther; it bares its teeth in an ugly grin.

47   INT. — PAULIE'S CAGE — NIGHT

It's covered but shaking a bit. PAULIE senses him, and the bird is
extremely upset. We may actually see the cover billow out a bit
where PAULIE strikes it in his swoops.

48   INT.   AT THE FOOT OF AMANDA'S BED, WITH THE
      CREATURE — NIGHT

It sticks its knife between its teeth like a pirate and climbs up onto
the bed, using the draped folds of the coverlet like a rope.

PAULIE'S CHEEPS are LOUDER. And now AMANDA MOANS.

THE CREATURE snaps its head around toward:

49   INT. — AMANDA, THE CREATURE'S POV — NIGHT

She's stirring, restless. PAULIE'S racket, we may assume.

50   *INT. — THE CREATURE — NIGHT*

For a moment it looks unsure. Then it slides down the bedspread to the floor. There is a tiny THUMP as its bare feet strike the wood.

51   *INT. — AMANDA'S BEDROOM, A WIDER SHOT — NIGHT*

THE CREATURE runs back across the floor, this time to the base of the birdcage. It stands there for a moment, looking up, then puts its knife between its teeth again and begins shinning up the wooden pole, using its fingernails and toenails to dig in like a telephone lineman.

52   *EXT. — THE SIDE LAWN, WITH GENERAL — NIGHT*

The cat looks agitated. It crosses the grass to the foot of the ivy trellis and looks up at:

53   *EXT. — AMANDA'S WINDOW, GENERAL'S POV — NIGHT*

This is, of course, an extreme up-angle, making AMANDA'S window look as high as Everest. Nonetheless, we can see the blowing curtains.

54   *EXT. — GENERAL, AT THE FOOT OF THE TRELLIS — NIGHT*

He *miaows*, almost surely upset.

55   *INT. — THE CREATURE AND PAULIE'S CAGE — NIGHT*

THE CREATURE reaches the bottom edge of the cage and hauls itself up. It lifts the cover and wriggles between the bars of the birdcage; it looks grotesquely like a little boy wriggling his way under the hem of a circus tent to steal a peek at the show.

The cover falls back into place.

56   *INT. — THE CREATURE, ECU — NIGHT*

It grins, revealing horrible fanged teeth in its pasty little face. The knife is back in its hand.

57   *INT. — PAULIE, CREATURE'S POV — NIGHT*

The poor little parakeet is flying around in a frenzy.

58   *INT. — THE CAGE — NIGHT*

We hear PAULIE. We see the cage moving with the force of his frenzied lunges.

(CONTINUED)

58   CONTINUED:

There's that CHITTERING SOUND . . . then a THUD that might
be THE CREATURE'S knife going home; then a CRUNCH that
might be small avian bones breaking.

Silence. And the cage stops moving. THE CAMERA HOLDS ON
THIS for a moment.

59   INT. — THE BOTTOM LIP OF THE CAGE, CLOSE — NIGHT

One small drop of blood slips out from beneath the cover and
glistens.

60   EXT. — THE IVY TRELLIS — NIGHT

GENERAL is climbing up.

61   INT. — THE POLE OF THE BIRDCAGE — NIGHT

THE CREATURE is coming down again. It is holding the knife in
its teeth. The blade gleams with blood.

It reaches the circular foot, takes the knife, and runs across to the
foot of the bed again; THE CAMERA FOLLOWS. It pauses for a
moment, CHITTERING with what might be triumph. Then it
climbs up.

62   INT. — AMANDA, CLOSE — NIGHT

Sleeping peacefully.

63   INT. — THE FOOT OF AMANDA'S BED — NIGHT

THE CREATURE'S face appears at the foot of the bed, a
grimacing bad dream come to life with the bloody knife in its teeth.

When it is safe on the bed, it takes the knife from its mouth and
slides it into its breechclout. It CHITTERS — a triumphant sound.
It starts forward. THE CAMERA FOLLOWS as it runs along the
shape of AMANDA'S body like a man running along the top of a
sand dune.

As it reaches her chest, it stops and squats down. It grins, cocks its
head as if listening, and then leans forward toward her face. Our
entire audience may not get this, but the hipper ones will catch the
drift: *Cats* may not steal breath, but *this* thing apparently *does*.

(CONTINUED)

63   *CONTINUED:*

       SOUND: A cat's growl of anger.

       THE CREATURE looks up, alarmed, toward:

64   *INT. — AMANDA'S WINDOW — NIGHT*

       GENERAL is crouched on the sill, eyes glowing a bright green, tail
       switching. He growls again — a low, warning sound.

65   *INT. — AMANDA'S BED, WITH THE CREATURE — NIGHT*

       It's alarmed — this wasn't supposed to happen. It bares its teeth
       and draws its knife. CHITTERS at the cat.

66   *INT. — AMANDA'S WINDOW, WITH GENERAL — NIGHT*

       GENERAL hisses — a sound like a radiator in overdrive — and
       leaps down.

67   *INT. — THE FOOT OF AMANDA'S BED — NIGHT*

       THE CREATURE comes sliding down, knife in mouth. The
       minute its ugly, long-nailed feet hit the floor it takes the knife out of
       its mouth and starts running for its hole.

68   *INT. — THE MIDDLE OF AMANDA'S ROOM, FLOOR
       LEVEL — NIGHT*

       This is the fight between GENERAL and THE CREATURE.
       Again, Faithful Director and Clever Special Effects Genius will
       decide the specifics, based on what they can do (and what the
       budget will allow). For these reasons, I have not even tried to break
       the action down into shots, but it should go something like this:

       The cat and the elf-thing meet somewhere near the Dolls of All
       Nations — GENERAL has succeeded in cutting THE
       CREATURE off from its hole, but not by a whole lot.

       GENERAL bats out at it with his paw, claws out, and knocks THE
       CREATURE sprawling. It comes to its feet, furious. It's bleeding
       from a number of slashes; its blood is green.

       It gestures at GENERAL with the knife — "Come on, then!"

       GENERAL feints. THE CREATURE slashes at him and misses.
                                    (MORE)
                                                            (CONTINUED)

68   CONTINUED:

The knife digs into the wood of the floor, pulling up a big splinter; something else for SALLY-ANN to moan about in the morning.

GENERAL swipes at THE CREATURE while it tries to pull its knife from the wood. THE CREATURE pulls back, CHITTERING. GENERAL misses; if he had gotten THE CREATURE that time, his claws probably would have taken the little beastie's head off.

The two of them circle, each looking for an opening. THE CREATURE is panting.

It cuts its eyes to one side and sees its hole, temptingly close. THE CREATURE breaks for it, and GENERAL rips his claws down THE CREATURE'S back, sending it sprawling again.

It's up in a moment, and whirls as GENERAL pounces on it.

69   *INT. — GENERAL AND THE CREATURE, CLOSE — NIGHT*

THE CREATURE stabs GENERAL in one shoulder — and then *bites*.

70   *INT. — GENERAL AND THE CREATURE, A WIDER SHOT — NIGHT*

HISSING AND SPITTING, GENERAL pulls away. The knife is hanging out of GENERAL'S shoulder. There's cat fur in THE CREATURE'S mouth.

In backing up, GENERAL strikes the post of PAULIE'S cage. The cage rocks. The knife drops out of GENERAL'S shoulder.

71   *INT. — THE CAGE — NIGHT*

It overbalances and falls with A TREMENDOUS CRASH.

72   *INT. — THE MASTER BEDROOM — NIGHT*

SALLY-ANN sits up with a gasp while HUGH is still coming soupily awake beside her.

                          SALLY-ANN
                    What was *that*?

But HUGH, soupy or not, is already swinging out of bed.
                                        (CONTINUED)

72   *CONTINUED:*

                                HUGH
                            Mandy's room.

73   *INT. — AMANDA'S BED — NIGHT*

          She sits up and looks around, still more asleep than awake.

                                AMANDA
                            General? That you?

74   *INT. — THE FLOOR, WITH THE CREATURE AND*
          GENERAL — NIGHT

          THE CREATURE runs for the hole in the baseboard again.
          GENERAL has been knocked asprawl by the falling birdcage, but
          he gives chase quickly nonetheless.

          This time he's a little too slow. THE CREATURE darts into its den.
          GENERAL tries to follow, but he's alerted by that wooden
          GRINDING SOUND and draws back in a hurry. We see he's
          bleeding quite freely from one shoulder.

          The wood slides together; THE CREATURE'S hole disappears.
          Nothing there now except the hole in the line of dolls where the
          Russian lady has once more fallen over.

75   *INT. — AMANDA, SITTING UP IN BED — NIGHT*

                                AMANDA
                        General, what are you doing in h —

          Her eyes fix on something else and widen, dismayed.

                                AMANDA
                                Paulie!

          She's out of bed in a flash.

76   *INT. — THE HALLWAY DOOR OF AMANDA'S ROOM — NIGHT*

          It opens, and there's HUGH, in his robe and pajamas. SALLY-ANN
          is behind him.

                                HUGH
                                Mandy?

                                            (CONTINUED)

76   CONTINUED:

                              SALLY-ANN
                         Honey? Are you — ?

                    AMANDA (voice, screaming)
                         Paulie! *Paulie!*

They run in, fast.

77   *INT. — AMANDA — NIGHT*

She's on the floor by the overturned birdcage. The cover has
either come partway off when the cage fell over or she has pulled
it up. Either way, the results are the same: AMANDA has seen
PAULIE'S remains, and she is sobbing hard.

HUGH and SALLY-ANN arrive.

                              SALLY-ANN
                         What happened?

                         AMANDA (sobbing)
             Paulie's dead! The monster in my wall killed Paulie!

HUGH bends down.

78   *INT. — PAULIE'S CAGE, HUGH'S POV — NIGHT*

The cover is still partly on and we can't see too much, but we can
see enough. Uck! Parakeet pizza.

79   *INT. — AMANDA, HUGH, SALLY-ANN — NIGHT*

There's distaste on the faces of the grown-ups; AMANDA is grief-
stricken.

HUGH holds the girl against his chest, getting her eye off
PAULIE'S remains. SALLY-ANN looks toward:

80   *INT. — THE PARTLY OPENED WINDOW — NIGHT*

81   *INT. — SALLY-ANN — NIGHT*

She goes to the window and looks down at:

82   *INT. — THE WINDOWSILL, SALLY-ANN'S POV — NIGHT*

There's blood there, and in some of it there are clear tracks. Cat
tracks.

83   *INT. — AMANDA, HUGH, SALLY-ANN — NIGHT*

SALLY-ANN slams the window down almost hard enough to break
the glass.

> SALLY-ANN (returning)
> There was a monster in here, all right. His name
> was General.

> AMANDA (shocked)
> Mommy! *No!* Not General!

AMANDA gasps, then begins to cry again.

> HUGH
> Get control of your tongue, Sally.

> SALLY-ANN
> I'm upset! I put the damned cat out and it
> crawled up that trellis and —

> HUGH
> I don't care how upset you are. Get control of
> your tongue.

> SALLY-ANN
> Don't tell me what —

> AMANDA (hysterically)
> *Stop it, both of you! Stop it!*

They have the good grace to look ashamed of their bickering, and
they try, as best they can, to comfort their weeping daughter.

84   *EXT. — THE BACK STOOP — MORNING*

SOUND: The school bus.

To the right of the stoop are two covered garbage cans.

The inner door to the kitchen is open; we hear HUGH and SALLY-
ANN through the screen.

> SALLY-ANN (voice)
> Okay, there's the bus. She's gone. Now get rid
> of it.

(CONTINUED)

84   CONTINUED:

> HUGH (voice)
> She's pretty convinced General didn't do it,
> babe.

GENERAL, the subject of this conversation, comes up on the back
porch and sits there silently, washing his feet. We can almost
believe he's listening to all of this.

> SALLY-ANN (voice)
> Yes, I know. *She's* convinced it was a troll that got
> tired of living under a bridge and came to live in
> her wall instead. But *she's* eight and you're thirty-
> eight and the fucking cat's tracks were on her
> windowsill. In Paulie's blood. Are you going to
> get rid of the bird, or am I?

> HUGH (voice)
> I'll do it.

Now the back door opens and HUGH comes out with a wrapped
newspaper package in one hand that must surely contain the
unfortunate PAULIE.

85   INT. — THE KITCHEN, WITH SALLY-ANN — MORNING

She's grim and distraught.

> SALLY-ANN (low)
> First the bird, then the goddam cat.

86   EXT. — ON THE BACK STOOP, WITH HUGH AND
          GENERAL — MORNING

HUGH looks at GENERAL, then drops the bird into the trash.

> HUGH
> Well, there he goes, Killer. I would have saved
> what was left, but I know how picky you are
> about leftovers.

GENERAL *miaows*. HUGH starts to turn away, then sees
something and does a double take. He squats and picks the
cat up.

87 *EXT. — GENERAL, IN HUGH'S HANDS, HUGH'S POV —
MORNING*

There is a small, clotted wound in GENERAL'S shoulder,
surrounded by flecks of dried blood. We see HUGH'S fingers
gently parting the fur to get a better look at the small slash.

88 *EXT. — THE BACK STOOP, WITH HUGH AND GENERAL —
MORNING*

He puts the cat down and stands up, frowning. After a moment he
goes inside.

89 *INT. — THE KITCHEN — MORNING*

> HUGH
> You know, it's just possible that General *didn't* do
> it, Sal. He's got a bloody place on one shoulder.

SALLY-ANN is doing dishes. She doesn't look around. Her mind is
made up.

> SALLY-ANN (snaps)
> So what?

> HUGH
> Well . . . I don't know . . .

> SALLY-ANN
> Paulie got one hit in before the cat killed him.
> Good for Paulie.

> HUGH
> Doesn't look like a peck. Looks like a slash.

> SALLY-ANN
> Crap.

HUGH has gone to the kitchen table and is drinking the last of his
coffee standing up. Now he looks toward her thoughtfully.

> HUGH
> Amanda said the other night that you didn't like
> General. I said you liked him fine. But I think she
> was closer on that one than I was.

(CONTINUED)

89   CONTINUED.

SALLY-ANN
You better hurry up. You'll be late for work.

He looks at her for a moment longer, but she doesn't look at him;
she doesn't want to discuss this.

90   INT./EXT. — THE DRIVEWAY — MORNING

We're looking out the living room window as HUGH backs his small
car down the driveway and into the street. He starts off to work.

91   INT. — THE LIVING ROOM, WITH SALLY-ANN — MORNING

She's been watching him go. Now she moves toward the kitchen.
Her face is purposeful . . . actually, rather grim.

92   INT. — THE KITCHEN COUNTER, WITH A PET DISH —
          MORNING

The dish is red plastic, and heaped with food — not just your
ordinary cat food either; a can of Three Diamonds Tuna stands
nearby. On the side of the dish, in yellow letters: GENERAL.

SOUND: Miaow!

93   INT./EXT. — GENERAL, ON THE BACK STOOP — MORNING

He's outside the screen, drawn by the smell of food.

94   INT. — THE KITCHEN — MORNING

We're looking toward an open pantry door. After a moment,
SALLY-ANN comes out. She's got a cat carrier in one hand, the
sort with a swinging door on the front.

She puts the cat carrier on the counter, opens the door, and places
the dish of tuna inside. She tosses the can in the trash and then puts
the cat carrier — now a baited trap — on the floor.

She crosses to the screen door and opens it. GENERAL doesn't
come right in; he sits on the stoop, tail twitching. What we see in his
green eyes might be distrust.

SALLY-ANN
Come on, stupid. Food. Not just your ordinary
(MORE)

(CONTINUED)

94   *CONTINUED:*

                  run-of-the-mill Calo either. We are talking big
                  time this morning.

95   *INT. — THE CAT CARRIER, GENERAL'S POV — MORNING*

       This is, of course, an extremely low angle — we see only SALLY-
ANN'S feet, and the open door of the carrier.

96   *INT. — SALLY-ANN AND GENERAL, AT THE SCREEN
DOOR — MORNING*

                      SALLY-ANN (exasperated)
                    Come *on*, you stupid thing!

GENERAL doesn't move.

SALLY-ANN starts to swing the screen door closed, very slowly.

                      SALLY-ANN
                    Going once . . .

GENERAL doesn't move. She swings the door farther and farther
closed.

                      SALLY-ANN
                    Going *twice* . . .

There's something very smelly about this. GENERAL knows it —
senses it, anyway — but he can no longer withstand the temptation.
He scoots through the closing door and trots across the linoleum
toward the cat carrier. He hesitates for a moment, then goes inside
and starts to eat.

97   *INT. — SALLY-ANN — MORNING*

       This is a basically nice woman, but in her triumph she looks rather
mean and ugly. She closes the cat carrier door and latches it tight.

                      SALLY-ANN
           There. Your bird-killing days are done, my friend.

98   *INT. — GENERAL, CU — MORNING*

       He turns and comes to the wires crisscrossing the front of the
carrier — he looks like a con in the pets' version of Attica. He
miaows.

99 *EXT. — A DOWNTOWN STREET — MORNING*

SALLY-ANN, driving the family station wagon, pulls up in front of a functional cinder block building. She gets out and goes around to the passenger side. She removes the cat carrier and starts up the walk to the door.

CAMERA PANS LEFT and we see a sign: CITY ANIMAL SHELTER.

100 *EXT. — AMANDA'S HOUSE — EVENING*

AMANDA (voice)
General! . . . General! . . . General!

101 *EXT. — THE BACK STOOP, WITH AMANDA — EVENING*

She's in her pajamas and is obviously upset.

AMANDA
General!

102 *EXT. — THE BACKYARD, AMANDA'S POV — NIGHT*

Nothing. Of course.

103 *EXT. — THE STOOP, WITH AMANDA — NIGHT*

SALLY-ANN (voice)
Hey, babe! Bedtime!

AMANDA
In a minute, Mom!

104 *EXT. — AMANDA, A REVERSE ANGLE — NIGHT*

She goes into the kitchen, and through the screen we see her unplug the can opener on the counter and bring it outside. There's a plug to the left of the stoop door, the kind with a cap to keep the rain out.

AMANDA squats down, lifts the cap, and plugs the can opener in. She holds it up and runs it on thin air, her face hopeful. After all, if there is a siren song for cats, it's the sound of an electric can opener.

105 *EXT. — THE YARD, AMANDA'S POV — NIGHT*

Nothing. Of course.

106   EXT. — THE BACK STOOP, WITH AMANDA — NIGHT

Little by little the hope goes out of her face.

SALLY-ANN comes to the screen door and opens it.

> SALLY-ANN (gentle)
> Come on, babe. Bedtime.

> AMANDA
> But *I* want General! I want to say good-night to
> him even if he can't come to bed with me!

> SALLY-ANN
> Well . . . he's probably off visiting his girlfriends,
> or something.

AMANDA slowly comes in, carrying the can opener.

107   INT. — THE KITCHEN — NIGHT

AMANDA takes the can opener back to the counter, puts it down,
and plugs it in.

> AMANDA
> What if he went away because you thought he
> killed Paulie?

> SALLY-ANN
> Mandy, cats don't *think*!

> AMANDA
> General does. And he knows you don't like him.
> He knows you think cats steal breath from kids
> even though they have their own. You know what
> I think? I think the monster in my wall killed
> Paulie just to get General in Dutch!

108   INT. — A KENNEL AT THE ANIMAL SHELTER — NIGHT

This is a dingy, unpleasant place. We're looking down a narrow
corridor lined with cages stacked three and four high. Dogs BARK,
cats YOWL. The place is crazy with noise.

An attendant is rolling a cart along this aisle. On the cart is a bag of
meal with a scoop in it. He opens cage after cage, takes out dishes,
fills them from the scoop, and puts them back in.

(CONTINUED)

108   CONTINUED:

Every now and then he consults a clipboard that swings from his cart, and several times he puts a red card on one of the cages.

He stops near the end of the row and takes his clipboard again.

109   INT. — THE ATTENDANT, CLOSER — NIGHT

ATTENDANT
Tomorrow's your big day, fella.

He removes a red card from his breast pocket.

110   INT. — THE CAGE, CLOSE-UP — NIGHT

The ATTENDANT'S hand slides the card into the grooves on the front of the cage. It reads: TERMINATION REQUESTED BY OWNER, FEE PAID. Below this: PET'S NAME: GENERAL.

CAMERA PANS DOWN to GENERAL, inside the cage. He appears to be sleeping.

111   INT. — THE ATTENDANT, AT GENERAL'S CAGE — NIGHT

He opens the cage to feed GENERAL . . . and GENERAL *springs* at him.

ATTENDANT (startled)
Hey!

For a moment there's a confusion of cat and man. The ATTENDANT is scratched. Then GENERAL hits the floor and runs around the far end of the aisle.

ATTENDANT
Billy! Hey, Billy!

112   INT. — ANOTHER CORRIDOR — NIGHT

This one is lined with cages on the left, cinder block on the right. At the end of it, a door stands open. There's an office beyond. We see the corner of a desk, and feet cocked up on it.

GENERAL goes streaking down this corridor and through the door.

113   INT. — THE OFFICE — NIGHT

The office is messy and rather sleazy; the walls are covered with
posters that deal with animal diseases and parasites, vaccinations,
rules, and regs. Messy and sleazy also pretty well describe BILLY,
who is behind the desk with his feet up. He's dressed in grungy
whites, and is reading a paperback porno novel. The cover shows a
scantily dressed woman with a French Poodle at her feet. Title:
Carla's Best Friend.

The door is standing open.

> ATTENDANT (voice)
> *Billy! Hey, Billy!*

BILLY puts his feet down and looks in the direction of the voice
just as GENERAL comes streaking through the office. He's out the
door in a flash.

> ATTENDANT (panting, cross)
> Goddamnit, Billy, that door isn't *ever* supposed to
> be open!

> BILLY (pretty vacant)
> Well . . . it was hot.

> ATTENDANT
> Goddamn. It's like he knew we were gonna give
> him the gas tomorrow. Close the door, Billy.

> BILLY
> Oh, yeah.

He starts for the door.

> ATTENDANT
> And give me my book.

He snatches it.

114   INT. — AMANDA'S BEDROOM — NIGHT

AMANDA is in bed. HUGH sits beside her. AMANDA is quite
sleepy, but she is also a very unhappy girl tonight. Her face is puffy,
her eyes red.

(CONTINUED)

114   *CONTINUED:*

> AMANDA
> Daddy, are you sure General's all right?

> HUGH (easily)
> Sure I'm sure, hon. Just out visiting his
> girlfriends.

> AMANDA
> Like Garfield.

> HUGH
> Yes! Like Garfield.

> AMANDA
> I'm scared, Daddy.

She rolls over onto her side, away from him. HUGH looks at her,
concerned.

> HUGH
> Amanda?
> (Pause)
> Mandy?

He leans over.

115   *INT. — AMANDA, CLOSE — NIGHT*

Her eyes are closed, her breathing smooth and regular.

SOUND: The creak of the bed as HUGH gets up, then footsteps as
he crosses to the door. The light diminishes on AMANDA'S face as
he closes the door.

In the dark, her eyes open and she looks very scared indeed.

116   *INT. — THE DOLLS ALONG THE BASEBOARD, AMANDA'S
POV — NIGHT*

Staring. Creepy. But not as creepy as what we *know* is in that wall.

117   *INT. — THE MASTER BEDROOM — NIGHT*

SALLY-ANN is sitting at a vanity table in her nightgown, rubbing
> (MORE)

(CONTINUED)

117   *CONTINUED:*

some sort of cream into her face. Her back is to us but we can see
her in the mirror. Speaking of her back, it's very straight, and her
movements are short, sharp, and curt. If HUGH wants to fight,
why, she'll give him what he wants.

HUGH comes in.

> HUGH
> Okay, where is he?

> SALLY-ANN
> I took him to the Animal Shelter. It was obvious
> to me that you were just going to let it slide.

> HUGH
> Didn't you think that was a little high-handed?

> SALLY-ANN (turns to him)
> No. General killing Paulie — I thought *that* was
> high-handed.

> HUGH
> I'm going down there and spring him tomorrow
> morning. As far as Mandy knows, he's just back
> from a night on the town. *Then* we can discuss
> things. But as a *family*.

> SALLY-ANN
> I am *not* Mussolini!

> HUGH
> Yeah? You could have fooled me. I'm going down
> to the Shelter and get the cat tomorrow, and
> that's it.

SALLY-ANN turns back to the mirror and resumes rubbing the
cream into her face. There is a whole stew of emotions on her
face — but not least among them is satisfaction.

> SALLY-ANN
> You do that.

118   EXT. — *AMANDA'S HOUSE — NIGHT*

All the lights are out — it's late.

119   *INT. — AMANDA'S BEDROOM — NIGHT*

She's sleeping. PAULIE'S cage has been removed. The window is tightly shut tonight.

SOUND: Groaning wood.

120   *INT — THE DOLLS ALONG THE BASEBOARD — NIGHT*

They tremble as if an earthquake was happening. This time several of them fall over at once.

The baseboard rips open. THE CREATURE steps out and looks around warily.

121   *INT. — AMANDA'S ROOM, UP-ANGLE, CREATURE'S POV — NIGHT*

THE CAMERA PANS from place to place in jerky, hurried fashion — THE CREATURE is looking for GENERAL.

122   *INT. — THE CREATURE — NIGHT*

Its wary look subsides. The cat is not here. It trots across the floor to AMANDA'S bed and begins climbing the folds of coverlet to the top.

123   *INT. — THE MASTER BEDROOM — NIGHT*

HUGH and SALLY-ANN are both deeply asleep. There will be no help from this quarter.

124   *INT. — AMANDA'S BED — NIGHT*

She's sleeping on her back. THE CREATURE again creeps up the shape of her body to her chest.

AMANDA moans. THE CREATURE grins.

It kneels down on her chest and puts its hands on her shoulders. It leans toward her face, as if to kiss her.

125   *INT. — AMANDA AND THE CREATURE, CLOSER — NIGHT*

THE CREATURE leans forward until its face is less than three inches from AMANDA'S. Then . . . it *sucks*. The resemblance to HUGH'S breakfast joke of the day before should be unmistakable.

(CONTINUED)

125   CONTINUED:

A dim, phosphorescent cloud begins to issue from AMANDA'S lips to THE CREATURE'S — it is her life, and the thing is quite literally sucking it out of her.

AMANDA moans again — a stifled, strangled sound — and struggles weakly. THE CREATURE holds on to her as she shifts in bed. It exhales, then leans forward again and once more *sucks*. That dully glowing cloud appears again.

AMANDA'S struggles weaken. We can see her growing paler and paler right in front of us. Now she begins to choke.

126   *INT. — AMANDA'S WINDOW — NIGHT*

GENERAL comes crashing through the window, spitting and yowling, his eyes furious green footballs. SLOW MOTION might be fun here.

127   *INT. — THE MASTER BEDROOM — NIGHT*

HUGH grunts. SALLY-ANN sits bolt upright.

                          SALLY-ANN
                       What was *that*?

128   *INT. — AMANDA'S BED, WITH THE CREATURE — NIGHT*

Its head whips around, its expression of glee turning to hate and fear.

129   *INT. — AMANDA'S ROOM, WITH GENERAL — NIGHT*

The cat comes loping across the floor at speed. It leaps up onto AMANDA'S bed.

AMANDA wakes up . . . and sees the grotesque CREATURE on her chest.

She SHRIEKS.

130   *INT. — THE UPSTAIRS HALL — NIGHT*

SALLY-ANN comes running, HUGH close behind her.

131   *INT. — AMANDA'S BED — NIGHT*

For a moment GENERAL and THE CREATURE are actually battling on top of the screaming AMANDA. THE CREATURE
                          (MORE)

                                              (CONTINUED)

131   CONTINUED:

whips its knife out and slashes GENERAL, who draws back on his haunches, spitting and clawing.

THE CREATURE runs, dives over the side of the bed. GENERAL follows.

132   INT. — THE FLOOR AT THE FOOT OF AMANDA'S BED — NIGHT

GENERAL leaps on THE CREATURE. The two of them roll across the floor in a spitting, chittering, spiteful ball.

133   INT. — AMANDA — NIGHT

She's sitting up in bed, too pale, screaming and gasping at the same time. There should be no doubt about one thing in our minds: This little girl almost died.

134   INT. — THE BEDROOM DOOR — NIGHT

SALLY-ANN and HUGH burst in.

                        SALLY-ANN
                    Honey, what's wrong?

                          HUGH
                    Christ, Mandy, what —

135   INT. — AMANDA, IN BED — NIGHT

                    AMANDA (shrieking)
          *General caught the monster! The monster was in
          bed with me! General caught the monster!*

And she looks toward:

136   INT. — THE BEDROOM FLOOR — NIGHT

THE CREATURE, terribly clawed, breaks away from GENERAL and runs for its hole.

GENERAL leaps after it, spitting.

137   INT. — HUGH AND SALLY-ANN — NIGHT

They are staring at this, both of them utterly flabbergasted.
                          (MORE)
                                              (CONTINUED)

137   *CONTINUED:*

AMANDA runs to them, embraces them both. She is still badly out
of breath as well as terrified.

> AMANDA
> It was in bed with me! General saved me!

> SALLY-ANN
> What is that thing? *Hugh, what is it?*

> HUGH
> I don't know.

138   *INT. — GENERAL AND THE CREATURE — NIGHT*

It has almost reached its lair when GENERAL pounces again. It
whirls and strikes the cat with the knife. No matter. GENERAL
is done messing around with this thing. He slashes (SLOW
MOTION?) and rips the thing wide open. It falls to the floor,
gushing green blood. The knife spills from its hand.

139   *INT. — AMANDA, HUGH, SALLY-ANN — NIGHT*

They stand just inside AMANDA'S bedroom door, staring, horrified.

> SALLY-ANN
> You know that old saying, "It came out of the
> woodwork?" That's just what it did, Hugh. It
> came out of the woodwork. It —

She begins to giggle helplessly and crams a fist into her mouth to
stop it. HUGH hugs her, not taking his eyes off the far wall.

140   *INT. — AMANDA, CLOSE — NIGHT*

> AMANDA
> Look! Mommy and Daddy! Look! It's going away!

141   *INT. — THE DOLL WALL, WITH GENERAL AND THE
CREATURE — NIGHT*

THE CREATURE is indeed disappearing . . . going up in smoke, it
seems. GENERAL backs away prudently.

Soon THE CREATURE is entirely gone, except for the croggly
little knife.

                                              (CONTINUED)

141   CONTINUED:

GENERAL approaches the knife as that WOODEN GRINDING
SOUND begins again. He bats it toward the irregular hole in the
wood several times. The last bat sends the evil little knife spinning
into the hole.

A moment later, the baseboard snaps shut like a bear trap.

142   INT. — AMANDA, HUGH, AND SALLY-ANN — NIGHT

> HUGH (awed)
> Holy Jesus Christ.

143   INT. — GENERAL — NIGHT

He trots across the floor.

144   INT. — AMANDA — NIGHT

Good old GENERAL! AMANDA runs to meet him and picks him
up. She makes much of him, petting him and crooning to him.

145   INT.   HUGH AND SALLY-ANN, BY THE DOOR — NIGHT

Both are still in a perfectly understandable state of shock.

> SALLY-ANN
> We're not going to say anything about this to
> anyone, Hugh — do you understand that? Not
> even if we are drunk. Not even if we are smoking
> funny cigarettes with the Whitsuns.

> HUGH
> *Talk* about it? I don't even want to *think* about it.

AMANDA joins them, holding GENERAL. The cat is purring loudly.

> SALLY ANN
> Amanda, I want you to promise me you won't talk
> about this with your friends.

> AMANDA
> Welll . . . that depends.

> SALLY-ANN
> Depends on what?

(CONTINUED)

145   *CONTINUED:*

> AMANDA (smiling)
> On whether or not General can sleep with me
> from now on.

> SALLY-ANN
> Amanda, that's blackmail!

> HUGH
> And we'll pay. But don't you want to spend the
> rest of tonight with us, honey?

> AMANDA
> Not if I can have General. I'll be safe if I have
> General.

> HUGH (to SALLY-ANN)
> I think she will be.

> SALLY-ANN
> Yes, I guess I do, too.

146   *INT. — THE MASTER BEDROOM — NIGHT*

HUGH and SALLY-ANN are back in bed. HUGH is lying on his
side with his eyes closed. SALLY-ANN is on her back with her eyes
open. She still looks very, very shaken.

> SALLY-ANN
> Did any of that happen, Hugh? Really?

> HUGH (doesn't open his eyes)
> Did any of *what* happen?

> SALLY-ANN
> Hugh . . .

> HUGH (kisses her)
> Go to sleep. It'll be easier not to believe in the
> morning.

She looks momentarily puzzled, then smiles. HUGH rolls over onto
his side again and closes his eyes. After a few moments, SALLY-
ANN follows suit.

147   *INT. — AMANDA'S ROOM   NIGHT*

All's peaceful; steady state has been restored. The Dolls of All
Nations have been set back up, GENERAL'S on AMANDA'S bed,
and all's right with the world.

THE CAMERA MOVES SLOWLY IN ON GENERAL.

IIc's not asleep, but in that sleepily watchful state that cats often fall
into. His eyes are very green (perhaps for this shot SFX can actually
hype that green).

SOUND: GENERAL, purring.

SLOW DISSOLVE, until all we can see are those green, watchful
cat's eyes on the screen.

SOUND: Purring.

FADE SLOWLY TO BLACK

THE LEGEND OF HELL HOUSE

‒ ‒ ‒ ‒ ‒ ‒ ‒ ‒ ‒

SCREENPLAY BY

RICHARD MATHESON

Based on his book *Hell House*

FADE IN:

1   *EXT. — DEUTSCH MANSION, ANGLE ON HOOD OF ROLLS-ROYCE — LATE AFTERNOON*

Hard rain drumming on the hood. TITLE: *December 18.* CAMERA PANS UP, REVEALING the CHAUFFEUR sitting behind the wheel, smoking a cigarette and reading a newspaper, CONTINUING UP ITS PAN UNTIL the mansion is revealed in B.G.

2   *INT. — ENTRY HALL, FULL SHOT — ANN BARRETT*

Looking small in the immense hall, sitting in a large wooden chair. Every object in sight is a museum piece.

3   *CLOSE ON ANN*

In her early thirties, a bright, attractive woman who, at the moment, is somewhat uncomfortable. She looks at her wristwatch, then gazes upward. CAMERA PANS UP UNTIL we see the second story.

4   *INT. — SECOND-STORY CORRIDOR   CLOSE ON CHRIS BARRETT'S POCKET WATCH*

Four-sixteen. CAMERA WITHDRAWS as he puts the watch away. CHRIS BARRETT is in his forties, one of today's variety of

(MORE)

(CONTINUED)

4   *CONTINUED:*

intellectuals — knowledgeable without being stuffy. He grimaces
with impatience; looks up as an O.S. door OPENS.

5   *POV SHOT — ANGLE ON DOOR TO DEUTSCH'S BEDROOM*

A harassed-looking SECRETARY shuts the door and moves along
the corridor, CAMERA PANNING WITH her, STOPPING when
Barrett is in B.G. He watches her walk out of frame, having opened
his mouth to speak, then remained silent. CAMERA MOVES IN
ON him as he makes a soft noise of restlessness. He looks toward
the O.S. door as it OPENS again.

> HANLEY (voice)
> Dr. Barrett?

Barrett stands and crosses the corridor, CAMERA PANNING WITH
him. HANLEY, a short, fussy-looking man in a black suit, waits for
him in the doorway. Stepping aside, he gestures for Barrett to enter.

6   *INT. — DEUTSCH'S BEDROOM, ANGLE ON DOORWAY*

Barrett ENTERS and HANLEY starts to close the door.

> DEUTSCH (voice) (sourly)
> Not you, Hanley.

The barest flicker of emotion crosses Hanley's face as he backs out
and shuts the door. Barrett waits.

> DEUTSCH (voice)
> Well, come here where I can see you.

Barrett crosses the huge room, CAMERA WITHDRAWING,
STOPPING as he stops at the foot of a large bed.

> BARRETT (unintimidated)
> Good afternoon.

7   *POV SHOT — DEUTSCH*

Eighty-seven, bald and skeletal; obviously ill. He gestures irritably
for Barrett to come yet closer. CAMERA DRAWS AROUND TO
INCLUDE Barrett as he moves to the side of the bed. Deutsch
eyes him with cold appraisal.

(CONTINUED)

7   CONTINUED:

                         DEUTSCH
            My people tell me you're one of the five best in
            your field.
                    (Cutting Barrett off)
            Your fee will be a hundred thousand dollars; your
            assignment, to establish the facts.

                    BARRETT (shaken by the offer)
                         Regarding what?

                         DEUTSCH
            Survival after death, of course. That *is* your field,
            isn't it?

                    BARRETT (tone stiffening)
            My "field" is *physics*, Mr. Deutsch.

                    DEUTSCH (scowling)
                         Whatever.
                       (Warningly)
            It isn't lies I'm looking for. I'll buy the answer
            either way so long as it's factual.

        Barrett wants the opportunity very much but has to speak the truth.

                         BARRETT
            Where am I to find these facts, Mr. Deutsch? In
            the twenty years I've studied parapsychology —

                    DEUTSCH (cutting in)
            If they exist at all you'll find them in the only
            house on earth that hasn't been explained away
            yet — the Belasco house in Maine.

        CAMERA MOVES IN QUICKLY ON Barrett's face as he reacts
        to this.

                         BARRETT
                       Hell House?

8   POV SHOT — DEUTSCH

        A man approaching death who wants, despite all hardheaded logic,
        to believe in survival. His voice betrays that want.

                                        (CONTINUED)

8   *CONTINUED:*

                              DEUTSCH
                              Hell House.

9   *TWO SHOT*

                              BARRETT (fascinated)
                   I thought Belasco's heirs had it sealed off after
                   what happened in —

                              DEUTSCH (interrupting)
                   That was twenty years ago. They need money
                   now; I've bought the place. Can you be there by
                   Monday?

        Barrett hesitates. Anger appears on Deutsch's face.

                              DEUTSCH
                         Well, *can* you or can't you?

                              BARRETT (impulsively)
                                   Yes.

                              DEUTSCH (nodding curtly)
                   There'll be two others with you. A woman named
                   Florence Tanner and —

                              BARRETT (breaking in)
                                  Tanner?

                              DEUTSCH
                         Something wrong with that?

                              BARRETT
                   She's practically a child. I mean —

                              DEUTSCH (interrupting)
                   My people tell me she's the best in her field, too.
                              (Threateningly)
                   If you don't think you can work with her . . .

        He doesn't finish; waits. Barrett has to retreat or lose the opportunity.

                              BARRETT
                         And the other one?

                                                      (CONTINUED)

9   *CONTINUED:*

                              DEUTSCH
                    A man named — uh —
                    (Beat; gesturing irritably)
                    The only survivor of the last attempt.

                         BARRETT (surprised)
                              Fischer?

                              DEUTSCH
          Between the three of you, I expect the answer in
          a week.

               BARRETT (positively stunned by this demand)
                              A *week*!

                         DEUTSCH (softly, fiercely)
          I am getting tired of your objections, Barrett.
          Take it or leave it.

                    BARRETT (pause; nodding once)
                         A week, then.

10   *INT. — HANLEY'S OFFICE, CLOSE ON SHEET OF PAPER —*
       LATER

       Hanley stabbing his pen point at each item of the list. As he reads it,
       CAMERA PANS UP AND WITHDRAWS TO REVEAL HIM and
       Barrett, a desk between them. Barrett is distracted, trying to
       conduct a conversation with Hanley and consider the suddenness of
       the project at the same time.

                              HANLEY
          A summation of all phenomena observed in the
          Belasco house. Restoration of electricity,
          Installation of telephone service. Transportation
          of your equipment. Is that it?

                              BARRETT
                    No, I'll need a certain —
                              (Beat)
          apparatus that is only partially constructed at the
          moment.

                                             (CONTINUED)

10   *CONTINUED:*

HANLEY
How long will it take to complete?

BARRETT
That depends on how many electronics experts
you put on it.

HANLEY (writing it down)
How soon will you need it?

BARRETT
No later than Wednesday.

HANLEY (looking up)
That it?

BARRETT
We haven't discussed living facilities.

HANLEY
Enough rooms have been renovated for your use.
A woman from Caribou Falls will deliver your
meals.
(Repressing a smile)
She's refused to sleep in the house, of course.

BARRETT
She'd only be in the way if she did.

HANLEY (beat)
Is that it?

BARRETT (hesitates; then must say it)
Is the choice of the other two irrevocable?

HANLEY
Why?

BARRETT
Because I feel that they'll be useless to the
project.
(Beat)
(MORE)

(CONTINUED)

10   CONTINUED: —2

> Fischer had incredible abilities as a boy, but after
> his stay at the house he had a complete breakdown
> and hasn't been heard of since; I even thought he
> was dead.
>   (Beat)
> As for Florence Tannor . . . despite her
> reputation as a mental medium, she's a dedicated
> spiritualist and a totally withdrawn and immature
> young lady in the bargain. I fail to see —

HANLEY (cutting in)
Their choices *are* irrevocable, Doctor.

Barrett gazes at him flatly for several moments, then speaks.

BARRETT
I see.

He gets up. Hanley rises from the desk and walks him toward the door,
CAMERA MOVING WITH them. They stop as the door is opened
sharply by a stout man in his forties — WILLIAM REINHARDT
DEUTSCH. He shuts it again to prevent Barrett from leaving.

W. DEUTSCH
I'm warning you right now. I don't intend to let
my father blow three hundred thousand dollars
plus expenses on a dying fancy.
            (Beat)
The *truth*. This is a waste of time, isn't it? Put it
in writing and I'll give you a check for ten
thousand dollars right now. There's no such thing
as the supernatural, is there?

BARRETT (unflustered)
That is correct.
(As Deutsch starts to smile)
The word is super*normal*.

W. DEUTSCH
What the hell's the difference?! It's superstition,
all of it!

(CONTINUED)

10   *CONTINUED: —3*

BARRETT
That is *not* correct.

He starts to leave but Deutsch grabs his arm.

W. DEUTSCH
Now look, you'd better drop this thing! I'll see
you never get that money!

BARRETT (pulling free; coldly)
Do what you will.
(With more control)
I'll proceed as planned unless I hear otherwise
from your father.

He opens the door and walks out of the office.

11   *INT. — CORRIDOR, MOVING SHOT — BARRETT*

CAMERA PULLING AHEAD as he walks down the corridor.
Deutsch comes out of the office to glare after him.

W. DEUTSCH
You'll never get a *nickel* of that money!

12   *INT. — ENTRY HALL, ANGLE ON ANN*

Looking around in surprise.

W. DEUTSCH (voice)
Not a goddamn nickel!

Barrett emerges from the corridor and heads for Ann. She stands
looking at him questioningly. He takes her arm, addressing her
sotto voce.

BARRETT
Time to go.

They move toward the front door, CAMERA PULLING AHEAD
of them. Ann looks at him, then glances across her shoulder at
Deutsch as he appears from the corridor, shouting after them.

W. DEUTSCH
You hear me, you fraudulent bastard!

(CONTINUED)

12   CONTINUED:

> ANN
> What's going *on*?

> BARRETT
> I'll tell you later.

> W. DEUTSCII
> *Not a goddamn nickel!*

13   EXT. — HIGHWAY, MOVING SHOT — ROLLS-ROYCE

Being driven through a lashing rain.

> ANN (voice)
> That's an awful lot of money, Chris.

> BARRETT (voice)
> Not to him. Especially when you consider that
> what he's paying for is an assurance of
> immortality.

14   INT. — CAR — BARRETT AND ANN

> ANN (confused)
> But surely he knows you don't believe —

> BARRETT
> Shhh; not so loud.
> (Smiling as she looks surprised)
> Of course he knows. He's not the sort of man
> who goes into anything without being totally
> informed.

> ANN
> I don't understand, then.

> BARRETT
> He's trying to convince himself that he's
> approaching this thing logically.
> (Beat)
> Obviously, though, he hopes the other two will be
> able to convince him of survival.

(CONTINUED)

14   *CONTINUED:*

ANN
Will they?

BARRETT
They'll be lucky if they come out with their skins.

ANN
Are they that inept?

BARRETT
Inept, no. Unbalanced, yes. The girl's a classic
case of divided consciousness. And Fischer *has* to
be a mental basket case. He almost died in that
house. He was only fifteen at the time.

ANN
Fifteen! My *God*.

BARRETT
My sentiment exactly.
(Pause; looking at her)
I'm wondering if I shouldn't go alone on this
one, Ann.

ANN (startled)
But I've *always* gone with you.
(As he doesn't answer)
Isn't this place just another so-called haunted
house?

BARRETT
No, it isn't. It's the Mount Everest of haunted
houses. There have been two attempts to
investigate it — one in 1931, the other in 1953.
Both were disasters, eight people killed,
committing suicide or going insane. Fischer was
the only one who survived and, as I say, I'm sure
he's incapacitated, sure he's lost whatever psychic
abilities he had.
(Pause)
(MORE)

(CONTINUED)

14   *CONTINUED: —2*

> If you do go with me, you're going to have to stay
> by my side at all times.

CAMERA MOVES IN ON her uneasy expression.

15   *EXT. — SKY, PRIVATE JETLINER — DAY*

Flying through the gray clouds, DEUTSCH ENTERPRISES
printed on its side. TITLE: *December 21.*

16   *INT. — JETLINER, CLOSE ON WINDOW*

Clouds swirling by outside. Reflected in the window is BENJAMIN
FRANKLIN FISCHER, 35. CAMERA WITHDRAWS TO
INCLUDE him staring out the window broodingly.

17   *CLOSE-UP, FISCHER*

Staring into his thoughts.

18   *SUBLIMINAL SHOT*

Fischer as a 15-year-old boy, lying naked on the front porch of Hell
House, curled up like a fetus, shivering and staring into space.

19   *CLOSE-UP, FISCHER*

Remembering.

20   *WHAT HE RECALLS*

A brief SHOT of him being put on a stretcher, screaming and
vomiting blood. CAMERA ZOOMS IN ON his staring eyes.

21   *CLOSE ON FISCHER'S EYES*

Closing them. CAMERA WITHDRAWS TO INCLUDE his rigid
features, HOLDS.

22   *EXT. — AIRPORT, ANGLE THROUGH CHAIN-LINK FENCE,
JETLINER*

Taxiing up to the fence and stopping. The door opens and Fischer
gets out, carrying his tote bag. CAMERA PANS him to the gate
where Barrett and Ann wait. As Fischer joins them, Barrett extends
his hand and introductions commence.

23   *EXT. — FOREST CROSSROAD INTERSECTION, DOWN
        ANGLE ON BLACK LIMOUSINE — DAY*

        Parked on the shoulder of one of the fog-shrouded roads.

24   *INT. — LIMOUSINE — BARRETT, ANN, AND FISCHER*

        Sitting in silence, Fischer on a pull-down seat, the Barretts on the
        backseat. Hanley sits in the front next to the chauffeur. Barrett takes
        out his pocket watch and looks at it, blows out impatient breath.

                                 ANN
                           Is she very late?

                   BARRETT (putting away the watch)
                                 Very.

                                 ANN
                 I don't understand why she didn't fly up.

                               BARRETT
                            She doesn't fly.

                         ANN (smiling faintly)
              That doesn't speak too well for her faith, does it?

        Barrett smiles a little in response. Ann glances at Fischer, sees that
        he isn't amused and stops smiling.

                                 ANN
                       Did that offend you, Mr. Fischer?
                           (As he looks at her)
                    I mean, if you're a spiritualist, too.

                               FISCHER
                               I'm not.

        They relapse into silence. After a while, Fischer slowly turns his
        head and looks along the O.S. road. Noticing, Barrett and Ann do
        the same. Seeing nothing, they look back at Fischer, then exchange
        a glance. Now they hear the sound of an APPROACHING CAR
        and look back toward the road. Ann glances at Fischer curiously,
        then turns toward the road once more.

25   *POV SHOT — CAR*

        Emerging from the fog, it pulls over to the shoulder and stops.

26   *INT. — CAR — THE THREE*

        Watching the O.S. car as its door OPENS and CLOSES.

27   *POV SHOT — FLORENCE TANNER*

        Indistinct in the fog, dressed in white with a white CAPE, looking
        very much like an approaching specter.

28   *INT. — CAR — THE THREE*

        Watching her approach, struck by her appearance.

29   *POV SHOT — FLORENCE*

        Coming closer, emerging from the fog.

30   *INT. — CAR, ANGLE PAST FISCHER, TOWARD THE
        BARRETTS*

        Fischer opens the door and Barrett and Ann shift over to make
        room for Florence as she sits on the backseat, CAMERA MOVING
        IN ON her face until it fills the screen, her expression one of
        curious serenity despite her youthful appearance. She smiles at
        them faintly.

                              FLORENCE
                          Good afternoon.

31   *EXT. — FOREST, TRACKING SHOT, LIMOUSINE — LATER*

        CAMERA FOLLOWING their progress along the road, which
        twists through the dense forest.

32   *INT. — LIMOUSINE — FLORENCE, BARRETT, AND ANN*

                              FLORENCE
                You really think it's safe to take your wife there,
                Doctor?

                       BARRETT (with a faint smile)
                I'd appreciate it, Miss Tanner, if you wouldn't
                alarm my wife unjustifiably.

                              FLORENCE
                     You *have* prepared her, though.
                                                    (CONTINUED)

32   *CONTINUED:*

>   BARRETT (patiently)
>   She's been advised that there will be . . .
>   *occurrences.*

Fischer's O.S. SNORT makes them look at him.

33   *FULL SHOT, INCLUDING FISCHER*

Looking at Barrett with cold amusement.

>   FISCHER
>   One way of putting it.

Barrett returns the look dispassionately, then looks back at
Florence.

>   BARRETT
>   She's also been advised that these occurrences
>   will not, in any way, signify the presence of
>   the dead.

>   FLORENCE (smiling sadly)
>   To each his own, Dr. Barrett.

>   BARRETT
>   Shall we just say that there's "something" there?

Florence shrugs, smiling.

>   ANN
>   How long will it take your Reversor to get rid of
>   it, Chris?

Fischer and Florence look at Barrett.

>   BARRETT
>   I'll explain it when we get a little further along.

Florence starts to say something, then they all look toward the
windows as the car angles downward.

>   BARRETT
>   We must be close.
>   (To Ann)
>   The house is in the Matawaskie Valley.

34   *POV SHOT — MATAWASKIE VALLEY*

Lying ahead, ringed by high hills, its floor obscured by fog.

35   *ANGLE PAST FISCHER, TOWARD THE OTHERS*

He looks at the valley ahead, his expression undecipherable. The car is suddenly immersed in fog.

> ANN
> Why would anyone build a house in a place
> like this?

> FISCHER
> This was sunshine to Belasco.

They all look at him, then stare through the windows in silence. It is as though they are in a submarine, navigating downward through a sea of curdled milk. Periodically, trees or bushes or boulder formations appear beside the car, then disappear. The only sound is the hum of the ENGINE.

36   *EXT. — MATAWASKIE VALLEY, MOVING SHOT — LIMOUSINE — LATER*

Moving slowly along the fogbound road. Soon the car stops.

37   *INT. — LIMOUSINE, ANGLE PAST THE FOUR, TOWARD HANLEY*

Getting out of the car, Ann looks around, perplexed.

> ANN
> This is *it*?

> BARRETT
> Must be.

> ANN
> I can't see a thing.

Hanley opens the door.

> HANLEY
> We're here.

> ANN (sotto voce)
> I don't believe it.

38–   *OMITTED*
39

40   *EXT. — LIMOUSINE, ANGLE ON LEFT SIDE*

Fischer gets out on the right side and walks out of frame. As Barrett
helps Ann out, she shivers convulsively.

> ANN
> *Cold.*

Florence joins them.

> HANLEY
> Your luggage is inside the house, the telephone
> has been connected, the electricity is on, and
> your rooms are ready. Supper will be delivered at
> six. We'll be back for you at five o'clock on the
> twenty-seventh. Any questions?

> BARRETT (clearing his throat)
> One minor one.
> (Beat)
> Where's the house?

He and Ann look toward the O.S. Fischer as Florence points
toward him.

41   *POV SHOT — FISCHER*

Standing motionless in the fog, hands in the pockets of his black pea
coat, looking toward the unseen house. Now he starts in that
direction.

42   *ANGLE PAST BARRETT, ANN, AND FLORENCE TOWARD
FISCHER*

Fischer already fading from view.

> BARRETT
> Ah, we're off. Thank you, Mr. Hanley.

> HANLEY
> Good-bye, Doctor.

They start after Fischer. Hanley gets back in the car.

(CONTINUED)

42   *CONTINUED:*

> ANN (softly)
> I trust he meant *au revoir*.

Barrett smiles.

43   *MOVING SHOT — FLORENCE*

Looking ahead with tense expectation.

44   *MOVING SHOT — ANGLE PAST FISCHER TOWARD THE OTHER THREE.*

Barrett, Ann, and Florence seen indistinctly in the B.G. Fischer starts along a gravel path, his shoes crunching on the stones. It is an extended walk before he stops. The others come up beside him and look in the same direction. CAMERA HOLDS.

45   *POV SHOT — HELL HOUSE*

A massive, looming specter of a house.

46   *ANGLE PAST FLORENCE TOWARD THE OTHER THREE*

Staring at the house. Ann narrows her eyes.

> ANN
> *It has no windows.*

> FISCHER
> He had them bricked up so no one could see in.

> FLORENCE
> Or out.

She walks OUT OF FRAME and the others follow, CAMERA PANNING TO FOLLOW their movement toward the house. They start up the wide porch steps.

47   *ANGLE ON STEPS*

Cracked with fungus and frosted grass sprouting from the fissures. The feet of the four move IN and OUT OF FRAME.

48   *ANGLE ON DOOR*

Massive and dark. The four ENTER FRAME and stop in front of it.

(CONTINUED)

48   *CONTINUED:*

                              ANN
                   If it opens by itself, I'm going home.

Barrett, smiling, removes a key from his pocket and slides it into the
lock, wiggling it back and forth to loosen the bolt. Abruptly, the key
turns and the heavy door begins to swing in. Ann glances aside as
Florence catches her breath. Barrett touches her shoulder and she
looks at him, his expression telling her not to be concerned. She
looks back at Florence.

49   *ANGLE PAST FLORENCE*

She is staring into the house, oblivious to the other three. Fischer
has been feeling inside for the light switch. He finds it now and
flicks it up and down without result.

                            FISCHER
                   So much for the restored electricity.

                            BARRETT
                   Obviously the generator hasn't been properly
                   restored.

                              ANN
                   Generator? Isn't there electrical service up
                   here?

                            BARRETT
                   There aren't enough houses in the valley to make
                   it worth the expense.

                              ANN
                   How could they put in a telephone, then?

                      BARRETT (looking into the house)
                   It's a field telephone.

50   *ANOTHER ANGLE*

                              ANN
                   So what are we going to do? Stay in Caribou Falls
                   until the new generator is installed?

                                              (CONTINUED)

50   *CONTINUED:*

> BARRETT
> That might take days. I'm sure there are some
> candles we can use while I take a look at the
> generator.

> ANN (wanly)
> Candles.

> BARRETT (smiling)
> Just for a while.

> ANN
> How do we find them?

Barrett takes a flashlight from his pocket and holds it up, grinning at
her. He moves inside.

51   *INT. — ENTRY HALL, ANGLE ON DOORWAY*

Stopping, Barrett looks around, then extends his hand through the
doorway. Ann comes in, grimacing, and making a sickened noise.

> ANN
> That *smell.*

> BARRETT
> Bricking up the windows wasn't the brightest idea
> Belasco ever had.

Florence, then Fischer COME IN with the guarded looks of
fighters entering a ring. They follow the flashlight beam as Barrett
plays it around. Ann makes an involuntary sound of awe.

52   *POV SHOT — FLASHLIGHT BEAM*

Moving around the dark immensity of the entry hall, the narrow
cone jumping from place to place, freezing momentarily on the
sparse furnishings now in a state of disarray as if the occupants had
fled in a hurry: huge, leaden-colored paintings; giant tapestries
filmed with dust; a staircase, broad and curving, leading upward
into blackness; a second-story corridor overlooking the entry hall —
and, far above, engulfed by shadows, a vast expanse of paneled
ceilings.

53   *THE FOUR*

                              BARRETT
                     Be it ever so humble.

                             FLORENCE
              It isn't humble at all. It reeks of arrogance.

Barrett glances at her critically.

                              BARRETT
                     It reeks, at any rate.
                 (Pointing the flashlight to his right)
                 According to the floor plan, the kitchen should be
                 that way.

They start in that direction, Barrett shining the flashlight ahead
of them.

54   *HIGH DOWN ANGLE SHOT — THE FOUR*

Moving across the entry hall, following the flashlight beam. They
can barely be seen, the sound of their footsteps loud on the
hardwood floor. As the CAMERA PANS, the lens begins to GLAZE
a little out of focus and the sound of their footsteps alters slightly.

55   *THE FOUR, FLORENCE FEATURED*

Stopping to look upward suddenly.

                             FLORENCE
                      It knows we're here.

Barrett gets a harried expression as Ann and Fischer look upward
automatically.

                              BARRETT
                       Miss *Tanner* . . .

                 FLORENCE (a little irritated at Barrett)
                 I'm sorry, I'll try to keep my observations to
                 myself.

They move forward again.

56   *INT. — KITCHEN, ANGLE THROUGH WINDOW OF RIGHT
        SWINGING DOOR*

                                              (CONTINUED)

56   CONTINUED:

The flashlight beam appears, approaching down the corridor.
Barrett pushes open the door, holds it ajar for the others to enter,
then comes in himself, shining the flashlight beam around the
kitchen.

ANN
Good God.

57   POV SHOT — KITCHEN

Huge, its perimeter rimmed by steel counters and dark paneled
cupboards; a long, double-basin sink; and a gigantic stove.

58   THE FOUR

Barrett moves to the nearest cupboard door and opens it, shining
the flashlight at shelves of dust-filmed liquor bottles. Fischer moves
OUT OF FRAME. Barrett pulls out a drawer and removes a sheet
of yellow-edge cardboard.

ANN
What's that?

BARRETT
One of their menus — dated March 27, 1928.
Shrimp bisque. Sweetbread in gravy. Stewed
capon in cream sauce. Creamed cauliflower.
Biscuits. For dessert, *amandes en crème:* crushed
almonds in whipped egg whites with heavy
cream. His guests must have all had heartburn.

FISCHER (voice)
The food wasn't aimed at their hearts.

They look around as he ENTERS FRAME, carrying some candles.

59   HIGH DOWN ANGLE SHOT, ENTRY HALL

Dark and still. FOOTSTEPS are heard and flickering candlelight
approaches. The four APPEAR from the side corridor, each
carrying a candleholder. Barrett starts toward the Great Hall
archway.

BARRETT
That would be the Great Hall.

60   *INT. — GREAT HALL, ANGLE THROUGH ARCHWAY*

The four approaching, Barrett in the lead. They move beneath the
archway and stop, Barrett grunting, impressed, as he holds up his
candle. The women react similarly.

61   *POV SHOT — THE GREAT HALL*

Enormous, its walls two stories high. Across the way is an immense
fireplace. The furnishings are antiques except for scattered chairs
and sofas in the fashion of the twenties. In the center of the hall
stands a circular table 20 feet in diameter with 16 highbacked chairs
around it and a large electrolier suspended over it.

62   *THE FOUR*

Only Fischer does not look impressed. Ann points toward a French-
style telephone receiver on a nearby table.

> BARRETT
> For use inside the house, I'm sure.
> (Pause)
> Well, let's push on.

63   *ANGLE PAST METAL BUST, TOWARD ARCHWAY*

The face of a strange-looking man with a disturbing smile on his
lips. In the B.G., the four move into the entry hall, the man's head
in silhouette as the candlelight fades.

64   *INT. — CORRIDOR, ANGLE TOWARD ENTRY HALL*

The four move beneath the overhanging staircase and down the
corridor. CAMERA PANS as they turn into another corridor and
start along it. Barrett points toward a staircase leading down.

> BARRETT
> That leads to the cellar, doesn't it, Mr. Fischer?

Fischer nods and Barrett looks at the door ahead.

> BARRETT
> What have we here?

> FISCHER
> The chapel.

(CONTINUED)

64   *CONTINUED:*

> BARRETT (appalled)
> *Chapel?*

As they near the door, Florence starts to make sounds of
apprehension. Ann looks at her uneasily. Barrett, opening the door,
looks around. The closer Florence gets to the door, the more
disturbed she gets. Finally, with a sickened noise, she turns away.

> FLORENCE
> I'm sorry, I can't right now. The atmosphere is
> more than I can bear.

> BARRETT
> We understand.

He takes Ann's arm and leads her into the chapel. Fischer watches
Florence for a second as she leans back against the chapel door,
then turns and follows the Barretts in. CAMERA MOVES IN on
Florence, her eyes are closed and she is breathing heavily. Suddenly
her eyes open, as she reacts to a sound O.S.

65   *INT. — CHAPEL, ANGLE TOWARD DOORWAY*

The walls are covered with murals in flagrant colors depicting mass
orgies; the faces distorted by lust. Barrett and Ann move slowly
down the middle aisle, Ann looking around warily. In the B.G.,
Fischer comes in and looks around. Ann looks confused.

> ANN
> Why couldn't she come in?

> BARRETT
> Her system is attuned to psychic energy.
> Obviously it's very strong here.

> ANN
> Why here?

> BARRETT
> Contrast perhaps. A church in hell; that sort of
> thing.

> ANN
> Why doesn't it bother him?

(CONTINUED)

65   *CONTINUED:*

> BARRETT
> Perhaps he knows how to protect himself better
> than she does.

66   *POV SHOT — THE ALTAR*

It is dominated by a giant crucifix in an upside-down position as
prescribed by devil worship. The figure of a near-nude man is
draped on the cross. CAMERA MOVES IN QUICKLY on the face
of the figure. It is a face of infinite evil, twisted and malignant
features of some demon incarnate — possibly Satan himself.

> ANN (shocked)
> He was sick.

> BARRETT
> *Yes, he was.*

He takes Ann's arm and escorts her along the aisle toward the door.
Fischer has already departed.

66A   *INT. — CORRIDOR*

Fischer is waiting for them.

> FISCHER
> She's gone.

> ANN (staring at him)
> How can she —

She breaks off suddenly, looking around.

> BARRETT
> I'm sure it's nothing.

> FISCHER (a bit angry)
> Are you?

> BARRETT (calling)
> Miss Tanner! Miss Tanner!

Ann and Fischer follow as he moves down the corridor.

> BARRETT (calling)
> Miss Tanner! Can you hear me?

(CONTINUED)

66A   CONTINUED:

FLORENCE (voice)
Yes! Here I am — in here.

Barrett smiles at Ann, then glances over at Fischer, whose
expression has not relaxed.

66B   INT. — GREAT HALL

Florence is standing on the far side of the hall as the Barretts and
Fischer enter.

BARRETT
You shouldn't have done that, Miss Tanner. You
caused us undue alarm.

FLORENCE
I'm sorry. I heard a voice in here.

Florence gestures toward the piece of furniture she is standing
beside, a phonograph inside a walnut Spanish cabinet. She reaches
down and places the arm of the needle on the record.

FLORENCE
Belasco.

BARRETT
His voice?

There is a crackling sound through the speaker, then a voice. It is
soft and mellow, yet terrifying.

BELASCO'S VOICE
Welcome to my house. I'm delighted you could
come, I am certain you will find your stay here
most illuminating. It is regrettable I cannot be
with you, but I had to leave before your arrival.
Think of me as your unseen host and believe that,
during your stay here, I shall be with you in spirit.
All your needs have been provided for, nothing
has been overlooked. Go where you will, and do
what you will — these are the cardinal precepts
(MORE)

(CONTINUED)

66B   *CONTINUED:*

> of my home. Feel free to function as you choose.
> There are no responsibilities, no rules. Each to
> his own devices shall be the only standard here.
> May you find the answer that you seek. It is here,
> I promise you.
>   (Pause)
>   And now . . . auf Wiedersehen.

The needle sticks and the voice repeats "auf Wiedersehen . . . auf
Wiedersehen . . . auf Wiedersehen . . ." until Florence removes it.
The Great Hall is now immensely still as the group reacts to what
they have just heard.

                    FLORENCE
          Auf Wiedersehen . . . until we meet again.

67   *INT. — GENERATOR ROOM, CLOSE ON FLORENCE*

A face of infinite good. CAMERA PANS TO Barrett working on the
generator. Abruptly, it starts running and an overhead light goes on.

                    BARRETT
               There we go.

68–   *SERIES OF SHOTS*
75

Showing various rooms of the house with the lights on: entry hall,
Great Hall, dining hall, kitchen, ballroom, second-floor corridor,
etc. It is a most impressive looking house.

76   *INT. — GREAT HALL, CLOSE ON WOODEN BOX — LATER*

As the top is levered up by means of hammer claws; the grating rasp
of the nails makes a jarring sound. CAMERA WITHDRAWS to
include Barrett and Ann standing by the round table, unloading
scientific equipment. There is a debris of wooden and cardboard
boxes on the floor. In the B.G. fireplace, a fire is burning.

77   *ANOTHER ANGLE, TOWARD ARCHWAY*

Fischer approaching, wearing a black turtleneck sweater, black
corduroy trousers, and a pair of scuffed tennis shoes.

                                        (CONTINUED)

77   CONTINUED:

FISCHER
Need help?

BARRETT
No, it's going fine, thank you.

Fischer watches. Barrett has removed a rack of lights from the wooden box and is wiping it off with a soft cloth. Ann tries to lift a wooden carton, but it is too heavy.

FISCHER
Here, I'll do it.

He picks up the box, grunting in surprise at its weight. He sets it on the table and watches as Barrett pries open the top and lifts out a cube-shaped instrument painted dark blue, a dial in front numbered from zero to 900, the needle at zero. Fischer looks at the inscription stenciled on top

78   INSERT: INSCRIPTION:

BARRETT-EMR

79   BACK TO SCENE

FISCHER (coldly amused)
That your Reversor?

BARRETT (ignoring Fischer's tone)
No.

They all turn toward the entry hall at the SOUND of Florence's approach

80   MOVING SHOT — FLORENCE

She has changed into a simpler outfit. She smiles at them.

FLORENCE
Hello.

CAMERA STOPS when all of them are INCLUDED in shot. She looks at Fischer after gazing at the array of instruments.

(CONTINUED)

80   *CONTINUED:*

FLORENCE
Would you walk with me, Mr. Fischer? I'd like to
see some more of the house.

FISCHER
If you like.

FLORENCE (to Barrett and Ann)
Will you excuse us?

Barrett gives her a quick, polite smile and returns to his work.
Fischer and Florence turn away and move toward the archway,
walking OUT OF FRAME. Ann returns to what she's doing. The
collection of instruments on the table now includes an astatic
galvanometer, a mirror galvanometer, a Crookes Balance, a
camera gauze cage, a manometer, a weighing platform, a tape
recorder, etc. Seeing Barrett remove an envelope from a wooden
box, tear it open, and lay a list on the table, Ann picks it up and
looks at it.

81   *INSERT: TOP OF LIST*

Observed Psychic Phenomena at the Belasco House. CAMERA
PANS DOWN the list, which reads: Apparitions, Apports, Asports,
Automatic Painting, Automatic Speaking, Automatic Writing,
Autoscopy, Bilocation, Biological phenomena, Book tests, Breezes,
Catalepsy, Chemical phenomena, Chemicographs, Clairvoyance,
Communication, Control, Crystal gazing, Dematerialization,
Direct drawing, Direct painting, Direct voice, Direct writing,
Divination, Dreams, Ectoplasm, Eidolons, Electrical phenomena,
Elongation, Emanations, Exteriorization of motricity, Extras,
Extratemporal perception, Ideoplasm, Impersonation,
Independent voice, Interpenetration of matter, Knot tying,
Levitation, Luminous phenomena, Materialization, Matter through
matter, Monition, Motor automatism, Obsession, Paraffin molds,
Parakinesis, Percussion, Phantasmata, Poltergeist phenomena,
Possession, Precognition, Prevision, Pseudopods, Psychic rods,
Psychokinesis, Psychometry, Radiesthesia, Raps, Retrocognition,
Sensory automatism, Skin writing, Slate writing, Transcendental
music, Transfiguration, Typtology, Voices, Water sprinkling,
Xenoglossy.

82   *CLOSE ON ANN*

Gaping at the list.

> ANN
> All these things happened here?

> BARRETT (repressing a smile)
> That's just the *verified* list.

He smiles at her expression.

83   *INT. — CORRIDOR, MOVING SHOT — FLORENCE AND*
      FISCHER

> FLORENCE
> What have you been doing since 1950, Mr.
> Fischer?

> FISCHER
> Surviving. What have you been doing?

> FLORENCE (with a slight smile)
> Working for God.

> FISCHER
> That right?
> (Beat)
> I'm not on His payroll anymore.

> FLORENCE
> Now, you know that —

She breaks off and the CAMERA STOPS. Florence's breathing
quickens, her expression altering to one of suffering.

> FLORENCE (cont'd)
> Yes . . . *yes* - - pain . . . sorrow.
> (Pause, as the feeling goes)
> Did you *feel* that?

No answer from Fischer. After an awkward silence, they move again.

> FLORENCE (cont'd)
> Have you read Dr. Barrett's article in which he
> compares us to Geiger counters?

(CONTINUED)

83   *CONTINUED:*

> FISCHER
> *Us?*

> FLORENCE (ignoring that)
> It's not a bad comparison. We *are* like Geiger
> counters in a way. Expose us to emanations and
> we tick. Of course, the difference is —

CAMERA ZOOMS IN ON her face as she jars to a halt, features
set in an expression of savage fury.

> ·FLORENCE (cont'd) (gutturally)
> *This-goddamn-sewer!*

She jolts and shakes away the feeling. CAMERA WITHDRAWS
TO INCLUDE Fischer.

> FLORENCE (cont'd)
> Oh, dear. Such fury, such destructive venom.
> (Inhaling deeply)
> A very hostile man. Yet who can blame him?
> (Pause)
> There seem to be so *many* spirits trapped in this
> house. What *happened* here?

> FISCHER
> A lot of things.
> (Beat)
> All of them bad.

84   *INT. — CELLAR CORRIDOR, UP ANGLE ON STAIRS*

Fischer and Florence descend the stairs, CAMERA PANNING
them to a pair of swinging metal doors. Fischer holds one of them
open for Florence.

> FISCHER
> Steam room's down the other end.

> FLORENCE
> We never had one of those in *our* cellar. Let's
> look at it.

85   *ANOTHER ANGLE — FISCHER AND FLORENCE*

As they start to move in the direction of the steam room, CAMERA
PANS SLOWLY, the lens GLAZING and the sound of their voices
and footsteps altering curiously.

> FLORENCE
> He must have been a very wealthy man.

86   *MOVING SHOT, CLOSE ON FISCHER AND FLORENCE*

Her expression growing blank as they walk. Abruptly, she stops.

> FLORENCE (whispering)
> *If thine eye offend thee . . .*

Fischer stops and looks at her. After several moments, she shakes
her head, her eyes refocusing.

> FLORENCE (cont'd)
> Did I say something?

> FISCHER (pause)
> No.

She gazes at him, her expression confused.

87   *ANGLE ON STEAM ROOM*

Fischer pulls open the heavy metal door and holds it ajar, directing
the flashlight beam inside. The steam room is 12 feet square; its
wall, floor, and ceiling tiled in white. Wooden benches line
the walls, and a length of green hose spirals across the floor leading
to a water outlet.

> FLORENCE (a grimace)
> Perverted in there.
> (Swallowing to clear her throat)
> But what?

Fischer lets the door swing shut, the closing echoing loudly.

88   *INT. — GREAT HALL, DOWN ANGLE ON FISCHER AND
FLORENCE*

Entering and stopping. Florence shakes her head.

(CONTINUED)

88   *CONTINUED:*

FLORENCE
This *house*.

CAMERA DRAWS BACK, PASSING one enormous chandelier,
then a second as Florence and Fischer walk across the dance floor.

FLORENCE (cont'd)
Can a great hall like this be a place of evil?

FISCHER
In this house it can.

CAMERA STOPS as Florence, then Fischer, stops.

FLORENCE (determinedly)
Evil has dwelt here long enough. It's time —

CAMERA MOVES IN QUICKLY ON the chandelier as several
pendants stir, making a tinkling noise.

89   *CLOSE DOWN ANGLE ON FISCHER AND FLORENCE*

As they jerk up their heads.

FLORENCE (whispering)
The challenge is met.

90   *UP ANGLE PAST FISCHER AND FLORENCE*

The parabola of heavy, hanging crystal motionless overhead, its
pendants refracting the candlelight, splaying colors of the spectrum
across the ceiling. Fischer turns to look at Florence, his voice hard.

FISCHER
Don't be so quick to accept it.

She turns to him, their faces in profile against the backdrop of the
chandelier.

FLORENCE
You're *blocking* it.
(Beat)
That's why you didn't get those impressions
before.

(CONTINUED)

90   *CONTINUED:*

> FISCHER (interrupting)
> I'm not blocking anything. I'm just not sticking
> my neck out like I did in 1953. This time I do it
> right.
>> (With a contemptuous sound)
> I was just like you in those days, No, worse. I
> really thought I was something. God's gift to
> psychic research at the age of fifteen.

> FLORENCE
> You were one of the most powerful physical
> mediums ever known.

> FISCHER
> Still am, Florence. Just more careful now, that's
> all, more with it. I suggest the same approach
> for you.

She puts her hand on his arm.

> FLORENCE
> Don't bury your talent, Mr Fischer.

With a disgusted sound, he pulls away from her.

> FISCHER
> *Bullshit*, kid. You're walking around this house
> like an open nerve. When you really do hit
> something it'll tear your insides out. This place
> isn't called Hell House for nothing, you know. So
> you'd damn well better learn to protect yourself
> or you'll just be another victim on the list!

Florence winces as he stalks OUT OF FRAME. She watches him in
distress, CAMERA HOLDING.

91   *LONG SHOT — DINING HALL — LATER*

CAMERA SHOOTING TOWARD a giant fireplace with a mantel
that reaches the ceiling. In the center of the hall is a 40-foot table
with 30 chairs around it. Spaced at intervals above the table are four

> (MORE)

                                    (CONTINUED)

91   *CONTINUED:*

hanging sanctuary lamps. The four are seated at the far end of the
table, Barrett at its head. CAMERA MOVES IN ON the table,
their voices rising in audibility. Florence is only drinking water.

> BARRETT
> Well, I must say that the house has scarcely lived
> up to its reputation so far.

> FISCHER (looking at his plate)
> It hasn't taken our measure yet.

Barrett glances at him, but does not respond.

> FLORENCE
> I think we'd be mistaken to consider the house as
> the haunting force. Quite evidently, the problem
> is created by multiple surviving personalities.

The look Barrett gives her makes her smile a little.

> FLORENCE (cont'd)
> You still don't accept survival, I take it.

> BARRETT
> It's a charming notion, no more.

> FLORENCE
> Have you any *alternative* to offer?

> BARRETT
> Oh, yes. An alternative far more complex and
> demanding. *The challenge of ourselves.* The
> undiscovered mysteries of the human spectrum:
> the infrared capacities of our bodies, the
> ultraviolet capacities of our brains.

> FLORENCE (pause; with a forced smile)
> We'll see.

> BARRETT
> Indeed we shall, Miss Tanner.

Ann speaks to break the tension.

                                                    (CONTINUED)

91   *CONTINUED: —2*

> ANN
> When was this house built, Chris?

> BARRETT
> I don't know.
> (Looking at him)
> Mr. Fischer?

> FISCHER
> Nineteen nineteen.

> BARRETT
> From several remarks you made today, I have the
> impression that you know quite a bit about
> Belasco. Would you care to share it with us?

Fischer is silent. Finally, he starts to talk in a flat voice.

> FISCHER
> Belasco, Emeric. Born March 23, 1879, the
> illegitimate son of Myron Sandler, an American
> munitions maker, and Noelle Belasco, an English
> actress. Took his mother's last name because
> his father was already married with a family of
> his own.

> ANN
> What did he look like?

For several moments, it appears that Fischer does not intend to go
on. Then he continues.

> FISCHER
> "His teeth are those of a carnivore. When he
> bares them in a smile it gives one the impression
> of a snarling animal. His face is white, for he
> despises the sun. He has astonishingly green eyes.
> His forehead is broad, his hair and short-trimmed
> beard jet black. Despite his handsomeness, his is
> a frightening visage; the face of some demon who
> has taken on a human aspect."

(CONTINUED)

91   *CONTINUED: —3*

> FLORENCE (impressed)
> Are you quoting?

> FISCHER
> His second wife.
> (Pause; looking up)
> She hanged herself from one of those lamps;
> in 1927.

His words have a chilling effect on them. Barrett ends it.

> BARRETT
> Was he tall or short?

> FISCHER
> Six-foot-five. The Roaring Giant, he was called.

> BARRETT
> Education?

> FISCHER
> New York. London. Paris. Berlin. Vienna. No
> specific course of study. Logic, ethics, religion,
> philosophy, psychology.

> BARRETT
> Just enough with which to rationalize his actions,
> I imagine.

> FISCHER (a cold contradiction)
> Wrong. He was a genius.
> (Pause; with a humorless smile)
> Of sorts.

> ANN (trying to keep Chris and Fischer from
> clashing now)
> What did he do to make this place so bad?

> FISCHER
> Converted it to Hell.

> ANN
> How?

(CONTINUED)

91   CONTINUED: —4

FLORENCE
Do we really want to know that, Mrs. Barrett?
Would it help us any?

BARRETT (ignoring her)
There was a lot of drug addiction, wasn't there?

CAMERA MOVES IN ON Florence's face, her expression
tightening as Fischer speaks.

FISCHER (slowly; with increasing emphasis)
Drug addiction. Alcoholism. Sadism. Bestiality.
Mutilation. Murder. Vampirism. Necrophilia.
Cannibalism.

Florence's face fills the screen now. She blinks.

92   SUBLIMINAL SHOT

Debauched-looking people eating at the table, a huge platter on the
table with a partially carved CORPSE on it.

93   BACK TO FLORENCE

Catching her breath.

94   FULL SHOT

The other three looking at her. Fischer's smile is thin.

FISCHER
Not to mention the gamut of sexual goodies; shall
I go on?

ANN (pause; shaken)
How did it end?

FISCHER (coldly)
If it had ended, would we be here?

BARRETT
It is *about* to end, Mr. Fischer.

Fischer only smiles dubiously. Ann swallows, staring at him.
(CONTINUED)

94   *CONTINUED:*

ANN (trying to ease the atmosphere)
What happened to Belasco?

FISCHER
No one knows. When relatives of some of his
guests had the house broken into in November
1929, everyone inside was dead from one cause
or another. Twenty-seven of them.
(As they react to this)
Belasco was not among them.

FLORENCE
If no one objects I'd like to try a sitting tonight.

BARRETT
I have no objection.
(Pause)
Would you care to sit in the morning, Mr. Fischer?

FISCHER
I'm not ready yet.

95   *INT. — GREAT HALL, CLOSE ON METAL BUST*

The face malignant, grinning. Florence ENTERS FRAME, her
body blocking off the bust. CAMERA PANS TO SHOW her
moving toward the round table at which the other three are waiting.
In addition to the equipment already mentioned, there is, now, also
a contact clock, an electroscope, standard and infrared lights,
thermometers, a hygroscope, a sthenometer, a phosphorescent
sulfide screen, an electric stove, a box of vessels and tubes, molding
equipment and cabinet equipment in a box. There is also a pitcher
of water and a glass.

96   *ANGLE ON TABLE*

FLORENCE
I'm ready now.

BARRETT (he'd rather do this someplace else)
You're certain this equipment isn't going to
bother you.

(CONTINUED)

96   *CONTINUED:*

> FLORENCE
> Not at all. For that matter, it might prove
> valuable for you to switch on your tape recorder
> when Fleurette starts to speak.
>   (To Ann)
> Your husband has explained to you that I'm a
> mental medium?

> ANN (nods)
> And Fleurette is your guide?

> FLORENCE
> My spirit guide, yes.

> ANN
> A French woman?

> FLORENCE
> A little girl. They're very spiritual, you know.
> Guides are usually children. Or Red Indians.
> Orientals, too.

> ANN
> Oh?

Barrett smiles at her expression and switches off the lights. There is
just enough illumination from the fireplace to see what transpires.
Florence sits at the table and clasps her hands on her lap.

> FLORENCE
> O Spirit of Love and Tenderness, we gather here
> tonight to communicate with those who walk in
> this house in torment. Help us bridge the chasm
> of death so faithfully that pain may be
> transformed into joy, sorrow into peace. All this
> we ask in the name of our Infinite Father. Amen.

97   *FLORENCE*

Starts to breathe deeply, making passes in front of her face. Soon,
she begins to rub both hands over her arms and shoulders, down
> (MORE)

              (CONTINUED)

97   *CONTINUED:*

across her breasts and over her stomach and thighs, her lips parted, her eyes half closed, her expression almost sensual.

98   *ANN AND BARRETT*

Ann's eyes widen, her mouth opening a little as she watches. Barrett, noticing, smiles.

99   *FISCHER*

Watching Florence, his face stonelike.

100   *ANGLE ON FOUR*

Florence has stopped rubbing herself. Her hands lie flaccidly in her lap. Her arms and legs twitch slightly. Bit by bit, her head leans back until it touches the chair. She draws in an extended, quavering breath, then is still. Moments pass. Abruptly, CAMERA MOVES IN ON her face as she lifts her head, eyes closed, her expression childlike.

FLORENCE
Je m'appelle Fleurette.

They stare at her in silence.

FLORENCE
Je m'appelle Fleurette.

BARRETT (wearily)
Good evening.

FLORENCE
Bon soir.

BARRETT
Will you speak in English, please.

FLORENCE
Oui.
(Haltingly; with a French accent)
If you wish.

BARRETT
We wish.

101   *ANGLE PAST FLORENCE, TOWARD THE THREE*

FLORENCE (nodding)
I . . . come from afar. Bring . . . greetings to you
from the realm of Eternal Peace. I am happy to
see you. Fleurette is always . . . happy to see
earthlings gather in a circle of belief. We are with
you always. Death is not the end of the road.
Death is but a doorway . . . to a world without end.

BARRETT
May we . . . ?

FLORENCE
Earthlings are souls in prison. Bound in dungeons
of flesh.

BARRETT
Yes, but may we . . . ?

FLORENCE
Death is the pardon, the release. Leaving behind
what a poet called the "muddy vesture of decay."

BARRETT (frowning)
How old are you?

FLORENCE
There is no age here.

BARRETT (grunts; beat)
Do you think we   ?

Ann lowers her head, pressing her lips together as Florence
interrupts again.

FLORENCE
Miss Tanner says put on machine, got her voice
on ribbon. I do not know what she means.

BARRETT (beat; surrendering)
Right.

He switches on the tape recorder and pushes the microphone
toward Florence. He opens his mouth to speak. Suddenly, the
(MORE)

(CONTINUED)

101   *CONTINUED:*

CAMERA MOVES IN CLOSE ON Florence's face as she turns to it, teeth bared, eyebrows pressing down, a sound of disapproval in her throat.

> FLORENCE
> This is a bad house. A place of sickness. Evil.
> (Pause; tilting her head up suddenly)
> There is a *man* here.

102   *ANN, BARRETT, AND FISCHER*

Ann drawing back unconsciously, looking where Florence is looking.

> FLORENCE (voice)
> An ugly man. Long hair. Dirt on his face.
> Scratches. Sores. Yellow teeth.

103   *FLORENCE*

As she speaks, CAMERA MOVES UP TO the spot she's looking at.

> FLORENCE (voice)
> Bent over. Twisted. Like an animal.

104   *FISCHER*

Staring at the spot.

> FLORENCE (voice)
> Breathing hard. In pain. So sick.

105   *SUBLIMINAL SHOT*

The man Florence has described.

106   *FISCHER*

Closing his eyes.

107   *ANGLE PAST ANN AND BARRETT, TOWARD FLORENCE*

Ann twitching as Florence raises her arm and points toward the entry hall.

> FLORENCE
> *Allez!* Leave this house!
> (MORE)

(CONTINUED)

107   CONTINUED:

> (Pause; turning back to the table)
> No good. He is here too long. Not listen. Not
> understand.

108   CLOSE ON FLORENCE

She touches her temple with an index finger.

> FLORENCE
> Too much sick inside.
> (A long pause; curiously)
> Limits. Nations. Terms. I do not know what that
> means. Extremes and limits. Terminations.
> Extremities.
> (Shaking her head)
> Not know.

She jerks around as though someone has grabbed her by the
shoulder.

109   ANN AND BARRETT

Ann starting. As Florence speaks, CAMERA PANS TO her, passing
Fischer.

> FLORENCE (voice)
> No. Go away.
> (Grunt)
> Young man stay here. Say . . . must talk . . .
> must talk.

CAMERA STOPS ON her. She is silent for several moments. Then,
abruptly, she begins to speak *with the voice of a young man,*
"looking" around the table, eyes still closed, expression one of rabid
agitation.

> FLORENCE
> I don't know you people! Why are you here? It
> does no good! Nothing ever changes; nothing!
> Get out of here or I'll hurt you! I can't help
> myself! Goddamn you filthy sons of bitches, can't
> you see I'm helpless!

110   *ANGLE PAST FISCHER, TOWARD BARRETT AND ANN*

Barrett interested in this phenomenon. Ann notices and looks
intently at Florence.

> FLORENCE (voice)
> I don't want to hurt you but I must! *I must!*

111   *CLOSE SHOT — FLORENCE*

CAMERA MOVES IN ON her savage expression, her lips drawn
back from clenching teeth.

> FLORENCE
> *Get out of this house before I kill you all.*

CAMERA ZOOMS BACK ON the table as a series of loud, staccato
RAPPINGS suddenly begins.

112   *ANGLE PAST FISCHER, TOWARD BARRETT AND ANN*

Fischer looks startled, Ann alarmed; Barrett suddenly fascinated.
Ann's voice is drowned out by the chain of savage BLOWS. It
sounds as though a berserk man is pounding a hammer on the
tabletop as hard and fast as he can.

> ANN
> What's that?

Barrett reaches for his instruments but the RAPPINGS suddenly
stop and Florence starts to groan. Barrett reaches into his jacket
pocket and removes a pencil flashlight. He shines a red beam at
Florence and CAMERA PANS TO her. Her head is lolling back
against the chair, her eyes still shut, mouth hanging open.

113   *THE FOUR*

Ann, looking down, stiffens.

> ANN (tightly)
> It's getting cold under the table.

Barrett tugs at the microphone wire, the scraping of the
microphone across the table setting Ann's teeth on edge. Florence
continues groaning. Barrett picks up the microphone.

(CONTINUED)

113   CONTINUED:

> BARRETT
>
> Temperature decline. Strictly tactile; no instrument
> reading yet. Phenomena commenced with series of
> severe percussions. Miss Tanner reacting
> erratically. Trance state retained but variable.
> Possible confusion at onset of unexpected physical
> phenomena. Absence of cabinet a probable factor.
> Will hand subject tube of uranium salt solution.

The red beam flicks over the tabletop. Barrett picks up the tube
and, standing, moves to press the tube into Florence's hand. The
tube lights up, then CAMERA MOVES IN ON her. Abruptly, she
sits up, opening her eyes.

> FLORENCE (her own voice)
> No.

114   ANGLE ON THE FOUR

> BARRETT (into the microphone; disappointedly)
> Subject out of trance.

He switches off the tape recorder and turns on a light, Florence
averting her face from it. Fischer pours her a glass of water and she
drinks it in a single swallow. Barrett starts to check his equipment to
see if any damage was done.

> FLORENCE (to Fischer)
> Thank you.
> (To Barrett)
> What happened?

> BARRETT
> You started manifesting physical phenomena.

> FLORENCE (startled)
> I'm not a physical medium.

> BARRETT
> You were just now.
> (Beat)
> The embryo of one, at any rate.

(CONTINUED)

114   *CONTINUED:*

> FLORENCE
> I don't understand.

> BARRETT (pause)
> We can work together if you like.

> FLORENCE
> I . . . guess.

> BARRETT
> I'll telephone Deutsch's man and have him
> arrange for the building of a cabinet tomorrow
> morning.
> (Finishing with his equipment and looking at her)
> You're sure, now?

> FLORENCE
> *Yes* . . . yes. It's just that . . . it's difficult for me to
> comprehend. All these years a mental medium.
> Now this.
> (Trying to smile)
> The Lord certainly *does* move in mysterious ways.

> FISCHER (coldly)
> *So does this house.*

They watch him as he strides away. Ann glances at Barrett, but he
doesn't notice. She looks at Fischer again. Florence is obviously
disturbed. Forcibly, she shakes herself out of it, CAMERA
MOVING IN CLOSE ON her.

> FLORENCE
> God's will, not mine.

> FISCHER
> The Lord may not have too much influence in
> Hell House.

115   *INT. — BARRETTS' ROOM*

Near the door is a large, carved bed, next to it a table with a lamp
(MORE)

(CONTINUED)

115   *CONTINUED*:

and a French-style telephone on it. Ann lies in the bed. Barrett
comes out of the bathroom and sits beside her, smiling.

                            BARRETT
                        Back to normal?
                        (As she nods)
                Those pounding noises *are* a bit unnerving the
                first time you hear them.

                            ANN
                        What causes them?

                            BARRETT
                Usually an invisible extrusion from the medium's
                solar plexus.

                        ANN (looking askance)
                        Aw, come on, Prof.

                        BARRETT (smiling)
                        You'll see.
                        (Beat)
                When it starts becoming visible.

She makes a sickened noise, tongue sticking out. Barrett smiles.

                            BARRETT
                I *hope* she keeps producing physical phenomena.
                I can do without that erudite little snot from
                France.

                            ANN
                Is she from — *was* she from France?

                            BARRETT
                I'll give you a hint where she's from.
                        (Beat)
                Fleurette translated into English is, *voilà*,
                Florence.

                            ANN
                        It's *her*?

                                                (CONTINUED)

115   CONTINUED: —2

                          BARRETT
              As I said, a classic case of divided consciousness.

116   INT. — FLORENCE'S ROOM, ANGLE ON BED

Florence kneeling in prayer beside it. CAMERA MOVES IN ON
her. Finishing, she turns off the light and gets in bed; prepares to
sleep. Silence for a while. Then she opens her eyes and turns her
head toward the O.S. door as it is OPENED and CLOSED quietly.
FOOTSTEPS approach, muffled on the rug. They reach the foot
of the bed and STOP. There is a sound of BREATHING at the
foot of the bed.

117   POV SHOT — FOOT OF BED

Dark. The sound of BREATHING.

118   CLOSE ON FLORENCE

                          FLORENCE
                          Who's there?

119   POV SHOT — FOOT OF BED

The BREATHING quickens.

120   CLOSE ON FLORENCE

                     FLORENCE (cont'd)
                       Speak to me.
                         (Pause)
                      Let me help you.

There is an O.S. SOB. She pushes up on an elbow.

            FLORENCE (cont'd) (compassionately)
                   Yes, I hear. I understand.
                         (Beat)
                   Tell me who you are.

121   OMIT

122   CLOSE ON FLORENCE

Reacting. Abruptly, the BREATHING sound stops and she reacts
again.

123   POV SHOT — FOOT OF BED

Nothing.

124   FLORENCE

She waits a while longer, then lies back down. CAMERA MOVES
IN ON her face. Abruptly, the answer occurs to her.

> FLORENCE (cont'd)
> Of course.

125   INT. — GREAT HALL, ANGLE OVER TABLE, TOWARD
        FISCHER

Sitting in a chair by the fireplace, staring at the table. CAMERA
MOVES IN ON him until his face fills the screen, his expression
carven, unreadable. He looks up slowly.

126   HIGH ANGLE SHOT — FISCHER

The GLAZED LENS effect again.

> FISCHER
> I know you're here, you bastards!
> (Beat)
> But you aren't going to get me this time!

CAMERA HOLDS. We hear the SOUND of a spoon clinking on a
platter.

127   INT. — DINING HALL, CLOSE ON PLATTER OF
        SCRAMBLED EGGS

As Barrett spoons some onto his plate. TITLE: December 22.
CAMERA WITHDRAWS to SHOW him and Ann at the table.
having breakfast. In the B.G. is the archway leading to the Great Hall.
They look around as Florence APPEARS, approaching the table.

> FLORENCE
> Good morning.

> ANN and BARRETT
> Good morning.

> FLORENCE (sitting; to Ann)
> Did you sleep all right?

(CONTINUED)

127   *CONTINUED:*

ANN
Fine. And you?

FLORENCE
I slept very well.

Barrett hands over the platter of eggs.

FLORENCE
Thank you.
(As she takes a small portion)
I think I have a partial answer to the haunting,
Doctor.

BARRETT (a bit startled)
Do you?

FLORENCE
Yes. That young man who warned us during the
sitting.
(Beat)
He came to my room last night.

Ann's hand freezes as she is lifting scrambled eggs to her mouth
with her fork.

FLORENCE (cont'd)
He's Belasco's son.

BARRETT (eating toast; casually)
Didn't know he had one.

FLORENCE
Yes. He's here — very young and very frightened.
And because he's frightened, very angry, very hostile.
I believe if I can convince him to move on, a good
portion of the haunting force will be eliminated.

BARRETT (casually)
Do it then, by all means.

Florence is about to speak, knowing that he doesn't believe a word
she's said. Before she can, however, there is a loud KNOCKING
(MORE)

(CONTINUED)

127   CONTINUED: —2

sound in the entry hall. Ann's hand twitches, spilling eggs from
her fork.

                    BARRETT (cont'd)
              That would be the carpenters.

Standing, he starts toward the Great Hall. Ann looks toward him.
He stops to regard her.

                    BARRETT (cont'd)
              Oh, I'm sure it's safe to leave you long enough to
              answer the door.

He starts away.

128   ENTRY HALL, MOVING SHOT — BARRETT

Coming out of the Great Hall and moving toward the front door. As he
does, he glances up to see Fischer descending the staircase in the B.G.

                    BARRETT
              Good morning.

Fischer doesn't answer.

129   ANGLE FROM FRONT DOOR, TOWARD FISCHER

He watches as Barrett opens the door. Outside, Hanley is standing
on the porch, an umbrella in his hand.

                    BARRETT
              Good Lord, it's raining.

                    HANLEY (coming in)
              I've got your carpenters.

CAMERA MOVES IN ON Barrett's look of satisfaction.

                    BARRETT
              Good! Now I can move.

130   INT. — CABINET, CLOSE ON FLORENCE — LATER

Eyes closed, head lolling; deep in trance. CAMERA WITHDRAWS
revealing the simple, three-sided, roofed cabinet, the front
                    (MORE)
                                        (CONTINUED)

130   *CONTINUED:*

opening of it covered by mosquito netting with small bells attached
to it. Florence is sitting on an armchair, wearing a pair of black
tights and a black smock, gloves on both hands held palms down on
metal plates attached to the chair arms. She has on special shoes
that rest on a pair of floor plates. In front of the cabinet is a small
table on top of which are a tambourine, a tea bell, and a bowl.
WITHDRAWING CAMERA reveals the rack of red and yellow
lights pointing at the table and melted paraffin wax in a pot on the
electric stove. Finally, CAMERA REVEALS Barrett with the tape
recorder microphone in his hand. His speech commences almost at
the beginning of the shot.

                         BARRETT
              Two thirty-eight P.M. Miss Tanner in apparent
              trance. Pulse rate 85. Respiration 15. Four
              electric contacts maintained. No change in
              temperature, steady at 73.2 degrees.
              Dynamometer reading 1,870.

131   *ANGLE PAST ANN, TOWARD FISCHER*

Both of them staring at the O.S. medium.

                     BARRETT (voice)
              Dynamometer reading decreased to 1,823 now.
              Temperature lowering — now at 69.6 degrees.
              Pulse rate 94.5 and rising.

CAMERA PANS to Florence lying back against the chair, eyes shut,
breathing faster and faster. Moments pass.

                     BARRETT (voice)
              Temperature drop now 12.3 degrees.
              Dynamometer tension reduced to 1,779.
              Pressurometer negative. Electric contacts still
              maintained.

132   *ANGLE ON THREE*

Watching Florence; Barrett checking his instruments.
                                                        (CONTINUED)

132   *CONTINUED:*

BARRETT
Rate of breath increasing — fifty . . . fifty-seven . . .
sixty — rising steadily.

Ann starts as the camera shutters CLICK O.S. CAMERA PANS
QUICKLY TO them.

BARRETT
Infrared rays broken, cameras activated.

The film winds itself automatically.

133   *CLOSE ON BARRETT*

BARRETT (an undercurrent of excitement in his
voice)
Evidence of EMR commencing.

134   *FISCHER*

Turning toward Barrett, curious.

BARRETT (voice)
Medium's respiration now 210. Dynamometer
1,460. Temperature —

ANN (voice)
What's that smell?

135   *ANGLE PAST ANN, TOWARD BARRETT AND FISCHER*

BARRETT (sniffs)
Evidence of ozone in the air.

Ann looks back at Florence. Soon, she starts to lean forward as if
uncertain what she's seeing.

136   *POV SHOT — FLORENCE*

CAMERA MOVES IN ON her right hand. Threads of pale white
viscous matter are oozing from the fingertips.

137   *ANGLE PAST FISCHER, TOWARD ANN AND BARRETT*

Fischer looks sickened, Ann awed.

(CONTINUED)

137   CONTINUED:

                            BARRETT
                        Teleplasm forming.

138   CLOSE ON FLORENCE'S RIGHT HAND

The threads getting longer and thicker, drifting out into the air.
CAMERA PANS TO her left hand. The same thing is happening to
it. CAMERA DRAWS BACK TO SHOW the separate threads from
each finger beginning to join, the two strands moving toward each
other.

                        BARRETT (voice)
            Separate filaments exuding from fingertips of
            both hands — uniting into two single strands.
                            (Pause)
            Two strands moving toward each other.

The two strands join and become one grayish, filmy tentacle that
gets longer, rippling in the air.

139   ANGLE PAST BARRETT, TOWARD FISCHER AND ANN

                            BARRETT
                Bypassing bell and tambourine in favor of
                specimen retrieval.

Fischer and Ann glance at him.

                            BARRETT
                Leave a specimen in the bowl, please.

Ann stares at him, amazed by the calmness of his tone. Then she
looks back at the teleplasm, winces.

140   ANGLE ON TENTACLE

Starting to rear up slowly like an eyeless serpent. Moments pass.

                        BARRETT (voice)
                Leave a specimen in the bowl, please.

The tentacle undulates in the air, then begins to glide toward
CAMERA until it fills the screen.

141   ANGLE PAST ANN, TOWARD FISCHER AND BARRETT

She stares at the tentacle with unblinking eyes. Her throat moves.

142   *MOVING SHOT — TENTACLE*

CAMERA WITHDRAWING FROM it as it glides through the air, through the net and toward the table. It inches its way across the table like a giant worm.

> BARRETT (voice)
> Teleplasmic stalk through net and moving toward table. Dynamometer reading 1,340, dropping steadily. Respiration 240. Electric contacts still maintained.

143   *FISCHER*

Staring at the tentacle, repulsed by it.

144   *SUBLIMINAL SHOT — THE BOY FISCHER*

A similar extrusion from his mouth.

145   *FISCHER*

Face hardening.

146   *TENTACLE*

Reaching the bowl and touching it, it recoils, rearing like a serpent again. The moist, filmy member sways back and forth like an undersea plant undulating in the current

147   *ANGLE PAST BARRETT, TOWARD ANN*

> BARRETT
> Leave a specimen in the bowl, please.

She looks at him, newly impressed by his calmness. He looks at the EMR Recorder and smiles excitedly. CAMERA PANS DOWN TO it. The needle has passed the 300 mark.

148   *TENTACLE*

Swaying down to the bowl, it slithers across the rim, recoils a little, then begins to coil itself with a languid, spiraling movement until it has filled the bowl. Abruptly, it disappears.

149   *ANGLE PAST ANN, TOWARD BARRETT AND FISCHER*

She starts in surprise. Barrett rises.

150   *ANGLE ON FLORENCE*

Barrett ENTERS FRAME and lifts the bowl off the table, moves
OUT OF FRAME again.

151   *ANGLE PAST BARRETT, TOWARD FISCHER AND ANN*

As Barrett reseats himself and sets the bowl on the table, picks up
the microphone again. Ann watches him; Fischer keeps his eyes on
Florence.

BARRETT

Specimen retained in bowl. No odor. Colorless
and slightly turbid.

FISCHER
Barrett.

Barrett glances at him, then toward the cabinet. Ann reacts as she
sees what's happening.

152   *POV SHOT — FLORENCE*

CAMERA MOVES IN FAST ON her face. Across the bottom half
of it, a cloudy mass is starting to form.

153   *ANGLE PAST BARRETT, TOWARD ANN AND FISCHER*

BARRETT

Teleplasmic matter being generated across lower
part of medium's face issuance from mouth and
nostrils.

(Impressed)
Remarkable.

154   *CLOSE ON FLORENCE*

The formation in front of her face now resembles a torn, grimy
handkerchief, the lower part of which hangs down in shreds. The
upper part is starting to rise, spreading with a swaying movement,
obscuring her nose, moving upward toward her eyes.

155   *THE THREE*

Watching

156   *CLOSE ON FLORENCE*

The teleplasmic formation covering her eyes now, moving upward toward her brow. In a few moments, her face is entirely cloaked, the teleplasm like a ragged veil through which her pale, tight features can be seen. Now the veil starts whitening.

BARRETT (voice)
Teleplasmic veil starting to condense

The texture of the mistlike veil curdles until Florence's face has vanished behind it. Gradually, her head, then upper shoulders are concealed beneath folds of what appears to be a soggy, grayish-white shroud. CAMERA WITHDRAWS TO SHOW the bottom of the dingy fabric descending toward her lap, lengthening into a solid strip several inches wide. As it descends, it begins to take on coloration.

BARRETT (voice)
Separate filaments extending downward, reddish
hue impinging on grayness.

157   *ANGLE PAST FISCHER, TOWARD ANN AND BARRETT*

His face like that of a statue as he watches. In the B.G., Ann observes uneasily.

BARRETT
Stretching tissue seems to be inflamed. Getting
brighter, brighter. The color of open flesh now.

158   *ANGLE ON FLORENCE*

A brief, startling shot of the open-fleshed look of the teleplasm.

159   *ANGLE PAST ANN, TOWARD BARRETT AND FISCHER*

Barrett glances over at her, notes her expression, then looks back at Florence. CAMERA MOVES IN ON Fischer as he stares at Florence, repelled by the sight and the memories it evokes from him.

160   *FLORENCE*

The shroud becoming more albescent every moment, starting to resemble linen dipped in white paint, transparent in some places,
(MORE)

(CONTINUED)

160   *CONTINUED:*

solid in others. Veil-like strips and patches are beginning to appear
at other spots on her body — her right arm and leg, her right breast,
the center of her lap. It looks as though a soiled bedsheet has been
dipped into some iridescent liquid, then torn apart, the fragments
thrown across her indiscriminately, the largest piece settling on her
head and shoulders. The teleplasmic sections start to coalesce. *Bit
by bit they start to assume a shape.* The filament, now pale again,
looks vaguely like an arm and wrist.

161   *ANGLE PAST THE THREE, TOWARD FLORENCE*

> BARRETT
> Something taking form.

Slowly, a figure forms, white, garbed in a shapeless robe, sexless,
incomplete, its hands like rudimentary claws. There is a mouth on
the head, two dark spots for nostrils, two elementary eyes.

> BARRETT (cont'd)
> Teleplasmic figure formed.
> (Beat)
> Imperfectly.

He breaks off as the figure CHUCKLES. CAMERA ZOOMS IN
ON the unfinished face as it begins to laugh, the mouth unmoving.
It is a rolling laugh, deep and resonant.

162   *ANGLE ON THREE*

Staring at the figure. CAMERA DRAWS BACK SLOWLY UNTIL
the figure's head is in F.G. It turns, the figure appearing to look at
them one by one. Ann is last. The figure keeps looking at her. She
draws back in her chair.

> BARRETT (cont'd)
> Easy.

Suddenly, the figure shoots toward Ann, CAMERA FOLLOWING.
Ann shrieks and she throws both arms across her face. With a noise
that sounds like the snapping of a giant rubber band, the figure
vanishes. Florence cries out in pain O.S. Fischer jumps to his feet.
> (CONTINUED)

THE LEGEND OF HELL HOUSE

162   CONTINUED:

>   BARRETT (cont'd)
>   Hold it!

Fischer stands rigidly as Barrett rises and moves to the cabinet, CAMERA WITHDRAWING UNTIL Florence's head is IN FRAME. Barrett shines the red beam of his pencil flashlight into her face, feels the pulse at her neck. He turns away.

>   BARRETT (cont'd)
>   Now.

Fischer pours a glass of water and brings it to Florence as Barrett returns to Ann, who is sitting frozen in her chair.

>   BARRETT (cont'd)
>   You all right?

She nods a little and he pats her shoulder.

>   BARRETT (cont'd)
>   That a girl.

As he picks up the microphone and starts talking, CAMERA MOVES IN ON the EMR Recorder.

>   BARRETT (cont'd)
>   Miss Tanner coming out of trance, premature
>   retraction of teleplasm causing brief systemic
>   shock. Conclusion of sitting: two forty-eight P.M.

The needle on the Recorder points to 403.

163   INT. – BARRETTS' BEDROOM — INSERT: MICROSCOPE
        SHOT

Motionless groups of shapeless forms and groups of oval and polygonal bodies. CAMERA PANS SLOWLY ACROSS them.

164   CLOSE ON ANN

As she opens her eyes. Turning her head on the pillow, she looks across the room.

165   POV SHOT — BARRETT

Sitting at an octagonal table, bent over a microscope.

166   *ANGLE PAST BARRETT, TOWARD BED*

Ann rises and walks to the table. Barrett looks around with a smile.

ANN
I apologize for what I did before.

BARRETT
No problem.

ANN
I spoiled your sitting, didn't I?

BARRETT
Not at all. I couldn't be more satisfied.
(Gesturing toward microscope)
Take a look.

She bends over to look into the eyepieces of the microscope.

167   *MICROSCOPE SHOT*

ANN (voice)
What is it?

BARRETT (cont'd)
A specimen of that teleplasm prepared in water.
(Beat)
You're looking at conglomerates of etiolated,
lamellar cohesive bodies, also single laminae of
varied forms resembling epithelium without nuclei.

168   *BACK TO SCENE*

Ann looks at him, straight-faced.

ANN
Would you like to run through that again?

BARRETT (chuckling)
Just showing off.
(Beat)
All right, we'll simplify it. Say the specimen
consists of cell detritus, epithelium cells, veils,
lamellae, filmy aggregates, isolated fat grains,
mucus, and so on.

(CONTINUED)

168   *CONTINUED:*

ANN
That's simplifying it?
(Pause; semi-humorously)
What does it *mean*, Chris?

BARRETT
It means that what the spiritualists refer to as
ectoplasm is derived almost entirely from the
medium's body, the remainder being admixtures
from the air and the medium's costume —
fibrous vegetable remains, bacterial spores, starch
grains, food and dust particles, etcetera. The bulk
of it, however, is organic, living matter.
(Beat; excitedly)
Think of it, Ann. *An organic externalization of
thought.* Mind reduced to matter.

ANN (awed)
She made that figure from her*self*?

BARRETT
Substantially —

ANN
Why?

BARRETT
To make a point, no doubt. We were supposed to
think that figure was Belasco's son.
(Amused)
A son who never existed outside of Miss
Tanner's mind.

169   *INT. — FLORENCE'S BATHROOM — FLORENCE*

Washing. Something FLAPS in the bedroom and she moves to the
doorway, looks in, reacting to the sight.

170   *POV SHOT — BED*

The comforter and blankets landing on the floor. CAMERA
(MORE)

(CONTINUED)

170   *CONTINUED:*

MOVES IN ON the top sheet. There seems to be a figure lying under it — the nude body of a man.

171   *FLORENCE*

Made uneasy by the man's nudity.

> FLORENCE
> So you're back.

She dries her face as she moves to the bed and stops. CAMERA MOVING WITH her. She looks down at the man's face, avoiding the look of his body.

> FLORENCE
> You have a nice face.

172   *UP ANGLE PAST FACE, TOWARD FLORENCE*

> FLORENCE
> What do you want?

Moments pass but nothing happens. Florence starts leaning over to see the face more clearly. She gets closer and closer to it. Suddenly, it makes a loud noise and the top sheet flies up into Florence's face. She rips it away. The air begins to ring with MOCKING LAUGHTER.

> FLORENCE (angrily)
> Very funny.

The LAUGHTER rises in pitch, taking on a frenetic quality.

> FLORENCE
> If you're all that clever, why are you a prisoner in
> this house?!

The LAUGHTER cuts off. Florence looks around, knowing something is about to happen. When the table lamp across the room flies off the table and breaks, she whirls with a gasp. She turns toward the door as angry FOOTSTEPS thud toward it.

173   *MOVING SHOT, ANGLE TOWARD FLORENCE*

CAMERA MOVING BACK TOWARD the door with the speed of
> (MORE)

(CONTINUED)

173   CONTINUED:

the FOOTSTEPS. The door is flung open so hard it crashes against the wall. Florence waits, then walks to the door and shuts it quietly.

> FLORENCE
> Such anger.
> (Pause)
> And yet it's more than anger.

She returns to the bed.

174   ANGLE OVER BED

She looks at the bed, then sits on it. She finds herself stroking the sheet where the man was lying and pulls her hand away, stands.

175   FULL SHOT

Florence standing by the bed uncomfortably.

176   INT. — DINING HALL, DOWN ANGLE SHOT, TABLE

The four eating supper in silence.

177   THE FOUR — BARRETT AND FLORENCE FEATURED

> FLORENCE
> I was visited by Belasco's son again this afternoon.

> BARRETT (somewhat carelessly)
> Were you?

Florence bristles at his tone. Barrett doesn't notice this but Fischer does. He watches curiously as anger builds on her face. At last, she speaks.

> FLORENCE
> Will it never end?

Barrett looks up at her. Seeing her glare, his eyebrows raise.

> BARRETT
> Were you talking to me?

> FLORENCE
> I was.

(CONTINUED)

177   *CONTINUED:*

>   BARRETT (pause)
>   Will what never end?
>
>   FLORENCE
>   This attitude of doubt. Distrust.
>
>   BARRETT
>   Distrust?
>
>   FLORENCE
>   *Yes.* Distrust . . .
>   (Beat)
>   That uncomfortable outfit you made me wear.
>   Those light plates on my palms and underneath
>   the shoes you made me wear. The clear
>   implication that, without your precautions, I'd
>   more than likely commit a fraud.
>
>   BARRETT (perplexed)
>   Miss —
>
>   FLORENCE (cutting in)
>   Why should mediums be expected to produce
>   phenomena only under conditions that science
>   dictates? We're not machines, we're human beings.
>   These rigid, unyielding demands by science —
>
>   BARRETT (cutting in)
>   What brought this on? Have I —
>
>   FLORENCE (cutting in)
>   I'm not a medium for the fun of it, you know. It's
>   often painful, often unrewarding.
>
>   BARRETT
>   Don't you think I —
>
>   FLORENCE (cutting in)
>   It just so happens I believe that mediumship is
>   God's manifestation in man. "When I speak with
>   thee, I will open thy mouth and thou shalt say to
>   them: Thus saith the Lord."

                                            (CONTINUED)

177   CONTINUED: —2

                              BARRETT (incredulous)
                              Miss *Tanner* —

                              FLORENCE (angrily)
              There is nothing in the Bible — not a single
              recorded phenomenon that does not occur today
              whether it be sights or sounds, shaking of the
              house, or coming through closed doors, rushing
              winds, levitations, automatic writing, or the
              speaking in tongues.

In the heavy silence, Florence glares at Barrett. Fischer and Ann
stare at her. Barrett is nonplussed. To cover his embarrassment for
her, he picks up the coffeepot and pours some into his cup. He puts
down the pot and picks up his cup. Lifting it to his mouth, he
pauses, looking at her.

                              BARRETT
              Miss Tanner, I have no idea at *all* what's
              bothering you but let me assure you —

CAMERA ZOOMS IN ON his right hand as the cup explodes,
spraying hot coffee on the table.

178   ANN

Jerking back in her chair with a gasp.

179   UP ANGLE ON BARRETT

Gaping at the shard of handle still in his fingers. Blood is starting to
drip from the cut in his thumb.

180   FLORENCE

Staring at Barrett, face taut.

181   FISCHER

Looking around the room tensely.

182   DOWN ANGLE ON TABLE

                              BARRETT
                       What in God's name —

                                                  (CONTINUED)

182   *CONTINUED:*

He breaks off as the glass beside his plate bursts apart; its fragments scattering across the table. Ann jerks her hand back as her plate leaps from the table, flipping over and dumping food across the floor before it lands and shatters. She recoils as the top part of her glass breaks off with a cracking noise and jumps across the table toward Barrett. Barrett, pulling out a handkerchief, twists to the side. The glass top thuds off his arm and tumbles to the floor. Fischer's glass explodes and he lurches in his chair, flinging an arm in front of his face. Florence's plate somersaults, scattering food over the table. She reaches out to grab it, then jolts back as the plate goes flying across the table toward Barrett. Barrett jerks his head aside. The plate sails past his ear and lands on its edge, rolling rapidly across the floor and OUT OF FRAME; it BREAKS O.S. Ann cries out as one of the serving dishes slides across the table toward her husband. Barrett jumps up, toppling his chair. He almost falls, then leans against the table. The serving dish slides off the table edge and crashes to the floor. Mashed potatoes splatter on his shoes and trouser cuffs. Fischer is on his feet now. He tries to turn from the table but is slammed against it as his chair lurches hard against his legs. His cup goes leaping across the table, spouting coffee over Barrett's shirtfront as it strikes him in the chest. Ann cries out again as Fischer's plate is catapulted from the tabletop, flying closely over her head. The chair slides back from Fischer and he crumples to his knees, face a mask of startlement. Barrett, still leaning on the table, tries to twist the handkerchief around his bleeding thumb. The coffeepot falls over and begins to spin across the table toward him, spouting coffee. Barrett lurches aside to avoid it, slips on the fallen potatoes, flails for balance, then goes onto his right side. CAMERA PULLS AWAY FROM the table to show the floor where he is lying.

The coffeepot falls off the table, bounding off his left calf; he cries out at the burning impact. Ann tries to stand to help him but her chair rocks backward, throwing her off balance. A knife and spoon go hurtling past her cheek. Only Florence hasn't moved, staring at another serving dish skidding across the table, heading for Barrett. Barrett sees it coming and scrabbles aside with a gasp. The serving dish crashes down beside him, the edge of its cover striking his shin. Ann has struggled to her feet by now.

(CONTINUED)

182   CONTINUED: —2

> FISCHER (to Ann)
> Get under the table!

Ann turns to Barrett and helps him under the table as Florence slides from her chair, falling to her knees and ducking under the table. Fischer flings himself beneath it, CAMERA MOVING DOWN AND IN to observe them closely. They look around in shock at the O.S. NOISE.

183   *POV SHOT — MONASTERY TABLE*

A heavy, silver chafing dish arcs across the room toward CAMERA.

183A   *THE FOUR*

Overhead, the chafing dish hits the table with tremendous impact. Ann gasps. Barrett turns to help her, then returns to wrapping the handkerchief around his thumb. A silver bowl comes hurtling across the hall from the monastery table, strikes a table leg, and spins around in a blur of movement. Florence glances at Fischer. He is on his knees, eyes staring, face a rigid mask. She starts to reach toward him, then looks up at the SOUND of the sanctuary lamps starting to swing back and forth. Two of them COLLIDE noisily.

The table starts to rock back and forth. The silver creamer lands nearby, its contents splattering across the floor. The sugar bowl falls beside it as the table rocks with mounting violence, legs crashing down like pounding horse hooves. Everyone looks in different directions like soldiers under a nightmare siege. Ann cries out as the table slides away from them suddenly, surging across the floor. They twist around to watch it as it shoots OUT OF FRAME.

184   *POV SHOT — TABLE*

Rushing across the floor to smash against the fire screen, bending it totally out of shape.

185   *DOWN ANGLE ON FOUR*

Looking up at the sanctuary lamps. CAMERA PULLS UP TO REVEAL them swinging violently back and forth, bouncing off

(MORE)

(CONTINUED)

185   *CONTINUED:*

each other, colliding with gigantic clanging noises. One of them
tears loose and hurtles off, creating a shower of sparks as it bounces
across the floor and off a wall. Heavy objects are flying all around,
sliding past them. A candelabra thuds against Barrett's side, making
him fall with a cry of pain. CAMERA ZOOMS IN ON Florence's
agitated face.

FLORENCE
No!

All O.S. movement stops abruptly. They look around.

186   *HIGH DOWN ANGLE SHOT*

Everything motionless, the four crouched amid debris.

187   *THE FOUR*

Barrett looks at Florence guardedly as he tries to rise, Ann helping
him. Florence is looking at Fischer.

FLORENCE
I think you should leave, Mr. Fischer.

FISCHER (turning to her abruptly)
What the hell are you talking about?

Florence looks at Barrett for support.

FLORENCE
Doctor . . .

BARRETT (interrupting)
Trying to get rid of us *both* now?

He and Ann start toward the Great Hall. Florence watches him,
confused.

FLORENCE
What do you mean?
(Pause)
Doctor, what do you *mean*?

BARRETT (overlapping; coldly)
I should think that was obvious, Miss Tanner.

(CONTINUED)

187   *CONTINUED:*

Stunned, Florence watches as the Barretts leave. Now she turns to
Fischer, who is wiping off his clothes with a napkin, his movements
angry.

> FLORENCE
> What is he saying?
> (Beat; incredulously)
> That *I* was responsible for —

> FISCHER (cutting in)
> You're the one who'd better leave this house,
> kid. You're the one who's being used, not me.

Slinging aside the napkin, he turns and strides off angrily. Florence
watches him go, her expression one of stricken disbelief.

188   *INT. — BARRETTS' ROOM, CLOSE ON BARRETT*

Sitting on his bed, unwrapping the handkerchief from his thumb.
CAMERA WITHDRAWS TO INCLUDE Ann bringing a first-aid
kit hurriedly. The sight of the deep, blood-oozing cut on his thumb
makes her hiss.

> ANN
> You need a doctor.

> BARRETT
> I'm all right.

Ann watches as he pours sulfa powder on the cut, wincing.

> ANN
> Chris, it needs *stitches*.

> BARRETT
> It's *all right*. Will you bandage it?
> (As she hesitates)
> Ann?

She begins to bandage the thumb.

> BARRETT (cont'd)
> Tight as you can.

(CONTINUED)

188   *CONTINUED:*

               ANN (a long pause)
               Do we have to stay?

               BARRETT (startled)
               Are you serious?

She gives him a hard look.

               BARRETT (cont'd)
               You know how important this is to me.

               ANN
               What if you're *hurt* again?

               BARRETT
               I won't be.

               ANN
               How do you *know*?

               BARRETT
               I'll *see* to it.
               (Beat)
Surely you noticed how it ended at a word from
her? How was I the only one hurt?
               (As she looks at him)
               I was the one who angered her.

               ANN (aghast)
               You're saying that Miss Tanner did all that?

               BARRETT
Not unassisted. There's a lot of power in this
house, Ann. She's the one who used it though,
directing it at me.
               (As she stares at him)
               The bandage?
               (As she bandages again)
I made a mistake. I accepted a quiet, polite
behavior toward me at face value. You can't do
that with a medium; you never know what's
underneath.

                                (CONTINUED)

188   *CONTINUED: —2*

He breaks off as there is a KNOCK on the B.G. door. Both of them
look around. Ann hesitates, then moves across the room and opens
the door. Florence stands there. She looks toward Barrett.

FLORENCE
May I speak to you?
(Noting his reluctance)
I'll only be a moment.

Ann looks toward Barrett to see what he wants. He hesitates; nods.
Florence comes in and she and Ann approach the bed.

FLORENCE (cont'd)
Were you badly hurt?

BARRETT
I'll manage.

FLORENCE
I know what happened now. It was Belasco's son.
(As Barrett reacts badly)
Don't you *see*? He wants to separate us. We're
less of a challenge to him that way.
(Pause)
You really think it was *me* who —

BARRETT (cutting in)
Not only think it, Miss Tanner, but know it. Now,
please. I'm in considerable pain.

FLORENCE
Doctor, I was not responsible! It was Belasco's son!

BARRETT (losing his temper)
Miss Tanner, *there is no such person!*

Florence draws back, stunned by what he's saying and the
vehemence of his tone.

BARRETT (cont'd) (tightly)
Please go, Miss Tanner.
(Pause)
Please go.

(CONTINUED)

188   *CONTINUED: —3*

ANN
Miss Tanner . . .

Florence looks at her. She wants to convince Barrett but the look on
Ann's face prevents her. She looks back at Barrett, starting to lose
control.

FLORENCE (weakly)
You're wrong.

She turns away.

189   *INT. — CORRIDOR, ANGLE ON DOOR TO BARRETTS' ROOM*

Florence comes out and shuts the door. She moves to the banister
rail, which overlooks the entry hall, CAMERA WITHDRAWING.
Her expression is one of anguish.

FLORENCE
You're wrong.
(Pause)
Don't you see you're *wrong*?

190   *HIGH ANGLE SHOT — FLORENCE*

The LENS GLAZES. This time there is a sound so subtle we
cannot be sure what it is, except that there is an element of
amusement in it. CAMERA HOLDS.

191   *INT. — KITCHEN, CLOSE ON BOURBON BOTTLE —
LATER*

Clinking on the lip of a glass as Fischer pours himself a drink.
CAMERA WITHDRAWS as he sets the bottle down, runs some
water into the glass, then sits on a counter, taking sips and looking
into his thoughts. In the B.G. one of the swinging doors opens and
Fischer jerks his head around. Florence ENTERS.

FISCHER (coldly)
What are you doing *now*?

FLORENCE (tightly)
Looking for something.

(CONTINUED)

191   CONTINUED:

                              FISCHER
                    Proof that Belasco's son existed?

                             FLORENCE
                   You don't believe me either, do you?

                              FISCHER
                 Does it really matter to you what I believe?

                        FLORENCE (turning away)
                    I'm sorry if I insulted you before.

Fischer starts to speak as she moves toward the dining hall, then
decides against it. She pushes through a swinging door into the
dining hall and disappears. He sits undecidedly for a while,
then slips off the counter and starts after her, leaving his drink.

192   INT. — DINING HALL, CLOSE ON DOOR TO KITCHEN

Fischer comes out and looks for her.

193   POV SHOT — DINING HALL

In a state of debris after the psychic attack. There is no sign of
Florence.

194   FISCHER

Moves toward the Great Hall, CAMERA PANNING TO
FOLLOW his movement.

195   DOWN ANGLE ON GREAT HALL, TOWARD ARCHWAY TO
        DINING HALL

Fischer comes out of the dining hall and looks around for Florence.
Not seeing her, he starts for the entry hall, CAMERA PANNING
WITH his movement.

196   INT. — ENTRY HALL, ANGLE ON ARCHWAY TO
        GREAT HALL

Fischer crosses to the archway and comes out into the entry hall,
looking around for Florence. He catches sight of her.

197   POV SHOT — FLORENCE

Just disappearing down the corridor.

198   *FISCHER*

Starting after her. CAMERA MOVES IN QUICKLY ON the back
of his head as he stops in his tracks and whirls, looking toward the
second floor. He gasps.

199   *POV SHOT — ANN*

Standing on the railing in her nightgown. CAMERA ZOOMS IN
ON her face, her eyes open, her expression blank.

200   *FISCHER*

Starts to call her name, then cuts himself off.

201   *UP ANGLE ON ANN*

Swaying back and forth on the railing.

202   *FISCHER*

Deciding abruptly, he lunges to the stairs and ascends them two
steps at a time, CAMERA MOVING WITH him. He keeps his eyes
on Ann.

203   *MOVING POV SHOT — ANN*

Swaying more and more on the railing.

204   *ANGLE PAST ANN'S FEET*

On the railing. In the B.G. Fischer reaches the top of the stairs,
races to Ann, and grabs her just before she is about to topple off.
CAMERA QUICKLY SHIFTS so that they are in a TIGHT TWO
SHOT. Ann stares at him.

FISCHER
You're all right, I've got you.

She does not respond, her face still blank.

FISCHER (cont'd)
Mrs. Barrett?
(Pause)
Mrs. Barrett?

Unexpectedly, she presses against him with a soft moan, sliding her
arms around his back.

(CONTINUED)

204   CONTINUED:

> ANN (softly; throatily)
> You.
> (Beat)
> Me.
> (Beat)
> The girl.
> (Beat)
> *Barrett.*

Fischer pulls back, looking at her intently. It is obvious that she is under some kind of mental control. As she speaks, her voice becomes more and more coarse until *it begins to resemble a different voice entirely.* Fischer stares at her, mesmerized.

> ANN (cont'd)
> All together.
> (Beat; a fierce whisper)
> *Naked.*
> (Beat; speeding up)
> *Drunk. Sweating. Clutching. Licking. Biting.*
> *Eating. Drinking. Blood!*

She breaks off with a gasp of shock as Fischer slaps her suddenly. She spins around with a gasp and almost falls. Fischer grabs her arm and pulls her to her feet. She stares at him in shock. Suddenly, she looks down at herself, reacts. She pulls back from him, frightened.

> FISCHER
> You were walking in your sleep. You almost
> jumped —

He breaks off as she turns and runs back toward her room, too alarmed to respond to his words. She runs OUT OF FRAME.

> FISCHER (cont'd)
> Mrs. Barrett!

He stops, watches her go.

205   INT. — BARRETT'S' ROOM, ANGLE ON DOOR

Ann comes in and shuts the door, leans back against it breathlessly, her expression one of fright. She looks around uneasily, then looks at Barrett.

206   *ANGLE PAST BED, TOWARD ANN*

Barrett is asleep. Ann moves over to the bed and sits on it. She
shudders convulsively, crosses her arms.

207   *SECOND-FLOOR CORRIDOR — FISCHER*

Still looking toward the Barretts' room. Now he looks toward the
downstairs area, starts to turn as though to follow Florence, then
changes his mind with a scowl.

FISCHER
Oh, to hell with her.

Turning again, he walks to his room, goes inside, and slams the
door.

208–   *SERIES OF SHOTS*
212

Florence moving through the downstairs part of the house,
searching anxiously. She cannot enter the chapel.

213   *CELLAR CORRIDOR, UP ANGLE ON STAIRS*

As Florence descends the stairs to F.G., exhausted but unwilling to
stop. As she reaches F.G., she stops abruptly, looking toward the
wine cellar door.

214   *POV SHOT — DOOR TO WINE CELLAR*

215   *CLOSE ON FLORENCE*

216   *SUBLIMINAL SHOT*

The young man standing in front of the door.

217   *FLORENCE*

CAMERA MOVES WITH her as she crosses to the wine cellar
door and opens it.

218   *INT. — WINE CELLAR, ANGLE ON DOORWAY, PAST
CEILING BULB*

Filmed with dust and grime as Florence switches it on. She looks
around the room with anticipation.

219   *POV SHOT — WINE CELLAR*

CAMERA MOVING AROUND as though it were Florence's eyes. O.S., we hear her quickening BREATH. The wine racks are empty. Across the room from the doorway is a brick wall. CAMERA MOVES PAST IT, THEN WHIP PANS BACK TO a certain area of it.

220   *CLOSE ON FLORENCE*

221   *SUBLIMINAL SHOT — THE YOUNG MAN*

In front of the area of brick wall.

222   *MOVING SHOT — CLOSE ON FLORENCE*

Moving to the wall, looking at it. She stops.

223   *POV SHOT — WALL*

CAMERA close to it.

224   *FLORENCE*

Staring at the wall.

225   *SUBLIMINAL SHOT*

The young man looking at CAMERA pleadingly. He is surrounded by lions

226   *ANGLE ON FLORENCE*

As she presses herself against the wall in what looks like a crucified position. She sobs with relief.

> FLORENCE
> *Daniel!*
> (Pause)
> I've *found* you!

Florence cries out as unseen hands clutch her by the throat. She reaches up and begins to grapple with them, grabbing them away and staggering to the side. Regaining direction, she lunges for the wall once more. Again the hands are on her, clutching her shoulders, hurling her away.

(CONTINUED)

226   *CONTINUED:*

> FLORENCE (cont'd) (catching her balance)
> Don't! I'm here to help. You *will not* deter me!

The unseen hands grab her again, then jerk free as she cries out:

> FLORENCE (cont'd)
> *In the name of the Father, the Son, and the Holy*
> *Ghost!*

Florence turns and searches frantically for an object to smash the wall, finds an iron bar, and in desperation hits it again and again against the wall, then stops suddenly, an awareness flooding her entire being. Calmly she presses her hand over a certain section of the wall, which starts moving to the right with a rumble. Shackled to the wall inside the narrow passage are the mummified remains of a man.

> FLORENCE (almost collapsing in tears)
> *Daniel! Oh, Daniel! Now your soul can rest in*
> *peace!*

227   *INT. — BARRETTS' ROOM, ANGLE ON ANN, TOWARD BARRETT*

Asleep. TITLE: *December 23.* There is KNOCKING on the O.S. door. Waking up, Ann looks around in alarm. The knocking is insistent. In the B.G. Barrett pushes up on an elbow. He starts to get up, then sinks back as his burned leg gives him pain. Ann rises quickly.

> ANN
> I'll get it.

CAMERA WITHDRAWS as she moves to the door and opens it. She shrinks back with a gasp.

228   *FLORENCE*

In the doorway, her clothes, face, and hands covered with mortar stains.

> FLORENCE
> Would you wake your husband, please.

229   INT. — WINE CELLAR, ANGLE ON DOOR TO CORRIDOR

As Florence ENTERS, followed by Barrett and Ann. Florence leads
them into F.G. where they stop. Abruptly, Ann makes a gagging
noise and averts her face; Barrett reacts. Only Florence looks
undisturbed.

230   POV SHOT — WALL OPENING

Crudely broken through with a crowbar. Inside, shackled to the
wall, are the remains of a man. CAMERA MOVES IN ON his
parchmentlike features, the eyes like hardened berries, the lips
drawn back in a soundless scream.

231   ANGLE ON THE FOUR

Florence looks at Barrett.

> BARRETT
> Shades of Poe.

> FLORENCE
> I told you he was real.
> (Waiting)
> Well?

> BARRETT
> Well, what?
> (As she stares at him)
> I see the mummified remains of a man. *Are you*
> *telling me it's Daniel Belasco?*

She gazes at him almost pityingly, then turns. Barrett watches as she
steps toward the opening.

232   ANGLE PAST BARRETT AND ANN, TOWARD FLORENCE

Reaching in through the opening, she removes a ring from the left
hand of the shackled figure. She carries it to Barrett, holds it out to
him. Barrett hesitates, Ann looking at him with a worried
expression. Then he takes the ring and looks at it. Immediately, he
hands it back.

> BARRETT (smiling thinly)
> Very good.

(CONTINUED)

232   *CONTINUED:*

                    FLORENCE
              Now do you believe me?

                  BARRETT (casually)
                        No.

               FLORENCE (incredulous)
                      No?

                     BARRETT
       Miss Tanner, I am not about to reverse the
       scientific convictions of a lifetime because of one
       cadaver with a ring.

              FLORENCE (overlapping)
       Doctor, I'm not *trying* to reverse your convictions.
       Can't you see that *both* of us can be right?

             BARRETT (shaking his head)
                  Absolutely not.
             (Pause; taking Ann's arm)
                     Let's go.

Ann looks back at Florence as Barrett leads her away. Florence
looks at the ring.

233   INSERT: RING

Made of gold with an oval crest. CAMERA MOVES IN ON it.
Across the crest in scroll-like letters are the initials D.B.

233A   INT. — FLORENCE'S ROOM, CLOSE ON RING

In Florence's right hand, the one found on the body. She turns the
face of it away from CAMERA as she revolves it in her fingers.
CAMERA PANS SLOWLY to her face. Her eyes are shut. She is
psychometrizing the ring. CAMERA MOVES IN ON the center of
her forehead toward the pineal gland area.

233B   WHAT SHE SEES

The only SOUND we hear is that of Florence's quickening breath
as we see a series of *rapidly flashing images* — strange, distorted: a
                      (MORE)
                                        (CONTINUED)

233B   *CONTINUED:*

dark-haired, handsome, young Daniel Belasco; laughing almost
hysterically, drinking wildly; making passionate love; sobbing in
anguish; plunging a hypodermic needle in his arm — frightened, as
a shadowy figure looms over him.

233C   *CLOSE ON FLORENCE'S FACE*

Tightening, her breath quickens further. CAMERA MOVES IN
ON her forehead again. It is dewed with sweat.

233D   *WHAT SHE SEES*

CAMERA MOVES IN ON the shadowy figure and on into
darkness, through a huge cavern to the edge of a pit, then down the
pit, moving faster and faster. Florence's breathing becomes
extremely agitated. Over this we HEAR a new sound. The sound of
a cat PURRING, which increases in volume like a crescendo.

233E   *CLOSE-UP — FLORENCE*

Her breathing suddenly cuts off as she snaps back to reality by the
sound. She looks to see what it is.

233F   *POV SHOT — THE CAT*

Lying at her feet, faint illumination from the bathroom revealing it.
CAMERA MOVES IN SHARPLY ON its head. Its eyes are
glistening, almost unnaturally so.

233G   *ANOTHER ANGLE — FLORENCE, CAT*

The purring continues. Florence's mood has changed quite
suddenly as she reacts to the animal's presence.

FLORENCE
What a lovely cat. *Where did you come from?*

She starts to bend down a little to pet it.

FLORENCE (cont'd)
Would you like a little milk?

The cat rears back, fur raised, then a hideous unnatural sound
comes from its throat — half human, half animal. There is no telling
whether it is a real cat or not.

233H   *ANGLE ON FLORENCE*

Staring at the O.S. cat. She starts to raise her right hand.

> FLORENCE (cont'd) (whispering)
> In the name of God . . .

With a savage yowl, the cat leaps INTO FRAME, jumping at her.

233I   *THE CAT ATTACK*

An array of rapid shots to include the following action: Florence
jerks back, both arms flung before her face. The cat thrashes into
her, sharp claws hooking into her arms. She cries out but cannot
pull it loose. Its teeth dig deeper, front claws almost buried in her
sweater and arms — the harsh, demented sound still issuing from
its throat. Florence jerks her left arm free and digs her fingers into
the fur and skin, trying to pull back its head. The teeth pull loose.
Instantly the cat's head lunges at her throat. Florence blocks its way
with her right arm and the cat's teeth sink into her flesh again. She
sobs in pain and tries to jerk its head away, which she succeeds in
doing, and it falls to the floor. In the faint light from the bathroom
we see the cat roll over and regain its feet. Florence lunges toward
the bathroom. The cat hurls itself against her legs, digging teeth and
claws into her calves. She cries out, almost falling. Struggling to
regain her balance, she staggers across the room, toppling against a
table, right arm crashing down on the telephone. She snatches up
the receiver and swings down at the cat with it. She begins to hit it
again and again, battering at its skull. Abruptly, the teeth jerk out.
Kicking the cat away, Florence spins around and dashes for the
bathroom. The cat darts after her. Lurching through the doorway,
she slams the door.

233J   *INT. — BATHROOM, CLOSE ON FLORENCE*

Leaning against the door. Outside, the cat CRASHES AGAINST
the door and starts clawing frenziedly at the wood. After a few
moments, Florence, panting, slowly sinks to her knees, CAMERA
MOVING IN ON her staring eyes. Outside the door, the cat keeps
raking its claws through the wood, making the horrible NOISE in
its throat. Suddenly, it stops. Florence starts, listening intently.
Then, when there are no more sounds, she opens the door
cautiously.

233K   *INT. — BEDROOM, ANGLE ON DOOR*

As Florence opens it and looks into the bedroom. Standing with
effort, she limps into the room and looks around.

233L   *POV SHOT — THE BEDROOM*

There is no sign of the cat anywhere.

233M   *FLORENCE*

Looking around the room, still dazed from the attack. Now, her
attention is drawn to the door and she looks down at it. CAMERA
PANS DOWN TO REVEAL the wood scratched and torn.

234   *INT. — GREAT HALL, MOVING SHOT — IMMENSE
         WOODEN CRATE*

Moving toward us; 4 × 12 feet, 7 feet high. CAMERA DRAWING
AROUND TO SHOW FOUR MEN moving the crate on several
pairs of dollies, Hanley keeping an eye on them.

Barrett and Ann watch by the circular table. The men place the
crate near the table and remove the dollies, take out crowbars to
open it.

> BARRETT
> I'll do that.
> (As they look at him)
> Thank you.

The four men move OUT OF FRAME, looking around, some
uneasily, some curiously.

> HANLEY
> Anything else?

> BARRETT
> Would you tell that woman to leave our meals in
> here from now on?

> HANLEY
> Something wrong with the dining hall?

> BARRETT (repressing a smile)
> Take a look.

                                                    (CONTINUED)

234   *CONTINUED:*

As Hanley moves OUT OF FRAME, Barrett picks up a crowbar
and starts to work on the crate. Ann watches him, still disturbed.
Barrett glances at her with a smile.

BARRETT (cont'd)
You're disturbed.

ANN
Aren't *you*?

BARRETT
Not at all.

ANN (pause; reluctantly)
There *was* a figure, Chris.

BARRETT (nodding)
Mm-hmm.

ANN (confused)
Doesn't that prove her story?

BARRETT
That's not the point, Ann.

ANN (totally in the dark)
What *is*?

He stops working and looks at her blank expression with a smile.

BARRETT

Item number one: Miss Tanner; a psychic of
considerable development. Item number two: A
vast residuum of power in this house to which she
has access. Put them together and what do you
get? A psychic who is able to create any number
of effects to validate her beliefs. She caused that
attack on me last night, then claimed it was
caused by Daniel Belasco. When I wouldn't
believe her she searched the house until she
found that body. That it may actually be the

(MORE)

(CONTINUED)

234   *CONTINUED: —2*

>remains of Daniel Belasco is irrelevant. What
>matters is that Miss Tanner is combining her own
>power with the power in the house to build a case
>for herself.
>>(Beat)
>A *false* case. Only one thing's going to conquer
>Hell House and here it stands.

CAMERA MOVES IN ON the crate as he rips off a board. On the
machine's side, we see stenciled the large letters EMR
REVERSOR.

235   *INT. — FISCHER'S ROOM, ANGLE ON BED, TOWARD DOOR*

Fischer lying on it, smoking, staring at the ceiling. He looks around
as there is a KNOCK on the door.

>>FISCHER
>>Yes?

Florence COMES IN, LOOKING PALE.

>>FLORENCE
>>May I speak to you?

>>FISCHER
>>What happened?

>>FLORENCE
>>Nothing . . .

Fischer's face tightens. He knows she's lying even though he can't
see any of her scratches.

>>FLORENCE (cont'd)
>>Nothing that matters.

He looks at her for a few moments without answering, then sits up.

>>FISCHER
>>What do you want, then?

She hesitates, then settles diffidently on the bed, a good distance
from him.

>>(CONTINUED)

235   CONTINUED:

                        FLORENCE (pause; hesitantly)
                    Would you do something for me?

                        FISCHER (suspicious)
                              What?

                            FLORENCE
            I've got to contact Daniel Belasco and trance is
            the quickest way. I'm uneasy about doing it alone,
            though. And Dr. Barrett won't sit with me.
                              (Pause)
                        Will you help me?
                              (Pause)
                            Please.

        He looks at her. Finally, he sighs, surrendering.

                        FLORENCE (cont'd)
                    Let me tell you what to ask.

236   INT. — FISCHER'S ROOM, CLOSE ON FLORENCE — LATER

        The room is dark.

237   TWO SHOT — FISCHER AND FLORENCE

        Sitting in wooden chairs, facing each other at a distance of
        three feet.

238   FISCHER

        Watching Florence, his expression stonelike.

239   FLORENCE

        As a strange, rattling noise is heard in her throat. Soon it stops.

240   TWO SHOT — FISCHER AND FACE

                            FISCHER
                          Who are you?

                    FLORENCE (in the young man's voice)
                        Daniel Belasco.

                                              (CONTINUED)

240   *CONTINUED:*

                    FISCHER
          Is it your body Miss Tanner found?

                    FLORENCE
                    Yes.

                    FISCHER
          Did you have anything to do with the attack in
          the dining hall last night?

                    FLORENCE
                    No.

                    FISCHER
          Who did, then?

There is no answer.

                    FISCHER (cont'd)
          Did you have anything to do with what happened
          in Miss Tanner's room before?

                    FLORENCE
                    No.

                    FISCHER
          Who did, then?

No answer.

                    FISCHER (cont'd)
          Who was the shadowy figure standing over you?

He tightens as there is a quickening of breath from the face.

                    FISCHER (cont'd)
                    Who was it?

                    FLORENCE
                    Cannot say.

                    FISCHER
                    Why not?

                                        (CONTINUED)

240   *CONTINUED: —2*

> FLORENCE
> Cannot.

> FISCHER
> *Why?*
> (Pause)
> You have to say.

> FLORENCE (pleadingly)
> Cannot.

> FISCHER
> Who was responsible?

> FLORENCE
> Please.

> FISCHER
> *Who?*

> FLORENCE
> I cannot say!

> FISCHER
> Who?

> FLORENCE
> *No.*

> FISCHER
> *Who?*

> FLORENCE (brokenly)
> Him.

> FISCHER
> Who's that?

> FLORENCE
> *Him.*

> FISCHER (shouting)
> *Who is that?!*

(CONTINUED)

240   CONTINUED: —3

CAMERA MOVES IN SUDDENLY ON the tortured face of the young man.

                    FLORENCE
                Him! The Giant!
                    (Beat)
                Father! Father!

241   INT. — FISCHER'S ROOM, CLOSE ON GLASS OF WATER —
        LATER

Being carried across the room, the lights back on. CAMERA WITHDRAWS to show Fischer handing it to Florence. She drinks it in one swallow, looks at Fischer.

                    FISCHER
        He said his father is responsible for the attack in
        the dining hall.

                FLORENCE (pause)
        Of *course*; I should have known. His father did
        those things to turn me against Daniel so I
        wouldn't help him.

242   CLOSE ON FLORENCE

                FLORENCE (cont'd)
        His father wants to keep him here.

243   INT. — FLORENCE'S ROOM — LATER

Florence walking back and forth, trying to evaluate this new problem. After a while, she sits tiredly on the bed. She starts to nod, falls asleep. As she sits there, her right hand twitches. Waking up, she stares at it. After a few moments, she realizes what has to be done and, reaching to the bedside table, pulls her purse onto her lap, opens it and takes out a pad and pencil, sets the purse aside. She puts the pencil point against the pad and closes her eyes.

                    FLORENCE
        How can I help you, Daniel?

                                    (CONTINUED)

243   *CONTINUED:*

CAMERA MOVES DOWN UNTIL the pencil is in F.G. Abruptly, she begins to write.It is a brief message. Florence opens her eyes and looks at what she has written. Immediately, her features tense with revulsion and, with a sickening cry, she crumples up the sheet and flings it to the floor.

She sits staring at the paper, shivering. CAMERA PANS DOWN TO it. All we see are the words *Let me —*

244   *INT. — GREAT HALL, REVERSOR*

Uncovered; very impressive-looking. CAMERA PANS TO Fischer sitting at the round table, drinking and morose. Serving dishes are on the table nearby. He looks around.

245   *ANOTHER ANGLE — INCLUDING BARRETT AND ANN*

Approaching the table, Barrett limping.

> BARRETT
> Good evening.

Fischer doesn't answer. Barrett and Ann start to put food onto plates, not sitting down, Ann careful not to look at Fischer. Her studied avoidance of him starts to irritate him.

> BARRETT (cont'd)
> We're going to eat in our room so I can rest my leg.

> FISCHER
> Are you?

> BARRETT
> I'm afraid I got a bit chewed up last night.

> FISCHER
> A *bit*.

Barrett starts to look at him, then decides to let it go.

> FISCHER (cont'd)
> How are *you*, Mrs. Barrett?

> ANN (quietly)
> Fine.

(CONTINUED)

245   *CONTINUED:*

                          FISCHER
                     Glad to hear it.

                          BARRETT
                Is something wrong, Mr. Fischer?

                          FISCHER
          No. Everything is *great.* I'm having a
          wonderful time.

                          BARRETT
                     If you can't —

                    FISCHER (cutting in)
          Have you thought about what happened last
          night, Barrett?

                  BARRETT (looking around)
                     Thought about it?

                          FISCHER
                Thought about it.
                        (Pause)
                Gotten the message.

                  BARRETT (guardedly)
          What message is that, Mr. Fischer?

                          FISCHER
          That the house is getting to you.

                    BARRETT (pause)
          I don't happen to believe that.

                          FISCHER
                     You don't.
                        (Beat)
          Just what the hell do you think is going on
          here, then?

                    BARRETT (coldly)
          What I think is going on is irrelevant to this
          conversation, Mr. Fischer.

                                        (CONTINUED)

245   CONTINUED: —2

ANN (softly)
Chris . . .

FISCHER (astounded)
Irrelevant!
(Beat)
Have you noticed *any*thing since we arrived here,
Barrett? Anything at all?!

Barrett regards him for several moments before he speaks.

BARRETT
A number of things, Mr. Fischer; foremost of
which is that Mr. Deutsch is wasting
approximately a third of his money.

He turns away followed by Ann. Fischer sits immobile, watching
them go. They are almost to the archway when he calls out angrily,
Ann glancing back.

FISCHER
What would you *like* me to do, commit
progressive suicide like you and Miss Tanner are
doing?

Barrett does not reply but moves out of sight. CAMERA MOVES
IN ON Fischer as he sits tensely. Abruptly, he shoves his glass off
the table and stands, striding toward the fireplace, CAMERA
MOVING WITH him. He leans against the mantel, staring at the
flames, expression hard with anger.

FISCHER (cont'd) (muttering)
If I'm not handling things the way they should be
handled, how come I'm the only one who hasn't
been touched yet?

He turns from the fireplace suddenly, his stricken face filling the
screen as the truth hits him. CAMERA WITHDRAWS FROM
him as he begins to stride restlessly around the hall. He stops in
CLOSE SHOT, a look of pain on his face; runs a shaking hand
through his hair.

(CONTINUED)

245   *CONTINUED: —3*

> FISCHER (cont'd)
> No, that isn't true.

He starts to pace again, the realization getting stronger. He shakes his head but can't deny it. He stops in F.G. again, face stricken.

> FISCHER (cont'd)
> She's right, *I've blocked it off.*
> (Pause; agonized)
> I'm *afraid* to open up!

His expression goes from self-revulsion to resistance to determination.

> FISCHER (cont'd)
> *No, I'm not.*

Moving to the nearest armchair, he sits down hurriedly. Closing his eyes, he begins to draw in deep breaths. After several moments of that, he stops. He waits for sensation to begin but nothing happens. He begins to draw in deep breaths again. After a while, he stops, sits motionless, as if listening. A look of concern begins to mar his face.

He draws in more deep breaths. CAMERA MOVES IN SLOWLY ON his face. His effort starts to work. He makes a sound of satisfaction, keeps inhaling deeply, going further into trance.

SOUNDS begin to rise in volume: the CRACKLING of the fire, the CREAKING of the chair he's sitting in, the sound of his BREATH soughing in and out. He begins to smile, keeps on drawing in deep breaths, then finally stops, waits. Nothing happens. His expression starts to change again, moving toward dread. Willfully, he forces himself into a deep trance. He is still for several moments. Then, abruptly, he strains forward in the chair, a sound of horror in his throat.

246   *LONG SHOT — FISCHER*

The GLAZED LENS effect and the shrill sound of unearthly amusement as the CAMERA ZOOMS AT Fischer. He tries to pull himself out of trance but has no time. As CAMERA REACHES
>   (MORE)

                                                            (CONTINUED)

246   *CONTINUED:*

him, he cries out hoarsely and his eyes leap open, staring, terror-stricken. Doubling over, he clamps both hands across his solar plexus. Something slams against him, hurling him sideways from the chair. He crashes against a table edge, is flung back with strangling gasp. He crumples to his knees, arms crossed, trying to resist the savage power that tries to rip his arms apart. He fights it, teeth clenched, face a stonelike mask, gurgling noises in his throat. Abruptly, the GLAZED LENS effect ends. Fischer totters on his knees, across his face the dazed expression of a man who has just been bayoneted in the stomach. He tries to hold himself erect but cannot. With a choking noise, he falls, landing on his side and drawing up his legs, bending forward until he has contracted to the fetal pose, eyes staring, body shivering uncontrollably.

247   *INT. — FLORENCE'S ROOM, DOWN ANGLE — FLORENCE*

Kneeling by her bed, praying. After a while, she straightens up with a groan. Standing, she looks at her wristwatch. Wearily, she moves into the bathroom, turns on the cold water. She opens the robe she wears over panties and a bra so that we see the scratches on her stomach, chest, and shoulders. She looks at herself in the mirror, then, grimacing, shuts her robe abruptly, and starts to rinse off her face.

248   *INT. — ENTRY HALL, MOVING SHOT — FLORENCE*

She wears an outfit that completely covers any trace of the encounter with the cat, and a scarf is tied around her throat.

Descending the staircase slowly, looking exhausted, drained. Almost to the bottom, she realizes how she's moving and thrusts back her shoulders, lifts her head.

249   *INT. — GREAT HALL, ANGLE ON TABLE*

Florence comes up to the table, touches the food to find it cold, then, sighing, serves herself a plate anyway. She is about to sit when she glances toward the fireplace.

250   *POV SHOT — FISCHER*

Slumped in a wooden armchair, staring into the fire.

251   *ANGLE PAST FISCHER, TOWARD FLORENCE*

She comes over to him, pulls a chair toward the fireplace and sits
on it.

> FLORENCE (tiredly)
> How are you?

Fischer doesn't speak. She looks at him, decides not to make
anything of his silence and continues speaking.

> FLORENCE (cont'd)
> I've been thinking —

She breaks off as Fischer turns his head and looks at her
apathetically. Florence's features tighten.

> FLORENCE (cont'd)
> What?

> FISCHER (turning back to the fire)
> Give up.

> FLORENCE (stunned)
> Give *up?*
> (Beat)
> When we've made such progress?

> FISCHER
> Toward what, our mutual graves?

> FLORENCE
> *No.* We've discovered much. How Belasco's
> son is —

> FISCHER (cutting her off)
> How do you know Belasco had a son? How do
> you know he isn't part of your imagination?

> FLORENCE
> The body.
> (Beat)
> The *ring.*

> FISCHER
> How do you know it's *his?*

(CONTINUED)

251   *CONTINUED:*

FLORENCE
The initials —

FISCHER
DB can stand for a hundred different names.

FLORENCE (shaking her head)
I know I'm right.

He stands with an angry, disgusted sound, begins to leave, then turns back to her.

FISCHER (with mounting savagery)
All of us in 1953 knew we were right, too. Grace
Lauter, a successful medium for twenty years,
who jumped from the second floor and shattered
her legs and spine and spilled her brains on the
entry hall floor. Dr. Graham, a hardheaded
physicist, who crawled out of the house, dead
drunk, to die of exposure in the woods. Professor
Rand, head of the chemistry department at
Fordham University, who was paralyzed and died
of a cerebral hemorrhage. Professor Fenley, an
experienced psychic investigator, who's crippled
and insane to this day. And me, the fifteen-year-
old genius of the séance room who was found on
the front porch, curled up like a fetus, both legs
broken, vomiting blood when they picked me up,
lying in a coma for three months in the hospital.
And all of us *knew we were right.*
(Beat)
Oh, what's the use?

Turning away, he stalks OUT OF FRAME. Florence watches him go in shock. CAMERA MOVES IN ON her as the impact of his words begins to work on her. She shakes her head.

FLORENCE
No.
(MORE)

(CONTINUED)

251   CONTINUED: —2

                              (Calling after him)
                        Daniel *does* exist! He *does*!
                              (Beat; to herself)
                        There has to be some way to prove it. some place
                        I can find . . .

         Her face is in CLOSE-UP now. Abruptly, she turns her head, a look
         of anxious anticipation on her face.

252   *LONG SHOT — CORRIDOR, ANGLE TOWARD GREAT HALL*

         After several moments Florence comes out of the Great Hall
         hurrying beneath the staircase and along the corridor toward
         CAMERA, which PANS as she turns the corner, heading for the
         chapel.

253   *ANGLE FROM CHAPEL DOOR*

         Florence runs into F.G., where the resistance begins. It is as though
         she is struggling with some unseen figure. She fights against it, lips
         moving as she prays. CAMERA MOVES IN ON her as her face
         breaks out in perspiration; her teeth clench, her eyes grow wide.
         She will not back off this time. Her breath gets faster, faster.
         Physically and mentally, she fights against the brutal force, her face
         distended by the effort. Bit by bit, she gets closer to the chapel
         door. Finally, she pushes open the door in triumph.

254   *INT. — CHAPEL, ANGLE ON DOORWAY*

         Florence comes in and switches on the lights. Leaning back against
         the door, she closes her eyes. Her face is bathed with sweat. After a
         while she opens her eyes and looks around the chapel. Then, slowly,
         she begins to move down the middle aisle, CAMERA
         WITHDRAWING FROM her UNTIL the crucifix is in F.G. As
         Florence reaches the foot of the aisle, she sees the face and stops,
         reacting. Clasping her hands, she bends over a little, pressing the
         hands to her forehead as she prays.

255   *CLOSE ON FLORENCE*

         She finishes praying and raises her head, lowering her hands. She
         looks at the altar area.

256   *POV SHOT — ALTAR AREA*

CAMERA MOVING as Florence looks at it. It SETTLES on a massive Bible lying on the altar.

257   *UP ANGLE PAST BIBLE, TOWARD FLORENCE*

Moving forward, she gazes at the Bible. She opens it; begins to turn the pages. Suddenly, her face is radiant.

258   *POV SHOT — BIBLE PAGE*

The top of it titled *Births*. CAMERA MOVES IN QUICKLY on the faded entry: *Daniel Myron Belasco was born at 2:00* A.M. *on November 4, 1903.*

259   *FLORENCE*

Her joy ends instantaneously as she whirls, reacting to the sight of —

260   *DANIEL BELASCO — FLORENCE'S POV*

Standing in the shadows, looking at her.

261   *FLORENCE*

Staring at him.

262   *DANIEL BELASCO*

Unmoving.

263   *FLORENCE*

She begins to shake her head, making soft noises of distress.

264   *DANIEL BELASCO*

Watching her.

265   *FLORENCE*

Becoming more and more disturbed. Suddenly, she cries out.

FLORENCE
No, Daniel!

She starts; stares across the chapel.

266   *POV SHOT*

Daniel is gone.

267   *FLORENCE*

Putting her hands over her face; shuddering.

                    FLORENCE (cont'd) (barely audible)
                            No, Daniel.

268   *INT. — ENTRY HALL, CLOSE ON UNCOVERED CIRCUIT*
        ASSEMBLY — LATER

CAMERA WITHDRAWS FROM the maze of wires and transistors
to REVEAL Barrett checking it, comparing it with the blueprint he
has taped to the side of the machine. CAMERA STOPS ON Ann
sitting nearby, watching. Barrett looks very tired.

                            ANN
                Anything I can do to help?

                BARRETT (pausing to look at her)
        I'm afraid not; it's just too complicated.
                        (Smiling)
                Thanks for asking, though.

He returns to his work. Ann watches in silence for a while before
speaking again.

                            ANN
                What's it going to do, Chris?

                        BARRETT
Well . . . you've heard me talk about the power in
the house.
                        (Beat)
It's *real power*, Ann. A field of measurable
energy. Energy that can be reversed, which is
exactly what I'm going to do.
                        (Pause)
By this time tomorrow, Hell House will be
drained . . . deenergized. You'll see —

They both whirl at the O.S. sound of slow, measured CLAPPING.

269   *FISCHER*

Standing in the archway, a bottle underneath his right arm as he claps.
                                        (CONTINUED)

269   *CONTINUED:*

FISCHER
Bravo.

270   *ANGLE PAST BARRETT AND ANN, TOWARD FISCHER*

He approaches them unevenly.

FISCHER (gesturing toward the machine)
That pile of junk you got there isn't going to do a
thing, Barrett. Belasco's going to spit in your eye.
They're all going to spit in your eye.
(A sound of contempt)
Deenergize, my ass.
(Looking at Ann almost angrily)
Get her out of here. Get yourself out. You haven't
got a chance.

BARRETT
Do you?

FISCHER
Oh yes. I know the score, Barrett. You don't fight
this place, it can't get at you. Hell House doesn't
mind a guest or two. What it doesn't like is
people who attack it. Belasco doesn't like it. All
his people, they don't like it, and they fight back
and they kill you or they make you kill yourself or
drive you mad.
(Pointing at Barrett; rabidly)
I'm *telling* you, *Barrett*! Leave that damn machine
alone, forget it! Spend your week here eating,
resting, doing nothing; and when Sunday comes,
tell the old fart anything he wants to hear and
bank your money! Hear me, Barrett? Try
anything more and you're a dead man!
(Looking at Ann)
With a dead wife by your side.
(Beat)
(MORE)

(CONTINUED)

270   *CONTINUED:*

> You know what your wife was doing last night?
> *Do* you?
>> (Beat)
> Standing on the second-story railing in the entry
> hall, just about to jump!
>> (As Barrott reacts)
> Oh, *gloriosky,* a reaction finally from the great big
> man of science.
>> (Turning)
> Oh, hell, why bother? No one listens.
>> (As he stumbles off)
> I was the only one to make it out alive and sane in
> 1953 and I'll be the only one to make it out alive
> and sane this time.

Ann watches him go fearfully. What he's said has gotten to her.
Barrett moves to her in concern.

> BARRETT
> Why didn't you *tell* me?

> ANN
> I wasn't sure myself. I thought . . .

> BARRETT
> Thought *what?*

> ANN (hesitates)
> I don't know.
>> (Beat; frightenedly)
> I don't *know,* Chris.

She begins to cry and he puts his arms around her.

> BARRETT
> Shh.
>> (Beat)
> It's all right, Ann.
>> (Beat)
> All right.

271   *INT. — FLORENCE'S ROOM, HIGH DOWN ANGLE —
       FLORENCE*

Kneeling by her bed again, praying. CAMERA MOVES DOWN
SLOWLY ON her.

> FLORENCE
> Daniel, please. You have to understand. What
> you ask is impossible. It isn't that I have no
> sympathy. I do. I've opened my heart to you
> completely. I *believe* in you. Now you must
> believe in me and let me save your soul. You
> don't have to stay in this house any longer. Not if
> you seek out those who have already progressed
> and take the help they offer. *Take* it, Daniel. You
> can be *free*. Believe it and it will be so. I pledge
> you this. *Trust* me, Daniel. Trust me and let go.
> Let *go*.

CAMERA STOPS as Florence is in CLOSE SHOT. Opening her
eyes, she pushes to her feet with infirm movements, her expression
one of sorrow as she looks around the room.

> FLORENCE (cont'd)
> Why won't you listen?

She starts for the bathroom when the O.S. phone begins to RING.
She stops and looks at it in disturbed surprise.

272   *POV SHOT — FRENCH TELEPHONE*

Ringing.

273   *FLORENCE*

Staring at it. The O.S. phone keeps RINGING, the shrill sound
making her nervous.

274   *TELEPHONE*

Ringing. Ringing.

275   *FLORENCE*

Getting more and more tense. Abruptly, she lurches forward.

276   *UP ANGLE OVER TELEPHONE*

Florence hurries INTO FRAME and jerks up the receiver,
dumping it on the table. She stares down at it, breathing hard.
Daniel's VOICE is heard from the receiver.

>   DANIEL (voice)
>   Florence?
>   (Pleading)
>   Florence?
>   (Pause; brokenly)
>   *Florence?*

With a faint sob, Florence picks up the receiver and puts it to her
ear, CAMERA MOVING IN ON her face. Daniel's voice is
heartbreaking.

>   FLORENCE
>   Why won't you go?

>   DANIEL (voice)
>   Please . . .

>   FLORENCE
>   No, Daniel! *No!*

>   DANIEL (voice)
>   Please.

>   FLORENCE (crying)
>   Daniel . . .

>   DANIEL (voice)
>   Please.

>   FLORENCE (eyes closed; whispering)
>   No.

>   DANIEL (voice)
>   *Please.*

>   FLORENCE (losing strength)
>   No, Daniel.

                          (CONTINUED)

276   *CONTINUED:*

> DANIEL (voice)
> *Please.*

> FLORENCE
> No, no.

> DANIEL (voice) (in utter anguish)
> *Please.*

> FLORENCE (crying)
> No.

> DANIEL (voice)
> Please. Please. Please.
> (Starting to cry)
> *Please.*

As he keeps repeating the word over and over, she begins to sob brokenly, getting weaker and weaker. Abruptly, she hangs up, a violent shudder racking her body.

> FLORENCE
> All right!

Kneeling beside the bed, she bows her head and clasps her hands together tightly.

> FLORENCE (cont'd)
> Reach down your hand and give me your
> protection. Help me, this night, to bring to your
> care, the tortured soul of Daniel Belasco.

Standing weakly, she turns off the lamp. Only the bathroom light provides illumination. Slowly, she undoes her robe and takes it off, lays it across a chair back. She draws her nightgown up across her head and puts it on the robe, her body silhouetted against the bathroom doorway. She looks down at herself. Then, drawing aside the bedclothes, she lies on her back. CAMERA MOVES IN SLOWLY ON her face until it is in CLOSE-UP.

> FLORENCE (whispering)
> Daniel.

Her eyes shift toward the door, she holds out her arms.

277–   OMIT
278

279   *DOWN ANGLE ON BED*

What appears to be the form of a man (Daniel Belasco) lies under the white satin sheets beside her, CAMERA MOVING IN ON them as they kiss long and tenderly. Then their embrace becomes more passionate. Closing her eyes, Florence turns onto her back, CAMERA MOVING IN ON her face. (*Note:* The style and staging of this scene to be at director's discretion.) Moments pass. Then his voice speaks ABOVE FRAME, cold and alien.

> DANIEL (voice)
> *Florence.*

She opens her eyes. Her features tighten.

280   *OMIT*

281   *FLORENCE*

Staring at the form over her. Suddenly, her face contorts with horror.

282   *POV SHOT — WHAT SHE SEES*

The face of a corpse, features in an advanced state of decomposition. Livid, scaly flesh is crumbling from his bones, his rotted lips are wreathed in a leering smile that shows discolored, jagged teeth, all of them decayed. Only the slanting yellow eyes are alive, regarding her with demoniacal glee. A leaden bluish light envelops the head.

283   *DOWN ANGLE PAST CORPSE, ON FLORENCE*

CAMERA MOVES IN FAST ON her face. Jolting suddenly, a scream of mindless shock comes flooding from her throat.

284   *INT. — FISCHER'S ROOM, ANGLE PAST BOTTLE ON TABLE*

Fischer jerks up on his elbow, gasping at the O.S. SCREAMING. For several moments, he is frozen by the sound; then, abruptly, flings himself to his feet and lunges OUT OF FRAME.

285   *INT. — CORRIDOR, ANGLE ON DOOR TO FISCHER'S ROOM*

Flinging open the door, he runs into the corridor and to the door of
(MORE)

(CONTINUED)

285   *CONTINUED:*

Florence's room, CAMERA PULLING AHEAD OF him. Twisting
the knob, he pushes at the door, but it is locked. Inside the room
Florence is still SCREAMING dementedly. In the B.G., the door to
the Barretts' room is opened and Ann peers out, her expression
stricken. Grabbing a heavy metal figure, Fischer starts to crash it
against the door. Ann and Barrett come out of their room,
approaching hurriedly. Inside the room, Florence's SCREAMING
stops. Fischer batters at the lock savagely. Suddenly, the jamb is
splintered and the door flies open.

286   *INT. — FLORENCE'S ROOM, ANGLE ON DOORWAY*

Fischer ENTERS and turns on the light switch. Barrett and Ann
follow him in. They all react to what they see, Ann averting her face
with sickened noise. She remains behind, face averted, as they move
to the bed, CAMERA WITHDRAWING FROM them. They stop,
looking down at Florence, their expressions stunned.

287   *DOWN ANGLE PAST BARRETT AND FISCHER — ON
FLORENCE*

Her body covered with scratches and bruises. CAMERA ZOOMS
IN ON her face. On her lips is a smile of hideous corruption.

288   *INT. — CHAPEL, ANGLE FROM DOORWAY, ON CRUCIFIX*

CAMERA ZOOMS IN ON the lips of the frightening visage.
HOLDING ON the smile; it is the same as that on Florence's lips.
The SOUND of demented amusement fills the air with a shrill,
keening sound.

289   *INT. — FLORENCE'S ROOM, DOWN ANGLE ON FLORENCE
AND FISCHER*

Total silence, Florence asleep in bed, Fischer slumped in an armchair
he has pulled to the side of the bed. TITLE: *December 24.*
CAMERA MOVES DOWN ON them, then IN ON Fischer. He is
staring at Florence, half asleep. Now he shudders, looking around.
Standing tiredly, he trudges into the bathroom, CAMERA
DRAWING AROUND to observe as he splashes cold water onto his
face, returning as he dries his face with a towel. As he draws the towel
down from his eyes, his movements freeze. He stares at Florence.

290   *POV SHOT — FLORENCE*

Eyes open, looking up at Fischer. Her face has no expression. It is as though she has never seen him before.

291   *TWO SHOT*

Fischer sits beside her on the bed. She continues staring at him without recognition.

> FISCHER
> Florence?

> FLORENCE (pause; swallowing dryly)
> Have you been here all night?

He nods. Her gaze holds on him for several moments, then shifts to the chair.

> FLORENCE (cont'd)
> There?

He nods again as she looks back at him. After a few moments, she makes a noise of cynical amusement.

> FLORENCE (cont'd)
> *Stupid.*
> (Beat)
> You could have slept with me.

He watches her guardedly. She pulls the covers down from her chest.

> FLORENCE (cont'd)
> Who put on my nightgown?

> FISCHER
> Mrs. Barrett.

> FLORENCE (with a wanton smile)
> Why didn't you?

He says nothing, staring at her. After a moment, something flares in her eyes and her body is convulsed by a wrenching shudder.

> FLORENCE (cont'd) (whispering)
> Oh, my God.
> (MORE)

(CONTINUED)

291   *CONTINUED:*

> (Sobbing)
> He's inside me.

Fischer takes her hands and holds them tightly.

> FISCHER
> We'll get rid of him.
> (As she shakes her head)
> We *will*, Florence.

> FLORENCE (brokenly)
> He lied to me. He said it was the only way.

> FISCHER (sickened)
> You still believe there's a Daniel . . .

> FLORENCE
> I know there is! I found the entry of his birth
> inside the chapel Bible!
> (As he reacts)
> Yes, I was there! I went inside and —
> (Breaks off with a gasp; tightly)
> He's *inside* me. Even as I'm speaking to you, I
> can feel him in there; waiting to take over.

She begins to shake so violently that Fischer pulls her up and puts
his arms around her.

> FISCHER
> *Shhh.* It's going to be all right. I'll take you out of
> here this morning.

> FLORENCE
> He won't let me go.

> FISCHER
> He can't stop you.

> FLORENCE
> Yes, he can; he *can*!

> FISCHER
> He can't stop *me*.

(CONTINUED)

291   *CONTINUED: —2*

She jerks away from him so quickly that she catches him completely
by surprise. Thumping back against the headboard, she looks at him
with furious contempt.

> FLORENCE (snarling)
> Who the hell are you, you bastard?
> (Beat)
> Maybe you were hot stuff when you were fifteen,
> but now you're shit! You hear me? *Shit!*

Fischer stares at her tensely. She glares at him in silence. Then a
flickering in her eyes reveals the change again. Instantly, she is
herself again; not as though emerging from amnesia, however, but,
instead, with total memory of what has just occurred.

> FLORENCE (cont'd) (barely able to speak)
> *Oh, God, please help me.*

He takes her in his arms again. She clings to him like a frightened
child, sobbing piteously.

> FISCHER (shaken)
> I will I will
> (Beat)
> I'll get you out of here.

292   *INT. — GREAT HALL, CLOSE ON COFFEEPOT*

As dark, steaming coffee runs into a cup. CAMERA WITHDRAWS
TO REVEAL Barrett and Ann sitting at the table. She hands
Barrett the cup of coffee.

> BARRETT
> Thank you.

Neither of them is eating. After a few moments they look around
toward the archway.

293   *ANOTHER ANGLE, INCLUDING FISCHER AND FLORENCE*

Approaching the table, wearing outdoor clothes, Florence looking
dazed, withdrawn. She walks somewhat stiffly as though something
is wrong with her legs.

(CONTINUED)

293   *CONTINUED:*

                          FISCHER
                I'm taking her to Caribou Falls.

                          BARRETT
                Good.
                (Beat)
                Have you called Hanley?

                          FISCHER
                Not yet.

                          BARRETT
                I'll call him for you then.
                (Gently)
                How are you, Miss Tanner?

                    FLORENCE (remotely)
                I'm all right.

                          BARRETT
                Are your legs bothering you?

                FLORENCE (throatily; tightly)
                          No.

Barrett, standing, looks at Fischer.

                          BARRETT
                You needn't come back if you don't want to, Mr.
                Fischer. The house will be clear by this afternoon.

CAMERA MOVES IN SUDDENLY ON Florence as she reacts.
Her voice and manner are very strange.

                          FLORENCE
                          Clear?

294   *BACK TO SCENE*

                    FLORENCE (cont'd)
                How?

                          FISCHER
                There isn't time for explanations.
                                              (CONTINUED)

294   *CONTINUED:*

> FLORENCE (stiffly)
> Yes, there is.
> (Pause)
> I won't leave until I know.

> FISCHER
> *Florence.*

> FLORENCE (with an undertone of impending
> hysteria)
> *I won't leave until I know.*

Fischer hesitates, then speaks, keeping his eyes on Florence.

> FISCHER
> Can you make it brief?

Barrett starts to object, then changes his mind, sits again.

> BARRETT
> All right; briefly, then. The human body emits a
> form of energy invisible to the eye. This energy
> can be expanded far beyond the borders of the
> body where it can create mechanical, chemical,
> and physical effects — percussions, odors,
> movement of objects, and the like, as we've
> experienced.

Florence listens intently, her expression becoming, somehow,
ominous.

> BARRETT
> The emanation I speak of *is a field of*
> *electromagnetic radiation.*

> FLORENCE (flatly)
> EMR.

> BARRETT
> Exactly. All living organisms emit this energy, its
> dynamo the brain. Such power must impinge
> itself on its surroundings, saturating its
> (MORE)

(CONTINUED)

environment. Is it any wonder, then, that Hell
House is the way it is? Consider the destructive
mental and physical radiations that have
impregnated its interior. In essence, the house is
a giant battery, the residual energy of which is
inevitably tapped by those who enter it.

                    FLORENCE
But can't you see this energy is what we survive
with after death?

                    BARRETT
No, Miss Tanner. The residue I speak of has
nothing whatever to do with the survival of
personality. The spirit of Emeric Belasco does not
prowl this house. Neither does that of his son or
any of the so-called entities you've believed
yourself in contact with. There is one thing in this
house and one thing only . . . *mindless,
directionless power.*

            FLORENCE (pause; with contempt)
            You're *wrong*, Dr. Barrett.

                    BARRETT
No, Miss Tanner, I'm right. This afternoon, my
Reversor will permeate the house with a massive
countercharge of electromagnetic radiation. Said
countercharge will oppose the polarity of the
atmosphere, reverse and dissipate it.
                    (Beat)
And Hell House will be exorcised.

                FLORENCE (strangely)
                I see.
                (Pause; calmly)
Well, there's nothing else to do, then, is there?

Her movement catches them by surprise. With a fluid turn she
rushes toward the Reversor. The three are frozen for a moment.
Then, simultaneously, Fischer starts after her and Barrett lurches
up from his chair, knocking it over in his haste.

295   *ANGLE FROM REVERSOR*

Fischer is halfway to her when Florence snatches up the crowbar
and swings it at the Reversor with all her might. Barrett, on his feet
now, jolts at the ringing SOUND of steel on steel, flinching as
though the blow were striking him instead.

BARRETT
No!

Florence swings again, battering at the front of the machine. The
glass face of a dial explodes beneath her blow. Barrett starts after
her, a look of horror on his face, moving as fast as his burned leg
will allow.

BARRETT (cont'd)
Stop her!

Reaching Florence, Fischer clutches at her shoulder and yanks her
back from the Reversor. She whirls and swings the crowbar at his
face, her expression one of manic rage.

Fischer dodges, the crowbar missing his head by inches. Lunging in,
he grabs her right arm, wrestling for possession of the bar. Florence
lurches back, snarling like a maddened animal. Fischer's face goes
blank as she flings her arms up, breaking his grasp. He grabs at
Florence's arms again. She heaves back and the two of them crash
against the front of the Reversor. She jerks her right arm free and
swings at him. Fischer ducks again, the crowbar smashing against
the metal face of the machine. He reaches for her arm again but her
next swing is incredibly fast. He throws his arms up, crying out as
the crowbar strikes him on the right wrist. He cannot avoid the next
blow. The crowbar hits his skull and drives him to his knees.
Florence raises the crowbar to hit him again. Then Barrett is on her,
the strength of frenzy in him. With a single, wrenching motion, he
jerks the crowbar from her grasp and hurls it aside. Florence whirls
and he slaps her violently across the face. She stares at him blankly;
then the eyes roll back in her head and she crumples to the floor.
CAMERA PULLS UP TO A DOWN ANGLE ON the four.
Fischer lies crumpled on the floor, unconscious, Florence lying
motionless a few feet from him. Barrett leans against the machine,
gripping his right wrist with his left hand, his face contorted by pain.
Ann starts to hurry toward him.

296   *DOWN ANGLE ON FOUR*

Through the GLAZED LENS. Again, the eerie SOUND of
amusement. CAMERA HOLDS.

297   *INT. — GREAT HALL, CLOSE ON FISCHER — MINUTES
LATER*

Still unconscious; CAMERA WITHDRAWS TO REVEAL him
lying on a sofa, PANS TO Florence lying unconscious on another
sofa, PANS TO Barrett and Ann walking toward the entry hall.

298   *INT. — ENTRY HALL, ANGLE ON FIELD TELEPHONE,
TOWARD GREAT HALL*

Barrett and Ann come over to the telephone, he takes the receiver
off the telephone and puts it to his head, waits. There is no answer.
He jiggles the cradle arm, making a face.

> BARRETT (angrily)
> A hell of a time for communication to be broken
> off.

He jiggles the cradle arm again, waits. He exhales irritably.

> BARRETT (cont'd)
> Come *on.*

He jiggles the cradle arm again, listens. He is about to hang up
when the receiver is LIFTED on the other end of the line.

> BARRETT (cont'd)
> This is Barrett. We need a car right away; an
> ambulance if possible.
> (Pause)
> Did you hear me?
> (Listens to VOICE)
> Would you have it sent out right away, then? Mr.
> Fischer and Miss Tanner require immediate
> hospitalization.
> (Pause)
> Do you *understand*?
> (Listens)
> (MORE)

                                              (CONTINUED)

298   *CONTINUED:*

What isn't fair?
(Listens to the VOICE for a longer interval;
shaken)
Weren't you even going to tell us?
(Pause)
Please have the goodness to send the car at
any rate.

He listens, then hangs up.

ANN
What is it?

Barrett looks at her, still stunned.

ANN (cont'd)
Chris?

BARRETT
It's finished.

ANN
What?

He acts as though he doesn't hear. Then a new look takes over his
face; one of resolution.

BARRETT
No, it isn't. I still have something.
(Beat; vengefully)
Something, hell, I still have *everything*.

He takes her by the arm and starts to lead her toward the Great
Hall, CAMERA MOVING WITH them.

ANN
Chris, what *is* it?

BARRETT
Deutsch is dead. His son has canceled the
project. There'll be no money.
(With a grim smile)
I got the Reversor out of him, though. He can't
take that away.

299   *INT. — GREAT HALL, MOVING SHOT — BARRETT AND ANN*

As they enter, Barrett leading her toward the Reversor.

> BARRETT (cont'd)
> I can use your help now.

They reach the Reversor and Barrett hands her a screwdriver.

> ANN (gesturing toward Florence and Fischer)
> What about them?

> BARRETT
> He said he'd send a car as soon as possible.
> (Beat)
> There's a plate marked A-A-Six on the back.
> Would you take it off?

She moves around the machine. Barrett examines the damage; looks relieved.

> BARRETT (cont'd)
> Thank God she didn't know what to hit.
> (Starting to work; with a grim smile)
> I should be flattered really. Her attack on the
> Reversor was her ultimate tribute to it.

CAMERA STARTS PANNING TOWARD the sofas.

> ANN (voice)
> I don't understand.

> BARRETT
> She knows I'm right — and there was nothing
> else to do; her very words if you recall.
> (Beat)
> She had to destroy *my* beliefs before they could
> destroy *hers*.

CAMERA MOVES IN CLOSE ON Florence. Abruptly, her eyes open.

300   *ANGLE PAST BARRETT, TOWARD ARCHWAY*

In the B.G. Florence rises without a sound and drifts across the Great Hall to the archway, disappearing from sight in the entry hall.

301   *MOVING SHOT — FLORENCE*

CAMERA DRAWS AHEAD of her as she moves across the entry hall, her face without expression, her eyes unblinking. She moves beneath the staircase and along the corridor, turns into the side corridor and moves to the chapel door. Opening it, she goes inside.

302   *INT. — CHAPEL*

CAMERA DRAWING AHEAD OF Florence as she moves stiffly down the center aisle and stops before the altar. CAMERA STOPS. She stands there, gazing blankly at the crucifix.

303   *POV SHOT — CRUCIFIX*

Looming overhead. After a few moments, it starts to move away from the wall, slowly pulling loose.

304   *CLOSE ON FLORENCE*

Staring up at the crucifix, no reaction on her face.

305   *POV SHOT — CRUCIFIX*

Pulling loose more and more, long nails rasping from the wall. Suddenly, it starts to topple toward CAMERA.

306   *DOWN ANGLE ON FLORENCE*

As the massive crucifix lands on her and knocks her to the floor, the crossbar crushing her legs, the upper portion of the upright bar crushing her stomach and lower chest.

CAMERA MOVES IN ON her face as her eyes blink and she regains her mind. Instantly, she groans in mortal agony. She tries to move but cannot. Abruptly, she looks toward the altar as the eerie SOUND of amusement begins O.S.

307   *WHAT SHE SEES*

A giant figure, very indistinct behind a darkness and a glazing effect.

308   *CLOSE ON FLORENCE*

Her expression contorting as sudden, horrendous realization is given to her. Desperately, she tries to pull free from beneath the crucifix. She cannot. The amused SOUND increases. Florence sobs

(MORE)

(CONTINUED)

308   *CONTINUED:*

in pain and frustration. Then her eyes catch sight of something on
the O.S. crossbar and she reaches out infirmly with her right hand,
forced to use every bit of remaining strength and willpower.
CAMERA PANS TO her hand as it inches across the bar until it
reaches a huge nail sticking out of it. Very slowly, she raises her
hand and lays her wrist on the nail point.

309   *CLOSE-UP — FLORENCE*

Eyes widening, gasping with pain as she jerks her wrist across the
point. The unearthly SOUND of amusement STOPS. In heavy
silence, Florence turns her head with agonizing slowness, looking at
the floor beside herself.

310   *FLOOR BESIDE HER*

Blood dripping onto it. Very slowly, her finger ENTERS FRAME
and starts using the blood to make a figure on the floor: a circle.

311   *CLOSE ON FLORENCE*

Eyes fixed, draining the last of her strength to make the O.S. figure.
As she does, she sings a spiritualist hymn beneath her breath, softly,
brokenly. CAMERA MOVES IN ON her dying face until it fills the
screen.

                                FLORENCE
                The world hath felt a quickening breath —
                from heaven's eternal shore.
                And souls triumphant over death
                Return to Earth once more.

312   *INT. — GREAT HALL, CLOSE ON FISCHER*

As he jars up to a sitting position, looking around dazedly. He tries
to stand, then reels, clutching at his head with both hands, uttering
a cry of pain.

313   *ANGLE PAST BARRETT, TOWARD FISCHER*

Barrett twists around from his work. Ann joins him.

                                FISCHER
                            Where *is* she?

                                        (CONTINUED)

313   CONTINUED:

> BARRETT (confused)
> She was lying there just a few minutes ago.

> FISCHER (lurching up)
> Why didn't you *watch* her?

He has only gone a step when he staggers, clutching at his head again, face distended by a look of agony.

> BARRETT
> You'd better sit.

He helps Fischer to a chair and seats him. Fischer rocks back and forth, hands over his face, groaning with pain.

> BARRETT (cont'd) (to Ann)
> We'd better look for her. She can't have gone far.

Abruptly, Fischer jerks down his hands, a look of stark realization on his face.

> BARRETT (cont'd)
> What is it?

CAMERA MOVES IN ON Fischer's face.

> FISCHER
> The chapel.

314   INT. — CHAPEL, ANGLE ON DOORWAY

As the three of them burst in. Ann cries out in reaction and twists away. Barrett puts his arms around her as Fischer walks forward unsteadily, CAMERA DRAWING BACK FROM HIM. Reaching the altar, he looks down at . . .

315   FLORENCE

Dead beneath the massive crucifix.

316   ANGLE ON THE THREE

Moving forward, Fischer crouches down beside the body, wincing at the pain it causes in his head. Recovering, he looks at Florence.

> (MORE)

(CONTINUED)

316   CONTINUED:

After a moment, his eyes shift to the floor; narrow. CAMERA
DOWN PANS to the symbol Florence has made on the floor with
her blood: a crude circle with the letter B inside it.

317   INT. — GREAT HALL, ANGLE ON MAIN SWITCH OF
REVERSOR — LATER

As Barrett throws it. CAMERA WITHDRAWS TO SHOW him
hastily setting dials. Inside the machine, a resonant HUM has
begun, making the floor vibrate.

318   ANN

Watching. The O.S. HUM rises in pitch and volume, the vibration
in the floor increasing. She starts to look alarmed.

319   ANGLE PAST ANN, TOWARD BARRETT

Hurriedly completing the setting of the Reversor. He backs off
toward her, turns and takes her by the arm.

BARRETT
Quickly.

320   INT. — ENTRY HALL, ANGLE FROM TABLE, TOWARD
GREAT HALL

Two coats lying on the table. In the B.G. Barrett and Ann hurry
from the Great Hall. The SOUND of the Reversor is becoming
painful to listen to. Reaching the table, Barrett helps her on with
her coat and pulls on his. Opening the door, he ushers her out and
follows, shutting it. CAMERA STARTS TO BOOM. The noise and
vibration of the Reversor increases steadily. A vase falls from its
table, breaking on the floor. A suit of armor crashes over. A corner
of a tapestry falls loose. Then, suddenly, the vibration ends, a new
SOUND is heard and, through the archway of the Great Hall, a
strange bluish glow of energy is seen. After a few moments it moves
into the entry hall like a strange, iridescent mist.

321–   SERIES OF SHOTS
325

The strange, luminescent mist moving through the house. On the
last SHOT we see it illuminate Florence's still face with something
akin to a holy radiance.

326   *EXT. — HOUSE — BARRETT, ANN, AND FISCHER*

Waiting . . . Barrett pacing restlessly. Inside the house, the NOISE of the Reversor can be faintly heard. CAMERA HOLDS.

327   *INT. — ENTRY HALL, ANGLE ON DOORWAY — LATER*

As the three come in and look around. CAMERA WITHDRAWS FROM them to show the damage caused by the Reversor. Barrett looks at Fischer questioningly. Fischer notices and looks at him.

BARRETT

You'll have to open yourself to it, Mr. Fischer.

Fischer moves away from them, looking around distrustingly, CAMERA DRAWING AHEAD of him. He stops. Barrett and Ann watch from the B.G.

BARRETT (cont'd)

Try, Mr. Fischer. I guarantee there'll be no
trouble.

Without responding or looking back, Fischer starts forward again, CAMERA WITHDRAWING FROM him. Barrett and Ann trail after him as he moves into the Great Hall, CAMERA DRAWING AROUND as he enters. CAMERA STOPS and he moves several yards more before stopping and looking around. The floor is littered with fallen objects; tapestries hang askew. After several moments, Barrett and Ann ENTER FRAME, stop.

BARRETT

Well?

328   *ANGLE PAST FISCHER, TOWARD BARRETT AND ANN*

He waves Barrett off impatiently, stands immobile, waiting, poised. Abruptly, then, he drops the barrier. Closing his eyes, he spreads his arms, his hands, his fingers. CAMERA MOVES IN ON his face. His eyes jump open, his expression one of bafflement. Then distrust returns. Turning, he moves past Barrett and Ann into the entry hall. They turn to watch as he moves OUT OF SCENE.

BARRETT

He's startled because there's nothing to pick up.

329–   SERIES OF SHOTS
338
Fischer striding to the center of the entry hall, stopping and opening
himself to impressions. Nothing. Moving down the corridor to the
chapel and shoving in the door. Nothing in the chapel. Descending
the steps to the cellar in leaps, straight-arming through the pool
doors, entering the pool area. Nothing. Bursting into the wine
cellar. Nothing. Dashing back up the stairs, gasping for breath. Into
the ballroom. Nothing. Into the kitchen, the dining hall. Nothing.

339   ANGLE PAST ANN AND BARRETT

Standing in the archway to the Great Hall. Fischer comes running
out of the dining hall, rocks to a dazed, panting halt in front of
them, starts to speak, then breaks into a run for the staircase,
lunging OUT OF FRAME.

> BARRETT (exultantly)
> Done.
> (Beat)
> It's *done*, Ann. *Done!*

Ann can scarcely believe it. She watches Fischer.

340   POV SHOT — FISCHER

Ascending the staircase two steps at a time, movements erratic.

341–   SERIES OF SHOTS
348
Fischer still running despite his increasing dizziness. Into
Florence's room. Nothing. Spinning with a gasp to run into the
corridor again. Into the Barretts' room. Nothing. Into his room.
Nothing. Into the bedrooms that have not been renovated.

349   LONG SHOT — SECOND-STORY CORRIDOR

Fischer comes around a corner, gasping for breath, perspiration on
his face as he runs weavingly into F.G., a look of amazement on his
face. His pain and dizziness hit him now and he staggers to the
nearest chair, dropping down on it, holding his head. CAMERA
MOVES IN ON his face. Despite his pain and grogginess, he is still
astonished.

(CONTINUED)

349   CONTINUED:

                          FISCHER
                   The house is *clear*.

He makes a hoarse sound of amusement.

                       FISCHER (cont'd)
          And I called it a pile of junk. Jesus God, a pile of
          junk!

350   INT. — BARRETTS' ROOM, ANGLE ON BATHROOM
        DOORWAY — LATER

Barrett emerges. Moving to the bed — CAMERA PANNING
WITH him — he sits on the edge of it. Ann is lying down, a
comforter pulled across her. Half asleep, she strokes his cheek.

                            ANN
                      How's the thumb?

                          BARRETT
          I'll have it checked as soon as we get home.

                            ANN
                          Home.
                          (Beat)
          I can't believe we're really going to see it again.

He leans over and kisses her gently on the lips, then straightens up;
smiles.

                        ANN (cont'd)
              How soon will we leave, do you think?

                          BARRETT
                 As soon as the car arrives.

                            ANN
                       If it arrives.

                      BARRETT (smiling)
                 If it doesn't, we'll walk.
                          (Beat)
          Get some sleep now. I'm going down to check my
          readings. I didn't have a chance before.

                                         (CONTINUED)

350   *CONTINUED:*

> ANN (smiling back)
> Now I know the house is clear. You're leaving me
> alone.

He smiles and strokes her hair, then stands and moves OUT OF
FRAME. Ann closes her eyes.

351   *INT. — ENTRY HALL, HIGH DOWN ANGLE, STAIRCASE*

Barrett descends. Reaching the bottom, he crosses toward the
Great Hall.

352   *INT. — GREAT HALL, ANGLE PAST REVERSOR, TOWARD
ARCHWAY*

Barrett comes into the Great Hall and approaches the Reversor.
Stopping in front of it, he regards the main dial with awe.

353   *INSERT: MAIN DIAL*

A reading of 114,780 on it.

354   *BACK TO SCENE*

After a few moments, he turns toward the table.

355   *ANGLE OVER EQUIPMENT ON TABLE, TOWARD REVERSOR*

Barrett comes over to the table and looks at the array of equipment.
He runs a finger over the top of the EMR Recorder.

356   *INSERT: EMR RECORDER*

Its needle stirs.

357   *BARRETT*

Frowns a little. He stares at the needle.

358   *INSERT: EMR RECORDER*

The needle motionless again.

359   *BARRETT*

After a moment, he twitches, looking at the needle.

360   *INSERT: EMR RECORDER*

The needle jumping across the dial. It flutters back to zero.

361   *UP ANGLE OVER RECORDER, TOWARD BARRETT*

After several moments, the CAMERA MOVES IN QUICKLY ON
his look of startlement.

362   *INSERT: EMR RECORDER*

The needle is moving slowly. It does not jump or flutter now but
creeps across the dial.

363   *BARRETT*

His expression one of aggravation.

364   *INSERT: EMR RECORDER*

The needle moving past the 100 mark, 150.

365   *UP ANGLE PAST RECORDER, TOWARD BARRETT*

He hits the top of the Recorder with his left palm.

A SOUND to his left makes him jerk his head in that direction.
CAMERA WHIP PANS TO the Dynamometer. Its needle is
beginning to turn.

366   *CLOSE ON BARRETT*

Still more angry than dismayed. His eyes shift quickly.

367   *INSERT: THERMOMETER*

Starting to record a drop in temperature.

368   *CLOSE ON BARRETT*

Face becoming a mask of malice. He gasps as the O.S. cameras
CLICK, looks at them abruptly.

369   *INSERT: CAMERAS*

The film inside them is wound, the lenses click again.

370   *BARRETT*

Starting sharply as his face is illuminated by colored lights. He looks
at them in shock.

371   *RACK OF LIGHTS*

Burning. Nearby, another rack of lights turns on.

372   *UP ANGLE ON BARRETT*

Face stiff with resistance.

> BARRETT
> This is *impossible*.

CAMERA ZOOMS BACK TO a rack of test tubes as one of them breaks in half and falls to the tabletop. Barrett starts to back off from the table as the test tubes start to break one by one, the electric stove begins to glow, all the equipment starts to function. Barrett shakes his head. CAMERA ZOOMS IN ON his face as he gasps at the EMR Recorder.

373   *INSERT: EMR RECORDER*

Starting to expand as though its sides and top are made of rubber instead of metal. The reading on the dial is almost to the 900 mark.

374   *ANGLE PAST BARRETT, TOWARD TABLE*

He backs off from it. The EMR Recorder keeps expanding.

> BARRETT (voice shaking)
> I do not accept this.
> (Pause; cracking)
> I DO NOT ACCEPT THIS!!

His voice is cut off by the sudden explosion of the recorder. Barrett whirls to CAMERA with a cry of agony, metal splinters buried in his face.

One of the cameras shoots up from the table, hits him in the back and knocks him to the floor, CAMERA MOVING DOWN WITH him. More equipment flies from the table and hits him as he struggles to his knees.

375   *POV SHOT — BARRETT*

The GLAZED LENS effect and the unearthly SOUND of amusement as CAMERA HURTLES toward him. He cries out in shock as the force jerks him from his feet as though he were a toy, propels him through the air and flings him violently against the front of the Reversor. His left leg snaps; he gasps in pain, body crashing to the floor. Instantly, the unseen force grabs hold of him again and starts to drag him across the hall.

376   *MOVING SHOT, BARRETT'S POV*

A shadow pulling him across the floor. A massive table blocks the way. Barrett cries out as he hits the table, then is yanked across it.

377   *MOVING SHOT — BARRETT*

The GLAZED LENS effect again, the SOUND of demoniacal amusement. Barrett crashes to the floor on the other side of the table, his right leg broken now. He has no power to fight against the brutal force that drags him into the entry hall, beneath the stairs and down the corridor.

378   *INT. — BARRETTS' ROOM, CLOSE ON ANN*

As she sits up with a gasp; looks around.

ANN
Chris?

No answer. She rises from the bed and moves toward the corridor door.

379   *INT. — SECOND-STORY CORRIDOR, ANGLE ON DOOR TO BARRETTS' ROOM*

Ann opens it and moves to the balcony rail, CAMERA WITHDRAWING FROM her.

ANN (cont'd)
Chris?

No answer. Ann moves to the staircase.

380   *INT. — GREAT HALL, ANGLE THROUGH ARCHWAY, TOWARD STAIRS*

Ann comes down the stairs and into F.G., looking into the Great Hall. She reacts, seeing the damage.

381   *POV SHOT — TABLE*

Broken equipment on the floor.

382   *BACK TO SCENE*

Ann looks around.

(CONTINUED)

382   CONTINUED:

                              ANN (worried)
                              Chris?

                         BARRETT (voice) (faintly)
                              Here!

She looks relieved, abruptly decides that his call came from the
corridor by the chapel and moves in that direction.

383   *ANGLE FROM SIDE CORRIDOR, TOWARD STAIRS*

Ann moves into F.G., stops, and looks down the side corridor. No
sight of Chris.

                              ANN (calling)
                              Where, Chris?

                         BARRETT (voice) (faintly)
                              Here!

The voice seems to come from the cellar area. Ann moves toward
the stairs uneasily.

384   *UP ANGLE ON STAIRS*

Ann appears and starts down them, CAMERA WITHDRAWING
AHEAD OF her. At the bottom of the stairs, she stops and looks
around.

                              ANN (calling)
                              Now where?

                           BARRETT (voice)
                              Here!

The voice seems to come from the area of the steam room. Ann
moves toward the swinging doors and proceeds in that direction.

385   *INT. — STEAM ROOM, ANGLE ON DOOR*

As she enters and looks around the room, which is obscured by
billows of steam.

                           ANN (voice breaking)
                              Chris!

                                                    (CONTINUED)

385   CONTINUED:

> BARRETT (voice) (nearby; *loudly*)
> Here!

She whirls and looks down; flings her hands to her head and shrieks with horror.

386   POV SHOT — BARRETT

The swirling steam clears away just enough to reveal Barrett's body, legs twisted and broken, dead eyes staring up at her.

387   ANN

Backing off, sounding as though she is about to strangle. Abruptly, with an animal groan, she twists around and staggers out the door.

388   INT. — CORRIDOR

Ann stumbling blindly to the staircase where she freezes, looking upward dumbly.

389   UP ANGLE ON STAIRCASE

A shadowy figure rushes down the stairs toward CAMERA. O.S. Ann starts to SCREAM. The figure blots out the screen.

390   INT — GREAT HALL, CLOSE ON ANN — LATER

Lying on a sofa, eyes shut. After a while, her eyes open; she begins to focus them.

391   POV SHOT — FISCHER

Sitting next to her. He comes INTO FOCUS, looking at her.

392   TWO SHOT

Ann stares at him in silence, then remembers, sits up suddenly.

> ANN
> *Chris.*

> FISCHER (restraining her)
> You don't want to see him.
> (As she struggles)
> You *don't* want to *see* him.

(CONTINUED)

392   *CONTINUED:*

Ann starts to cry and Fischer puts his arms around her. Ann weeps
uncontrollably against him. After a while, she draws away from him
abruptly, an embittered look on her face.

ANN

Oh, God, let's get *out* of here.

Fischer shakes his head slowly.

ANN (appalled)

Aren't *two deaths enough*?

FISCHER (overlapping)

I have to do it, Mrs. Barrett.

ANN

Why?

FISCHER

While your husband and Florence were doing
everything they could to solve the haunting,
I was —

ANN (interrupting)

But they *didn't* solve it! There's no *way* to
solve it!

393   *FISCHER*

Regarding her in silence for a while before he replies.

FISCHER

Then I'll die trying.

394   *ANN*

Staring at him. After a while, she presses the palms of her hands
over her eyes.

395   *DOWN ANGLE ON FISCHER AND ANN*

Motionless on the sofa. After a while, Fischer rises suddenly.

FISCHER

I don't understand. The house *still* feels clear.

396–   OMITTED
400

401   UP ANGLE ON STAIRCASE — FISCHER AND ANN

Stopping in F.G., Fischer looking angrily confused.

FISCHER
But there has to be *something* left. *Some*where.

He gets an idea and turns his head toward the corridor that leads to
the chapel; stares in that direction. Ann looks at him.

402   INT. — CHAPEL, ANGLE ON DOOR

As Fischer opens it and he and Ann COME INSIDE. He looks
around; begins to tense.

FISCHER
It's *here*.
(Beat)
The entire house is clear except for this one
place.
(Pause; baffled)
But *why*?

CAMERA MOVES WITH him as he walks down the center aisle,
looking around. Ann remains behind, watching him. He stops by the
fallen crucifix and looks at it.

403   CLOSE SHOT — FISCHER

Eyes shifting to the floor beside the crucifix.

404   POV SHOT — SYMBOL ON FLOOR

Florence's body and — the letter *B* inside the circle.

405   CLOSE-UP — FISCHER

Beginning to understand the symbol.

406   CLOSE SHOT — SYMBOL

407   TIGHTER CLOSE-UP — FISCHER

Staring at the symbol; almost to its answer now.

408   *CLOSE-UP — SYMBOL*

409   *TIGHTER CLOSE-UP — FISCHER*

Face filling the screen as he suddenly gets the answer.

> FISCHER
> My *God*.

He looks up quickly, face stiffening with dread as the SOUND of unearthly amusement is heard O.S. from the altar.

410   *ANN*

Freezing with dread, looking toward the altar.

411   *POV SHOT — SHADOW*

Rushing at CAMERA from behind the altar, filling the screen, the SOUND becoming painful to hear.

412   *CLOSE-UP — FISCHER*

Jolting with shock; then, abruptly, going blank-faced. Sudden silence. CAMERA WITHDRAWS FROM Fischer as he turns after a while and walks toward the door.

> ANN
> What is it?
> (Beat)
> Mr. Fischer, what . . .

She breaks off, startled, as he walks by her as though she's invisible.

413   *INT. — CORRIDOR, ANGLE ON CHAPEL DOOR*

Fischer comes out and walks into F.G., his expression staring, masklike. Ann moves after him and grabs his arm.

> ANN (cont'd)
> Mr. Fischer?

She breaks off as he pulls free and continues on.

414   *INT. — ENTRY HALL, DOWN ANGLE PAST SECOND-FLOOR BANISTER RAIL*

Fischer walks from the corridor and toward the stairs. Ann runs after him and grabs his arm again.

(CONTINUED)

414   *CONTINUED:*

> ANN (cont'd)
> Mr. *Fischer.*

415   *CLOSE ON THEM.*

He pulls free of her grip and slings her aside. She almost falls, then regains her balance, staring at him in shock. Fearfully, she runs after him, trying to stop him.

> ANN (cont'd)
> Mr. Fischer!

He throws her aside again and starts up the stairs. Ann falls and hurts herself, tries to stand but can't.

> ANN (cont'd)
> Mr. *Fischer!*

Despite the pain in her ankle, she forces herself to pursue him hobblingly . . . CAMERA PANNING TO FOLLOW their movement to the second floor. Walking into F.G., face impassive, Fischer begins to climb on the railing. Ann reaches him and pulls him back. They wrestle until she suddenly remembers herself in the same situation and, abruptly, pulls her right hand free and slaps his face hard.

416   *ANGLE ON FISCHER*

As he jerks back with a gasp, slips, and sprawls onto the floor, stunned by what has almost happened. Ann kneels beside him. He stares at her, panting. She isn't sure if he has regained his senses or not.

> ANN (cont'd)
> Mr. Fischer?

> FISCHER (still panting)
> He caught me again.

> ANN
> *He?*

> FISCHER
> Belasco.
> (MORE)

> (CONTINUED)

416   *CONTINUED:*

                              (Pause; starting to regain his breath)
                         That's what the *B* inside the circle means.
                              (Beat)
                         She was trying to tell us that it's been Belasco all
                         along.
                              (Beat)
                         No wonder the haunting was never solved.
                         Everyone's been going at it in the wrong direction;
                         thinking in terms of multiple sources when, all the
                         time, there was only one. One entity pretending to
                         be dozens. That's where the answer lies.
                              (Beat)
                         But what's the key?
                              (Pause)
                         The *key*.

           CAMERA MOVES IN QUICKLY ON his face.

417   *SUBLIMINAL SHOT*

           The tape recorder.

418   *BACK TO FISCHER AND ANN*

           Abruptly he rises and hurries OUT OF FRAME. Ann hesitates,
           then follows him, CAMERA PANNING TO SHOW them running
           toward the Great Hall.

419   *INT. — GREAT HALL, ANGLE OVER TABLE, TOWARD
           ARCHWAY*

           Fischer runs into the hall and over to the table, followed by Ann.
           He picks up the tape recorder and puts it on the table, tries it. It
           works. "Teleplasmic veil beginning to condense," Barrett's VOICE
           says on it. Ann shudders. Fischer reverses the spool and switches
           the recorder to PLAY again. "Medium's respiration now two
           hundred and ten," Barrett's VOICE says. Fischer reverses the spool
           again, lets it run for several moments.

                                        ANN
                              What are you doing?

                                                            (CONTINUED)

419   *CONTINUED:*

He waves her off, puts the recorder on PLAY again. Barrett's
VOICE says: "Sitters Dr. and Mrs. Christopher Barrett, Mr.
Benjamin —" He reverses the spool again, stops and plays it. "Don't
want to hurt you but I must!" says Florence's VOICE.

> FISCHER
> *Damn* it.

Again he reverses the spool and plays it. Florence's VOICE is
heard, speaking like her guide. "Leave this house!" Pause. "No
good," says the VOICE. "He is here too long. Not listen." With a
muffled curse, Fischer reverses the spool again, puts it on PLAY.
Florence's VOICE says, "Nations. Terms. I do not know what that
means. Extremes and limits. Terminations. Extremities." Pause.
"Not know." Grimacing, Fischer reverses the spool again, puts it
on PLAY. As he listens, CAMERA MOVES IN ON him. He has
gotten the message but failed to absorb it, and the failure starts
to work on him as Florence's VOICE is heard: ". . . greetings to
you from the realm of Eternal Peace. I am happy to see you.
Fleurette is always happy to see earthlings gather in a circle of
belief."

> FISCHER (over the above)
> Wait a second.

He stops the spool and moves it forward. CAMERA WITHDRAWS
TO INCLUDE Ann as Florence's VOICE is heard saying, "Not
understand. Too much sick inside." Silence for several moments.
Fischer leans across the tape recorder tensely. Florence's VOICE is
heard again, saying, "Limits. Nations. Terms. I do not know what
that means. Extremes and limits. Terminations. Extremities."
Fischer reverses the tape a little. Again, Florence's VOICE says,
"Extremes and limits. Terminations. Extremities." Fischer switches
off the tape recorder.

> FISCHER
> Extremities.
> (Pause)
> *Legs.*
> (MORE)

                                                        (CONTINUED)

419   *CONTINUED: —2*

> (Pause; thinking hard)
> Grace Lauter . . . shattering her legs and spine.
> (Beat; with increasing excitement)
> Dr. Graham — *crawling*. Professor Rand —
> *paralyzed*. Professor Fenley — *crippled*.
> Florence's legs — *crushed*. Your husband's
> legs — twisted — broken.

Suddenly, he remembers something.

420   *CLOSE ON FLORENCE'S LIPS*

> FLORENCE (whispering)
> *If thine eye offend thee.*

421   *CLOSE ON FISCHER*

He runs OUT OF FRAME

422   *ANN*

She hesitates, then runs after him, CAMERA PANNING TO
SHOW them moving into the entry hall.

423   *INT. — CHAPEL, ANGLE ON DOOR*

Total silence. Then, faintly, the sound of Fischer's running
FOOTSTEPS can be heard coming closer and closer. Abruptly, he
flings open the door and lunges inside.

> FISCHER
> *Belasco!*

Ann runs in, stunned by what he's doing.

> FISCHER (cont'd)
> Here I am again! Destroy me if you can!
> (Pause)
> Come *on*! Don't leave the job half done! I'm
> here! We're *both* here! *Kill* us!

Heavy silence except for Fischer's breathing. Ann starts to speak to
him, then looks toward the altar. A faint SOUND is beginning,
unidentifiable.

424   *POV SHOT — ALTAR*

The SOUND increasing in volume little by little; the hideous sound of amusement.

425   *FISCHER AND ANN*

Looking at the altar. The O.S. sound gets louder, louder.

                          FISCHER
                      That's it; that's it.

Ann glances at him frightenedly, then stares back at the altar.

426   *POV SHOT — ALTAR*

The SOUND getting louder every moment. The floor begins to shake. CAMERA MOVES IN ON the altar.

427   *FISCHER AND ANN*

Ann starts drawing back. Fischer grabs her arm and holds her, an expression of maniacal intent on his face. She looks at him again, then back at the altar. The sound is becoming deafening, the entire chapel shaking. CAMERA WITHDRAWS FROM them. The SOUND gets closer, closer. The chapel shudders. Now the altar is in F.G., trembling violently as the SOUND gets louder, louder. Suddenly CAMERA ZOOMS IN ON Fischer and Ann as the SOUND stops. Ann recoils but Fischer holds her. His voice is taut with excitement.

                          FISCHER
                  This is a special moment.
                          (Beat)
                   Meet Emeric Belasco.

428   *POV SHOT — EMERIC BELASCO*

Enormous, dressed in black, his face is the demoniac visage from the crucifix. CAMERA MOVES IN ON his terrifying face.

429   *ANGLE PAST FISCHER AND ANN, TOWARD BELASCO*

                   FISCHER (with tight control)
             Tell me something, Belasco. Why didn't you ever
                          (MORE)

                                              (CONTINUED)

429   *CONTINUED:*

            leave this house when you were alive? Why did
            you despise the sunlight?
                        (Cuttingly)
            Was it *better* hiding in the shadows?

Ann draws back, horrified, as the figure starts toward them, moving
stiffly. To her renewed shock, Fischer lets go of her and starts
approaching Belasco.

430   *MOVING SHOT — FISCHER*

Ann watching from the B.G., terrified.

                    FISCHER (with cold contempt)
            No one could really get a good look at you then,
            could they? No one could find out your secret.

431   *POV SHOT — BELASCO*

Moving stiffly toward CAMERA, a look of savage intent on his face.

432   *MOVING SHOT — FISCHER*

Still advancing.

                    FISCHER (cont'd)
            Well, I know what that secret is, Belasco.

433   *POV SHOT — BELASCO*

Starting to slow down, eyeing Fischer with feral suspicion.

434   *FISCHER*

Still advancing.

                    FISCHER (cont'd)
            You walk with a labored tread, Belasco. Just as
            you did in life, *correct*?
                        (Beat)
            Why is that?
                        (Beat; sadistically)
            Why did you always go for their legs, I wonder.
            Was it because you couldn't stand to see them
                        (MORE)
                                            (CONTINUED)

434   *CONTINUED:*

> walking like *you* never could? Was *that* it,
> Belasco? Was that why you always had to *get* their
> *legs* in some way when you killed them?
> (With a sudden, mocking cackle)
> The Roaring Giant?! *You?*

435   *CLOSE ON ANN*

Her expression one of awe as she looks at Belasco.

436   *POV SHOT — FISCHER AND BELASCO*

Belasco is moving backward and *is not as big as he was before.*

437   *MOVING SHOT, ANGLE PAST BELASCO, TOWARD
        FISCHER*

Fischer advancing implacably on Belasco, who keeps retreating;
keeps getting smaller.

> FISCHER (cont'd)
> You *funny little bastard*!

He freezes as a SOUND of rage is heard from the dwindling figure.
For several moments, Fischer cannot react. Then the cruel smile
returns.

The figure draws back past the altar toward the wall on which the
crucifix had hung.

> FISCHER (cont'd)
> What a funny, little, hobbling bug of a *bastard*.
> (Beat)
> You weren't a genius. You were a *fraud*. A *sick,
> degenerate fraud*.

438   *ANGLE PAST FISCHER, TOWARD BELASCO*

Belasco keeps retreating; Fischer keeps advancing.

> FISCHER (cont'd) (contemptuously)
> How tall were you really? Five-foot-one? Two?
> (Beat)
> *Or were you even five feet tall?*

(CONTINUED)

438   *CONTINUED:*

As Belasco backs through the altar wall, Fischer breaks into a run
for it.

439   *ANN*

Watching Fischer startledly.

440   *FISCHER*

Reaching the wall, he throws his weight against the wall, which
makes a portion of it swing in.

441   *INT — CHAMBER, ANGLE ON OPENING*

Fischer moves inside, stopping to adjust his eyes to the gloomy
light. Now he sees Belasco.

442   *POV SHOT — BELASCO*

Backing slowly across the chamber, a small, shadowy figure.

443   *MOVING SHOT — FISCHER*

Advancing on Belasco again. In the B.G., Ann approaches the
opening.

                              FISCHER
                What was wrong with them, Belasco?

A hideous WAIL begins to come from Belasco.

              FISCHER (cont'd) (tightening the screws)
                Were they just *stunted*? A boy's legs holding up
                the body of a man?

The WAIL increases.

                          FISCHER (cont'd)
                FUNNY . . . LITTLE . . . BASTARD-D-D!

He stops abruptly, features washed of fury as the WAILING sound
becomes more than he can bear. He stares at Belasco.

444   *POV SHOT — BELASCO*

Cowering at the foot of a shadowy dais on which something dark
and formless is seen. The WAIL of defeat weakens; chokes off.

445   *FISCHER*

Looking at Belasco with sickened pity.

> FISCHER (cont'd)
> God help your crippled soul, Belasco.

His face tightens.

446   *POV SHOT — DAIS*

The figure is gone. A wailing sound is heard that fades into silence.

447   *ANGLE PAST FISCHER, TOWARD WALL OPENING*

As he stares at the dais, Ann APPEARS in the wall opening, making a sound in the heavy stillness. Fischer looks around. Moving to her, he takes her hand and leads her across the chamber, CAMERA DRAWING AHEAD OF them. They stop by the dais, looking upward.

Fischer takes a book of matches from his pocket and lights one. Ann gasps in shock. CAMERA WHIP PANS TO a figure sitting in a large wooden armchair on top of the dais: the mummified remains of Emeric Belasco.

CAMERA MOVES IN ON Belasco's face, open-eyed, glaring at them from death.

448   *FISCHER AND ANN*

Ann lowers her gaze; reacts.

> ANN
> His *legs*.

449   *UP ANGLE ON BELASCO*

CAMERA DOWN PANS SLOWLY TO his legs. They are immense in proportion to his body. O.S. FOOTSTEPS. CAMERA WITHDRAWS AS Fischer lights a second match and leans over Belasco's corpse, Ann watching. She gasps as he wrenches loose one of the legs, straightens up.

> FISCHER
> If thine eye offend thee — *pluck it out.*
> (MORE)

(CONTINUED)

449   *CONTINUED:*

> (Beat)
> He so despised his shortness that he had his own
> legs *cut off at the hips* and wore these instead to
> give him height.

He puts down the leg and descends the steps of the dais, starts to
move around the chamber.

> FISCHER (cont'd) (beat)
> This time he overextended himself, though.
> Because your husband really *did* have part of the
> answer. And Florence had part of it. And, with
> your help, I finally found the last part of that
> answer.
> (Beat)
> The part Belasco's giant ego couldn't face.

Stopping at a wall, he lights another match and checks it closely.

> FISCHER (cont'd) (impressed)
> Maybe he *was* a genius after all.

> ANN
> What do you mean?

> FISCHER (still to himself)
> That's why he stayed in here. That's why the
> Reversor didn't destroy *his* power.
> (Looking around at her)
> *The walls are sheathed with lead.*
> (Pause; looking toward Belasco)
> He knew what was coming more than forty years
> before it came.

CAMERA PANS TO Belasco's face and HOLDS.

> DISSOLVE TO:

450   *EXT. — HOUSE, ANGLE ON FRONT DOOR — LATER*

As Fischer pulls it shut and the lock catches. He turns to Ann; stops.

451   *ANN*

An odd expression on her face.

452   *TWO SHOT*

> FISCHER (gently)
> What is it?

> ANN (swallows; faintly)
> It's Christmas Eve.

They move away from CAMERA. As they do, a limousine starts appearing from the thinning fog.

FADE OUT

MOONLIGHTING

- - - - - - - - -

WRITTEN BY

HARLAN ELLISON

Adapted from his published story "Ormond Always Pays His Bills"

FADE IN:

1   *BLACK FRAME. CAMERA PULLS BACK FROM BLACK AS TITLES RUN.*

DURING SLOW PULL-BACK we HEAR a VOICE-OVER. The VOICE of MRS. KAY, a middle-aged woman. The VOICE is filled with deep anguish and a vengeful madness.

> MRS. KAY'S VOICE (over)
> You made a fool of the law, but you're not going
> to escape justice.
> > (cold and flat)
> All those kids dead . . . the whole school building
> collapsed . . . did you see all those little bodies?
> *Did you?*

PULL-BACK reveals the BLACK FRAME was looking down the barrel of a handgun. We pull back out of the muzzle as the VOICE OVER CONTINUES. (NOTE: Suggest use of a Colt Automatic "Commander" in the polished nickel model; or alternately a .38 Colt Super or .45 ACP. Suggest 3/4-inch barrel shorter than standard; polished nickel for shot that follows.)

(CONTINUED)

1   *CONTINUED:*

> MRS. KAY'S VOICE (CONT'D)
> You cut corners on the material, the construction
> was rotten . . . everybody knows it, even if you
> bought off the politicians at the hearing . . .

CAMERA HAS PULLED BACK to feature the handgun LARGE
IN F.G. As CAMERA MOVES AROUND the gun we see reflected
in the flat, highly polished nickel surface of its bulk the man at
whom the gun is aimed. He looks terrified.

> MRS. KAY'S VOICE (CONT'D)
> You don't get away with it . . . there's a due bill on
> sixteen dead kids . . .

CAMERA has PULLED BACK sufficiently to show us the gun held
by a tearful, coldly angry, fortyish woman on whose face is written a
memory of crushing sorrow. CAMERA AROUND HER and
HOLDS HER LARGE IN F.G. to show the man sitting behind the
desk, the man we saw reflected in the side of the gun. The large
logo on the wall behind him reads:

> COLONY CONSTRUCTION COMPANY
> Sonny Canoga, Pres.

SONNY CANOGA is in his early forties but retains the rugged self-
centered good looks of a college wingback; and he's as big across
the shoulders as one. He is extremely good-looking in the manner of
a comic book superhero: blond, expensive haircut, formidable jaw,
clear blue eyes, silk shirt open to the sternum, one discreet gold
chain: Mr. Wonderful, who could sell sandboxes to Arabs and get
away with it. But now he's showing another aspect of his nature: his
cowardice. He's terrified with this woman pointing the gun
unwaveringly at his head. Nervously, he toys with a long LETTER
OPENER that has a replica of the distinctive Colony Construction
logo at one end. We see now that we are in:

2   *INT. CONSTRUCTION OFFICE — NIGHT — ON SONNY*

Sweating, toying with the opener, he tries to reason with her, tries
to be forthright, but we can tell from his manner he's lying, just
babbling to stop her from firing.

                                                    (CONTINUED)

2   *CONTINUED:*

> SONNY (dissembles)
> This isn't right, Mrs. Kay . . . this isn't fair! You
> can't come in here and make threats like that . . .
> I'm not responsible!
> (beat, swallows)
> I didn't pick the land they used to build on. It was
> soft ground, it settled, the school went down from
> landfill, not what my company did!

3   *MOVING CAMERA AROUND SONNY TO MRS. KAY IN B.G.*

She holds the gun level, straight out in front of her, *not* with both
hands gripped around the butt as TV cops do it, but steadily, with
one hand.

> MRS. KAY (flatly)
> Say: Giselle.

> SONNY (uncomprehending)
> What?

> MRS. KAY
> Say it. Say: Giselle.

> SONNY (slowly)
> Giselle . . .

> MRS. KAY
> Again. Say: Giselle; and say: I'm sorry.

> SONNY   MRS. KAY
> (almost together)
> Why do you . . . ? *Say it!*

> SONNY
> Giselle . . . I'm, I'm sorry . . .

> MRS. KAY (softly)
> My daughter. I want her name on your lips when
> you die, Mr. Canoga.
> (beat)
> (MORE)

(CONTINUED)

3   *CONTINUED:*

> Her death is on your hands, I want her name on
> your lips.

Through preceding dialogue CAMERA COMES AROUND to
POV from BEHIND Sonny. Suddenly the door to the construction
office bursts open and a large man in uniform, STATE TROOPER
FRED LAMONT, smashes through as CAMERA ANGLE
WIDENS to FULL SHOT. Another woman is behind him.

4   *FULL SHOT — ANOTHER ANGLE — ON ACTION*

As Trooper Lamont wrestles with the slight Mrs. Kay, who seems to
possess the deranged power of a dozen men. He has grabbed her
from behind and wrenches her arm toward the fiberboard ceiling.
The gun goes off.

                                                    CUT TO:

5   *INTERCUT*

The logo on the wall above Sonny's head explodes from the random
shot. He dives out of the chair.

                                            CUT BACK TO:

6   *SAME AS 4 — WITH THE ACTION*

Trooper Lamont wrestles the gun away from her.

                                                    CUT TO:

7   *INTERCUT — THE OTHER WOMAN*

Still standing in the doorway, trying to swallow her fist. SARAH
BIEBER, an extremely plain-looking, very thin woman of
indeterminate years, but past the bloom of youth, though her wildly
inappropriate hairstyle tries to fly a flag of effort in that ebullience.
It just looks pathetic. She's what used to be called a spinster. She
stares wide-eyed.

                                            CUT BACK TO:

8   *MEDIUM SHOT — TROOPER & MRS. KAY*

As she lands a hard, short one over his heart. The trooper gasps and
                              (MORE)

                                            (CONTINUED)

8   *CONTINUED:*

(CONT'D)

manhandles her across the room to the sofa, gets her down with difficulty, and manages to cuff her. She is hysterical now, crying, trying to beg the trooper:

MRS. KAY (tearful, pleading)
Oh please . . . please don't stop me   please . . .
he *has* to pay . . . please . . .

9   *WITH SONNY — MEDIUM SHOT TO FULL SCENE*

as he gets off the floor, the letter opener still in his hand. He is wild-eyed and furious, reacting to being almost a dead thing. He comes for her, the letter opener held aloft.

SONNY (wild)
You lousy, crazy, stinking old bat! I oughtta pull
your damned *head* off!

Trooper Lamont steps in front of him, calms him with his body. He takes the letter opener away from him. He speaks calmly.

LAMONT
It's a good thing Miz Dieber came in late to work on
your books, Mr. Canoga. She called us just in time.

SONNY (furious)
I'm gonna press charges! She tried to kill me! You
saw her, both of you saw her; you're witnesses!

Mrs. Kay is slumped over her knees, sobbing softly.

10   *ANOTHER ANGLE FEATURING SARAH*

as we see the scene through her. Her reactions of intense concern for Sonny underline the action.

LAMONT
Take it easy now, Mr. Canoga. You're okay. This
is bad, but no sense in getting yourself all unlaced.

Sonny starts to harangue him, but pulls up short. There is a mean twist to his otherwise extraordinary good looks. He breathes deeply,

(MORE)

(CONTINUED)

composes himself, and becomes the trained smoothyguts again. He
smiles one of those buttery smiles.

> LAMONT (CONT'D)
> I'm going to take her by St. Anne's for a quick
> stop in the emergency . . . and she'll be at the
> station when you get ready to sign the complaint.

> SONNY (thin smile)
> You're right. Absolutely.
> (beat)
> And I want you to know the State Police'll be
> getting some terrific glowing story about you,
> Trooper. Your commandant's gonna know you
> saved my life. There'll be a big promotion in this
> one, you can bet on it. I give you my word!

Lamont frowns at all this unctuousness. He tries to be polite. But he
obviously doesn't like the way Sonny is sucking up to him.

> LAMONT
> Well, that'll be just fine, sir. I'm just glad we got
> here in time.
> (beat)
> Oh . . . here . . .

He hands him the letter opener. Sonny refuses it.

> SONNY
> No indeed. You keep it. A nothing little gift. Just
> one of our new giveaways with the storm
> windows. My appreciation.

The trooper places it on the desk with a smile.

> LAMONT
> Thanks anyway, Mr. Canoga. I don't get much
> mail.

He goes to the weeping woman and gently, kindly, raises her from
the sofa till he's almost hugging her. We get the feeling he is

> (MORE)

(CONTINUED)

10   *CONTINUED: —2*

sympathetic to her actions. He turns her to the door and they move off, passing Sarah Bieber, who still stands frozen, eyes wide. As they pass out the door . . . over his shoulder:

> LAMONT (CONT'D)
> I'll see you at the station, sir.

Then they're gone.

11   *LONG SHOT — PAST SONNY TO SARAH*

As she stares at him, still wide-eyed. Then suddenly the membrane breaks and she rushes to him in F.G. She flies into his arms, trembling. She hugs him tightly. Her words of adoration and concern are AD LIB muffled and run-on, incoherent. He kisses her. He pats her back as he holds her, strokes her hair.

> SONNY
> It's all right . . . it's okay . . . I'm fine . . . you saved
> my life.
> (¹/₂ beat)
> Again.

CLOSE ON THEM as they stand together. She comes up for air, looks at him intensely.

> SARAH
> Oh, my God, I was so frightened. I came in to . . .
> you know . . . to do just a little more work on the
> loose ends in the books   just in case they
> subpoena . . .

His face tightens. He grips her shoulders too tightly.

> SONNY (snake smooth)
> Now c'mon, Sarah, honey. You can't just be
> mentioning that all the time. You gotta make it
> one of those things we know and don't say. I love
> you, so it's okay, isn't that right?

She looks away and in EXTREME CU we see she is tormented.

> SARAH (confused)
> I . . . I . . . don't know . . .

                                                        (CONTINUED)

11   *CONTINUED:*

> SONNY (tougher)
> It's *love*, Sarah. I'm not talkin' about what we do
> here on the sofa, I'm talkin' about *love*!

He has an almost tv evangelist tone to his voice.

> SONNY (CONT'D)
> How many people ever feel this in their life,
> darlin'? How many do you think?

She's mesmerized. A cobra at a mongoose rally. Sonny keeps pressing.

> SONNY (CONT'D)
> I promised you, didn't I? Didn't I give you my
> bounden word the nights on the sofa would come
> to an end? Soon as this is all past I tell Darleen I
> want a divorce, there's no kids, legally I got it
> arranged so the settlement won't hurt —

> SARAH
> But I'm so frightened!
> (beat, with awe)
> I've *never* been involved in such things . . .
> with you . . . the hearings . . . now that woman
> trying to —

> SONNY (getting miffed)
> Can't you let it sleep?!?

> SARAH
> Oh, Sonny . . . those terrible things she was
> saying! So many people in town whisper behind
> my back when I go in the stores.

> SONNY (soothes her)
> It's okay, dumplin'. It's just nothin' but okay.
> Commission said I was clean, they can't shake
> back at that, comes right down to it.

> SARAH
> But Sonny, if that's so, why couldn't I find the
> proper specs on that job, the bills of lading, all
> the docu —

                                    (CONTINUED)

11   *CONTINUED: —2*

> SONNY (toughly)
> I said it don't *matter*! As long as the books are
> squeaky, it's just a lotta wind they're raising.

Then he is very businesslike. He puts her from him and starts to roll
down his sleeves.

> SONNY (CONT'D)
> I build roads, and bridges, and buildings, and
> whole damned tracts of houses. Let'm say what
> they want. As long as I got you, you little whiz, I
> got the world in an egg-cup!

> SARAH (goofy-eyed)
> Oh, I do love you more than any thing I ever
> knew, Sonny.

> SONNY (distracted)
> And I love you, too, babe. But if I don't get home
> Darleen'll be comin' after me with a blowtorch.
> (beat)
> Now I'm just fine, just *fine*. You stay on, work a
> bit on those books, and come in late tomorrow.

He shrugs into his all-weather padded vest, zips up, and gives her a
honey-dripping grin. He opens his arms and like a puppy she moves
to him, hungry for the smallest touch, and as he embraces her
passionately the CAMERA MOVES PAST THEM toward the
window of the construction company office, as the first few drops of
rain spatter on the pane.

> SONNY'S VOICE
> (Over)
> Can you imagine the *gall* of that damned woman?
> Makin' me say her dead kid's name!

As Sonny's VO speaks, lightning splits the sky, the rain starts to
come down torrentially, and CAMERA GOES INTO WINDOW as
the thunder rattles ominously around the night.

> CUT TO:

12   *EXT. CONSTRUCTION COMPANY — NIGHT*
          — REVERSE FULL SHOT

From the edge of the woods CAMERA ESTABLISHES the
small, three-room construction company offices sitting in the
middle of a small clearing at the side of the highway. Tall woods
all around. Floodlights illuminate a sign near the road with the
Colony Construction name and logo prominent. In the otherwise
empty parking area — turning to mud as the rain comes down —
we see a fancy current-model pickup truck: a behemoth RV with
a rack of spotlights on the cab, gargantuan tires, painted in *very
distinctive* candy-flake colors, the Colony logo on the door.
There is also a modest sedan, perhaps three years old, sitting
near the RV, looking pathetic next to the high-rise RV. The small
grounds of the office are neatly manicured, the lights are on in
two of the offices. As we watch, one of the lights goes off, Sonny
comes out of the building, pauses a second to gauge the rain
as he stands on the porch of the frame office, then he hunches
his shoulders, dashes down the steps, rushes through the
pelting rain as lightning and thunder crash, leaps up to the
runningboard of the RV, gets in quickly. The RV lights go on,
throwing cones of brilliance across the highway to the woods.
Then the motor revs like a waking dragon and, spewing mud in a
wide swath, he tools out of the lot, turns onto the highway, and is
gone, as CAMERA PANS LEFT to follow the action. Rain falls
heavily. CAMERA HOLDS a moment then PANS BACK and
BEGINS TO MOVE IN SLOWLY on the office building where
the single light glows. Lightning illuminates the woods briefly as
CAMERA CONTINUES TO MOVE IN STEADILY toward the
window until we can see Sarah inside, poring over the ledgers
and we

                                        LAP-DISSOLVE THRU:

13   *SARAH — EXT. & INT. SHOTS*
and
14   DIFFERENT ANGLE THAN SHOT 12. On the woman working
          by lamplight, ledgers in duplicate before her, altering figures,
                              (MORE)
                                        (CONTINUED)

13
and
14

CONTINUED:

changing dates. We need not see exactly what she is writing, but
should get the impression that time is passing. CAMERA
CONTINUES MOVING IN ON WINDOW

THRU TO:

INT. OFFICE — ANOTHER ANGLE — SAME SCENE
As she works. Hours have passed. And we CONTINUE

LAP-DISSOLVE TO:

15   EXT. CONSTRUCTION COMPANY — NIGHT

Rain has now turned the parking lot to a series of small lakes.
ANOTHER ANGLE THAN SHOT 12 as the single light goes off in
the building, the door opens and Sarah Bieber emerges, locks up
quickly, pulls her collar around her neck, and dashes to her car.
CAMERA IN as she tries to start the old vehicle. It revs a few
times, then catches. CAMERA TO CAR as she pulls away, spraying
water, and CAMERA HOLDS on her retreat as she swings onto the
highway, going in the same direction Sonny took, and her taillights
are lost in the rain.

CUT TO:

16   INT. SARAH'S CAR — NIGHT — HER POV

Past her to show the road barely visible through the sheeting rain. She
swabs at the windshield. The wipers work fitfully. Her lights swerve on
the road picking up nothing but rain, and the occasional center-stripe.

17
thru
19

SERIES OF EXT. ANGLES — TRAVELING SHOTS

On her car as it skids. We see her go off the road onto the berm
several times. Not many cars pass her going the other way, but each
time a car swooshes past, the water from the highway inundates her
vehicle. On LAST SHOT of SEQUENCE CAMERA HOLDS as
car passes through to:

20   INT. CAR

As suddenly a gigantic semi looms up, lights glaring, booms past,
(MORE)

(CONTINUED)

20   *CONTINUED:*

water rises over her like a tidal wave, she starts to skid badly, spins
the wheel . . .

INTERCUT TO:

21   *EXT. HIGHWAY — NIGHT — RAIN*

As the vehicle fishtails wildly, swerving across the line and back and we

CUT BACK TO:

22   *SAME AS 20*

As she struggles with the wheel, the road and trees flashing in the
windshield. Then, as she manages to get the car under control, she
sees THRU WINDSHIELD the glow of neon lights, red and yellow
and flashing at her. She turns toward them, as CAMERA HOLDS
HER POV, until she is right under the lights and we can see it's the
gaudy road sign of the old sort, circa Forties, that flash on and off
with the message:

HI OLD TIME
ROADHOUSE   DANCING
EATS

23   *EXT. ROADHOUSE — NIGHT — HIGH SHOT*

On Sarah's car as she pulls past the sign and into the muddy parking
lot. Her car is covered with mud, windshield obscured. She pulls into
the lot, near the few RVs and cars and 4-wheel-drive vehicles. The Hi
Old Time is one of those ratty-looking, utterly disreputable joints that
features greasy food, redneck music, sawdust on the floor, and
probably a congeries of small rooms upstairs in which the totality of
furniture is a bed, a hat rack, and a sink, if you get the meaning. Sarah
pulls to a stop near some vehicles. NOTE: we should not be able to
make out one vehicle from another. ANGLE to obscure this element.

24   *INT. SARAH'S CAR*

CLOSE ON DASH CLOCK. Two A.M. CAMERA PULLS BACK
to ANGLE on SARAH as she looks at the Hi Old Time. She makes
(MORE)

(CONTINUED)

24   *CONTINUED:*

a disgusted sound, the sort of sound a good churchgoing woman
would make at the doorway to Sodom. It is clear that she reviles this
sinkhole of depravity. She reaches into her glove compartment,
brings out a small squeegee and sponge implement, and opens the
door on the rain.

25   *EXT. ROADHOUSE PARKING LOT — CLOSE ON CAR —*
HAND-HELD CAMERA — STEADICAM

As Sarah steps out. She is lit by the neon that goes on and off with
eerie colors washing her. She slams the door and begins
squeegeeing her windshield, removing the mud that covers the
glass. Then she stops. CAMERA HOLDS HER as she looks across
the hood of the car and CAMERA ANGLE TILTS to show us the
vehicle parked next to her. It rises above her car and as we SHOOT
PAST HER we are full on the Colony Corporation logo. It is on the
side of Sonny's RV. It can be no other vehicle. We know that
trashwagon appearance from scene 12. She looks around, obviously
confused to see the vehicle here. Wasn't Sonny going straight home
to his wife . . . to the police station in town . . . what's going on
here? Concern, querulousness.

CAMERA HAND HELD — WITH HER

Still holding the squeegee, she slogs through the rain and mud to
the roadhouse, opens the front door and steps inside.

26   *INT. ROADHOUSE — ANGLE ON DARK ENTRANCEWAY*

As Sarah moves out of shadow with the door closing behind her,
coming TO CAMERA. CLOSE ON HER as we see her looking
into CAMERA. The SOUND of pseudo-disco-cum-country music,
achingly bad and cheap music, OVER THIS SCENE. EXTREME
CU as she REACTS to what she sees.

                                                                CUT TO:

27   *REVERSE ANGLE — SARAH'S POV — WHAT SHE SEES*

The usual stereotyped roadhouse scene, with neon beer signs
bubbling, a bar, tables and chairs, the band platform empty but the
                              (MORE)
                                                        (CONTINUED)

27   *CONTINUED:*

jukebox blaring. And in the middle of the room, Sonny is slow
dancing with a pair of, well, to put it politely, a PAIR of BIMBOS.
Acres of eyeshadow and blonde hair, short black leather skirts,
spiked heels an assassin would envy. Not easy dancing with two
women at the same time. CAMERA MOVES IN CLOSER to show
the technique Sonny uses for dancing: his hands where they
shouldn't oughtta be, and mouth-to-mouth resuscitation, first one
lady, then the other. And heads thrown back with laughter.

CUT BACK TO:

28   *SAME AS 26*

CAMERA MOVING IN STEADILY, CALMLY, ANGRILY on
mousy Sarah's face as she stares in wide-eyed disbelief . . . then a
pain so clear, so obvious, that even an Easter Island statue would
melt at her angst . . . then a rapidly dawning and blossoming and
burning hatred. We can *see* betrayal in her expression, and her
clenched fist underlines it.

28A   *CLOSE ON SONNY & WOMEN*

They do not attempt to keep their voices down, yet they are saying
double-entendre as if it were sotto voce:

SONNY (lecherously)
Swear I haven't been around such prime beef
since I was locked in overnight at the meat market.

1ST BIMBO (archly)
You look like a filet mignon type to me, Sonny.

2ND BIMBO
Don'tchoo get no prime filet to home, honey?

SONNY
Ground round, nothin' but ground round.

1ST BIMBO
Dog meat.

2ND BIMBO
Imported kangarooooooo . . . !

(CONTINUED)

28A   CONTINUED:

SONNY
Everywhere I put my hands . . .
(and he puts his hands)
I get hamburger, when my soul cries out for
USDA prime cut!

The bimbos squeal and writhe under his pawing, as they dance.
Sonny begins to chant, and they take it up:

SONNY (CONT'D) (chanting)
I wanna double burger . . . I wanna double
burger . . . I wanna

1ST BIMBO (joins in)	2ND BIMBO (joins in)
I wanna double burger . . . I wanna double burger . . .	I wanna double burger . . . I wanna double burger . . .

28B   SAME AS 28

CAMERA MOVING IN on Sarah, whose teeth are clenched.

SARAH (murmurs softly)
"I better get home before my wife comes after
me with a blowtorch . . ."

29   ANGLE PAST SARAH — TO BARROOM

As she stands there. She cannot take her eyes off the squalid scene.
Suddenly the women dancing with Sonny begin to drag him toward
the shadowy foyer. Sonny, half resisting, grabs up his padded vest
from the back of a chair, screams a goodbye to an unseen
bartender, and they all careen toward the spot where Sarah
watches. But the spot is empty, and we see the front door slowly
closing.

30   EXT. PARKING LOT — THE SCENE

As the reeling trio emerge, the women holding their coats over their
heads. They rush to the RV. He is about to unlock the RV when a
particularly BRIGHT BLAZE OF LIGHTNING and
accompanying thunder illuminates the scene.

31   *INTERCUTS BETWEEN SONNY & SARAH IN CU*
thru
34   His eyes widen. Rain washes his face as he stares in disbelief.

                                                          CUT TO:

ANGLE across the RV and Sarah's car, beside each other, to Sarah
staring at him with naked hatred as she stands with her door
unlocked and open.

                                                          CUT TO:

Sonny dropping the mask. His amazement vanishes and his lips skin
back in a growl. He utters a low growl.

                                                        · CUT TO:

Sarah throws the squeegee at him and gets in the car, starts it
instantly and PULLS OUT OF FRAME as we

                                                          CUT TO:

35   *FULL SHOT — THE SCENE*

As Sonny ignores the women, leaves them standing beside the still-
locked passenger side of the RV, dashes around the vehicle as
Sarah's car roars out of the muddy parking lot and heads *back
toward the office* (and the orientation should be clear from previous
shots). He unlocks quickly, jumps up and slams the door, guns the
motor and burns rubber, spraying mud everywhichway. He takes off
after her as CAMERA COMES IN CLOSE on the two ladies of the
evening, now utterly drenched, doing a kind of all-over wet
T-shirt performance, furious at his abandonment. The RV's
taillights wink, and he's gone.

36   *THE HIGHWAY — MOVING SHOT — NIGHT*
thru
40   First Sarah's car, careening down the flooded road, skidding,
swerving, Sarah in tears if an INTERIOR SHOT is needed, holding
the road only by a miracle as she recklessly rushes away from the
roadhouse. Then Sonny coming after her, at full throttle, flooding a
car passing on the other side, Sonny cursing, pounding the steering
wheel if an INTERIOR SHOT is needed, determined to catch her.
                              (MORE)

                                                    (CONTINUED)

36
thru
40

CONTINUED:

End sequence with Sonny as he skids sidewise into the parking area
of the Colony Construction offices. Sarah's car is close to the front
steps, door open, pulled up onto the neatly landscaped display area
right in front. The light is on in the car, headlights still glowing, and
the front door of the offices is standing ajar. We see all of this in the
brilliant glare of Sonny's RV headlights.

41   *EXT. CONSTRUCTION COMPANY*

As Sonny sluices to a halt, jumps out, rushes up the steps, and
through the doorway.

42   *INT. SONNY'S OFFICE — THE SCENE — FAVORING
            DOORWAY*

as Sonny rushes in, dripping wet, looking like a raging behemoth.
Sarah has the desk lamp on, and she is using the letter opener to pry
open a locked desk drawer. As he storms in, big as a house, filling
the doorway, lit by the single lamp in terrifying immediacy, she
pulls the ledgers from the drawer and looks up. Her face is filthy
with tear-tracks and mud.

> SARAH (betrayed, in pain)
> Ogod, Ogod, what a fool I am!

> SONNY
> Sarah, darlin', listen to me . . .

> SARAH
> No! No more lies!

He comes to the desk, stands on the other side, fists balled, trying to
finesse a way out of this.

> SONNY (smoothly)
> Now don't do anythin' with the books you're
> gonna regret later.

> SARAH (runs on)
> I did terrible things for you. I didn't want to
> believe them, but I knew, down inside I *knew* . . .
> but I lied for you . . .
> (MORE)

(CONTINUED)

42   *CONTINUED:*

(beat)
All the pain you caused . . . the dead children . . .
I *saw* them on the TV, and I *lied* for you.

SONNY
No, you're wrong . . . I . . .

SARAH (screams)
You *did*! You did what they said! You shaved the
specs, used inferior material, my God, they weren't
even galvanized *nails*; the first rain everything ran
with rust! Why didn't I see what you are? I'm a
decent woman . . . what I let you do to me . . .

Then she gets very cold and calm. She clutches the ledgers and
starts around the desk. The letter opener lies there prominently.

SARAH (CONT'D)
But no more. This is for me and for that poor
Mrs. Kay . . .

As she passes him we

SHARP CUT TO:

43   *INTERCUT*

As Sonny's hand comes down and picks up the letter opener with its
prominent logo of the Colony Corporation sculpted at the end of
the hilt.

CUT BACK TO:

44   *MURDER SEQUENCE — VARIOUS ANGLES*
thru
49   (NOTE: Suggest this be shot and edited as one would a music
video, extreme close-ups, tilt angles, slam-cuts, all with misdirection
so we never actually see the murder. In much the same way
Hitchcock shot the shower sequence in *Psycho*.)

Bodies frozen as Sarah tries to get around him. As she passes, one
muscular shirt-soaked arm whips out, grabs her by the hair. He
(MORE)

(CONTINUED)

44
thru
49

CONTINUED:

swings her around. The ledgers go flying. The desk lamp is knocked
over. The light washes up the wall. The letter opener rises, vanishes
from frame. Again. And on the third stroke we see the letter opener
is broken off halfway up its length. Sarah falls, the plastic raincoat
she still wears streaked and stained with blood *inside*. No blood on
the hardwood floor.

50
thru
55

WITH SONNY

As he drops the broken letter opener, the logo shining in the fallen
desk lamp's light. He stands there heaving with labored breathing.
He wipes his hand over his face, the rainwater still dripping off him.
His expressions rush through a gaunt of emotions: SERIES OF
RAPID LAP-DISSOLVES:

SONNY'S FACE IN MEDIUM CU: Horror: I'm a murderer!
                            Remorse: Oh, Sarah, you fool.
                            Panic: What'll I do?
                            Fear: They use the lethal
                               injection in this state!

And finally . . . a nasty little smile comes over his face.

> SONNY (calmly)
> Well, *okay*. Of course.

56

THE SCENE

As he folds the plastic raincoat around her, leaves her for a moment
to exit the office and CAMERA HOLDS ON THE BODY. He
comes back quickly from the next room, with a small tarpaulin. He
lays it out, rolls her into it, folds it around her, and tapes it at the
ends with industrial strapping tape from a dispenser on the desk.
Then he hoists the body and puts her over his shoulder, and leaves
through the doorway.

57

BLACK FRAME — INT. CONSTRUCTION SHED — NIGHT

As the overhead swinging-bulb light clicks on. HOLD FULL SHOT
OF SCENE as Sonny lays the body down, takes off his vest, rolls up
(MORE)

(CONTINUED)

57   *CONTINUED:*

his sleeves, and begins mixing a batch of cement from bags of sand
and clay and limestone sitting around the shed. He mixes them in a
metal trough, using a hose connected to the wall. He mixes a six-foot-
long troughful. Then, after a bit, he drops the tarp-encased shape
into the thickening soup. A few bubbles as it settles. He stares down.

                          SONNY
              Consider it your Christmas bonus, darlin'.

                                            DISSOLVE TO:

58   *EXT. LAKE — NIGHT — FULL SHOT*

The black rain slants down. The RV is parked at the edge of the
lake. Sonny is lowering a block of cement onto a small hand-truck.
He gets down, tilts it back with some straining of his muscular body,
and backs toward the dock. CAMERA MOVES IN to show Sonny
easing the block off the dolly, into a skiff tied up at the side.

                                            DISSOLVE TO:

59   *EXT. LAKE — LONG SHOT — DAWN*

Across the forested area to the body of the lake. It is just coming to
light in the sky. We can see a shape out there, and we know it's the
skiff. There is movement in the small craft, something goes over,
there is a DIM BUT DISTINCT SPLASH and we

                                            DISSOLVE TO:

60   *INT. CANOGA HOME — BEDROOM — EARLY MORNING*

CLOSE ON SONNY as he sleeps. We HEAR the insistent ringing
of a strident doorbell. It rings. Rings again. Rouses him from sleep.
He turns over and shouts.

                          SONNY (yells)
              Dammit, Darleen, answer the door!

The ringing continues. No one answers it. Sonny curses and throws
the bedclothes off. He sleeps in pajama bottoms, still wearing his
discreet gold chain. He snorts, rubs his hair, and goes to the
bedroom door.

                                                CUT TO:

61   *INT. CANOGA HOME — FRONT FOYER — DAY*

As Sonny comes stumbling downstairs toward the front door. The doorbell continues its caterwauling. Barefoot, he reaches the door.

> SONNY
> Hold yer water, I'm comin'!

He throws open the door. Standing there very large and ominous, is Trooper Fred Lamont.

> LAMONT
> Morning, Mr. Canoga. Got a spare minute?

Sonny looks confused, but gathers his wits.

> SONNY
> Yeah, sure. Come on in.
> (beat)
> What's up?

He closes the door. Lamont steps farther inside and removes his Smokey Bear hat.

> LAMONT
> I understand your bookkeeper, Miz Bieber,
> hasn't been to work for about ten days.

> SONNY (cheerful but careful)
> That's right. She went to see her sister in, uh, I
> think it's Omaha. She's gonna have a kid and
> Sarah went to help.

> LAMONT (firmly, shaking his head)
> No.

> SONNY
> No?

> LAMONT
> Definitely no.

> SONNY
> Well, that's what she told *me*.

(CONTINUED)

61   *CONTINUED:*

> LAMONT
> I don't think so.

Trooper Lamont holds up the broken letter opener. CAMERA
ANGLES to include Trooper and Sonny and the doorway to the
kitchen nearby.

> LAMONT
> I found this in the trash barrel behind your office.
> (beat)
> The other half was in Sarah Bieber's back.

At that moment, a woman in her mid-thirties, once pretty but now a
trifle careworn from living with Sonny, comes out of the kitchen
carrying a plastic clothes basket filled with wash and clothespins.
She stares openmouthed as Trooper Lamont unships his handcuffs.

> LAMONT (CONT'D)
> Let's go, Sonny.

Sonny starts to say something, but Lamont gives him a look.

> LAMONT (CONT'D)
> You really want to make a statement now? *Before*
> I read you your rights? I don't think so.

Sonny folds. Lamont cuffs him. He opens the door.

> SONNY
> But . . . how . . . ?

Lamont looks at him coldly. Then he pushes him out the door.

62   *EXT. CANOGA HOME — DRIVEWAY — DAY*

FEATURING STATE PATROL CAR IN F.G. as Sonny in cuffs
and the Trooper come to it. Darleen stands in the doorway, just
watching. They come to F.G. and as Lamont opens the rear door
and bends Sonny, protecting his head to put him in the back seat,
their faces are very close in EXTREME CU.

> LAMONT
> Damn stupid of you to use your own materials,
> Sonny.
> (MORE)

                                      (CONTINUED)

62   *CONTINUED:*
                                    (beat)
                    She floated to the top this morning.
                                    (beat)
                    Any fool knows that much sand in the mix won't
                    hold together.

Sonny's face falls apart. The horror of his own stupidity overwhelms him. His face slides down the frame in the back seat as the car door is slammed. He stares out the window. He stares back at the house.

                                                    QUICK CUT TO:

63   *CLOSE ON DARLEEN IN DOORWAY*

The veriest hint of a soft smile appears around her mouth and we

                                                    CUT BACK TO:

64   *STREET SHOT*

As the State Patrol car pulls away, with the face of Sonny Canoga, petrified with fear, still staring out at us. On his way to a lethal injection.

                                            FADE TO BLACK
                                                and
                                            FADE OUT.

KILLING BERNSTEIN

— — — — — — — —

TELEPLAY BY

HARLAN ELLISON

Based on his short story

FADE IN:

1   *NIGHT — ESTABLISHING SHOT — INT. NETTA'S APT.*

CAMERA HOLDS for **SEVERAL BEATS** to show a tastefully decorated singles apartment. Lights are low; a bright red chiffon scarf draped over the shade of a lamp casts sultry crimson shadows across the room. There is a pronounced Art Nouveau look to the room, elegant but not ostentatious. We **HEAR** the subdued strains of Tchaikovsky's Symphony #4 in F minor as CAMERA MOVES IN through the living room of the apartment.

CAMERA TRAVELS around the room and we see incongruous toys lying here and there . . . on the coffee table a child's peg-and-wooden mallet set lies atop a long yellow pad of notepaper filled with comments, a pencil on the pad as if the writing had been interrupted . . . a space war–type ray gun on the desk under a Tiffany lamp . . . a teddy bear at the foot of the sofa . . .

CAMERA TRACKS around living room — avoiding the short hallway leading to the bedroom. Now CAMERA DRIFTS over to HOLD on the dark passageway to the bedroom, as we **HEAR**:

> NETTA'S VOICE (from bedroom)
> Jimmy . . . Jimmy . . . I love you . . .

(CONTINUED)

1   *CONTINUED:*

CAMERA MOVES IN SLOWLY through the passageway to the
bedroom. NETTA'S VOICE professing love is heard UNDER and
now JIMMY'S VOICE IN ECHO is HEARD OVER.

> JIMMY (ECHO)
> It shouldn't have been so easy to kill Netta
> Bernstein.

CAMERA DOWN PASSAGE into the darkness. The only SOUND
WE HEAR is the music under and the sounds of love from the
bedroom:

> NETTA'S VOICE (from darkness)
> Jimmy . . . Jimmy . . .

CAMERA INTO BEDROOM. We HEAR Netta and Jimmy
making love, but the bed is empty. Rumpled sheets, signs of a
passionate scene now done, but Netta's voice languidly speaking his
name over and over. CAMERA HOLDS on empty bed.

> JIMMY (ECHO)
> Too easy. It was too easy killing Netta . . . *the first*
> *time* . . .

As he says the last three words CAMERA WHIP-PANS across the
dimly lit bedroom and in SOFT FOCUS with VASELINE ON
LENS and WITHOUT SOUND (except the SOUND UNDER of
Tchaikovsky's music and Netta's love-words) we see a man and a
woman struggling. He is about thirty-five, extremely good-looking in
a smooth, country club, well-manicured way. The sort of man
women make fools of themselves over . . . for a little while . . . before
they learn better. She has one of those Audrey Hepburn faces that
reflects remarkable genes: no lines, no pouches, no shadows. An
ageless, beautiful face that one might find on a twenty-year-old, and
again at thirty-five, and again at fifty. She is perhaps in her early
twenties, but she might be a gamin eighteen, or a spectacular thirty-
seven. Ageless. The man wears pants, sport jacket, and an open
shirt; the woman is in a lounging negligee. The fight is a strenuous
one. The man is JIMMY DUNCASTER. The woman is NETTA
                                  (MORE)
                                                        (CONTINUED)

1   *CONTINUED:* —2

BERNSTEIN, and she is holding her own. They are approximately
the same height and she is a hardy woman, so Jimmy isn't just
knocking her around. She fights back. They are against a wall beside
the half-open door of the closet. As they struggle, they force open
the door and in a moment are half-in, half-out of the closet.
CAMERA MOVES IN so we see them struggling.

                          JIMMY (ECHO)
               The first time I killed her . . .

2   *CAMERA CLOSE*

As they struggle in the closet. Clothes hanging in heavy plastic
garment bags are knocked off their hangers. The hangers are thick
wooden forms. One hanger comes to hand and Jimmy grabs it.
Netta's eyes widen as Jimmy raises it to strike her. CAMERA IN
CLOSE-UP on Netta's face so we see her thick auburn hair, her
lovely features. And FREEZE.

                          JIMMY (ECHO)
          That night she said my name a hundred times in a
          minute . . . and the next day at the office . . .

CAMERA CLOSE FREEZE on Netta's face as we

                          RAPID MATCH DISSOLVE TO:

3   *INT. NETTA'S OFFICE — DAY*

FREEZE CLOSEUP on Netta's face as DISSOLVE ENDS and
FRAME UNFREEZES. Netta's expression is now one of
annoyance, not fear, as she speaks.

                             NETTA
                 What is it now, Duncaster?

CAMERA PULLS BACK TO MEDIUM SHOT showing the
office. It is the psychological testing office of a major toy company.
Shelves are filled with toys that are tagged with different colored
notes. Several racks of psych books; charts on the wall. A large
photo of what must be the plant, with a clearly readable sign that
                            (MORE)
                                                        (CONTINUED)

3   *CONTINUED:*

        says *MyToy Corporation*. CAMERA BACK to show a one-way glass
        partition in the wall, and on the other side a half-dozen children in a
        playroom setting, fooling around with various games and toys. And
        SHOT INCLUDES Jimmy standing just inside the office door,
        looking at Netta with amazement.

4   *ON JIMMY*

        Startled by her tone of voice.

                              JIMMY
                Duncaster? It wasn't Duncaster last night,
                Princess.

        He moves toward her, to embrace her. She has a large coloring book
        in her hands, which she has been rolling into a tube. Now she thrusts
        it in front of her, and it stops against his chest as he gets within range.

                              NETTA
                It's *Doctor* Bernstein, not Princess. And you're
                not my idea of Prince Charming.

                         JIMMY (genuinely confused)
                What the hell's the matter with you? Was it
                something I said?

                              NETTA
                Back off, Duncaster. I've got testing to do.

                              JIMMY
                But last night . . . !

        Her eyes narrow. She is getting really angry.

                              NETTA
                What last night? I went to the ballet last night.
                And it wasn't *The Sleeping Princess*.

5   *SHOT THROUGH OFFICE DOOR — NETTA & JIMMY*

        as they stand there arguing, the coloring book still wedged against
        his chest. We cannot hear them but their postures are clearly
        antagonistic. And WE HEAR OVER the VOICE OF NETTA:
                                              (CONTINUED)

5   *CONTINUED:*

                            NETTA'S VOICE
                             (echo over)
                   I love you, Jimmy . . . I love you . . .

                                                        CUT BACK TO:

6   *INT. OFFICE — ANOTHER ANGLE — FAVORING JIMMY*

He is now reconciled to the weirdness of what's happening. He may
not know *what* is happening, but he knows this woman doesn't like
him.

                               JIMMY
                   Okay! Then *forget* last night! Can I just have
                   those test results on my projects and I'll go about
                   my business?

                            NETTA (cold)
                   You know I don't disburse test stats till the
                   meeting. You'll get them at three o'clock, the
                   same as everyone else.

                           JIMMY (horrified)
                               But . . .

                               NETTA
                           Will that be all?

He starts to say something, but stops. His face gets nasty. He starts
to turn, spins back, and slams the coloring book out of her hand.
They stare at each other a moment and Jimmy almost bares his
teeth. But she stares him down, he turns and goes, slamming the
door. She looks after him a moment with dislike evident in her
expression; then she turns to the one-way glass and watches the
children playing with the toys.

7   *WITH JIMMY — STEADICAM*

as he storms down the corridor TOWARD CAMERA from Netta's
office. We get a long look at Jimmy. Now we see the amoral face
usually hidden by corporate charm. The walls are yellow and at the
                               (MORE)
                                                        (CONTINUED)

7   *CONTINUED:*

end of the corridor is a yellow fire-door with a large red circle and
the legend SECURITY WING in the center of the circle. An armed
guard in uniform, wearing a clearance badge in yellow, stands in
front of the door. Jimmy approaches fast.

GUARD
Morning, Mr. Duncaster.

JIMMY
Just open the door!

The guard looks surly, his courtesy having been rebuffed; but he
inserts a long flat code-key in the wing door and swings it open.
Jimmy starts to go through, but the guard stops him.

GUARD
Your clearance badge for security wing . . . *sir.*

Jimmy gives him a dirty look, fishes in his pocket, comes up with the
badge—yellow with a red circle—and clips it to his jacket lapel. The
guard ceremoniously steps aside.

GUARD
Have a good one, Mr. Duncaster.

Jimmy nods and passes into the wing.

7A   *REVERSE SHOT — FROM PERSONNEL OFFICE — DOWN*
       CORRIDOR

as Jimmy comes through the security door, the glass-fronted door of
the personnel office opens. A plaque on the wall beside the door
reads LEN WINCH, DIRECTOR OF PERSONNEL. Like Jimmy,
he is in his middle thirties, but smaller and rounder, softer, perhaps
a bit on the weak side; but there is a similarity of manner and style.

LEN
Jimmy . . . got a minute?

Duncaster almost passes him. Still florid from Netta's treatment of
him, he stops, looks confused for a moment, then recognizes Winch
and shoves past him into the Personnel Office.

8   *DELETED*

9   *INT. WINCH'S OFFICE*

Files, charts, a poster showing new MyToy products such as
Gumball, Destruction Derby, Change-A-Face. Jimmy storms
around the office, trying to find a place to light. Len closes the door
carefully, perches on the edge of the desk. He watches Duncaster
restlessly moving, waits. Jimmy finally stops, turns to him.

                          JIMMY
           She's hanging me out to dry. You think that little
           prick Barrett got to her?

                          LEN
                   You're getting paranoid.

                          JIMMY
           I'll tell you how paranoid I am: Last night she was
           dynamite, told me I didn't have a thing to worry
           about, she was sure the tests on the kids would
           come up positive for the Goodie Two Shoes doll.

He picks up one of the ray-gun models (as we saw in scene 1) lying
on a table filled with MyToy product, and begins hefting it, as if it
were a real weapon. Len watches.

                      JIMMY (CONT'D)
           And this morning she's like a different woman.
           Like some kind of demento. Says she went to the
           ballet last night . . . and when I asked her for the
           test stats she told me to go take a flying leap.
                          (beat)
           I'm tellin' you, Len, Barrett got to her. They're
           trying to force me out.

Len walks over, takes the ray-gun away from Duncaster.

                          LEN
           Take a breath, willya! You're still Director
           of Market Research. You're still the guy who
           brought Gumball to MyToy . . . and Destruction
           Derby and —

He has been waving at the posters. Jimmy cuts him off.

                                        (CONTINUED)

9   *CONTINUED:*

                                    JIMMY
                    That was five years ago! And Barrett came over
                    from Ideal with half a *dozen* knockoff designs.
                                    (beat)
                    He's going for my job, Len. That's a hundred
                    sixty grand a year . . . and I'm out dancing for
                    dimes on Wilshire Boulevard.

                                                        SMASH-CUT TO:

10   *INTERCUT — NETTA'S CLOSET — OMINOUS MOOD*

        CAMERA MOVING IN SLOWLY in the darkened bedroom,
        toward the closet where Jimmy fought with Netta. The door is ajar.
        CAMERA TOWARD IT as we HEAR:

                            NETTA'S VOICE (echo)
                    I love you, Jimmy . . . I love you so much . . .

                                                              CUT TO:

11   *INT. CONFERENCE ROOM — LATER SAME DAY*

        Paneled big business meeting room. Ornate and expensive logo on
        the wall with the name MyTOY CORPORATION evident. Long
        table, eight or ten men and women seated, poring over clipboards,
        stat sheets, graphs, conferring with each other prior to
        commencement of the meeting. Jimmy comes in as CAMERA
        GOES WITH HIM. A number of chairs are empty. Len Winch is in
        place. Jimmy goes to his seat as the double doors at the far end of
        the room open and "The Old Man," SLOAN, enters. He is sixtyish,
        extremely trim, tanned, an older version of the Ted Turner business
        magnate still in good shape and into vital action on everything he
        surveys. He comes in fast, no nonsense. And right behind him,
        clutching a thick sheaf of stats and her clipboard . . . Netta Bernstein.

                                                        INTERCUT TO:

12   *INTERCUT — JIMMY*

        CLOSE on his face as he sees Netta. He is astonished. She
        shouldn't be with Sloan. Jimmy's head turns and PAST HIM we see
                                    (MORE)

                                                        (CONTINUED)

12   CONTINUED:

        Len down the table. He also looks startled, spreads his hands, and
        arches his eyebrows as if to say "Don't ask me."

                                                                    CUT BACK TO:

13   SAME AS 11 — ON SLOAN

        as he takes his seat at the head of the conference table. At his left
        hand is a sharp-featured, feral little man, MARV BARRETT. Netta
        sits down at Sloan's right hand.

                                    SLOAN
                        All right, let's get at it.
                                    (beat)
                Barrett, what progress is there on the Lexington,
                Kentucky, plant site?

                                    BARRETT
                Mr. Sloan, you'll be delighted to know . . .

        His VOICE FADES till we RUN SILENT as we HEAR:

                            NETTA'S VOICE (echo)
                Jimmy . . Jimmy . . . say you love me, Jimmy . . .

                                                                SMASH-CUT TO:

14   SAME AS 10

        THE CLOSET. CAMERA COMING IN, closer now than in
        previous shot of this scene. Toward the door of the closet. Ajar.
        Ominous. We *know* there's something terrible in there.

                                                                    CUT BACK TO:

15   INT. CONFERENCE ROOM — INCLUDING JIMMY
        AND SLOAN

        CAMERA OUT OF FOCUS. As it RERACKS INTO FOCUS and
        Sloan speaks, Jimmy seems to shake himself awake from a reverie
        (it is preshadowing, not memory):

                                    SLOAN
                Then that solves *that* problem. Now let us get
                                    (MORE)

                                                                    (CONTINUED)

15   *CONTINUED:*

                    down to the crunch point. Fisher-Price and
                    Mattel ran past us last quarter.
                              (beat)
                    The natives are restless. I want dynamism, folks!
                              (beat)
                    Ms. Bernstein: let's have your test results from
                    the children on the new designs.

16   *REACTION SHOTS — JIMMY ♂ NETTA*
♂
17   He looks at her pointedly. She refuses to look at him. She unclips
        the first batch of reports. As she does so another, younger woman,
        Netta's assistant, GWEN, gets up and hurriedly assembles toys from
        a rolling bin at the side of the room on a display table that also rolls
        up to the conference area. The first batch of toys are dolls. As Netta
        speaks, Gwen puts one doll after another in the forefront,
        illustrating Netta's comments. Show-and-tell.

                              NETTA
                    Let's start with Mr. Duncaster's Little Miss
                    Goodie Two-Shoes doll.

18-28   *DELETED*

29   *CLOSE ON NETTA — VASELINE ON LENS — JIMMY'S POV*

        as seen through Jimmy's eyes and his paranoia, his fear. She is like a
        hunter closing in on its prey. A meat-eater going for a bloody meal.
        Her wide eyes sparkle. Her lush mouth is moist. Her full figure
        seemingly buoyed up with unbridled passion for the nasty job ahead.
        The charming, sweet lovely face altered by Jimmy's twisted POV.

                                                    INTERCUT TO:

30   *CLOSE ON JIMMY*

        for just a second, a beat, a *heart*beat. His eyes bright and terrified.

                         JIMMY'S VOICE OVER
                              (echo)
                    Please . . . gimme a break . . .
                              (MORE)

                                                    (CONTINUED)

30   *CONTINUED:*

                                        (beat)
                              Love, Netta . . . love . . .

                                                              CUT BACK TO:

31   *MEDIUM CLOSE ON NETTA*

         holding the Little Miss Goodie Two-Shoes by the neck.

                                  NETTA
                         This is one of the most dangerous toys I've ever
                         tested.
                                        (beat)
                         A baby doll containing a voice-activated tape
                         loop. When you say to the doll, "Good dolly,
                         you're a good dolly," or a similar affectionate
                         phrase, the doll goes "Mmmmmm."
                                        (beat)
                         But when you say, "Bad dolly, you've been a bad
                         dolly," or a similar hostile phrase, the dolly whimpers.
                                        (beat)
                              But unfortunately . . . and horribly . . .

         She looks at Jimmy with scorn and loathing . . .

                              NETTA (CONT'D)
                         The tape loop isn't the only thing activated by
                         hostile phrases.

         She snaps her fingers and Gwen hits a switch that throws the
         conference room into darkness while simultaneously starting a film
         that is shown on a section of white wall we did not realize was also a
         movie screen. As she says the preceding sentence and snaps her
         fingers, she turns HALF-AWAY FROM CAMERA affording us a
         VIEW OF THE SCREEN. The remainder of this scene is shot with
         Netta in F.G., a large dark shadowy shape that speaks, as we watch:

31A   *WHAT WE SEE ON THE SCREEN — FULL SHOT*
         BURN-IN INSERT

         The children's playroom setup we saw through the glass window of
         Netta's office in shots 3 & 6.

                                                              (CONTINUED)

31A   *CONTINUED:*

Four or five children, boys and girls, playing with models of Little Miss Goodie Two-Shoes. CUT FROM ONE CHILD TO ANOTHER with ACTION PARALLELING DIALOGUE.

> NETTA (CONT'D) (coldly, incisively)
> My tests, over a four-month period — with a statistically larger group of children than I would ordinarily have charted . . .
> > (beat)
> Cross-checked through our independent testing group at Harvard . . .
> > (beat)
> Clearly show that this toy activates unhealthy aggression in children, triggering the worst in them . . .
> > (snarling tone)
> and *feeding* it, *encouraging* it!

We see the children's escalating brutality to the dolls. It should not be overly dramatic, or hokey; just coldly chilling as we realize the potential for viciousness in any human being, which lies close to the surface in children who are less sophisticated. We should see progressive violence on the toys. We should shudder.

> NETTA (CONT'D)
> They were brutal with the dolls. Tormenting them, savaging them, tearing them apart when merely chiding them, or spanking them, or throwing them against the walls failed to satisfy their *need to hear* the whimpering . . .

As the FILM RUNS behind her, Netta turns back INTO CAMERA for the capper:

> NETTA (CONT'D)
> If we care about children at all . . . if we care about anything except making a buck . . . if we have any sense of responsibility . . . if we don't want lawsuits and wretched publicity and the
> > (MORE)

                                               (CONTINUED)

31A   *CONTINUED: —2*

> Religious Right and all the child-watchdog
> agencies coming after us . . .
>> (beat)
> we'll reject this toy.

She snaps her fingers. The lights go on as NETTA GOES OUT OF
FRAME as CAMERA MOVES AROUND HER to show Sloan. He
says nothing, looks toward Jimmy Duncaster and his lips *do not
move* as we HEAR his VOICE OVER in ECHO:

>> SLOAN'S OVER VOICE
>> (echo)
> There's blood in the water, Duncaster;
> blood and sharks.

CUT TO:

32   *JIMMY — CLOSE*

He looks as if he's been struck repeatedly by a ball-peen hammer.
He looks sick. Green. As if he wants to get rid of his expensive
expense-account lunch. We HOLD that sick expression and

SMASH MATCH-CUT TO:

33   *JIMMY — CLOSE*

as the sick expression solidifies and he TURNS FROM CAMERA
so we can see the INTERIOR of the EXECUTIVE WASHROOM
in the MIRROR where Jimmy's face was just reflected. He has
dropped from FRAME and we HEAR the SOUNDS of dry
heaving (*Not* violent, *not* obnoxious, just wrenching.) Then we
HEAR the SOUND of water running in the wash basin. We HOLD
on mirror and reflection of opposite wall, and Jimmy comes back up
into FRAME, laving his face with handfuls of water as he stares at
his ruined countenance in the glass.

>> JIMMY (hoarsely)
> Dancing for dimes . . . on Wilshire Boulevard . . .
>> (beat)
>> Oh . . . God . . .

DISSOLVE THRU:

34   *INT. JIMMY'S BEDROOM — NIGHT — HIGH SHOT*

DOWN-ANGLE FROM ABOVE on Jimmy thrashing in the
sheets. He is naked to the waist, covered with sweat, an ominous
light bathing him from an unseen source. He is asleep and in the
tormented grip of a living nightmare. He rolls his head from side to
side, wets his dry lips. The pillow is wet from his matted hair.

                    JIMMY (in sleep)
        Oh . . . God . . . a break . . . gimme a break . . .

CAMERA COMES DOWN STEADILY on his tormented,
sleeping face as we

                                        DISSOLVE THRU TO:

35   *JIMMY — CLOSE — MyTOY EXECUTIVE ELEVATOR*

Now awake. Looking like hell. But at least shaved, clean, alert, as we
HEAR the SOUND of ELEVATOR DOORS OPENING and
CAMERA PULLS BACK to show Jimmy now dressed in a suit, in
control of himself. Obviously the next day. The elevator doors open
and in walks Netta Bernstein, carrying a sheaf of reports close to her
chest, looking more radiant and softer than we've seen her before. She
smiles brightly at him. The doors close. They are alone in the elevator.

                    NETTA (sultry)
                New in town, sailor?

His expression cannot be described. Amazement. Hatred. Absolute
confusion. Disorientation. This is the woman who, just yesterday,
viciously hung him out to dry; the woman who is probably in
league with Barrett and maybe even Len Winch to ruin his career,
blight his life. *And now she's coming* on *to him!?!* Now she's
smiling at him!?! What the hell is going *on* here? You can't
describe the expression of a man who is totally unmanned,
disarmed, floundering with confusion. We can *see* it, but we can't
describe it.

                    NETTA (conspiratorially)
            Eight o'clock? My place? Prime rib, creamed
            horseradish, spinach soufflé . . . a real Yorkshire
            pudding, not one of those concrete popovers . . . ?
                                        (CONTINUED)

35   *CONTINUED:*

She moves close to him. She rubs up against him, looking absolutely edible herself. He nods . . . dumbly . . . without realizing he's accepting . . . bewildered. She lifts on her toes to kiss him as he leans back against the elevator wall. Then the elevator stops, the doors open, and she's gone, leaving him standing there, mouth half-open with befuddlement and, as we HOLD on Jimmy's FACE and CAMERA COMES IN TIGHTER, the expression turns to one of murderous tension and foreshadowed violence. We HEAR

NETTA'S VOICE OVER
(echo)
I love you, Jimmy . . . I love you . . .

And CAMERA COMES IN TIGHTER and TIGHTER as we

MATCH-DISSOLVE TO:

36   *INT. NETTA'S APARTMENT — NIGHT — CLOSE ON JIMMY*

as MATCH DISSOLVES THRU to JIMMY'S FACE IN CLOSE-UP we see the look of hatred more clearly and CAMERA PULLS BACK so we realize we are in Netta's apartment. It is the same as in scene 1 (except scene 1 was devoid of people). We see the smart living room with its Art Nouveau look peppered with toys. One of them is Jimmy's Little Miss Goodie Two-Shoes doll; another is a copy of the ray-gun Jimmy played with in Winch's office in scene 9. We HEAR Tchaikovsky's Symphony #4 OVER. The bright red chiffon scarf drapes over the leaded glass dragonfly-design shade of the Tiffany lamp we remember from scene 1. And we realize what we saw earlier was the foreshadowing of things to come. Things to come . . . *now!*

NETTA'S VOICE O.S.
You've barely said a word all night . . . and you
hardly ate a thing . . .

Jimmy's face is a frozen mask of tension. He is caught in the 'twixt and 'tween. Now he speaks with deadly cold control as CAMERA BACK to show Netta in a lounging negligee — the one we saw her wearing in the violent scene 1. She is putting away a gateleg table
(MORE)

(CONTINUED)

CONTINUED:

that was obviously the place where she had served dinner. She
covers it with a fringed shawl of the twenties, and places a piece of
Handel nouveau statuary on it. Then she turns to Jimmy as he
speaks.

> JIMMY (cold, tight)
> What the hell are you trying to do to me . . . are
> you trying to drive me crazy . . . ?

She looks concerned, moves toward him to hold him. He slaps her
hands away petulantly. He backs away from her, leaving her with
outstretched arms.

> JIMMY (CONT'D)
> I don't *believe* you . . .

> NETTA (soothingly)
> Jimmy, you know how I feel about you . . .
> but sometimes, in business . . .

He rages away from her around the living room, his fists balled, his
movements sharp and jerky, beginning gestures that, if completed,
would shatter the fine Tiffany glass, would clear the tables of their
objects, would smash bookcases and framed pictures. Gestures
begun but arrested in mid-air. Fury needing to explode, but being
held back.

> JIMMY (paranoiacally)
> It's Barrett, isn't it? That little maggot . . . he's got
> you on the pad, doesn't he?

> NETTA
> What?

> JIMMY
> The pad. The take. On the line. In his pocket!
> What's he promised you for making me look like
> a cripple in front of Sloan?
> (beat)
> Expanded department? Stock shares? Vice
> presidency? What's the blue sky for cutting my
> throat? You screwing him, too?

(CONTINUED)

36   *CONTINUED: —2*

> NETTA (coolly)
> I don't know what you're talking about. I have no
> dealings with Barrett. None.

Her eyes flash and she turns, storms away from him, down the long
corridor toward the bedroom, into darkness. He watches after her,
as Tchaikovsky plays in B.G. Then he goes after her. He vanishes
into darkness, saying:

> JIMMY (pissed off)
> Don't you goddam walk away from me when I'm
> talking to you!

CAMERA BEGINS TO MOVE SLOWLY INTO CORRIDOR as it
did in previous scenes 1/10/14/26, and now we understand that all
those former slow moves in on the ominous bedroom were
foreshadowing this moment of real time. We HEAR their VOICES
O.S. from the bedroom as CAMERA MOVES SLOWLY DOWN
THE CORRIDOR, with Tchaikovsky under.

JIMMY	NETTA
	(simultaneously)
You're like two different women.	I *do* love you. Why can't you
Night before last you said you	*believe* that? I love you and
loved me and everything was	want you to be happy. There
terrific . . . and yesterday you	are just some things you'll have
stuck it in my back and killed	to take on faith . . . it can all be
me with Sloan . . .vicious . . .	fixed at the office . . . let me *try*
mean . . . just plain rotten mean	to fix it for you . . .
. . .*fix it?* . . . are you crazy?	

CAMERA RETRACES the path it took in Scene 1 except now we
hear no sounds of love, we HEAR the real conversation of hurt and
anger and viciousness. And as the CAMERA PANS across the bed,
it is not rumpled as it was in Scene 1. It is still neatly made, never
having been touched; but as CAMERA PANS across bedroom we
see Jimmy slap Netta for the first time; and now the struggle begins
that we saw in Scene 1, played exactly as we saw it previously in
foreshadowing . . . but this time it's real.

37   *THE SCENE — FOLLOW THE ACTION TO CLOSE SHOT*

as they struggle, Netta giving as good as she gets. They slide along
the wall, strike the half-open door of the closet, fall inside, we see
feet and the CAMERA COMES to the closet, hovers above them as
they fight and struggle among the clothes. Jimmy reaches back, his
hand strikes the heavy wooden hanger just as we saw it in Scene 2.
He grabs the hanger and raises it above his head and CAMERA
COMES IN ON CLOSEUP of Netta's face in terror as she
screams:

NETTA (screams)
Jimmy . . . no . . . I love y —

His violent motion in one direction is COUNTERED BY
CAMERA WHIP-PANNING IN OPPOSITE DIRECTION. We
HEAR a thud sound. Camera holds on the empty bed and we
HEAR, trailing off as if on the wind . . .

NETTA'S VOICE (echo)
I love you, Jimmy . . . I love you . . .

38   *INT. LIVING ROOM — CLOSE ON TURNTABLE —*
STEADICAM FOR HAND-HELD TILTS

SHOT CLOSE on Tchaikovsky record as it comes to an end, tone
arm rejects, slides back, begins to replay, then stops on the record
as the turntable stops. Silence. CAMERA (HAND HELD) PANS
SLOWLY across living room as we have seen it previously, moves
down corridor to bedroom, MOVES ACROSS empty bed, comes to
rest in MEDIUM SHOT of Jimmy sitting in the corner, trembling,
back to the wall; like a kid who has broken something belonging to
his parents, knowing he's gonna get it when Pop comes home; in
one hand the heavy wooden hanger . . . broken; he chews the
fingernails of the other hand; he stares into the darkening middle
distance. CAMERA HOLDS ON HIM long enough for us to know
he has gone too far. He didn't want anything like this to happen, the
poor sonofabitch. Then the CAMERA moves toward the half-open
door of the closet . . . where something ominous waits. CAMERA
INTO MEDIUM SHOT of the interior of the closet and we see all
the clothes and plastic bags and hangers have been pulled off the

(MORE)

(CONTINUED)

38   *CONTINUED:*

transverse bar and have been heaped in a corner of the closet. All
the shoes, all the clothes, pushed into a rising mound in the far
corner. No blood, no body, no signs of violence . . . just a mound of
clothing and a hand and forearm lying palm-up, protruding from
under the clothes that Netta Bernstein will never again wear.

CAMERA DOES NOT MOVE but the interior of the closet begins
to RECEDE INTO DARKNESS like the IRIS FADE of an old-
time film. Back and back, growing smaller and smaller, into
darkness as we begin to HEAR the SOUND of WATER
CASCADING IN A SHOWER and we

FADE TO BLACK.

39   *FADE BACK IN FROM DARKNESS*

to the increasing SOUND of a SHOWER. Something light back
there in the darkness, getting larger, coming toward us, the light in
the center of the tunnel seems to expand and we see

39A   *EXT. OLYMPIC PENINSULA, WASHINGTON STATE—*
&   *(MEASURE) — NIGHT*
40

(NOTE: Stock footage should be used to cheat a segué into
Scene 40. MEASURE FOOTAGE to DISSOLVE into new footage
to be shot in the Los Angeles Forest.)

Up beyond the vicinity of Seattle-Tacoma in STOCK FOOTAGE.
Virgin wilderness. Huge stands of Douglas fir and whitebark alder,
the leaves reddish-brown at the top. The Olympic Range and the
Cascades and Mt. Rainier in the FAR b.g. And DISSOLVE INTO
mist and fog streaming past like quicksand. The forest, and Jimmy
running, running, running AWAY FROM CAMERA, running as
fast as he can, arms upthrown against the branches and the moisture
dripping off the trees and the fog eerily lit from a light source far
ahead and to the right . . . an unearthly corona illuminating the
scene as light rushes at Jimmy through the cathedral forest.

CAMERA MOVES IN CLOSE BEHIND JIMMY and shoots
PAST HIM up a slight incline, a slope in the forest. Up there, in the
(MORE)

(CONTINUED)

39A *CONTINUED:*
ↄ
40 glare of the light streaming over the crest of the hill, in a clearing
uncluttered by trees, stands something. It could be a person. The
light streams around it, as if blown toward CAMERA by a gigantic
wind machine. And as we — and Jimmy — stare at that shape that
could be a person, it begins to STROBE. (SPECIAL EFFECT:
key-strobe technique of duplicate image over itself [print every
third frame]; image atop image without reproducing b.g.; Quantel
multiple exposure recommended w/Chromakey.)

Jimmy's movements slow. Not full slow-motion, but 40 FRAMES
PER SECOND so he seems to be laboring forward toward the
multiple image figure above him.

The LIGHT GLARES MORE BRIGHTLY until Jimmy is washed
out in the blaze of it, and we continue to HEAR the SOUND of
WATER in a SHOWER as we GO INTO LIGHT-GLARE and

                                        MATCH-DISSOLVE THRU:

41 *SHOWER — MATCH LIGHT-GLARE*

as we COME OUT OF LIGHT-GLARE it becomes water
cascading down out of a showerhead and CAMERA BACK to show
Jimmy trying to wash out his sins. The water has a powerful,
thundering presence, and Jimmy's face is wide open and tilted up,
hammering at him, hurting him as we see him lean against shower
wall, eyes closed and

                                        DISSOLVE TO:

42 *INT. CORRIDOR — MyTOY CORPORATION — DAY*

WITH JIMMY as he strides past office after office. He passes various
staff members, hurrying here and there, carrying papers, pushing
carts with toys in them, standing at cross-corridors talking. CAMERA
STAYS WITH JIMMY as he is greeted by this one and that one.

                        1st CLERK
                Morning, Mr. Duncaster.

No answer. Jimmy's face is a mask. He keeps moving.
                                        (CONTINUED)

42   CONTINUED:

2nd CLERK
Morning, Mr. Duncaster.

Nothing. Jimmy looks precise and incredibly clean.

3rd and 4th CLERKS
Good morning, Mr. Duncaster.

He says nothing. Clean. Hours in the shower. Absolutely unblemished.
Lady Macbeth just didn't stay at it long enough. But Jimmy Duncaster
did. Now he's clean. And no one can tell from his appearance what he
did last night. As he comes abreast of Sloan's office, the door opens
and the boss emerges. Jimmy almost bumps into him.

INTERCUT TO:

43   INTERCUT — SOLARIZED FOR EFFECT — EERIE EFFECT

SHOT WITH FISH-EYE LENS FOR DISTORTION. Sloan comes
two steps forward and Jimmy can now see the COPS behind him.
They have their pistols drawn and aimed at him. Sloan's face is
almost inhuman with vindictiveness and fury. He points a meaty
finger at Jimmy and the lens-distortion makes the finger as menacing
as the muzzles of the .32 Police Positives and the Colt Python .357
Magnums held by the merciless-looking quartet of cops behind him.

SLOAN'S VOICE (echo)
That's him, officers! The one who wanted us to
sell a demon doll. He killed our research
psychologist because she was on to him! Bashed
in her head and left her stuffed in a closet till he
could think of some way to get rid of the body.

The cops move out from behind Sloan, they move into the corridor.
All of this SHOT IS SOLARIZED IN EERIE COLOR.

SLOAN (CONT'D)
(echo)
Beautiful young woman; I loved her like a
daughter; brilliant; Netta Bernstein. Killed her.
She adored him and he smashed her skull. Take
(MORE)

(CONTINUED)

43   CONTINUED:

> his yellow color-coded badge with the red
> security dot in the middle, and get him the hell
> out of here!

Jimmy's face contorts in terror as the savage-looking cops and the deranged Sloan converge on him as we

CUT BACK TO:

44   SAME AS 42

As Sloan stares at him. There are no cops. NORMAL SHOT with solarization gone and fish-eye lens gone. Just a perfectly normal scene . . . except that Jimmy is about to faint. He's clean, but beaded with cold sweat.

> SLOAN
> You look like hell, Duncaster.

> JIMMY (off-key)
> Bad night, J.R. You didn't make it easy for me
> the other day.

> SLOAN
> Not my job, Duncaster. My job is making
> your life tough. How else would you know I
> appreciate you like crazy?

He laughs, claps Jimmy on the shoulder and strides away. Jimmy turns away from camera, leans against the wall, running the back of his hand over his desert-dry lips. He stands there a beat, then turns so we can see a relieved, exonerated smile begin to come over his face. He's regaining his old Jimmy-the-Mover look. Self-assured. *He got away with it!* He shakes his head, licks his lips to regain some composure, and walks on a little bit unsteadily. As he comes to Len Winch's office he is stopped by Len, who has obviously been waiting for him. Len bangs on the glass window, startling Jimmy. Duncaster pauses for a moment, allowing Len to open the door and pop his head out.

> LEN (abashed)
> Hey, uh, Jimmy . . . I, uh . . . about Tuesday, er, I,
> (MORE)

(CONTINUED)

44   *CONTINUED:*

> uh, wanted to tell you I was as shocked as you
> when Bernstein did what she did to you. Jesus,
> man, that was just brutal . . . I mean . . .

Jimmy's face goes cold and hard. His business face. He isn't at all
sure he can trust Len Winch any more. He keeps moving down the
corridor toward the Security Section door.

> JIMMY
> I'll knit you a gold watch for your
> retirement, Len.

And he GOES AS CAMERA FOLLOWS to the security door, hits
the lockbar that opens the door without assistance from a guard —
as opposed to other side of the door in which corridor section the
armed guard waits — and passes through. CAMERA HOLDS ON
DOOR as it closes.

45   *CORRIDOR OUTSIDE NETTA'S OFFICE — SAME AS 7*

ANGLE DOWN CORRIDOR as Jimmy comes through the
security door. The Guard we saw in shot 7 is there again. But now
Jimmy has a jaunty manner as he pauses way down there at the
other end of the passage. We HEAR him speak, but it's a distance
and the voices are soft.

> JIMMY (to Guard)
> Ben? Is it Ben? Yeah, well, we both know I owe
> you an apology. Tuesday . . . remember . . . yeah,
> you remember. I was acting like the north end of
> a southbound horse.

> GUARD
> No need to apologize, Mr. Duncaster . . . we all
> have bad ones every once in a while . . .

> JIMMY (starts to move)
> You're okay, Ben. Just the same, I'm gonna be on
> good behavior for a while . . .

He waves, Ben smiles, Jimmy comes toward CAMERA as
CAMERA SWINGS SLOWLY to an ANGLE that will enable us to
(MORE)

(CONTINUED)

45   *CONTINUED:*

see inside Netta Bernstein's glass-fronted office. As Jimmy gets
closer he can be seen to MOVE SLOWLY (40 FRAMES PER
SECOND AS IN SCENE 40) and his expression is one of a man
girding himself to look nonchalant as he passes an *empty office*.
That's the key to this scene. We expect to see an empty office. So
does Jimmy. Has to be empty, doesn't it? Netta Bernstein is dead,
ain't she? Stuffed into a clothes closet, right?

46   *REVERSE ANGLE — WITH JIMMY IN F.G.*

as he comes up on the office with the NETTA BERNSTEIN plaque
on the wall. He *casually* looks inside.

Netta is in the office, talking to Gwen.

Jimmy reels back, his hands fly up as if to ward off a blow and we
HEAR the SOUND of a REVERBERATION like an underwater
explosion. He staggers back against the opposite wall of the
corridor, his legs are about to go out from under him. Ben the
Guard, seeing this, comes running. STAY WITH JIMMY!

GUARD
Mr. Duncaster! You okay?

Jimmy is making random movements against the air with his hand,
as if trying to clear away invisible webbing. He swats at the Guard.

JIMMY
Get away from me . . . just get the hell away . . .

The Guard gives him a look that would stun a police dog and stalks
away, back to his post, cursing under his breath.

47   *ANGLE FROM JIMMY THRU OFFICE WINDOW*

as he stares at Netta Bernstein — whom he killed the night
before — talking to Gwen. They are poring over a chart. Jimmy
stares and as he does, WE DOUBLE-EXPOSE THE SCENE and
replay the struggle in the closet, the hand striking the wooden
hanger, the arm coming up to strike, Netta's face in a rictus of
terror, the arm coming down, Jimmy sitting on the floor, and at last,
as CAMERA MOVES IN, the pile of clothing with the hand
sticking out from underneath.

(CONTINUED)

47   *CONTINUED:*

And at that moment both Netta and Gwen emerge from her office, as if to go down the corridor. They stop as they see Jimmy half-leaning, half-kneeling against the wall.

> NETTA (annoyed)
> *Well*, Duncaster? What sort of goofy game are
> you up to this time?

Gwen giggles, catches herself. Netta looks at him coldly.

> NETTA (CONT'D)
> You look like hell. Do you need a doctor?

Jimmy tries to speak, merely mumbles, keeps making motions vaguely with his hand.

> NETTA (CONT'D)
> (to Gwen)
> Human speech is not his natural tongue.

She shakes her head disgustedly, motions Gwen, and they walk away, leaving Jimmy as CAMERA COMES IN CLOSE and we see a tear begin to glide down his cheek. This is a man who is scared out of his ever-loving mind!

18   *LONG SHOT — THE CORRIDOR — FROM GUARD TO JIMMY*

Ben the Guard in f.g. watches as Jimmy Duncaster, half-crawling, half-slipping and sliding, scrabbles up the wall and dashes out of the door at the other end.

> GUARD (softly)
> Creep.
> (beat)
> Have a nice day.

CUT TO:

49   *INT. NETTA'S APARTMENT — DAY*

CAMERA MOVING IN on the front door as we HEAR the
SOUND of a key clattering in the lock, as if being used by someone
> (MORE)

(CONTINUED)

49   *CONTINUED:*

who isn't used to it. Someone like Jimmy using the key he'd taken from Netta's handbag after he killed her, knowing he'd need it to get the body out today.

The door opens and Jimmy slips inside. He has a tire iron in his hand, and he looks like something almost neanderthalic as he stands there against the closed door, listening. Silence. The apartment is silent. Sunlight casts beams of light through which dust motes tumble. And that's the totality of movement. Still. Silent.

50   *WITH JIMMY — HAND HELD MOVEMENT — STEADICAM*

as he moves through the living room into the hallway and into the bedroom. The bed is still neatly made. Silent. He goes slowly to the closet. It is closed. He stands there and in the b.g. we HEAR the faintest last lingering SOUND of Netta saying "I love you, Jimmy," in a whisper so dim we know it's gone forever. He reaches for the knob, tire iron ready to strike. He opens the door slowly and we see . . .

The closet is empty of body. The clothes are neatly hung on the transverse bar. The shoes are arrayed neatly. No pile in the corner, no hand sticking out, no blood. *It is as if it never happened.*

51   *CLOSE ON JIMMY'S FACE*

as he struggles to stay sane. He *knows* he killed her. Or at least he *thinks* he knows for sure. We HOLD on his face as he wrinkles his brow, thinks back, and we can HEAR the SOUNDS OF THE STRUGGLE from the night before, very faintly. Then his features straighten, his eyes clear, and his jaw sets. He nods gently, and closes the closet door.

> JIMMY (smoothly, softly)
> Well, *oh*-kay. If it ain't what it was, then it gotta
> be what it wasn't.
> (beat)
> And I will sit me down and wait. Well, *oh*-kay.

And he sits down in a small rocking chair in the bedroom, lays the tire iron across his lap, closes his eyes, and waits, as we

DISSOLVE THRU:

52   *SAME SCENE — LATER IN DAY*

Jimmy waiting patiently as the light visibly dims, dims, dims. As we watch the hours go by either on the bedstand clock or simply by the passage of the sun through the window, till darkness approaches and we

DISSOLVE THRU TO:

53   *SAME SCENE — NIGHT*

as Jimmy sits in the darkness. A good darkness — not the usual day-for-night darkness of the soundstage. A darkness that lets us see Jimmy only faintly, in the wan glow of the light from outside the window, perhaps a streetlamp. A silence and a darkness that are now broken as we HEAR the SOUND of another KEY TURNING IN THE LOCK. Jimmy is up, swiftly, smoothly and CAMERA STAYS CLOSE WITH HIM as he sweeps out of the bedroom, down the hall, into the dark living room, and positions himself behind the front door.

CLOSE WITH JIMMY as he raises the tire iron over his head.

54   *DOORWAY — MEDIUM SHOT*

as Netta Bernstein stands framed for a long moment in the light from the hallway outside the apartment. We can see it is Netta, beautiful Netta, carrying an attaché case. She reaches in and around for the light switch as a hand suddenly thrusts itself around the door, grabs her by the lapel of her jacket, and propels her inside the apartment. No light. She never got to the switch.

55   *INTERCUTS*
thru
58   NETTA'S FACE as she sees Jimmy,

JIMMY'S FACE as he swings the tire iron.

CLOSE on the Art Nouveau lamp with the red scarf still draping the shade. We HEAR the SOUND of a blow landing as the tire iron keeps on coming around in FRAME and hits the lamp. We do not see any violence. We may HEAR it, but the shattering of the lamp is as close as we get to seeing anything nasty.

Final INTERCUT TO JIMMY again. He is looking down. His face is wet with sweat. He is fighting to catch his breath.

(CONTINUED)

58   *CONTINUED:*

> JIMMY (looking down scrutinizing)
> A job worth doing is a job worth doing well.
> Trifles make perfection and perfection is no trifle.

His head nods slowly, keeps nodding up and down in a movement that means yes, this time I did it right, no mistakes, it's okay, definitely o and kay. HOLD his trembling face as we

SLOW LAP-DISSOLVE THRU:

59   *MEDIUM CLOSE — THE ACTION — STEADICAM*

which is: Jimmy pulling down the shower curtain in the bathroom and, in the faint light from the window of the bedroom, rolling something into the shower curtain, tying it up with strapping tape from a big roll, tossing it over his shoulder, bowing under the weight and, in FOLLOWING SHOT CAMERA POV, opening the door of the apartment, going out, closing the door, coming to the end of a dark passage in the garage, where his car stands with trunk open, putting the weighted shape inside, closing the lid, turning and going back into the passage, waiting moments until he returns with an IBM Selectric typewriter and a length of tire chain, opening the trunk, tossing the items inside, closing the trunk, getting in the car, and driving away. COMPLETE THE LAP-DISSOLVE as we

DISSOLVE TO:

60   *EXT. THE PIER — NIGHT*

As Jimmy's car drives out slowly onto the structure, its lights off. He coasts, no motor sounds. Perhaps in the b.g. we HEAR Tchaikovsky's Fourth. The car comes right to the end of the pier. Jimmy's door on the driver's side opens and he gets out, pulls his collar up around his neck, looks out across the water as we HEAR a foghorn in the distance, and perhaps THUNDER; Jimmy goes to the trunk of the car as CAMERA COMES AROUND THE OTHER WAY. He opens the trunk, looks around carefully for observers, reaches down and takes out the chain and typewriter, carries them to the end of the pier. He returns, gets the shape in the shower curtain, lifts it awkwardly and carries it out to the edge of the pier and lays it down

(MORE)

(CONTINUED)

60   *CONTINUED:*

gently next to the other items. CAMERA ANGLE ON JIMMY'S
UPPER BODY as he works attaching the chain and typewriter to the
shape in the curtain. We do not see the actual job being done, but
from the way he grunts and spaces his words as he works, we know
he is doing a workmanlike job.

> JIMMY
> Take my word for it, Netta, this time it is
> bye-bye baby.
> > (beat)
> Maybe you thought I'd sit and wait for you to drop
> the net on me. Maybe you thought I'd be so scared
> I'd let you walk into my office with the cops.
> > (beat)
> > Wrong, and wrong, Princess.
> > (beat, almost rap-rhyming)
> Good and *tight* . . . and out of *sight*. For keeps.

CAMERA BACK as he rolls the shape off the end of the pier. It hits
the water and sinks out of sight instantly. Jimmy turns and walks
INTO CAMERA as we

CUT TO:

61   *INT. MyTOY CORRIDOR — DAY*

as Jimmy walks away from CAMERA almost to the spot where he
saw Netta in her office the previous day. He is in a fine mood, he is
whistling, and he casually looks into the glass-fronted office and sees:

62   *JIMMY'S POV — WHAT HE SEES*

Netta Bernstein, talking to a small CHILD. She has the kid up on
the desk and she is chattering away with the tot, who is laughing and
pointing and covering his/her eyes from time to time.

63   *SAME AS 61*

Jimmy begins to tremble.

> JIMMY (moans softly)
> Oh . . . God, oh God, oh jeezus . . . no . . .

DISSOLVE TO:

64   *INT. NETTA'S APARTMENT — NIGHT*

as the door opens, and we see Netta, with a stack of reports, backlit
by a source in the hallway. As she reaches for the light switch, the
arm is grabbed, she is dragged inside, the door slams shut and we
HOLD on Netta's face as she registers shock and then quick
annoyance:

> NETTA
> Duncaster, what the hell . . .

There is the SOUND of WATER RUSHING as it did in the shower
in scene 41 and the CAMERA WHIP-PANS LEFT as a snowfall of
MyToy reports cascades through the air like thin, white, frantic
birds. And as CAMERA WHIP-PANS BACK RIGHT we

CUT TO:

65   *SAME AS 40 — FOREST, OLYMPIC PENINSULA — NIGHT*

Exactly what we saw before. Jimmy running slowly, the fog
dripping, the bright light through the trees, the shape that
multiplies itself again and again STROBELIKE. And we

CUT TO:

66   *TOPANGA CANYON — WASTELAND — NIGHT*

CAMERA HIGH and COMING DOWN on Jimmy burying Netta.
He is at the final stages, throwing the last of the dirt into the hole,
holding the hammer and looking at it, shivering, and then throwing
that into the hole, laying the dirt in and then replacing the sod he
has neatly cut out in sections, having laid them on a blanket. He
puts the sod back, rolls up the blanket and, as CAMERA DOWN
INTO CLOSE-UP he looks up at the stars in cold Topanga
and says:

> JIMMY
> Third time's the charm, Netta. Please, please,
> please let third time be the charm . . .

And he walks away, out of FRAME as CAMERA HOLDS the
grave.

DISSOLVE TO:

67   INT. CORRIDOR — MyTOY CORPORATION —
        SAME AS 42 & 44

The other side of the Security Door from Netta's office. As Jimmy
approaches Len Winch's office. He stares at the Security Door for a
long moment, then goes into Winch's personnel office. HOLD ON
OPEN DOOR as Winch looks up from behind desk, then Jimmy
enters and closes door.

68   SAME AS SCENE 9 — INT. — WINCH'S OFFICE — DAY

Len doesn't get up as Jimmy enters. He is eating an apple, feet up
on the desk. But there is a cautious, almost frightened tone to his
waiting. Jimmy's been acting weird since Tuesday's bloodbath. He
watches as Jimmy walks around the office, seemingly casual, but
with a spring in his step that makes Len Winch wary. Finally Jimmy
sits on the table against the wall, swinging his legs. He just stares.

                    LEN (nervous)
          I heard the Old Man was friendly yesterday . . .
                       (beat)
          After that horror show last week . . .

                    JIMMY (coldly)
          What'd Barrett promise you, Len? What was your
          price to sell my ass out?

                    LEN
          Hey, kiddo! Honest to Mego, I didn't . . .

Jimmy cuts him off sharply. His tone is menacing.

                    JIMMY (nasty)
          I don't mind if you *think* I'm a schmuck, Len.
          What grinds my gears is when you *talk to me* as if
          you think I'm a schmuck.

Len looks hopeless. He starts to speak, then purses his lips, shrugs,
and nods with resignation. Jimmy has caught him. He sits, vulnerable,
waiting to hear the threats. Jimmy nods in satisfaction. He stares at
him for a long moment as if trying to work out the program, then he
gets off the table and walks around the office as if in full command,
talking to the walls and ceiling . . . but really to Winch.

                                        (CONTINUED)

68   *CONTINUED:*

> JIMMY
>
> Okay. It looks like Sloan was only barking to get
> me nervous, see if I'd perform.
>> (beat)
>
> That's fine. Shows he's not entirely convinced
> Barrett is the answer to MyToy's problems. He
> wants us to square off at each other. Good
> business thinking; he wins, whichever of us comes
> out of the grinder.

> LEN (false cheer)
>
> Man, you're certainly bouncing back from that . . .

> JIMMY
>
> Shut up. When I want syrup poured on me I'll
> lie down and play waffle. Sloan's no problem;
> and neither is Barrett now that I know he's after
> my job.
>> (beat)
>> So I just go to war.
>> (beat)
>
> But you're another piece of business, Len, old chum
> buddy pal. What do I do with a skunk turd like you?

> LEN
>
> Jimmy, c'mon, cut me a break here, willya!

> JIMMY (toying with him)
>
> How about I take you off just above the knees.
> Maybe with a cheese grater. Howzabout I fix it so
> you come all unglued in your job and snaffle things
> oh-so-bad. That way I can look out the window
> and watch *you* dancing for dimes on the street.

> LEN
>
> For God's sake, Jimmy . . . we've known each
> other ten years . . . I . . .

> JIMMY
>
> Maybe I'll just knit you a spine for Christmas.
>> (MORE)

(CONTINUED)

68   CONTINUED: —2

(beat; warning, mean)
Get back in line, old chum. I'm on the rise again, and
this time I don't have any problems, not even you.

LEN (last spark of defiance)
Don't count on it. There's always Netta Bernstein.

Jimmy smiles, then catches himself. There is almost a ruminative
quality in his voice, something light and ethereal, as he replies.

JIMMY
We had a talk. She's decided not to be such a
pain in the —

LEN (cuts in)
Fat chance. When she left the letter for Sloan this
morning she mumbled something about teaching
you a lesson you'd never forget.

INTERCUT:

69   SAME AS 40 — OLYMPIC PENINSULA — NIGHT

The night, the streamers of fog, mist hanging low, the forest, Jimmy
running but seeming to get nowhere, the light roaring out of the
distance, cascading through the trees, and that shape on the slope
above him, strobing and reproducing itself as we

CUT BACK TO:

70   CLOSE ON JIMMY — ANOTHER ANGLE IN WINCH'S OFFICE

The look on his face. Naked horror. Dachau. Lye pits. Vivisection
chambers. Death Row at major prisons. In Jimmy's expression we
see all the nameless terrors that come after all of us. This man is at
the breaking point. All his bravado, all his cool, all his new plans "on
the rise" have turned to suet with one random remark from Winch.
Jimmy clutches for the edge of Len's desk. He can barely speak.

JIMMY (hoarsely)
This . . . morning . . . ?

LEN (has no idea what terror he's released)
Yeah. Left a letter for Sloan. Left it with me.

(CONTINUED)

70   *CONTINUED:*

>   JIMMY
>   You . . . *saw* . . . her?
>
>   LEN
>   Yeah.
>
>   JIMMY
>   Right here. Right in this office? You actually
>   *saw* her? *Today?*
>
>   LEN (c'mon already)
>   *Yeah!* I said so, didn't I?

Jimmy lurches across the desk, scattering toys and papers. He gets a
hand around Winch's throat. Not choking, just trying to drag him
across the desk.

>   JIMMY
>   You're lying, dammit!
>   (beat)
>   It was a phone call . . . someone *called* and said
>   it was Netta and you talked to *someone* you
>   *thought* was Netta Bernstein!
>   (beat)
>   You didn't actually *see* her, did you? Admit it, you
>   little shit, you didn't really *see* her here, moving in
>   this room, did you?

Len wrenches himself away. He rolls back in his chair, gets to his
feet, trying to stay away from Jimmy, who is hysterical.

>   LEN
>   Geeeezus, man! I did! She was! She walked in
>   with her overnight bag and asked me to give this
>   letter to Sloan when he got in, and said she was
>   taking off for a few days . . .
>
>   JIMMY
>   Where?
>
>   LEN (screaming now)
>   How the hell should *I* know?

                                          (CONTINUED)

70   *CONTINUED: —2*

Jimmy comes around the desk. Len moves into a space where he's
trapped between wall and filing cabinets.

> JIMMY
> Gimme the letter!

Len starts to object. Jimmy cocks back his fist.

> JIMMY (CONT'D)
> I'll chew on your heart! Gimme that damned letter.

Len folds. He inches past Jimmy, still standing legs apart, fist
cocked to take off his head. He reaches into his desk, pulls out the
letter, hands it to Jimmy. CAMERA IN ON JIMMY as he tears it
open and reads it. One typed sheet, a short message. We don't see
what it is. Jimmy's jaw muscles tremble as he stares into the middle
distance for several beats. Then he says, in a cold, low voice:

> JIMMY (CONT'D)
> Give me Netta Bernstein's personnel file. Don't
> say a word, don't blow any smoke, just *do* it, Len.

His tone is so cold, so menacing, Len Winch goes to one of the file
cabinets, leafs through files, comes up with a folder and CAMERA
IN ON HIS HAND as he extends the folder to Jimmy and we

>   MATCH-CUT TO:

71   *EXTREME CLOSEUP — INTERIOR L.A. INTERNATIONAL
          —TICKET COUNTER — DAY*

MATCH-SHOT WITH PRECEDING SHOT of Len's hand
extending file folder. CUT TO female TICKET CLERK handing
over a ticket folder. PULL BACK to show Jimmy receiving the flight
folder.

> TICKET CLERK
> That's our flight number twelve-oh-five to
> Seattle-Tacoma, leaving from gate eighty-one in
> forty minutes, arriving Sea-Tac Airport at . . .

But Jimmy isn't listening. He's already gone as we

>   CUT TO:

72   *CLOSE ON JIMMY — INTERIOR 727 JETLINER — LATE DAY*

We can see the sun setting over the wing of the Boeing 727 as
Jimmy sits alone in a three-across, poring over the Netta Bernstein
file folder he dragooned from Winch. His dinner sits untouched on
the tray-table to his right. He is in the window seat. The sun goes
down and the cabin grows dark as Jimmy reaches up and clicks on
the overhead light. CAMERA COMES IN SLOWLY as we HEAR
JIMMY'S VOICE OVER.

> JIMMY O.S. (intimate)
> Netta Bernstein. Thirty-seven years old. Graduate,
> University of Washington. Degree in psychology,
> majored in child therapy. Married at age eighteen
> while an undergraduate, to one of her professors.
> (beat)
> Thirty-seven years old? Gotta be a mistake . . .
> *twenty*-seven maybe . . .
> (beat)
> Soon after marriage professor left university for
> position with Merck, Sharp, and Dohme, drug
> company, New Jersey. Took his child-bride with.

He riffles some pages, looks closely at next entry.

> JIMMY O.S. (CONT'D) (deeply interested)
> Stayed with him when he got a federal grant for
> research project . . .
> (beat)
> project . . . project . . . what kind of project?
> Nothing. Classified. Had to be national defense–
> oriented, eyes only . . . damn . . . oh well . . .
> (goes back to reading)
> . . . moved to Olympic peninsula of Washington
> state to work on project . . . remote area . . . Grays
> Harbor County . . . stayed there next sixteen
> years . . . husband died three years ago . . . yeah,
> that's thirty-seven, but she sure don't look it . . .
> Netta hired by Baylor Medical School, Houston,
> department of biochemistry . . . research on RNA
> (MORE)

                                                            (CONTINUED)

72   *CONTINUED:*

> messenger molecules . . . something . . . ah . . .
> related to autistic children. Left Baylor, came to
> MyToy thirteen months ago . . .

CAMERA HOLDS ON JIMMY as he closes the folder and picks up
the letter Netta left with Winch. It has been lying on the next seat.
He reads it again. This time we HEAR what it says in VOICE
OVER:

> JIMMY O.S. (CONT'D)
> Dear Mr. Sloan. A personal emergency compells my
> immediate attention. I'll need a week to ten days'
> leave. In the event of some problem I can be
> reached at my home in Grays Harbor County. The
> number is unlisted, but you will find it in my
> personnel file. Thank you for your understanding . . .
> Netta Bernstein.

His jaw muscles tense again. He crushes the letter, looks out the port as we

DISSOLVE THRU:

73   *AIRPORT RENTAL AREA — EVENING*

Still a little bit of light. Not fully dark yet. Jimmy emerges from the
rent-a-car office, sees a guy with a baseball cap with the company
emblem on it and hails him. This is silent. The ATTENDANT points
down the row of cars to a sedan. Jimmy hustles to it. He has no suitcase.

DISSOLVE THRU:

74   *MOVING SHOTS — HIGHWAY — NIGHT*
thru
82   As Jimmy's car roars through. Various shots that lead farther and
farther toward the high mountains of the Olympics and Cascades.
Shot with Mount Rainier in the b.g. Going toward deep forest.
More inhospitable. Colder. Fog starting to appear in the headlight
beams. Jimmy can be seen straining his eyes, wiping the windshield.
Fog, lots of ominous fog. Tchaikovsky in the b.g. maybe. West from
Olympia toward Aberdeen. North on Highway 101. A map in
Jimmy's hands. Light on inside the car. A right turn into a dirt road,
                    (MORE)

                              (CONTINUED)

82   *CONTINUED:*

frozen solid. Driving over bumpy corduroy road. Another road. He
misses it, it's so damned small and obscure. Backing and filling to
turn to get to it. A road practically a path. Driving slowly, beams on
high. Forest, deep forest all around. Mist and fog suffusing
everything in the darkness. Driving up a road so narrow the trees
scrape against both sides of the car.

83   *INT. CAR — NIGHT — ANGLE ON JIMMY AND FRONT
WINDSHIELD*

Suddenly the car's headlights reveal a high wire fence of
heavyweight dimensions. Silence outside. Everything swathed in
moist, eerie fog and mist. Dark shapes of trees. So suddenly does
the car come through the trees that have hidden the fence, that
within the beat of a second it is not there . . . then it is! Jimmy slams
on the brakes and the car digs to a halt. So suddenly that Jimmy
pitches forward, hitting his head against the steering wheel. A small
cut is opened over his left eye. He blinks, swipes at the blood,
curses softly. Then he opens the car door and fog rushes in.

84   *EXTERIOR FOREST — ON CAR — NIGHT*

As Jimmy gets out. He isn't wearing an overcoat, just what he had
on at the MyToy offices. It is colder than hell up here. And wet. In
moments he's dappled by wet and mist. And he's shivering. Blood is
running into his eye from the tiny cut. He wipes it away, looks at the
fence.

85   *REVERSE ANGLE — THROUGH FENCE — TO JIMMY*

He looks at the heavy link chain. This is no bullshit fence, but a
massively constructed barrier. The kind of thing you would find at a
military emplacement. Nonetheless, he looks at it with lips tensed,
rubs his hand over his forehead, brings it away bloody, gets a mean,
tough look on his face at sight of his own blood, puts up his collar,
and rubs the blood into his pants. Then he takes a few steps back to
get a running start, dashes for the fence and hits it at top speed,
reaching as high as he can INTO CAMERA. His fingers close on the
loops, he pulls himself up and up, and in a few moments scrambles

(MORE)

(CONTINUED)

85   *CONTINUED:*

over. CAMERA HAS PULLED BACK and DROPPED to provide
an UP-ANGLE ON THE FENCE and Jimmy up there at the top.
He is poised there for a moment, then jumps INTO CAMERA as we

CUT TO:

86   *SAME AS 40 — FOREST, OLYMPIC PENINSULA — NIGHT*

Now it's not foreshadowing, though we can see by the repetition
that this is the real time of the scene we have been seeing since the
middle of the story. He sloughs his way through the woods, cold,
the mist and fog all around, and the light suddenly streaming over
the slope above him. He climbs, climbs, sliding and sliding. *We do*
NOT *see that ominous strobe figure reproducing itself.*

Otherwise it is exactly the scene we have been seeing so often
previously.

87   *ANOTHER ANGLE — THE FOREST*

AT THE TOP OF THE SLOPE as Jimmy reaches the low summit.
There, on the other side, sitting on a small plateau, surrounded by
perimeter lights that have been casting the eerie glow through the
forest, lies Netta Bernstein's home. A long, low, almost research
lab–like structure. Very clean, very modern. Isolated. Nothing
around but deep forest and the mist and the night.

88   *PAST JIMMY*

as he stares at the building. He stands there for a very long moment
as we HEAR in the b.g.:

NETTA'S VOICE (echo)
I . . . love . . . you . . . Jimmy . . .

He looks down the slope to the building, then with broken-field
expertise, keeping low, he rushes down the slope as CAMERA
HOLDS the LONG SHOT of JIMMY RUNNING AWAY FROM
CAMERA. Stay on the summit as we see him circling the building,
keeping out of the pools of light that lie on the chilly ground.
Finally, we see a square of light in the darkness and we realize

(MORE)

(CONTINUED)

88   *CONTINUED:*

Jimmy has found a way inside. CAMERA MEASUREDLY ZOOMS
down the slope and to Jimmy as he stands beside the open door. He
wipes blood from his eye and with CAMERA IN CLOSE he now
slips inside the building. As he slips inside, the storm that has been
building with the fog suddenly bursts, and a CRACK OF
LIGHTNING rips down the night to accentuate his quietly closing
the door behind him. As if marking finis to freedom.

89   *INT. CORRIDOR — THE LAB*

It is ultramodern. No furniture. Onyx. Long and faintly lit. A limbo
set. CAMERA HOLDS ON JIMMY as he moves catlike through
the shrouding darkness. The floors are highly polished, like onyx.
The walls are dim in the glow of hidden lights. The source of light
cannot be traced. And in the middle of it all . . . Jimmy.

> NETTA'S VOICE O.S.
> Going to kill me again, Jimmy?

He spins. No one in sight. He almost drops to a commando crouch.
No one! He's alone! From another direction comes Netta's voice
again.

> NETTA'S VOICE O.S.
> Why did I know you'd get the letter from Len
> Winch? Why are you so damned predictable . . . ?

He turns in the other direction. Like a trapped animal. No one!
He's alone here. From another direction we HEAR:

> NETTA'S VOICE O.S.
> I suggest Jimmy Duncaster get squashed like the
> botulism he is.

> NETTA'S VOICE O.S
> (immediately, from another direction)
> Squash? No. How about a tire iron, or a closet
> hanger, or maybe a ball peen hammer!

Jimmy turns and turns and turns, starting, stopping, trapped in the
net of voices — all of which are Netta's — from every corner of the
room without walls, without dimensional reference. Frantic,
trapped, terrified!

90   *ANOTHER ANGLE — ON JIMMY*

As a beam of light stabs out of the darkness, pooling at Jimmy's feet.
He stands now, pinned by the circle of brilliance, surrounded by
darkness and voices . . .

> NETTA'S VOICE O.S.
> Maybe it would have been simpler not to cut the
> power in the fence. I think sixteen hundred volts
> would have taken care of the problem.

Jimmy strains his eyes into the darkness outside the circle. The
beam of light blinds him. He shades his eyes, tries to see a way of
getting away. Blood in his left eye from cut. Scared. More than a
touch of cowardice surfacing.

> NETTA'S VOICE O.S.
> (loathing)
> What a putrescent piece of human garbage you
> are, Duncaster . . .
> (beat, with a sorrowful catch in the voice)
> Did you even love her a *little* bit? Even a touch?
> Was it in you to love her just a little?

Jimmy grabs for the opportunity to flim-flam his way out of
things . . . maybe. The con man of the corporation rises.

> JIMMY
> I *loved* you . . . of *course* I . . .

He stops. She didn't say "did you love *me*" — she said "did you love
her"!

> NETTA'S VOICE OVER
> (echo)
> Did you love *her* . . . love *her* . . . *her* . . .

> JIMMY (panicked)
> How did you do it? How did you come back three
> times? I put you away *three* times! I *know* I did!?!
> (now screaming)
> You're no ghost, how do you do it? Tell me . . .
> *tell me . . . !*

                                                        (CONTINUED)

90   *CONTINUED:*

And the pool of light widens, the darkness recedes, as they step into
the edge of the light, shadows falling around them. They step out
one by one as CAMERA COMES IN ON JIMMY.

91   *THE SCENE — HAND HELD — CIRCULAR SHOT*

FEATURE JIMMY'S HEAD, PROFILE IN CLOSE F.G. with
FOCUS at the edge of the circle of light. As Netta Bernstein steps
into the misty edge of the light pool. Jimmy looks at her. Then
movement to her right and Jimmy's head turns slowly as a 2nd
NETTA steps to the edge of light. Then movement to her right
and Jimmy's head follows as a 3rd NETTA comes to the
shimmering edge of illumination. And the process is repeated and
repeated, slowly, in stately fashion as we reach this climactic
moment . . . until a DOZEN NETTA BERNSTEINS ring him,
circle him, hold him immobile in the intensity of their hatred and
presence. And we realize that for some time now we have been
HEARING THE SOUND OF JIMMY MOANING low in his
throat, like a whipped dog; a terrified, uncomprehending,
bewitched creature.

1st NETTA
Daddy was a geneticist.

2nd NETTA
Fell in love with an eighteen-year-old, auburn-
haired, green-eyed undergraduate who stared at
him all through his lecture with unabashed
adoration.

CAMERA CIRCLES as they speak, following the edge of the pool
of light. Each is dressed differently, otherwise they are identical,
down to the hairstyle and eye makeup. One dozen — count 'em,
twelve — Netta Bernsteins. A dozen beautiful, nineteen-year-old
replicas. CAMERA AROUND AND AROUND as Jimmy's soft
moan runs underneath like a hidden river.

3rd NETTA
Daddy took the cutting from Mama and ran off
fifteen of us. Here, far away from all prying eyes.

(CONTINUED)

91   *CONTINUED:*

> 4th NETTA
> Raised us from infancy, stone righteous copies of
> our beautiful Mama. And we grew so fast and so
> well, just like the Five Little Peppers.

> 2nd NETTA
> Little Women

> 1st NETTA
> Bobbsey Twins times seven and a half.

> 5th NETTA
> And Mama grew older so gracefully.

> 6th NETTA (with disagreeing tone)
> Well . . .

> 5th NETTA (stern)
> *Gracefully!* Mama grew older *very gracefully*. So
> when Daddy died three years ago . . .

> 6th NETTA (bitterly)
> Leaving the thirty-four-year-old original with
> fifteen daughters . . .

> 7th NETTA
> . . . with fifteen *sisters* . . .

> 8th NETTA
> With fifteen sisters, fifteen daughters, all
> duplicates just sweet sixteen years old, Mama
> trained us here in this lab to go out and take her
> place.

> 9th NETTA
> To be in a dozen places at once.

> 10th NETTA
> Because we had to pay the rent and feed the
> mouths.

> 7th NETTA
> To make ends meet.

(CONTINUED)

91   CONTINUED: —2

> 6th NETTA
> Because a girl has to live, has to keep bodies and
> souls together,
>> (beat, bitter)
> has to take care of Mama the way Mama took
> care of us . . .

> 11th NETTA
> Shut up!

> 6th NETTA (fights back)
> If Sister hadn't risked our situation, falling in love
> with this slug, we wouldn't *have* to worry what to
> do about him!

> JIMMY (barely breathes words)
> You're clones . . . Netta times twelve . . .

> 4th NETTA
> Recombinant DNA.

> 3rd NETTA (playful)
> RNA . . . DNA . . . AOK . . . D!O!A!

> JIMMY (stunned)
> Netta, times twelve . . .

> 6th NETTA
> Times fifteen. But, then, you've *killed* us three
> times, haven't you, Duncaster?

> 12th NETTA
> All right, enough! We know what we have to do
> with him. How?

> 3rd NETTA
> I say we each get a try at him!

Then a VOICE of NETTA FROM THE DARKNESS is heard. But
it is quite different from the others. It is eerie, strange and
whispery, the voice of someone who has gone over the edge.
Heathcliff's wife, the Madwoman of Chaillot. All the clone Nettas
turn their heads to stare out of the light.

(CONTINUED)

91   *CONTINUED: —3*

NETTA'S VOICE (like a retarded child)
Oh . . . don't hurt him . . . isn't he lovely . . .

They stare into the darkness as a figure in a long white nightgown
comes toward the circle. The bride of Dracula. IT IS IMPERATIVE
THAT SHE REMAIN IN SHADOW, THAT WE NEVER
ACTUALLY SEE HER IN CLOSEUP OR REAL DETAIL. Just
an ephemeral, graceful, but oddly erratic, disturbing figure.

3rd NETTA
Mama . . . we didn't mean to wake you . . .
(beat, angrily)
Who was supposed to stay with Mama?

NETTA
That's all right, dear.
(beat)
Isn't he lovely . . .
(beat)
It's been so long since we've had company . . .

The 6th Netta turns back to Jimmy. Her voice is cold.

6th NETTA
One of the wonders of the human condition. The
child becomes the parent . . . the parent becomes
the child . . .

Now the 1st Netta turns and looks at Jimmy with calculation.

1st NETTA
Maybe we *don't* kill him . . . Mama might want
him. If *one* of us was sick enough to love him . . .

They all turn to stare at Jimmy.

JIMMY
You've gotta let me out of here . . . people will be
looking for —

3rd NETTA
Would you like him, Mama . . . ?

(CONTINUED)

91   *CONTINUED: —4*

NETTA
Oh, yes. He's *so* lovely . . .

JIMMY
What's wrong with her? I . . . I can't see her . . .

All but the 6th Netta turn back to the figure outside the circle.

6th NETTA
Wrong? Nothing's *wrong* with our mama. It's
just . . . raising fifteen copies of yourself can be . . .
(beat)
disturbing to your mama . . .

1st NETTA
Mama . . . pretty Mama . . . we've got a little
present for you . . .

And they all turn back, as one, to stare at Jimmy.

92   *THE SCENE — BOOM SHOT — FROM ABOVE*

as the circle of Nettas opens before Mama in shadow. An opening
just big enough for Jimmy. And the circle draws in around him as
CAMERA RISES and Jimmy is inexorably moved toward the
opening, toward the shrouded figure. As CAMERA MOVES UP
AND AWAY we HEAR two things: Tchaikovsky's Symphony #4 and

NETTA'S VOICE (echo)
I love you, Jimmy . . . I'll *always* love you . . .

JIMMY'S VOICE O.S. (echo)
Killing Netta was impossible. They'd found her in
the closet and taken her away.
(beat)
One of them had loved me.
(beat)
Here, the rain and the mist are sanctified . . . and
there's music . . . and they don't harm me . . .
(beat)
And one of them had loved me.
(MORE)

(CONTINUED)

92   *CONTINUED:*

> > > (beat)
> > Some day, maybe some day, they'll let me go.
> > And maybe, some day, they'll clone again . . . and
> > perhaps I'll get blessed again . . .
> > > (beat)
> > . . . and one of them will love me.

CAMERA UP and UP as shadows close in on circle of clones and
the doomed love-object that is Jimmy Duncaster.

93   *DOWN-ANGLE FROM ABOVE — SPECIAL EFFECT*

At the last moment, with JIMMY'S VOICE OVER, ringing like a
silver whisper, the shadowy figure in the white gown BEGINS TO
STROBE like the figure in scene 40. It begins to reproduce itself
like ripples in a pool, out and out and out, till FRAME GOES TO
BLINDING LIGHT and we

> > > > > CUT TO BLACK
> > > > > and
> > > > > FADE OUT.

DEAD IN THE WEST
(A WEIRD WESTERN)

BY
JOE R. LANSDALE
Based on his novel, *Dead in the West*

FADE IN:

LOGO AGAINST COMPLETE DARKNESS:

EAST TEXAS, 1870s

DARKNESS

SOUNDS OF LOVEMAKING

An abrupt wedge of light as a door is opened on a darkened room, revealing a man and woman in bed, making love.

Framed in the light of the doorway, a big BEARDED MAN.

ON THE BED

The light lies heavy on THE REVEREND and a WOMAN. The Reverend is a lean, hard-faced man in his mid-thirties. Woman is young and attractive. Reverend rolls off the woman, turns toward —

BEARDED MAN
You!

BEARDED MAN

Draws a revolver from under his coat, points it at the Reverend.

BACK TO SCENE

WOMAN
No, Able!

Reverend leaps to the side of the bed, reaches for his revolver, which lies on top of a Bible on the nightstand. Woman shrieks.

Bearded Man FIRES.

Woman takes the slug meant for Reverend in the chest, melts back dead and bleeding onto the sheets.

REVEREND

hand on the .36 Navy, wheels, FIRES THREE AMAZINGLY QUICK SHOTS as Bearded Man's bullet cuts across his cheek and slams into bed's headboard.

BEARDED MAN

He's got three holes in his forehead. They aren't more than a thumb-nail apart. HOLD ON HIS AMAZED FACE, then he collapses, and we —

CUT TO:

EXT. — A CHURCH — NIGHT — LATER

A horse tied out front, saddled and laden with gear.

A sign that reads:

THE CHURCH OF OUR LORD'S MERCY
Reverend Jebidiah Mercer
Gladewater, Texas

Backing out of the church is the Reverend, wearing pants and boots and no shirt. His revolver is stuck in his waistband. He has a torch and a barrel of kerosene. He's pouring from the barrel as he backs away. Outside, he drops the barrel, boots it inside, tosses the torch in after it.

FLAMES POOF LOUDLY TO LIFE AND LICK OUT THE DOORWAY, lap at the Reverend, who stumbles backward, away from the heat. He finds a safe distance, watches as the flames start to consume the church.

Reverend goes over to the church sign, grabs it, groans, tugs it to the earth, falls on top of it with his knees.

CLOSE ON REVEREND

as tears crawl down his face. Lifts his head to God and yells —

REVEREND
I'm a sinner! A sinner!

DARK CLOUDS

hint of RUMBLING THUNDER. A BURST OF LIGHTNING, and it's a strange configuration, like A READY KILOWATT SPIDER. HOLDS HOT AND WHITE for a long instant, then —

BACK TO THE REVEREND

as sudden RAIN hits his face, washes his hair in his eyes, mixes with the tears.

Slowly the Reverend rises, unties the horse, swings into the saddle, starts riding away.

DISSOLVE TO:

The rain and the night, and the SOUND OF THE RAIN DIES, and the night becomes RICH DARKNESS.

HOLD THAT DARKNESS UNTIL —

SCREEN LOGO APPEARS.

ONE YEAR LATER

OUT OF THE DARKNESS A LIGHT

WIDEN OUR VIEW

so we see the light is the MOON looking like a big plate with gravy stains on it.

TRACK DOWN

from the moon, and the moonlight reveals —

A NARROW, TREE-LINED TRAIL

Moonlit and shadow-marked, the trail bends to the left around a forest of tall pines, and we HEAR before we see, NOLAN.

> NOLAN (O.S.) (Gradually becomes more audible
> with each word.)
> You goddamned, shit-eating, wind-breaking
> excuses for mules. Git on, you contrary
> sonsabitches.

A RUMBLE, and around the bend comes a stagecoach, lanterns attached to both sides of the driver's seat. They swing left and right like huge fireflies.

DRIVER'S SEAT

is occupied by two men. NOLAN and THE SHOTGUNNER. Nolan looks
like Gabby Hayes but there's something about his expression makes you
think he might have a strand of barbwire up his ass. He's grizzled and wears
a slouchy hat and an eye patch.

His partner is long and lean and goofy-looking. He doesn't look smart enough
to outwit his dinner. If he didn't have ears, his hat would be over his face and
he wouldn't notice. A double-barrel shotgun rests in a gun boot between them.

> SHOTGUNNER
> I can't hold it much longer, Nolan. I'm gonna wet
> myself.

> NOLAN
> Goddamn, you pick the worst times to piss.
> Whoa! Whoa!

Stage slows, stops at the side of the road.

> NOLAN
> Hurry up, will you? We're late.

Shotgunner drops to the ground, starts into the woods.

> NOLAN (shouting)
> Why you got to —

INT. — COACH

> NOLAN (O.S.)
> — go so far?

LULU, a seedy dance-hall gal is inside. She's wearing too much war paint
and the hat she's got on has everything on it but a fart and train schedule.

Beside her is a GAMBLER dressed up in card table duds. Oily face.
Overgrown sideburns. Bowler. Black suit. Checked vest. A waxed mustache.
He looks as if he'd probe a dead man's asshole for a nickel.

Across from them is a mother, FLORENCE, with a young girl, MIGNON,
asleep in her lap. The mother looks nervous and innocent. The child hugs a
rag doll.

We see all this in the moment we HEAR Shotgunner respond to Nolan's
question.

SHOTGUNNER (O.S)
Lady present.

Lulu, feeling flattered, tries to look very proper when she hears this, and the Gambler tries to look pleasant as well, but their faces turn sour, when —

NOLAN (O.S.)
You ain't askin' her to hold your pecker for you,
you jackass.

EXT. — COACH

Gambler's head juts out the coach window and he yells at Nolan and Nolan turns to look.

GAMBLER
Mind your mouth, Mister. You've been nothing
but a verbal cesspool since this trip started. There
are ladies present.

NOLAN
Yeah. I keep hearing that. Let me tell you
somethin' Mr. Tin Horn Gambler. The "lady"
sittin' next to you, Lulu McGill, would suck and
blow your asshole for four bits.

Lulu sticks her head out the opposite coach window, and Nolan responds by leaning to her side for a look.

LULU
Goddamn you, Nolan. I ain't never done the like
for no four bits, and you know it. Right now I'm a
lady. Hear?

NOLAN
Can't help but hear you.

Gambler, really tough now.

GAMBLER
And there's a young girl and her mother in here,
too. Hush that mouth of yours, or you'll have me
to deal with.

Nolan leans from the driver's seat toward the Gambler's window. He has the double-barrel shotgun. He puts the tip of it over the Gambler's nose, cocks back the hammers.

> NOLAN
> I know who's inside, Mr. Tin Horn. Now listen
> tight. I'd hate to blow your stupid head off and
> disturb that little girl. So git in there and shut up.

INT. — COACH

Gambler jerks back inside, looks embarrassed. Lulu and the mother give him
a disgusted look.

> LULU
> Ain't you the Top Dog?

EXT. — THE WOODS — MOMENTS LATER

Shotgunner taking a leak. There are lots of shadows falling across the scene,
but one of the shadows is strange. It's looped. It's right in front of
Shotgunner, and he's pissing through the loop. He turns and looks toward
the tree where the shadow originates, and we see a noose.

Shotgunner shakes the dew off his lily, packs it away, goes over to the rope.
He takes hold of the rope, runs his hand over it, and is rewarded with a rope
burn. He jerks his hand back and shoots his injured finger into his mouth to
suck on it.

> SHOTGUNNER
> Damn hemp.

Shotgunner turns to start back toward the coach, sucking his finger, and
behind him —

CLOSE ON THE ROPE

Coming down the length of it, an oddball spider with a white skull marking
its back. It scurries down one side of the loop, and we go —

CLOSER

so we can see there's blood on the noose, and the spider is easing up to the
blood, and it becomes obvious that it's tasting the blood, and it begins to
GROW AND GROW AND GROW . . .

SWOLLEN SPIDER

drops from the rope to the ground, swells as if it's being pumped full of air.
Its legs twitch; the leaves rattle beneath its legs. This dude is big, and it's
really got too many legs for a spider now. It's slightly nebulous. A bad dream
that moves in the shadows.

SHOTGUNNER

hears something, turns. Nothing is there. He studies the woods behind him for a moment. Empty of life. Just the trees, the leaves, and the shadows. He sighs. Turns.

And the giant spider-thing is in his face. Its legs grab Shotgunner and jerk him into its mouth and it bites, and a BRIGHT BURST OF BLOOD EXPLODES into —

A MATCH

being struck, and the match illuminates Nolan's face, and we PULL BACK and see he is relighting one of the lanterns on the coach. Then he carefully lights the other.

> NOLAN
> Goddamn wind. Goddamn cheap-ass lanterns.

Nolan takes out his pocket watch and holds the match close to the watch so he can see the time. His face takes on an even more disgusted look.

> NOLAN
> Damn idiot. Why couldn't he piss in the wind like
> a real man?

A SHADOW falls over Nolan and he jerks his head toward it, and we see the SPIDER'S FACE, close enough it blows its breath in Nolan's whiskers and makes them rustle.

Match goes out and Nolan yells, and the weak lantern light on either side of Nolan is extinguished as the shape of the spider takes their place, blocking our view of Nolan.

A SOUND LIKE A WALNUT CRACKING between a plier's jaws and the shape of the spider shifts to something not quite as identifiable; shifts as if it is made of India ink and mercury.

GAMBLER

sticks his head out the window. From his angle he can see Nolan's right arm and shoulder.

> GAMBLER
> What's all that racket? We goin' to Mud Creek or
> not?

INT. — COACH

> LULU (disdainful)
> I just love it when you take charge, Mr. Tin Horn.

Gambler turns his head inside to look at her, frowns. Sticks his head and arm out the window —

EXT. — COACH

as Gambler beats on the side of the stage.

> GAMBLER
> Hey. Let's go! I'm a paying passenger here.

Action of beating on the side of the coach causes Nolan to lean farther to the right. Gambler, afraid a gun will be pulled again, flinches. Then —

NOLAN'S BODY

falls to the side, and with his feet hung in the boot sheath, he dangles there, his face twisted toward us. There's a seriously nasty bite out of the side of the old man's jaw. No one would mistake it for acne.

> GAMBLER (almost wistfully)
> Uh oh.

A FLOWING SHAPE-SHIFTING SHADOW

comes down on the Gambler and the women inside SCREAM, and we CUT TO —

EXT. — MUD CREEK, MAIN STREET — DEAD OF NIGHT

TOMB SILENCE

Empty street. At the far end of the street, coming toward us, seeming to melt out of the dark, SLOW MOTION, comes the stage. Both of its lanterns are extinguished, but it is clearly visible, ghostlike. Horses are frothing. Their hoofs are pounding up dust. In the moonlight, the dust looks like snow.

A big man — from here on out we'll call him THE INDIAN — is driving the team. His face isn't visible. It's shadowed by the night and he wears a hat.

Stage continues in SLOW MOTION until it is CLOSE, then it stops before the livery, which bears this sign: BILLY JACK RHINE, BLACKSMITH AND LIVERY. Then we're —

NO LONGER IN SLOW MOTION AND DEAD SILENCE

The Indian pulls the brake. Jumps down, lithe as a cat. He seems to glide around to the back of the stage.

Out from beneath the luggage flap he pulls a long wooden crate — coffin-size. He holds the crate as lightly as a shoe box. He glides around until he stands before the livery.

The doors are closed and there's a huge padlock on them. The Indian moves his hand slightly. The padlock — without coming open — drips to the earth, à la *The Brides of Dracula*. The doors blow open with a creak.

The Indian slips inside. The doors close behind him. The padlock jumps into place.

HOLD A BEAT as we HEAR a distant rumble of THUNDER beyond the blue-black, East Texas woodlands.

DISSOLVE TO:

CREDITS AGAINST A HOT, RED SUN

rising over the East Texas landscape, which is mostly trees, and this grass-covered rise, and riding up to it, as if riding out of the sun, is a man on a horse dark as the devil's asshole.

FRONTAL SHOT, CLOSE ON THE REVEREND

He looks better than when we saw him last, but he has a haunted look. His face looks sterner, as if it's been chipped out of flint with a dull chisel. Handsome in an almost too masculine way. Eyes the color of revolver steel. He's wearing a black hat and black suit with a white shirt and a black string tie. Visible in his waistband is an ivory-handled, converted .36 Navy pistol. A large, worn Bible juts out of one of his coat pockets. He looks tired, ready to drop. He's not a man you'd expect to smile a lot.

REVEREND'S POV

The town stretched out in the distance between huge oaks and pines. Sighing, the Reverend opens his saddlebag, takes out a whisky bottle, pulls the cork, takes a swig, and returns the bottle. He starts the horse down the rise toward the town.

THE TOWN

as the Reverend rides in, past a sign that reads: MUD CREEK. People give him looks as he comes in. He looks as much like a shootist as a preacher.

TRACK REVEREND

taking in the town, until he stops his horse in front of —

BILLY JACK RHINE'S LIVERY

as we FINISH CREDITS. There's a boy standing out front. A Huck Finn type. His name is DAVID. He looks as if he'd rather be anywhere than where he is. He looks hot and bothered. He's cleaning his fingernails with a large jackknife. He lazily lifts his head and he and the Reverend eye each other.

> DAVID
> Yeah. Whatcha want?

> REVEREND
> Provided you don't think it'll tire you too much,
> I'd like my horse groomed.

> DAVID
> Six bits. Now.

> REVEREND
> I want him groomed, not shampooed, you little
> crook. What's your name, son? I'd like to know
> who to avoid from here on out.

> DAVID
> David.

> REVEREND
> At least you've got a fine biblical name, even if
> you do look like a loafer to me.

> DAVID
> And you look like a preacher.

The Reverend studies David. He likes the boy's spunk.

> REVEREND
> That supposed to be an insult? You say it as if the
> word is poison.

> DAVID
> You look like a preacher, but you got that gun.

The Reverend dismounts, takes money from his pocket, and hands it to the boy. As he removes his saddlebags from the horse, tosses them over his shoulder, he talks.

> REVEREND
> I AM a preacher, boy. Name is Mercer. Reverend
> Mercer to you. Perhaps you'll groom my horse
> sometime between now and tomorrow.

BILLY JACK RHINE enters scene.

He's a big, pot-bellied man with huge arm muscles and a face like a clenched
fist. His bald head is pink and beaded with sweat. He's carrying a
blacksmith's hammer in his hand. He looks like he could eat a bucket of
tacks and shit you a toolbox. With tools inside.

> BILLY JACK
> Boy talking you to death, Mister?

Rhine's voice strikes the boy like a blow. He immediately goes stiff, looks wary.
The Reverend takes note of this. It's clear there's tension between the two.

> REVEREND
> We were just making a deal on the grooming of
> my horse. You must be the owner.

> BILLY JACK
> Billy Jack Rhine. Boy charge you two bits like he's
> supposed to?

David swallows. He looks at the Reverend.

> REVEREND
> I'm satisfied.

David smiles, leads the Reverend's horse inside the livery. Rhine, wearing a
disgusted look, watches the boy lead the horse away, turns back to the
Reverend with a frown.

> RHINE (snide)
> Boy's like his mother. A dreamer. Have to beat
> respect into him now and then. Damn sure wasn't
> born with any.

> REVEREND
> Boys have their own ways. Where's the best place
> to stay around here?

> RHINE
> Ain't but one. The Hotel Montclaire. Git a room

with a window. You don't, you'll be hotter than a
bitch dog in heat.

> REVEREND
> Obliged.

Reverend crosses the street heading toward the HOTEL MONTCLAIRE.

INT. — HOTEL MONTCLAIRE

A real firetrap of a building. Stairway. Ragged furniture. JACK
MONTCLAIRE at the check-in desk. Montclaire is a balding fat man in a
too-small shirt with his elbow on the desk and his oily, sweat-beaded head in
his hand. He looks like a guy who could grow penicillin under his arms. He's
snoozing, snoring like a busted accordion. Flies buzz around his head,
looking for a safe place to land.

A HAND

comes down on a desk bell in front of Montclaire, jumping him awake.

> MONTCLAIRE
> Huh? What?

WIDER VIEW

so we see it's the Reverend who has rung the bell.

> MONTCLAIRE
> Sorry. Jack Montclaire at your service. Caught me
> sleeping. It's the heat.

Reverend nods. Montclaire opens the register book. The Reverend signs in.

> MONTCLAIRE
> Six bits a night. Clean sheets every third day.
> Provided you stay three days.

> REVEREND
> I will. Meals extra?

> MONTCLAIRE
> Would be if I served them. I don't. You want to
> eat, try Molly McGuire's Cafe. Biscuits taste like
> dried cow shit, but the rest of what they got's all
> right . . . You ain't got no bags, do you?

Reverend pats saddlebags slung over his shoulder.

> MONTCLAIRE
> Room Thirteen all right with you?

> REVEREND
> Any number is fine with me, as long as it has a
> window that opens.

Reverend tosses the pen on top of the register. Montclaire turns the register around and reads it.

> MONTCLAIRE
> Reverend Jebidiah Mercer. Ain't never seen no
> Reverend carries a gun. I mean, a man of the
> Holy Word and Peace and all.

> REVEREND
> Who said the Lord's work was peaceable? Devil
> brings a sword, and I bring a sword back to him.

Montclaire pulls the room key from one of the wall boxes and hands it to the Reverend. Montclaire points toward stairs.

> MONTCLAIRE
> I suppose that's one way to see it.

Reverend starts up the stairs.

> REVEREND (without looking at Montclaire)
> No supposing about it.

When the Reverend is out of sight and earshot.

CLOSE MONTCLAIRE

> MONTCLAIRE (soft as a falling snowflake)
> Self-righteous asshole.

INT. — HOTEL ROOM 13

Reverend unlocks the door and enters.

WIDER VIEW

It's a simple room. Curtained window across the way. The curtains are the color of dust on white and they are blowing slightly because the window is open.

The bed is sagging. On a small table to the side of the bed is a washbasin with wash materials. Chair. Mirror with a crack down the center. The wallpaper is flyspecked and dirty.

Reverend goes to the window, pushes aside the curtains, puts his head out.

REVEREND'S POV

Street. Wagon rattles by. A man on muleback rides along. A woman, ABBY PEEKNER, walks from the hotel side of the street to the opposite side. She's wearing a bright dress and bonnet. When she reaches the other side, she stops, turns to face the hotel, takes off her bonnet, and as if drawn to it, lifts her face to the Reverend's window, and we —

GO CLOSE ON ABBY

She's so goddamn beautiful she breaks your heart.

CLOSE ON THE REVEREND

He's still stern-looking, but it's clear he likes what he sees. At this moment, Jesus is not foremost on his mind.

REVEREND'S POV

as Abby disappears inside a building.

REVEREND

pulls inside, leaves the curtains and window open. He walks to the bed, tosses the saddlebags on it, takes off his coat, hangs it on a bedpost, and tops it off with his hat. He takes the bottle of whisky out of the saddlebags, uncorks it, swigs. He lies back on the bed with his back resting against the headboard, crosses his feet, and begins to drink. He closes his eyes for a moment —

QUICK FLASH ON BEARDED MAN TAKING THREE BULLETS

ANOTHER FLASH. The Reverend on his knees in the rain. The dark sky and THE ELECTRIC-SPIDER STITCHED BY LIGHTNING.

BACK TO NOW, REVEREND WINCING

Eyes pop open. A hard breath. As Reverend tips the bottle up we go to —

REVEREND'S POV

A fat spider on the ceiling.

RETURN TO SCENE

as Reverend switches the bottle to his left hand, and then, SNAKE-STRIKE FAST, he draws the .36 Navy from his waistband and shoots the spider. The ceiling rains plaster.

LOBBY

Montclaire leaps from his chair, rushes out from behind the desk, then runs back and gets a revolver out of a drawer, starts cautiously up the stairs.

He steps into the hallway, just as the Reverend appears in the doorway of his room, the .36 Navy dangling from his hand. Other doors open down the way. A few heads peek out.

Montclaire moves toward the Reverend.

> MONTCLAIRE (cautious)
> You okay, Reverend?

The Reverend looks at Montclaire and nods. His face is flushed and oily.

> REVEREND
> A spider. The devil's own creature. I cannot
> abide them.

> MONTCLAIRE
> You shot a spider?

> REVEREND (wry)
> Right between the eyes.

Reverend stands aside as Montclaire looks into the room. He sees the plaster dripping down from the ceiling onto the bed. He looks up.

MONTCLAIRE'S POV

A BULLET HOLE in the ceiling, and positioned around it on the ceiling are the SPIDER'S LEGS.

BACK TO SCENE

Montclaire steps out of the room to face the Reverend.

> MONTCLAIRE
> Preacher or not. I can't have you shootin' up my
> place. There'd been a third floor, a gent might
> have caught a blue whistler in the asshole. That'd

been some price to pay for a spider. This place is
respectable —

The Reverend digs into his pants pocket, comes up with some money. He
shoves it at Montclaire.

> REVEREND
> It's an outhouse and you know it. Here's a dollar
> for the spider. Five for the hole. That's
> respectable spider bounty. Take it or leave it,
> windbag.

Montclaire knows the truth when he hears it. He studies the money. Briefly.
Then grabs it faster than a crow picking corn kernels from a pile of shit.

> MONTCLAIRE
> Well, all right, but —

The Reverend steps back inside the room and slams the door. Montclaire
looks indignant for a moment, pockets the money, looks down the hall at the
faces sticking out of doorways.

> MONTCLAIRE
> Go on and mind your own business.

The observers draw back inside their rooms. Montclaire starts toward the
stairs.

INT. — REVEREND'S ROOM

He picks the bottle off the washstand and takes a swig. He sits on the end of
the bed, swigs again, and as he lowers the bottle he sees his coat hanging on
the bedpost and the top of his Bible sticking out of the coat pocket.

He takes the Bible from the coat and holds it like he would a poisonous
reptile.

> REVEREND
> Why, Lord, hast thou forsaken me?

Long pause as the Reverend seems to wait for an answer. He smiles a slow
ugly smile.

> REVEREND
> That's what I thought you'd say.
> (Lifting the bottle in toast)
> Same to you.

MATT
Watch your mouth.

CALEB
Her sister and her brat turn up dead, hell, Matt
you can go out there and comfort her. There's a
good side to everything.

MATT
You're gonna push once too often, Caleb.

Caleb smiles. It's not the smile of a worried man.

CALEB
Come on, Matt. You ain't got idea one about that
stage, do you?

Matt frowns, shakes his head.

MATT
No. Rode out the stage trail this morning. Didn't
see hide nor hair of the passengers. And I lied to
Millie. Didn't want to upset her needlessly. I did
get an answer to my wire. They didn't stop off
anywhere. They're just plain ole gone. Could
have been Indians, I guess. Or robbers.

CALEB
You're grabbin' at farts, Matt. You know well as I
do ain't been no Indian trouble around here in
years. 'Cept that medicine show fella and his
woman, and he damn sure ain't no trouble now.

MATT
You hung him, Caleb. Not me. I wasn't even
there.

CALEB
Judas didn't nail up Jesus neither . . . You gave
him to us, Matt. It's the same thing. And it ain't
nothing to feel guilty about.

MATT
He was an innocent man.

CALEB

Shit, he was an Injun and his wife was a nigger.
Red niggers, black niggers, Meskin niggers.
They're all the same. But it don't matter now.
They're both boilin' with worms. But we was
talkin' about the stage. It wasn't no Indians or
robbers and you know it. They wouldn't have
been polite enough to bring the stage in and put
on the brake. Somethin' else goin' on here, and it
stinks badder'n my ass in wintertime britches.

MATT

I'd reckon nothing stinks that bad.

Reverend enters scene, tips his hat.

REVEREND

Reverend Jebidiah Mercer, Sheriff. I'm a man of
God. I travel from town to town teaching and
spreading the word —

CALEB

And filling your offering plates.

Reverend turns to look at Caleb, who's rolling a smoke, tobacco raining ever
which way.

REVEREND

Like you, sir, I must eat. But I bring something
with me besides a sermon. I bring the word of
our Lord and eternal salvation.

MATT

No disrespect, Reverend, but you think we could
cut through the horseshit and get down to cases?
What can I do for you?

REVEREND

I would like to rent a tent and, with your
permission, hold a night of gospel singing, prayer,
and bringing lost souls to Jesus.

CALEB

And passin' that offerin' plate.

Caleb lights his cigarette and puffs a little cloud and smiles at the Reverend. The Reverend isn't bothered.

> MATT
> It's all right with me. I drink on Sundays. But we got a preacher already. Reverend Calhoun. You ought to walk down and check with him. I think he's got one of them tents like you want.

> REVEREND
> Obliged. I shall do just that.

> MATT
> Main Street forks at the north end. You'll see the church there. Calhoun's most likely around.

Reverend touches his hat in thanks, heads for the door.

CLOSE ON CALEB

> CALEB (to no one in particular)
> Goddamn God hounds. Sorriest bastards ever squatted to shit over a pair of boots.

EXT. — CAFE

Reverend steps onto the boardwalk, and there's the beautiful woman, Abby, going inside with a puffy-laced, elderly man with a shock of white hair creeping out from under his hat like dead grass rotting under a rock.

Reverend and Abby hold each other's gaze. Obvious attraction. He tips his hat. She smiles, and goes past with the old man into the cafe, but not before turning for a last look.

ON REVEREND

As he walks past the livery, he pauses suddenly, turns his head toward it. The doors are locked. No one's around. As he looks at the livery we —

CUT TO:

INT. — LIVERY

CAMERA ROAMS

and zeros in on the crate resting on the loft beneath a thin sheath of hay. The crate shifts abruptly, as if pointing toward the Reverend.

BACK TO THE REVEREND

He continues down the street, pauses, looks back at the livery, shakes as if ice has been dropped down his spine, then proceeds.

EXT. — CHURCH

CALHOUN, an old man with a long white beard, dressed in overalls, is hoeing inside a little fenced garden next to the church.

The Reverend goes to the gate in the fence and calls out to the old man.

> REVEREND
> Reverend Calhoun?

Calhoun lifts from his hoeing, eyes the Reverend.

> REVEREND (cont'd)
> Good day, sir. I'm Reverend Mercer. I've come to
> ask you a favor. One any good Christian could not
> refuse.

Calhoun straightens his back and leans on the hoe. He's a quarrelsome-looking old man.

> CALHOUN
> We'll see about that.

The Reverend opens the gate and comes inside the garden. Calhoun eyes him warily.

> CALHOUN (cont'd)
> Mind your feet.

> REVEREND
> Sheriff said if it's all right with you, I might hold a
> night of gospel singing and preaching here in
> Mud Creek. He also said you might have a tent
> you could rent me. I'm willing to pay nicely.

> CALHOUN
> How nicely?

> REVEREND
> You name it.

> CALHOUN
> Six bits.

> REVEREND
> A popular price.

> CALHOUN
> And I choose Saturday night for you to hold your
> meeting.

> REVEREND
> Sir, that's the worst night of the week. The saloon
> will be filled.

> CALHOUN
> Take it or leave it.

> REVEREND
> I reckon I'll take it.

Calhoun pauses to eye the Reverend more carefully.

> CALHOUN
> Sure you're a preacher? You got that pistol. That's
> hardly a tool of the Lord.

> REVEREND
> Even the Lord allowed Samson to smote the
> Philistines. He gave Samson the jawbone of an
> ass. He has given me a revolver.

Calhoun doesn't appreciate this remark. He looks even more sour, drops
the hoe.

> CALHOUN
> Mighty high on yourself, boy. You want the tent,
> let's do it. I have work to do

> REVEREND
> No less than I, I assure you, sir.

INT. — CHURCH

Reverend and Calhoun. They're walking down the pew-lined aisle toward
the pulpit. They go around it and to the back of the church and Calhoun
opens a door.

STORAGE ROOM

Calhoun and Reverend framed there. Calhoun takes a lantern from a shelf
and lights it. They proceed down the stairs. Calhoun says —

CALHOUN
Watch your step.

He waves lantern at a missing stair step.

CALHOUN (cont'd)
Rot got that one. Got to fix it one of these days.

Down into the darkened, cob-web infested storage room. At the bottom of
the stairs, stacked all around, are crates with the words COLT,
WINCHESTER, and AMMUNITION written on the sides. A fistful of rifles
and shotguns are strewn about. There's also the barrel of a Gatling gun
poking out from under a tarp. The Reverend stops, peels back the tarp and
we get a good look at the Gatling. The Reverend drops the tarp back,
reaches for a loose double-barrel shotgun, feels the balance in his hands.

REVEREND
For a man who dislikes guns, you certainly have a
few on hand.

CALHOUN
Don't be snide with me, mister. When they built
this church it was sort of a fortress against outlaws
and Indians. We never had much of either, but
the guns are still here, same as there's still bars on
the windows. Come on. Tent's back here.

Reverend lays the shotgun aside, follows Calhoun to a dusty corner where a
molded canvas tent lies folded in a heap.

REVEREND
Any spots on it not rotten?

CALHOUN
Take it or leave it.

Reverend sighs, pulls six bits from his pocket.

REVEREND
I'll take it. I'll send someone for it, shortly.

Calhoun takes the money and waves the Reverend up the stairs.

CALHOUN
Remember the step.

Reverend starts up the steps, pauses, turns to Calhoun.

> REVEREND
>
> One theologian to another. A question of theology?

> CALHOUN
>
> Very well.

> REVEREND
>
> Do you believe the Lord truly forgives us our sins
> here on earth?

Calhoun is a little taken aback.

> CALHOUN
>
> The little ones, yes. The big ones? Perhaps in
> heaven, but not on this earth. This is where we
> pay, Reverend Mercer. I'm not a believer in a
> merciful God.

> REVEREND (slowly)
>
> Nor am I.

Reverend turns, proceeds up the stairs.

INT. — HOTEL MONTCLAIRE, REVEREND'S ROOM — LATE DAY

The Reverend reading his Bible. He's naked, sitting on the bed by the little table and he's got the whisky bottle nearby. He reaches for it, pulls a long drink, and there's a KNOCK at the door. The Reverend pulls on his pants and answers the door. It's David.

> REVEREND
>
> Let me guess. The price of my horse has gone up
> and I supply the curry comb.

David sniffs.

> DAVID
>
> Smells like a drunk's nest in here. And like maybe
> you been greasing your axle.

> REVEREND
>
> I've been known to pull it from time to time.
> That's natural. A boy your age ought to know
> about that.

DAVID
Yeah. But I got an excuse. I'm too young for
women.

The Reverend leaves the door open and goes back to his position on the bed,
picks up the whisky bottle and chugs it. David watches him carefully, comes
inside, and closes the door.

DAVID
Thought you preachers don't approve of strong
drink.

The Reverend takes another slug from the bottle.

REVEREND
I don't. But I drink it anyway. Medicinal
purposes. Something I can do for you, boy, or you
just come over here to give me a temperance
lecture and find out if I pull my joint?

David grins.

DAVID
Sure you're a preacher?

REVEREND
Sure as I am that you're a nosy, bothersome boy.
Git to it, or git out.

DAVID
You any good with that pistol?

REVEREND
I generally hit what I aim at.

DAVID
Figured you did. I want a shooting lesson. I'd pay
for it.

The Reverend studies David for a moment.

REVEREND
Why you want to learn so bad?

DAVID
Papa says I ain't much at the things a man ought
to know. Says I'm a dreamer.

REVEREND
My father said the same about me.

DAVID
Did he beat the hell out of you regularlike?

REVEREND
He beat hell into me, son. He didn't think I
measured up.

DAVID
Shootin' is something a man ought to know. And I
might even be interested in that. Papa won't
teach me because he thinks I'm too stupid to
shoot a gun. He thinks the thing I'm best for is
shoveling horse poop.

REVEREND
And you want to show him?

David nods and the Reverend takes another long swig from the bottle.

DAVID
I wouldn't have figured you for a drunk, Reverend.
You look . . . I don't know. Special. Like you really
are the right hand of the Lord. You know?

This distresses the Reverend.

REVEREND (snappy)
No, I don't know. Look, I'll give you a shootin'
lesson. Tomorrow morning. I don't want your
money. I got a sermon to do Saturday night, and I
want you to get some boys, go over to the church,
and get a tent I've paid for. Cut me some poles,
and put the tent up on that hill just outside of
town. Pass out some handbills I've had made up.

DAVID
Let me see. Get the tent, cut some poles, put the
tent up, and pass out some handbills. Want me to
just go on and preach your sermon for you, too?

REVEREND
Very funny. I'll pay all the boys two bits. You get a

shooting lesson. Now go on, I've had about all of
you I can handle.

David smiles, tips his hat, and starts out.

REVEREND
Whoa. Wait!

Reverend stands, digs money from his pants, gives it to David.

REVEREND
Hire a rig from your papa. Extra dollar is for you.
We'll go out in the country and fire a few rounds.

DAVID
Thanks, Reverend.

REVEREND
Tell your pa I'm hiring you for some work. He
looks like a man likes to know his son is sweating.

David grins, goes out, shuts the door. The Reverend smiles, then the smile
slowly fades. He lifts the bottle, starts to drink. He sees himself in the
cracked mirror, the bottle uplifted, his face split in two by the crack. One
side of his face looks distorted. Perhaps it's the dust. The light. Whatever,
the Reverend stares for a BEAT, doesn't like what he sees. He jerks the
bottle from his lips and throws it at the mirror. Glass flies. Whisky splatters.

REVEREND (distressed)
I'm trying, Lord! I'm trying!

INT. — RHINE'S LIVERY — NEAR EVENING

LOFT

as the crate shifts subtly.

FULL VIEW

Billy Jack Rhine is pounding a horseshoe. Every once in a while he pauses.
Looks around furtively. Listens. SOUND of the crate moving slightly. Hay
drifts down. Rhine looks up at the loft.

RHINE
David?

Nothing. Rhine clenches the hammer, goes to the ladder, starts cautiously
up. The higher he gets, the more frightened he looks. He starts to blow his

breath, tremble slightly. He looks like a man coming down with the flu. He hurries down the ladder.

>   RHINE (cont'd)
>   David, that's you, I'll beat the hide off ya.

A BEAT. No answer. SLIGHT CREAKING SOUND.

Rhine drops the hammer, tosses a bucket of water on the forge, grabs his hat off a peg, and goes out the livery's double doors.

EXT. — LIVERY

Rhine pushes the door shut and locks it. As soon as that's done, he looks relieved.

>   RHINE (cont'd)
>   Rats. Goddamn rats.

He turns, walks briskly down the street.

EXT. — SKY — MOMENTS LATER

Clouds darken. Wind picks up. All along the street townsfolk look alarmed. They rush inside or hurry about their business. The sky continues to darken until it's as black as tar paper.

>   TIME DISSOLVE TO:

EXT. — LIVERY — CLOSE ON PADLOCK ON DOOR

Padlock drops off the latch and falls to the ground. The doors blow open.

INT — LIVERY

CREAKING SOUND as we FOCUS on crate. The lid thrown back and wobbling as if it's just been lifted. Hay is twirling in the wind.

EXT. — LIVERY

A black cloud BLUSTERS out of the livery and into the street and BLOWS away with a SCREAMING noise.

Livery doors SLAM shut.

Latch closes.

Padlock jumps into place.

Wind slows. Dies.

Sky lightens. Clears.

It's NIGHT and the MOON floats HIGH and BRIGHT.

EXT. — MUD CREEK ALLEYWAY — A LITTLE LATER

NATE FOSTER, a well-dressed banker with a beard and top hat, comes out of the bank and locks the door. It's obvious he's drunk as a skunk. He's singing "Buffalo Gals" and is walking a little too carefully. He takes a metal flask from his coat pocket, opens it, and sucks at it.

TRACK NATE

until he comes to a dark alley and goes in. He puts the flask away, uses the alley wall for support, goes down a ways, stops next to a large trash crate with this written on it: MOLLY'S TRASH ONLY. The crate is overflowing. A lot of what we see are uneaten biscuits from Molly's, the biscuits Montclaire warned the Reverend about.

Nate turns to face the wall and works with his fly. He takes a leak. When he's finished, he turns and trips over something.

                              NATE
                         Goddamn it!

Nate carefully lights a match, and has some difficulty doing it, due to his condition. What he sees in the match glow is a —

BIG UGLY DOG

It's dead, and its throat is ripped out.

BACK TO SCENE

                         NATE (cont'd)
                           Sheeeit!

Nate wobbles to his feet. Match burns his fingers. He drops it. Sticks his finger in his mouth. He reaches into his coat pocket and gets out the metal flask. He unscrews it, dips his burned finger into the bottle, licks the finger. He takes a swig from the bottle. He points and speaks to the dog.

                         NATE (cont'd)
               Somethin' damn sure got your ass, Rover.

                  VOICE (O.S.) (sandpaper and gravel)
                           Sure did.

Nate wheels toward the voice, and it's a big dark shape of a man. We know him as the INDIAN. The Indian wears a wide-brimmed hat and a black serape. He's big and steeped in shadow. He's tall, as in REAL TALL.

NATE (terrified)
You! No!

Frightened, Nate scrunches up his face, bends over, pukes all over the man shape. All we can see of the Indian is a dim outline of features and his eyes glowing like two fanned coals. Indian looks down at himself, at Nate's puke. He takes Nate's head in his hands.

INDIAN
Not nice. Not nice at all.

Indian squeezes Nate's head so hard the eyeballs pop out like golf balls, the teeth jump like popcorn, and the brains leap from his skull like overboiled cauliflower; it's one big red, gray, and white blossom that SPRINKLES the scene, and we —

CUT TO:

EXT. — STAGE TRAIL — NIGHT

Moonlit. Trees stand like sentinels.

CAMERA WANDERS off the trail, into the woods. There's a cracking sound beneath the trees, then, like a Polaris missile going off, Nolan's head POPS out of the ground, tossing dirt. His eye patch is turned up, the empty eye socket is full of dirt. The wound on his face is really ugly now. It writhes with happy worms.

Hands and arms work at the dirt next to Nolan. The Gambler tears his way out of the dirt, wobbles to his feet dripping grubs. His neck is broken and his head hangs well over on his shoulder; looks like a half-filled sack of onions. His neck is elongated, like pulled taffy.

Lulu works her way free, dried leaves falling off of her. She actually looks kind of happy.

Then up comes Shotgunner. He doesn't look any dumber dead than he did alive. As he comes out of the ground and stands, a big mound of dirt and leaves on his belly sheds, and beneath it, clinging to him like a straw monkey, is the little girl, Mignon. She's holding her rag doll. Shotgunner rakes her off. She hits the ground and rolls. We get our first good look at her face. It's one nasty face. Being dead does not become her.

Now Florence is pulling out of the ground. She looks oddly sweet-faced, considering her mouth and nostrils are filled with dirt. She's missing a shoe.

Nolan and Gambler bump into each other, exchange hairy eyeballs. Nolan hauls off and hits the Gambler so hard his rubbery neck swings his head far right, then left, and back again. It comes to rest on the Gambler's opposite shoulder.

Mignon, still clutching her rag doll, tries to climb up Shotgunner's leg. He reaches down, grabs her by the leg, starts walking, carrying her so that her head hangs upside down. She accepts this, dangles in his grasp, holding her doll the way she's held.

The Dead Folk walk out of the woods, onto the stage trail, and head toward town.

INT. — SHERIFF'S OFFICE

Matt and Caleb sharing a bottle of whisky.

> CALEB
> Tonight reminds me of the time we hung that
> Injun. Great hangin' weather. Crisp and cool.

> MATT
> Don't start, Caleb.

Caleb reaches inside his shirt, produces a strand of rawhide from around his neck. The strand is decorated with beads and a small, human ear.

> CALEB
> Real pretty, don't you think? I get a gun barrel
> just thinkin' about it.

> MATT
> Jesus. Put that thing away.

> CALEB
> Getting squeamish in your old age, ain't you, Matt?

Matt pushes his chair back, gets up, and grabs his hat off the hat rack. As he puts it on

> MATT
> Tired of seeing it is all. Why in hell I tolerate your
> company is beyond me. I'm gonna make my
> rounds.

> CALEB
> Do that. Me, I'm gonna sit right here and keep
> this bottle company. It's a hell of a lot more
> entertainin' than you are anyway.

EXT. SHERIFF'S OFFICE — NIGHT — MOMENTS LATER

Matt adjusts his hat, looks out at the night. His expression changes as we go —

CLOSE ON MATT

closing his eyes, and we HOLD A BEAT.

MATT OPENS HIS EYES

and we've FALLEN BACK IN MEMORY TO —

PULL BACK WIDE

Matt is dressed differently and the street is filled by a crowd. Caleb is leading them. Rhine, Shotgunner, Nolan, Nate, town familiars are here.

Crowd is moving toward Matt who has his hand on his revolver butt. They look less than friendly.

> CALEB
> Let us by, Matt. We want that Injun and his
> nigger, and we aim to have 'em.

> MATT
> They deserve a fair trial. I can't do that.

> CALEB
> Sure you can, Matt. Can't he, boys?

Crowd crows in agreement.

> MATT
> It's for the law to decide.

DAVID WEBB

a distraught fella wearing a long billed cap, steps to the forefront.

> WEBB
> It was my daughter they murdered, Sheriff. What
> kind 'a trial's needed for that? Now, you step
> aside and let justice be done. Ain't no one gonna
> think less of you for doin' what you oughta.

MATT

holds his ground, but gradually loses his resolve. He puts his revolver away, hangs his head, steps aside.

CROWD

rushes the jail.

MATT

lifts his head, OPENS HIS EYES, and we're —

BACK TO THE PRESENT

Face beaded with sweat, Matt shakes as if chilled, steps into the street, starts to walk. He goes by the DEAD DOG SALOON. We HEAR a tinny piano and a DRUNK WHORE SINGING.

Matt continues past storefronts, grabbing the knobs, shaking them, checking to make sure they're locked. He comes to the alley that runs alongside Molly McGuire's, not paying that much attention.

ALLEY

A SHADOW CRAWLS up the wall, swells into the shape of a large man wearing a flat-brimmed hat.

BACK TO SCENE

Matt senses something, snaps a look down the alley, sees nothing. He doesn't notice the shadow on the wall. It's too close to him, too big for him to really discern what it looks like. But we see it looming over him, leaning away from the wall, as if at any moment it will drop down on him like a bird of prey.

A NOISE like something SLITHERING.

Matt jerks his revolver.

WE SEE THE SHADOW

change shape, appear to be a great taloned hand, and the talons reach out quickly and flow away into the greater darkness of the alley.

MATT

jerks a look at the wall.

No shadow.

Matt is getting seriously worked up at all this rustling and movement he can't quite discern. He looks back down the alley, tries to peer into the darkness.

                                MATT
                             Who's there?

Out of the darkness, along the alley floor, in a RUSH, flows the shadow, a shadow like a liquid version of the man in the flat-brimmed hat. The shadow washes up close to Matt's boots.

Matt jumps back, points the revolver at —

A SHAPELESS BLOB OF SHADOW at his feet.

Matt breathes a deep sigh of relief. He relaxes. He puts the revolver away.

FROM THE DARKNESS, a VOICE that sounds as if it's made of glass and asphalt —

                             VOICE (O.S.)
                        You are not forgotten.

Shadow at Matt's feet MOVES and CLUTCHES one of his boots.

Matt panics, jerks the boot loose, bolts up the street.

TRACKING MATT

Nothing is visible behind him, but the walls along the street show his RUNNING SHADOW, and the CLOSE SHAPE-SHIFTING SHADOW of his pursuer blowing along.

The shadow is like a chameleon silhouetting the inhabitants of hell. Sometimes a MAN SHAPE, sometimes a SPIDER SHAPE, sometimes a WOLF SHAPE, yet not quite any of these things.

It's in hot pursuit of Matt, who is picking up his pace. Behind him the SHADOW BECOMES a LARGE SET OF TEETH-FILLED JAWS SNAPPING at his head. A wind HOWLS behind him like a hungry wolf. Dust KICKS UP in the street as the thing gives chase.

THE CHURCH

looms before Matt at the end of the street, the cross on the steeple forms its own shadow, and it falls toward Matt.

Matt runs toward the church, losing his hat. He charges onto the church steps, turns with his back to the door, pulling his revolver.

MATT'S POV

Nothing.

Street is empty.

The moon is high and bright.

BACK TO SCENE

Matt slowly calms. He begins to smile, weakly.

>   MATT
>   I'm a damn fool. Jumpin' at shadows.

Matt holsters his revolver, wanders out into the street. He picks up his hat, turns it over. CROWN HAS BEEN BITTEN out of it.

>   MATT (cont'd)
>   Jesus Christ and two disciples!

WIND makes a SOUND LIKE LAUGHTER, then —

>   STONE DEAD SILENCE.

EXT. — RHINE'S LIVERY

As a monstrous INDIAN-SHAPED SHADOW, black as the pit, flows across the screen and starts to fall apart like wet construction paper, strikes the ground, glides like oil toward the livery, and —

ON THE DOORS

Lock drops.

Doors fly open with a sigh.

Oily Shadow flows inside and joins the darkness there.

Doors close.

Lock jumps into place.

INT. — LIVERY

Flowing blackness takes shape halfway up the ladder and becomes the Indian, at least so we know it's him but not so we really get a good look at his face yet. Indian finishes off his climbing. Lid to the crate opens, and —

INSIDE THE CRATE

is a nude, mauled, female body.

BACK TO SCENE

Indian steps into the crate, adjusts the corpse into his arms, stretches out inside, and though we're still not going to get a clear look at his entire face, we go —

CLOSE ON ONE OF THE INDIAN'S EYES

A tear squeezes out. Runs down his cheek. A shadow slowly covers his face as the lid to the crate comes down, as if pulled shut by a ghostly hand.

EXT. — STAGE TRAIL — MOMENTS LATER

The Dead Folk, and they're gettin' it on. The Gambler is the best walker, and it's almost as if it's a race. He looks behind him now and then to check the position of the others. Positions noted, he picks up his pace, smiles stupidly. He's got just enough brain to be happy he's ahead.

A partial lightening in the trees. The sun is rising. The Dead Folk note this, make excited grunting noises. They start looking left and right. All except the Gambler, he's too into being first. He's really hoofing it now.

Florence stops suddenly, looks through the trees. There's a house out there. She cocks her head like a curious puppy.

FLORENCE
Sisssder   Sisssder . . . Millie . . . Millie . . .

Florence starts toward the house, steps in a hole, falls down. Gets up. She has a mouth full of dirt from the fall.

The sun is coming up fast now. Florence nears the house. Smoke starts to rise off of her. She begins to get agitated. She sees a root cellar and makes for it, throws open the doors and starts inside.

INT. — ROOT CELLAR

Dark and half full of brackish water. Mason jars of food float about. Water moccasins swim about. Florence comes down the steps, letting the root cellar doors fall shut behind her. She goes into the water, sinks out of sight beneath it. A huge water moccasin swims over the spot where she went down.

EXT. — STAGE TRAIL.

Except for the Gambler, who is out of sight, the other Dead Folk have abandoned their walk. They're off the trail, smoking in the emerging sunlight, digging frantically in the dirt, tossing it and leaves over them.

ON DOWN THE TRAIL

Gambler is going around a bend. He's lost the others. He looks back and is
as happy as if he had good sense. Smoke is starting to rise up from the top of
his head. Mud Creek is visible in the distance.

INT. — REVEREND'S ROOM

He's up and washing his face in the water basin, looking at himself in a
fragment of the mirror. He doesn't like what he sees. He dries off, goes to
the window, looks out.

REVEREND'S POV

Sees Gambler shuffling down the street, little trails of smoke rising up from
him like a half-crushed cigarette.

He watches as Gambler goes to the saloon. It's locked. Gambler grabs the
doorknob and begins to pull on it. He looks frantically about. The sun is hot
and yellow now.

Gambler panics. He's starting to smoke like chicken left too long on the grill.
Little bursts of flames lick around his head and hands. He grabs the knob
and jerks hard.

His arm comes off at the elbow with a RIP, his hand still clutching the knob.

> GAMBLER (gargle-spoken)
> Dang.

Gambler uses his good hand to pry the arm loose. He sticks it in his coat
pocket, elbow down. He's really cooking now. He turns, bolts into the street.
He bursts into flames, starts to fall apart. He begins to look as if he is made
of oatmeal and Gummy Bears. He falls flat in the street with a SPLATTING
SOUND.

REVEREND

has run out of the hotel and is in the street. He goes over to the smoking
mess that was Gambler, reaches down, touches him. He recoils in horror.
His hand is dripping flesh the consistency of snot.

> REVEREND
> By the saints.

A HAND

on the Reverend's shoulder —

AND WE'RE TALKING CHAIN LIGHTNING WITH A HOT COAT
HANGER UP ITS ASS, as the REVEREND WHEELS, comes to a crouch
with his revolver drawn, fitting it snugly over the tip of a man's nose. It's the
older man who was with Abby. Hereafter known as DOC.

Standing nearby is Abby.

>   DOC
>   Whoa! We're Good Samaritans like yourself. We
>   saw him fall . . . Lord, but you're fast.

Reverend slowly replaces the .36 Navy in his waistband. His eyes go to Abby.

>   REVEREND
>   Sorry. Guess I'm a bit jumpy.

Doc leaning over the body.

>   DOC
>   Looks like he's been dead a week.

>   REVEREND
>   Listen! That man was walking.

>   DOC
>   Don't mess yourself, son. I know that. Somehow
>   the sun did this to him. Wait here. I'll be right
>   back.

Doc goes off, Reverend turns to look at Abby. She smiles. They look at the
dead man, smoking pleasantly in the sunlight. An eyeball rolls out of the
Gambler's head and swirls on the ground like a top, goes still. Reverend
turns back to Abby, nods in the direction the Doc went.

>   REVEREND
>   Your father.

>   ABBY (nodding)
>   He's a doctor.

Reverend looks at the decimated Gambler, whose teeth are falling out of his
head, one at a time, like hardened corn from an old cob.

>   REVEREND
>   Seems a little late to me for that.

Doc hoofs back into the scene pushing a wheelbarrow with a shovel in it.

> DOC
> Shovel him into the 'barrow, son, and try not to
> get too much dirt with him.

Reverend takes the shovel and moves toward the mess.

> DOC
> By the way. I didn't get your name. I'm Doc
> Peekner. This is my daughter, Abby.

As the Reverend scoops up the first steaming shovelful of Gambler.

> REVEREND
> Reverend Jebidiah Mercer. Glad to meet you, I'm
> sure.

INT. — DOCTOR'S OFFICE

The office is attached to living quarters. There's a table and most of the Gambler is heaped there. He's still steaming and gurgling and popping, but it's slowing down. Abby and the Reverend stand by the table watching in amazement. Doc has a trowel and he's scraping the trowel loudly along the sides of the wheelbarrow, getting what residue he can. The Gambler's clothes dangle on the side of the wheelbarrow. The Gambler's boots are beside the wheelbarrow.

Doc finishes scraping and slaps a big slab of goo off the trowel onto the table. He drops the trowel, grabs the Gambler's boots, sets them on the edge of the table, and delicately removes the socks from inside the boots with tongs, gets the socks by the toes, upends them. Dissolving bone, flesh, and blood the consistency of cough syrup slides out of the socks onto the table.

> DOC
> What a mess. You two go make some coffee. I'll
> finish up here. I'll probably have to wring his
> clothes out. I want as much of him as I can find.

DOC'S KITCHEN

Abby is pouring a cup of coffee for the Reverend, who is sitting at the table. She pours herself a cup, perches on a counter. She looks very fetching there, and the Reverend can't keep his eyes off of her.

> ABBY
> With my father being a doctor, I've been around

death all my life. Been his nurse since I was
sixteen. But I've never seen anything like that.

Even as the Reverend talks, his eyes stick to Abby like flypaper.

> REVEREND
> Closest thing I've seen is a slug. You pour salt on
> a slug, it'll do like that.

> ABBY (smiling)
> Do you usually look this dreamy when you talk
> about salting slugs, or do you have something else
> in mind?

The Reverend, embarrassed.

> REVEREND
> Sorry. You're a very attractive woman.

> ABBY
> I know. Every man in town has told me. At least
> twice. I thought perhaps you might have a fresh
> approach.

The Reverend, looking stupid.

> REVEREND
> I suppose not.

> ABBY
> You never did answer my question. Do you have
> something in mind?

> REVEREND
> Perhaps. But I'm not sure it's proper to
> mention it.

> ABBY
> Don't be such a stuffed shirt, Reverend.

> REVEREND
> Calling me Jeb ought to help.

> ABBY
> Jeb then.

Reverend looks as if he might actually say what's on his mind. But instead —

> REVEREND
> I'd better be going. I promised a boy a shooting
> lesson this morning. We'll be driving out of town,
> so I need to get started.

> ABBY
> Sounds wonderful. What say I invite myself
> along? We'll make a picnic of it.

Before Reverend can respond, Doc enters scene drying his hands on a towel.

> DOC
> It's not like anything I've seen or heard of. I don't
> think it's a disease of some kind. And I've never
> heard of anyone being that sensitive to the sun.

> REVEREND
> Then what is it?

> DOC
> I've got some ideas . . . But they're just ideas. I'll
> need some time to think on it. Do some research.

Doc wanders over to the stove, picks up the coffeepot, and pours himself a cup. He's obviously distracted. Abby slips off the counter and moves next to the Reverend.

> ABBY
> Dad, the Reverend and I were discussing going
> on a picnic, weren't we, Reverend?

The Reverend hesitates only a moment.

> REVEREND
> Yes. We thought that might be a nice idea.

> DOC
> Can't abide them. Damn ants and dirt. Critters
> gettin' in the food —

> ABBY
> Dad?

> DOC
> What?

> ABBY
> You weren't invited.

Doc turns to see Abby taking the Reverend's arm as he rises from the chair.

> DOC
> Oh.

EXT. — MAIN STREET — WAGON TRAVELING — LATER

Reverend is holding the reins and Abby is sitting next to him. In the back of the wagon is David, looking sullen.

> DAVID
> You didn't say nothin' about no girl.

Reverend and Abby ignore him, smile to each other.

EXT. — STAGE TRAIL — LATER

Abby is laying out a blanket under a tree, preparing the picnic goods. Reverend is standing next to the stage trail, looking across it.

On the other side, David is finishing jabbing sticks into the ground. He runs back to the Reverend's side. In one hand he's holding more short, sharpened sticks.

When David is next to him, the Reverend removes his revolver from his waistband.

> REVEREND
> This is a thirty-six Navy revolver; eighteen sixty-
> one model.

> DAVID
> I don't care what it is. I just want to shoot it.

> REVEREND
> Always know your weapon, David. It has been
> converted from cap and ball to modern
> ammunition.

> DAVID
> Why don't you just get a new one?

> REVEREND
> This one has done well by me.

Abby has finished laying out the picnic goods. She's watching them.

                              ABBY
          You two going to shoot or talk those sticks to
          death?

Reverend looks back at Abby and smiles.

                            REVEREND
                            Good point.

The Reverend wheels, and he's FAST, VERY, VERY FAST, and the Navy
barks. BLAM! BLAM! BLAM! BLAM! BLAM!, and the sticks fly in half,
and David, mouth wide open, looks in amazement at what's been done. The
echo of gunfire is still dying as the Reverend removes the empty shell casings
from the Navy, drops them in his pocket, starts to reload.

David cranks his mouth up.

                             DAVID
                        God All Mighty!

                       REVEREND (casual)
          Watch your language, son. The Lord is not nearly
          as enthused with good shooting as we are.

                             DAVID
          You must be as good as Wild Bill Hickok was.

                   REVEREND (matter of factly)
          Most likely better. Your turn. Go put up some
          more sticks.

Abby comes over.

                              ABBY
                 You're pretty sure of yourself.

                            REVEREND
             Yes, I am. On the matter of shooting, anyway.

The Reverend accidentally drops a shell casing on the ground, bends to
retrieve it, spies —

A SPIDER

on the ground.

BACK TO SCENE

Reverend jerks up and stomps the spider, good and hard, too
enthusiastically. He's a little breathless.

> ABBY
> I take it you don't like spiders.

> REVEREND
> Despise them. When I was a boy, my father
> locked me in a closet as punishment for some
> childhood silliness that I forget. He was like that.
> A stern man. The closet was full of spiders.

Reverend picks up the casing, drops it in his pocket, finishes loading the gun.

> ABBY
> I'm sorry, Jeb.

> REVEREND
> I was bitten several times. I can't see one, or
> anything that looks like one, without feeling a
> certain . . . alarm. Queasiness.

David comes running back. The Reverend gets behind him, leans over a
shoulder and hands him the revolver, guiding his hand with his own.

> REVEREND
> Don't aim. Just imagine you're lifting a finger and
> pointing at one of the sticks. Soft squeeze on the
> trigger.

VIEW FROM THE STICKS

as David fires three times in quick succession, missing wildly.

BACK TO SCENE

As the Reverend takes the revolver and takes out the spent casings and
reloads with fresh shells.

> REVEREND
> You're trying too hard. You've got to become one
> with the gun.

> DAVID
> Can I put it in my belt and draw it?

REVEREND
Only if you want to lose your manhood.

DAVID
You mean I might shoot my pecker off?

REVEREND
Precisely.

Abby chuckles. David takes note.

DAVID
Sorry, ma'am. I forgot you were there.

ABBY
Quite all right.

The Reverend turns toward the targets.

REVEREND
You've got to kinda feel into it. Like this!

Smoke and thunder. Hot sulphur blisters on a clear, blue sky. The Reverend jerks the revolver up, fires three times, POW! POW! POW! Three sticks jump apart close to the ground.

Reverend tosses gun to his other hand. Three more shots. Three more twigs jump to pieces.

The Reverend twirls the gun, tosses it, catches it with the other hand, twirls it, sticks it in his waistband.

DAVID
Wow!

Abby strolls over, looks falsely stern.

ABBY
Show-off.

The Reverend doesn't miss a beat.

REVEREND
Vanity's a sin, Abby. I wouldn't want to teach the
boy bad habits. I'm just showing him the
mechanics of the gun.

ABBY (smiling)
I think you're showing me the mechanics.

> REVEREND
> That, too. David, run see how I did.

David squatting over the sticks. He's counting them.

> DAVID
> One. Two. Three. Four. Five. Six . . .

David notes that one of the sticks is not a stick. It's smoking. He leans close for a look.

INSERT WHAT DAVID SEES

A dirty finger shot off at the second knuckle. Smoke drifts up from it.

> DAVID
> Reverend! Come quick!

BACK TO SCENE

Reverend and Abby come running. The Reverend bends down, digs around the finger, reveals a human hand. He digs some more, uncovers part of the corpse's chest, then the face. The face is full of happy, white grubs. The wound on his face is the most active part. This is in fact the ballroom of the grubs. The face begins to steam.

> DAVID
> It's Nolan, the missing stage driver.

> REVEREND
> Run back to the wagon, David. Get a blanket.
> Quick!

EXT. — STAGE TRAIL   THE WAGON TRAVELING

Reverend and Abby on the front seat. The body is in the back with the blanket over it. David is sitting on the open tail end of the wagon as it rumbles along.

> DAVID (to self)
> Some picnic. Some shootin' lesson.

INT. — WAGON — ON BLANKET COVERED CORPSE

One hand is outside the blanket. It's smoking in the sunlight. Flesh is falling off of it in meaty, green strips. Unseen by anyone, the hand slithers beneath the blanket to safety.

EXT. — MUD CREEK — LATER

Wagon with Reverend driving pulls up in front of the Doc's office. Reverend gets down off the wagon, helps Abby down. As he walks to the back of the wagon, he speaks to David.

> REVEREND
> Better get this rig back to your father. I'm going
> to haul the body in to Doc Peekner.

Reverend bundles the blanket around the corpse, pulls it out of the wagon, bends and hangs the body over his shoulder.

> DAVID
> What about the shooting lesson?

Reverend stepping onto the boardwalk, followed by Abby.

> REVEREND
> That was the first. Consider on it. Right now, you
> have a tent to get up, boy.

David climbs into the driver's seat, takes the reins, releases the brake. He looks a little dejected.

> DAVID
> I think I got the short end of this stick.

INT. — DOC'S OFFICE — LATER

Doc. Abby. Reverend. They're bending over Nolan's corpse, which is on a table. In a large tub, on ice, is the naked body of Nate Foster. Nate's head looks as if it's been in a vise. He's got dissolved patches of skin all over, as if acid has been dropped on him. Doc nods toward the tub.

> DOC
> They brought the banker, Nate Foster, in after
> ya'll left. Wanted me to look him over before the
> undertaker got hold of him.

> ABBY
> What could have done that to his head?

> DOC
> I don't know. They found him out back of
> Molly's. There was a dead dog found nearby.

Sheriff thought the dog did that to him. But teeth
didn't crush Nate's head. It's more like he's had it
in a vise. And if somehow it was the dog, how'd
the dog get dead. Suicide? Ripped out its own
throat? Another thing. Watch this.

Doc goes over and pulls a heavy curtain open. Sharp sunlight hits Nate in the
tub and Nate starts to sizzle. Flesh drips off of him.

> DOC
> That was startin' to happen to him in the alley. I
> got him in here, out of direct sunlight, it stopped.
> Watch Nolan now.

Doc pulls the curtain wider, so that the sunlight hits the table where Nolan
lies. Nolan starts to drip flesh, like liver sliding off porcelain.

Doc drops the curtain over the window. Dissolving ceases.

> DOC
> Sunlight's poison to their flesh.

> REVEREND
> Same as the man this morning.

> DOC
> Correct. Though that old boy had a considerably
> more generous dose.

Doc directs their attention to a shelf full of very large specimen jars.

TRIO'S POV

Jars have crude paper labels glued to them. The labels read, and the jars
contain: HEAD FRAGMENTS. LEG FRAGMENTS. TOES. PENIS.
TESTICLES. SOMETHING OR ANOTHER. BRAIN. GUTS. Etc.

BACK TO SCENE

> DOC
> Except for the man this morning, I don't believe
> sunlight is what did them in though. Nate's head
> was crushed.
> (Nods at Nolan)
> Nolan was bitten by something. An animal maybe.
> Though it's not like any bite I've seen. There's

been a serious loss of blood . . . Another curious
point is sunlight affects them dead or alive.

REVEREND
So you're not any closer to a solution?

DOC
Perhaps . . . Not sure I want to tell you this,
Reverend, but you're a man who deals with
immortal souls, and I think you're the one to hear
it. Reverend, do you believe the dead can walk?

ABBY
What?

Doc ignores her. He keeps his eyes on the Reverend, observing his reactions.

REVEREND
I suppose so. Lazarus walked.

DOC
I'm talking about the Living Dead, not returning
from the dead.

REVEREND
You mean Nosferatu? Ghouls? Zombies? I've
read of such things.

DOC
God help me, Reverend. That's exactly what I
mean. Do you think I'm crazy?

REVEREND
In God's universe I dismiss nothing. But I've
been known to doubt.

DOC
The man who fell apart in the street . . . He was
dead before he fell.

ABBY
Dad, that's ridiculous.

DOC
I been telling myself that all afternoon. But I
examined pieces of him under the microscope,

performed a couple of tests. His body was dead
decaying flesh before he fell. The sun speeded
up the decay, but I tell you, he was a walking
dead man.

                          ABBY
Dad, you know better. That defies all the laws of
science.

                          DOC
That it does. Reverend, how about curses. You
believe in those?

This one hits the Reverend in a personal manner. Something moves behind
his eyes.

                        REVEREND
                          I do.

Doc sits on the side of the tub containing Nate.

                          DOC
Both of you. Sit down.

Reverend and Abby look for a place to sit. The place is pretty well taken up
with bodies and parts, but they eventually find accommodations.

                      DOC (cont'd)
Mud Creek has a curse on it, Reverend. And I
fear everyone in this town is gonna die like a bug-
stung tomato. And the moment I saw you, sir, I
knew you were part of this thing. It was like you
were the last ingredient in the stew. You're what
finally set it all in motion . . . I think maybe you
know that.

On the Reverend, and it shows on his face that he does know.

The Doc continues talking, and as he does we —

                  TIME DISSOLVE TO FLASHBACK:

EXT. — MUD CREEK, MAIN STREET — ONE MONTH EARLIER

A medicine-show wagon. Driving is the Indian. He looks better here than
the way we've seen him. Healthier. Human. Beside him is a beautiful light-

skinned African-American woman, hereafter known as THE INDIAN'S
WOMAN.

The wagon's sideboard reads:

> Good Medicine, Fortunes, and Cures

The street is full of people and they're turning to check this unusual wagon
and couple out.

> DOC'S VOICE
> About a month ago, this wagon rolled into town.
> An Indian was driving. He was huge. Powerful-
> looking. Had a good-lookin' high-yeller woman
> with him.

JUST OUTSIDE OF TOWN BENEATH A LARGE OAK

The Indian's Woman is sitting at a table under the oak, reading an elderly
woman's palm. She's talking. We can't hear what she's saying, but it's obvious
the elderly woman is engrossed. Nearby, the Indian is selling bottles of
medicine, lickety-split, to eager customers.

> DOC'S VOICE
> Bein' Indian and Colored, they might have got
> run out the first day they showed up, if they
> hadn't been such a curiosity . . . The Negress read
> palms, the Indian sold medicine, and it wasn't
> alcohol laced with sugar and vinegar. It was
> medicine that worked.

MUD CREEK, MAIN STREET

An older lady, Mrs. Jameson, is holding out her hands to a circle of surprised
townsfolk. The Doc is among them.

> DOC'S VOICE
> Mrs. Jameson was just one of many examples.

> MRS. JAMESON
> Look! Look! You've all seen 'em before. Like
> knotted plow lines.

She rushes to Doc Peekner, holds her hands out to him.

> MRS. JAMESON (cont'd)
> You know how they was, Doc. Wasn't nothin' you

could do helped. But look at them. He gave me a
salve, and it worked.

Doc takes her hands, looks at them amazed.

> DOC 'S VOICE
> She'd had the misery for years, and in a week's
> time of using the Indian's medicine, she had
> hands like a twenty-year-old.

INDIAN'S WAGON   NIGHT

There's a campfire. The horses are tied nearby. The Indian is leaning against
the wagon, watching the Doc like a hawk. Doc, hat in hand, is talking to the
Indian's Woman. She's listening intently. She has a friendly look on her face.
We can't hear them, but we hear his V.O.

> DOC 'S VOICE
> That Indian being able to do what he did sort of
> got my goat, I'm not ashamed to say it. After
> they'd been around a few days, I went out to
> thank them for what they'd done for the town.

Indian and Doc exchange glances. The Indian's look is one of distrust. The
Doc looks nervous. Doc finishes talking to the woman, puts on his hat.

> DOC 'S VOICE
> The Indian saw right through me. Figured I was
> hoping to latch onto a few of his healing secrets,
> which I admit I was.

Doc climbing into his buckboard, looking back at the Indian's Woman. She
looks very fetching there in the firelight.

> DOC 'S VOICE
> And the woman . . . I'm embarrassed to say this
> with Abby here, but I was attracted to her. Even
> at my age, I felt a stirring I didn't know I was
> capable of anymore. She was bewitching.

DOC IN BED

The Indian's Woman is in bed with him. It's all very surreal. Shadows jump.
Sometimes Doc seems to be rolling between the woman's legs. Other
moments a huge serpent with a woman's arms and head writhes about
his body.

>   DOC 'S VOICE
>   I had dreams about her. Not polite dreams.
>   Strange dreams.

Serpent tail wraps around his throat, starts to choke him, and —

>   DOC 'S VOICE
>   They seemed remarkably real.

DOC

sits bolt upright in bed. His face is a sweaty mess. But the scene looks
different. Normal. He's the only one in bed.

Doc realizes it was a dream, sighs, swings his legs off the side of the bed and
puts his head in his hands.

EXT. — MUD CREEK — ANOTHER NIGHT

It's raining hard. Puddles swell in the streets. Lightning cracks, jumps hot
and white in the sky. Thunder rolls. David Webb is running across the street
with a girl child in his arms.

>   DOC 'S VOICE
>   Few days later, it began to rain. Folks caught the
>   summer sickness. And, of course, they went to
>   the Indian for help.

DOC'S OFFICE — MOMENTS LATER

As David Webb bursts into the office with his rain-drenched daughter in
his arms.

>   WEBB
>   Doc, that Indian gave her somethin', and she's
>   gone limp. She's worse than she was.

Doc takes the child, puts her on a table, looks her over, touches her with a
stethoscope. He lifts here eyelids for a look. He puts a mirror to her mouth.
He turns to Webb, sadly shakes his head. Webb SCREAMS —

INT. — SALOON — LATER

Webb standing on the bar top. His daughter's body lies on the bar top beside
him, partially covered with a blanket. Webb is yelling still, crying. Pointing at
the body of his child. There's a crowd listening to him. Caleb is in the

forefront, but Nate, drunk as a loon, wobbling a little, is there, too. As are
Rhine, Nolan, Shotgunner, and Lulu.

> DOC 'S VOICE
>
> In an instant, every good thing the couple had
> done was forgotten.

> WEBB
>
> That Indian and his nigger. They poisoned my
> child. Ain't no tellin' who else they'll poison. I
> trusted them with her life, and they mocked me.
> They killed her for spite, the goddamned
> heathens. Are we gonna stand for that?

Nolan becomes prominent.

> NOLAN
>
> Hell, no.

Crowd yelling, mumbling, rushing out of the saloon, Caleb in the lead.

EXT. — JAIL.

Crowd crossing the street toward the jail. Matt steps outside of the jail, ready
to defend it against attack.

> DOC 'S VOICE
>
> The Sheriff got wind of what was happening,
> brought the couple into protective custody.

INT. — JAIL

The Indian and the Indian's Woman sitting on a cot in an open cell. The
noise outside causes the Indian to stand, to come to the open doorway of
the cell.

EXT.   JAIL

Matt, defeated, steps aside.

> DOC 'S VOICE
>
> But he didn't have enough iron in his spine.

INT. — JAIL

Crowd storms in, Lulu yelling for the men to —

LULU
Get those murderous vermin!

— and the Indian puts up a fight. A good fight. He throws men around like a
kid tossing Cracker Jacks. But he is overwhelmed. Crowd pushes over his
downed body and they grab the woman who tries to fight, but she's quickly
overcome.

EXT. — THE WOODS NEAR STAGE TRAIL — A SHORT TIME LATER

Drunken crowd has Indian perched on top of the wagon with a rope around
his neck, the other end tied to the overhanging limb of a huge oak. The
horses are hooked to the wagon. The Indian has really been worked over.
His shirt is torn, revealing on his chest a strange, hairy, uplifted mole in the
shape of a spider with a white skull-shape on its back.

Some of the thugs, Caleb and Rhine among them, come out of the woods
chuckling, carrying something bloody in a blanket. They toss the blanket on
the ground and the Indian's Woman rolls out into the dust. She's nude.
Mutilated.

Caleb holds up his blood-wet knife, waves it at the Indian. From Caleb's
wrist dangles a rawhide thong with an ear on it. The Indian looks at what
they've done to the woman. He swallows hard, but he has tremendous
composure, courage.

CALEB
This here ear's gonna make me a damn fine
necklace, Injun. I might even make me a backer
sack out your pickle, boy.

Laughter from thugs. The Indian with a countenance of steel.

WEBB
Any last words, child killer?

INDIAN

Eyes like chipped flint.

INDIAN
We did nothing to you. My woman is dead, but
you're daughter is not dead.

NOLAN
I reckon we know dead when we see it.

INDIAN
With my death, you seal your own.

The Indian raises his head to the sky. Rain splatters on his face. Lightning moves in the heavens. A drumroll of thunder.

INDIAN (cont'd)
I offer my soul to the dark one. Yogsith. Yuggoth . . .
(Trails off into unintelligible mumbles)

Rain picks up. Wind howls like a wolf with its balls in a vise.

Rhine, pushing forward out of the crowd.

RHINE
Nuff of this mumbo jumbo.

Caleb jumps forward, slaps the horses hooked to the wagon, and they bolt. The Indian swings, kicks once or twice, goes still.

LIGHTNING

hot as Satan's breath, forked as his tongue, cracks out of the wet sky and strikes the Indian, and the world goes —

WHITE for a long searing instant. Then —

Our eyes adjust, and in the Indian's place is —

THE SMOKING NOOSE. EMPTY.

But then we see something scuttling up it, heading for the sanctuary of the oak. A small but odd-looking spider with a white skull-shape on its back.

SLOW DISSOLVE TO:

EXT. — THE WOODS — LATER THAT NIGHT

Doc with a shovel, digging a grave. He has a crate by the grave and there's a lantern setting on the crate, illuminating the scene.

DOC 'S VOICE
When I heard what had happened, I hitched up
the wagon and went out and got the woman's
body and buried it in an old plow crate in the
woods.

Doc finishes off the hole. He places the lantern on the ground, drags the crate into the hole. Starts covering it up.

EXT. — MUD CREEK — STILL LATER

Doc driving his buckboard into town. There's a crowd in the street and
David Webb is frantically loading some bags of supplies into a wagon. Caleb
and the others in the crowd are mumbling to each other.

Doc stops the buckboard and stares angrily at the crowd.

> DOC
> You folks happy with what you've done? You
> bastards. Why'd you do her that way?

Webb looks up. His face is coated with sweat and fear. His eyes are as wild
as birds in flight. He stares at Doc a long instant, then picks up the last bag,
tosses it in the wagon.

Next instant, out of one of the buildings comes Webb's wife, ELVIRA
WEBB. She's carrying their daughter. Who is ALIVE and smiling.

The Doc is astonished.

> DOC
> She's alive . . .

Elvira, frantic as a pig on slaughter day.

> ELVIRA
> The medicine just put her to sleep. Deep
> sleep. She came out of it an hour ago, fit as a
> fiddle. It's your fault. You said she was dead. You
> started the whole thing. You drove my man mad.

> DOC
> She was . . . dead.

> ELVIRA
> Well, she ain't.

Webb climbs onto the wagon seat, extends a hand and pulls his daughter up.
Elvira climbs up. Webb turns to the Doc.

> WEBB
> If the medicine worked, I figure the curse he put
> on the town'll work. I'm gettin' out now. Spend
> the rest of my life makin' this up. Not that it can
> be made up.

> (Almost as an afterthought)
> Ain't your fault, Doc. I done what I done of my
> own free will.

Webb turns, clicks to the horses, the wagon starts to move.

ON CALEB

> CALEB
> Well, I ain't runnin' from a goddamned thing.
> Way I figure, one less nigger and Injun is one less
> nigger and Injun, mumbo jumbo or not, and I
> ain't gonna miss neither of 'em.

Caleb pulls the rawhide thong out of his shirt and out from around his neck
and holds it up, displaying the bloody ear.

> CALEB (cont'd)
> They're dead. Both of 'em. One got cooked to
> spit by lightning, the other'n we funned to death.
> And that's the end of that mystery. I'm gonna get
> a drink.

Caleb stalks off.

INT. — DOC'S HOUSE, BEDROOM — LATER THAT NIGHT

> DOC'S VOICE
> That night I believe the Indian sent me a sign.
> Just in case I felt free of all that had happened.
> A little reminder, that in a way, what Caleb
> and Webb and the others had done was all my
> fault.

Doc in bed. He's tossing and turning.

Lightning FLASHES outside the window.

A PEAL of thunder. Doc rolls over.

A FLASH of lightning.

QUICK LOOK at bed and the mutilated corpse of the Indian's Woman
lying, smiling, beside him.

Doc rolls with a YELL, hits the floor. Rises up slowly and looks at —

THE EMPTY BED

CLOSE ON DOC

His expression shows us he feels something nearby. He turns his head toward the window —

FLASH OF LIGHTNING —

ON THE INDIAN'S FACE

at the glass, backed by a white explosion of heavenly light.

> INDIAN'S VOICE (as if from the ether)
> Do you like the dream I sent you?

Lightning is gone. There's nothing at the window. But there is the sound of laughter. It sounds as if it's falling down a tunnel.

Then it's gone.

BACK TO THE PRESENT

Doc looks drained, frightened.

> DOC
> Sometimes I believe it was only my imagination.

> ABBY
> Dad, it was.

Doc puts his attention on the Reverend.

> DOC
> But what I believe now is this: I believe it's you
> he's been waiting for to start the ball rolling. I
> don't know why, but I feel it in my gut.

The Reverend listens, absorbs, and —

DISSOLVE TO:

DOC'S KITCHEN

Reverend and Abby.

> ABBY
> You have to forgive Dad his mumbo jumbo. I fear
> he's gotten fanatic about it since Mom died. He

reads nothing but old books on witchcraft and
demonology.

> REVEREND
> It might be said the Bible is full of that, and I
> believe it. So, why not? As for your father, I think
> he's a fascinating man . . . I find his daughter
> fascinating as well.

Abby likes that. She smiles.

> ABBY
> Perhaps this is a little undignified, Jeb. Forward.
> But I'd like to see you again.

> REVEREND
> You will. Tonight I give a sermon. Will you come?

> ABBY
> Of course . . . Jeb, what my father said about you
> being the last ingredient . . .

> REVEREND
> I believe your father is right. The Lord brought
> me here for a reason yet to be revealed. I know
> that. I've seen the signs. I accept it, and I wait. I
> had better go.

> ABBY
> Am I too forward now?

Abby grabs him, pulls him to her, and kisses him. He likes it. He kisses back.
He forces himself to pull away from her.

The Reverend. Embarrassed. Nervous.

> REVEREND
> I better go.

Reverend turns to leave. Stops.

> REVEREND
> I'm not as righteous as I pretend, Abby. Until this
> town, until you, I had begun to doubt my faith. I
> have things in my past. The Lord is trying me.

Rightfully so. I violated my calling. Even used it to
manage a sin. A sin that led to another, greater sin.

> ABBY
> It doesn't matter. Not to me.

> REVEREND
> It matters to me. It matters to God. God's
> righteous curse on me versus the evil of this town,
> and the evil curse the Indian gave the town in
> return.
> (Wry)
> God prefers to do his own damage. No help from
> devils required.

> ABBY
> You don't believe that.

> REVEREND
> I do. I must go. I have a sermon to prepare.

Before the Reverend shuts the door on his way out, he pauses to look at the
lovely, worried Abby. He smiles. Then he's gone.

ESTABLISH SUN SLOWLY SINKING

EXT. — HILL OVERLOOKING MUD CREEK

In the dying sunlight David, with several other boys, is putting up the
Reverend's tent. They're trying to raise a central pole in the middle of the
tent. They're not having an easy time of it. We can see legs scuttling like
centipedes as the partially rolled tent tangles around the boys inside.

A few boys are outside, trying to pull the sides of the tent. David is
ramroding things. He's outside yelling orders.

> DAVID
> Come on. We're running out of daylight. We'll be
> puttin' it up around him preachin', rate ya'll are
> goin'.

From inside the tent, legs only visible.

> A BOY'S VOICE
> Way you run your mouth, you ought to be
> preachin'.

> ANOTHER BOY'S VOICE
> What you ought to be doin' is using some of that
> hot air to lift this here tent up.

David, disgusted, lifts the flap, goes under the tent to help.

EXT. — STAGE TRAIL

Ground trembles, breaks open.

Fingers.

A face.

A wiggling foot.

INT. — ROOT CELLAR

Florence surfaces from the dank water. A moccasin sees her, strikes, hits her cheek, can't withdraw its fangs, flaps there like a worm on a hot griddle.

Florence, the reptile dangling from her cheek, goes up the ladder, cracks the cellar, sees red rays of the dying sun, lets the doors slam back. She looks anxious, hungry. She cocks her head. An idea has floated into her waterlogged brain.

> FLORENCE
> Millllie . . . Milllllie
> (Louder)
> Millie . . . Millie . . . Sisssder . . .

EXT. — FRONT OF MILLIE'S HOUSE

Millie is out front killing a chicken to be dressed. She has it by the feet and has its head on a chopping block. She brings down a hatchet. Off goes the chicken's head. She lets go of its feet, and it runs around headless, squirting blood, then falls dead with a quiver.

She picks up the dead chicken, starts towards the house, and the sunlight plays out and the scene turns GRAY, and we HEAR —

> FLORENCE (O.S.)
> Milllllie . . . Milllie . . .

Millie stops. Drops the chicken. Listens.

> MILLIE (tentative)
> Florence?

As Florence continues to call, Millie sticks the ax in the stump and goes around to the back of the house.

The sound is coming from the root cellar.

> FLORENCE (O.S.)
> Millllieeee . . . Milllieeee . . . Milllieee . . .

Millie walks slowly over to the root cellar.

> MILLIE
> Florence? Is that you, sister? You in there?

> FLORENCE (O.S.) (softly)
> I'm tired, Flory. I'm cold. Wet.

Millie leaps toward the root cellar doors, jerks them open.

DOWN ON FLORENCE

standing at the top of the steps. A face like death warmed over, the snake still dangling.

SHOCKED REACTION FROM MILLIE

BACK TO SCENE

as Florence shoots out an arm, grabs Millie by the throat, pulls her down as if she were made of crepe paper, simultaneously saying —

> FLORENCE
> and hungry!

Florence, clutching the surprised Millie by the throat, walks backward down the steps, the snake flapping. Millie struggles like one of the chickens. The tops of her shoes scraping on the steps. Florence backs until she pulls Millie beneath the water.

Moonlight shines through the open cellar doors, floats on the rippled water that begins to churn and boil and turn blood-red in its center.

After a moment one of Millie's legs pokes up. Kicks. Disappears.

More blood on the water.

A large bubble that swells and pops and causes a massive ripple.

Ripple subsides.

Calm water. Spreading blood.

EXT. — STAGE TRAIL

Dead Folk shuffling along, lickety-split. These aren't the drag-your-ass-mummy-style walkers. These guys have got stiff joints, but they can truck.

Mignon wanders off the road, starts through a pasture. She steps in a cow plop. Stops. Looks at what's swelling around her foot. She lifts her foot, drags a finger through the shit, pokes it in her mouth, tastes, kind of turns her head side to side like she can't make up her mind if it's okay. Decides it isn't. Continues walking.

EXT. — A HOUSE

Standing in the fresh moonlight.

INT. — THE HOUSE

An OLD WOMAN in a rocking chair, knitting. An OLD MAN in an armchair, smoking a corncob pipe, reading the Bible.

A KNOCK at the door. Old couple stop what they're doing.

> OLD WOMAN
> Well, who could that be?

> OLD MAN
> We can sit here and guess, or open the door.

Old Woman gives Old Man a "you smartass" look. She gets up. Opens the door.

DOORWAY

stark against the night, Mignon and her doll. She smiles. Her teeth are full of dirt and cow plop.

BACK TO SCENE

> OLD WOMAN
> I'll swan. It's a little girl.

Old man comes to the door, looks at the child. Mignon shows him her smile. It's big and wide.

> OLD MAN
> She smells like cow shit.

> OLD WOMAN
> Watch your mouth. She's a child. She's lost.

OLD MAN
She still smells like cow shit . . . Look there. She's
got it on her shoes.

Old Woman really gives Old Man a look.

OLD WOMAN
It'll clean up . . . Come in, baby.

Mignon looks tentatively inside. Smile goes away momentarily. She steps
inside.

Old Woman bends down to her, says —

OLD WOMAN
Hungry?

The little girl nods —

AND LEAPS.

She's like a giant, starved rat. She grabs the old woman by the shoulders and
starts biting her face, and the Old Woman screams, leaps, runs around the
room, rolls on the floor. The kid hangs with her, tight as a cancerous mole.
Blood is flying.

Old Man watches in amazement. He looks around. He grabs a fireplace tool.
He goes after them.

Old Woman is lying on the floor with the little girl on top of her, tearing
savagely at her with her shit-stained teeth.

OLD MAN
Let her go, you brat!

Old Man brings the tool down hard on the back of Mignon's head. It sticks
there. Little girl freezes. Old Woman has quit moving. Old Man starts trying
to work the tool free. As he yanks and works it back and forth, it makes a
sound like someone walking while wearing tight shoes full of water.

Mignon turns slowly to look unpleasantly at the Old Man, and as she does,
the tool tears free of her flesh.

Old Man swings down with the tool again.

Mignon catches it with one hand, pulls it away from him.

And BAM! Mignon hits him on the foot with it, drops it, leaps on him, leaving the bleeding, barely moving Old Woman lying there, a pool of blood forming around her.

Old Man runs around the room with Mignon holding on to him. She climbs him, clings to his back. Old Man runs into a wall and goes down, and the little girl finishes him with a —

CLOSE FLASH OF NASTY KID TEETH AND A SPRAY OF RED —

and we're gone to MUD CREEK where we —

ESTABLISH BLACKIE MERTZ FUNERAL PARLOR AND COFFIN MAKER SHOP — THIS SAME NIGHT AND TIME, and we —

DISSOLVE TO:

INT. — FUNERAL PARLOR

Naked bodies of Nate Foster and Nolan are in cheap, open, pine coffins perched on sawhorses. The mortician, BLACKIE MERTZ, a skinny, hook-nosed man, who has been drinking, carries clothes over to Nolan's box. He puts the clothes on the side of the coffin, lifts Nolan up, starts to put the shirt, which is split down the back for convenience, on him. It's a bitch of a job anyway.

>   BLACKIE
>   Hope you boys 'ppreciate all I've done for you.
>   (Pauses)
>   Course, who the hell's gonna see you?

Blackie suddenly drops Nolan back in the box with a THUD.

>   BLACKIE (cont'd)
>   And that being the case, and since nothin's gonna
>   make you pretty, why in hell am I wastin' my time?

Blackie tosses the clothes into the box on top of Nolan.

>   BLACKIE (cont'd)
>   Keep 'em. You done stunk up the shirt.

Blackie goes around to Nate's coffin. There are dress clothes hung on the side of the box. Boots on the floor. Blackie looks inside the coffin.

>   BLACKIE (cont'd)
>   You'll do just fine way you are, too. Ain't like
>   anybody's comin' to the funeral. 'Cept worms and

flies. So you can go back the way you come in.
With your bare ass hangin' out.

Blackie chuckles to himself. He looks down at the boots.

> BLACKIE (cont'd)
> I might even be able to see your boots get
> proper wear.

Blackie picks up a boot and measures it against his own foot. Looks as if it might fit.

A NOISE BEHIND BLACKIE.

Blackie doesn't like this.

He turns slowly, still holding the boot.

NOLAN

is sitting up in his coffin, struggling frantically to get the shirt on.

> BLACKIE
> No. You're dead as hell.

Nolan still struggling with the shirt. He's getting frantic.

> NOLAN
> Don't fit.

Nolan struggles to get the shirt on, overturns the coffin. Nolan rolls out. He gets up and stands in front of Blackie. He seems more concerned with the shirt that's hanging off of him.

> BLACKIE
> But you're dead!

> NOLAN
> Still don't fit.

HANDS

from behind Blackie. They belong to —

FOSTER

who grabs Blackie by the neck.

> FOSTER
> My boots!

A RED MOMENT

as Nolan grabs Blackie from the front and teeth begin to SNAP AND RIP.

INT. — DOC PEEKNER'S OFFICE

Doc sitting at his desk. He's reading a book. It is bound in leather. The title of it is *The Necronomicon.* On the desk beside him, spine out, we glimpse *De Vermis Mysteriis, Cabal of Saboth, Book of Doches.*

CAMERA MOVES PAST DOC, TOWARD LAB DOOR.

DISSOLVES TO:

INT. — LABORATORY

PAN LABORATORY

Shelves containing Gambler's body parts in jars.

Jars rattle.

Flesh and goodies inside jars crawl.

Lids on the jars turn from the inside as blobs of flesh try to unscrew them.

DOC'S OFFICE

As there is a CRASH from the lab.

Doc lifts his head, turns slowly in his chair. Listens.

ANOTHER CRASH.

SEVERAL OTHERS.

SOUNDS OF CRUNCHING BONE. SLURPING.

Doc opens his desk drawer, removes a big horse pistol, gets up, moves toward the lab.

He stops at the door.

Puts his ear to it. Listens.

CRACKLING AND SLURPING NOISES.

LABORATORY

as the door opens and we see Doc framed by his office light. He steps inside, into the shadows. He shoves the pistol into his belt, picks up a lantern and lights it.

Lantern throws a —

BEAM OF LIGHT ON SHELVES

Shelves are empty. Except for one jar containing skeletal hands. The hands
are pushing at the jar from the inside. It rocks. Falls.

We HEAR the jar BURST behind a table and supplies.

BACK TO SCENE

Doc pulls the pistol with his free hand, moves cautiously around the table.
As he gets to one end of it, starts to peer around —

ON SKELETAL HANDS

as they SCUTTLE away, sneaking around to the other side of the table.

Doc HEARS the SCUTTLE but sees nothing except broken glass. He turns
and looks around on the other side of the table. Quickly.

NOTHING. But we hear the bony fingers scuttling. They've dodged him
again.

Doc, scared, sets the lantern on the table, turns it up, eases around the table
with the gun —

AND HANDS JUMP OUT OF THE SHADOWS AND GRAB

his pants leg and start scrambling up his body until they grab at his throat
and try to choke him.

Doc SCREAMS, drops the pistol, jerks at the hands. They come free. He
tosses them across the room.

ON HANDS

as they hit the floor and slide into a mess of something writhing.

DOC'S POV

as he snatches up the lantern for a look. And is shocked to see that the hands
have slid into a heap of maggot infested flesh that wobbles like meat on a fat
man's ass.

The skull is reassembling itself like a puzzle being snapped together.

Eyeballs roll into the skull's mouth, poke through the skull eye sockets,
adjust themselves like roulette balls coming to a stop.

Flesh leaps to the bone and the bone clicks together with a sound like dice in a Yahtzee cup.

Hair pokes out of the head.

A tongue crawls into the mouth, turns, finds its place. Flaps a few times as if tasting the air.

AND THIS MESS

starts to rise to its feet, one of which is on backward.

The monstrosity is on the major homely side. I mean, we're talking a seriously ugly patchwork dude here, known hereafter as PATCHES. Hair is poking out of the face. The skull has bare bone sections. The flesh is haphazard, and there's a nose under its chin. A few teeth stick out of its face, but there are enough in place for Patches's jaws to click together like castanets.

Patches takes in Doc with his wet, roll-around-marble eyes. He hunches a little, smiles with what it's got to smile with, and waddles toward Doc. Teeth chatter. It drags the foot that's on backward.

DOC AND PATCHES

Doc grabs up the pistol. He starts to back way. He fires off a round, and the round hits Patches in the chest, and the back of Patches's body bursts open with a leap of flesh, and the —

FLESH

hits the wall, and worms fall out of it, and the flesh slides slowly down the wall like a tossed pizza.

PATCHES

pokes a finger in the hole in his chest, and isn't happy. He's not hurt. He's pissed.

Once again, Patches starts walking.

DOC AND PATCHES

DOC gets behind the table. Patches lunges for him over the table, surprises us by how far he can reach. He clamps those bony, hair-spotted hands on the Doc's shoulders, and digs his fingers in.

Doc lets out a yell as Patches's face comes forward to bite him. Doc pokes his revolver forward, quicklike, and —

WE'RE ON PATCHES'S MOUTH

as the revolver slips right in and Patches clamps down on the gun, hard. Teeth fly out of Patches's rotten head like hot popcorn, and the barrel slides down his throat like a Deep Throat trick, and —

BLAM!

DOC AND PATCHES

as the revolver bucks and a chunk of skull leaps away, and Patches hits the floor faster than a second-rate boxer with a mob connection.

Doc leaps back, slams himself into the shelf. Shelf wobbles.

On the table edge we see Patches's ugly hands appear, grabbing, pulling himself upright.

And now he's up. Half his skull is gone, and there are some brains wobbling in the cup of his head, like oatmeal mixed with moldy Jell-O, and the brains drip out in plops and glops, and Patches, he's got one eye left, and it is on strands of tendons that dangle down around its chin.

Patches puts both skeletal palms on the table and leans forward and HISSESSSSS.

Doc grabs the lantern, tosses it. Patches ducks. Lantern hits the far wall, explodes into flames on the floor.

Patches glares at Doc, opens his mouth in a confident smile, sticks out that ugly tongue and flaps it like a curtain blowing in a breeze.

Doc leaps to the side, by the shelf, grabs it, pushes it forward, and down it comes —

PATCHES

as his one remaining eyeball lifts on its tendons for a look. His nasty bottom jaw drops like a steam shovel opening up. He tries to step away from the table, but he's too slow, and —

> PATCHES (resigned)
> Shit.

Shelf comes down hard, hits Patches in what is left of his head, drives it down to the edge of the table, clips it off clean as the guillotine that gave Robespierre the trim.

HOLD ON the table and Patches a BEAT. Patches's brains start to ooze out from between the shelf and table and drip onto the floor.

ANOTHER ANGLE ON SCENE

Doc goes around for a look. He pulls the shelf back. It's ugly under there.

He runs over and stomps out the fire made by the lantern, grabs another lantern, fires it up, hangs it on a peg.

By lantern light, he drags the corpse over to the large tub that had contained Nate Foster. He throws the body inside, grabs a bucket and trowel, scoops up Patches's brains and skull fragments on and beneath the table, dumps them in the bucket, hurries them to the tub, pours them inside.

ABBY

enters the scene carrying a candle as Doc is pouring lantern fuel in the tub. She gives the room a once over.

                    ABBY
        Dad, what in the name of heaven . . . ?

Doc takes the candle from her.

                    DOC
        Heaven had nothing to do with it.

Doc drops the candle in the tub. Flames jump. The mutilated corpse burns. Abby looks at the tub's contents with surprise.

                    ABBY
              My God!

CLOSE ON THE TUB

and the black smoke, and gradually we realize we are no longer looking at black smoke, but instead a —

DARK COTTONY CLOUD

and the cloud rolls away and reveals the moon.

PAN DOWN TO

THE HILL

Moonlight in the wind-blown trees. The tent writhing like a living thing.

BENEATH THE TENT

where all the boys are struggling to raise it. They're having a bad time of it, and the wind isn't helping. The tent flaps and heaves. David is trying to encourage everyone to lift at the same time, pushing up on a tent pole. Then, out of the corner of his eye —

DAVID'S POV

Glimpse of someone's legs outside of the tent.

ANOTHER ANGLE ON SCENE

as David waits for the wind to flap the tent up again.

The wind comes. The tent flap moves.

There's nothing out there.

Down goes the flap.

Wind again. Flap goes up.

Someone's out there. Slightly different spot. Shotgunner and Lulu. They don't look good.

Down goes the flap.

DAVID
Someone's here already.

ONE OF THE BOYS
Maybe he could just preach under a tree.

David fights the wind-blown canvas, struggles from beneath the tent.

EXT. — THE HILL

No one's there.

David glances to his left. Sees the bottom of Lulu's shoe as it pulls beneath the tent.

A SCREAM.

A SERIES OF SCREAMS and VICIOUS NOISES.

Tent shakes, starts to fall. The wind blows hard, catches the tent, fills it with air, carries it away and down the hill and out of sight.

Lulu and Shotgunner are revealed. They've got a boy apiece, and the boys are obviously dead, their necks twisted like coat-hanger wire. Lulu and Shotgunner are biting big chunks out of them.

The other boys are in a terrified heap. Now, free of the tent, they bolt down the hill like frightened mice.

David, startled, turns to follow them. Runs like the wind.

LULU AND SHOTGUNNER

enjoying their meal.

EXT. — STAGE TRAIL

Mignon and Old Man and Old Woman stumbling along. Ahead of them we see Mud Creek.

CLOSER ON MUD CREEK

and farther down the trail. Florence and Millie, dripping water, shoes slurping like sucking wounds. Florence still has that water moccasin on her face. It's flapping, trying to get out of her face. It finally grows tired and just dangles.

EXT.   MUD CREEK, MAIN STREET

Dead Folk are starting to show up in town. There's Nolan and Foster and new folks, too. Nolan has the burial shirt on now, and nothing else. And he's right about the shirt. It doesn't fit. Nate is naked except for a pair of boots.

Blackie Mertz has joined their ranks. He doesn't have a hook to his nose now. In fact, he doesn't have a nose.

And stumbling down the street in his long handles is David's father, Billy Jack Rhine. The trap door is open and his naked butt moons us.

The dead clutch up in the middle of the street. Some are coming out of buildings, dragging living victims. Like the boys who were with David. Other townsfolk.

When fresh meat arrives, the crowd gets down on them like ducks on june bugs.

FEEDING FRENZY

Flash of hands and teeth. Red gleams. Meat between teeth. One ghoul, Rhine, crunches an eyeball like a grape.

Crowd backs off, moves down the street. The recently mauled lie there. Some of the bodies are little more than raggedy skeletons.

SHOT OF THE MOON

rolling happily in the heavens.

PAN DOWN TO MAIN STREET

A bony corpse twitches. Opens its eyes. Well, one eye. The other got sucked out of its head. Corpse stands. It's sort of like a cheap erector set being pulled upright by strings.

The other corpses twitch. They struggle to stand. They seem stunned. Amazed. They start to wander down the street in search of meat. They rattle doors.

EXT. — SHERIFF'S OFFICE

Caleb running up to the door. He grabs the knob, pulls —

Locked.

He turns, looks behind him.

Dead Folk are coming toward him, and they look happy to see him.

> CALEB
> Matt! Open the door! Matt! Open the
> goddamned door!

> MATT (O.S.)
> Go the hell away. I got a headache.

Caleb glancing behind. The dead are close now. He turns back to the door, tugs.

> CALEB
> Matt! You goddamned sonofabitch. Quit pullin'
> your dick. Let me in! They're after me.

Caleb takes another look, draws his revolver, leans his back against the door.

> CALEB
> All right, then. Come and get me, you stinky-ass
> sonsabitches!

Door opens. Light. Caleb falls back and inside, just as hands snatch the air.

INT. — SHERIFF'S OFFICE

Matt stares amazed at the dead faces in the doorway as Caleb stumbles back, regains his balance, kicks one of the Dead Folk in the chest and knocks them back, upsetting some of the others like bowling pins.

> **CALEB**
> Out of the way, goddamnit!

Caleb pushes Matt aside, slams the door, bolts it.

Matt is stunned.

> **MATT**
> What in the world?

Pounding on the door.

> **CALEB**
> Well, it damned sure ain't the welcome wagon.
> Those bastards wanted to eat my ass. They're
> eatin' sonsabitches all over town. And they ain't
> cookin' 'em.

Caleb grabs one of the Winchesters out of the rack, goes over to the barred window for a look.

CALEB'S POV

Quite a crowd. It looks like a cemetery occupant convention. They're milling, moaning, watching.

> **CALEB**
> Jesus Christ with a wooden dick.

BACK TO SCENE

as Matt joins Caleb for a look.

> **MATT**
> My God, they're dead.

Caleb gives Matt a special look.

> **CALEB**
> Reckon that's why you're sheriff. You're so
> goddamned observant.

                              MATT
                          Wha . . . How?

                              CALEB
              That goddamned Indian, I reckon. That curse.
              Webb was right.

                              MATT
              What are they waiting on? What do they want?

                              CALEB
              They want supper. And we're it. As for what
              they're waitin' on, I ain't got a figure. Maybe one
              of 'em went to get the salt.

ON THE DEAD FOLK

Waiting. Milling. Drooling.

INT. — DOC'S LABORATORY

Doc and Abby are stirring what's left of Patches with a stick. There's nothing
in the tub but ashes.

                              DOC
              Only way I could stop him was destroyin' his
              brain. Whatever controls them, makes them walk,
              it comes from there, way it would if they was livin'.

                              ABBY
              But how can they live at all?

                              DOC
              They don't live. They're undead. Ghouls. It's the
              Indian, like I thought. I've been researching his
              curse. From what I can tell it comes out of the
              cult of Chtuhulu. The Indian may in fact call it
              something else, but it's the same thing. He has
              been given powers by the Old Ones to manage
              his revenge, and he, in turn, will give them his
              soul. And the souls of others. These dark gods of
              his are eaters of souls.

A CRASH FROM DOC'S OFFICE

Doc grabs the horse pistol and rushes in there. Abby follows.

DOC'S OFFICE WINDOW

It's broken and a hand is reaching in from the outside, waving around, trying to grab anything. It grabs the curtains. Pulls them down.

At the window. Nate Foster.

Doc fires a perfect shot, hits Foster dead center of the forehead. Like a board, Nate falls back.

Doc leaps to his desk, grabs a box of shells.

DOC
Get the Winchester, Abby.

INT. — REVEREND'S ROOM

He's sitting on the bed reading the Bible. He pauses, looks at his watch. He rises, casually pulls on his coat, straightens it.

NOISE at the door. The doorknob RATTLES. BANGING on the door.

The Reverend goes over and opens the door and David rushes in, almost knocking him down. Reverend grabs him by the shoulders.

REVEREND
Whoa! Whoa, boy.

DAVID
Reverend! There's a problem.

REVEREND
You got the tent up?

DAVID
Hell with the tent. There ain't gonna be no
preachin' tonight.

REVEREND
What are you saying, boy? You're father out to
whip you?

David, frightened, trying to hold it together.

DAVID
Worse. He wants to eat me. They all want to eat
me. And Daddy's in his underwear.

Reverend gives David a quizzical look.

> REVEREND
> You been nipping your old man's shine?

Reverend grabs David's chin, bends close to his face, and sniffs his breath.

Frustrated, David grabs the Reverend's arm and pulls him to the window.

> DAVID
> Look!

Reverend looks. Street is full of people, in all manner of dress and undress. They're in the process of tearing a man apart, feasting on him.

A gnawed leg flashes in the moonlight.

An arm.

A boy bursts from the frenzied huddle, runs off on all fours with a head in his mouth, his teeth clamped around an ear.

> REVEREND
> What in God's name?

> DAVID
> They're back from the dead, Reverend. And they
> want'a eat. They ain't a bit sociable neither.

REVEREND AND DAVID'S POV

From the side of Doc's office comes a HEYAH noise. Someone yelling to horses. From around the building's side, charging like steeds from hell, two horses appear pulling a buckboard. Doc's driving. Abby's in the back. She has a rifle and she's wearing bandoleers across her chest. Dead Folk are jumping onto the buckboard. She's firing damn near point-blank, blowing skulls to hell. She kicks one in the head, knocks him loose of the buckboard as the buckboard makes a corner practically on two wheels, rights itself, smashes a Dead Folk beneath a wheel rim, squirting his head in all directions.

Buckboard darts down Main Street. Dead Folk make a wall in front of the horses, foam over the buggy. Abby's still popping these suckers, one hand cocking the Winchester.

Dead woman leaps onto a horse, starts biting at its neck. Blood flies. Horse wobbles.

BACK TO SCENE

> REVEREND
> Abby!

Reverend grabs his .36 Navy off the washbasin, charges for the door.

> DAVID
> No, Reverend. No! They'll eat you.

But the Reverend's gone.

David stands where he is a moment, glances out the window.

DAVID'S POV

Horses down, kicking, screaming, their guts are being ripped and dragged out of their bodies like coils of steaming wet rope. Abby and Doc being surrounded by enthusiastic and hungry Dead Folk.

BACK TO SCENE

> DAVID
> Oh, hell.

David turns, rushes out of the room.

EXT. STREET — AND WE'RE GONNA HOT WIRE THIS BABY FROM HERE ON OUT

Dead Folk have the stranded buckboard enveloped. It's as if Abby and Doc are becalmed amid a sea of boat-climbing sharks.

Doc has his horse pistol, and he's firing it close range. Dead Folk's heads explode like overripe cantaloupes.

Abby is down to swinging the Winchester. She cracks heads. Some Dead Folk go down. Others just take the blow and keep climbing.

CLOSE ON DOC AND ABBY

back to back as the Dead Folk's hands reach for them. Dead Folk's faces circle Doc and Abby as if they are planets and their Dead Folk are orbital craft being pulled groundward by their gravity.

SUDDENLY, Dead Folk fly backward. The wall of Dead Folk starts to collapse. An opening is made, and it shows us —

THE REVEREND

He's snatching them by the hair, collars, necks, slinging them back. He kicks them and throws them. He slams the Navy against heads.

FULL SCENE

Doc, slams his horse pistol down on a woman's head so hard it creases it almost to the nose.

> DOC
> You got to destroy their brains.

Reverend shoots one of the Dead Folk through the head, and the Dead Folk does a little pirouette, goes down for a big finish.

A DEAD MAN IN OVERALLS about to grab the Reverend, who's preoccupied kicking a ravenous child away from his feet. As the child soars like a football, Dead Man in Overalls grabs the Reverend's shoulders —

ANGLE ON DEAD MAN IN OVERALLS

as an arm goes around his neck from behind, and legs wrap around his hips and a knife flashes and stabs Dead Man in Overalls in the eye.

This doesn't bother Dead Man in Overalls in the least, but it saves the Reverend, because Dead Man in Overalls lets go of him and becomes preoccupied with his rider.

Dead Man in Overalls is spinning, trying to shake what's on his back, and what's on his back is David. As they whirl around, the Reverend reaches out and snatches David free of the Dead Man in Overalls and puts a .36 Navy slug through the dead man's head, dropping him.

Our defenders have a little gap now, and they make for it, except David. He's frozen.

In front of him is

BILLY JACK RHINE

his father, his long handle flap hanging open, his butt gathering moonlight. And he's smiling, and he's turning his head from side to side as if he's trying to recognize the boy.

BEAT.

Rhine shows recognition. He takes off his belt, comes for David. Past experience holds David sure as a vise.

> DAVID (soft and sad)
> No, Daddy.

> RHINE
> Hit. Then eat. Like your mama.

> DAVID
> Mama. No!

CLOSE ON RHINE

Then his head flies apart and he falls forward, revealing —

THE REVEREND

looking over his smoking pistol.

FULL SCENE

Reverend grabs David, drags him back, and we —

TRACK

as our team makes like track stars up the street —

> DOC (yelling)
> Run for the church! It's holy ground.

Dead Folk coming. They're not Olympic material, but they're not slow either. You wouldn't want to stop and tie your shoe, in other words.

David cuts in front of Reverend. They collide, go down, Reverend flies into Doc who flies into Abby. Bowling pin reaction. They're all in the dirt.

Dead Folk let out a gasp of excitement. Things look good. Lunch is down. They start really hoofing.

Reverend rises to a knee, picks off a couple of leaders. Bullets through the brains.

Abby, Doc, and David scramble to their feet and run.

Reverend backing, reloading, firing at a few more, hitting dead center of their heads, covering his comrades' exit.

Abby and others on the church porch. Doc frantically trying to open the door, which is locked.

Abby is reloading her Winchester. David runs around to a window, beats on it —

> DAVID (yelling)
> Reverend Calhoun! Let us in, Reverend!

Doc, winded, yells to David —

> DOC
> Try around back, where he lives.

David darts away, around the side of the church.

Abby's loaded up. She makes a one-hand swing, cocking the Winchester lever. She fires.

POW. A Dead Folk down.

Abby, three times in succession SWING COCKS THE WINCHESTER AND DELIVERS FAST FIRE.

BLAM! BLAM! BLAM! Three Dead Folk eat dirt.

Reverend on the church steps now, reloading.

> REVEREND (to Abby)
> I thought you said I was a show-off.

> ABBY (laconically)
> Takes one to know one.

Dead Folk gathering like locust for the last grains of wheat. Doc looks out over the closing multitude of Dead Folk. They're happy and slobbery.

> DOC
> Looks like it's die dog or eat the hatchet.

Reverend, Abby, Doc pressed against the door.

> REVEREND
> I hope David keeps goin'.

A Dead Folk puts a boot on the porch —

AND BURSTS INTO BLUE AND RED AND YELLOW FLAMES.

> DOC
> Holy ground!

> REVEREND
> The power of God Almighty.

Door behind them opens. David and Calhoun in the light. Calhoun looks a little like a rabbit in the headlights. He can't believe what's lurking below his front porch.

Our team rushes in, closes the door, throws the heavy wooden bar.

> CALHOUN
> I'm sorry. I heard you. I thought it was them.
> They been here once already. I heard them
> outside, calling. I saw them take down poor Mrs.
> O'Fee. Oh, Jesus, they tore her apart. They
> tossed her head through a window.

Calhoun gestures. Mrs. O'Fee's head lies beneath a window of shattered glass.

> CALHOUN
> I saw what they were doin'. I wanted to help.
> There was nothing I could do. I wanted to help.

> REVEREND
> You did right. There was nothing you could do.

> ABBY (to her dad)
> Are we safe here, on holy ground?

Doc finds a pew, sits, puts his head between his hands.

> DOC
> For a time. Until their master comes.

> CALHOUN
> Master?

> DOC
> That Indian. That's what it's about, Calhoun. That
> curse he put on the town for what was done.

> CALHOUN
> But I didn't do anything. I didn't touch either
> of them.

> DOC
> It's as much for what we didn't do as what we did.
> As far as the Indian's concerned, we're all guilty.
> The whole damn town . . . And I'm not sure he's
> wrong.

REVEREND
What do you mean, we're safe until their master
comes? God stands against the power of the
devil. Whether it's the devil's lacky or the devil
himself.

Doc looks up, wears a wan smile.

DOC
You seem to think there's only one god involved
here, my friend.

REVEREND
I'll not listen to blasphemy.

Doc stands, angrily points to the door.

DOC
The blasphemy is outside that door, Reverend. And
it's got teeth. Now, do you want to hear the truth,
or do you want to talk about God's good grace?

REVEREND
Very well.

DOC
As it nears morning, the Indian loses strength.
But he's stronger than these folks he's made his
own. When he comes he will give it all he has.
Our trappings of religion will only hold him so
long. You may not believe this, but his powers of
darkness are equal to God's powers of light.

REVEREND
Even the devil bows to God.

DOC
The things that give the Indian his powers owe
nothing to the devil. Pardon me, Reverend, but the
Indian's demons would make your devil piss blood.
You don't get it, do you, Reverend? Your God.
Your devil. They're but one of many gods and
devils fighting for dominance in this world. And
they don't never get together to have no tea party.

What this town did. Who you are. Who you
represent — the Christian God. It's all been
ordained. The forces of your God against the
forces of his. It's as much a chess game between
deities as anything else. With our lives as the
stakes.
　　We're pawns, Reverend. Rooks and bishops
and knights. You're the white king. The Indian
the dark king.

The Reverend doesn't like hearing this. But he forces himself to ask.

                    REVEREND
　　Can we stop the Indian? It? Can God stop it?

                      DOC
　　The only thing that will truly contain him is the
　　sunlight. God's greatest power. But now, in the
　　dark, the Indian is nearly all powerful. The best
　　we can do is hold him until the Lord's powers are
　　at their peak.

Doc pops open his pocket watch, stares at the face of it.

                  DOC (cont'd)
　　And until daylight . . . Well, we have quite a ways
　　to go.

MEANWHILE . . .

EXT. — SHERIFF'S OFFICE

Dead Folk all over, looking through the barred windows, pushing at
the door.

INT. — SHERIFF'S OFFICE

Matt and Caleb, armed, watching hands and faces at the barred windows.

                     MATT
　　What are we gonna do?

                     CALEB
　　Unless you can chew a hole through the floor
　　with your asshole big enough for us to crawl
　　down, we're gonna fight.

A SOUND from outside. The hive sighing of the Dead Folk. Hands and faces move away from the window.

> CALEB
> What in hell?

> MATT
> Maybe they're givin' up.

Caleb moves to the window, followed by Matt.

THEIR POV

as the crowd of Dead Folk parts like the Red Sea. And there, visible through the rift of Dead Folk, is a thick cloud of insects. Fat, black flies. In their midst is the crate, supported by and surrounded by flies.

THE FLIES

consolidate to form the shape of a man, then they become solid. Abruptly, they are the Indian, walking effortlessly, carrying the big crate on his shoulder as easily as a baseball bat.

MATT AND CALEB

> CALEB
> I been to a shitload of rodeos, but I ain't never
> seen nothing like that.

> MATT
> Can't be.

> CALEB
> Better start dealing with what is, boy, 'stead of
> what you think can't be. We're about to step off
> in some deep shit, and you goddamn better be
> well ready to swim and eat turd at the same time.

EXT. — ON INDIAN

He sets the crate on the ground, long side up. He waves a hand. The lid of the crate POPS off.

INSIDE THE CRATE

The Indian's Woman. What a mess.

BACK TO SCENE

The Indian just stands there. Dead Folk crowd around him. Grovel at his feet. Touch him.

INT. — SHERIFF'S OFFICE

> MATT
> What's he doin'?

> CALEB
> Showin' us what got us in trouble in the first place. That gal of his.

> MATT
> But I tried to stop you. I tried to stop all of you.

> CALEB
> Take it up with him.

Caleb grabs the window bars, yells angrily —

> CALEB (cont'd)
> You red nigger! Git on back to hell!

ON INDIAN

suddenly gliding across the ground, Dead Folk scrambling.

Indian reaches the Sheriff's Office door, draws back his fist.

INT. — SHERIFF'S OFFICE

As the fist STRIKES, and INDIAN'S FIST slams through the wood, jerks side to side, splintering lumber. Hand grabs the wooden cross bar, flips it away.

Matt grabs a double-barrel shotgun from the rack, a fistful of shells. He and Caleb back toward the jail cells as Dead Folk peer around the Indian like shy kids looking around a parent.

Matt's got the shotgun loaded. He's backing up, holding it, waiting for the right moment.

Caleb switches the Winchester to his left hand, draws his revolver, and calmly FIRES SIX TIMES in rapid succession at the Indian as his hands move VERY FAST, plucking the bullets from the air.

Indian smiles. Opens his clenched fists.

INSERT: FISTS

He's got all of Caleb's bullets.

Closes his hands.

Opens them again.

Six plump bluebottle flies buzz up from his palms and fly away.

BACK TO SCENE

Matt cuts loose with both barrels of the shotgun.

Blasts hit the Indian. Chunks fly out of him, splatter all over the Dead Folk behind him.

CLOSE ON INDIAN

as the gaping wounds reseal themselves. His clothes rethread.

BACK TO CALEB AND MATT

Caleb tosses down his revolver and pumps Winchester shots at the Indian with no effect. He grabs the Winchester by the barrel.

Caleb rushes the Indian and swings the Winchester. Indian's hand goes up like a fat dove taking flight, grabs the barrel of the Winchester, jerks it away from Caleb, and tosses it.

Caleb slugs the Indian. Indian isn't bothered.

Caleb swings again. Indian grabs Caleb's arm, twists, snaps it off at the shoulder. Caleb SCREAMING. BLOOD FLYING.

Indian begins to beat Caleb with the arm. He goes savage. Caleb goes down. The Indian pulls the ear necklace from Caleb's neck, pushes it lovingly into his shirt pocket.

The Dead Folk, like dogs given the signal, leap forward and start ripping, biting and tearing at Caleb, jerking his chest apart, exposing his ribs and his still-beating heart —

INDIAN

stabs his hand between Caleb's rib cage, jerks out the heart. He bites a plug from the heart and tosses it at —

MATT

who it strikes right in the mouth.

Matt turns to run into the cell row. He finds an open cage and goes inside and slams the door. He backs up until he's on one of the bunks.

ANOTHER ANGLE ON SCENE

Indian at the bars. The dead gather behind him, chewing on parts of Caleb.

Matt empties the shotgun again. Same lack of effect.

Indian smiles.

And smiles.

And smiles.

His mouth is WAY TOO WIDE, and goddamn grandma, what great big teeth you have!

And then the Indian grabs the bars and starts to bend them apart as if they're made of chewing gum.

> MATT
> Jumpin' dog shit.

Matt drops the empty shotgun. Draws his pistol. He puts the gun to his head, starts to fire —

BUT THEN THE INDIAN'S THERE. Faster than you can say "Uh oh" he's on Matt like a wart. Grabs the gun, stops Matt from taking his own life. Indian squeezes the gun to a buttery pulp. He grabs Matt by both ears, jerks him forward, and opening his mouth to the size of a bear trap, bites away Matt's face.

Indian grabs Matt up, tosses him toward the bars where they have not been stretched. Tosses him so hard Matt hits them and goes through like cheese through a grater. Dead Folk are knocked over. They spring up and scramble for Matt's remains.

ON INDIAN

shaking his head like a dog worrying a bone as his TOO MANY GODDAMN TEETH chew up Matt's face, sucking down the eyeballs as if they're olives.

He lifts his head to the ceiling and his lips stretch into a snout like a wolf and his teeth drip goo, and he lets out with a triumphant HOWL, and as the HOWL CONTINUES, we —

CUT TO:

A HAND

snatching the tarp off the Gatling gun.

PULL BACK

INT. — CHURCH, BASEMENT

It's the Reverend's hand. He's in the basement with Doc and Calhoun, who have their arms full of shotguns and ammunition. They are frozen as the HOWL goes on and on. Then stops.

> CALHOUN
> I don't suppose that was a dog?

DISSOLVE TO:

A VIEW THROUGH A NARROW SLIT

where WE SEE the Dead Folk outside the church, standing still and silent, as if waiting for a train.

A BOARD COMES INTO VIEW, FILLS OUR VISION

PULL BACK

and we see Abby pushing the board into place so Doc can nail it up. We were looking through a gap in the boards being nailed over the church window.

FULL VIEW, INT. — CHURCH

Front door is blockaded with several pews. Abby and David are at the windows, holding boards — utilized from pews — while Doc and Calhoun nail them up. All of their belts bristle with revolvers and against the wall lean shotguns and rifles.

Reverend is finishing up mounting the Gatling gun on its support. (This is one of the later versions with ten barrels, developed after the Civil War. It can fire 400 rounds a minute. It is fired by rotating the barrels with a crank so that bullets are fed into the gun by a tall clip.)

There is a stockpile of weapons in two pews that have been pulled up close to the Gatling. Other pews have been heaped three feet high in front of the Gatling as a barrier. They are pulled around in a semi-circle till they reach the wall. Behind all this is the open door to the basement.

Reverend cranks the Gatling to see how it rotates. Then he pushes a clip into place. Pauses suddenly as we again HEAR THE HOWL. It sounds both sad and triumphant.

Doc and others are finishing the nailing. They pause to listen as the HOWL COMES AGAIN. They find places to look through the boards to the outside.

DOC
The bastard has us treed.

AS HOWL ENDS, Reverend grabs a double-barrel shotgun from one of the pews, hustles over the barricade to the window. He looks out through a split in the boards.

REVEREND'S POV

The dead start to move aside, forming an alley. But there's nothing in the alley but darkness.

Then stepping out of the darkness, as if from a crack between our world and another, is the Indian with the crate, lidded. We glimpse something in that moment, something in the crack. Something dark and evil and writhing, but it's just a glimpse, then it's gone. The crack is closed.

BACK TO SCENE

DAVID
What was that?

DOC
I don't know. And I'd rather not know.

OUR GANG'S POV

The Indian sets the crate down on one end, throws off the lid. The Indian's Woman doesn't look any better than when we saw her last.

BACK TO SCENE

DOC
He's making it clear what this is all about.

CALHOUN
How come she's not like one of . . . them?

REVEREND
Simple. He's the one in control, and he doesn't
want her to be like one of them.

ABBY
He loved her. He really loved her. Even in death.

DAVID
Yeah, but he don't love us none.

CALHOUN
What do we do?

REVEREND
Our best. This is our first line of defense. The
church doesn't hold them —

DOC
It won't. Not for long.

REVEREND
— then we back toward the Gatling. We make a
stand back there behind it. They get through us
there, we make one last-ditch effort. The
basement. Comments?

DOC
Shoot for the head. You can tear them apart with
that Gatling, but it doesn't matter, you don't
destroy their brains. That's what stops them.
That's where the Indian's power lies. If one of
them gets to you, bites you, save a bullet for
yourself.

Our defenders pause on that cheery note. Abby goes to the Reverend. They
kiss. For a long time.

DAVID
Sorry, Reverend. Abby. But you'll have to break it
up. We got company.

Reverend goes to the window, stands by David, looks through a crack in the
boards.

DEFENDERS' POV

Dead Folk are coming. Their feet are smoking as they come up the church
steps, get closer to the church itself. But they keep coming. The Indian is
directing them as if he's a conductor. Waving his hands, gesturing.

Flames wrap around the feet of the Dead Folk. They try to fade back. The Indian gestures wildly, lets out a HISSSSSSS of displeasure that makes your ears hurt. He grabs up one of the flaming Dead Folk, and throws him like a spear at the door.

INT. — CHURCH DOOR

as DEAD MAN'S HEAD slams through it. Dead Man looks as surprised as the defenders. His teeth start to snap at midair.

Doc lifts his shotgun, blows the Dead Man's head to shards of flesh and bone. Messy brains drip down the door.

EXT. — CHURCH

As the Dead Folk HOWL and CHARGE the church!

INT. — CHURCH

as bodies slam against the structure, vibrating the boards at the windows, shaking the door.

> DAVID
> Nice knowin' you, Reverend

> REVEREND
> Don't count yourself out till it's over. You got to
> hang in there to your last fiber. Trust in God and
> your weapons.

DEFENDER'S SIGHTS AND SOUNDS:

BATTERING AT THE DOOR.

BATTERING AT THE WINDOWS, FRONT AND SIDE.

SHATTERING GLASS.

CRACKING BOARDS.

FACES AT THE WINDOWS. HANDS ON THE BARS AT THE WINDOWS, PULLING, TUGGING, BITING. BODIES SQUIRMING THROUGH GAPS. ALMOST INSIDE.

> REVEREND
> I love you, boy.

David hugs the Reverend.

DAVID
I love you, too. I'm scared.

Abby reaches out and touches David, gently.

REVEREND
We're all scared, but we can't let it take us.
Courage is not absence of fear. It's control of
fear. Using it to your advantage.

Reverend lets go, smiles at David.

REVEREND (cont'd)
Hallowed be the name of the Lord, and shotgun
do your stuff.

David smiles. Smile melts as —

— dem ole debil Dead Folk, they be a smokin' as that holy ground lights
them up, and they're HITTING the windows and PULLING at the bars and
BANGING at the door, and TEARING at the gap the tossed Dead Folk's
head made in the door, and we see in glimpses through the windows, the
Indian, outside, walking around SNATCHING at the bars in the windows,
removing them as easy as jerking pesky nose hairs —

AND THE DEAD ARE COMING THROUGH, and they done got them
that smorgasbord smile.

DEFENDERS' GUNS

rock with a one-two rhythm, and the Dead are ceasing to smoke. They're
coming through gaps, pushing through windows. They're strong now. They
look happy and powerful.

DOC (yelling)
Holy ground ain't shit to 'em no more.

REVEREND
Back up.

LAST STAND

Defenders are pumping shotgun loads, and Dead Folk are banging apart,
and when their heads remain intact, their flesh tries to come back to them,
crawling up their legs, looking for home.

Some Dead Folk's guts fall out like huge strands of spaghetti, drag behind them to be stepped on and pulled free by others. Guts coil and writhe like snakes, seek their owners, try to rejoin by writhing up their legs, heading for body cavities.

Defenders don't have time to reload as they back up and the dead do that We Sho Is Hungry Shuffle, and Defenders are drawing their revolvers, and the revolvers are barking like angry dogs, and the Dead Folk take loads in the heads and go down, but right behind them, MORE OF THE SAME.

Defenders make the semi-circle of pews just ahead of Dead Folk, grab shotguns or Winchesters and the ROCKING RHYTHM returns. Now, dear hearts, it's ALAMO TIME, and the Dead Folk are boiling over those pews like ants on gingerbread, and it's seriously elbows and assholes as Defenders kick Dead Folk back and swing rifles and shotgun stocks, popping Dead Folk's heads open like they're cracking rotten walnuts.

Reverend on the Gatling, and he starts to crank that baby and the Dead be a poppin' and hoppin' to the gunsmoke tune. And he swings that ole Gatling, and chunks of Dead Folk meat flys every which way, and ole Caleb, little more than a head and rib cage mounted on legs, gets cut off at the waist, and he's pulling himself across the floor, trying to drag himself over the pews —

Calhoun reloading, and Caleb grabs him by the sleeve, pulls him down, and Caleb reaches up with his other hand and grabs Calhoun by the hair and yanks his partial body up, and it's bite city.

Abby throws down an empty shotgun, draws a revolver, sees Calhoun in shock as Caleb nibbles, and she takes Caleb out with a revolver shot to the head.

Calhoun turns, looks at her, happy. Then his face changes as his hand darts to his cheek and the wounds Caleb made. Then a horde of Dead Folk rise and GRAB HIM, bite him, pull him back.

Abby mercifully shoots Calhoun right between the eyes. Moment of regret, then she pulls another revolver from her belt. Two-gun Abby. 44s bark and bite.

Swarm of Dead Folk on the Gatling, and Reverend has to relinquish. Grabs up an empty shotgun and starts swinging the stock, trying for home runs.

REVEREND
Move back to the storage room. Now!

Doc has a Winchester and he's COCKING AND FIRING faster than a rabbit can mate, and —

David pokes a pistol forward and shoots Florence. Down she goes.

Montclaire, looking really nasty, reaches out and grabs David's pistol, and David pulls back, and Montclaire really pulls, dragging David over the pews, and —

WE'RE CLOSE ON THIS DISASTER IN THE MAKING

and it looks like that's all she wrote for young David, when —

A SHOTGUN STOCK

comes down on Montclaire's head BAM! BAM AGAIN. Brains ooze out of his ears like creek mud between clutched fingers.

FULL VIEW

Reverend snatches David from Montclaire's hands, even as Montclaire collapses, and the Dead Folk all start over the pews, and our team is crabbing for that open storage room door.

UGLY FAT DEAD SUMBITCH

grabs Abby by the waist from behind, picks her up, and she twists around and shoots him in the head, and down they both go, tumbling over the pews into the Dead Folk, Ugly Fat Dead Sumbitch on top, spurting brains, writhing like a snake without a head.

Abby's pistol flies from her hand, and she's trapped beneath this "horizontally impaired" Dead Fella, and now there are shadows as a crowd of Dead Folk come down on her.

ABBY

jerks out from under Ugly Fat Dead Sumbitch just in time to dive for her pistol, but the Dead, they done got her. They drop down on her faster than two-dollar whores at the Mardi Gras, and bite her all over.

Abby yells in pain, raises her head —

SEES THE REVEREND

and his mouth falls open because he knows she's doomed, and she yells —

ABBY
I love you.

— grits her teeth, sticks the revolver in her mouth. BAM!!!!! She checks out.

DOC

loses it, jumps over the pews —

> DOC (yelling)
> Abby! Abby!

Then he's just yelling cause **THEY GOT HIM.**

HORDE OF DEAD FOLK

on Doc, grabbing and biting. All that's visible amid the spider web of their arms is his shocked face.

REVEREND

jerks up the .36 Navy, fires and we **FLASH TO —**

DOC

as he takes the bullet twixt the peepers, then we **JUMP TO —**

REVEREND AND DAVID

armed with a pistol apiece, easing back into the —

STORAGE ROOM

Reverend slams the door, pinching off a Dead Folk's fingers. He throws the wooden bar in place as Dead Folk SLAM against it. Reverend grows weak, he leans against the door.

> REVEREND
> Oh God. Abby.

David touches his arm.

> DAVID
> Wasn't nothin' you could do, Reverend.

> REVEREND
> Seems like there never is.

WHAM! WHAP! SMACK! The door is taking some licks.

> DAVID
> Single-minded sumbitches, ain't they?

Reverend takes the lantern off the shelf and lights it. He and David hustle down the stairway, and the Reverend restrains David long enough to hold the lantern over the missing step.

They step over it, hurry down into the storeroom proper. They start reloading their revolvers. Their hands shake. David drops a bullet on the floor, scuttles after it, loads.

REVEREND'S POV

A window. A curtain held by a strand of rope is over it. Reverend grabs a nail keg, climbs on it, pulls back the curtain, and we got —

Bars.

> REVEREND
> Damn!

REVEREND'S POV THROUGH BARS

The sky is lightening.

> REVEREND
> It's near morning.

BACK TO SCENE

> DAVID
> Almost don't count for nothin'.

TOP OF STAIRS

Door heaves like a chest pulling in air. Wooden bar stretches, cracks.

REVEREND AND DAVID

Reverend jumps down from the keg. He and David watch the bar expand and crack.

> REVEREND
> This is our last stand, boy. Be sure you got one in
> that gun for yourself things get final.

> DAVID
> I don't know I can.

> REVEREND
> Think about if you don't.

>   (Softer)
> Just put it dead center of your forehead and pull
> the trigger, quick. Don't think. Just do it. You'll
> leap on over to the other side, and you'll be there
> with Jesus.

>   DAVID
> I'll be dead is what I'll be.

SOUND OF DOOR CRACKING.

TOP OF STAIRS

EXPLOSION OF THE WOODEN BAR.

The Indian framed in the light at the top of the stairs. On his shoulder, like a
parrot, sits Mignon. She smiles, and she's got a major set of teeth here.
These babies would make a crocodile proud.

>   MIGNON (not a little girl's voice)
>   *Boo,* Preacher Man.

REVEREND AND DAVID

flinch. Then they look disgusted with themselves.

MIGNON

cackles, bites a chunk out of her doll's rag head, she's so frenzied.

DEAD FOLK

try to push around the Indian, they're so anxious to eat.

CLOSE ON INDIAN

He HISSES, speaks. And it is the VOICE OF DOOM.

>   INDIAN
>   *Back! They're mine!*

TRACKING INDIAN

He comes down the stairs, and he's about to reach the missing step —

REACTION SHOT, REVEREND AND DAVID

Hopeful.

INDIAN

steps where the step ought to be, and —

Nothing.

He steps on MIDAIR and keeps right on keepin' on.

REVEREND AND DAVID

disappointed.

> REVEREND
> Figures.

MIGNON

She cackles. Waves her chewed doll.

> MIGNON
> You've had it now, Preacher Boy.

FULL SCENE

Reverend pissed, jerks up his revolver and shoots Mignon's eye out. Her head goes back, then she falls forward, her doll leaving her hand. The doll bumps down the stairs, and Mignon bumps after it, lands in a similar heap.

Indian becomes the Shadow Spider with a semi-human head and face, and he Fast Flows the rest of the way down and he comes at the Reverend in a rush, and the —

Reverend, freezes momentarily, and he's got that ole spider bugaboo on his mind, and you can see it on his face, but he YELLS in defiance, jerks up the revolver, FIRES, hits Indian in the forehead, dead center —

— and the Indian isn't fazed, comes on jetlike, grabs the Reverend by the throat with one of his prehensile legs, smiles, sticks his face close to the Reverend's so that we're —

CLOSE ENOUGH ON INDIAN TO COUNT TEETH

> INDIAN
> That shit don't work on me, God's underling. I'm
> gonna swallow you like a snake swallows an egg.

Spider Image melts away. Demonic-reptile look. Yellow eyes with black slits. A flash of lizard tail. Clawed hands. Indian's mouth opens and unhinges, and he pulls the Reverend forward for a spit bath, pauses —

INDIAN
But it's the spider you fear, isn't it, Reverend?

Transformation to the spider-thing. But God, Almighty, it's never looked this nasty.

DAVID

jumps forward, kicks the Indian. Indian flicks him across the room with a spider limb. David's revolver slides away from him, out of sight under junk.

INDIAN AND REVEREND

INDIAN
I'm gonna chew your soul, Mister Preacher.

WIDEN VIEW

to include David as he jerks the jackknife out of his pocket, runs at the Indian SCREAMING. The Indian has just put his spider mouth over the Reverend's head, saliva dripping like snot.

But David's yelling causes him to pause. He pulls the Reverend's dripping head from his mouth. Turns to stare at David.

David, almost on the Indian, dives low, drives the jackknife through one of the Indian's spider legs, pins it to the floor.

Indian looks down at his leg, looks at David. He can't believe how stupid the kid is. He smiles. And with that mouth, it is a SMILE. WET AND RED AND SHARP.

REVEREND

dangling. Choking. His wind is going. He roves an eye to his right.

REVEREND'S POV

The curtained window. A red ray of sunlight.

BACK TO SCENE

Reverend lifts his Navy, FIRES. He hits the windowsill. FIRES AGAIN as —

Indian's knife-trapped spider leg comes free and he spreads his spider-demon jaws WIDE to finish Reverend —

— and Reverend's shot hits the rope holding the curtain, and the curtain swings down, and a —

RAY OF SUNLIGHT

slices into the room and cuts through the Indian's arm smooth as a laser beam. The arm falls off, and the Reverend is dropped to the floor.

REVEREND

rolls, snatches the dead hand, for it is now a hand, away from his throat.

INDIAN

staggers, starts to disintegrate.

He's lost the spider transformation.

He tries to transform into a wolf. No luck. Just a glimpse of that.

Reptilian form. Nope. That won't get it either. Forked tail thrashes, disappears.

Various transformations flap by, but they don't hold. Nothing's working here.

Indian in human form starts to crawl up the stairway, his back smoking.

THE LIGHT

from sunrise is expanding. It fills the storage room, falls on the INDIAN who bursts into flames. He rolls down the stairs, tries to get beneath them, out of the light.

REVEREND

grabs a keg, charges the stairs, bangs some of the plank steps to pieces. No shade for the Indian.

LIGHT

falls on the Indian full force again. He bursts into brighter flames, and the flames lick up through the steps, and —

DEAD FOLK

at the top of the stairs cringe as the light expands to include them, and we —

FOLLOW DEAD FOLK

wheeling from storage room, running throughout the church. Sunrise is coming through the windows and the breaks in the door and walls, and it's lighting them up like Christians at the Coliseum on the emperor's birthday.

BACK TO STORAGE ROOM

David looks at the gap in the steps. Flames are leaping up and licking the steps and catching them on fire, and it looks bad. They're trapped.

Reverend grabs David by the collar and the seat of the pants.

> DAVID
> Hey!

Reverend tosses David toward the higher steps, through the flames.

David grabs hold.

Flames lick at him.

He YELLS, scrambles up the steps, away from the flames. Almost to the top.

He turns, looks down at the Reverend through the smoke and flames.

> DAVID
> Reverend!

> REVEREND
> Go, boy! Go!

> DAVID
> Not without you.

Steps sag. Flames lick up and around David's feet.

Reverend sees he means it. He grabs an ammo box, puts it on the one surviving lower step. He backs up, jumps his foot onto the box, springs.

Charred step crumbles under the weight, but —

— the Reverend makes it, grabs the step high above him.

Flames bite him.

He YELLS.

David grabs him.

Reverend, with David's aid, pulls himself up with a gasp. His clothes are on fire. David helps him beat out the flames.

Fire washes up from below, and with a surge, the flame expands and takes on the form of THE INDIAN'S HAND, which then takes the form of a huge tarantula, and the Tarantula/Hand GRABS the Reverend's foot.

Reverend jerks free, and the Tarantula/Hand falls back into flames, and the flames take the stairs.

Reverend and David race up to the church. Behind them, the steps are dissolved by fire.

INDIAN

He looks like a humanoid-hunk of green shit on fire.

HOWLLLLLLLLLLLLL OF PAIN AND DISAPPOINTMENT.

AMMO BOX

explodes and blows the flaming Indian into several sticky, burning pieces.

CHURCH

Smoking. Burning. Dead Folk running together. Falling down.

The Reverend grabs up a shattered piece of pew planking, and with David behind him, he swings it, batting aside the Dead Folk who are only interested in trying to find shade. Some of them are crawling under pews, dropping to their knees, pushing their heads to the floor and trying to protect themselves with their hands. They're burning anyway, bursting into flames as they are poisoned by the sunlight.

TRACK REVEREND AND DAVID

as they battle their way to —

EXT. — CHURCH

Sunlight. Hot and yellow. Reverend and David practically tumble out of the church, flames at their backs.

A couple of Dead Folk fall out behind them, but they're not dangerous now. Food is the least of their worries. They drop down near the crate containing the Indian's Woman and blaze into charred ruins. It's all over for the Dead Folk.

David collapses to the ground, breathing hard. The Reverend stands, watching the church.

                                    REVEREND
                            Abby. Abby . . .

ON THE CHURCH

A ROAR OF COLORFUL FLAME licks out of all the windows. Then

there's a sound like THE GODDAMNEST SCREAM IN CREATION, and
the FLAMES LICK HIGH, HIGH, HIGH, and they have the GENERAL
SHAPE OF THE INDIAN, and they FLICKER in that position
momentarily, then FALL TO EARTH with a BANG and the church goes in
all directions, and —

SILENCE.

The church is black smoking rubble.

REVEREND

looks at the body in the crate. He lowers the crate back so that it lies on the
ground like an open coffin. He removes his jacket and takes out the Bible.
He lifts the woman's head gently. He places the jacket under her.

He pulls a burning brand out of the debris of the church. He places the Bible
on the dead woman's body. He sets the torch to the jacket. It takes a couple of
tries before the jacket catches and her head is enveloped, followed by her body.

REVEREND
God take and rest your soul.

DAVID
Is it over, Reverend?

Holding the torch, the Reverend turns to David.

REVEREND
As much as it's ever over. Come, son. No rest for
the wicked, and the good don't need any.
(He looks at the burning torch)
We have some cleansing to do.

EXT. — THE HILL — LONG VIEW — LATER

The hill and the hot yellow sun rising above it.

Then the Reverend and David appear, riding double on horseback. They
ride slowly up the hill. At its peak they stop, and we go —

CLOSE ON REVEREND AND DAVID

As they look back at the town.

THEIR POV — THE ENTIRE TOWN

is on fire.

BACK TO SCENE

David watches silently as the Reverend lifts his head to the heavens, asks loudly —

                        REVEREND
                     Am I redeemed?

LONG PAUSE.

NOTHING.

Reverend smiles sadly.

                        REVEREND
                     Thy will be done.

Reverend touches his heels to the horse, and they ride down the hill, and disappear from sight and into history.

HOLD FOR A MOMENT ON

The empty hill. The hot yellow sun.

                                         SLOW DISSOLVE TO:

BURNING TOWN

A quick camera tour. This place is most definitely scourged.

DOLLY SLOWLY DOWN MAIN STREET

as the flames lick this way and that. Arrive at the remains of the church and go —

CLOSE ON CHURCH RUBBLE

A spider, the exact shape of the hairy mole on the Indian's chest, skull design and all, wobbles over the debris. The spider smokes as if on fire. It weakly scuttles toward a small dark hole near where the church steps still stand. The spider tumbles into the hole. A wisp of white smoke boils out of the hole to mark its passing.

PULL BACK FOR THE COMPLETE VIEW

The smoking hole.

The town blazing.

The sun, high and bright. And we —

                                         FADE OUT

TRACK DOWN

‒ ‒ ‒ ‒ ‒ ‒ ‒ ‒ ‒ ‒

SCREENPLAY BY

ED GORMAN

Based on his novel

As we FADE IN we think we're in the opening scene of a western.
RICHARD DADE is a big handsome middle-aged man, just a bit gone to fat
but still powerful and intimidating. We are SHOOTING DOWN on him as
he paces away from the camera, clearly ready to turn, snatch his Colt .45 from
the holster he has strapped gunslinger style . . . fire off several deadly rounds.
The western motif holds right down to his clothes — western style shirt and
trousers with fancy piping and a flat-brimmed hat.

He paces off four . . . five . . . six steps. And then turns directly at the
audience and fires.

The echoes of gunfire . . . drifting cloud of gunsmoke . . . fix our attention
while Dade remains in his firing crouch, a glowering man of heroic
proportions.

Then he straightens out of his crouch and speaks to somebody we don't yet see.

> DADE
> The ladies go crazy for shit like that. You want to
> get yourself a girl, you just show her a little fancy
> shootin'.

We pull back to see a sixteen-year old, JAMES BANNION. He's a nice kid,
quiet, with a certain air of brooding about him. He's got a great smile, that
being his ticket into the company of human beings. They trust a smile like
that — there's warmth and just a bit of pain in it.

> DADE
> Your turn, Jimmy.

Jimmy is dressed in a blue workshirt and jeans. He could very easily have
been in the western movie we set up in the opening shot. But now we see
that he's sitting on a black Honda motorcycle. Dade walks over to him and
hands him the .45 butt first. Jimmy looks at it but doesn't touch it.

> JIMMY
> You be pissed if I don't shoot it, Uncle Richard? I
> guess I never got into guns.

> DADE
> If your dad was alive, you'd be into guns. You'd
> be a goddamned marksman is what you'd be.
> Instead of a piano player, I mean.

Jimmy grins. This is how he plays off his uncle's ferocity sometimes — just
kind of lazily smiles in the face of all that torment and tumult.

> JIMMY
> My mom's done a pretty good job of raising me,
> Uncle Richard.

Jimmy looks away at the green Iowa countryside. Looks back to Dade.

> JIMMY
> I guess I'd rather not remember him that way,
> Uncle Richard. I mean, when he came back, he
> was pretty screwed up. He wasn't a very happy
> man, Uncle Richard. Then when he had that
> heart attack and died —

Dade raises the .45 and looks at it glint in the sunlight. It seems to glow with
an inner light.

> DADE
> Don't ever belittle what your father did. I was
> with him over there, Jimmy. He was the bravest
> son-of-a-bitch in the whole company. The whole
> company.

Dade holds the gun out to Jimmy. Jimmy looks at it and sighs, knowing that
there's no placating his uncle unless he fires the weapon.

Dade goes up and sets some new Pepsi bottles up on the corral fence —
pushing off the six broken bottles he himself just shot up.

Jimmy takes his place, raises the gun, aims and starts firing. He shoots all his
shots in a burst and because we're watching him directly, we see how the
gun jumps in his hand.

> DADE
> You were closing your goddamned eyes again,
> Jimmy.
>> (Shakes his head.)

Dade glares at him a long moment, then goes over to the motorcycle and
climbs on. He angrily starts the engine. Because of the proprietary way he
was sitting on it, the bike looked like Jimmy's. But now all Jimmy can do is
climb on the back. Dade tears away.

Credits over farm montage:

This is a portrait of James David Bannion as a farm boy.

He is scrubbing out cow dung from the dairy barn. He accidentally slides his
hand into a fresh cow pie and makes a face.

He is feeding a baby lamb and gives her a hug.

He is working hay up in the mow and he accidentally, through his own
clumsiness, falls backward out of the mow door — right into a deep fall
breaking pile of hay. He grins.

He is trying to drive a tractor with his impatient uncle sitting right
alongside — but all he can do is grind gears.

He is riding a horse that almost bucks him off.

He is milking a cow that squirts him in the eye.

He is sitting up on the porch roof with his telescope, looking out at the
summer stars.

He is toweling off after a shower and looking at a framed photo of himself
and his father. He lifts the photo up for a closer look and we can see that he
is touched by memory.

                                                                              CUT TO:

Dade lies against the headboard of his bed while SONIA, a very attractive middle-aged woman, is making love to him by sitting on his lap. Dade is really into it. His eyes are closed and he's breathing heavily.

> DADE
> Oh, God, do that thing with your hips, will you?

She kind of gives him her hula girl special. Dade comes and then she comes right after, then slumps against him

CUT TO:

Sonia stands before the mirror in Dade's bedroom, putting on her skirt and blouse.

> SONIA
> You think your sister-in-law knows I do more
> than clean your house?

Dade comes out of the master bedroom, tucking his shirt back in.

> DADE
> Are you kidding? She's a very sweet lady and I
> honest-to-God love her, but she's about as naïve
> as you can get.
>   (He comes over and cups her big breasts.)
> Between you and me, I was always a little
> disappointed when Tom married her. She comes
> from a very big society family over in the valley.
> Went to a private school and all that shit.

He starts dry humping her from behind. She starts to get into it again, too. But then she stops. Laughs.

> SONIA
> Just because you're the richest farmer in the valley
> doesn't mean I *always* have to do what you say.
> Now I've got to get down there and make dinner.

> DADE
> Why don't you stay and make something else?

Sonia finishes up by putting a colorful scarf in her hair.

> SONIA
> You want my opinion, Richard, she's doing a good
> job of raising that boy all alone. He's a nice kid.

> DADE
That's the problem. He's *too* nice, Not enough
backbone.

Walks over to the window. Looks out at the countryside, then to himself
more than Sonia:

> DADE
But I'm gonna take care of that.

CUT TO:

A long, well-appointed dining room with just a hint of the Old West about it.
Dade sits across from Louise, who is a very beautiful and somewhat delicate
forty-three-year-old — but this isn't to suggest a wilting flower. There's steel
and irony in her. Sonia is pouring them wine.

> LOUISE
I wish we could stay for the country fair, Richard,
but we can't. I told you I'd be here just to pick
him up and take him back — two days.

> DADE
I still think he'd be better off skipping college for
a year and working here on the farm.

> LOUISE (ironically)
Turn him into a real he-man, I suppose.
(A bit of resentment here.)
The way you were always trying to turn my
husband into a he-man?

> DADE
I'm still glad I talked my brother into going to
Nam with me. Gave him a chance to prove he
was a man.

> LOUISE
You forget Johnny had a Master's Degree in
history, did you also forget that he didn't want to
go? He was a scholar.

> DADE
Scholars might impress you. They don't do a hell
of a lot for me

Just as Sonia finishes up pouring the wine, Jimmy comes in. He seats himself and then looks at his mother and uncle. He grins.

> JIMMY
> Oh, God, you aren't talking about my sex life
> again, are you?

His mother smiles. So, in the doorway, does Sonia.

> JIMMY
> Uncle Richard is afraid I don't like girls.

Puts his napkin on. Picks up his wine glass and guns it right down. His mother looks as if she wants to stop him. When he puts his glass down, he belches.

> JIMMY
> Well, I'm here to tell you, Uncle Richard, that
> there's nothing I enjoy more than a glass of wine
> and a good piece of ass.

Uncle Richard laughs.

> LOUISE
> Jimmy!

> DADE (smiling)
> Music to my ears when you talk like that.

> JIMMY
> In fact, Uncle Richard, I'd like to take the
> motorcycle into town tonight.

> LOUISE
> You don't even have a license.

> DADE
> Hell, Louise, your husband and I used to drive all
> over this part of the state without a license.

> LOUISE
> He couldn't even get it started the other day.

> DADE
> Only one way to learn.

> JIMMY
> I'll be fine, Mom. I really will.

LOUISE
What's in town, anyway? I just got here today. I'd
think you'd want to spend more time with me.

DADE (winks at Jimmy)
Yeah, have a harpsichord recital in the parlor.

CUT TO:

Night. Jimmy in the front yard. Trying to start the motorcycle but without
much luck. He isn't doing it right. Louise and Dade peek at him through the
curtains.

LOUISE
I told you he didn't know how to ride that thing.

DADE
And I told you, Louise, there's only one way he's
going to learn.

Takes her gently by the arms and holds her close. There's even a hint of the
romantic in this — on his part, anyway.

DADE
You don't seem to understand, Louise. I *love* that
boy. To me, he's my very own son. Since Kathryn
got killed —

And then he stops. Walks away. He tears up. This is a powerful moment,
seeing a big man like this struck dumb and aggrieved.

She walks over to him and very tenderly puts her elegant fingers on his
rough cheeks . . . and wipes away the lone tears that course down his face.

DADE
He's my own very son, Louise. I protect him
every way I can —

Snuffles his nose, wipes his own tears.

DADE
And one way I protect him is by not
overprotecting him. He's got to get into the fray,
Louise. He's got to start becoming a man, the way
Johnny would have wanted him to. You need a
man around,

(takes her arms from behind, romantically).
You're a fine-looking woman. And we'd make a
fine-looking couple.

LOUISE (turns and faces him)
You tried to get me in bed when your brother was
still alive. I've never forgotten that, Richard.

DADE
I was drunk.

LOUISE (angry)
He was your own *brother*.

Just then they hear the motorcycle in the front yard. They race to the
window.

He's actually got it started. He takes off in a wobbly fashion and not more
than a hundred feet away, he spills it, the bike falling on him.

LOUISE
Oh, God, is he all right?

DADE
Of course he's all right.

LOUISE
Maybe I'd better go see if —

Dade nods out the window.

DADE
Look.

She turns back to the window and peers out.

LOUISE
He's getting up.

DADE
'Course he's getting up.

LOUISE
And he doesn't seem injured

DADE
'Course he isn't injured.

LOUISE
But what happens if he gets out on the highway
and —

Dade takes her hand playfully, the way a lover would, and pulls her toward
the living room.

DADE
Let him be, woman. Let him be.

CUT TO:

On the road with Jimmy . . . who doesn't know how to ride this damned
thing at all. He's a-wiggling, he's a-wobbling, he's a-waggling.

Car comes tearing up behind him on the two-lane highway and nearly runs
him down. Terrifying moment. As the car goes out around him, a couple of
farm boys flip him the bird and yell "Asshole!" at him.

Jimmy is so scared by the incident that he loses control and pitches right into
a shallow ditch on the side of the highway.

We see him slowly get up. Moan.

JIMMY
Oh, fuck me. Fuck me.

He hobbles around, favoring the pain in his knee, wincing at the sharpness
of it.

Goes back over to the motorcycle and kicks it as if it was a human being who
did him wrong.

JIMMY
You son of a bitch. You fucking son of a bitch.

Then he favors his knee again, starts wincing, and begins hobbling around
once more.

CUT TO:

Jimmy cruises into Black River Falls, a small Midwestern town at night.
Teenagers drive up and down the main drag on this summer night, and most
of the stores on the town square are lit up.

Jimmy is still riding the motorcycle in wobbly fashion. At a stoplight, he kills
the engine and then has a hard time getting it started again. Two cute
teenage girls in a convertible watch him and smirk.

After he gets going again, Jimmy pulls up to a Baskin-Robbins-style ice cream parlor. Kids mill around outside the door. They watch him and smile. The sign says *Pete's Place* above the door.

> GIRL #1
> He still doesn't know how to ride that thing.

> GIRL #2
> Yeah, but he's kind've cute in a helpless sort
> of way.

> GIRL #1 (nods to red-haired girl inside)
> If he keeps messing around with Sue, he really *is*
> gonna be helpless. Bobby'll kill him.

Jimmy gets off his bike and walks inside, self-conscious about the other kids watching him.

> GIRL #1
> My brother can teach you how to ride that thing
> and he'll only charge you twenty-five bucks.

> GIRL #2
> My brother'll teach you for just twenty bucks.
> Plus I'll even let you take me for a ride.

Jimmy smiles and goes inside the ice cream shop.

Sixteen-year-old Sue, a very pretty and competent-looking girl in a T-shirt and jeans, is piling up scoops of ice cream on a fragile-looking cone while a mouthy twelve-year-old kid watches her.

> KID
> You can do better than that. Two more scoops at
> least.

> SUE
> Yeah, right.

She hands it over to him. It's piled so high, it's practically falling apart.

Kid looks at Jimmy.

> KID
> Here's that weird city kid who has a crush on you.

Sue looks embarrassed.

> SUE
> That'll be seventy-five cents.

> KID
> You give me a discount. You didn't put enough
> scoops on.

> SUE
> Seventy-five cents or I'll tell everybody that I saw
> you kissing old Mrs. Fenwick the other night.

> KID
> You're warped, you know that?

Digs in his pocket and hands over seventy-five cents. Then he looks at
Jimmy.

> KID
> You tell him what Bobby told you last night?

> SUE
> I don't think that's any of your business. Now get
> the hell out of here.

> KID
> I'm gonna tell your boss you swore at a customer.

He takes one more good look at Jimmy, then leaves. The bell above the door
rings when he goes out.

> JIMMY
> Bobby tell you something last night?

> SUE
> Yeah. I'm afraid so.

She starts cleaning up the counter as they talk.

> JIMMY
> Afraid?

> SUE
> Yeah. He found out you walked me home after
> work the other night.

> JIMMY
> Oh.

SUE (looks at him)
You better get out of here, Jimmy.

JIMMY
I've been lifting weights with my uncle all
summer. I'm not afraid of him.

SUE (smiling)
Maybe you're not, but I am. I've seen him mad.
Especially when he's trying to impress those
stupid friends of his.

Door opens and a heavy older lady comes in.

Jimmy stands back and watches Sue wait on her. She's a sweet, lively girl, Sue.

WOMAN
I'm supposed to be on a diet.

SUE
We're all supposed to be on something, Mrs.
Fenwick. But I wouldn't worry about it.

WOMAN (laughs)
Well, in that case, give me *two* scoops tonight.

SUE
Butter-brickle?

WOMAN
Is there any other kind?

The woman looks at Jimmy.

WOMAN
Is this your boyfriend, Sue? You make a nice
looking couple.

Jimmy smiles shyly.

CUT TO:

We're inside a car and cruising a small-town nighttime street of taverns.

Three men stand in front of one of the taverns, talking.

A still camera with a telephoto lens comes into the frame and snaps several
photos of them from a distance of perhaps a quarter of a block.

CUT TO:

A very tired and aged stripper with preposterous silicone bazooms does a tired strip and we pull back from her to see a mostly empty cocktail lounge.

A middle-aged private investigator named Murphy sits watching her a moment, then lights a cigarette, takes a long pull on his drink, and then gets up, throws money down on the table. He looks as tired and aged as the stripper. Soulmates maybe.

We follow him outside to a glass phone booth. It's pretty smashed up, pissed in, puked in, the phone book torn out. Murphy makes a sour face when he picks up the stench. He feeds a quarter into the phone and then dials a blur of numbers.

> MURPHY
> Operator, I'd like to make a collect call.
> (Beat)
> To Mr. Richard Dade. My name is Murphy.

He stands looking out at the night. Then takes some black-and-white photos from the pocket of his short-sleeved shirt.

The photos show the three guys he photographed earlier tonight.

> MURPHY
> Thank you, operator.
> (Beat)
> I've got some good news for you, Mr. Dade. All
> three of them are in town for the next couple
> of days.
> (Beat)
> I even got some photos of them for you.

CUT TO:

Dade's den. Dade sits at the desk. For the first time we see Kathryn, a beautiful fourteen-year-old girl who has the aura of a princess about her.

Her framed photograph sits on the corner of his massive oak desk. As he talks, he lifts it up and looks at it reverently.

> DADE
> You don't have any doubts that they're the ones.

MURPHY (O.C.)
No doubt at all, Mr. Dade. I've spent a long time
working on this thing, remember. I tracked them
to this little burb — and here they are. They've
just gone on with their lives like nothing
happened.

DADE
Yes, I know. I've been paying your bills.

MURPHY
I never said I came cheap, Mr. Dade.
(Beat)
I've been working hard.

DADE
It isn't the money I'm worried about — it's
making sure they're the right ones.

MURPHY
Like I said, they're the right ones, Mr. Dade. I
told you I thought they might be from a nearby
town. I just had to find the right town.

DADE
You know something? You've never asked me
why I wanted to find them.

Stares at Kathryn's photo again.

MURPHY
I figure that's your business, Mr. Dade. My
business was to find them for you. Then I turn the
whole thing over to you. I'm sorry it took so long.
(Laughs)
They were about an hour away all the time.

DADE
There'll be a bonus in your next check,
Murphy. You've done a damned good job, and I
appreciate it.

MURPHY
And I appreciate the bonus, Mr. Dade. I
appreciate it very much.

CUT TO:

EXT. — OF THE ICE CREAM SHOP. LIGHTS GOING OUT. SUE AND JIMMY APPEAR. SUE LOCKS UP.

They walk over to the motorcycle.

> SUE
> You getting any better at this?

> JIMMY
> A little.

> SUE
> You want me to drive it?

> JIMMY
> Yeah, that'd look real cool. Me on the back end.

> SUE (smiling)
> Yeah, I guess that wouldn't do too much for your image, would it?

> JIMMY
> Oh, my mom said to say hi. She really liked you the couple of times she stopped into the ice cream parlor.

> SUE
> She's nice.

> JIMMY (smiling)
> So are you.

They get on the bike. He tries to start it. Doesn't have much luck.

Sue climbs off the back of the bike.

> SUE
> Watch this. Just like my older brother showed me.

She gets on. Gets it started right away.

> SUE
> You see what I did?

> JIMMY
> I think so.

SUE
Watch.

She turns off the engine. Runs through the whole thing again.

He gets on the bike and tries it. The engine kicks over right away.

He looks around, as if people are watching.

JIMMY
I hope nobody was watching.

SUE
There's nothing wrong with not knowing how to
ride a motorcycle. You've just been doing other
stuff.

JIMMY
Yeah, wimpy stuff.

SUE
You're not a wimp.

JIMMY
I'm not?

SUE
You're a nice, kind, decent guy.

JIMMY (laughs)
You make me sound pretty exciting.

SUE
C'mon. Take me home.

CUT TO:

A few more hair-raising motorcycle sequences as Jimmy nearly gets them
run over by a truck and then comically misses an S-turn and takes the
motorcycle into the bushes.

Then they're back on the road and driving down a nice residential
street when —

From nowhere there are three of them on big powerful motorcycles —

They surround Jimmy, almost forcing him to dump his motorcycle.

This could only be Sue's ex-boyfriend Bobby and two of his buddies.

They follow Jimmy all the way home to Sue's driveway next to a large Colonial-style home.

Bobby and his friends pull in right behind them. Jimmy gets off his motorcycle and starts walking Sue to the front door.

Bobby gets off his motorcycle and starts following them, Bobby being much bigger and older than Jimmy.

> BOBBY
> We need to talk, man. Now turn around here and face me.

> SUE (stage whispers)
> Don't pay attention to him. Just keep walking.

> BOBBY
> You hear me, man? I said we need to talk. You better fucking face me when I'm talking to you. Understand?

They keep walking. Sue takes Jimmy's hand.

Bobby lunges for Jimmy then, spins him around and smashes him hard in the face.

Then Bobby grabs him and throws him on the ground, Bobby's friends all excited about the fight that's about to take place.

> SUE
> You leave him alone, Bobby, or I'll go in and phone the police.

But Bobby is crazed. Shouts down at Jimmy.

> BOBBY
> You're willin' to fuck her but not fight for her is the deal, faggot? Well, I'm gonna *make* you fight for her, faggot — you understand?

Jimmy gets up and startles everybody by kicking Bobby in the balls.

Bobby clutches his groin, Jimmy decks him.

> CUT TO:

Dade's den. He sits in his deep leather armchair facing the big screen TV.

He lifts up the remote control and then punches up a video tape. The only real light in the room comes from the flickering images on the TV set.

A hand-lettered signs says (scratchy 8 mm film pre-home video):

KATHRYN'S 10TH BIRTHDAY

We see a younger version of Dade; a beautiful woman, obviously his wife; and an even more beautiful young girl. The girl is trying to blow out all her candles on her birthday cake. All three of them wear corny birthday hats. Dade is blowing on a noise-maker.

KATHRYN'S 12TH BIRTHDAY

Same three people except they all look a little older. They're all making faces at the camera.

KATHRYN'S 14TH BIRTHDAY

Here we see a country club party with Dade in a dinner jacket and Kathryn all dressed up. They're dancing in the center of the floor with the other guests watching them. Kathryn is beautiful.

Then at the same party, we see Jimmy and Kathryn dancing. And then the film jumps to various other scenes: Jimmy and Kathryn playing Frisbee with the dog; Jimmy and Kathryn riding horses together; Jimmy and Kathryn playing basketball.

The film jumps again. This time to front steps of a church where the casket is being brought down to a waiting black hearse. Coming behind the pallbearers and the casket is Dade. He is alone and looks terrible. Jimmy and Louise are right behind him.

We reverse angles — watch Dade as he sits in his chair, taking all of this in.

Behind him, the den door opens and we see Sonia in the doorway. She comes in silently and comes over to his chair and sits on the arm of it and takes his head the way she would comfort a child.

He does not try to hide or impede the tears that run down his face as the TV commences to flicker colors as images across his face.

DADE
Murphy called tonight.

SONIA
You need to forget about Murphy.

> DADE
> He found them.

He stares at the TV.

Dade reaches over and takes her hand.

Looks at the TV.

> SONIA
> I don't want you to do anything crazy

> DADE
> I want to see them. They're only about an
> hour away.

> SONIA
> If you're sure he's right, Murphy I mean, you
> should go to the police.

Stares at the TV — the image is now of Kathryn and Jimmy playing Frisbee with a handsome dog.

> DADE
> They were like brother and sister. You should've
> heard him cry when I told him Kathryn was dead.
> Same way Louise cried twenty years ago when I
> told her my wife died in cancer surgery.

> SONIA
> You really think it's a good idea to take him
> with you?

> DADE (looks up at her)
> He loved her as much as I did. He'll want to go
> along.

> SONIA
> I just don't want you to get in any trouble, Dade.
> I love you too much for that.

> CUT TO:

Sue hurls herself on Bobby's back and gets him around the neck and tries pulling him off Jimmy. Enraged, Bobby gets up, throws her off, then crouches as if he's going to hit her.

> SUE
> You gonna hit me, Bobby?

Bobby turns on Jimmy, who is still on the ground. Kicks him in the side very hard. Sue grabs him, slaps him.

> BOBBY
> Wish I could get a girl to do my fightin'
> for me.

> SUE
> Get out of here, Bobby. Get out of here now.

Jimmy has struggled to his feet, looks ashamed.

> BOBBY
> Maybe I didn't give him a fair chance.

> SUE
> I just want you out of here, Bobby.

But Bobby is enraged again. He walks over to Jimmy.

> BOBBY
> I'm givin' you your chance, faggot. Just c'mon and
> hit me. I won't even hit you back.

> SUE
> Bobby!

She starts toward him, but one of Bobby's friends grabs her and stops her.

> BOBBY
> C'mon faggot. Hit me. C'mon.

> CUT TO:

Al's Duck Inn Tavern is a working man's place where men go to get drunk and shoot pool. It is dingy and dark.

Three men sit at a table in the rear. TOM PITTMAN is a husky working man with a beard; STEVE WINDERS is a skinny, balding guy with long sideburns; RICK BRYANT is a short, powerful-looking man. They're all about mid-thirties. They're all drinking bottled beer.

These are the three whose photograph private investigator Murphy took earlier tonight.

                              TOM
                    You sure it was Wyman?

                              RICK
                         Pretty sure.

                              TOM
                   And he was in your garage?

                              RICK
                     Yeah. Just after sun-up.

                             STEVE
              I told ya that son-of-a-bitch has been on to us all
              along — ever since it happened.

                              TOM
              Yeah, but if he had any proof, he would've
              arrested us by now.

                             STEVE
              Way he was lookin' around my garage this
              mornin', he's tryin' real hard to nail our ass.

After a silence.

                              TOM
                 The worst thing is, we didn't even mean to do it.

                             STEVE
              Yeah? You think a jury gonna give a shit that we
              didn't mean it? The girl died. That's all they give
              a damn about.

                              RICK
              Been a year now. If Wyman hasn't gotten
              anything yet —

                           STEVE (after a silence)
                       I keep seein' her face.

                              TOM
                          Me, too.

                              RICK
                     She was really pretty.

(Miserably)
Oh, shit, the gun just fell out of my hand and hit
the floor and went off. It's just I was so scared —
I keep thinking of that poor girl —

TOM
Shit — look.

They turn to look and there in the doorway of the tavern stands Chief
Howard Wyman, a big sheepdog of a man with a solemn but kind face and a
great air of melancholy competence. He's seen many things in this job that
have changed him in ways he didn't want to be changed. His khaki uniform
suggests the Old West, Wm Holden in "The Wild Bunch," perhaps.

He goes over to the bar.

WYMAN
Diet Pepsi, please.

The bartender reaches behind the bar and produces a can of Diet Pepsi and
a glass.

TOM
What the hell's he doing here? He never comes
in here.

RICK
Well, he was never in my garage until this morning.

STEVE
He's got a hair up his ass, no doubt about it.

Wyman picks up his Diet Pepsi and glass and walks over to them.

WYMAN
Mind a little company?

TOM
I don't. You guys?

They shake their heads.

WYMAN
Appreciate it.

Sits down and makes a fuss over pouring his Diet Pepsi. They watch him,
scared but transfixed.

What the hell kind of game is he playing anyway?

> WYMAN
> Suppose Rick here told you he saw me in his
> garage this morning?

They look at each other.

> WYMAN
> You hear I'm retiring?
> (He looks at them)
> Went in for some tests and I've got to have a
> heart bypass operation. Guess now's as good a
> time as any to hand in the badge. But I've got one
> piece of unfinished business.
> (Looks at them again.)

Pours himself some Diet Pepsi.

> WYMAN
> Never thought I could get used to this diet stuff,
> but I guess I did.

Takes a long drink.

> WYMAN
> Anyway, my theory on that robbery has always
> been this. Remember when the tire factory closed
> down here two years ago and about 1,000 people
> got put out of work? Well, the way I see this
> robbery is that these three guys were probably
> decent, hard-working men who were just desperate
> for money. Their unemployment insurance was
> running out. There weren't any other jobs to have.
> And they had families to feed and bills to pay. And
> so what they did was they put masks on and they
> went in and robbed this convenience store over in
> Lawlor. Now like I say, these are basically decent
> men. They just wanted to get the money and get
> out of there without anybody getting hurt. In fact,
> the very last thing these men had on their minds
> was to hurt somebody, especially a young girl like
> that. Hell, they have kids of their own.

>   (Looks around at them again)
>   They're family men.

He pours the last of his Diet Pepsi into the glass.

>   WYMAN
> What these three guys couldn't know was that a
> year later somebody would come along and buy
> the tire factory and put everybody back to work
> again. Now these three are doing pretty well
> again — but they've got this thing with that poor
> girl in the background.

>   RICK
> I kind've feel sorry for them, the robbers I mean.

>   WYMAN
> I feel sorry for everybody involved — the girl and
> her father — and even the men. They shouldn't
> have stuck up the place no matter how desperate
> they were — but I don't believe they meant to
> hurt anybody.
>   (Looks at them again)
> And I think a jury would understand that, that it
> was an accident, I mean.

Looks at his wristwatch.

>   WYMAN
> Oh, hell, I'm covering for one of my deputies
> tonight. I'm supposed to be making the rounds in
> the business district.

Eyes each one of them.

>   WYMAN
> Appreciate you men letting me run my mouth a
> little. That's the one case I want to get all
> wrapped up before I retire in a couple of weeks.

Smiles at them and puts on his western-style hat.

>   WYMAN
> Give my best to your families. Nobody
> appreciates kin like an old widower like me.

Stands up.

WYMAN
Night.

They chorus:

MEN
Night.

They watch him walk back to the bar and set his glass and empty Diet Pepsi can down.

Then he walks out without looking back at them.

RICK
What the hell we gonna do? He knows it's us.

TOM
Well, I'll tell you one thing we're not gonna do.
We're not gonna panic. You understand?
(Looks at them both)
You understand?

They both nod.

CUT TO:

Sue's front yard. Jimmy and Sue on the front porch.

SUE
You sure you don't want me to just run a
washcloth over your face? He hit you a lot.

JIMMY (smiles)
You see me kick him in the balls?

SUE (returns smile)
Yeah, it was pretty cool, actually.

JIMMY (sits up straight)
I didn't know what else to do. I mean, I tried
to swing back at him, but it didn't seem to
work.

SUE
So you're not a fighter. It's not a big deal.

JIMMY
It is to my uncle. He doesn't think I'll ever grow
up and be a man.
(Remembering)
He was the same with her. Wanting her to shoot
and hunt and everything. And she was a girl.

SUE
Your cousin Kathryn?

JIMMY
Uh-huh. She was my best friend.

SUE
You didn't see her that often, did you?

JIMMY
No, but we spent a lot of time on the phone. She
was great.
(Beat)
And then she got killed. Those fuckers.

SUE
Everybody said it was an accident.

JIMMY
Yeah, but there wouldn't have been an accident if
they hadn't been there in the first place.

SUE
I guess that's true.

Her father comes to the front door.

FATHER
Time to come in.

SUE
Couple more minutes, Dad. Then I'll be in.

Her father nods and goes back inside.

JIMMY
You want to watch me try and start the
motorcycle again?

> SUE
> You'll get the hang of it, Jimmy.

They walk over to the motorcycle.

> JIMMY
> Uncle Richard says it's all those music lessons my
> mom made me take — rotted my brain.

He has some trouble starting the motorcycle at first, but then it roars
into life.

> SUE
> See, I told you.

He looks at her longingly for a moment, then holds out his arm and takes her
to him. They have a tender kiss.

> JIMMY
> Oh, shit.

> SUE
> Boy, I knew I was a bad kisser, but —

> JIMMY
> My face is more bruised than I thought.

> SUE
> Well, I'm gonna bruise it a little more then.

She kisses him as the motorcycle idles.

Then he takes off, waving to her in the darkness.

> CUT TO:

Jimmy sneaking up the broad staircase to the second floor of his uncle's
house.

Screen left, we can see Louise and Uncle Richard in the TV room watching
the tube.

> LOUISE (calls up to Jimmy)
> Aren't you at least going to say goodnight?

> JIMMY
> Night, Mom. Uncle Richard.

> LOUISE
> Why don't you come down a second? Uncle
> Richard's got a surprise for you.

> JIMMY
> I'm kinda tired, Mom. I think I'll just go
> to bed.

Louise and Uncle Richard give each other strange looks.

Uncle Richard gets up and comes out into the hall.

> DADE
> You all right, Jimmy?

> JIMMY
> Yeah, I'm fine.

> DADE
> You don't sound fine. And why do you keep
> holding your face away from me?

Louise comes out, stands just behind Uncle Richard, looks afraid. Then she puts her hand on Uncle Richard's arm.

> DADE
> I want you to come down here, Jimmy.

> LOUISE
> Maybe he's sick. Maybe he'd rather go upstairs.

Uncle Richard brushes Louise's hand away and stalks over to the stairway.

> DADE
> You come down here right now and let me
> see you.

After a long pause, Jimmy turns around and faces them. His face is a mess of cuts and bruises.

> LOUISE
> Jimmy! What happened?

> DADE
> You got in a fight, didn't you?

Jimmy nods.

LOUISE
A fight! Jimmy's never been in a fight in his life.

Playing against the moment, Uncle Richard erupts with laughter and slaps Jimmy manfully on the back.

DADE
Then it's damned well time!

LOUISE
But maybe he's hurt. Maybe he's —

DADE
You leave him to me, Louise. You leave him to
old Uncle Richard. Right, Jimmy?

He hugs Jimmy.

DADE
You just leave him to old Uncle Richard.

CUT TO:

A shadowy bedroom. Tom Pittman lies on top of his wife BRENDA as if they're making love. But then he rolls off her.

BRENDA
I guess Little Chuckie just doesn't want to come
out tonight and play.

Tom stares up at the ceiling.

BRENDA
Honey, according to the magazines I read, this
happens to most men every once in a while.

TOM
That's not what I'm thinking about.

BRENDA
Oh?

TOM
Wyman came into the tavern tonight.

BRENDA (afraid)
Wyman?

                              TOM
          He said that he's going to retire and that there's
          one case he wants to wrap up before he does.

                            BRENDA
                      The girl who got killed?

                              TOM
                            Exactly.

                            BRENDA
                        Then he knows?

          She sits up now, looks down at her husband.

                              TOM
                      Oh, he knows, all right.

                            BRENDA
                  What do you think he's going to do?

                              TOM
          That's the hell of it. I don't have any idea at all
          what he's going to do.

                                                    CUT TO:

          A very large, well-appointed bathroom. Jimmy sits on the toilet lid as Uncle
          Richard, like a cut man in a boxing match, works over his face with a
          washcloth. Once, Dade picks up a fifth of whiskey and soaks a washrag with
          it and applies it to Jimmy's face. It smarts. There are also two glasses sitting
          next to the fifth. For Dade, this is a celebration of sorts.

                              DADE
                    He got you some good ones.

                            JIMMY
                        He sure did.

                              DADE
                      You get him back?

          Jimmy kind of shrugs.

                            JIMMY
                    I kicked him in the balls.

> DADE
> Hard?

> JIMMY
> Real hard.

> DADE
> Good boy.

Reaches down and takes Jimmy's hands. Holds them closer to the light.

> DADE
> You didn't punch him, though.

> JIMMY
> Guess I didn't.

There is a long silence, then Dade goes over and pours himself a drink of whiskey. He guns it and then pours himself another. He guns this one, too.

Then he pours himself another one — and one for Jimmy, too. He hands it to Jimmy.

> JIMMY
> Maybe I better not, Uncle Richard.

> DADE
> Yeah, you wouldn't want to be hung over for your
> music lessons tomorrow, now would you?

Grabs the drink and pushes it in Jimmy's face.

> DADE
> C'mon, you little pussy, you take this fucking
> drink and be a man for once on your life!

Jimmy reluctantly takes the drink. He sips at it at first. We can see that he's not used to liquor. He makes faces.

Then he looks up resentfully at his uncle and guns the drink down. He's angry now; his pride has been deeply hurt.

> JIMMY
> Give me another one.

> DADE
> What?

JIMMY
You fucking heard me. I want another drink.

Uncle Richard pours him another drink.

Jimmy knocks it back. The whole thing.

JIMMY
Gimme another one.

DADE
Jimmy, I didn't have any right to call you a pussy.
I just lost my temper, son.

Jimmy glares at him.

JIMMY
Give me another fucking drink.

DADE
Your mother's gonna kick my ass.

JIMMY
If she doesn't, I will.

They look at each other a long moment and then break out laughing.

DADE (delighted)
So you're gonna kick my ass, huh?

JIMMY
Damned right I am.

He grabs the bottle and takes a long pull on it.

Dade watches him. And then he seems to come to a conclusion he's been
struggling with.

DADE
You know your mom said I had a surprise
for you?

JIMMY
Right.

DADE
Well, I'm giving you the motorcycle to take
back home.

JIMMY
God, thanks, Uncle Richard.

DADE
But now I've got another surprise. How'd you like
to take a trip with me?

JIMMY
A trip?

DADE
Just a little business trip. I've got to look over
some livestock.
(Looks out the window)
Plus, I thought we could stop by Kathryn's grave.
Before we go, I mean.
(Turns back to Jimmy)
Tomorrow would've been her birthday.

JIMMY
I'd like to go, Uncle Richard. I really would.

Uncle Richard comes over to him and musses his hair.

DADE
I'm really sorry for what I said.

JIMMY
I know you are.

DADE
We'll have a good time on this trip — then when
we get back, you can take that motorcycle of
yours on home.

JIMMY
I really appreciate it, Uncle Richard.

Uncle Richard opens the door. Louise has been standing out there all along.

DADE
This son of yours is gonna make it yet, Louise.
He's just like his Uncle Richard — you wait
and see.

Louise smiles nervously.

CUT TO:

In the morning, early, Jimmy is up and shaving. A soft knock at the door. Louise comes in.

He continues shaving. She watches him.

LOUISE
I like to watch you shave.
(Beat)
I just can't believe it's my same little boy.

JIMMY (smiling)
Better not let Uncle Richard hear you say that.

LOUISE

He means well. I mean, look at how he's taken care of us since your father died.

JIMMY

I know he means well, Mom. It's just that sometimes —

LOUISE

He just doesn't understand that there are different ways to be a man, I guess. He's got this John Wayne thing.

Jimmy has a face white with shaving foam. He grins in the mirror.

JIMMY (sardonically)

I think we're going to bond on this trip we're taking. He'll probably make me kill a moose with my bare hands and then eat the meat raw.

LOUISE

He wasn't always this bad. But since Kathryn was killed —

She comes over and kisses him on the ear. She still gets some foam on her face.

LOUISE
I just wanted to say goodbye, honey.

CUT TO:

Dade's shiny new Cadillac pulls up on the road in a cemetery. He gets out carrying fresh-cut flowers.

Dade and Jimmy go over to Kathryn's grave. Dade sets the flowers down in the appropriate place and then he kneels down next to the grave. When Jimmy doesn't kneel, Dade glares at him. Jimmy kneels down.

Dade's eyes fill with tears. We watch as his big loose hands become hard, tight fists.

Then Dade stands up, face hard, eyes still wet, and silently walks back to the car.

                                                                       END ACT ONE

Inside the car. Traveling.

                          DADE
          I always wished you and Kathryn weren't related.

                          JIMMY
                        How come?

                          DADE
          So you could have gotten married.

                    JIMMY (smiles)
          I *did* have this crush on her when we were little.
          There was this older kid down the block where I
          lived. He was always taking his girlfriend to the
          movies. So I always dreamed about taking
          Kathryn to the movies.

                          DADE
          She had a crush on you, too. One day she asked
          her mom if cousins could marry each other.

Suddenly reaches out and touches Jimmy's shoulder.

                          DADE
          I appreciate all the time you spent with her —
          and how much you loved her.

                          JIMMY
          It was my pleasure, Uncle Richard. God, she was
          my best friend. She really was.

Dade nods solemnly and drives on.

CUT TO:

Dade is driving through countryside.

> DADE
> Reach in the cooler back there and fish me out a
> beer, would you, please?

> JIMMY
> I thought it was against the law to have an open
> beer in a car.

> DADE
> Well, I suspect you're right, Jimmy. But there are
> laws and there are laws.

> JIMMY (smiles)
> I guess that clears it up.

Reaches in back and fishes out a beer for his uncle. Hands it to him.

> DADE
> Thank you. You don't want one for yourself?

> JIMMY
> Not right now.

Jimmy sits back and closes his eyes.

> DADE
> That mother of yours ever told you about
> higher law?

> JIMMY
> I don't think so.

Keeps his eyes closed.

> DADE
> Sometimes there are higher laws than the man-
> made ones. And sometimes, even if it means
> *breaking* the man-made ones, you have to honor
> the higher ones.

> JIMMY (smiling)
> Like drinking a beer?

> DADE (angry)
> This isn't time for one of your little fucking
> smirks, Jimmy.

Jimmy opens his eyes, sees how angry his uncle is.

Jimmy sits up, looks out the window.

After a long time, Dade speaks.

> DADE
> I didn't mean to snap at you.

> JIMMY
> At least you didn't call me a pussy this time,
> Uncle Richard.
> (Smiles)
> You're getting better.

Dade reaches over and musses Jimmy's hair.

> DADE (laughing)
> You little pecker.

CUT TO:

Dade's car drives past a sign that says:

WELCOME TO ARDMORE

CUT TO:

Jimmy watches through windshield as Dade is in MOTEL office.

CUT TO:

Darkness. Dade pushes open door. In the light stream, Dade and Jimmy
enter the room. Jimmy opens the blind.

> DADE (seeming serious)
> Dammit. Where are they?

> JIMMY (looking confused)
> Where are who?

> DADE
> Who? The broads, of course.

> JIMMY
> You mean girls?

> DADE
> They promised there'd be two of them.
> (Grins)
> Two for me and two for you!

Gives Jimmy a good-natured shove.

> DADE
> I had you goin' there, didn't I?

> JIMMY
> Yeah, you did.

They start laying their stuff down on their respective beds.

> DADE
> You're gonna have a big night tonight.

> JIMMY
> Oh?

> DADE
> You're going to lose your virginity.

> JIMMY
> You ever think maybe I'm not a virgin?

> DADE
> You're a virgin, all right. And it's time for you to
> grow up.

Takes a sportcoat out of his garment bag and carries it over and hangs it up.

> DADE
> Don't worry about them health-wise. They get
> tests for everything including AIDS, and they're
> just about the sexiest girls I've ever seen.

> JIMMY
> God, you're serious, aren't you?

> DADE
> Sure, I'm serious. And you should be, too. No
> way a boy your age should be a virgin.

CUT TO:

Chief of Police Wyman is sitting in his office with a big, angry man.

WYMAN
I went up and saw your wife this morning,
Tolliver. You broke her nose, her right arm, and
three fingers. Personally, I wouldn't think a frail
little 275-pounder like you could beat the shit out
of a dangerous 95-pounder like your wife — but
you did. And I'm proud of you. What'd she do
this time, burn your toast?

TOLLIVER
That fuckin' bitch ain't got no respect for men.

WYMAN
Maybe she would if she ever met one.

Knock on his partly open door. A female khaki-clad deputy sticks her head in
the door.

DEPUTY
Excuse me, Chief.

Wyman looks at her.

DEPUTY
Susan over at the motel? She said she was
supposed to call you if that Richard Dade ever
checked in? Well, she said he checked in about
twenty minutes ago.

WYMAN
Thanks, Ellen.

Deputy nods, withdraws from doorway.

WYMAN
Tolliver, you crossed the Pecos this time. I'm
gonna ask the judge to throw your ass in county
for a year.

TOLLIVER
A year? She won't be able to last a year
without me.

> WYMAN
> Yeah, I could see where a woman might get
> lonely for you.
> (Smiles)
> Nice sensitive guy like you.

Picks up phone and dials.

> WYMAN
> Judge Helen Hartly, please. Thank you.
> (Cups receiver)
> You hear about our new woman judge, Tolliver?
> (Smiles)
> You know how those women stick together.

CUT TO:

Motel room. Dade putting on his hat.

> DADE
> I'm going to run out and take a look at some
> horses.

> JIMMY
> Want me to go with you?

> DADE
> Old friend of mine. We'll probably end up talkin'
> 'bout old times. Probably just bore your ass off.

Goes to door.

> DADE
> I'll be back in a little while.

CUT TO:

A schoolyard. A few teachers play among a small group of retarded children.

Rick Bryant, one of the three robbers, stands with his wife Connie, watching the children.

A particularly retarded five-year-old girl comes over to them, followed by her teacher.

> TEACHER
> Your daughter's been very creative this week.

(Shows Crayola drawing)
Look at this.

Rick gets down on his haunches and hugs his daughter to him. It's easy to
see how much he loves her.

> TEACHER (to Connie)
> She'll be going home with you in a few more
> weeks.

> RICK
> Y'hear that, Ellie? You'll be comin' back home
> with us.

He hugs her again.

CUT TO:

Dade sits in his car across the street, watching Rick and his wife and daughter.

> DADE (to himself)
> I had a daughter, too, you cocksucker.

CUT TO:

Chief Wyman standing outside motel room door. Knocks.

Jimmy opens the door.

> JIMMY
> Help you?

> WYMAN
> I'm looking for a Mr. Richard Dade.

> JIMMY
> He's my uncle.

> WYMAN
> He isn't here right now?

> JIMMY
> No, but he should be back in a while.
> (Suspicious)
> He isn't in any trouble, is he?

> WYMAN (smiles)
> No, nothing like that. Just want to ask him a
> couple of questions.

(Beat)
Say, mind if I step in? Maybe you can help me.

JIMMY
Sure. I guess that'd be all right.

Wyman goes inside the motel room.

CUT TO:

Dade's den. Sonia is dusting. Louise comes to the door. Walks in.

LOUISE
There's a delivery man to see you, Sonia.

SONIA
The freezer?

LOUISE
I think so.

SONIA
Finally. The old one hasn't worked right for years.

Louise walks around. It's a beautiful room.

LOUISE
This is such a nice room. Almost like a sanctuary.

SONIA
He spends more and more time in here since —
since Kathryn passed on.
(Looks melancholy)
I'd better go let him in.

Louise walks around some more, then stops over at the desk and looks at the folder there that reads:

MURPHY INVESTIGATIONS INC.

She looks curious. Opens the folder.

She sees the individual photos of the three robbers.

Lifts a letter on letterhead. Reads it:

LOUISE (V.O.)
"3 Feb. Dear Mr. Dade: Pursuant to the matter

of your daughter's death, I believe I have located
the three individuals we have been looking for."

She picks up another letter. Reads it:

> LOUISE (V.O.)
> "12 March. Dear Mr. Dade: I have finally been
> able to complete background checks on the three
> individuals we have been investigating. I enclose
> a b.g. on each one."

She picks up a third letter. Reads it:

> LOUISE (V.O.)
> "6 May. Dear Mr. Dade: I am checking up on the
> three individuals once a month. All are employed
> at the tire factory again and all seem to be going
> about their lives in a normal fashion."

She picks up a fourth letter. Reads it:

> LOUISE (V.O.)
> "If your plans involve anything illegal, I should
> warn you that it is my sworn duty to contact law
> enforcement and so inform them of your plans.
> For that reason, I must advise you not to even
> bring up the matter we touched upon in our
> last conversation. What you do with the
> information I have gathered for you is entirely
> up to you."

She sets the letter down. Then picks up the photos of the men again.

Suddenly, she looks very worried.

CUT TO:

The motel room. Jimmy opens a can of Pepsi and leans on the edge of the
bureau.

> WYMAN
> You just kind of on a little vacation?

> JIMMY
> Yeah, just a business trip.

                          WYMAN
I just want to make sure I've got the right man.
Your uncle's daughter was named Kathryn?

                          JIMMY
                    Right. She was —

                          WYMAN
                         Killed.

                          JIMMY
            Right. How'd you know that?

                          WYMAN
You know a private investigator named Murphy?

                    JIMMY (Grins)
        I don't know *any* private investigators.
                          (Beat)
            How'd you know about Kathryn?

Wyman walks back to the closet where Dade hung his clothes. Keeps his
back to Jimmy.

                          WYMAN
That why he said you were coming here?
Business trip?

                          JIMMY
Yeah. That's what he said. But how'd you know
about Kathryn?

Turns back from the closet.

                          WYMAN
I checked out this Murphy. He was looking into
Kathryn's death for your uncle.

                          JIMMY
                        He was?

                          WYMAN
Yeah. That's why I need to talk to you uncle.

                          JIMMY
When he comes back, I'll tell him to call you.

Wyman opens the door.

> WYMAN
> You tell him for me if his daughter was anything
> like you, she must've been a very nice girl.

> JIMMY
> Thanks.

Wyman stares at him.

> WYMAN
> Nothin' to be scared of, kid. But I really do need
> to talk to him.

He walks out.

CUT TO:

Dade sitting in his car in front of GENTLE CARE NURSING HOME.
Steve Winders, the third robber, is walking his white-haired mother around
the grounds.

She stumbles and falls to one knee. We see in Winders' panic reaction how
close he is to her.

Dade watches all this without expression. Then he drives away.

CUT TO:

Wyman parks his car in a gravel lot behind the police station. He's just
walking up to the front door when he sees Tom Pittman on the street.

> WYMAN
> Hey, Pittman.

Waves him over.

Pittman comes over.

> WYMAN
> There's a man in town that seems to have a
> special interest in you and your two friends. Even
> had a private investigator check you out.

> TOM
> Yeah. And who would that be?

> WYMAN
> That would be Mr. Richard Dade, the father of
> the girl you accidentally killed when you stuck up
> that convenience store.

> TOM
> We don't have anything to hide.

> WYMAN
> I'm not sure Mr. Dade shares that opinion. I just
> wanted to give you fair warning.

Wyman stares at him a long moment.

> WYMAN
> You could always say thanks for me warning you.

Tom looks back at him. Then drops the tough-guy bullshit. Sighs.

> TOM
> Thanks, Chief.

CUT TO:

In the hotel room, Jimmy is propped up on his bed reading a Dean Koontz novel.

Dade comes in. He takes out a fifth of Jack Daniels from a paper bag and shows it to Jimmy.

> DADE
> Brought us a present.

> JIMMY
> I think I'll skip it, Uncle Richard. I had plenty last
> night.

> DADE
> Last night? Hell, that wasn't anything.

Dade goes in the can and pees. We watch this from behind. When he's done, he washes his hands with hot water and soap. Then he picks up two paper-wrapped glasses and fills them half full with sour mash.

He carries the drinks out, along with the bottle, and sits on the bed opposite Jimmy.

> DADE
> You'll have to drink this one, my friend. I'm
> saluting Kathryn on her birthday.

Jimmy looks at him. Sees how sad he looks.

> JIMMY
> Aw, hell, Uncle Richard. I guess I could have
> one. For Kathryn.

Dade hands him the glass.

> DADE
> For Kathryn.

Jimmy drinks as much as he can. It really burns going down.

> JIMMY
> Wow.

> DADE
> You'll get used to it. Then you'll start appreciatin' it.
> (He hoists his glass)
> To the best little girl a man could ever have.

Then he's suddenly on his feet, hurling the glass against the wall.

> DADE
> Those cocksuckers!

Turns to Jimmy.

> DADE
> I know who they are. I'll tell you that. I have the
> names of every fucking one of them! Every
> fucking one!

Dade is seized by grief. He stoops over and begins sobbing.

Jimmy just watches him for a time. Then he goes over to Dade.

> DADE
> Uncle Richard? Uncle Richard, why don't you
> come over and sit down?

Slowly, he leads Dade over to the bed and sits him down on the edge of it.

JIMMY
I'm gonna get you another drink, all right? You
just sit right there.

Jimmy goes into the toilet and gets another glass. He brings it out and pours
Dade a good stiff one.

JIMMY
Take this, Uncle Richard.
(Beat)
C'mon now. Take it.

DADE
She would've been sixteen fucking years old
today. Sixteen fucking years old.

Jimmy goes over and sits on the edge of his bed and just looks sadly at his
uncle.

DADE
Sixteen fucking years old.

CUT TO:

Dade's kitchen. Louise and Sonia are sitting at the table. Sonia is smoking a
cigarette. Starts coughing.

SONIA
Dade wants me to give these up.

LOUISE
You should.

SONIA (smiles)
I'm one of those people who should probably do
a lot of things.

Louise picks up the private investigator's folder.

LOUISE
This scares me.

SONIA
Yeah, me, too.

Sonia picks it up and looks at it.

SONIA
Maybe we're overreacting.

LOUISE
Looks like he found the men who killed Kathryn.

SONIA
That doesn't necessarily mean he's going to do
anything about it.

LOUISE
If he wasn't, he would've turned all this over to
the law.

SONIA (checks watch)
I'll give him a call after dinner. See how he
sounds.

LOUISE
I'm worried about Jimmy.

SONIA
If you knew how much he loves that boy, you
wouldn't be worried at all.

Louise reaches out and takes Sonia's hand.

LOUISE
That's nice to hear.

SONIA
He always tells people that Jimmy is "his son."
Since Kathryn died — well, Jimmy took her
place.

Looks at the file.

SONIA
But I'm still going to give Richard a call after
dinner. See what's going on.

CUT TO:

Uncle Richard is in the motel room bathroom.

We see him from behind, washing his face, wetting his hair, running a comb
through it. Then pouring himself a fresh drink from the bottle on the sink.

> DADE
>
> Sorry I turned into such a pussy on you, Jimmy.

Jimmy comes and stands in the doorway.

> JIMMY
>
> I loved her, too, Uncle Richard. I know how you feel about those bastards. If I had half a chance, I'd tear their fucking faces off for what they did to her.

Dade turns around and looks at Jimmy.

> DADE
>
> I never heard you talk like that before.

> JIMMY
>
> I mean it, Uncle Richard. I hate those motherfuckers.

Dade is all lit up. Jimmy is the kind of kid he wants him to be, after all.

> DADE
>
> You gotta have another drink with me.

Jimmy smiles.

> JIMMY
>
> Yeah, you're right. I think I do.

Dade pours him a drink.

Jimmy downs it, choking. But he keeps on drinking anyway.

> DADE
>
> You're like my own god damned son, Jimmy, you know that?
>
> (Gets teary again)
>
> My own god damned son.

They embrace.

CUT TO:

Wyman's car pulls up in front of Tom's trailer. At night, the place doesn't look so bad. But it is very isolated out here on the prairie.

Wyman walks up to the door and knocks. Brenda answers the door. She's carrying "the little one" as she calls him. He's in nice fresh diapers.

> WYMAN
> Evening, Brenda.

> BRENDA
> Evening, Chief.

> WYMAN
> Looks like you've got your hands full as usual.

> BRENDA (smiles nervously)
> Yup. As usual.

She looks back into the trailer as the other kids make noise.

> BRENDA
> You two stop that and go get ready for bed.

Looks back at Wyman.

> BRENDA
> They're regular dynamos.

> WYMAN
> Was wondering if Tom might be home, Brenda.

> BRENDA
> 'Fraid not, Chief.

> WYMAN
> Any idea where I might find him?

> BRENDA
> Bowling alley. This is his league night.

> WYMAN
> Darn it, I forgot about that. Being his league
> night, I mean.

> BRENDA
> I don't think you did, Chief. I think you knew it
> was his league night. I think you came here to
> see me.

> WYMAN (smiles)
> I must be slippin' in my old age. I used to be
> pretty good at stuff like this.

> BRENDA

Bein' a good liar ain't nothin' to be proud of,
Chief.

> WYMAN

No, I guess it isn't, is it?
(Stares directly at her)
I'm afraid there could be some trouble, Brenda.
I'm gonna need your help talkin' some sense into
your husband.

The little one in her arms starts to cry.

> BRENDA

Place is a pit. Enter at your own risk, as Tom
always likes to say.

> WYMAN

Should see my place since the Mrs. died. Your
place couldn't look half as bad as mine.

> BRENDA

All's I got to offer is coffee.

> WYMAN

Cup of coffee would be darned good right now.

He steps up into the trailer. The doors closes, shutting the night into
darkness again.

> CUT TO:

A very decent if somewhat plain restaurant. Jimmy and Dade are at a table.
A pretty, middle-aged waitress stands at their table.

> WAITRESS

Would you like a few minutes?

> DADE

If I told you what I'd really like, you might be
surprised.

> WAITRESS (flirting back)

I bet I wouldn't. Be surprised, I mean.
(Hands them menus)

Dade folds them up and hands them back.

> DADE
> Don't need 'em, honey. Know just what we want.

He shapes his hands to make big invisible steaks.

> DADE
> Two steaks medium rare. Biggest and best you
> got. French fries and salads with both of 'em. And
> a Cutty Sark and a water for me and a bottle of
> Heineken's for my boy here.

> WAITRESS
> Oh, sweetie. I can't serve your boy no beer. We'd
> lose our license.

Jimmy starts to speak — looking very uncomfortable — but Dade holds up
his hand.

> DADE
> Put your hand out, honey.

> WAITRESS
> My hand?

> DADE
> Yes'm, and palm up.

She puts her hand out, palm up.

From his shirt pocket, Dade takes a piece of currency and lays it in the palm
of her hand.

> WAITRESS (stunned)
> Is this real?

> DADE
> It sure is.

> WAITRESS
> A fifty dollar bill?

> DADE
> It sure is. Now how about that Cutty and
> that beer?

> WAITRESS
> You bet.

The waitress goes away.

> DADE
> Money talks.

> JIMMY
> Couldn't she get in trouble?

> DADE
> She took the money, didn't she? She gets in
> trouble, it's her problem.

> JIMMY
> She seems like a nice woman.

> DADE
> That's the way it works, Jimmy. I wanted
> something and she wanted something. So we
> made our little trade. I gave her money and she
> gave you your bottle of beer.

The waitress comes back. Sets down their drinks.

> WAITRESS
> Got a grandson with a birthday coming up,
> mister. I really appreciate that tip.
> (Smiles)
> Though I still wonder if it's real.

Dade pats her on the ass. She doesn't seem to mind at all.

> WAITRESS
> Be a little while yet with your food.

The waitress goes away.

> DADE
> Grandson with a birthday coming up. Still think
> I'm a big asshole?

> JIMMY
> I just don't want to see her get in trouble is all,
> Uncle Richard.

Looks at his beer.

> DADE
> It won't bite ya.

> JIMMY
> Beer on top of that whiskey. I don't want to
> get sick.

> DADE
> And I don't want you to get sick. You got to save
> yourself till later.

> JIMMY
> Later?

> DADE
> You'll see. So tell me more about this hayseed
> sheriff. What'd he say his name was?

> JIMMY
> Wyman?

> DADE
> And why'd he want to talk to me? That's the part
> you haven't told me yet.

> JIMMY
> That's the part I didn't understand. Something
> about some investigator named Murphy.

Dade looks suddenly angry.

> DADE
> How the hell'd he find out about Murphy?

> JIMMY
> Who is Murphy, anyway, Uncle Richard?

> DADE (to himself)
> Nosy son-of-a-bitch.

> JIMMY
> Who's a nosy son-of-a-bitch, Uncle Richard?
> Murphy or Wyman?

But Dade isn't listening. He's up on his feet.

JIMMY
You stay here. I gotta go make a call.

Storms away.

CUT TO:

Wyman sits in Brenda's living room with his cup of coffee in his lap. The children play quietly in the background. Brenda has the baby in her lap.

WYMAN
You make good coffee.

BRENDA
You didn't come here to tell me about my coffee.
(Stares at him)
You got me scared, Chief Wyman.

WYMAN
In a way, that's what I want to do.

BRENDA
Scare me?

WYMAN
Fine pair of boys back there. Lucky to have parents as good as you and Tom.

BRENDA
You really mean that, about Tom being a good parent?

WYMAN
I sure do. And that's why I'm here.

Leans forward and speaks low so the boys won't hear him.

WYMAN
Tom's in some trouble.

BRENDA (obviously lying)
I guess I don't know what you're talking about.

Wyman sits back in his chair and shakes his head.

WYMAN
I knew your folks real good.

BRENDA
I know you did. And they liked you a lot, too.

WYMAN
In fact, I was at your christening.

BRENDA
I guess I don't know what you're getting at, Chief
Wyman.

WYMAN
What I'm getting at is that you can trust me,
know that I'm acting in your best interest.
(Stares at her)
I am, you know.

BRENDA
Anything I'd say about — the trouble you
mentioned — I couldn't say nothing without Tom
being here.

WYMAN
There's a man.

BRENDA
A man?

WYMAN
A man named Richard Dade.

BRENDA
Dade?

WYMAN
It's real hard talking when you keep on
pretending you don't know what I'm saying.

Still, she says nothing.

WYMAN
The girl's father. The girl who was accidentally
killed. And I sincerely believe her death was an
accident. And I also sincerely believe that the
county attorney wouldn't press for anything more
than involuntary manslaughter. If Tom and the
others —

Stares at her.

> WYMAN
> You really aren't going to help me on this, are
> you, Brenda? Even though it's for your own good.

> BRENDA
> Tom has to speak for himself, Chief.

The baby starts to fuss.

> BRENDA
> He's tired. I think he needs to be put to bed.

> WYMAN
> This Dade went to an awful lot of trouble to find
> out about Tom and his friends. I'm not sure what
> he's doing in town exactly.

> BRENDA
> Maybe you should tell Tom this instead of me.

> WYMAN
> I told Tom. Earlier today.

> BRENDA (surprised)
> You did?

The baby is really fussing now.

> BRENDA
> What'd he say?

> WYMAN
> Not much. He's like you. Pretends he doesn't
> know what I'm talking about.

Wyman stands up.

> BRENDA
> Well, you got your way, Chief Wyman.

> WYMAN
> Oh, how's that?

> BRENDA
> You succeeded in scarin' me.

> WYMAN
> Good. Then maybe you can scare that husband of
> yours into having a talk with me. An honest talk.
> We're past the point where we can afford to lie to
> each other anymore.

> BRENDA
> You think this Dade might really hurt Tom?

> WYMAN
> I sure do, Brenda. I sure do.

CUT TO:

Dade is in a phone booth at the back of the restaurant.

> DADE
> Well, there's a chief of police here who sure
> seems to know a lot about me — for you never
> having talked to him or anything.
> (Beat)
> Don't bullshit me, Murphy. Just tell me the truth.

CUT TO:

Murphy on a bed in a cheap apartment. He's in boxer shorts and an
undershirt. A blowzy bottle blonde in bra and panties lies next to him, idly
playing with his dick as he talks.

> MURPHY (sighs)
> He broke into my room one night, this Chief of
> Police son-of-a-bitch. I didn't know it but I guess
> he followed me around questioning the people I
> questioned. I guess he wanted to find out what I
> was doin' in his little town.

He takes the woman's hand and slides it in the opening of his boxer shorts.

> MURPHY
> So anyway, one rainy night I get back to my motel
> room and I see this flashlight inside and I go in
> there with my gun and all that cowboy shit — and
> it turns out to be this fucking chief of police,
> right? So I ask this asshole what he's doing and he
> shows me this warrant. These hayseeds stick

together. I didn't tell him shit. Not shit. Anything
he learned about you, he picked up entirely on
his own.

There is a pause. We hear Dade shouting into the receiver.

> MURPHY
> I didn't tell you because I didn't think it was
> important.
> (Beat)
> Why didn't I think it was important? Figure it out
> for your fucking self, Dade. I figure you were
> going to turn all the information I got over to the
> cops where the girl was shot — and let them take
> it from there.

She begins to jack him off.

Dade's shouting into the receiver again.

> MURPHY
> Mr. Dade, if you didn't have some stupid fucking
> TV idea about handling this yourself, then you
> wouldn't have to worry about the Chief of Police
> now, would you?

Leans back. She's really going at him now. He rolls his eyes in pleasure.

> MURPHY
> (Dade shouts at him some more)
> Well, I don't want to work with you anymore
> either, Dade. Your bill's paid up so I can tell you
> what a psycho asshole you really are.
> (Dade shouts at him some more)
> And I can also have the pleasure of slamming the
> fucking phone in your fucking ear.

He slams the phone.

He looks down at the woman. He speaks in baby talk.

> MURPHY
> How about giving little John Henry a kiss? He's
> real lonely tonight.

She starts to go down on him.

CUT TO:

Dade comes back to the table. Sits down. Takes a swallow.

> ### JIMMY
> He just said he wanted to talk to you. And he
> mentioned Murphy.

> ### DADE (scowls)
> Murphy! All the money I spent on that son-of-a-
> bitch and then he sells me out.

> ### JIMMY
> Sells you out? Whaddayou mean?

> ### DADE
> It means he's like most people runnin' around on
> this planet. No balls. No backbone. No honor.

He picks up his drink, finishes it off, and then looks around for the waitress.

She's waiting on a table.

Dade shouts at her.

> ### DADE
> You think we could get a little god damned
> service over here.

She looks embarrassed.

Jimmy squirms in his seat.

> ### JIMMY
> She's a nice lady, Uncle Richard.

> ### DADE
> Nice lady, huh? Bet if I gave her $100 she'd get
> right down on her knees and blow me. Right
> here. Right now. You wanna bet me $25?

Takes a small roll of bills from his western shirt and plunks it down on the table.

> ### DADE
> You want to test my theory, boy?

JIMMY
Don't ask her, Uncle Richard. Please.

Dade looks at him for a time.

DADE
You really are a pussy sometimes, you know that?
I give a woman a goddamned $50 tip, least I can
expect is some service.

The waitress arrives.

WAITRESS
I just got kinda busy is all. I didn't mean to
neglect you.
(She looks sad and nervous. She's as Jimmy says
she is, a nice decent woman)

But Dade is having one of his moments. He looks at Jimmy and then he
looks at the waitress. Then he takes his roll out and slaps a $100 bill on the
table, all the time looking up at the waitress.

DADE
The boy and I here have a bet going.

WAITRESS
Bet?

DADE
Yeah. I bet him $25 that you'd —

JIMMY
Uncle Richard!

Jimmy accidentally knocks his beer over, he's so angry. People in the
restaurant turn to watch.

JIMMY
Leave her alone!

The waitress looks first at Dade and then at Jimmy. She knows what Dade
was going to say.

WAITRESS
Let me get that for you.

She picks up the beer and the glass and starts to wipe up the spilled beer.

WAITRESS
I appreciate you being such a gentleman and all,
young man.

Jimmy still looks miserable.

Dade glowers at him.

Just as the waitress finishes up, she reaches into her apron and plucks out the
fifty dollar bill and drops it on the table.

WAITRESS
I don't believe I care to accept this.

DADE
No skin off my ass.

But Jimmy picks up the money and puts it in her hand.

JIMMY
He isn't usually like this, ma'am. He's just kinda
down. His daughter — she died. And he's having
a hard time is all.

The waitress' face softens as she listens to Jimmy talk.

WAITRESS
I'm sorry about your daughter.

DADE
He shouldn't have told you about it. It's family
business. My family.

She looks at the money in her hand. Jimmy closes her hand around the
money. The waitress leaves.

DADE
I don't need you to defend me.

JIMMY
I just didn't want her to think —

DADE
Why should I give a shit what some kind of
waitress thinks of me?

Jimmy just looks at him.

> JIMMY
Maybe you should go see that policeman, Uncle
Richard.

> DADE
And maybe you should just shut your fuckin'
mouth, you ever think of that?

He stands up, digs in his shirt pocket, rips off several bills and throws them
down on the table. Then he stalks off, leaving Jimmy sitting alone.

After a time, the waitress comes back over.

> WAITRESS
You gonna be all right?

> JIMMY
Yeah, I'll be fine. I just don't want you to think
that he's like that all the time.

> WAITRESS (smiles)
I'll bet he's a regular saint most of the time.

> JIMMY
He's got a bad temper.

> WAITRESS
Yeah, I kind've noticed that.

> JIMMY
But he's not bad — in here.
(Taps his heart)

She looks at him.

> WAITRESS
I was gonna say something real stupid.

> JIMMY
Yeah? Like what?

> WAITRESS
I was gonna say I hope you stay as sweet as you
are — but you can't. They won't let you.
(Sadly)
They won't be satisfied till you're just like them.

CUT TO:

The parking lot of the restaurant. Dade leans against the grill of his car. He looks despondent. Jimmy sees him, then stops. He's just slightly afraid.

Dade looks up.

> DADE
> Well, I sure did it in there, didn't I?

> JIMMY
> Yeah, you sure did.
> (Beat)
> She didn't have it coming, Uncle Richard.

> DADE
> You want me to go in and apologize?

> JIMMY
> Nah. That's all right.

He walks over to the car.

> DADE
> I'm gonna make it up to you tonight, Jimmy. I've got one hell of a time planned for us.

> JIMMY
> You gonna see that cop?

> DADE
> You want me to?

> JIMMY
> Yeah. He seemed like a nice guy.

> DADE (sardonic)
> Like that waitress, huh? Nice?

> JIMMY
> Yeah, Uncle Richard. Nice — just like that waitress.

There's an edge in Jimmy's voice and in his eyes. We see him subtly stand up to Dade for the very first time.

> JIMMY
> I mean, you know she's nice, right?

> DADE (smirks)
> I wish I had your faith in humanity, kiddo.

> JIMMY
> I want you to tell me that you think she's a nice
> woman.

Dade sees that Jimmy isn't about to take any more shit from him, not at that
moment anyhow.

> DADE
> She's a nice woman, Jimmy. A damned nice
> woman, in fact.

They stare at each other.

> DADE
> Let's go see that cop and get it over with, all right?

Dade hesitantly extends his arm to Jimmy's shoulder — will Jimmy shrug it off?

But Jimmy lets Dade slide his arm over his shoulder.

> DADE
> I love you, Jimmy. I hope you know that.

> JIMMY
> Yeah, that's what makes you so hard to
> understand sometimes — I know you love me but
> you still treat me like shit sometimes . . . just the
> way you did Kathryn.

> DADE
> You don't have any goddamn right to talk to me
> that way!
> (Beat)

He seems miserable now—but not angry.

> DADE
> That's somethin' I'll take to my grave, Jimmy, the
> way I treated her sometimes.
> (Beat)
> She always said I was better at hating than loving,
> and maybe she was right.

CUT TO:

Wyman's office. Wyman is at his desk, writing out forms. A uniformed officer goes to the window and looks out.

> COP
> I'll be damned.

> WYMAN
> What?

> COP
> It's him.

> WYMAN
> You gonna give me a clue?

> COP
> That Richard Dade.

> WYMAN
> Coming here?

> COP
> Uh-huh. Big as you please.

> WYMAN
> That boy with him?

> COP
> Huh-uh. He's alone.

> WYMAN
> Nice kid. Damned nice.

> COP
> Here he comes.

Rushes over to his desk, sits down and pretends to be working.

Dade comes in. He is not the least intimidated. His walk contains his usual swagger, and his gaze, as always, is mildly disapproving of everything he encounters.

> DADE
> Evening.

> COP
> Evening. Help you with something?

                          DADE
I'm looking for the chief. Wyman, I think his
name is.

                          WYMAN
                  That'd be me, Mr. Dade.

                      DADE (smiles)
         Jimmy was right. You *do* know who I am.

Wyman comes over and puts forth his hand.

                          WYMAN
Sorry about your girl, Dade. Lost a wife here not
long ago so I've got some sense of what you're
going through.

                          DADE
                         Cancer?

                          WYMAN
                          Yeah.

                          DADE
Me, too. That's how I lost my wife. Eight years
ago it was.

                          WYMAN
I've got a more private office in the back, Mr.
Dade. Why don't we kind've drift back that way?

                          DADE
                          Fine.

Dade follows him back along a narrow corridor.

                          WYMAN
Kind of a dump, this place, but I'm gonna miss it.

                          DADE
                      You retiring?

                          WYMAN
                   Yup. And real soon.

They enter the office and sit down. Instead of a lot of patriotic stuff, Wyman
has a lot of family pictures on the wall.

DADE
Don't you hate to turn it over to some young pup
who doesn't know half as much as you do?

Pours them coffee from a Mr. Coffee sitting next to his desk.

WYMAN
Are you kidding? That young one out front? Got a
Masters in Criminology. He knows a hell of a lot
more about law enforcement than I ever will.

Pushes Dade's cup of coffee to him.

WYMAN
Where's the boy?

DADE
He decided to wait out in the car.

WYMAN
Nice kid.

DADE
His mama raised him all by herself. You know
how boys like that can be.

WYMAN
My mama raised me all by herself, Mr. Dade.

DADE (smiles)
There I go again. Stickin' my dick in the light
socket. No offense meant, Chief.

WYMAN
None taken.
(Beat)
I kept pretty close to Murphy while he was here.
Not often a little town like this gets a big city
private investigator snoopin' around.

DADE
Don't think he don't charge for snoopin' around,
either.

WYMAN
Can we cut the bullshit, Mr. Dade?

DADE
I wasn't aware of any bullshit.

WYMAN
Three men accidentally killed your daughter in
the commission of a robbery. Murphy tracked
them here and told you about them. I want to
know why you're here, Mr. Dade.

DADE
You know these men?

WYMAN
I do.

DADE
And you agree with Murphy that they're the men
who killed her?

WYMAN
I do.

Rage in Dade. Slams his fist on the desk.

DADE
Then why the hell don't you arrest them!

WYMAN
Because I can't *prove* they did it. And short of
that, I need a confession.

DADE
So they just go free?

Wyman stands up and walks over to a window and looks out at the night.

WYMAN
I'm going to say something that's really going to
piss you off, Mr. Dade.

DADE
Oh?

WYMAN
I'm going to tell you that they're basically decent
men. The tire factory closed down here and the
whole town went a little crazy. People started

losing everything they had. These three men,
they were the same. First, the bank took their
cars back. And then they started leaning on them
about the mortgages. These men couldn't even
get part-time jobs. So they did something foolish.

> DADE
> They killed my daughter.

> WYMAN
> No, they didn't, Mr. Dade. Not in the way you
> mean. They robbed a store and one of them
> dropped his gun in panic and it misfired. As a
> result, your daughter was killed.

Dade is once again enraged.

> DADE
> I can't believe this shit! You're defending cold-
> blooded murderers!

Wyman comes back and sits behind his desk.

> WYMAN
> I believe they should be sent to prison for
> involuntary manslaughter. They shouldn't have
> stuck up that store, and your daughter wouldn't
> be dead if they hadn't. But they're not killers in
> the sense you mean, Mr. Dade. And if you just
> have a little patience, they'll confess.

> DADE
> They will?

> WYMAN
> Yeah, they will. Because they can't deal with what
> they did. You can see that in their faces.
> (Leans forward on his elbows)
> Mr. Dade, why don't you get in that fancy-ass car
> of yours and go back home where you belong?
> And take that nice young kid with you? I've
> already started leaning on them about a
> confession. Told them that that's the one
> unfinished piece of business I plan to finish up
> before I retire — getting that confession.

(Beat)
I can handle this in my own way, Mr. Dade.
(Looks at him)
And I'm very sorry about your daughter. It was
hard enough losing a wife —
(shakes his head)
— but losing a young girl . . .

He stands up. He picks up Dade's hat and hands it to him as he comes
around the desk. Dade stands up.

WYMAN
I don't imagine you like me very much right now,
do you, Mr. Dade?

DADE
No, I don't imagine I do.

Walks him down to the door.

WYMAN
It's better if we handle this my way, Mr. Dade.

DADE
You really think you're going to get a confession?

WYMAN
I really do, Mr. Dade.

Dade turns to face him.

WYMAN
Now why don't you get a good night's sleep at
the motel and in the morning, get up and head
back home?

DADE
I guess that's something to think about, isn't it?

Wyman smiles. We see the small-town politician in him now.

WYMAN
It sure is something to think about, Mr. Dade. It
sure is.

                                                    CUT TO:

Phone booth across the street from Dade's car. Jimmy's in there talking.

                              JIMMY
          You're getting busy. I can hear a lot of voices.
                              (Beat)
          I wish I had one of those ice cream cones of yours
          right now.
                              (Beat)
          I just wanted to thank you for last night. I mean,
          the way you handled it and all.
                              (Smiles)
          You were just afraid I'd kill him if I ever started
          hitting him.
                              (Beat)
          You think I could call you at home? I'd like to talk
          to you.
                              (Smiles)
          Great. I'll call you tomorrow night then.

He looks across the street

                              JIMMY
              There's my uncle. I better haul ass.
                              (Beat)
          Haul ass? It's just something we say in Cedar
          Rapids.
                              (Grins)
          Yeah, we *are* pretty cool in Cedar Rapids. 'Night.

Hangs up. He's got that first-love look on his face. He leaves the booth and
walks across the street to Dade's car.

                              JIMMY
              How'd it go with Wyman?

Dade just shrugs.

                              DADE
          Kind of a hayseed, but I don't think he wants any
          trouble. Just kinda checking me out, I guess.

They get in the car and drive off.

                                                          CUT TO:

Dade pulls into the parking lot of a liquor store.

> DADE
> You know what Wild Turkey is?

> JIMMY
> Kind of like Jack Daniels?

> DADE
> Kinda. But better.

He punches Jimmy on the arm playfully.

> DADE
> I'm gettin' you your own bottle.

CUT TO:

Wyman's back office, where he talked to Dade a few minutes ago. Wyman's in his chair, feet up on his desk when the young cop comes to the door.

> COP
> What'd you think of him?

Comes in and pours himself a cup of coffee.

> WYMAN
> I take it you're referring to Mr. Dade?

Cop nods.

> WYMAN
> I'm not sure. On the one hand, I feel sorry for
> him, losing a daughter like that. On the other —

Stops and thinks.

> COP
> You ever going to get around to finishing that
> sentence?

Wyman takes his feet down. Sits up.

> WYMAN
> I'm not sure *how* to finish it. Like I said, on the
> one hand, I feel sorry for him. I don't think you
> ever recover from losing a child. My sister had a
> boy who drowned when he was seven. In a lot of
> ways, we buried her the same day we buried him.

COP
You think Dade's like that?

WYMAN
A little bit. On the other hand —

COP
That's the part you haven't finished yet.

WYMAN
On the other hand, he's a cold, arrogant guy
who's used to having his own way in everything
he does. That's my sense of him, anyway.

COP
You think he's going to cause any trouble?

WYMAN
That's the part I'm not sure of.
(Beat)
And that's the part that makes me nervous.

CUT TO:

A two-story farmhouse. Newly painted. Nice-looking. Four or five cars in the
driveway. Loud rock music. The impression is there's a party going on.

JIMMY (smiles)
Now you going to tell me why we came here?

DADE
Huh-uh. First, I'm going to give you this bottle of
Wild Turkey.

Hands it over ceremoniously.

DADE
You drink this over the next twenty-four hours,
Jimmy, you'll have completed the first half of
Uncle Richard's sure-fire manhood ritual.

JIMMY
Sure-fire manhood ritual?

DADE
Same thing my father did for me, same thing his
father did for him. You know, the Plains Indians

used to make their young men stay out in the
woods alone for several days. If they survived,
they were accepted as braves.

JIMMY
And if they didn't survive —

DADE
And if they didn't survive, they were a bunch of
candy-asses who were better off dead anyway.

Bends down to peer through the windshield at the house.

JIMMY
What kinda place you say this was, Uncle
Richard?

CUT TO:

It's this kinda place: a whorehouse. There are six girls and most of them have
paid their visit to Dr. Jiggle, the silicone merchant. They wear halter tops
that emphasize their jiggling breasts, and Levi cutoffs. Couple of farmboys
are already here, drunk and a little bit rowdy, but not hurting anybody. All
this is overseen by Jenny, a crippled middle-aged woman with a cane and an
eyepatch. She wears a prim dress with a high frilly collar. It's much too hot
for such a dress.

Dade knocks on the outside door, but he knows they can't hear him for the
music. He opens the door and goes inside to the vestibule. He's carrying his
bottle of Wild Turkey, just as Jimmy is carrying his.

Once they're in the room, they see that the farmboys are celebrating a
birthday. There's a big cake. Hooker #1 speaks.

HOOKER #1
You want me to blow out that candle for you?

FARMBOY (laughs)
I'll take care of the candles. You just worry
about me!

JENNY
Good evening, Mr. Dade.

DADE
Evening, Jenny. I'm gonna have a quick drink

with the boy here, and then we'll send him
upstairs.

> JENNY
> Sounds good to me.

They walk into another room while the party gets more raucous
behind them.

> FARMBOY (to Hooker #1)
> Why don't you do me while I do the candles!

> JENNY
> If you do, I want to be sure to get a picture of it.

Jimmy and Dade go into a room with a couch and armchairs and a big-
screen TV. They sit at a small table. Dade grabs two glasses and pours them
each drinks. He pushes one of them to Jimmy.

> DADE
> I just want you to know that it's natural to be
> nervous the first time.

> JIMMY
> But Uncle Richard —

> DADE
> My old man was nervous, too. One night when he
> was drunk, he told me he could barely get it up
> that first time.
> (Looks straight at Jimmy)
> So whatever you're worried about — it's natural.

But before he can finish, there's another outburst of laughter.

> FARMBOY (O.C.)
> C'mon, Jenny, you gotta get a picture of this. I
> got a pretty good sized one, don't you think?

More laughter.

> DADE
> You know how my old man put it to me when he
> brought me to a place like this?

> JIMMY
> Uncle Richard —

But Dade is finished talking. He pours them each another drink and hoists his glass.

> DADE
> Your dad was the best friend I ever had, Jimmy.
> Now you're the best friend I've got. And that
> means a hell of a lot to me. Drink up.

Jimmy sees that he doesn't have any choice. He knocks back his drink, coughing and sputtering after he does so.

> DADE
> Went down the wrong pipe, huh?

> JIMMY
> I thought you said this was real smooth whiskey.

> DADE
> It is.
> (Winks)
> If you're used to drinkin' whiskey.

Another geyser of laughter from the other room.

> DADE
> I'm goin' upstairs, too. I'll walk with you.

> JIMMY
> Uncle Richard, there's really something I should
> tell you about me.

Dade looks worried.

> DADE
> Nothing — perverted or anything?

Jimmy stares at him a moment and then shakes his head.

> JIMMY
> Never mind, Uncle Richard. Let's just go
> upstairs.

>   CUT TO:

Hallway upstairs. There are several doors along the hall, and each one is closed.

DADE
There used to be a little Mexican gal who
worked here —

JIMMY
This wasn't when Aunt Helen was alive, was it?

DADE
I was havin' fun, Jimmy. Fun. The way men do
sometimes. It didn't mean diddly squat to me.
(Defensive)
I *loved* your aunt, Jimmy, and I never would've
done anything to harm our marriage. Never.
(Looks up and down the hall)
You're in Room D. You want me to check her out
first?

Jimmy still looks and sounds a little crushed about Dade being unfaithful.

JIMMY
I'll be all right.

DADE
You sure?

JIMMY
I'm sure.

DADE
Remember — you're going up the stairs a boy —

JIMMY
but coming down the stairs a man. I
remember it, Uncle Richard. I really do.

DADE
I asked for a nice, young juicy one for you
(Nudges him)
Hope mine's half as good as yours. And you know
the nice thing — I got both of them for the whole
night. You can get drunk and pass out if you want
and nobody'll hassle you. Nobody.

Jimmy still looks very skeptical about all this but he walks over to Room D,
knocks quietly.

MISTY
Come in.

Jimmy looks at Dade.

DADE
A nice, juicy young one.

Jimmy opens the door and goes in. The room is in shadow. There is a brass
bed and a bureau and a darkened TV. Everything is feminine in a futzy
contrived way — too many frills. Next to the window stands Misty, who is
twenty and with a pretty but overly madeup face. Like the room, she is
dressed in a way that is almost a parody of sexy femininity — Frederick's of
Hollywood run amok.

MISTY
I was thinkin' maybe you backed out.

JIMMY
No, ma'am.

MISTY
Your uncle paid a lot of money for me. He really
wants you to enjoy this.

She smiles, as if reading his mind.

MISTY
He said you'd be nervous. You want to have a
drink and maybe a massage first?

JIMMY
I think I'd just like to sit down for a while.

MISTY
Maybe he picked the wrong one.

JIMMY
Ma'am?

MISTY
I wish you'd quit callin' me that. I'm not much
older than you.
(Beat)
Maybe he picked the wrong one — I mean,

maybe you don't think I'm . . . Maybe I don't turn
you on.

> JIMMY
> It isn't you — it's me.
> (Beat)
> Could I just sit down for a while?

She doesn't answer. He goes over and sits in a straight back chair and stares
out the rear window. At different intervals, we hear laughter and music
exploding downstairs.

She comes over and lifts the bottle from his hand.

> MISTY
> Wow. Wild Turkey.

> JIMMY
> Help yourself.

> MISTY (tenderly)
> Thanks for not calling me ma'am.

Smiles at her.

> JIMMY
> My pleasure.

She pours them both a drink. Brings it over.

> JIMMY
> I'm really going to get drunk tonight.

> MISTY
> How many drinks've you had?

> JIMMY
> Four — more than I've ever had in my life

> MISTY
> Well, I'll be glad to help you finish that bottle if
> that's what's worryin' you. Don't get Wild Turkey
> very often.

She walks behind him, sets her drink down and starts massaging his
shoulders.

> JIMMY
> I wish you wouldn't do that.

> MISTY
> I just had a very uncharitable thought.

> JIMMY
> Oh?

> MISTY
> Yeah. I just thought — maybe you're one of those
> boys who don't like women.

She lets that significant statement hang in the air.

CUT TO:

Two rooms down the hall, Dade is having no problems with his woman. He's taking her from behind while she's got her arms spread wide over the bureau she's clutching as he's pounding into her. When he comes, it's almost an act of violence, so much jamming motion, so harsh the grunts and groans.

He slips to the floor, naked, his chest heaving, his skin slick with sweat. His breath comes in gasps.

BONNIE lies down next to him.

> BONNIE
> I wish you came here more often.

> DADE
> Darlin', I'm a busy man.

> BONNIE
> Never saw you before three weeks ago — but
> you've been here seven times since. You must've
> taken a liking to our little town.

> DADE
> Yeah. Somethin' like that.

He rolls away from her. She rolls over and touches him on the shoulder.

> BONNIE
> You all right, Mr. Dade?

> DADE
> Keep your fuckin' hand off me, you whore.

> BONNIE
> I was just tryin' to —

> DADE
> I know what you were tryin' to do. And I told you
> to keep your hand off me.

He gets up, slips into his boxer shorts, and goes over to the small table and starts to work on his Wild Turkey. He drinks right from the bottle.

> DADE
> Get your clothes on and get over here. I don't
> feel like drinkin' alone right now.

> BONNIE
> Well, maybe I don't feel like drinkin' with a man
> who just called me a whore.

> DADE
> You tryin' to tell me you're not a whore?

Bonnie is slipping into her bra and panties.

> BONNIE
> It's what I do, not what I am.

Then she goes over and yanks the bottle from his mouth and guns down a drink of her own.

CUT TO:

Room D. Misty and Jimmy lying on their backs on the bed.

> MISTY
> You're really not kiddin' me?

> JIMMY
> I'm really not kidding you.

> MISTY
> Your uncle set this all up so you'd lose your
> virginity tonight — and you lost it —

> JIMMY
> — when I was fourteen years old.

> MISTY
> And you been doin' it regular?

JIMMY
Well, I wouldn't say regular.
(Smiles)
But whenever I get the chance.

MISTY
You're gonna spoil his whole evening for him.

JIMMY
'I went up the stairs a boy and came down the
stairs a man.' That's what I'm going to tell him.

MISTY
Boy, that's corny.

JIMMY
Yeah, but he loves it.

They lie there in silence.

MISTY
I'll give you a blowjob if you want. I mean, I know
you said you were in love with that girl and
wanted to be faithful — but a blowjob isn't really
like cheatin'.

JIMMY
Yes, it is.

MISTY
Is a handjob cheatin'?

JIMMY
Yeah. Yeah, it is.

MISTY
Would you just feel me up a little so I don't feel
like a freak?

JIMMY (smiles)
Strictly for medicinal purposes?

MISTY
Huh?

JIMMY
Nothing.

MISTY
Then you want to get a little sleep? He rented me
till morning.

He gives her a very passionate kiss.

CUT TO:

Bonnie and Dade at the same table where we last saw them. We hear rain
pocking the roof and ground.

BONNIE
Listen to the rain. It always makes me sad.
(Sips whiskey)
You know what time it is? You've been telling me
about your daughter all night. It's almost five
o'clock.

From here on out, Dade is drunk, but it's a scary, sober drunk — a crazed,
angry drunkenness.

BONNIE
Almost five o'clock.

DADE
I gotta get goin'.

BONNIE
What about Jimmy?

DADE
I'll let him sleep. I'll come back for him.

He stands. As he tries to tug on his cowboy boots, we see that he's really
loaded. She tries to steady him, but the moment she lays a hand on his arm,
he slaps her suddenly and viciously, and she falls back into the wall.

DADE
Next time I want some whore to help me, I'll let
you know.

CUT TO:

Dade sneaking down the cathouse stairs in back. When he gets there, he
peeks out the back door window and sees Wyman sitting in his car, watching
the whorehouse. Rain is pouring down and will pour down for the rest of the
picture.

DADE
Son-of-a-bitch.

He tiptoes to the front of the house and then goes down the steps of the
front door.

CUT TO:

Dade sneaking along the side of the house, so he can get in the back of
Wyman's car that is parked next to the garage.

CUT TO:

Dade getting behind the garage and then peeking out along the edge. He
picks up a good-sized rock and then hurls it against Wyman's back window.

CUT TO:

Wyman in his car. When the rock hits, he nearly jumps out of his skin. What
the hell is going on? He gets out of the car, gun drawn.

CUT TO:

Wyman working his way, gun at the ready, along the front of the garage.

CUT TO:

Dade ready to leap on him — leaps. Even with the gun, Wyman is no match
for the rage and brutality of Dade. Dade twists his gun from his hand, hurls
him up against the garage, slams him to the ground, and then kicks him once
very hard in the face. Then he goes around to the squad car, takes the keys,
and throws them in the bushes. Then he starts running.

CUT TO:

Dade jumping in his car and speeding away. From under the seat, he takes
Murphy's file folder with the black-and-white pictures of the three men. He
spreads them out on the seat.

END ACT TWO

Jimmy wakes up in bed with Misty. There's a commotion in the hallway.
Heavy pounding on the door.

JENNY
You get down here right away, Kid. The chief
wants to talk to you.

Jimmy looks over at Misty, dazed and confused.

> **MISTY**
> I wonder what the hell happened.

CUT TO:

The kitchen, the girls stand around half-dressed. The chief has his head under the sink faucet while one of the girls looks at his wound.

> **HOOKER**
> He got you a good one, Chief. Bet your head hurts.

She gives him a towel to wipe his hair just as Jimmy enters the kitchen.

Wyman speaks to the hooker.

> **WYMAN**
> That kid would appreciate a cup of coffee and so would I.

To Jimmy.

> **WYMAN**
> Why don't you have a seat there, son?

Jenny stage whispers to one of the hookers.

> **JENNY**
> I *thought* that Dade was a crazy son-of-a-bitch.

Wyman goes over and sits down at the table where Jimmy sits. Hooker brings over their coffees.

> **WYMAN**
> Now, son, I want you to tell me why you came to our little town, and where I can find your uncle.

> **JIMMY**
> He do that to you? Your head, I mean? My uncle?

Wyman nods painfully. Jimmy shakes his head solemnly.

CUT TO:

Dade is parked down the street from Tom's trailer. Tom comes out in the rain and gets into his truck. After a time, Dade starts to follow him.

CUT TO:

Tom sees he's being followed, speeds up.

CUT TO:

Dade speeds up. They're on an open stretch of road. Dade overtakes him and then picks up the mother of all double-barreled sawed-off shotguns and shoots through his open window. He blows the tire out on Tom's truck. Tom fights to keep the truck on the road, but can't. Goes into a ditch. Dade gets out with shotgun and forces Tom, bloody and shaken, into his truck.

> TOM
> Where you taking me?

> DADE
> The old fishing cabin you boys use in the
> summer.

> TOM
> How'd you know about that?

> DADE
> There're a lot of things I know, you son-of-a-
> bitch.

CUT TO:

Kitchen. Jimmy and Wyman are the only two in the room now.

> WYMAN
> You figured it out yet, son?

> JIMMY
> Figured out what, Chief?

> WYMAN
> Why he came here?

> JIMMY
> He said he wanted to see some livestock. I think
> he also wanted to see if — well, see if I liked girls.

> WYMAN
> That why he brought you here to Jenny's?

> JIMMY
> Uh-huh.

Chief sips his coffee, sets the cup down.

                              WYMAN
              He's going to kill the three men who were
              involved in his daughter's death. I called all of
              them early this morning and told them to be
              careful. You wouldn't happen to have any idea
              where I could find him, would you?

                              JIMMY
                             No, sir.

                              WYMAN
                     And I can believe that?

                              JIMMY
          Yessir. I don't want to see anybody else get killed.
                        (Looks miserable)
          When his daughter died — Well, he was always
          sort of mean and crazy. But after Kathryn —
                        (Looks at Chief)
                 I'm scared for him, Chief.

                              WYMAN
              I'm scared for all of us, Jimmy. For all of us.

Jenny peeks her head in.

                              JENNY
          Excuse me, Chief, one of your deputies called
          and said that he found Tom Pittman's truck in the
          ditch out near Hartson's Creek. Said Tom wasn't
          there but his window had been shot out.

                              WYMAN
          C'mon, son. I'll give you a ride back to your motel.

                                                        CUT TO:

Dade pulling down a road to a battered old isolated fishing cabin.

                              TOM
                 What're you gonna do to me?

                              DADE
               What'd you do to my daughter?

> TOM
> You got the wrong guy. Honest, mister.

> DADE
> I do, huh?

CUT TO:

Jimmy sitting on the edge of his motel bed with the telephone receiver in his hand.

> JIMMY
> I'm glad you're home — I needed to talk to
> somebody, Sue. My uncle — it's like he's gone
> crazy or something. I mean, what I just told you
> about him beating up the Chief of Police and
> all —
> (Beat)
> No, they don't know where he is. They'd arrest
> him if they did. I think the Chief thinks I have
> something to do with it.
> (Beat)
> No, you'd better get ready to go to work. I'll call
> you tonight when I get the chance. I-I'm thinking
> about you a lot. When I get back there, I want to
> take you out for dinner.
> (Beat)
> Thanks for saying that. That's how I feel, too.

Hangs up. Goes in bathroom. Washes up. The phone rings. He comes out. Picks it up.

CUT TO:

Dade in a phone booth in the boonies.

> DADE
> Just listen to me, Jimmy. I'm going to pick you up
> in five minutes in back of the cattle barn we
> stopped at yesterday. You remember where it is?
> (Beat)
> I don't have time to go into that now.
> (Beat)

I didn't hurt him much. I could've killed him if
I'd wanted to.
(Beat)
Just be there, Jimmy. Five minutes.

He hangs up the phone.

CUT TO:

Jimmy in room. Presses down the telephone buttons.

VOICE (O.C.)
Front desk.

JIMMY
Could you connect me with the police station?

VOICE
Sure. Hold on.

Jimmy looks tense while he waits.

VOICE #2
Police station.

JIMMY
Is Chief Wyman there?

VOICE #2
Not at the moment. Can I ask who's speaking?

JIMMY
I'll just call back.

Hangs up.

CUT TO:

Jimmy in back of big wholesale cattle barn. Standing under the overhang
while rain pelts the earth.

Dade comes hurtling up in his car. Leans over and opens the door.

Jimmy gets in. Says nothing. Dade peels out. Jimmy looks down at the
sawed-off double-barreled shotgun sitting on the seat between them.

A man carrying a pail of water looks out from the cattle barn and sees Dade.
Man sets the pail down and runs to a phone.

CUT TO:

Wyman looking at Tom Pittman's truck in the ditch. Leans in and touches fingers to the steering wheel. Looks at the smudge. Blood.

> PATROLMAN #1
> You think Dade shot him?

> WYMAN
> Don't think so. Seem like there would've been a
> lot more blood than this.

Wyman looks back at his car. The two-way is squawking excitedly about something.

> PATROLMAN #1
> I'll check on that.

Runs back in his poncho in the rain. Reaches inside the squad car and picks up the two-way microphone. Listens. The rain drowns out the words.

The patrolman runs back to the chief. The patrolman looks excited.

> PATROLMAN #1
> Patterson over at the cattle barn says he thinks he
> just saw Dade heading out Highway 2.

> WYMAN
> Maybe we can catch him.

They head back for their car.

CUT TO:

Jimmy and Dade approach the fishing cabin. Dade throws open the door. In the middle of the only room sits Tom Pittman, bound to a chair.

Dade crosses the room with his double-barreled shotgun, going directly to Tom. He brings the butt of the shotgun down across Pittman's jaw. Pittman screams.

> DADE
> You see this boy here, Pittman? He loved my
> daughter just as much as I do — and he hates you
> just as much as I do. Isn't that right, Jimmy?

> JIMMY
> Uncle Richard, I —

DADE (shouts insanely)
Isn't that right, Jimmy?

JIMMY
That's right, Uncle Richard.

TOM
Kid, he's crazy. You can see that, can't you. Run
and get Chief Wyman, will you? He's gonna kill
me, kid. He's gonna kill me right now.

DADE
You chickenshit son-of-a-bitch. Listen to you. You
didn't show my little girl any mercy and I'm not
going to show you any mercy either.

From his belt, he takes a Colt .45, tosses it to Jimmy. Jimmy stares down at it
as if he's never seen anything like it before.

DADE
It's the one you practice on, Jimmy. I figured
you'd be more comfortable with it.
(To Tom)
He's gonna fire the first couple shots, then I'm
gonna take over.
(To Jimmy)
Just wound him, Jimmy. Leave the rest to me.

TOM
You see, kid? You see? He's gonna kill me! He's
gonna kill me!

DADE
Damn right I'm gonna kill you, you scumbag son-
of a bitch. And then I'm gonna kill your two
buddies, too.
(To Jimmy)
Shoot him, Jimmy. Shoot him in the leg.

Silence in the cabin. The three figures seem frozen. The only sound is of the
rain pelting the roof.

JIMMY (softly)
I want to help you, Uncle Richard.

DADE

You want to help me, Jimmy, then you shoot the
bastard. Right now.

TOM

See, he don't want to do it, he knows it's wrong.
It's wrong, isn't it, kid?

But Jimmy is focused only on his uncle.

JIMMY

I know how much you loved her, Uncle Richard.
I really do. But she wouldn't want you to do this.
She really wouldn't.

Jimmy takes a step closer to his uncle.

JIMMY

Why don't you hand me the shotgun, Uncle
Richard?

TOM

Keep talkin' to him, kid. Maybe you'll get through
to him.

Jimmy takes another step.

JIMMY

Please, Uncle Richard. Just hand me —

DADE

You never loved her, Jimmy. You're too much of
a pussy to love anybody. Lovin' people's hard —
and you don't understand hard.

Dade puts his hand out.

DADE

Put the gun there, Jimmy.

TOM

Don't give him the gun, kid. Keep the gun. Make
him go see Wyman. Make him go right now.

DADE

You never loved her. And I should have seen that
right from the start.

With his free hand, he slaps Jimmy with incredible fury.

> DADE
> Now get the hell out of here before I kill you, too,
> Jimmy.

> TOM
> Go get Wyman, kid. Go get Wyman right now.

But Jimmy just stares at him, then stares at his uncle. Then he leaves silently and goes out into the chill morning rain.

CUT TO:

Interior of a car on the highway. Louise is driving. Sonia in the passenger seat. Sue leans over the back seat.

> LOUISE
> I really appreciate you calling us, Sue. I just hope
> everything's all right. We've still got a half hour
> before we get there.

> SONIA
> I was afraid of something like this, Louise. I
> didn't want to scare you. But I was afraid —

> LOUISE (pats her hand)
> It's all right.

CUT TO:

The rain on the hill just outside the cabin. Jimmy stands soaked and unprotected in it, but doesn't seem to notice. He turns and looks back at the cabin. Again, the only sound is that of the rain.

And then the two shots. BOOM (Beat) BOOM,

Another long silence ensues and then Dade comes out of the cabin, double-barreled shotgun dangling from his hand, and walks up the hill to stand next to Jimmy.

> JIMMY
> I want to help you, Uncle Richard.

> DADE
> You wanted to help me, you would've taken your
> turn shootin' that son-of-a-bitch.

JIMMY

I'll drive you back to town. We'll get you some
help. I-I don't want anybody to hurt you, Uncle
Richard. That's what scares me. That somebody'll
hurt you.

DADE (snorts)

Who, that lawman Wyman?
(Stares at Jimmy)
You never loved her, did you, Jimmy? When it
came right down to it, you never loved her.

JIMMY

Please let me help you, Uncle Richard. Please
let me.

DADE

The only thing you can do for me now is to stay
out of my way.

He starts to walk up the hill in the rain.

Jimmy goes after him.

JIMMY

They'll kill you, Uncle Richard, they really will!

Catches up to his uncle and grabs at his shoulder.

DADE

You had your chance to prove you loved her,
Jimmy, and you didn't take it! Now leave me
alone!

And with that, he brings the butt of his shotgun down hard across Jimmy's
jaw, knocking him out.

Dade walks the rest of the way up the hill alone.

CUT TO:

The curve of the hill at the top. No sign of anybody. Rain continues to pour.
Over the top we see Wyman and the patrolman coming.

As they get down the hill a ways, they see Jimmy lying down near the base of
it. Wyman goes down and revives him. The patrolman goes into the cabin
and then comes back. Jimmy gets to his feet.

PATROLMAN #1

Tom Pittman's in there, Chief. He took two shots
right in the face. He's a mess.

WYMAN

You go alert everybody that Dade'll be looking for
the other two. Make sure their houses have got
protection.

The patrolman runs up the hill.

Jimmy and Wyman walk at a more leisurely pace.

JIMMY

I'm scared somebody's going to kill him. It's just
Kathryn — it made him crazy. He's a good man.
He really is.

WYMAN

You know, it's a funny thing about men.
Sometimes they love their uncles more than their
own fathers.

JIMMY

Please don't kill him, Chief. Please don't kill him.

CUT TO:

We're in tight on a black-and-white photo of the retarded girl we saw earlier.
Rick Bryant is looking at it on the wall of his kitchen.

RICK

Couple more weeks and she'll be home with us
for a little while, hon.

WIFE

Maybe you should stay home today, hon. Wyman
sounded real upset when he called — about that
man Dade running around looking for you three.

RICK

I'll be fine. Wyman's got a man posted out in the
garage. He'll ride to work with me.

Eloise, a seven-year-old beauty, comes out in a cotton nightgown, rubbing
her eyes.

ELOISE
Can I get a kiss, Daddy?

RICK
Oh, I think that can be arranged.

Lifts her up, carries her to the door.

WIFE (hugging him)
I sure love you.

CUT TO:

Uniformed lawman in garage. Holding rifle. Looking around. Dade comes
up behind him, knocks him out.

CUT TO:

Rick comes out of the door, his wife and daughter right behind him. Dade
steps from the garage into the rain.

DADE
Your turn, Bryant. Get your ass out here. And
bring your little girl.

He sees that Bryant doesn't want to take his daughter along.

DADE
You either bring her or I'll kill your wife right now.

WIFE
Leave us alone.

DADE
This has nothing to do with you, ma'am. This is
between your husband and me. Now get out
here, Bryant.

Bryant comes down off the back porch and walks through the rain to Dade.

DADE
Get in the garage.

Bryant walks inside, carrying his daughter.

CUT TO:

Interior of Wyman's car. Wyman just hanging up two-way.

WYMAN
They just found him, son. He's over at Rick Bryant's
place. Got Rick in the garage. And Rick's daughter.

JIMMY
His daughter?

WYMAN
That's what they said.

CUT TO:

We're looking down on the Bryant house and backyard. The area is
surrounded by police and emergency vehicles in the rain. And dozens of
onlookers. There is nothing more vicariously exciting than a hostage drama.
Like the best stories, you're just never sure how it's going to turn out.

We see Jimmy and Wyman get out of their car and go up to the scene.
Wyman talks to a couple of the officers and then picks up a bullhorn and
walks over to the back of the house, directly in front of the garage.

WYMAN
I'd like to talk to you, Mr. Dade. I don't mean you
any harm. Your nephew Jimmy's here and can
vouch for that.

CUT TO:

Louise comes walking quickly from the police station. Gets into the car.

LOUISE
One of the policemen just gave me directions to
where they are.

SOPHIA
Something's wrong, isn't it?

Louise nods somberly.

CUT TO:

Dade has Bryant backed up to the wall.

DADE
At least be man enough to admit you killed her.

BRYANT
It was an accident, mister. It really was.

DADE

Yeah, well let's see how you feel when I kill *your* daughter.

Hear Wyman's voice over the bullhorn.

WYMAN

We want to make sure that nobody else gets hurt, Mr. Dade. And that includes you.

Bryant sees that Dade is momentarily distracted. He makes for the door. But Dade grabs him and slams him up against the wall.

CUT TO:

Bryant's wife stands next to Wyman in the rain.

WIFE

You've got to do something, Chief. You've got to.

WYMAN

We're doing all we can. Now Please go back inside and sit down.

Jimmy comes up.

JIMMY

I'm going into the garage.

WYMAN

What if he tries to kill you?

JIMMY

He won't.

WYMAN

Son, your uncle's not himself right now. We can't be sure what he'll do.

JIMMY

I'm still going in there.

WYMAN

Then I'm going with you.

They start toward the garage.

Dade shouts from inside.

DADE
Stay out of here! Both of you!

JIMMY
I want to talk to you, Uncle Richard!

DADE
Don't push me, Jimmy. Just stay away!

But they both keep walking.

And then Dade shoots, getting Wyman right in the shoulder.

Wyman falls to his knees.

JIMMY
I'm still coming in, Uncle Richard.

He walks into the garage.

Silence except for the rain as Jimmy sees Bryant and his daughter huddled in the back, Uncle Richard training his double-barreled shotgun on them.

JIMMY
Let them go, Uncle Richard.

DADE
You never loved her. Never. You're takin' the side
of the men who killed her and you don't seem to
understand that.

BRYANT
At least let Eloise go, mister. At least let her go.

DADE
Let her go? The way you let my daughter go,
you mean?

Jimmy looks down at his belt and sees the Colt .45 there. Bryant watches him.

But before anybody can do anything, Dade grabs Eloise and puts the shotgun to her head.

DADE
How's that feel, Mr. Bryant? How do you like it
when it's *your* daughter?

BRYANT
Oh, God, Dade, please don't!

ELOISE
I'm so scared, Daddy! I'm so scared!

DADE
Now you're gonna know what it really feels like,
Bryant.

He pulls back the hammer.

ELOISE
Daddy! Daddy!

JIMMY
Let her go, Uncle Richard.

Jimmy points the .45 right at Dade.

JIMMY
I don't want to shoot you, Uncle Richard.

DADE
You won't shoot me, Jimmy. You're too scared.

JIMMY
Just let her go.

DADE
Don't come any closer.

But Jimmy keeps walking toward him.

JIMMY
Let her go, Uncle Richard.

DADE
One more step and I'll kill you!

He pulls the shotgun from the little girl and points it right at Jimmy.

DADE
One more step, Jimmy, and I swear to God
you're dead.

Jimmy starts to take a step and then dives for the little girl, throwing her free
of Dade.

Eloise runs to her daddy, who gets her out of the garage.

Now Jimmy and Dade are standing facing each other, each one armed.

DADE

Thanks for stopping me, Jimmy. I didn't really
want to kill that little girl.
(Wipes a hand on his face)
I killed a man a little while ago. You know that?
Shot him in cold blood.

JIMMY

Let me help you, Uncle Richard.

DADE

You really want to help me, Jimmy?

JIMMY

You know I do.

DADE

Then shoot me, Jimmy. I haven't wanted to live
since Kathryn died, anyway.

JIMMY

You know I couldn't do that, Uncle Richard.

DADE

You want to see me in prison? You want to see
me in the electric chair? You want to see me alive
when I want to be dead?

JIMMY

But Uncle Richard —

Dade throws down his shotgun and starts walking to Jimmy.

DADE

I need you to be a man, Jimmy, goddamn you, to
be a grownup man. I don't have the guts enough
to do it myself. Isn't that funny? I hate livin' so
much but I'm scared to die.

Jimmy just stands there watching Dade come closer and closer. The Colt .45
trembles in Jimmy's hand.

DADE

I need you to be man enough for both of us,
Jimmy.

Then he lunges at Jimmy and they wrestle and the gun fires and Dade sinks to the ground.

Louise and Sonia and Sue and a bloody Wyman come rushing into the garage and find Dade lying on the floor and Jimmy standing there with the .45 still in his hand.

Jimmy lets the gun drop from his hand and then looks down mournfully at his uncle and then walks alone out of the garage and out past the gawkers.

Just walking. Alone. As the camera rises in a crane shot.

Just walking. Alone.

THE HUNTED

BY

RICHARD LAYMON

FADE IN:

EXT. — A CITY PARK — EARLY MORNING

KIM SANDERS is running gracefully over the grass. She is a slim, attractive woman in her mid-twenties. Her shoulder-length blond hair streams behind her in the breeze. She wears a gray "Late Show with David Letterman" sweatshirt, its sleeves cut off at the shoulders. She wears blue gym shorts. Her legs are bare. As she runs along, she is clearly at peace with herself. She seems to be enjoying the fresh, early-morning air.

CUT TO:

LARGE DOG sniffing the grass. Its head suddenly jerks up. The dog springs into a run.

CUT TO:

Kim striding over the field past a deserted playground. The dog comes charging at her from the side, SNARLING and BARKING. Kim, still running, looks at it. Her face remains calm, though the dog appears eager to rip her apart.

Kim halts, turns to the dog, and crouches low. She reaches out for it. The dog skids to a stop, hunches down, and GROWLS at her.

KIM (pleasantly)
Morning there, fella. What's your story, huh?

She pats the side of her thigh. Dog approaches warily. Kim ruffles the fur at the side of its neck.

The dog begins to wag its tail. Kim continues to stroke it.

> KIM (gently)
> Yeah, yeah, Aren't you the tough guy? Yes, you are.

The dog flops onto its side, rolls onto its back, and Kim scratches its stomach.

FADE OUT:

FADE IN:

INT. — AN OFFICE

Kim is alone in a small office cubicle, tipped back in a swivel chair, her shoeless feet propped up on the cluttered top of her desk. The desk is strewn with case files. Kim is wearing a prim white blouse and a straight gray skirt. She is talking on the telephone.

> KIM (patiently)
> Yes.
> (Pause)
> Yes, I understand that. But I think their offer is
> reasonable and it's my advice that you accept it.

Nodding as she listens, Kim glances at the digital clock on her desk. It shows 7:28 P.M.

> KIM
> Yes, of course a jury might give you more, but it's
> also possible that they'll find for the defendant. The
> liability just isn't all that clear-cut, and even if all
> the facts *were* in your favor, it'd still be a gamble. A
> trial is *always* a gamble. And always expensive.
> (Pause)
> I'm not saying we *won't* win . . .

FADE OUT:

FADE IN:

INT. — KIM'S APARTMENT — NIGHT

Kim steps out of the bathroom wearing a robe. She is drying her hair with a towel.

MOVING SHOT

as Kim walks up a short hallway to her bedroom.

CUT TO:

INT. — KIM'S BEDROOM — NIGHT

She enters her bedroom and tosses the towel onto the bed. It falls among the casual disarray of clothes she had discarded before showering: a white slip, bra and panties, and the straight skirt and blouse she had been wearing in the office.

Kim finds her hairbrush on top of the cluttered dresser.

CUT TO:

THE MIRROR, showing Kim's reflection. She begins to brush her hair. She appears confident and cheerful, and hums a current tune.

THE TELEPHONE suddenly RINGS. Kim doesn't appear startled by the sudden noise. Instead, she looks pleasantly surprised.

CUT TO:

Kim as she heads for the telephone on the nightstand beside her bed. The TELEPHONE KEEPS RINGING. On her way to answer it, Kim steps over her discarded pantyhose and high-heeled shoes on the bedroom floor.

She picks up the telephone.

KIM
Hello?

She is clearly pleased when she recognizes the voice on the line.

KIM (cont'd)
Just got out of the shower.
(A pause and she smiles)
Oh, I'm sure you would. Too late for that, buster.
Missed your big chance. But how about coming
over? It's been a while, you know?
(Pause)
Well, I've been busy, too. But I think I could've
found a few minutes to squeeze you in.
(Listens a moment, then laughs)
Think I'm *that* kind of girl, do you?

(Pause)
Tomorrow?
(She listen, occasionally nodding)
Tahoe'd be great, but it's awfully short notice.
What happened, did somebody else bail out
on you?
(Pause)
I know, I know. I was just kidding, Jerry.
(Pause)
Well, I was working late and then I had to stop by
the supermarket. But that's beside the point,
don't you think? You've go to admit, Friday
night's pretty late to be asking someone to jump
on a plane with you at ten o'clock the next
morning.
(Pause)
Sure, I want to go. But it wouldn't have killed you
to ask me a few days ago. Or last week, maybe?
(Pause)
Right, spur of the moment.
(Kim looks at the clock on her nightstand.)

CUT TO:

THE CLOCK

It shows 9:45.

CUT TO:

Kim, who is smiling and shaking her head a bit.

KIM (cont'd)
Uh-huh. Impetuous. You're impetuous, and I'll
probably be up half the night. When I don't get
any sleep, I'm a real bitch.
(Pause)
Oh, a few minor things like do my hair, figure out
what I'm going to wear . . .
(Listens a moment and chuckles)
Oh, yes I do. I don't think they'd let me through
airport security that way.

(Pause. She nods and smiles)
Okay, well, I'd better start putting my stuff
together.
(Pause).
Right, see you at eight.
(Another pause. Then, in a softer voice)
Good-night, Jerry.

Kim hangs up. She stares at the phone, shakes her head, smiles, and sighs.

Dropping to her knees, she reaches under the bed and pulls out a suitcase. She swings it onto the mattress, opens the empty case, and strides to her dresser. She pulls open the dresser's top drawer.

CUT TO:

INSIDE THE DRESSER DRAWER. Except for a single pair of pink underpants and two bras, the drawer is empty.

KIM (frustrated)
Great. Just great.

FADE OUT:

FADE IN:

INT — CORRIDOR OF KIM'S APARTMENT BUILDING — NIGHT

Kim, now dressed in a T-shirt, red gym shorts, and sneakers, is carrying a basket full of dirty clothes down the corridor. Atop the heap of clothing rests a box of laundry detergent.

CUT TO:

LAUNDRY ROOM as Kim enters. She flicks a light switch. The small room has a single washing machine and one dryer.

CUT TO:

SIGN ON WASHING MACHINE. The cardboard sign, hand-lettered, reads "OUT OF ORDER."

CUT TO:

Kim as she reads the sign. A wry smile comes to her face. She looks as if she is somewhat amused by the latest complication.

FADE OUT:

FADE IN:

EXT. — LAUNDROMAT PARKING LOT — NIGHT

KIM'S CAR, a rather old and beat-up compact, swings off a deserted street and enters the parking lot of a LAUNDROMAT. Several other shops that share the lot (such as a meat market, a bakery, a card shop, a beauty parlor) are all closed for the night.

The Laundromat is fronted by a glass door and a wall of windows. It is brightly lighted inside. The several parking spaces facing the Laundromat are taken. Kim parks her car on the street side of the lot. She gets out of her car and removes her laundry basket from the trunk.

As she crosses the small lot, a MAN and WOMAN exit the Laundromat and carry their wash to a car.

Kim enters the Laundromat.

CUT TO:

INT. — LAUNDROMAT — NIGHT

There are few people inside. One, a HEAVYSET WOMAN in curlers and a housecoat, is removing her clothes from a dryer. She will obviously be leaving soon. A young man, BRADLEY, is sitting atop a machine while he waits for his clothes to be done.

Bradley smiles at Kim and gives her an interested once-over with his eyes. Bradley appears to be in his early twenties. He is big, and dressed like a jock. He wears a sleeveless sweatshirt that has been cut off at mid-chest level, red gym shorts similar to those worn by Kim, gray sweatpants *under* the shorts, and sneakers.

CUT TO:

Kim as she crouches in front of a washer, opens it, and begins to throw in her laundry.

FADE OUT:

FADE IN:

INT. — LAUNDROMAT — NIGHT

Kim is seated on a chair near the front corner of the Laundromat, her back to a wall, the windows to her right. She glances through a magazine while she waits. Looking up from the magazine, she watches a MIDDLE-AGED COUPLE carry their laundry bags out to the car.

CUT TO:

THE COUPLE as they exit. They are seen through the window as they go to their car. As the car leaves, we see that only two cars remain in the lot: Kim's on the far side, and Bradley's, which is the last one facing the Laundromat.

ANOTHER CAR pulls into the lot. It is a rather old, dirty, full-size sedan. It swings toward the window and moves slowly forward, straight toward Kim, its headlights shining on the glass.

CUT TO:

Kim, who squints and turns her head away from the glare of the headlights. The lights die and the motor goes silent. Kim glances at her wristwatch, then resumes browsing through the magazine.

After a few moments, a puzzled expression crosses her face. She looks out the window again.

KIM'S POV

as she looks at the car. The driver, CARSON, can be seen vaguely through the windshield. He appears to be large and rough-looking. He sits motionless behind the steering wheel. He seems to be staring at Kim.

CUT TO:

Kim as she turns her face away, clearly uneasy. She glances at the magazine, then scans the Laundromat.

ANGLE ON LAUNDROMAT

Except for Bradley, still sitting on top of a machine, the place is deserted.

CUT TO:

Kim, again glancing out the window.

KIM'S POV

Carson is still motionless in his car, still staring at her.

CUT TO:

Kim, setting the magazine aside, picking up her handbag, and striding to the washer.

Bradley watches her approach and smiles.

Kim nods a silent greeting to Bradley. She stops at the washer, finds that it has finished, and unloads her damp garments. She piles them into the laundry basket, carries them to a nearby dryer, and begins to toss them in.

PULL BACK

As Kim loads the dryer, Bradley hops down from his perch. Kim looks over her shoulder at him. Bradley goes to a dryer not far from Kim, opens it, and begins transferring his laundry into a bag.

CUT TO:

Kim as she realizes that Bradley is about to depart, leaving her alone in the Laundromat. Her face is worried. She swings the dryer door shut, starts the machine with a coin, and looks toward the front of the Laundromat.

KIM'S POV

looking at the car. It is still there, Carson faintly visible behind the windshield.

BACK TO SCENE

Kim turns toward Bradley. She looks nervous, and forces a smile onto her face.

Bradley closes his laundry bag, rises, and notices that Kim is watching him. He appears a little shy, but pleased by the attention.

Kim walks closer to Bradley. They face each other. She leans against a machine and tries to hold onto her smile.

                    KIM (hesitant)
                        Hi.

            BRADLEY (shy and eager to please)
                      Hello.

                       KIM
        I'm sorry to bother you, but I was wondering if
        you could do me a favor.

                     BRADLEY
                      Yeah?

BRADLEY'S POV

He sneaks a look down her body, noting her T-shirt (her bra visible through the fabric), her shorts, her slim bare legs and tennis shoes. Then his gaze scoots back up to her face.

BACK TO SCENE

Bradley, smiling and nodding, is obviously attracted to Kim and ready for any suggestion.

> BRADLEY
> What sort of favor?

Kim shrugs, looking a little embarrassed.

> KIM
> It's nothing much, really. I just don't want to be
> left alone in here. I was wondering if you might
> be able to stick around for a few minutes and
> keep me company till my clothes are finished.
> Won't take very long.

> BRADLEY
> That's all?

> KIM
> Well, if you could walk me out to my car when
> I'm done . . .

> BRADLEY
> No problem.

> KIM (relieved)
> Great. I really appreciate it.

> BRADLEY (a bit nervous)
> By the way, my name's Bradley.

Nodding, Kim takes a step toward him and offers her hand. They shake.

> KIM
> I'm Kim. I sure appreciate this.

> BRADLEY
> Like I told you, no problem.

KIM
Won't be long.

She steps across the aisle and boosts herself up onto one of the machines in the middle row. As she does so, she glances over her right shoulder toward the front of the Laundromat.

KIM'S POV

as she looks out at Carson's car. Carson is still visible through the windshield. He is motionless, and seems to be staring at her.

BACK TO SCENE

Kim faces Bradley again, and he quickly lifts his gaze from her breasts to her face. Kim slumps forward slightly to loosen the pull of her T-shirt across her chest. She cups her knees with her hands and smiles.

BRADLEY
You live near here?

KIM
A few blocks away. Are you a student?

BRADLEY
A senior. I live off-campus. I've got my own apartment.
(Pause a beat)
Do you come here often?

KIM
First time.
(Wrinkling her nose)
Kind of spooky here, this late.

BRADLEY
I guess. If you're a gal.

KIM
Oh, I am.

Bradley nods agreement, smiling at her remark.

KIM
At least there's no waiting for the machines.
(A wry smile)
Famous last words.

BRADLEY
Nothing to worry about.

KIM
Hope not.

Again, she looks over her shoulder.

CLOSE ON BRADLEY

as he follows her gaze.

BRADLEY'S POV

We again see Carson sitting in the car.

ANGLE ON BOTH

BRADLEY
You worried about that guy out there?

KIM
Well, yeah. A little, I guess.
(Grimaces)
I think he's watching me.

Bradley glares in Carson's direction.

KIM (cringing)
Don't! Jesus! Just pretend he's not there.

BRADLEY (showing his macho)
Maybe I ought to go out and . . .

KIM
No!

Silence as Bradley frowns, considering the situation.

BRADLEY
You don't know who the guy is?

KIM
I've never seen him before.

BRADLEY
No wonder you're upset.

Kim rubs her arms as if feeling a sudden chill. She shrugs.

> KIM (trying to calm herself)
I'm sure it's nothing. He probably just likes to
look at women.

> BRADLEY
Hell, *I* like to look at women. That doesn't mean I
hang around Laundromats like a goddamn pervert.

> KIM
He's probably harmless.

> BRADLEY
Doesn't look harmless to me. Who's to say he
isn't some kind of freak like the Butcher?

Kim makes a face, clearly bothered by the suggestion.

> KIM
Hey, come on.

CLOSE ON BRADLEY

as he suddenly looks distressed. His eyes move down and up, again taking in
Kim's appearance. This time, however, he does so without any pleasure. He
looks as if he does not like what he is seeing.

> CUT TO KIM:

> KIM (alarmed by the change in him)
What is it?

ANGLE ON BOTH

> BRADLEY
Christ. I hate to tell you this, but . . .

> KIM
What?

> BRADLEY
You . . . you're a dead match for his victim profile.

> KIM (smirking)
So I've heard.

> BRADLEY
I mean, really. You *are*. He's had five victims, and

they all . . . They were eighteen to twenty-five
years old, maybe not as pretty as you, but almost.
And slim, and they all had blond hair. Just like
yours. You look so much like the others that you
could all be sisters.

KIM

How come *you're* such an expert?

BRADLEY

Well, I used to go with a girl who kind of fit the
profile. Not as much as you do, but it had me
worried. I was afraid, you know, she might end up
raped and mutilated like . . . Is there a back way
out of here?

Bradley turns to study the rear of the Laundromat.

KIM

Hey, come on. You're really . . .

BRADLEY (with growing urgency)
I'm not kidding.

KIM

I know, but . . . It probably isn't him. Right? I
mean, he hasn't . . .

BRADLEY

He hasn't nailed anyone in a month. Not since
that gal the campers found. I know what the cops
say: He left the area, or died or something. But
they don't *know*. They're just trying to calm
everyone down, saying stuff like that.
(Gazes hard into Kim's eyes)
Have you ever been up around Mount Bolton?

Kim shakes her head. She is looking sick.

BRADLEY

I tell you, it's one big mean wilderness. A guy
could hide out for years if he knew what he was
doing. So maybe the Butcher laid low for a while,
and maybe now the urge has gotten the best of

him, and . . . Not much of anyone goes up there
anymore. If he wanted a new victim, he might
come down into town for one.

KIM
This is really starting to give me the creeps.

BRADLEY
Just sit there a minute. I'll check out back.

KIM'S POV

as she watches Bradley walk up the aisle between the rows of silent washers
and dryers. He disappears into a recessed area at the rear of the room, is out
of sight for a few moments, then reappears. He shakes his head. He returns
to Kim, not once looking toward the front windows — obviously taking great
care to avoid alerting Carson that they are aware of him.

BRADLEY
Nothing but a utility room. The front's the only
way out.
(Pause)
You think your stuff's about ready?

ANGLE ON BOTH

Kim shakes her head. She no longer cares whether her clothes are dry. She
hops off the machine. Bradley picks up his laundry bag and stays at her side
as she goes to the dryer. The dryer shuts off when she opens its door.
Crouching, she begins to pull out damp garments and toss them into her
basket.

BRADLEY'S POV

taking in a view of Kim's tight T-shirt. A band of bare skin shows between
the bottom of her shirt and the waistband of her shorts.

CLOSE ON BRADLEY

as he stares. His expression is ambiguous, but suggests the possibility that he
might like to screw her. As he speaks, he becomes more agitated.

BRADLEY
Your car's in the lot?

KIM
Yeah.

> BRADLEY
> I'll get in with you. We'll stay together.

> KIM
> Okay.

> BRADLEY
> If he follows us when we leave, maybe we can lose
> him. But at least you won't be alone. As long as I'm
> with you, he'll think twice before he tries anything.

CUT TO:

Kim as she looks up at Bradley.

> KIM
> I really appreciate this.

ANGLE ON BOTH

> BRADLEY
> I'm just glad that I'm here to help.

> KIM
> He's probably not the Butcher, anyway.

CLOSE ON KIM'S FACE

as she reaches into the dryer for the last of her clothes. Something awful
occurs to her. Something that stuns her. Her eyes widen, her mouth drops
open. She shakes her head slightly, trying to banish the thought.

ANGLE ON BOTH

Kim swings the dryer door shut, stands up straight, and faces Bradley. She
regards him with wariness and distrust that she is unable to conceal. Bradley
looks confused by her obvious change in attitude.

> BRADLEY
> What's wrong?

Kim shakes her head. She sets her box of detergent onto the heaped clothes,
and bends down to pick up the basket.

CUT TO:

LAUNDRY BASKET full of damp garments, detergent box resting on top of
them, as Kim begins to lift it.

> BRADLEY (a low murmur)
> Oh, my God.

CUT TO:

Bradley, his face slack with shock as he gazes toward the front of the Laundromat.

CUT TO:

Kim, stunned by Bradley's reaction. She drops the basket and whirls around.

CUT TO:

Carson filling the Laundromat's doorway, coming toward them with long, sure strides. He doesn't look like a serial killer — more like a commando about to kick ass.

Carson wears a dark stocking cap. His face is streaked with black makeup. His black T-shirt looks swollen with mounds and slabs of muscle. The sling of a rifle crosses his chest. So do the straps of a harness that holds a sheathed knife, handle down, against the left side of his rib cage. Circling his waist is a web belt loaded with canvas cases, a water bottle, and a holster. He wears baggy camouflage pants. Their cuffs are tucked into high-topped boots.

Carson is Death, and he is marching straight toward Kim and Bradley.

BACK TO SCENE

Kim stands frozen. Carson approaches steadily, his face grim.

Bradley suddenly darts past Kim and blocks Carson's way.

> BRADLEY (trying to be brave, booms out)
> Stop right there, mister!

Bradley assumes a fighting stance, ready to defend Kim. Carson keeps coming. A blow to the midsection drops Bradley to his knees. A knee to the forehead hurls him backward. He hits the floor, sliding, and comes to a stop, unconscious, at Kim's feet.

Carson keeps coming.

Kim whirls away to run. Carson's hand snatches the shoulder of her T-shirt, and he tries to jerk her to a stop. The neck band and shoulder of the shirt stretch, then rip away from Kim's shoulder as the yank twists her sideways. Her feet tangle. She crashes to the floor.

Kim scurries, trying to get up. Carson grabs both of her ankles. He tugs her flat. He drops onto her back. He slips an arm across her throat and applies pressure.

CLOSE ON KIM

as her head is raised by the choking arm. Her eyes bulge. She tries to pull at the arm. Her face is a mask of agony and terror.

FADE OUT:

FADE IN:

EXT. — LAUNDROMAT PARKING LOT — NIGHT

Carson carries Kim's limp body out to his car. The trunk lid is already up, waiting for her. Carson throws her into the trunk, and slams the lid shut.

He returns to the Laundromat.

CUT TO:

INT. — LAUNDROMAT — NIGHT

Carson goes to Bradley, who is still unconscious on the floor. Bradley's keys and wallet are tucked under the waistband of his shorts. Carson takes the keys, then hefts Bradley and carries him outside.

CUT TO:

EXT. — LAUNDROMAT PARKING LOT — NIGHT

Carson carries Bradley to the nearest car. He tries the keys on the trunk. This turns out to be Bradley's car. Carson opens the trunk, flings Bradley into it, tosses the keys in after him, and slams the trunk shut.

He returns to his own car, where he opens the driver's door. He unslings the rifle, puts it into his car, and gets in behind the steering wheel. He drives slowly out of the parking lot and turns onto the street.

FADE OUT:

FADE IN:

EXT. — A STREET — NIGHT

ANGLE ON CARSON'S CAR

as it drives slowly through the BUSINESS DISTRICT of a town. The street is nearly deserted. Most of the town's businesses are closed for the night.

FADE OUT:

FADE IN:

EXT. — A HIGHWAY — NIGHT

Only a few cars are traveling on the highway, which passes through a wooded countryside. Carson's car speeds by.

FADE OUT:

FADE IN:

EXT. — THE HIGHWAY — NIGHT

ANGLE ON HIGHWAY SIGN that reads "MOUNT BOLTON ROAD"

ANGLE ON CARSON'S CAR

as it passes the SIGN and takes the OFF RAMP.

FADE OUT:

FADE IN:

EXT. — A COUNTRY ROAD — NIGHT

This is a winding two-lane road bordered by thick forest. It has an uphill grade. Carson's car appears, passes, then disappears around a bend.

FADE OUT:

FADE IN:

INT. — CARSON'S CAR — NIGHT

VIEW THROUGH THE WINDSHIELD

We see the headlight beams pushing their way along the road. Carson's car slows, and turns onto an unpaved road that is little more than a set of tire ruts. The ride becomes bumpy. Undergrowth presses in closely. Branches scrape along the sides of the car.

FADE OUT:

FADE IN:

EXT. — THE WOODS — NIGHT

ANGLE ON CAR

as it comes up the rutted track. It arrives at a clearing, and lurches off the unpaved road. It begins to move slowly over the forest floor, dodging trees and clumps of bushes.

FADE OUT:

FADE IN:

EXT. — THE WOODS — NIGHT

Carson's car rocks and bounces as it makes a U-turn around a tree. Completing the turn, its headlights find the CAMERA. The car moves closer, then stops. The headlights go dead. The engine goes silent.

Carson climbs out, slings the rifle onto his back, and strides to the trunk.

CUT TO:

TRUNK of Carson's car as it opens. Kim is lying on her side, curled up, her back to Carson. She appears to be unconscious. Except for Kim, the trunk is completely empty: no spare tire, no jack or tools or flares — nothing she might use for a weapon.

BACK TO SCENE

Carson bends over the trunk. He jams one hand under Kim's side beneath her armpit. He shoves his other hand between her legs. With no sign of effort, Carson lifts Kim from the trunk.

He pivots, swinging Kim clear of the car, and hurls her away from him. Kim, who'd been playing possum, GASPS with alarm as she is thrown. She tumbles through the air, flinging her arms and legs about as if she hopes to break her fall.

ANGLE ON KIM

as she hits the ground hard. She GRUNTS with the impact. The force of Carson's throw sends her scooting and rolling over the forest floor. When she stops, she is sprawled on her back. She suddenly thrusts herself into a sitting position, drawing her feet in, preparing to spring up. Just as suddenly, she freezes.

PULL BACK

to show Carson, straight in front of Kim, aiming the rifle at her face.

CLOSE ON KIM

She looks like a kid who is being tormented by a playground bully but is determined not to cry.

BACK TO SCENE

> CARSON (calm, but stern)
> Get up.

Kim gets to her feet. She is dirty and a little scratched from her rough tumble across the ground. Her T-shirt (torn at the Laundromat) hangs off her right shoulder, showing some of her bra. Kim stands a little taller. Glaring at Carson, she lifts the flap of her T-shirt and holds it in place.

> CARSON
> What's your name?

> KIM (hanging tough)
> Fuck you.

Carson's face, smeared with black makeup, is grim for a moment. Then his mouth twists with a sneer.

> CARSON
> Take a look around.

> CUT TO:

Kim, facing Carson and the rear of his car. She begins to turn, scanning the area.

KIM'S POV

She is standing in a small, moonlit clearing. There are thick woods all around except directly behind her, where she sees fairly open ground for some distance. She turns all the way around until she is again facing Carson.

BACK TO SCENE

> KIM
> Yeah? So?

> CARSON
> Know where we are?

> KIM
> Got a pretty good guess.

> CARSON
> You're a tough little bitch, aren't you.

> KIM
> What've I got to lose?

> CARSON (another sneer)
> Not a thing.

Carson raises his left hand and studies his wristwatch.

> CARSON
> You've a five-minute headstart.

CLOSE ON KIM

looking surprised and wary.

> KIM
> What are you talking about?

> CUT TO:

Carson, still looking at his wristwatch.

> CARSON
> Go.

> CUT TO:

Kim, who stands there and shakes her head.

> KIM
> What is this?

BACK TO SCENE

> CARSON
> The hunt.
> (Pause a beat)
> Your time is running.

CLOSE ON KIM

as she frowns, confused and suspicious, but suddenly understanding. She glances at her own wristwatch.

PULL BACK

to show Kim whirl away from Carson and run. This is no girlish flight with flapping arms. She tucks her head down and dashes like a sprinter.

KIM'S POV — MOVING SHOT

The area ahead of her is sometimes moonlit; sometimes dark. We see bushes, rocks, and a few tree trunks as she races for her life. She leaps some obstacles, dodges others. She glances back and sees the distant, dim form of Carson still standing at the rear of his car. She looks forward again. Just ahead is a sparsely wooded downhill slope.

ANGLE ON KIM

as she starts down the slope. She shortens her strides, waves her arms for balance, but only makes it about halfway down before she loses her footing. She takes a hard fall, tumbling and sliding. When she stops, she is sprawled on her back. She lies there for a few moments, grimacing with pain and exhaustion, PANTING for breath and GROANING. She sits up and looks around her.

KIM'S POV

Beyond the bottom of the slope, the woods remain sparse. There are few trees to provide cover for her. To either side, however, the forest is thick and dark. She raises her left hand so the face of her watch catches the moonlight. From the desperate sound of her MOAN, the news is not good.

ANGLE ON KIM

scurrying to her feet. She looks toward the top of the hill, then traverses the slope, rushing, staying low in a crouch. She reaches the area where the forest is dense, and she vanishes into the darkness among the trees.

FADE OUT:

FADE IN:

EXT. — SOMEWHERE IN THE WOODS — NIGHT

Nothing is in sight except trees, bushes, and a few scattered rocks touched by flecks of moonlight. We hear the SOUNDS OF NIGHT BIRDS, INSECTS, CRICKETS, etc. And then come the faint SOUNDS of a PERSON RUSHING THROUGH FOLIAGE, painfully GASPING FOR BREATH. The sounds of the person grow louder.

Kim enters the scene, jogging but clearly tired. It is obvious that she has been running for quite a while since we last saw her. HUFFING, she slumps backward against a tree trunk. She lifts the bottom of her T-shirt and wipes the sweat off her face.

As she rests, she peers in the direction from which she had come. She glances this way and that. There is no indication that Carson is anywhere nearby. Kim wipes her face again. Then she steps around the tree and continues on her way. She takes a few steps, walking, then quickens her pace, and breaks into a slow run that carries her out of the scene.

FADE OUT:

FADE IN:

EXT. — THE WOODS — NIGHT

Kim appears, jogging, weaving her way around bushes and trees.

FADE OUT:

FADE IN:

EXT. — THE WOODS — NIGHT

Kim jogs into view from the darkness of the trees. She steps into the moonlight of a small clearing, and halts.

KIM'S POV

A short distance ahead of Kim is a DEADFALL. This is a large, dead tree stretched across the forest floor. At one end is the clump of its roots, as high as Kim's head. The root cluster holds up the base of the trunk, creating a gap between the bottom of the trunk and the ground. The gap is clear. A short distance to the right, however, the gap is concealed by branches of the dead tree and by heavy growth that has climbed the sides of the trunk.

CUT TO KIM:

as she approaches the deadfall. She moves toward the root area. Where the trunk is elevated off the ground, she crouches down. She peers into the dark gap. Then, she gets down on her hands and knees, and enters the space. She crawls to the right.

KIM'S POV

The trunk above Kim slants gradually toward the ground. Looking to her right, she has a view of the clearing she has just crossed. Just ahead, however, limbs and undergrowth provide a wall of foliage that will conceal her.

ANGLE ON KIM

sinking onto her belly and squirming forward until the slant of the trunk prevents her from going farther. She is sandwiched between the tree and the ground. She lies there, motionless, her head turned to the right.

KIM'S POV

Though it is very dark under here, she can see the dead branches and tangles of undergrowth, and bits of moonlight from beyond the thick mass along the trunk. Obviously she is now well-hidden. She takes a few trembling BREATHS, trying to settle down. We hear the quiet, peaceful SOUNDS OF A SOFT BREEZE AND FOREST CREATURES. Very calming. Kim is safe.

Suddenly comes a LOUD SCURRYING NOISE as if some small animal is clambering through the thicket *very close to Kim*, maybe just inches from her face.

KIM (quietly, but with alarm)
Shit!

ANGLE ON DEADFALL

No sign of Kim, but plenty of RUSTLING NOISES and quiet WHIMPERS from her. Then she comes into view, squirming backward beneath the trunk. She scurries clear and staggers to her feet.

CUT TO:

Kim, a little freaked out, backing away from the deadfall and staring at it as if she expects a troop of rats to come scampering out from under it. In a frenzy, she brushes debris off her T-shirt, arms, and shorts.

CLOSE ON KIM'S THIGH

where a SPIDER is about to disappear up the leg hole of her shorts. With a soft YELP, she knocks the spider away.

BACK TO SCENE

Kim bends over, furiously swiping at her legs. Then she begins raking fingers through her tangled hair as if she's afraid something may have nested there.

Suddenly, she seems to remember Carson. She jerks around and stands motionless, scanning the forest.

Satisfied that she is alone, Kim hurries around the deadfall's root cluster and continues on her way.

As she walks along, she never stops trying to rid herself of whatever may have gotten onto her under the tree. She flutters her T-shirt, shakes her hair, rubs her arms and legs, looks inside the front of her shirt, slips hands under her shorts to feel around.

FADE OUT:

FADE IN:

EXT. — THE WOODS — NIGHT

Kim is making her way up a steep slope. It is not an easy ascent. She sometimes uses bushes or tree roots for handholds. At last, she reaches the top. She flops onto her back, GASPING.

> KIM (exhausted, depressed, but hasn't lost her
> sense of humor)
> Where are the cops when you need 'em?

She rolls over, pushes herself up, staggers to her feet, and moves on.

FADE OUT:

FADE IN:

EXT. — THE WOODS — NIGHT

Kim, weary, is walking through the forest. She sits down and leans back against the trunk of a tree. While resting, she sees a SQUIRREL some distance away.

KIM'S POV

The squirrel scoots up the trunk of a tree. We follow its progress until it vanishes in the upper branches.

CLOSE ON KIM

who has been watching it. Her expression changes as she suddenly gets a good idea.

> KIM (murmurs)
> Yeah.

ANGLE ON KIM

as she gets to her feet and starts walking forward, studying the trees ahead of her. She approaches a few of them and inspects their trunks. Stopping in front of one that has enough low branches to make climbing easy, she nods. She reaches up for a handhold, then stops and turns away from the tree. She scans the ground.

Stepping away from the tree, she searches until she finds a chunk of rock. It is as large as a baseball. She tosses it and catches it a few times as if testing its weight, then nods with satisfaction.

Kim scans the forest around her as if trying to spot Carson.

Then, she continues her search until she has found a dozen good-sized rocks. Cradling them in her arms, she returns to the tree. She drops them to the ground.

She pulls off her T-shirt. She knots it at the bottom to form a bag. Crouching, she drops the rocks inside. She lifts the makeshift sack. She slips her left arm through the T-shirt's neck hole and left sleeve, pulls the shirt up to her shoulder and swings it behind her. Now the T-shirt loaded with rocks hangs by her shoulder against the back of her left side. She has her weapons, and her hands are free.

Kim starts climbing the tree. She makes her way slowly up the trunk, pulling herself up by branches, sometimes shinnying, standing on limbs and reaching for higher ones.

PULL BACK

to show Kim vanish among the surrounding branches and leaves.

CUT TO:

Kim, still climbing. Then she stops. Standing on a branch and holding onto a higher one, she leans forward and looks down.

KIM'S POV

Below her, there is only the tree. She is very high in it. The ground cannot be seen because of the lower foliage and darkness.

ANGLE ON KIM

as she resumes climbing.

KIM'S POV

Looking forward and slightly upward, she sees the starry night beyond the leaves of her tree.

CLOSE ON KIM

Her face is dimly lighted by a patch of moonlight. She has the look of someone who has lasted a round with the champ. She is exhausted and grim, but pleased with herself. She has survived this far, but the fight is far from over.

PULL BACK

Kim is standing on a fairly thick branch. With her right arm wrapped around the trunk, she shrugs the T-shirt off her left shoulder. The sleeve slides down her arm, and she catches it with her hand. She drapes the rock-loaded shirt like saddlebags over a nearby branch.

Holding the trunk with both hands, Kim eases herself down. She straddles the branch on which she had been standing, scoots forward, scissors her legs around the trunk, then wraps her arms around it.

HOLD ON KIM

embracing the tree, safe for now.

FADE OUT:

FADE IN:

EXT. — THE WOODS — DAY

We see the forest, the nearby mountain, and the sky as dawn comes.

ANGLE ON A STAND OF TREES

Several are clustered close together.

ANGLE ON KIM'S TREE

in the middle of the stand. She is out of sight.

CUT TO KIM:

FRONTAL VIEW reveals Kim leaning forward against the trunk. Her face rests against its side. She is asleep. Her arms and legs are no longer wrapped around the tree. They hang limp. She is sitting astride the branch, leaning against the trunk, holding nothing at all.

CLOSER ON KIM

AND CLOSER

until we are mere inches from her shut eyes and can see that her eyes are darting from side to side under her lids. She is in REM sleep, dreaming.

CUT TO:

INT. — A BEDROOM — DAY

Kim rushes into the bedroom, whirls around and SLAMS the door shut. She
rests her back against it, panting. She is wearing a white, diaphanous
nightgown.

KIM'S POV

She looks at her boyfriend, JERRY, who is still asleep on the bed in spite of
the noise of the slamming door.

> KIM (near panic)
> JERRY! JERRY, WAKE UP!

He doesn't stir.

BACK TO SCENE

Kim shoves herself off the door, grabs a straight-backed chair, and jams its
back under the doorknob.

She rushes to the bed. She throws the covers off Jerry. He is sleeping
facedown, wearing only undershorts. Kim shakes him, tugs him onto
his back.

Jerry wakes up. Still groggy, he smiles up at her. He is in his late twenties,
handsome, but more of a self-centered playboy than a man of action.

> JERRY
> Kim. Am I ever glad to see you.

He wraps his arms around her, pulls her down gently against him, and
kisses her.

Kim pushes herself away from him.

> KIM
> There's no time for that.

> JERRY
> Sure there is. The plane doesn't leave till . . .
> (suddenly perplexed)
> Hey, where's your suitcase? Why aren't you
> dressed?

> KIM
> Tahoe's out.

She looks over her shoulder at the barricaded door.

> KIM
> The Butcher's after me.

> JERRY
> Huh?

> KIM
> Where's your gun? He'll be here any minute.

The urgency of the situation doesn't sink into Jerry. He remains pleasant and sleepy.

> JERRY
> We're going to the Sahara. You won't need
> my gun.

> KIM
> The BUTCHER'S after me!

> JERRY
> Who?

Kim suddenly produces a newspaper and sticks it in front of his face.

CLOSE ON NEWSPAPER

A HEADLINE reads "BUTCHER STALKS KIM STANLEY." There are photographs of five young women, all of whom bear some resemblance to Kim. Below the lineup of victim photos is a LARGE PHOTO of Kim. This one is labeled "BUTCHER'S NEXT VICTIM."

BACK TO SCENE

> KIM (losing patience)
> Get it?

> JERRY
> You mean he's after you now?

> KIM
> Yes!

Jerry, still unconcerned, suddenly looks hopeful.

JERRY
There's probably time for a quickie before he
gets here.

He slips the nightgown straps off Kim's shoulders. She springs away
from him.

KIM (urgently)
Where's your damn gun, Jerry?

He nods toward his dresser.

CUT TO:

Kim as she dashes to his dresser and jerks open the top drawer. It is filled
with HER CLOTHES: bras, panties, stockings, a garter belt. She looks at
them for a moment, perplexed.

SLOW MOTION

as Kim hurls the clothes out of the drawer, tossing them back over her
shoulder. Many of the garments appear to be the same clothes she had been
unloading from the dryer at the Laundromat. They fly slowly over her
shoulder and drift to the floor.

While she flings the clothes, POUNDING on the door as if someone is
kicking it from the other side. She continues to hurl clothes over her
shoulder. The drawer seems bottomless.

When the last of the clothing is flung away, JERRY'S PISTOL is seen resting
on the bottom of the empty drawer.

BACK TO REAL SPEED

Kim snatches the pistol from the drawer and whirls around.

CUT TO BEDROOM DOOR:

as it SMASHES DOWN, ripped from its hinges. It disintegrates the chair
that had been bracing it. It CRASHES to the floor.

BACK TO SCENE

Carson marches into the room, stepping over the door, coming straight
at her.

Kim FIRES at him. The pistol makes of soft PFWUT! A bullet comes slowly
out of the barrel, flies sluggishly for a few feet, and drops to the floor.

KIM (shouts)
Jerry!

CLOSE ON JERRY

He shrugs, looking perplexed but unconcerned, ignoring Carson's presence.

JERRY
Must be old ammo.

BACK TO SCENE

Carson, marching toward Kim, pulls the huge knife from its sheath.

Kim whirls away. She dashes toward the bedroom window, leaps, and dives through its glass.

CUT TO:

EXT. — OTHER SIDE OF BEDROOM WINDOW — DAY

Kim explodes through the glass and is falling, falling, her nightgown flowing around her as she plunges toward the distant ground.

CUT TO:

EXT. — THE WOODS — DAY

Kim is sitting on the tree branch, leaning against the trunk as before — arms and legs hanging. But now she is WHIMPERING and GASPING in her sleep. She moves slightly. She tips sideways just a bit.

Then a bit more. When a fall seems imminent, she wakes up with a YELP, clutches the trunk, and rights herself. Alarmed by her close call, she hugs the tree in terror for a few moments.

After she has recovered, she eases her hold and scoots backward slightly.

CLOSE ON KIM

her face shows agony.

PULL BACK

to show Kim struggle to rise from her perch. Her legs don't work right. Grimacing, she manages to stand by pulling herself up the trunk until she is able to grab an upper limb. Clutching the limb to support her weight, she shakes one leg, then the other. When she has recovered the use of her legs, she releases the limb with one hand and rubs her rear end through the seat of her shorts. She SIGHS.

Still on her feet, she returns to the trunk. She presses herself against the trunk and gazes out past its side.

KIM'S POV

The leafy limbs, this high, are sparse. She has a fairly clear view of the morning sky, the tops of nearby trees, the peak of a distant mountain, and the woods. Lowering her gaze, she sees small areas of the forest near her tree. There is no sign of anyone.

CLOSE ON KIM

frowning, deep in thought. Then she comes to a decision, and shakes her head.

> KIM (muttering)
> No way.

PULL BACK

to show Kim lowering herself carefully onto her branch. This time, she sits on it as if it is a bench. She scoots until her side is against the tree, and wraps one arm around the trunk. Settled on her perch, she leans forward and peers down between her knees.

KIM'S POV

The ground is barely visible through the branches below her. It is *very far* down.

CLOSE ON KIM

She wrinkles her nose, looking almost amused by her position.

> KIM (wryly)
> Isn't *this* wonderful.

FADE OUT:

FADE IN:

EXT. — THE WOODS — DAY

ANGLE ON THE GLARING MIDDAY SUN

CLOSE ON KIM

Her head is drooping, her eyes half-shut. Tangles of wet hair cling to her brow and the sides of her head. Her face drips with perspiration. She licks her lips. She is clearly suffering. As a fly buzzes her face, Kim sticks out her lower lip and blows some breath at it.

PULL BACK

to show that Kim is hanging by her hands from the upper limb, standing on her usual perch. Her bra is dirty and wet. Her filthy red shorts hang low on her hips. Her bare skin gleams with moisture.

FADE OUT:

FADE IN:

EXT. — KIM'S TREE — DAY

Kim is on her back, resting on the limb, the tree trunk between her thighs. Her legs dangle. Her feet are bare. Her SNEAKERS, tied together with their laces, hang over a nearby branch. Kim's hands are folded beneath her head. Her eyes are tightly shut, her mouth open and grimacing as she pants for breath.

CLOSE ON KIM'S MOUTH

Her lips are dry and cracked. She explores them gently with the tip of her tongue.

FADE OUT:

FADE IN.

EXT. — KIM'S TREE — DAY

ANGLE ON KIM'S BACK

She is standing again, hanging onto the higher limb. Now, she is naked. Her bra, shorts, and underpants are draped over a nearby branch. Her hair is a wet mat against the back of her head and neck. Her skin gleams as if slicked with oil.

FADE OUT:

FADE IN:

EXT. — KIM'S TREE — DUSK

ANGLE ON KIM

She is dressed, wearing her sneakers, and sitting with her back against the trunk, her legs straddling the branch. Now that the heat of the day has passed, she appears haggard but is no longer suffering and sweaty. She tips her head back and looks toward the dimming sky.

FADE OUT:

FADE IN:

EXT. — KIM'S TREE — NIGHT

Kim swings down from her perch and begins to descend the tree. She has made her way down a short distance when she stops.

> KIM (muttering, disgusted)
> Great.

She begins climbing UPWARD.

Soon, she is back where she started. She reaches out and plucks her rock-filled T-shirt off the branch where she had deposited it the night before.

> KIM
> Guess I won't be needing you fellas.

With that, she upends the shirt and lets the rocks fall. They THUD against lower branches, and make SOFT SOUNDS as they hit the distant ground.

Kim tucks the T-shirt under the waistband at the rear of her shorts, so it hangs behind her. She resumes her descent.

FADE OUT:

FADE IN:

EXT. — KIM'S TREE — NIGHT

Kim struggles down to the lowest branch of her tree. She eases herself down, clinging to it, then lets herself drop to the ground. There, she turns around and scans the woods.

KIM'S POV

Her gaze moves slowly as she studies the dark woods in every direction. There is no sign of anyone.

ANGLE ON KIM

She starts walking, heading in the same general direction as earlier — away from the place where she had fled from Carson.

She stumbles along, worn out, dragging.

FADE OUT:

FADE IN:

EXT. — THE WOODS — NIGHT

Kim is making her weary way through the woods. As she staggers along, she plucks her T-shirt from the back of her shorts. She wipes her face with it, and tucks it again under her waistband.

Abruptly, she halts and straightens up.

CLOSE ON KIM

She looks amazed.

There is the RUSHING SOUND of a stream.

MOVING SHOT

Kim runs past bushes, dodges trees, and comes upon a narrow, swift-moving stream. With a WEARY CRY of delight, she throws herself into the water. She submerges herself in it, disappearing.

CAMERA MOVES IN

on the moonlit stream. Kim bursts to the surface, gasping. On her knees, she cups water to her mouth.

CLOSE ON KIM'S HEAD

as she fiercely drinks handful after handful of water. A hand suddenly darts from behind and grabs the hair at the back of Kim's head.

ANGLE ON KIM ONLY

She CRIES OUT in fear and pain as the hand yanks her upward by the hair. She reaches overhead and grabs the wrist. A bare arm crosses her belly. She is lifted, kicking, from the stream.

KIM'S POV

as she is carried from the stream by the ATTACKER. Once ashore, she is hurled down. The ground flies up to meet her face.

ANGLE ON KIM'S BACK

She is sprawled facedown on the ground, trying to push herself up. A fist pounds the side of her head. Stunned by the blow, she sags. The hands of Attacker rip open the catch of her bra and break the shoulder straps. They feverishly rub her bare back. They hook the waistband of her shorts, and drag the shorts down.

CLOSE ON KIM'S FEET

Her shorts are yanked off over her sneakers. The hands of Attacker grab her ankles, lift them. With a scissoring motion of the ankles, he flips Kim onto her back.

KIM'S POV

As she is rolled over, she sees the man standing above her. He holds her ankles against his hips.

This is not Carson.

Attacker is thin, with a leering, cadaverous face. His head is hairless. He wears ragged, cut-off jeans and no shirt. Around his waist is a belt that holds a huge hunting knife.

CLOSE ON ATTACKER'S FACE

> ATTACKER (squealing with delight)
> Whew! Got me a good 'un! Some fun! Whaaah!

CRACK OF HIGH-POWERED RIFLE

ATTACKER'S HEAD is kicked sideways as the bullet punches through his temple. The other side of his head explodes in a spray of gore.

KIM'S POV

She sees Attacker still standing there, holding her upraised legs by the ankles. Then he lets go. As her legs fall toward the ground, the man drops straight backward.

ANGLE ON KIM

Pressing the bra to her breasts, she sits up and snaps her head to the left.

KIM'S POV

The dim shape of a man appears among the trees. He is striding toward her, rifle in his arms. He enters a moonlit area. The man who killed her Attacker is Carson.

ANGLE ON KIM

GASPING, frightened, confused, she scurries over the ground. She snatches up her shorts and T-shirt, and glances back at Carson.

CUT TO:

Carson, who marches straight up to the body of the attacker and FIRES TWO MORE ROUNDS into him.

CUT TO:

Kim, whirling around on her knees, clutching the clothes to her body, a look of shock on her face as she gazes at Carson standing over the body.

> KIM (stunned)
> Jesus.

CLOSE ON CARSON

as he casts her a grim look.

> CARSON
> Nope. Just me.
> (Pause)
> Go on, get dressed. I'll give you a lift back to
> town.

ANGLE ON BOTH

Kim is suspicious, perplexed.

> KIM
> What do you mean?

> CARSON
> I mean, It's over. All done. Butcher canceled.
> Mission accomplished.

> KIM
> You're not the Butcher?

> CARSON
> Nope.

Carson slings the rifle onto his back, squats down, and picks up the body. He throws it over his shoulder. Then he starts to walk away.

CARSON
You coming?

KIM
No way.

Carson carries the body away, heading in the direction from which he had come.

Kim remains sitting on the ground, holding her clothes, staring after Carson.

FADE OUT:

FADE IN:

EXT. — THE WOODS — NIGHT

Carson is carrying the body. SOUNDS OF RUSHING PERSON behind him. Casually, he turns around.

CUT TO:

Kim, in her T-shirt and shorts, hurrying forward to catch up with Carson.

ANGLE ON BOTH

as Kim comes up beside Carson. She is on the side away from body.

CARSON
Changed your mind.

KIM
Who *are* you?

CARSON
Hired hand.

KIM
Like . . . a mercenary or something?

CARSON
You got it.

They walk along in silence for a few steps. Suddenly, Kim grabs his arm and gives it a hard jerk. Carson, stopping, turns toward her. She backsteps fast to avoid the feet of the body draped over his shoulder.

KIM (enraged)
Why did you *do* this to me.

> CARSON (matter-of-fact)
> Needed bait. You were it. Just his type.

Kim throws a roundhouse at Carson. Her fist just misses the rump of the body. It lands solidly on Carson's chin. The blow doesn't seem to bother him. But he doesn't hesitate. His right arm shoots out and he smashes his fist against the side of Kim's face. Her head snaps sideways, and the impact hurls her backward. She slams against a nearby tree trunk, strikes the back of her head against it, bounces off and flops facedown on the ground. She lies there, out cold.

> CUT TO:

Carson as he glances at her, shakes his head, and starts walking again. He leaves her behind.

> FADE OUT:

> FADE IN:

EXT. — THE WOODS — NIGHT

Kim regains consciousness and slowly gets to her hands and knees. She looks this way and that. No sign of Carson. She gets to her feet, wincing and holding her head. After a few wobbly steps, she calls out.

> KIM
> Hello!
> (Pause)
> Hey! You rat, where are you?

No answer comes. Kim keeps walking.

> KIM (muttering)
> Rotten bastard. Bait. Fucker used me for bait.

Walks a little farther, muttering to herself.

> KIM (yelling into the woods)
> I COULDA BEEN KILLED, YOU SHIT!

> CARSON (O.S.) (nearby)
> Some loss.

Startled, Kim whirls sideways.

KIM'S POV

as she watches Carson approach from some nearby trees, still lugging the body.

                    CARSON (a little amused)
         If you want to tag along, you'd better learn how to
         behave.

ANGLE ON BOTH

as they again start walking together.

                    KIM (mutters)
                    Fuckin' Rambo.

                    CARSON
                    Just clam up.

                    KIM (pushing it)
         Oh, really? Or what? You gonna punch me out
         again? Or maybe this time you'll put a couple of
         slugs in my head. You seem to excel in that.

                    CARSON
         Should've let him have you, I guess. Bagged him
         after he got done.

Silence for a while as they continue walking through the woods. Then, Kim
looks up at Carson.

                    KIM (somewhat subdued)
         Your timing *was* pretty good. I'll give you credit
         for that.

                    CARSON
                    Why thank you, ma'am.

                    KIM
                    How did you find me?

                    CARSON (amused)
                    Find you? Hell, I never *lost* you.

                    KIM
                    I'll bet.

                    CARSON
         Climbing that tree was a pretty good gimmick.
         Showed you were using your head. Showed some
         real brains, too, sticking it out till after dark.

> KIM (still with disbelief)
> This is bull. I lost you.

> CARSON
> I'm not gonna argue the point.

Silence for a while as they continue walking.

> KIM (a little concerned)
> Could you see me up there in the tree?

> CARSON
> Could *you* see *me*?

Kim glares at him.

> CARSON (cont'd)
> I was the guy with the binoculars in the tree
> next door.

> KIM
> Wonderful. Just great.
> (Disgusted)
> Hope you enjoyed yourself.

> CARSON
> Mighty hot up there.

> KIM
> You're a real prize, you know that?

> CARSON
> Got my man.

> KIM
> Whoop-dee-doo.

> CARSON
> Maybe "whoop-dee-doo" to you, tiger. To me, it's
> fifty grand.

> KIM (astonished)
> *Fifty thousand dollars?*

> CARSON
> On delivery.

He pats the rump of Attacker.

> KIM
> Somebody paid you to come out and kill him?

> CARSON
> Asshole made the mistake of nailing a gal with a
> rich papa.

FADE OUT:

FADE IN:

EXT. — THE WOODS — NIGHT

Kim and Carson enter a clearing. Carson throws the body to the ground.

> KIM (worried)
> What are you doing?

Carson doesn't answer. He sits down on the back of the corpse, opens a
pouch on his web belt, and takes out a pack of cigarettes and a lighter.
He shakes out a cigarette, pokes it into his mouth, and raises the pack
toward Kim.

Kim, standing near him, shakes her head.

CLOSE ON CARSON

as he lights his smoke, the glow of the lighter fluttering on his
black-smeared face.

ANGLE ON BOTH

Kim watches him.

> KIM (hesitant)
> Have you got anything to eat?

> CARSON
> Yep.

He just sits there, puffing on his cigarette.

> KIM
> Well, give me something, damnit.

> CARSON
> What's the magic word?

> KIM
> Fuck you.

> CARSON
> That ain't it.

> KIM
> You *kidnapped* me, you bastard! You pounded
> that poor guy, Bradley . . .

> CARSON (calmly, puffing)
> Got in my way . . .

> KIM
> You *choked me out* and threw me in your trunk
> like a sack of trash and dragged me to this
> goddamn place to help you nail your goddamn
> *maniac* who damn near *raped* me, and NOW
> YOU'RE GIVING ME SHIT ABOUT FOOD!

Kim kicks the ground, sending a bunch of dead leaves and twigs flying
against Carson's boots and camouflage pants.

> CARSON (amused)
> You're a scrapper, all right.

Kim kicks some more forest debris at Carson. She jams a finger toward him.

> KIM
> You OWE me!

> CARSON
> Where's that magic word?

> KIM
> Go to Hell.

> CARSON
> Wrong again.

Finished with his smoke, Carson extinguishes the glowing butt by jabbing it
against the bare shoulder of the corpse.

CLOSE ON KIM

wincing, shaking her head, disgusted.

> KIM
> Pig.

ANGLE ON BOTH

> CARSON
> Don't hear *him* complaining.

With that, Carson gets to his feet. He hefts the body and throws it over his shoulder.

They leave the clearing, Kim following at a short distance.

FADE OUT:

FADE IN:

EXT. — THE WOODS — NIGHT

Carson is carrying the body through the forest. Kim enters the scene, still keeping her distance. They come to another clearing, and again Carson drops the body to the ground. It lands flat on its back, legs together, arms straight out at its sides.

> KIM
> Now what?

> CARSON
> A little R and R.

Carson unslings his rifle and lies down, rifle at his side, his head resting on the back of the corpse.

Kim, standing nearby, stares down at Carson and shakes her head.

> KIM
> You've gotta be kidding.

> CARSON
> Nope.

> KIM (frustrated)
> Come on, we can't be that far from the car.

> CARSON
> Far enough.
> (Folds his hands on his stomach)
> Got no shut-eye last night.

KIM (sighing, annoyed)
At least give me something to eat before you
settle down for your goddamn nap.

CARSON
Please?

KIM
Kiss my ass.

CARSON
Tempting.

CLOSE ON KIM

suddenly uneasy as she realizes Carson *might* try something with her.

ANGLE ON BOTH

Kim steps away from Carson. A few yards off, she sits down with her back to
a tree trunk. She draws her legs up, and wraps her arms around them.

Kim stares at Carson. He is stretched out, motionless.

ANGLE ON KIM

staring at Carson from behind her upraised knees. HOLD on her.

FADE OUT:

FADE IN:

EXT. — THE SAME CLEARING — DAY

Kim is sprawled on the ground near the trunk of the tree, face up, asleep.
She looks a wreck: her hair is tangled; her face is bruised; her arms and legs
are scratched; her knees have abrasions and grass stains. The flap of her torn
T-shirt hangs down, baring her right shoulder and the top of her breast.

The SOUND OF FOOTSTEPS approach her, crunching softly on the forest
floor.

CARSON'S BOOTS enter the scene. They stop near one of Kim's feet. For a
few moments, Carson just stands there. We see only his boots and Kim
sprawled in front of him asleep, vulnerable.

A PACK OF TWINKIES drops onto her belly.

Kim flinches awake. Groggy, she looks up at Carson. She makes a face as if he is the last person she wants to see. MOANING, she braces herself up on her elbows.

KIM'S POV

She sees the Twinkies resting on her stomach, then looks again at Carson. He no longer wears the stocking cap. His hair is very short. The black makeup is gone. His face is rugged, handsome. But not friendly.

BACK TO SCENE

Kim pushes herself to a sitting position, Twinkies slipping onto her lap, and scoots backward to lean against the tree trunk. She picks up the Twinkies. Unwrapping them, she looks up at Carson.

> KIM (wryly)
> Twinkies?

> CARSON
> Breakfast of champions.

Kim actually smiles for a moment. Then, the smile falters. Carson's unexpected gesture of kindness moves her.

> KIM
> Thank you.

> CARSON
> Just don't want you keeling over on me. We've
> got some ground to cover.

> KIM
> Appreciate it, anyway.

Her trembling, grimy hands rip open the package. She lifts a Twinkie to her mouth, takes a big bite of it, and begins to chew. She shuts her eyes. From the look on her face, this is the best meal she has ever tasted.

Carson looms over Kim, watching her eat. He removes a plastic WATER BOTTLE from his belt and tosses it to the ground beside her. Then he turns away.

Carson strides across the clearing toward the body of Attacker. The body is in the same position it landed in last night, when Carson threw it down. It is face up, feet together, arms spread out almost straight from its sides. Carson stares down at it, then turns to Kim.

CARSON
Let's move out.

Kim nods as she chews.

KIM
How far to the car?

CARSON
Far enough. You covered a lot of ground for a gal.

KIM (her feminist feathers ruffled)
For a *gal*, huh.

CARSON
Don't get your shorts in a knot.

Kim scowls at him, then takes a drink from the water bottle. Holding onto the bottle and the second Twinkie, she struggles to her feet. She grimaces as if she aches all over. MOANING, she stretches to get the kinks out. Then she walks stiffly toward Carson.

She watches Carson crouch over the body, shove his hands beneath it, and lift it. The body is rigid, arms still sticking out as he picks it up.

CLOSE ON KIM

upset by the grim sight.

KIM
My God.

ANGLE ON BOTH

as Carson turns to face her, holding the body at chest level. He looks a little annoyed.

KIM (grossed out)
Can't you do something about that?

CARSON
He'll soften up after a while. Rigor's like a hard-on: it comes and goes.

KIM (not appreciating the comparison)
I had a client like you once. He's doing life
without parole.

                              CARSON (amused)
                        You a goddamn ambulance chaser?

                                    KIM
                         Beats killing people for a living.

                                  CARSON
                       Known you were a lawyer, I'd of let the guy
                       have you.

                                    KIM
                            Surprised you didn't.

                                  CARSON
                            Chivalry ain't dead.

Carson turns away, and starts walking. Kim follows.

                              KIM (mutters)
                        Sure. You and Lancelot. My ass.

KIM'S POV

as she looks from the grotesque, rigid body to the Twinkie in her hand.

CLOSE ON KIM

She looks at the Twinkie as if it has metamorphosed into a turd. Then a
what-the-hell look comes to her face, and she bites into it.

ANGLE ON BOTH

as Kim follows Carson across the clearing. Carson approaches some trees.
He has to turn sideways to carry the body between the trunks.

                                                            FADE OUT:

                                                             FADE IN:

EXT. — THE WOODS — DAY

Carson is walking through the forest. Kim, behind him, has finished eating,
and the water bottle is back in place on Carson's belt. The strain of carrying
the stiff corpse cradled in his arms shows on Carson's face. He stops and
turns to Kim.

                                  CARSON
                          Give me a hand with this.

KIM
You're kidding.

CARSON
Take his feet.

KIM
No way.

CARSON (stern)
Take his feet.

KIM
He's your meal ticket. You carry him.

CARSON
I'll strip you both naked and *tie* you to him.

CLOSE ON KIM

stunned that he would even think of such a thing.

KIM (doubtful, but pressing it)
You wouldn't.

CLOSE ON CARSON

He doesn't have to say a thing. The look on his face makes it clear that he *would*. And he just might enjoy it.

ANGLE ON BOTH

Disgust on her face, Kim approaches. She touches the bare ankles of the corpse, then jerks her hands back. Nose wrinkled, she wipes her hands on her shorts.

CARSON
Now.

Kim steels herself, and again takes hold of the ankles. Carson shifts position, jostling the corpse until he has it by the shoulders, its head against his belly.

CARSON
Go first.

Kim turns around so that she holds the feet behind her. She begins to walk. This is like carrying the body on a stretcher — without the benefit of the stretcher. The arms still stick out straight from its sides.

Kim turns her head.

> KIM (with distaste)
> You're sick, you know that?

> CARSON
> Feel just fine, thanks.

> KIM
> You oughta be committed. You've got loose
> screws.

> CARSON
> More than likely. But I'm getting fifty grand, and
> you're not.

> KIM
> You know what a sociopath is?

> CARSON
> I got a feeling you might tell me.

> KIM
> Just look in the mirror.

> CARSON
> Not just a lawyer, but a shrink, too. I'm
> impressed.

> KIM
> Maybe *you* oughta try working for a living.

> CARSON
> This feels like work to me.

> KIM
> How many people *have* you killed?

> CARSON
> Enough.

> KIM
> And it doesn't bother you at all?

> CARSON
> Why should it? I'm gonna lose sleep 'cause I drop

a hairball like this guy? You got any idea what he
had in mind for you?

> KIM
> I read the papers.

> CARSON
> Okay, then.

> KIM
> The bastard wouldn't have touched me if you
> hadn't dragged me out here.

> CARSON
> I hadn't dragged you out here, he'd still be
> roaming around looking for action. He'd have
> gotten another gal. Sooner or later. Now, he
> won't.

> KIM
> So, you're a great humanitarian.

> CARSON
> I get the job done.

> KIM
> Even if you've gotta kidnap someone . . .

> CARSON
> You do what it takes.

FADE OUT:

FADE IN:

EXT. — THE WOODS — DAY

Kim is still in the lead, carrying the corpse by its ankles. The strain of lugging
the weight shows on her.

She is breathing heavily, dripping with sweat.

She glances to her right.

KIM'S POV

She sees that they are walking along the crest of a hill. The rather steep slope
is just a couple of yards away.

ANGLE ON BOTH

as Kim faces forward again.

> KIM
> You hire out to anyone who can pay the price?

> CARSON
> What do you think?

> KIM
> I imagine so.

> CARSON
> Do *you*?

> KIM
> What's that supposed to mean?

> CARSON
> You already told me you defended a killer. The
> guy that got life?

> KIM
> I stopped doing criminal work.

> CARSON
> Conscience get the better of you?

> KIM
> Everyone's entitled to a fair trial. Even that killer
> I defended.

> CARSON
> He give his victim a fair trial?

> KIM
> That's not the point.

> CARSON
> Shit. You'd probably defend *this* piece of garbage
> if you got the chance.

> KIM
> Gimme a break.

> CARSON
> Too bad I spoiled your chance.

(Grim, satisfied smile)
This is one guy won't get off on a technicality.

KIM

Yeah? Well, technically, you killed an
innocent man.

CARSON

This here innocent man was ready to jump your
bones, and that would've been the *best* part of it.
He would've spent *hours* on you, after that.
(Pause)
No goddamn lawyer's gonna get him off the hook,
now. Nope. He's doing his time in Hell.

KIM'S POV

A couple of yards in front of her, GEORGE springs out from behind a bush.
He is identical to Attacker (obviously his twin brother) except that he sports
the tattoo of a skull on his chest. He wears ragged old jeans and a rope belt.
A knife is tucked under the rope at his hip.

In his hands is a double-barrel SHOTGUN.

SHRIEKING WITH RAGE, George shoulders the shotgun at the same
instant he leaps into sight. He aims it straight at Kim.

CUT TO:

Kim, YELLING with alarm, hurling herself aside as the

SHOTGUN ROARS

CUT TO:

Carson, catching the blast full in his face, flopping backward dead.

CUT TO:

George swinging his shotgun toward Kim.

CUT TO:

Kim throwing herself over the hill's edge as the shotgun BLASTS.

MOVING SHOT

follows Kim as she begins her wild tumble down the slope, twisting,
somersaulting, rolling.

CUT TO:

George, reloading as he rushes to the rim of the slope. He FIRES BOTH BARRELS down at Kim.

CUT TO:

Kim, still tumbling down the slope. She comes to a stop near the bottom, and looks up.

KIM'S POV

She sees George at the top, snapping the breach of his shotgun shut after reloading again. He looks furious, crazed. He starts rushing down the slope toward her.

GEORGE (a mad wail)
Y'KILLED HIM! Y'KILLED EARL!

CUT TO:

Kim, frantic, scurries to her feet and rushes farther down the slope. Another GUNSHOT. BARK flies off the trunk of a tree beside her. She races past the tree.

CUT TO:

George as he lowers the shotgun and continues after her, leaping down the slope in his frenzy, somehow miraculously staying on his feet.

MOVING SHOT

of Kim, now on flat ground, racing for her life. She is GASPING, WHIMPERING. She dodges trees, crashes through bushes. Her face is twisted with terror and agony. She glances over her shoulder.

KIM'S POV

George, about fifty feet behind Kim, halts and raises his shotgun.

CUT TO:

Kim diving for the ground as the gun BLASTS.

CUT TO:

George as he breaks open his shotgun. He flicks the spent shells from the double chambers. He digs a hand into a pocket of his jeans for fresh shells.

None there. He switches the shotgun to his other arm, and searches his other pocket. No shells there either. He scowls toward Kim.

GEORGE (enraged)
GONNA HAVE YOU, BITCH! GONNA SKIN
YER SWEET ASS!

He hurls his shotgun aside. He jerks the huge hunting knife from its sheath, rips the air with it, shakes the blade at the sky, and bolts after Kim.

MOVING SHOT

as Kim rushes through the woods. She dodges some obstacles, leaps others, rams her way through undergrowth.

FADE OUT:

FADE IN:

EXT. — THE WOODS — DAY

Kim dashes into scene, GASPING and frantic. She glances over her shoulder. George is out of sight, but we HEAR him PLUNGING through BUSHES, and GRUNTING. Kim keeps running. Then she halts.

KIM'S POV

A short distance ahead of her is a DEADFALL. She is coming up from behind the same deadfall that she had tried to hide under the first night.

CUT TO:

Kim as she races for the deadfall, which is blocking her way. Her face is a sweaty, grimy mask of fear and pain. She is struggling to suck in enough air. But she seems to recognize the deadfall. She looks over her shoulder again.

KIM'S POV

George isn't in sight, but we STILL HEAR HIM. He is not far away.

ANGLE ON

Kim from behind as she dashes the final distance to the deadfall. The top of the fallen trunk is about as high as her head. She flings herself against the trunk and climbs over it.

CUT TO:

George, lurching into sight from behind bushes.

GEORGE'S POV

He sees Kim scurry over the top of the deadfall, leap down, and vanish.

CUT TO:

George, wild-eyed and grinning. He runs toward the deadfall, brandishing his knife.

GEORGE
I gotcha. I gotcha, sweet thing. You're mine!

He climbs over the top of it, and leaps.

CUT TO:

OTHER SIDE OF DEADFALL

George lands on his feet. Hunched over slightly, teeth bared, he jerks his head from side to side, scanning the area ahead.

GEORGE (in a teasing voice)
Come out, come out, wherever you are.

GEORGE'S POV

He sees only the clearing, bushes, and trees. No sign of Kim.

CUT TO:

George, front view. He is still hunched over, looking this way and that. Cocking his head sideways as he listens. The only sounds are his WHEEZY GASPS for air, and the normal forest sounds of the breeze, birds, and insects.

GEORGE
I know yer here. Can't fool George. C'mon, sweet
thing.
(Keeps looking)
Got somethin' for ya. Got somethin' big 'n hard.
C'mon and get yer taste.

While he stands there, the deadfall at his back is clearly visible. We see the gap into which Kim had crawled to hide that first night in the woods.

CLOSE ON GEORGE

as a sneaky grin comes to his face. His eyes roll upward. He *knows*.

BACK TO SCENE

George whirls around and lurches to the gap under the deadfall. As he drops to his hands and knees . . .

GEORGE (excited)
Wheee! Yer mine!

He crawls forward and peers into the space between the trunk and the ground.

GEORGE'S POV

as he peers into shadows under the deadfall. Kim isn't there.

GEORGE (disappointed)
Aww, piss!

CUT TO:

Kim stepping into view from the place where she has concealed herself beside the deadfall's root clump. She has a section of branch the size of a baseball bat. Club raised overhead, she sneaks toward George.

CUT TO:

George, finished looking, backs out from under the deadfall on his hands and knees.

ANGLE ON BOTH

Kim rushes George from behind. He hears her coming. As she swings the club sideways at his head, he twists around, braces himself up with his right hand (which grips the knife) and blocks the blow with his left arm. He CRIES OUT in pain and rage. The impact knocks him onto his back. Kim raises the club high, ready to swing it straight down at his head. But George kicks out. His foot smashes against Kim's leg. Losing her balance, she staggers backward and falls.

George scrambles up and rushes Kim. She is on her back. The club is on the ground beside her, but she still holds it in one hand.

CUT TO:

George, GROWLING, as he makes a dive onto Kim with his knife ready to rip her.

BACK TO SCENE

Kim jerks the club up. One end is planted against the ground beneath her armpit. The other rises just in time to catch George in the chest as he dives onto her. He SQUEALS. Instead of smashing down on Kim, he is propped up by the club and sails over her like a mad pole-vaulter. He kicks at the air, somersaults past Kim's head, and lands on his back. His breath is knocked out.

ANGLE ON GEORGE

His face is twisted horribly as he tries to breathe. We glimpse the skull tattooed on his chest. The jagged end of Kim's branch has torn a shallow wound in the skull's eye. George clasps a hand to the wound.

BACK TO SCENE

Kim scurries to her feet. She lifts the club and approaches George. He looks all done in: breathless, holding his wound. But his crazed eyes are fixed on her. Wary of his feet, Kim moves cautiously to George's side. She stays back, out of reach of reach for a moment.

Then, fierce and determined to end it right here, Kim suddenly raises her club, takes a big step toward George, and swings it down at his face.

George catches the club with both hands, wrenches it from Kim's grip, and as he throws it aside . . .

GEORGE (yelling with triumph)
YAH! NOW!

Kim is shocked to find herself suddenly without her weapon.

KIM (in anguish at her fate)
NO!

And she scrambles backward as George rolls toward her and slashes the knife at her shin. He misses. Kim whirls around and runs.

She runs in the direction from which she had come. She dashes around the root clump of the deadfall and out of sight.

CUT TO:

George as he gets to his feet. The knife is in his right hand. He looks down at his chest. Blood has spilled down his bare torso from the gouged flesh at the eye of the skull tattoo. The fingers of his left hand go to the wound. As he touches it, he lets out a QUIET, MAD GIGGLE.

FADE OUT:

FADE IN:

EXT. — THE WOODS — DAY

Kim runs through the forest. She is clearly exhausted, struggling for breath and slowing down. But she no longer appears terrified. Her face shows grim determination. She keeps plowing ahead.

KIM'S POV

We see the forest in front of Kim jarring and jolting in her vision as she runs. Shadows, patches of sunlight. We hear her HARSH GASPS for breath. She seems to be heading straight for the trunk of a tree. The trunk looms closer, closer. Just when Kim is about to crash into it, her arms thrust into view and she catches the trunk.

ANGLE ON KIM'S BACK

as she jerks to a halt, arms straight out against the trunk. She bends over slightly, GASPING, hanging her head between her arms. Her filthy, sodden T-shirt clings to her back.

A few moments pass. Then, Kim lifts her head. Wearily, she straightens up and pushes herself away from the tree.

She turns around and scans the area of woods from which she has come. We hear no one approaching. Kim lifts the bottom of her T-shirt and wipes her dripping face. She is still PANTING, but not as harshly now.

CLOSE ON KIM'S FACE

Determined, wary. Her eyes are narrowed as her gaze slowly sweeps the woods.

CUT TO:

CLOSE ON GEORGE'S FACE

as he runs. He is not panting. He seems gleeful. His face is streaked with red bands: He has used the blood from his chest wound to give himself war paint.

CAMERA PULLS BACK

to show a frontal view of George loping easily through the woods, knife brandished in his right hand.

GEORGE'S POV

Ahead of him, but a short distance to the right, is the same tree where Kim was resting moments ago. On the ground in front of it is one of her sneakers.

BACK TO SCENE

George grins when he spots the sneaker. He changes course, and jogs toward the tree. He is a couple of yards from the tree when Kim springs out from behind its trunk. Her face looks fierce: eyes wild, twisted lips baring her teeth in a snarl. She HURLS A ROCK point-blank at George's face.

The rock strikes his mouth and bounces off. He staggers to a stop but doesn't go down.

CLOSE ON GEORGE'S FACE

His lips are mashed, torn, bleeding. Gazing wide-eyed at Kim, he spits out pieces of teeth. He grins, showing her a mouth of bloody teeth.

CUT TO:

Kim — shocked that George is still on his feet. But without hesitation, she fires a SECOND ROCK at him.

BACK TO SCENE

The second rock clips George's ear and flies on by. With a SAVAGE CRY, he raises his knife overhead and rushes Kim. She whirls around and runs. George is close behind her, YELLING.

CLOSE ON KNIFE

as the huge blade plunges downward at Kim's back. It almost misses. But not quite. The point rips her clinging T-shirt and cuts a downward slice on her skin about three inches long.

But George has stabbed hard. He expected the knife to ram deep into Kim's back. He wasn't prepared for a miss. Taken by surprise, he isn't quick enough to stop the downward course of his knife. The blade plunges hard into his own right thigh.

ANGLE ON BOTH

George, SHRIEKING with pain, jerks the knife out of his leg and falls to the ground. Kim keeps on running as blood spreads down the back of her T-shirt.

FADE OUT:

FADE IN:

EXT. — THE HILLSIDE — DAY

Kim, the back of her shirt and shorts soaked with blood, is making her way up the wooded hillside. This is the same slope she had tumbled down immediately after the shooting of Carson.

Kim is missing one shoe. She struggles toward the top of the slope, sometimes crawling, sometimes grabbing bushes or tree roots to pull herself higher.

CUT TO:

George sitting on the ground where he fell after stabbing himself. His legs are stretched out in front of him. He is working on his thigh. He has already cut off the leg of his jeans near the inseam, and is wrapping the denim around his thigh. He uses his rope belt to bind the makeshift bandage in place.

GASPING and SNARLING through his demolished mouth, George gets to his feet. Knife in hand, he begins to limp forward.

FADE OUT:

FADE IN:

EXT. — THE HILLTOP CLEARING — DAY

CLOSE ON KIM'S BACK WOUND

The skin around her wound is bare. The shallow cut is low enough on Kim's back to allow her to reach it. Her hands come into view. They press an actual bandage (a clean white pad of gauze) against the wound, and move out of sight.

PULL BACK

to show Kim from behind, wearing only her shorts. She is standing near the bodies of Carson and Earl. A small first-aid kit (from Carson's belt) lies open by her feet. Next to the kit is her balled-up T-shirt. On top of her T-shirt rests Carson's automatic. She wears a sneaker on one foot. The other foot is bare. Her bloody shorts are clinging to her rump.

CUT TO:

KIM's face, grim and determined, eyes narrow.

MUSIC SWELLS AS

CAMERA SLOWLY PULLS BACK

to show Kim from the front. She is standing sturdy, feet slightly spread, with the bearing of a proud warrior. She is wearing her T-shirt and shorts. Both her feet are bare. Carson's web belt is looped over her left shoulder and hangs across her chest like a bandolier. The holstered automatic, attached to the belt, is at her right hip. She holds Carson's rifle at port arms.

She turns slowly in a full circle, scanning the area. When we see her back, there is Carson's knife sheathed on the web belt low on her back so that she would be able to reach behind herself with her right hand and grab its hilt.

FADE OUT:

FADE IN:

EXT. — THE WOODS — DAY

MOVING SHOT

of George in the forest below the hillside, favoring his right leg as he runs. The knife is in his hand. He is GASPING for air through his open, bloody mouth.

FADE OUT:

FADE IN:

EXT. — THE HILLTOP CLEARING — DAY

Kim steps over to Carson's body. Squatting beside it, she sets down the rifle. She pats the front pockets of Carson's pants. When she pats his right pocket, there is a quiet JANGLING SOUND. Kim digs her hand into the pocket, and pulls out his car keys.

FADE OUT:

FADE IN:

EXT. — THE WOODS — DAY

KIM'S POV

as viewed through Carson's binoculars from the top of the slope. Her gaze roams slowly through the woods along the bottom of the hillside, and searches the area beyond. Foliage stirs in the gentle breeze. There are quiet sounds of the BREEZE, BIRDS, INSECTS. No sign of George. Not yet.

The binoculars sweep back across the same area. This time, we see George hobbling out from behind a tree. The VIEW HOLDS on him.

George makes his way forward, squinting this way and that as he hunts for Kim.

The VIEW SHRINKS as the binoculars are lowered from Kim's eyes. But we are still seeing what Kim sees — George limping closer, searching.

CUT TO:

George as he approaches the bottom of the slope. He is scowling, angry that he can't find Kim. He stumbles around, turning, scanning every direction.

ROAR OF A GUNSHOT

George jumps as if scared witless. The shot kicks up forest debris near his feet. At the SECOND BLAST, he turns his back to the hillside, ducks slightly, covers his head with both arms like a kid being pelted with snowballs, and lopes for the safety of a tree.

SEVERAL SHOTS RAPID FIRE

Bullets smack the woods around George as he flees. He dives to the ground and scurries behind a trunk.

> KIM (O.S.) (frustrated)
> Shit.

CUT TO:

Kim, sprawled on the ground at the top of the slope, in the standard prone shooting position. Rolling onto her side, she removes the empty magazine from Carson's rifle and puts in a full one. She chambers a fresh round, resumes the prone position, and sights in on the place where she last saw George.

KIM'S POV

as George, far below, peeks around side of tree trunk where he has taken shelter. Nothing happens, so he moves a little farther into view.

CUT TO:

Kim emptying the magazine at him, RIFLE ROARING, jerking in her grip, each shot jolting the length of her body, brass shells flipping high.

After she stops firing, she doesn't move for a moment. Then she raises her head as if to see better.

KIM'S POV

George is sprawled flat on his back beside the tree where he had taken cover. But he is far away.

CUT TO:

Kim lifting the binoculars to her eyes.

KIM'S POV

A CLOSE VIEW THROUGH THE BINOCULARS of the tree trunk, pocked in a few places where the bullets blasted its bark away. The view moves sideways. There is George, flat on his back. His ruined mouth hangs open and his wide eyes seem to be staring straight upward. He sure looks dead. But there is no apparent new wound on his body.

> KIM (O.S.) (mutters)
> So where's the damn hole?

CUT TO:

Kim, getting to her feet, but leaving the rifle on the ground. She draws Carson's automatic from the holster at her hip, and starts down the slope.

MOVING SHOT

as Kim moves down the hillside. She is in no hurry. She makes her way carefully, trying to keep her eyes on the body but sometimes glancing down to check the ground ahead of her. There is nothing of fear about her. She appears calm and grim. She is no longer anybody's prey. She is the hunter.

KIM'S POV

As she reaches the bottom of the slope. She strides toward George, who is several yards straight ahead of her. He is still on his back, and still appears dead.

CLOSE ON KIM'S FACE

Her eyes narrow. She nods slightly.

CLOSE ON PISTOL

Kim jacks a cartridge into the chamber.

CUT TO:

Kim standing motionless, spreading her legs slightly, taking careful aim with the pistol.

CUT TO:

George as he bolts to a sitting position, YELLING and hurling his knife at Kim as the pistol BLASTS and kicks up earth where his head had been just a moment ago.

CUT TO:

Kim diving sideways. The KNIFE flies by, just missing her. She hits the ground, skidding. She rolls, gets to her knees, and brings the pistol up.

KIM'S POV

She glimpses George running, but he is only visible an instant at a time because of trees that block the view. Each time he appears between trees, Kim fires and misses. Then, George is gone.

CUT TO:

Kim, shaking her head, angry at herself for letting him get away. She rises to her feet, and searches the ground nearby until she finds his knife. She picks it up with her left hand, then throws it far up onto the slope, where it disappears in the undergrowth.

Turning away from the slope, she starts walking.

FADE OUT:

FADE IN:

EXT. — THE WOODS — DAY

Kim approaches the deadfall, the same one as earlier. She appears weary, but calm. She is not running, not breathing heavily. But she glances this way and that, on guard, as she walks to the deadfall.

She climbs onto the top of the trunk. Standing there, she scans the area. Then she sits down and crosses her legs. She brushes some crumbs of leaves and pine needles off the bottoms of her feet. Her feet are dirty, but show no damage from traveling barefoot through the woods.

She takes the web belt off her shoulder and spreads it across her lap. She unholsters the pistol and sets it down on her right thigh. After removing the water bottle, she drinks. Then she searches some of the canvas pouches attached to the belt. She finds more ammo in one. She opens another and finds a pack of GORP and a pack of TWINKIES.

CLOSE ON KIM'S FACE

as she looks at the Twinkies. She shows regret, even a little sorrow.

CLOSE ON KIM'S HANDS

Her filthy hands are steady as she starts to rip open the Twinkies.

FADE OUT:

FADE IN:

EXT. — THE WOODS — DAY

FRONT VIEW OF KIM

standing on the deadfall, feet apart. The belt again hangs across her chest. The pistol is in her right hand.

She leaps to the ground, landing in front of the GAP. She strides forward in a relaxed, ambling way, pretty much at ease with the present situation. After a few steps, she halts and looks back at the opening beneath the deadfall.

It is clear that she has not forgotten about George. But neither is she terribly concerned about him. After all, she is armed to the teeth and he is without any weapon at all. She doesn't bother to inspect the opening. With a shrug, she turns away and resumes walking.

FADE OUT:

FADE IN:

EXT. — THE WOODS — DAY

Kim walks into the scene, looking hot and weary. Then she stops. She turns her head from side to side, frowning slightly as she scans the forest.

> KIM (mutters)
> Can't be far.

She resumes walking. As she approaches a tree, she tips back her head to make sure that George isn't perched up there, ready to pounce. She passes that tree. As she comes to the next, she also checks it.

ANGLE ON KIM'S BACK

She keeps walking slowly forward, head turning and lifting as she checks the areas ahead and above her.

FADE OUT:

FADE IN:

EXT. — THE WOODS — DAY

KIM is sitting under a tree, knees up, back against the trunk. She has taken off the belt, and it rests on the ground at her right side. The pistol is on top of the belt, within easy reach. Kim drinks from the water bottle, then pours some water into her cupped hand and rubs her face with it. She plucks at the torn front of her T-shirt, peeling the fabric away from her skin, and dribbles some water down her chest. Her eyes close and she sighs at the good feel of it.

FADE OUT:

FADE IN:

EXT. — A CLEARING IN THE WOODS — DAY

Kim enters a clearing, and squints in the brilliant sunlight. She appears haggard. The pistol in her right hand hangs at her side, swaying at the end of her limp arm as she walks.

KIM'S POV

looking forward. There are a few scattered bushes and trees in the near distance. Farther on, the woods are thick again. SCAN to the right. The clear area continues, sloping gently downward. CAMERA follows her gaze as Kim turns her head forward again, then to the left.

To the left is a rather steep uphill SLOPE. The slope is sparsely wooded. This is not the same hill from which Kim ambushed George. It IS the slope she descended shortly after running from Carson's car.

CLOSE ON KIM'S FACE

She looks agonized with hope.

CAMERA PULLS BACK

to show Kim turning to the left, walking slowly toward the bottom of the slope, then walking more quickly. She shoves the pistol into its holster.

MOVING SHOT

Hands free, Kim begins jogging, and then she is sprinting. She attacks the slope full-speed and bounds up it like an eager kid taking stairs three at a time. She chugs up the slope, gasping for breath, arms and legs pumping, teeth bared.

ANGLE DOWNWARD

from the top of the slope, straight down at Kim. She is really moving, ignoring her agony, eyes fixed on the goal.

KIM'S POV

her vision bouncing and jerking on the rim of the hill just above her. And then she sees over the top. There are trees, bushes. Then CARSON'S CAR comes into view.

CUT TO:

KIM staggering over the crest. She stands there, HUFFING, grimacing, blinking sweat from her eyes. She bends over and holds her knees, but keeps her head up, keeps staring at the car. After a few moments, she straightens up.

CUT TO:

CARSON'S CAR in the distance, a few trees partly blocking the view.

CLOSE ON KIM

Her T-SHIRT is wadded in her hands and she is rubbing her face with it.

PULL BACK

as Kim raises her arms and puts the shirt on again. She is still BREATHING HEAVILY, but is no longer entirely winded. She bends down, picks up the belt at her feet, and hangs it over her shoulder. With trembling hands, she unsnaps a canvas case on the belt and takes out the car keys. She holds the keys in her left hand. Her right hand draws the pistol from the holster at her hip. She starts walking cautiously toward the car.

KIM'S POV

She makes her way toward the car, gaze moving from the car to the clearing on both sides, to the heavier growth of trees along the borders of the clearing.

CUT TO:

Kim, halting about 30 feet from the rear of the car. She peers at it, her eyes narrow, suspicious. Her head moves from side to side. She nibbles her lower lip. Then, she lifts the keys to her mouth. Holding them in her teeth, she uses both hands to work on the pistol.

She jacks a live round out of the chamber and releases the clip. She takes a close look at the top of the clip, where a couple of staggered rounds are visible.

Squatting, she picks up the live round. She blows and rubs some dirt off it, then feeds it into the clip. She slides the clip back into place in the handle of the pistol, and jacks a round into the chamber.

CLOSE ON KIM'S FACE

as she takes the keys from between her teeth. She looks grim, a little worried, but determined.

PULL BACK

to show Kim carefully walking the final distance to the car. She holds the pistol ready. Her eyes dart this way and that. About six feet from the rear of the car, she stops again.

KIM'S POV

quickly sweeping the area around the car, then lingering on the car.

ANGLE ON KIM

She moves slowly forward. Tense and watchful, she makes a complete circle around the car. She checks not only the area close to the car, but leans forward and peers into its windows.

She halts near the driver's door. She switches the pistol to her left hand, the keys to her right. Then she glances over her shoulder for a final look behind her.

She turns again to the door. Her trembling right hand tries the first key on the lock. The key doesn't fit.

CLOSE ON KIM'S RIGHT HAND

She fumbles out a second key. Because of her shaking hand, she has trouble finding the lock with its tip. Finally, the key slides in. She twists it.

CLOSE ON LOCK BUTTON

through the window of the driver's door. The button pops up.

ANGLE ON KIM

She has a look, not of joy, but of suffering that has come to a merciful end.

She pulls the key from the lock, grips the door handle, and steps backward as she opens the door.

She moves forward slightly. Standing between the inner side of the door and the exposed driver's seat, she tosses the keys onto the seat. She uses her right hand to pull the belt over her head. She tosses it into the car.

ANGLE ON BELT

as it sails into the car and lands on the passenger seat. Carson's knife, sheathed at the back of the belt, is now in the car.

CUT TO:

Kim giving final glances all around her. Then, she steps closer to the side of the car. She leans into the car to pick up the keys.

ANGLE ON KIM'S FEET

Her right foot is on the ground at the very edge of the gap beneath the car. Her left foot is farther back.

GEORGE'S HAND DARTS OUT from under the car, grabs her right foot, and jerks it forward. Kim's shin smashes against the doorsill.

ANGLE ON KIM

CRYING OUT in pain and alarm. She is thrown backward, Her side strikes the open door. She hits the ground, sprawling on her back, arms flung out to either side.

Even as she strikes the ground, she is being dragged under the car. In an instant, both her knees are out of sight. Squirming and squealing, she is dragged under to the hips. The pistol is still in her left hand. She flings her right arm up and hooks it against the doorsill as she is jerked farther under the car. She struggles to hold herself there. But George is too strong. Her arm is pulled away from the doorsill.

Except for her right hand, Kim is out of sight beneath the car. Her hand is fiercely gripping the edge of the undercarriage. Then it loses its hold, and seems to be sucked into the space beneath the car.

CUT TO OTHER SIDE OF CAR

George is clear of the car, on his knees, dragging Kim by her right ankle. She is coming out crooked, her left leg off to the side. When she is visible to the waist, her left leg bends, knee rising. She digs her heel into the ground, trying to stop herself.

George keeps tugging. Kim is dragged clear of the car. Her face is a mask of terror. Her T-shirt is rucked up around her chest. She raises her head off the ground and swings the pistol toward George.

George, YELLING as he sees Kim aim the pistol, releases her ankle and dives at her.

She gets off ONE SHOT. The bullet rips off a corner of George's ear as he drops onto her. He grabs the wrist of her gun hand, and drives the hand down against the ground as ANOTHER SHOT ROARS.

George is now sprawled on top of Kim, pinning her gun hand to the ground. She squirms and bucks under his weight. George pins down her other hand. He pushes himself up and sits on her belly, still clamping her hands to the ground.

CLOSE ON GEORGE'S FACE

He leers down at her, his mashed lips twisting into a grin that shows his broken teeth.

> GEORGE
> Gotcha!

CLOSE ON KIM'S FACE

Snarling.

ANGLE ON BOTH

as Kim drives a knee up, smashing it against George's back. George GRUNTS from the impact. Kim's knee slams into him again, and again. George is hurting. He releases Kim's right hand and drives a punch at her face. The blow jars her, knocks her head sideways.

Kim's eyes shut and she goes limp.

CLOSE ON GEORGE'S FACE

looking eager.

CLOSE ON KIM'S LEFT HAND

George takes the pistol from her limp fingers and flings it aside.

ANGLE ON BOTH

Kim is sprawled limp beneath him. George's hands go to her breasts. They rub her breasts through the T-shirt, squeeze them. He breathes heavily. He moans. Kim lies motionless as the fondling continues. With both hands, George grabs the torn neck of her T-shirt. As he rips the shirt . . .

This is the moment Kim has waited for.

SHE THRUSTS UP BOTH HANDS AND DIGS HER THUMBS INTO HIS EYES.

CLOSE ON GEORGE'S FACE

as KIM'S THUMBS JAM IN, GOUGING BOTH HIS EYES. Gore explodes from the demolished orbs. He SHRIEKS. Kim's thumbs go deep into his sockets.

ANGLE ON BOTH

Kim is beneath him, both arms up, hands clutching the sides of his head, thumbs in his sockets. SCREAMING, George reaches for his face.

Kim swings him sideways by his head. He tumbles off her, and she rolls onto her side, keeping her grip. Then she jerks her thumbs from his sockets with WET, SUCKING SOUNDS.

While George holds his face and rolls in a fit of agony, Kim scurries for the gun. She snatches it off the ground, whirls around and fires.

ANGLE ON

George lurching as a bullet punches through his head.

CUT TO:

Kim on her knees, eyes wild, pistol bucking in her hand as she RAPID FIRES until the pistol is empty.

HOLD ON KIM

Motionless on her knees, still aiming the pistol at George.

SLOW DISSOLVE TO BLACK

FADE IN:

EXT. — STREET — NIGHT

A police car stops at the curb in front of Kim's apartment building. The passenger door opens, and Kim climbs out. She leans into the car for a moment, speaking to the officer.

In the glow of the streetlamps, we see that she is still wearing her filthy T-shirt and shorts.

She shuts the car door, and the police car moves slowly away.

Kim turns toward her building.

KIM'S POV

as she sees her own car parked in one of the car ports alongside the front of the apartment house. Someone is *in* the car. Its door opens, and BRADLEY steps out. He is nicely dressed in a sport shirt and slacks. He walks toward Kim, carrying her handbag.

BACK TO SCENE

Kim, surprised to see him, smiles.

> KIM
> Bradley?

> BRADLEY (holding out the handbag)
> Thought you might need your stuff. Your laundry's in the trunk.

She takes the bag from him. They stand facing each other.

> KIM
> Thanks.
> (Shakes her head)
> Are you okay?

> BRADLEY
> Fine. God, I've been worried about you.

> KIM
> I'm really sorry I got you involved.

> BRADLEY
> I'm just sorry I wasn't any help. I went to the cops as soon as I could, but . . . I guess they didn't do you much good either.

> KIM
> Big area to cover.

BRADLEY (uncomfortable)
Yeah.

KIM
You been waiting around here for long?

BRADLEY (shrugs)
I came over when I heard about you on the radio.

CLOSE ON BRADLEY

He suddenly looks as if he might start to cry. He presses his lips tightly
together and shakes his head.

BRADLEY
I thought for sure you were a goner.

BACK TO SCENE

Kim, moved by his emotion, steps closer to Bradley and rubs his shoulder.

KIM (gently)
Let's not just stand here all night. Come on in.
I'll get cleaned up, and maybe we can grab a bite
to eat.

BRADLEY (eager but shy)
I don't want to intrude.

Kim takes hold of his arm, and leads him toward the building.

FADE OUT:

FADE IN:

INT. — KIM'S APARTMENT — NIGHT

CLOSE ON KIM

talking on the telephone. Her face is bruised and scratched but clean. Her
hair is damp.

KIM (annoyed)
No, I'm not upset. I'm thrilled you had a good
time at Tahoe. Tickled pink.
(Pause as she listens)
No, I don't think so.
(Pause)

> Not then either.
> (Pause)
> Right, call me again in a few days. Good-bye.

PULL BACK

as Kim hangs up the phone. She is seated on her living room sofa beside Bradley. He is still dressed as in previous scene. Kim is wearing her bathrobe. She faces Bradley and smiles.

> KIM
> Former boyfriend. So . . . does pizza sound good
> to you?

> BRADLEY
> Sure. Whatever.

Kim pats his leg.

> KIM
> Pizza it is. Let's have it delivered. I don't feel
> much like running around town.

FADE OUT:

FADE IN:

INT. — KIM'S APARTMENT — NIGHT

Kim is asleep in her dark bedroom, a soft breeze stirring the curtains. She is sprawled facedown, covered to the shoulders by a sheet. THE DOORBELL RINGS. Kim moans, stirs in her sleep. The BELL RINGS again and again. Someone is very persistent. The BELL CONTINUES TO RING as Kim wakes up.

She tosses back the sheet, swings her legs off the bed, and sits on the edge of the bed. Reaching up, she turns on the lamp. She looks groggy, but somewhat concerned. In the lamplight, we see that Kim is wearing a white, diaphanous nightgown. Her hair, though mussed a little, looks glossy and golden. She appears to be completely healed from her ordeal. She looks radiant, gorgeous.

As she gets up and walks across the room, the RINGING DOORBELL STOPS.

MOVING SHOT

as Kim walks down the dark hallway. She enters the living room, turns on a light, and goes to the door.

> KIM (calm, but a little worried)
> Who is it?
> (Pause)
> Brad?
> (Another pause)
> Who's there?

Still getting no response, Kim steps up close to the peephole. She peers out.

KIM'S POV

looking through the peephole. The corridor appears to be deserted.

CUT TO:

Kim, frowning slightly as she removes the guard chain and opens the door.

ANGLE FROM CORRIDOR

shows the door swing open. A paper-wrapped PACKAGE the size of a brick in on the floor in front of her feet. Kim leans into the corridor and glances both ways. Then she crouches and picks up the package.

KIM'S POV

On the wrapping paper is written with a marking pen, "TO KIM SANDERS — MY APOLOGIES AND MY GRATITUDE."

She rips open the paper. In her hands is a block of GREENBACKS bound together by a rubber band. She thumbs through the thick bulk.

CLOSE ON BUNDLE OF MONEY

All $100 bills. About four inches of them.

CLOSE ON KIM'S FACE

She stares at the MONEY. She is frowning, thinking, her lips slightly pursed. She appears amazed, but troubled.

CUT TO:

INT. — KIM'S APARTMENT

CLOSE ON BUNDLE OF MONEY

which is airborne, rising in SLOW MOTION toward the ceiling, twirling.

CUT TO:

Kim gazing upward, frowning at the tossed MONEY as it rises. Then she whirls in SLOW MOTION, the nightgown flowing around her. She spins in a full circle, drops gracefully to one knee, reaches out, and, smiling, makes the catch.

FREEZE ON KIM

down on one knee, holding the money she has just caught, beaming.

FINAL FADE OUT